SECOND EDITION

802.11® Wireless Networks
The Definitive Guide

Matthew S. Gast

Beijing · Cambridge · Farnham · Köln · Paris · Sebastopol · Taipei · Tokyo

802.11® Wireless Networks: The Definitive Guide, Second Edition
by Matthew S. Gast

Copyright © 2005 Matthew S. Gast. All rights reserved.
Printed in the United States of America.

Published by O'Reilly Media, Inc., 1005 Gravenstein Highway North, Sebastopol, CA 95472.

O'Reilly books may be purchased for educational, business, or sales promotional use. Online editions are also available for most titles (*safari.oreilly.com*). For more information, contact our corporate/institutional sales department: (800) 998-9938 or *corporate@oreilly.com*.

Editor:	Mike Loukides
Production Editor:	Colleen Gorman
Cover Designer:	Ellie Volckhausen
Interior Designer:	David Futato

Printing History:

April 2002:	First Edition.
April 2005:	Second Edition.

 This book uses RepKover™, a durable and flexible lay-flat binding.

ISBN-10: 0-596-10052-3
ISBN-13: 978-0-596-10052-0
[M]   [02/07]

Table of Contents

Foreword

Matthew Gast was my mentor long before I met him. I began reporting on wireless data networking in October 2000 when I discovered that Apple's claims for its 802.11b-based AirPort Base Station were actually true.

I'd been burned with another form of wireless networking that used infrared, and had spent many fruitless hours using other "interesting" networking technologies that led to dead ends. I figured 802.11b was just another one. Was I glad I was wrong!

This discovery took me down a path that led, inexorably, to the first edition of *802.11 Wireless Networks*. How did this stuff actually work as advertised? I knew plenty about the ISO model, TCP/IP, and Ethernet frames, but I couldn't reconcile a medium in which all parties talked in the same space with what I knew about Ethernet's methods of coping with shared contention.

Matthew taught me through words and figures that I didn't originally understand, but returned to again and again as I descended further into technical detail in my attempts to explain Wi-Fi to a broader and broader audience through articles in *The New York Times*, *The Seattle Times*, *PC World*, and my own Wi-Fi Networking News (*http://www.wifinetnews.com*) site over the last five years.

I starting learning acronyms from *802.11 Wireless Networks* and used Matthew's book to go beyond expanding WDS into Wireless Distribution System into understanding precisely how two access points could exchange data with each other through a built-in 802.11 mechanism that allowed four parties to a packet's transit.

Now as time went by and the 802.11 family grew and became baroque, the first edition of this title started feeling a little out of date—although it remained surprising how many "new" innovations were firmly rooted in developments of the early to mid-1990s. The alphabet soup of the first edition was gruel compared to the mulligatawny of 2005.

Matthew filled the gap between the book and contemporary wireless reality through his ongoing writing at O'Reilly's Wireless DevCenter, which I read avidly. And somewhere in there I was introduced to Matthew at a Wi-Fi Planet conference. We hit it off immediately: I started pestering him for details about 802.1X, if I remember correctly, and he wanted to talk about books and business. (I wound up writing two editions of a general market Wi-Fi book, neither of which did nearly as well as Matthew's extraordinarily technical one.)

Since then, I have been in the rare and privileged position to be the recipient of Matthew's generosity with his knowledge and humble insight. Matthew isn't one who assumes; he researches. His natural curiosity compels him to dig until he gets an answer that's technically and logically consistent.

Take, for instance, the incredibly political and complicated evolution of the 802.1X standard. (I know, from Matthew, that it's properly capitalized since it's a freestanding standard not reliant on other specifications. Even the IEEE makes this mistake, and it's their rule for capitalization that we're both following.)

802.1X is simple enough in its use of the Extensible Authentication Protocol, a generic method of passing messages among parties to authentication. But the ways in which EAP is secured are, quite frankly, insane—reflecting Microsoft and Cisco's parallel but conflicting attempts to control support of legacy protocols in a way that only damages easy access to its higher level of security.

Matthew eschewed the religious debate and spelled out the various methods, difficulties, and interoperability issues in an O'Reilly Network article that's the nugget of the expanded coverage in this book. I defy any reader to find as cogent and exhaustive an explanation before this book was published. There's nothing as clear, comprehensive, and unaffected by market politics.

At times, Matthew bemoaned the delays that led to the gap between editions of this book, due partly to his joining a startup wireless LAN switch company, but I think readers are better served through his very hard-won, late-night, long-hours knowledge.

Matthew's relationship with 802.11 might have previously been considered that of a handy man who knew his way around the infrastructure of his house. If a toilet was running, he could replace a valve. If the living room needed new outlets, he could research the process and wire them in.

But Matthew's new job took him allegorically from a weekend household warrior to a jack-of-all-tradesman. Matthew can tear out those inner walls, reframe, plumb, and wire them, all the while bitching about the local building code.

It's been a pleasure knowing Matthew, and it's even more a pleasure to introduce you to his book, and let you all in on what I and others have been more private recipients of for the last few years.

—Glenn Fleishman
Seattle, Washington
February 2005

Preface

People move. Networks don't.

More than anything else, these two statements can explain the explosion of wireless LAN hardware. In just a few years, wireless LANs have grown from a high-priced, alpha-geek curiosity to mainstream technology.

By removing the network port from the equation, wireless networks separate user connectivity from a direct physical location at the end of a cord. To abstract the user location from the network, however, requires a great deal of protocol engineering. For users to have location-independent services, the network must become much more aware of their location.

This book has been written on more airplanes, in more airports, and on more trains than I care to count. Much of the research involved in distilling evolving network technology into a book depends on Internet access. It is safe to say that without ubiquitous network access, the arrival of this book would have been much delayed.

The advantages of wireless networks has made them a fast-growing multibillion dollar equipment market. Wireless LANs are now a fixture on the networking landscape, which means you need to learn to deal with them.

Prometheus Untethered: The Possibilities of Wireless LANs

Wireless networks offer several advantages over fixed (or "wired") networks:

Mobility
> Users move, but data is usually stored centrally, enabling users to access data while they are in motion can lead to large productivity gains. Networks are built because they offer valuable services to users. In the past, network designers have focused on working with network ports because that is what typically maps to a user. With wireless, there are no ports, and the network can be designed around user identity.

Ease and speed of deployment

Many areas are difficult to wire for traditional wired LANs. Older buildings are often a problem; running cable through the walls of an older stone building to which the blueprints have been lost can be a challenge. In many places, historic preservation laws make it difficult to carry out new LAN installations in older buildings. Even in modern facilities, contracting for cable installation can be expensive and time-consuming.

Flexibility

No cables means no recabling. Wireless networks allow users to quickly form amorphous, small group networks for a meeting, and wireless networking makes moving between cubicles and offices a snap. Expansion with wireless networks is easy because the network medium is already everywhere. There are no cables to pull, connect, or trip over. Flexibility is the big selling point for the "hot spot" market, composed mainly of hotels, airports, train stations (and even trains themselves!), libraries, and cafes.

Cost

In some cases, costs can be reduced by using wireless technology. As an example, 802.11® equipment can be used to create a wireless bridge between two buildings. Setting up a wireless bridge requires some initial capital cost in terms of outdoor equipment, access points, and wireless interfaces. After the initial capital expenditure, however, an 802.11-based, line-of-sight network will have only a negligible recurring monthly operating cost. Over time, point-to-point wireless links are far cheaper than leasing capacity from the telephone company.

Until the completion of the 802.11 standard in 1997, however, users wanting to take advantage of these attributes were forced to adopt single-vendor solutions with all of the risk that entailed. Once 802.11 started the ball rolling, speeds quickly increased from 2 Mbps to 11 Mbps to 54 Mbps. Standardized wireless interfaces and antennas have made it much easier to build wireless networks. Several service providers have jumped at the idea, and enthusiastic bands of volunteers in most major cities have started to build public wireless networks based on 802.11.

802.11 has become something of a universally assumed connectivity method as well. Rather than wiring public access ports up with Ethernet, a collection of access points can provide connectivity to guests. In the years since 802.11 was standardized, so-called "hot spots" have gone from an exotic curiosity in venues that do not move, to technology that is providing connectivity even while in transit. By coupling 802.11 access with a satellite uplink, it is possible to provide Internet access even while moving quickly. Several commuter rail systems provide mobile hot-spots, and Boeing's Connexion service can do the same for an airplane, even at a cruising speed of 550 miles per hour.

Audience

This book is intended for readers who need to learn more about the technical aspects of wireless LANs, from operations to deployment to monitoring:

- Network architects contemplating rolling out 802.11 equipment onto networks or building networks based on 802.11
- Network administrators responsible for building and maintaining 802.11 networks
- Security professionals concerned about the exposure from deployment of 802.11 equipment and interested in measures to reduce the security headaches

The book assumes that you have a solid background in computer networks. You should have a basic understanding of IEEE 802 networks (particularly Ethernet), the OSI reference model, and the TCP/IP protocols, in addition to any other protocols on your network. Wireless LANs are not totally new ground for most network administrators, but there will be new concepts, particularly involving radio transmissions.

Overture for Book in Black and White, Opus 2

Part of the difficulty in writing a book on a technology that is evolving quickly is that you are never quite sure what to include. The years between the first and second edition were filled with many developments in security, and updating the security-related information was one of the major parts of this revision. This book has two main purposes: it is meant to teach the reader about the 802.11 standard itself, and it offers practical advice on building wireless LANs with 802.11 equipment. These two purposes are meant to be independent of each other so you can easily find what interests you. To help you decide what to read first and to give you a better idea of the layout, the following are brief summaries of all the chapters.

Chapter 1, *Introduction to Wireless Networking*, lists ways in which wireless networks are different from traditional wired networks and discusses the challenges faced when adapting to fuzzy boundaries and unreliable media. Wireless LANs are perhaps the most interesting illustration of Christian Huitema's assertion that the Internet has no center, just an ever-expanding edge. With wireless LAN technology becoming commonplace, that edge is now blurring.

Chapter 2, *Overview of 802.11 Networks*, describes the overall architecture of 802.11 wireless LANs. 802.11 is somewhat like Ethernet but with a number of new network components and a lot of new acronyms. This chapter introduces you to the network components that you'll work with. Broadly speaking, these components are stations (mobile devices with wireless cards), access points (glorified bridges between the stations and the distribution system), and the distribution system itself (the wired backbone network). Stations are grouped logically into Basic Service Sets (BSSs). When no access point is present, the network is a loose, ad-hoc confederation called an independent BSS (IBSS). Access points allow more structure by connecting disparate physical BSSs into a further logical grouping called an Extended Service Set (ESS).

Chapter 3, *802.11 MAC Fundamentals*, describes the Media Access Control (MAC) layer of the 802.11 standard in detail. 802.11, like all IEEE 802 networks, splits the MAC-layer functionality from the physical medium access. Several physical layers exist for 802.11, but the MAC is the same across all of them. The main mode for accessing the network medium is a traditional contention-based access method, though it employs collision avoidance (CSMA/CA) rather than collision detection (CSMA/CD). The chapter also discusses data encapsulation in 802.11 frames and helps network administrators understand the frame sequences used to transfer data.

Chapter 4, *802.11 Framing in Detail*, builds on the end of Chapter 3 by describing the various frame types and where they are used. This chapter is intended more as a reference than actual reading material. It describes the three major frame classes. Data frames are the workhorse of 802.11. Control frames serve supervisory purposes. Management frames assist in performing the extended operations of the 802.11 MAC. Beacons announce the existence of an 802.11 network, assist in the association process, and are used for authenticating stations.

Chapter 5, *Wired Equivalent Privacy (WEP)*, describes the Wired Equivalent Privacy protocol. In spite of its flaws, WEP is the basis for much of the following work in wireless LAN security. This chapter discusses what WEP is, how it works, and why you can't rely on it for any meaningful privacy or security.

Chapter 6, *User Authentication with 802.1X*, describes the 802.1X authentication framework. In conjunction with the Extensible Authentication Protocol, 802.1X provides strong authentication solutions and improved encryption on Wireless LANs.

Chapter 7, *802.11i: Robust Security Networks, TKIP, and CCMP*, describes the 802.11i standard for wireless LAN security. In recognition of the fundamental flaws of WEP, two new link-layer encryption protocols were designed, complete with new mechanisms to derive and distribute keys.

Chapter 8, *Management Operations*, describes the management operations on 802.11 networks. To find networks to join, stations scan for active networks announced by access points or the IBSS creator. Before sending data, stations must associate with an access point. This chapter also discusses the power-management features incorporated into the MAC that allow battery-powered stations to sleep and pick up buffered traffic at periodic intervals.

Chapter 9, *Contention-Free Service with the PCF*, describes the point coordination function. The PCF is not widely implemented, so this chapter can be skipped for most purposes. The PCF is the basis for contention-free access to the wireless medium. Contention-free access is like a centrally controlled, token-based medium, where access points provide the "token" function.

Chapter 10, *Physical Layer Overview*, describes the general architecture of the physical layer (PHY) in the 802.11 model. The PHY itself is broken down into two "sublayers." The Physical Layer Convergence Procedure (PLCP) adds a preamble to form the complete frame and its own header, while the Physical Medium Dependent (PMD) sublayer includes modulation details. The most common PHYs use radio frequency (RF) as the wireless medium, so the chapter closes with a short discussion on RF systems and technology that can be applied to any PHY discussed in the book.

Chapter 11, *The Frequency-Hopping (FH) PHY*, describes the oldest physical layer with 802.11. Products based on the FH PHY are no longer widely sold, but a great deal of early 802.11 equipment was based on them. Organizations with a long history of involvement with 802.11 technology may need to be familiar with this PHY.

Chapter 12, *The Direct Sequence PHYs: DSSS and HR/DSSS (802.11b)*, describes two physical layers based on direct sequence spread spectrum technology. The initial 802.11 standard included a layer which offered speeds of 1 Mbps and 2 Mbps. While interesting, it was not until 802.11b added 5.5 Mbps and 11 Mbps data rates that the technology really took off. This chapter describes the two closely-related PHYs as a single package.

Chapter 13, *802.11a and 802.11j: 5-GHz OFDM PHY*, describes the 5-GHz PHY standardized with 802.11a, which operates at 54 Mbps. This physical layer uses another modulation technique known as orthogonal frequency division multiplexing (OFDM). Slight modifications were required to use this PHY in Japan, which were made by the 802.11j standard.

Chapter 14, *802.11g: The Extended-Rate PHY (ERP)*, describes a PHY which uses OFDM technology, but in the 2.4 GHz frequency band shared by 802.11b. It has largely supplanted 802.11b, and is a common option for built-in connectivity with new notebook computers. The PHY itself is almost identical to the 802.11a PHY. The differences are in allowing for backwards compatibility with older equipment sharing the same frequency band.

Chapter 15, *A Peek Ahead at 802.11n: MIMO-OFDM*, describes the PHY currently in development. 802.11n uses a PHY based on multiple-input/multiple-output (MIMO) technology for much higher speed. At the time this book went to press, two proposed standards were dueling in the committee. This chapter describes both.

Chapter 16, *802.11 Hardware*, begins the transition from theoretical matters based on the standards to how the standards are implemented. 802.11 is a relatively loose standard, and allows a large number of implementation choices. Cards may differ in their specified performance, or in the manner in which certain protocols are implemented. Many of these variations are based on how they are built.

Chapter 17, *Using 802.11 on Windows*, describes the basic driver installation procedure in Windows, and how to configure security settings.

Chapter 18, *802.11 on the Macintosh*, describes how to use the AirPort card on MacOS X to connect to 802.11 networks. It focuses on Mac OS X 10.3, which was the first software version to include 802.1X support.

Chapter 19, *Using 802.11 on Linux*, discusses how to install 802.11 support on a Linux system. After discussing how to add PC Card support to the operating system, it shows how to use the wireless extensions API. It discusses two common drivers, one for the older Orinoco 802.11b card, and the MADwifi driver for newer cards based on chipsets from Atheros Communications. Finally, it shows how to configure 802.1X security using xsupplicant.

Chapter 20, *Using 802.11 Access Points*, describes the equipment used on the infrastructure end of 802.11 networks. Commercial access point products have varying features. This chapter describes the common features of access points, offers buying advice, and presents two practical configuration examples.

Chapter 21, *Logical Wireless Network Architecture*, marks the third transition in the book, from the implementation of 802.11 on the scale of an individual device, to how to build 802.11 networks on a larger scale. There are several major styles that can be used to build the network, each with its advantages and disadvantages. This chapter sorts through the common types of network topologies and offers advice on selecting one.

Chapter 22, *Security Architecture*, should be read in tandem with the previous chapter. Maintaining network security while offering network access on an open medium is a major challenge. Security choices and architecture choices are mutually influential. This chapter addresses the major choices to be made in designing a network: what type of authentication will be used and how it integrates with existing user databases, how to encrypt traffic to keep it safe, and how to deal with unauthorized access point deployment.

Chapter 23, *Site Planning and Project Management*, is the final component of the book for network administrators. Designing a large-scale wireless network is difficult because there is great user demand for access. Ensuring that the network has sufficient capacity to satisfy user demands in all the locations where it will be used requires some planning. Choosing locations for access points depends a great deal on the radio environment, and has traditionally been one of the most time-consuming tasks in building a network.

Chapter 24, *802.11 Network Analysis*, teaches administrators how to recognize what's going on with their wireless LANs. Network analyzers have proven their worth time and time again on wired networks. Wireless network analyzers are just as valuable a tool for 802.11 networks. This chapter discusses how to use wireless network analyzers and what certain symptoms may indicate. It also describes how to build an analyzer using Ethereal, and what to look for to troubleshoot common problems.

Chapter 25, *802.11 Performance Tuning*, describes how network administrators can increase throughput. It begins by describing how to calculate overall throughput for payload data, and common ways of increasing performance. In rare cases, it may make sense to change commonly exposed 802.11 parameters.

Chapter 26, *Conclusions and Predictions*, summarizes current standards work in the 802.11 working group. After summarizing the work in progress, I get to prognosticate and hope that I don't have to revise this too extensively in future editions.

Major Changes from the First Edition

The three years between 2002 and 2005 saw a great deal of change in wireless LANs. The standards themselves continued to evolve to provide greater security and interoperability. Following the typical technology path of "faster, better, and cheaper," the data rate of most 802.11 interfaces has shot from 2 or 11 Mbps with 802.11b to 54 Mbps with 802.11a and 802.11g. Increased speed with backwards compatibility has proved to be a commercially successful formula for 802.11g, even if it has limitations when used for large-scale networks. The coming standardization of 802.11n is set to boost speeds even farther. New developments in PHY technology are anxiously awaited by users, as shown by the popular releases of pre-standard technology. Two entirely new chapters are devoted to 802.11g and 802.11n. European adoption of 802.11a was contingent on the development of spectrum management in 802.11h, which resulted in extensive revisions to the management chapter.

When the first edition was released in 2002, the perception of insecurity dominated discussions of the technology. WEP was clearly insufficient, but there was no good alternative. Most network administrators were making do with remote access systems turned inward, rather than their natural outward orientation. The development of 802.11i was done a great deal to simplify network security. Security is now built in to the specification, rather than something which must be added on after getting the network right. Security improvements permeate the book, from new chapters showing how the new protocols work, to showing how they can be used on the client side, to how to sort through different options when building a network. Sorting through security options is much more complex now than it was three years ago, and made it necessary to expand a section of the deployment discussion in the first edition into its own chapter.

Three years ago, most access points were expensive devices that did not work well in large numbers. Network deployment was often an exercise in working around the limitations of the devices of the time. Three years later, vastly more capable devices allow much more flexible deployment models. Rather than just a "one size fits all" deployment model, there are now multiple options to sort through. Security protocols have improved enough that discussions of deploying technology are based on what it can do for the organization, not on fear and how to keep it controlled. As a result, the original chapter on network deployment has grown into three, each tackling a major part of the deployment process.

Conventions Used in This Book

Italic is used for:

- Pathnames, filenames, class names, and directories
- New terms where they are defined
- Internet addresses, such as domain names and URLs

Bold is used for:

- GUI components

`Constant Width` is used for:

- Command lines and options that should be typed verbatim on the screen
- All code listings

`Constant Width Italic` is used for:

- General placeholders that indicate that an item should be replaced by some actual value in your own program

`Constant Width Bold` is used for:

- Text that is typed in code examples by the user

 Indicates a tip, suggestion, or general note

 Indicates a warning or caution

How to Contact Us

Please address comments and questions concerning this book to the publisher:

O'Reilly Media, Inc.
1005 Gravenstein Highway North
Sebastopol, CA 95472
(800) 998-9938 (in the U.S. or Canada)
(707) 829-0515 (international/local)
(707) 829-0104 (fax)

There is a web site for the book, where errata and any additional information will be listed. You can access this page at:

> *http://www.oreilly.com/catalog/802dot112/*

In a fast-moving field, smaller articles bridge the gap between contemporary practice and the last version of the printed book. You can access my weblog and articles at:

> *http://weblogs.oreillynet.com/pub/au/692/*

To comment or ask technical questions about this book, send email to:

> *bookquestions@oreilly.com*

For more information about our books, conferences, software, Resource Centers, and the O'Reilly Network, see our web site at:

> *http://www.oreilly.com/*

Safari Enabled

 When you see a Safari® Enabled icon on the cover of your favorite technology book, it means the book is available online through the O'Reilly Network Safari Bookshelf.

Safari offers a solution that's better than e-books. It's a virtual library that lets you easily search thousands of top technology books, cut and paste code samples, download chapters, and find quick answers when you need the most accurate, current information. Try it for free at *http://safari.oreilly.com*.

Acknowledgments

As much as I would like to believe that you are reading this book for its entertainment value, I know better. Technical books are valued because they get the details right, and convey them in an easier fashion than the unadorned technical specification. Behind every technical book, there is a review team that saw the first draft and helped to improve it. My review team caught numerous mistakes and made the book significantly better. Dr. Malik Audeh of Tropos Networks is, for lack of a better term, my radio conscience. I am no radio expert—what I know about radio, I learned because of my interest in 802.11. Malik knew radio technology before 802.11, and I have been privileged to share in his insight. Gerry Creager of Texas A&M offered insight into the FCC rules and regulations for unlicensed devices, which was valuable because wireless LANs have been upending the rules in recent years. When Glenn Fleishman agreed to write the foreword, I had no idea that he would offer so much help in placing 802.11 within its larger context. Many of the details he suggested were references to articles that had run in the past years on his own Wi-Fi Networking News site. As a writer himself, Glenn also pointed out several locations where better examples would make my points much clearer. Finally, Terry Simons of the Open1X project has worked extensively with 802.11 on Linux, and with nearly every 802.1X supplicant on the major operating systems. Terry also is one of the architects of the wireless authentication system at the University of Utah. His expertise can be felt throughout the early part of the book on security specifications, as well as in the practical matter of using supplicants and building an authentication system.

I am also indebted to many others who help keep me abreast of current developments in 802.11, and share their knowledge with me. Since 2002, I have been privileged to participate in the Interop Labs initiatives related to wireless security and 802.1X. The real world is far too messy for the classroom. Every year, I learn more about the state of the art by volunteering than I ever could by taking a prepared class. Through the Interop Labs, I met Chris Hessing, the development lead for xsupplicant. Chris has always generously explained how all the keying bits move around in 802.11, which is no small feat! Sudheer Matta, a colleague of mine, always has time to explain what is happening in the standards world, and how the minute details of the MAC work.

The large supporting cast at O'Reilly was tremendously helpful in a wide variety of ways. Ellie Volckhausen designed a stunning cover that has adorned my cubicle as well as most of the personal electronics devices I own since 2001, when I began writing the first edition. (It even looks good as the wallpaper on my mobile telephone!) Jessamyn Read took a huge mass of raw sketches and converted every last one into something that is worth looking at, and did so on a grueling schedule. I do not know how many hours Colleen Gorman, the production editor, put into this book to get it finished, but I hope her family and her cat, Phineas, forgive me. And, as always, I am thankful for the wisdom of Mike Loukides, the editor. Mike kept this project moving forward in the innumerable ways I have been accustomed to from our past collaborations, and his background as a ham radio operator proved especially useful when I started writing about the dark and forbidding world of antennas and RF transmission. (Among many, many other items, you have him to thank for the footnote on the gain of the Aricebo radio telescope!)

As with so much in life, the devil of writing is in the details. Getting it right means rewriting, and then probably rewriting some more. I did not attempt a large writing project until college, when I took Brad Bateman's U.S. Financial System class. Although I certainly learned about the flow of money through the economy and the tools that the Federal Reserve uses in formulating policy, what I most value in retrospect was the highly structured process of writing a lengthy paper throughout the semester. In addition to simply producing a large document, Dr. Bateman stressed the revision process, a skill that I had to use repeatedly in the preparation of this book and its second edition. It would be a mistake, however, for me to simply credit

Dr. Bateman as an outstanding writing teacher or an economist gifted with the ability to explain complex subjects to his students. Dr. Bateman is not shackled by his narrow academic expertise. During the preparation of the second edition of this book, I attended a lecture of his about the social history of my alma mater. In a captivating hour, he traced the history of the institution and its intersection with wider social movements, which explained its present-day culture in far more depth than I ever appreciated while a student. Not all professors teach to prepare students for graduate school, and not all professors confine their teaching to the classroom. I am a far better writer, economist, and citizen for his influence.

When writing a book, it is easy to acknowledge the tangible contributions of others. Behind every author, though, there is a supportive cast of relatives and friends. As always, my wife Ali continued to indulge my writing habit with extremely good humor, especially considering the number of weekends that were sacrificed to this book. Many of my friends informally supported this project with a great deal of encouragement and support; my thanks must go to (in alphabetical order) Annie, Aramazd, Brian, Dameon, Kevin, and Nick.

—Matthew Gast
San Francisco, California
February 2005

## CHAPTER 1

Introduction to Wireless Networking

Over the past five years, the world has become increasingly mobile. As a result, traditional ways of networking the world have proven inadequate to meet the challenges posed by our new collective lifestyle. If users must be connected to a network by physical cables, their movement is dramatically reduced. Wireless connectivity, however, poses no such restriction and allows a great deal more free movement on the part of the network user. As a result, wireless technologies are encroaching on the traditional realm of "fixed" or "wired" networks. This change is obvious to anybody who drives on a regular basis. One of the "life and death" challenges to those of us who drive on a regular basis is the daily gauntlet of erratically driven cars containing mobile phone users in the driver's seat.

Wireless connectivity for voice telephony has created a whole new industry. Adding mobile connectivity into the mix for telephony has had profound influences on the business of delivering voice calls because callers could be connected to people, not devices. We are on the cusp of an equally profound change in computer networking. Wireless telephony has been successful because it enables people to connect with each other regardless of location. New technologies targeted at computer networks promise to do the same for Internet connectivity. The most successful wireless data networking technology this far has been 802.11.

In the first edition of this book, I wrote about 802.11 being the tip of the trend in mobile data networking. At the time, 802.11 and third-generation mobile technologies were duking it out for mindshare, but 802.11 has unquestionably been more successful to date.

Why Wireless?

To dive into a specific technology at this point is getting a bit ahead of the story, though. Wireless networks share several important advantages, no matter how the protocols are designed, or even what type of data they carry.

The most obvious advantage of wireless networking is *mobility*. Wireless network users can connect to existing networks and are then allowed to roam freely. A mobile telephone user can drive miles in the course of a single conversation because the phone connects the user through cell towers. Initially, mobile telephony was expensive. Costs restricted its use to highly mobile professionals such as sales managers and important executive decision makers who might need to be reached at a moment's notice regardless of their location. Mobile telephony has proven to be a useful service, however, and now it is relatively common in the United States and extremely common among Europeans.*

Likewise, wireless data networks free software developers from the tethers of an Ethernet cable at a desk. Developers can work in the library, in a conference room, in the parking lot, or even in the coffee house across the street. As long as the wireless users remain within the range of the base station, they can take advantage of the network. Commonly available equipment can easily cover a corporate campus; with some work, more exotic equipment, and favorable terrain, you can extend the range of an 802.11 network up to a few miles.

Wireless networks typically have a great deal of *flexibility*, which can translate into rapid deployment. Wireless networks use a number of base stations to connect users to an existing network. (In an 802.11 network, the base stations are called *access points*.) The infrastructure side of a wireless network, however, is qualitatively the same whether you are connecting one user or a million users. To offer service in a given area, you need base stations and antennas in place. Once that infrastructure is built, however, adding a user to a wireless network is mostly a matter of authorization. With the infrastructure built, it must be configured to recognize and offer services to the new users, but authorization does not require more infrastructure. Adding a user to a wireless network is a matter of configuring the infrastructure, but it does not involve running cables, punching down terminals, and patching in a new jack.†

Flexibility is an important attribute for service providers. One of the markets that many 802.11 equipment vendors have been chasing is the so-called "hot spot" connectivity market. Airports and train stations are likely to have itinerant business travelers interested in network access during connection delays. Coffeehouses and other public gathering spots are social venues in which network access is desirable. Many cafes already offer Internet access; offering Internet access over a wireless network is a natural extension of the existing Internet connectivity. While it is possible to serve a fluid group of users with Ethernet jacks, supplying access over a wired network is problematic for several reasons. Running cables is time-consuming and expensive

---

* While most of my colleagues, acquaintances, and family in the U.S. have mobile telephones, it is still possible to be a holdout. In Europe, it seems as if everybody has a mobile phone—one cab driver in Finland I spoke with while writing the first edition of this book took great pride in the fact that his family of four had six mobile telephones!

† This simple example ignores the challenges of scale. Naturally, if the new users will overload the existing infrastructure, the infrastructure itself will need to be beefed up. Infrastructure expansion can be expensive and time-consuming, especially if it involves legal and regulatory approval. However, my basic point holds: adding a user to a wireless network can often be reduced to a matter of configuration (moving or changing bits) while adding a user to a fixed network requires making physical connections (moving atoms), and moving bits is easier than moving atoms.

and may also require construction. Properly guessing the correct number of cable drops is more an art than a science. With a wireless network, though, there is no need to suffer through construction or make educated (or wild) guesses about demand. A simple wired infrastructure connects to the Internet, and then the wireless network can accommodate as many users as needed. Although wireless LANs have somewhat limited bandwidth, the limiting factor in networking a small hot spot is likely to be the cost of WAN bandwidth to the supporting infrastructure.

Flexibility may be particularly important in older buildings because it reduces the need for construction. Once a building is declared historical, remodeling can be particularly difficult. In addition to meeting owner requirements, historical preservation agencies must be satisfied that new construction is not desecrating the past. Wireless networks can be deployed extremely rapidly in such environments because there is only a small wired network to install.

Flexibility has also led to the development of grassroots community networks. With the rapid price erosion of 802.11 equipment, bands of volunteers are setting up shared wireless networks open to visitors. Community networks are also extending the range of Internet access past the limitations for DSL into communities where high-speed Internet access has been only a dream. Community networks have been particularly successful in out-of-the way places that are too rugged for traditional wireline approaches.

Like all networks, wireless networks transmit data over a network medium. The medium is a form of electromagnetic radiation.* To be well-suited for use on mobile networks, the medium must be able to cover a wide area so clients can move throughout a coverage area. Early wireless networks used infrared light. However, infrared light has limitations; it is easily blocked by walls, partitions, and other office construction. Radio waves can penetrate most office obstructions and offer a wider coverage range. It is no surprise that most, if not all, 802.11 products on the market use the radio wave physical layer.

Radio Spectrum: The Key Resource

Wireless devices are constrained to operate in a certain frequency band. Each band has an associated *bandwidth*, which is simply the amount of frequency space in the band. Bandwidth has acquired a connotation of being a measure of the data capacity of a link. A great deal of mathematics, information theory, and signal processing can be used to show that higher-bandwidth slices can be used to transmit more information. As an example, an analog mobile telephony channel requires a 20-kHz bandwidth. TV signals are vastly more complex and have a correspondingly larger bandwidth of 6 MHz.

---

* Laser light is also used by some wireless networking applications, but the extreme focus of a laser beam makes it suited only for applications in which the ends are stationary. "Fixed wireless" applications, in which lasers replace other access technology such as leased telephone circuits, are a common application.

Early Adoption of 802.11

802.11's explosive advance has not been even. Some markets have evolved more quickly than others because the value of wireless networks is more pronounced in some markets. In general, the higher the value placed on mobility and flexibility, the greater the interest in wireless LANs.

Logistics organizations responsible for moving goods around (think UPS, FedEx, or airlines), were perhaps the earliest adopters of 802.11. Well before the advent of 802.11, package tracking was done with proprietary wireless LANs. Standardized products lowered the price and enabled competition between suppliers of network equipment, and it was an easy decision to replace proprietary products with standardized ones.

Health care has been an early adopter of wireless networks because of the great flexibility that is often required of health care equipment. Patients can be moved throughout a hospital, and the health care professionals that spend time with patients are among some of the most mobile workers in the economy. Technologically advanced health care organizations have adopted wireless LANs to make patient information available over wireless LANs to improve patient care by making information more accessible to doctors. Computerized records can be transferred between departments without the requirement to decipher the legendarily illegible doctor scrawls. In the cluttered environments of an emergency room, rapid access to imaging data can quite literally be a lifesaver. Several hospitals have deployed PCs to make radiology images available over wireless LANs on specially-equipped "crash carts" that offer instant access to X-rays, allowing doctors to make quick decisions without waiting for film to be developed.

Many eductional institutions have enthusiastically adopted wireless LANs. 10 years ago, colleges competed for students based on how "wired" the campus was. More high speed data ports everywhere was assumed to be better. Nowadays, the leading stories in education are the colleges using wireless LANs to blanket coverage throughout the campus. Students are highly mobile network users, and can benefit greatly from network access between classes or in their "homes away from home" (the library, studio, or science lab, depending on major).

Radio spectrum allocation is rigorously controlled by regulatory authorities through *licensing* processes. Most countries have their own regulatory bodies, though regional regulators do exist. In the U.S., regulation is done by the Federal Communications Commission (FCC). Many FCC rules are adopted by other countries throughout the Americas. European allocation is performed by the European Radiocommunications Office (ERO). Other allocation work is done by the International Telecommunications Union (ITU). To prevent overlapping uses of the radio waves, frequency is allocated in bands, which are simply ranges of frequencies available to specified applications. Table 1-1 lists some common frequency bands used in the U.S.[*]

---

[*] The full spectrum allocation map is available from the National Telecommunications and Information Administration at *http://www.ntia.doc.gov/osmhome/allochrt.pdf*.

Table 1-1. Common U.S. frequency bands

Band	Frequency range
UHF ISM	902–928 MHz
S-Band	2–4 GHz
S-Band ISM	2.4–2.5 GHz
C-Band	4–8 GHz
C-Band satellite downlink	3.7–4.2 GHz
C-Band Radar (weather)	5.25–5.925 GHz
C-Band ISM	5.725–5.875 GHz
C-Band satellite uplink	5.925–6.425 GHz
X-Band	8–12 GHz
X-Band Radar (police/weather)	8.5–10.55 GHz
Ku-Band	12–18 GHz
Ku-Band Radar (police)	13.4–14 GHz 15.7–17.7 GHz

The ISM bands

In Table 1-1, there are three bands labeled ISM, which is an abbreviation for *industrial, scientific, and medical*. ISM bands are set aside for equipment that, broadly speaking, is related to industrial or scientific processes or is used by medical equipment. Perhaps the most familiar ISM-band device is the microwave oven, which operates in the 2.4-GHz ISM band because electromagnetic radiation at that frequency is particularly effective for heating water.

I pay special attention to the ISM bands in the table because those bands allow license-free operation, provided the devices comply with power constraints. 802.11 operates in the ISM bands, along with many other devices. Common cordless phones operate in the ISM bands as well. 802.11b and 802.11g devices operate within the 2.4 GHz ISM band, while 802.11a devices operate in the 5 GHz band.

The more common 802.11b/g devices operate in S-band ISM. The ISM bands are generally license-free, provided that devices are low-power. How much sense does it make to require a license for microwave ovens, after all? Likewise, you don't need a license to set up and operate a low-power wireless LAN.

What Makes Wireless Networks Different

Wireless networks are an excellent complement to fixed networks, but they are not a replacment technology. Just as mobile telephones complement fixed-line telephony, wireless LANs complement existing fixed networks by providing mobility to users. Servers and other data center equipment must access data, but the physical location of the server is irrelevant. As long as the servers do not move, they may as well be connected to wires that do not move. At the other end of the spectrum, wireless networks must be designed to cover large areas to accommodate fast-moving clients. Typical 802.11 access points do not cover large areas, and would have a hard time coping with users on rapidly-moving vehicles.

Lack of Physical Boundary

Traditional network security places a great deal of emphasis on physical security of the network components. Data on the network travels over well-defined pathways, usually of copper or fiber, and the network infrastructure is protected by strong physical access control. Equipment is safely locked away in wiring closets, and set up so that it cannot be reconfigured by users. Basic security stems from the (admittedly marginal) security of the physical layer. Although it is possible to tap or redirect signals, physical access control makes it much harder for an intruder to gain surreptitious access to the network.

Wireless networks have a much more open network medium. By definition, the network medium in a wireless network is not a well-defined path consisting of a physical cable, but a radio link with a particular encoding and modulation. Signals can be sent or received by anybody in possession of the radio techniques, which are of course well known because they are open standards. Interception of data is child's play, given that the medium is open to anybody with the right network interface, and the network interface can be purchased for less than $50 at your local consumer electronics store. Careful shopping online may get you cards for half of that.

Furthermore, radio waves tend to travel outside their intended location. There is no abrupt physical boundary of the network medium, and the range at which transmissions can be received can be extended with high-gain antennas on either side. When building a wireless network, you must carefully consider how to secure the connection to prevent unauthorized use, traffic injection, and traffic analysis. With the maturation of wireless protocols, the tools to authenticate wireless users and properly encrypt traffic are now well within reach.

Dynamic Physical Medium

Once a wired network is put in place, it tends to be boring, which is to say, predictable. Once the cables have been put in place, they tend to do the same thing day in and day out. Provided the network has been designed according to the engineering rules laid out in the specification, the network should function as expected. Capacity can be added to a wired network easily by upgrading the switches in the wiring closet.

In contrast, the physical medium on wireless LANs is much more dynamic. Radio waves bounce off objects, penetrate through walls, and can often behave somewhat unpredictably. Radio waves can suffer from a number of propagation problems that may interrupt the radio link, such as multipath interference and shadows. Without a reliable network medium, wireless networks must carefully validate received frames to guard against frame loss. Positive acknowledgment, the tactic used by 802.11, does an excellent job at assuring delivery at some cost to throughput.

Radio links are subject to several additional constraints that fixed networks are not. Because radio spectrum is a relatively scarce resource, it is carefully regulated. Two ways exist to make radio networks go faster. Either more spectrum can be allocated, or the encoding on the link can be made more sensitive so that it packs more data in per unit of time. Additional spectrum allocations are relatively rare, especially for license-free networks. 802.11 networks have kept the bandwidth of a station's radio channel to approximately 30 MHz, while developing vastly improved encoding to improve the speed. Faster coding methods can increase the speed, but do have one potential drawback. Because the faster coding method depends on the receiver to pick out subtle signal differences, much greater signal-to-noise ratios are required. Higher data rates therefore require the station to be located closer to its access point. Table 1-2 shows the standardized physical layers in 802.11 and their respective speeds.

Table 1-2. Comparison of 802.11 physical layers (PHYs)

IEEE standard	Speed	Frequency band	Notes
802.11	1 Mbps 2 Mbps	2.4 GHz	First PHY standard (1997). Featured both frequency-hopping and direct-sequence modulation techniques.
802.11a	Up to 54 Mbps	5 GHz	Second PHY standard (1999), but products not released until late 2000.
802.11b	5.5 Mbps 11 Mbps	2.4 GHz	Third PHY standard, but second wave of products. The most common 802.11 equipment as the first edition of this book was written, and the majority of the legacy installed base at the time the second edition was written.
802.11g	Up to 54 Mbps	2.4 GHz	Fourth PHY standard (2003). Applies the coding techniques of 802.11a for higher speed in the 2.4 GHz band, while retaining backwards compatibility with existing 802.11b networks. The most common technology included with laptops in 2005.

Radio is inherently a broadcast medium. When one station transmits, all other stations must listen. Access points act much like old shared Ethernet hubs in that there is a fixed amount of transmission capacity per access point, and it must be shared by all the attached users. Adding capacity requires that the network administrator add access points while simultaneously reducing the coverage area of existing access points.

Security

Many wireless networks are based on radio waves, which makes the network medium inherently open to interception. Properly protecting radio transmissions on any network is always a concern for protocol designers. 802.11 did not build in much in the way of security protocols. Coping with the inherent unreliability of the wireless medium and mobility required several protocol features to confirm frame delivery, save power, and offer mobility. Security was quite far down the list, and proved inadequate in the early specifications.

Wireless networks must be strongly authenticated to prevent use by unauthorized users, and authenticated connections must be strongly encrypted to prevent traffic interception and injection by unauthorized parties. Technologies that offer strong encryption and authentication have emerged since the first edition of this book, and are a major component of the revisions for the second edition.

A Network by Any Other Name...

Wireless networking is a hot industry segment. Several wireless technologies have been targeted primarily for data transmission. Bluetooth is a standard used to build small networks between peripherals: a form of "wireless wires," if you will. Most people in the industry are familiar with the hype surrounding Bluetooth, though it seems to have died down as real devices have been brought to market. In the first edition, I wrote that I have not met many people who have used Bluetooth devices, but it is much more common these days. (I use a Bluetooth headset on a regular basis.)

Post-second-generation (2.5G) and third-generation (3G) mobile telephony networks are also a familiar wireless technology. They promise data rates of megabits per cell, as well as the "always on" connections that have proven to be quite valuable to DSL and cable modem customers. After many years of hype and press from 3G equipment vendors, the rollout of commercial 3G services is finally underway. 2.5G services like GPRS, EDGE, and 1xRTT are now widely available, and third-generation networks based on UMTS or EV-DO are quickly being built. (I recently subscribed to an unlimited GPRS service to get connected during my train trips between my office and my home.) Many articles quote peak speeds for these technologies in the hundreds of kilobits per second or even megabits, but this capacity must be shared between all users in a cell. Real-world downstream speeds are roughly comparable to dial-up modem connections and cannot touch an 802.11 hot spot.

This is a book about 802.11 networks. 802.11 goes by a variety of names, depending on who is talking about it. Some people call 802.11 *wireless Ethernet*, to emphasize its shared lineage with the traditional wired Ethernet (802.3). A second name which has grown dramatically in popularity since the first edition of this book is *Wi-Fi*, from the interoperability certification program run by the Wi-Fi Alliance, the major trade assocation of 802.11 equipment vendors. The Wi-Fi Alliance, formerly known as the Wireless Ethernet Compatibility Alliance (WECA), will test member products for compatibility with 802.11 standards.* Other organizations will perform compati-

---

* More details on the Wi-Fi Alliance and its certification program can be found at *http://www.wi-fi.org/*.

bility testing as well; the University of New Hampshire's InterOperability Lab (IOL) recently launched a wireless test consortium.

The Wonderful Thing About Standards...

Several standards groups are involved in 802.11-related standardization efforts because 802.11 cuts across many formerly distinct boundaries in networking. Most of the effort remains concentrated in the IEEE, but important contributions to wireless LAN standards have come from several major locations.

The first is the *Institute of Electronics and Electrical Engineers* (IEEE). In addition to its activities as a professional society, the IEEE works on standardizing electrical equipment, including several types of communication technology. IEEE standardization efforts are organized by *projects*, each of which is assigned a number. By far the most famous IEEE project is the IEEE 802 project to develop LAN standards. Within a project, individual *working groups* develop standards to address a particular facet of the problem. Working groups are also given a number, which is written after the decimal point for the corresponding projects. Ethernet, the most widely used IEEE LAN technology, was standardized by the third working group, 802.3. Wireless LANs were the eleventh working group formed, hence the name 802.11.

Within a working group, *task groups* form to revise particular aspects of the standard or add on to the general area of functionality. Task groups are assigned a letter beneath the working group, and the document produced by a task group combines the project and working group number, followed by the letter from the task group. (Some letters that are subject to easy confusion with letters, such as the lowercase "l," are not used.) In wireless networking, the first task group to gain wide recognition was Task Group B (TGb), which produced the 802.11b specification. Table 1-3 is a basic listing of the different 802.11 standards.

Interestingly enough, the case of the letter in a standards revision encodes information. Lowercase letters indicate dependent standards that cannot stand alone from their parent, while uppercase letters indicate full-fledged standalone specifications.

802.11b adds a new clause to 802.11, but cannot stand alone, so the "b" is written in lowercase. In contrast, standards like 802.1Q and 802.1X are standalone specifications that are completely self-contained in one document, and therefore use uppercase letters.

At periodic intervals, the additions from dependent task groups will be "rolled up" into the main parent specification. The initial revision of 802.11 came out in 1997. Minor changes to the text were released as 802.11-1999, which was the baseline standard for quite some time. The most recent rollup is 802.11-2003.

Table 1-3. standards

IEEE standard	Notes
802.11	First standard (1997). Specified the MAC and the original slower frequency-hopping and direct-sequence modulation techniques.
802.11a	Second physical layer standard (1999), but products not released until late 2000.
802.11b	Third physical layer standard (1999), but second wave of products. The most common 802.11 equipment as the first book was written.
TGc	Task group that produced a correction to the example encoding in 802.11a. Since the only product was a correction, there is no 802.11c.
802.11d	Extends frequency-hopping PHY for use across multiple regulatory domains
TGe (future 802.11e)	Task group producing quality-of-service (QoS) extensions for the MAC. An interim snapshot called Wi-Fi Multi-Media (WMM) is likely to be implemented before the standard is complete.
802.11F	Inter-access point protocol to improve roaming between directly attached access points
802.11g	Most recently standardized (2003) PHY for networks in the ISM band.
802.11h	Standard to make 802.11a compatible with European radio emissions regulations. Other regulators have adopted its mechanisms for different purposes.
802.11i	Improvements to security at the link layer.
802.11j	Enhancements to 802.11a to conform to Japanese radio emission regulations.
TGk (future 802.11k)	Task group to enhance communication between clients and network to better manage scarce radio use.
TGm	Task group to incorporate changes made by 802.11a, 802.11b, and 802.11d, as well as changes made by TGc into the main 802.11 specification. (Think "m" for maintenance.)
TGn (future 802.11n)	Task group founded to create a high-throughput standard. The design goal is throughput in excess of 100 Mbps, and the resulting standard will be called 802.11n.
TGp (future 802.11p)	Task group adopting 802.11 for use in automobiles. The initial use is likely to be a standard protocol used to collect tolls.
TGr (future 802.11r)	Enhancements to roaming performance.
TGs (future 802.11s)	Task group enhancing 802.11 for use as mesh networking technology.
TGT (future 802.11T)	Task group designing test and measurement specification for 802.11. Its result will be standalone, hence the uppercase letter.
TGu (future 802.11u)	Task group modifying 802.11 to assist in interworking with other network technologies.

When it became clear that authentication on wireless networks was fundamentally broken, the IEEE adopted several authentication standards originally developed by the *Internet Engineering Task Force* (IETF). Wireless LAN authentication depends heavily on protocols defined by the IETF.

The *Wi-Fi Alliance* is a combination of a trade association, testing organization, and standardization organization. Most of the Wi-Fi Alliance's emphasis is on acting as a trade association for its members, though it also well-known for the *Wi-Fi* certification program. Products are tested for interoperability with a testbed consisting of products from major vendors, and products that pass the test suite are awarded the right to use the Wi-Fi mark.

The Wi-Fi Alliance's standardization efforts are done in support of the IEEE. When the security of wireless networks was called into question, the Wi-Fi Alliance produced an interim security specification called *Wi-Fi Protected Access* (WPA). WPA was essentially a snapshot of the work done by the IEEE security task group. It is more of a marketing standard than a technical standard, since the technology was developed by the IEEE. However, it serves a role in accelerating the development of secure wireless LAN solutions.

CHAPTER 2
Overview of 802.11 Networks

Before studying the details of anything, it often helps to get a general "lay of the land."
A basic introduction is often necessary when studying networking topics because the
number of acronyms can be overwhelming. Unfortunately, 802.11 takes acronyms to
new heights, which makes the introduction that much more important. To understand 802.11 on anything more than a superficial basis, you must get comfortable with
some esoteric terminology and a herd of three-letter acronyms. This chapter is the glue
that binds the entire book together. Read it for a basic understanding of 802.11, the
concepts that will likely be important to users, and how the protocol is designed to
provide an experience as much like Ethernet as possible. After that, move on to the
low-level protocol details or deployment, depending on your interests and needs.

Part of the reason this introduction is important is because it introduces the acronyms
used throughout the book. With 802.11, the introduction serves another important
purpose. 802.11 is superficially similar to Ethernet. Understanding the background of
Ethernet helps slightly with 802.11, but there is a host of additional background
needed to appreciate how 802.11 adapts traditional Ethernet technology to a wireless
world. To account for the differences between wired networks and the wireless media
used by 802.11, a number of additional management features were added. At the heart
of 802.11 is a white lie about the meaning of media access control (MAC). Wireless
network interface cards are assigned 48-bit MAC addresses, and, for all practical purposes, they look like Ethernet network interface cards. In fact, the MAC address
assignment is done from the same address pool so that 802.11 cards have unique
addresses even when deployed into a network with wired Ethernet stations.

To outside network devices, these MAC addresses appear to be fixed, just as in other
IEEE 802 networks; 802.11 MAC addresses go into ARP tables alongside Ethernet
addresses, use the same set of vendor prefixes, and are otherwise indistinguishable
from Ethernet addresses. The devices that comprise an 802.11 network (access points
and other 802.11 devices) know better. There are many differences between an 802.11
device and an Ethernet device, but the most obvious is that 802.11 devices are mobile;

they can easily move from one part of the network to another. The 802.11 devices on your network understand this and deliver frames to the current location of the mobile station.

IEEE 802 Network Technology Family Tree

802.11 is a member of the IEEE 802 family, which is a series of specifications for local area network (LAN) technologies. Figure 2-1 shows the relationship between the various components of the 802 family and their place in the OSI model.

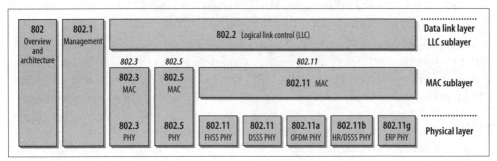

Figure 2-1. The IEEE 802 family and its relation to the OSI model

IEEE 802 specifications are focused on the two lowest layers of the OSI model because they incorporate both physical and data link components. All 802 networks have both a MAC and a Physical (PHY) component. The MAC is a set of rules to determine how to access the medium and send data, but the details of transmission and reception are left to the PHY.

Individual specifications in the 802 series are identified by a second number. For example, 802.3 is the specification for a Carrier Sense Multiple Access network with Collision Detection (CSMA/CD), which is related to (and often mistakenly called) Ethernet, and 802.5 is the Token Ring specification. Other specifications describe other parts of the 802 protocol stack. 802.2 specifies a common link layer, the Logical Link Control (LLC), which can be used by any lower-layer LAN technology. Management features for 802 networks are specified in 802.1. Among 802.1's many provisions are bridging (802.1D) and virtual LANs, or VLANs (802.1Q).

802.11 is just another link layer that can use the 802.2/LLC encapsulation. The base 802.11 specification includes the 802.11 MAC and two physical layers: a frequency-hopping spread-spectrum (FHSS) physical layer and a direct-sequence spread-spectrum (DSSS) link layer. Later revisions to 802.11 added additional physical layers. 802.11b specifies a high-rate direct-sequence layer (HR/DSSS); products based on 802.11b hit the marketplace in 1999 and was the first mass-market PHY. 802.11a describes a physical layer based on orthogonal frequency division multiplexing

(OFDM); products based on 802.11a were released as the first edition of this book was completed. 802.11g is the newest physical layer on the block. It offers higher speed through the use of OFDM, but with backwards compatibility with 802.11b. Backwards compatibility is not without a price, though. When 802.11b and 802.11g users coexist on the same access point, additional protocol overhead is required, reducing the maximum speed for 802.11g users.

To say that 802.11 is "just another link layer for 802.2" is to omit the details in the rest of this book, but 802.11 is exciting precisely because of these details. 802.11 allows for mobile network access; in accomplishing this goal, a number of additional features were incorporated into the MAC. As a result, the 802.11 MAC may seem baroquely complex compared to other IEEE 802 MAC specifications.

The use of radio waves as a physical layer requires a relatively complex PHY, as well. 802.11 splits the PHY into two generic PMcomponents: the Physical Layer Convergence Procedure (PLCP), to map the MAC frames onto the medium, and a Physical Medium Dependent (PMD) system to transmit those frames. The PLCP straddles the boundary of the MAC and physical layers, as shown in Figure 2-2. In 802.11, the PLCP adds a number of fields to the frame as it is transmitted "in the air."

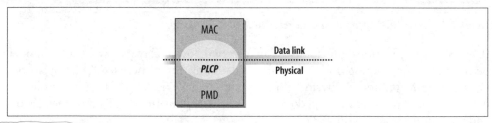

Figure 2-2. PHY components

All this complexity begs the question of how much you actually need to know. As with any technology, the more you know, the better off you will be. The 802.11 protocols have many knobs and dials that you can tweak, but most 802.11 implementations hide this complexity. Many of the features of the standard come into their own only when the network is congested, either with a lot of traffic or with a large number of wireless stations. Networks are increasingly pushing the limits in both respects. At any rate, I can't blame you for wanting to skip the chapters about the protocols and jump ahead to the chapters about planning and installing an 802.11 network. After you've read this chapter, you can skip ahead to Chapters 17–23 and return to the chapters on the protocol's inner workings when you need (or want) to know more.

802.11 Nomenclature and Design

802.11 networks consist of four major physical components, which are summarized in Figure 2-3.

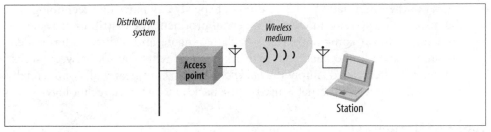

Figure 2-3. Components of 802.11 LANs

The components are:

Stations

Networks are built to transfer data between *stations*. Stations are computing devices with wireless network interfaces. Typically, stations are battery-operated laptop or handheld computers. There is no reason why stations must be portable computing devices, though. In some environments, wireless networking is used to avoid pulling new cable, and desktops are connected by wireless LANs. Large open areas may also benefit from wireless networking, such as a manufacturing floor using a wireless LAN to connect components. 802.11 is fast becoming a *de facto* standard for linking together consumer electronics. Apple's AirPort Express connects computers to stereos via 802.11. TiVos can connect to wireless networks. Several consumer electronics companies have joined the 802.11 working group, apparently with the intent of enabling high-speed media transfers over 802.11.

Access points

Frames on an 802.11 network must be converted to another type of frame for delivery to the rest of the world. Devices called *access points* perform the wireless-to-wired bridging function. (Access points perform a number of other functions, but bridging is by far the most important.) Initially, access point functions were put into standalone devices, though several newer products are dividing the 802.11 protocol between "thin" access points and AP controllers.

Wireless medium

To move frames from station to station, the standard uses a wireless medium. Several different physical layers are defined; the architecture allows multiple physical layers to be developed to support the 802.11 MAC. Initially, two radio frequency (RF) physical layers and one infrared physical layer were standardized, though the RF layers have proven far more popular. Several additional RF layers have been standardized as well.

Distribution system

When several access points are connected to form a large coverage area, they must communicate with each other to track the movements of mobile stations. The distribution system is the logical component of 802.11 used to forward frames to their destination. 802.11 does not specify any particular technology for the distribution system. In most commercial products, the distribution system is implemented as a combination of a bridging engine and a distribution system medium, which is the backbone network used to relay frames between access points; it is often called simply the *backbone network*. In nearly all commercially successful products, Ethernet is used as the backbone network technology.

Types of Networks

The basic building block of an 802.11 network is the *basic service set* (BSS), which is simply a group of stations that communicate with each other. Communications take place within a somewhat fuzzy area, called the *basic service area*, defined by the propagation characteristics of the wireless medium.* When a station is in the basic service area, it can communicate with the other members of the BSS. BSSs come in two flavors, both of which are illustrated in Figure 2-4.

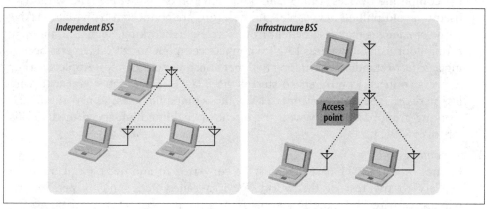

Figure 2-4. Independent and infrastructure BSSs

Independent networks

On the left is an independent BSS (IBSS). Stations in an IBSS communicate directly with each other and thus must be within direct communication range. The smallest possible 802.11 network is an IBSS with two stations. Typically, IBSSs are composed of a small number of stations set up for a specific purpose and for a short period of time. One common use is to create a short-lived network to support a single meeting in a conference room. As the meeting begins, the participants create an IBSS to share data. When the meeting ends, the IBSS is dissolved.† Due to their short duration, small size, and focused purpose, IBSSs are sometimes referred to as *ad hoc BSSs* or *ad hoc networks*.

---

* All of the wireless media used will propagate in three dimensions. From that perspective, the service area should perhaps be called the service *volume*. However, the term area is widely used and accepted.

† IBSSs have found a similar use at LAN parties throughout the world.

Infrastructure networks

On the right side of Figure 2-4 is an *infrastructure BSS*. (To avoid overloading the acronym, an infrastructure BSS is never called an IBSS). Infrastructure networks are distinguished by the use of an access point. Access points are used for all communications in infrastructure networks, including communication between mobile nodes in the same service area. If one mobile station in an infrastructure BSS needs to communicate with a second mobile station, the communication must take two hops. First, the originating mobile station transfers the frame to the access point. Second, the access point transfers the frame to the destination station. With all communications relayed through an access point, the basic service area corresponding to an infrastructure BSS is defined by the points in which transmissions from the access point can be received. Although the multihop transmission takes more transmission capacity than a directed frame from the sender to the receiver, it has two major advantages:

- An infrastructure BSS is defined by the distance from the access point. All mobile stations are required to be within reach of the access point, but no restriction is placed on the distance between mobile stations themselves. Allowing direct communication between mobile stations would save transmission capacity but at the cost of increased physical layer complexity because mobile stations would need to maintain neighbor relationships with all other mobile stations within the service area.

- Access points in infrastructure networks are in a position to assist with stations attempting to save power. Access points can note when a station enters a power-saving mode and buffer frames for it. Battery-operated stations can turn the wireless transceiver off and power it up only to transmit and retrieve buffered frames from the access point.

In an infrastructure network, stations must *associate* with an access point to obtain network services. Association is the process by which mobile station joins an 802.11 network; it is logically equivalent to plugging in the network cable on an Ethernet. It is not a symmetric process. Mobile stations always initiate the association process, and access points may choose to grant or deny access based on the contents of an association request. Associations are also exclusive on the part of the mobile station: a mobile station can be associated with only one access point.* The 802.11 standard places no limit on the number of mobile stations that an access point may serve. Implementation considerations may, of course, limit the number of mobile stations an access point may serve. In practice, however, the relatively low throughput of wireless networks is far more likely to limit the number of stations placed on a wireless network.

---

* One reviewer noted that a similar restriction was present in traditional Ethernet networks until the development of VLANs and specifically asked how long this restriction was likely to last. I am not intimately involved with the standardization work, so I cannot speak to the issue directly. I do, however, agree that it is an interesting question.

Extended service areas

BSSs can create coverage in small offices and homes, but they cannot provide network coverage to larger areas. 802.11 allows wireless networks of arbitrarily large size to be created by linking BSSs into an *extended service set* (ESS). An ESS is created by chaining BSSs together with a backbone network. All the access points in an ESS are given the same *service set identifier* (SSID), which serves as a network "name" for the users.

802.11 does not specify a particular backbone technology; it requires only that the backbone provide a specified set of services. In Figure 2-5, the ESS is the union of the four BSSs (provided that all the access points are configured to be part of the same ESS). In real-world deployments, the degree of overlap between the BSSs would probably be much greater than the overlap in Figure 2-5. In real life, you would want to offer continuous coverage within the extended service area; you wouldn't want to require that users walk through the area covered by BSS3 when en route from BSS1 to BSS2.

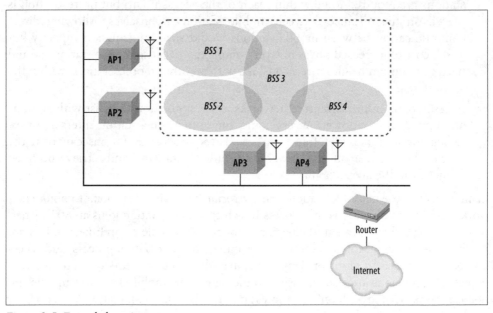

Figure 2-5. Extended service set

Stations within the same ESS may communicate with each other, even though these stations may be in different basic service areas and may even be moving between basic service areas. For stations in an ESS to communicate with each other, the wireless medium must act like a single layer 2 connection. Access points act as bridges, so direct communication between stations in an ESS requires that the backbone network also look like a layer 2 connection. First-generation access points required direct layer 2 connections through hubs or virtual LANs; newer products implement a variety of tunneling technologies to emulate the layer 2 environment.

802.11 supplies link-layer mobility within an ESS, but only if the back-bone network appears to be a single link-layer domain. This important constraint on mobility is often a major factor in the way that wireless LANs are deployed, and one of the major ways that vendors differentiate their products.

Early access points required that the backbone network be a single hub or VLAN, but newer products can interface directly with the backbone. Many can support multiple VLANs simultaneously with 802.1Q tags, and some can even dynamically instantiate VLANs based on authentication information.

Extended service areas are the highest-level abstraction supported by 802.11 networks. Access points in an ESS operate in concert to allow the outside world to use the station's MAC address to talk to a station no matter what its location is within the ESS. In Figure 2-5, the router uses the station's MAC address as the destination to deliver frames to a mobile station; only the access point with which that mobile station is associated delivers the frame. The router remains ignorant of the location of the mobile station and relies on the access points to deliver the frame.

Multi-BSS environments: "virtual APs"

Early 802.11 radio chips had the ability to create a single basic service set. An AP could have connect users to only one "wireless network," and all users on that network had similar, if not identical, privileges. In early deployments with limited user counts, a single logical network was sufficient. As wireless networking grew in popularity, one network no longer sufficed.

As an example, most organizations get regular visitors, many of whom have 802.11 equipment and need (or strongly desire) Internet access. Guests are not trusted users. One common way of coping with guest access is to create two extended service sets on the same physical infrastructure. Current 802.11 chipsets can create multiple networks with the same radio. Using modern chipsets, each access point hardware device can create two BSSs, one for the network named *guest*, and one for the network named *internal*. Within the AP, each SSIDs is associated with a VLAN. The guest network is connected to a VLAN prepared for public access by unknown and untrusted users, and is almost certainly attached outside the firewall.

Wireless devices see two separate networks in the radio domain, and can connect to whatever one suits their needs. (Naturally, the internal network is probably protected by authentication prevent unauthorized use.) Users who connect to the wireless network named *guest* will be placed on the guest VLAN, while users who connect to the wireless network named *internal* will be authenticated and placed on the internal network.

This somewhat contrived example illustrates the development of what many call *virtual access points*. Each BSS acts like its own self-contained AP, with its own ESSID,

MAC address, authentication configuration, and encryption settings. Virtual APs are also used to create parallel networks with different security levels, a configuration that will be discussed in Chapter 22. Current 802.11 radio chipsets have the ability to create 32 or even 64 BSSes, which is adequate for nearly every configuration.

Robust security networks (RSNs)

Early wireless LANs proved to have feeble built-in security. 802.11i, which was ratified in June 2004, specifies a set of improved security mechanisms that provide *robust security network associations* (RSNAs). Robust security network associations are formed when improved the authentication and confidentiality protocols defined in 802.11i are in use. Support for 802.11i may be composed of hardware, software, or both, depending on the exact architecture of a particular device. Hardware which does not support the improved protocols is referred to as *pre-RSN capable*. Many recent pre-RSN capable devices may be upgradeable to support 802.11i, but most older devices will not be upgradeable.

The Distribution System, Revisited

With an understanding of how an extended service set is built, I'd like to return to the concept of the distribution system. 802.11 describes the distribution system in terms of the services it provides to wireless stations. While these services will be described in more detail later in this chapter, it is worth describing their operation at a high level. The distribution system provides mobility by connecting access points. When a frame is given to the distribution system, it is delivered to the right access point and relayed by that access point to the intended destination.

The distribution system is responsible for tracking where a station is physically located and delivering frames appropriately. When a frame is sent to a mobile station, the distribution system is charged with the task of delivering it to the access point serving the mobile station. As an example, consider the router in Figure 2-5. The router simply uses the MAC address of a mobile station as its destination. The distribution system of the ESS pictured in Figure 2-5 must deliver the frame to the right access point. Obviously, part of the delivery mechanism is the backbone Ethernet, but the backbone network cannot be the entire distribution system because it has no way of choosing between access points. In the language of 802.11, the backbone Ethernet is the *distribution system medium*, but it is not the entire distribution system.

To find the rest of the distribution system, we need to look to the access points themselves. Most access points currently on the market operate as bridges. They have at least one wireless network interface and at least one Ethernet network interface. The Ethernet side can be connected to an existing network, and the wireless side becomes an extension of that network. Relaying frames between the two network media is controlled by a bridging engine.

Figure 2-6 illustrates the relationship between the access point, the backbone network, and the distribution system. The access point has two interfaces connected by a bridging engine. Arrows indicate the potential paths to and from the bridging engine. Frames may be sent by the bridge to the wireless network; any frames sent by the bridge's wireless port are transmitted to all associated stations. Each associated station can transmit frames to the access point. Finally, the backbone port on the bridge can interact directly with the backbone network. The distribution system in Figure 2-6 is composed of the bridging engine plus the wired backbone network.

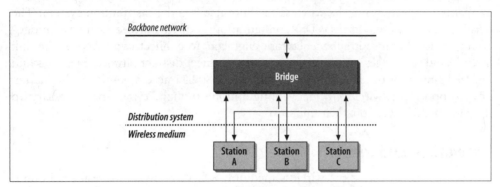

Figure 2-6. Distribution system in common 802.11 access point implementations

Every frame sent by a mobile station in an infrastructure network must use the distribution system. It is easy to understand why interaction with hosts on the backbone network must use the distribution system. After all, they are connected to the distribution system medium. Wireless stations in an infrastructure network depend on the distribution system to communicate with each other because they are not directly connected to each other. The only way for station A to send a frame to station B is by relaying the frame through the bridging engine in the access point. However, the bridge is a component of the distribution system. While what exactly makes up the distribution system may seem like a narrow technical concern, there are some features of the 802.11 MAC that are closely tied to its interaction with the distribution system.

Interaccess point communication as part of the distribution system

Included with this distribution system is a method to manage associations. A wireless station is associated with only one access point at a time. If a station is associated with one access point, all the other access points in the ESS need to learn about that station. In Figure 2-5, AP4 must know about all the stations associated with AP1. If a wireless station associated with AP4 sends a frame to a station associated with AP1, the bridging engine inside AP4 must send the frame over the backbone Ethernet to AP1 so it can be delivered to its ultimate destination. To fully implement the distribution system, access points must inform other access points of associated stations. Naturally, many access points on the market use an interaccess point protocol (IAPP) over the backbone medium. Many vendors developed proprietary protocols between access points to carry association data. A standard IAPP was produced as 802.11F, but I am not aware of its use in any products.

Wireless bridges and the distribution system

Up to this point, I have tacitly assumed that the distribution system medium was an existing fixed network. While this will often be the case, the 802.11 specification explicitly supports using the wireless medium itself as the distribution system. The *wireless distribution system* (WDS) configuration is often called a "wireless bridge" configuration because it allows network engineers to connect two LANs at the link layer. Wireless bridges can be used to quickly connect distinct physical locations and are well-suited for use by access providers. Most 802.11 access points on the market now support the wireless bridge configuration, though it may be necessary to upgrade the firmware on older units.

Network Boundaries

Because of the nature of the wireless medium, 802.11 networks have fuzzy boundaries. In fact, some degree of fuzziness is desirable. As with mobile telephone networks, allowing basic service areas to overlap increases the probability of successful transitions between basic service areas and offers the highest level of network coverage. The basic service areas on the right of Figure 2-7 overlap significantly. This means that a station moving from BSS2 to BSS4 is not likely to lose coverage; it also means that AP3 (or, for that matter, AP4) can fail without compromising the network too badly. On the other hand, if AP2 fails, the network is cut into two disjoint parts, and stations in BSS1 lose connectivity when moving out of BSS1 and into BSS3 or BSS4. Coping with "coverage holes" from access point failures is a task that requires attention during the network design phase; many newer products offer dynamic radio tuning capabilities to automatically fill in holes that develop during network operation.

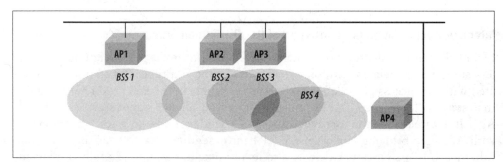

Figure 2-7. Overlapping BSSs in an ESS

Different types of 802.11 networks may also overlap. Independent BSSs may be created within the basic service area of an access point. Figure 2-8 illustrates spatial overlap. An access point appears at the top of the figure; its basic service area is shaded. Two stations are operating in infrastructure mode and communicate only with the access point. Three stations have been set up as an independent BSS and communicate with each other. Although the five stations are assigned to two different BSSs, they may share the same wireless medium. Stations may obtain access to the medium only by using the rules specified in the 802.11 MAC; these rules were carefully designed to enable multiple 802.11 networks to coexist in the same spatial area. Both BSSs must share the capacity of a single radio channel, so there may be adverse performance implications from co-located BSSs.

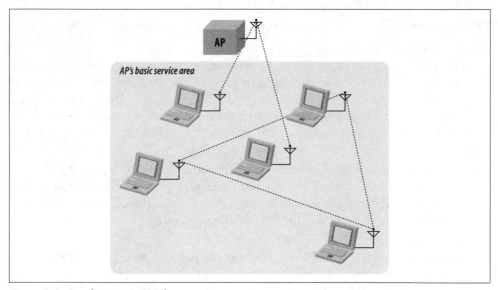

Figure 2-8. Overlapping network types

802.11 Network Operations

From the outset, 802.11 was designed to be just another link layer to higher-layer protocols. Network administrators familiar with Ethernet will be immediately comfortable with 802.11. The shared heritage is deep enough that 802.11 is sometimes referred to as "wireless Ethernet."

The core elements present in Ethernet are present in 802.11. Stations are identified by 48-bit IEEE 802 MAC addresses. Conceptually, frames are delivered based on the MAC address. Frame delivery is unreliable, though 802.11 incorporates some basic reliability mechanisms to overcome the inherently poor qualities of the radio channels it uses.[*]

---

[*] I don't mean "poor" in an absolute sense. But the reliability of wireless transmission is really not comparable to the reliability of a wired network.

From a user's perspective, 802.11 might just as well be Ethernet. Network administrators, however, need to be conversant with 802.11 at a much deeper level. Providing MAC-layer mobility while following the path blazed by previous 802 standards requires a number of additional services and more complex framing.

Network Services

One way to define a network technology is to define the services it offers and allow equipment vendors to implement those services in whatever way they see fit. 802.11 provides nine services. Only three of the services are used for moving data; the remaining six are management operations that allow the network to keep track of the mobile nodes and deliver frames accordingly.

The services are described in the following list and summarized in Table 2-1:

Distribution

> This service is used by mobile stations in an infrastructure network every time they send data. Once a frame has been accepted by an access point, it uses the distribution service to deliver the frame to its destination. Any communication that uses an access point travels through the distribution service, including communications between two mobile stations associated with the same access point.

Integration

> Integration is a service provided by the distribution system; it allows the connection of the distribution system to a non-IEEE 802.11 network. The integration function is specific to the distribution system used and therefore is not specified by 802.11, except in terms of the services it must offer.

Association

> Delivery of frames to mobile stations is made possible because mobile stations register, or associate, with access points. The distribution system can then use the registration information to determine which access point to use for any mobile station. Unassociated stations are not "on the network," much like workstations with unplugged Ethernet cables. 802.11 specifies the function that must be provided by the distribution system using the association data, but it does not mandate any particular implementation. When robust security network protocols are in use, association is a precursor to authentication. Prior to the completion of authentication, an access point will drop all network protocol traffic from a station.

Reassociation

> When a mobile station moves between basic service areas within a single extended service area, it must evaluate signal strength and perhaps switch the access point with which it is associated. Reassociations are initiated by mobile stations when signal conditions indicate that a different association would be beneficial; they are never initiated directly by the access point. (Some APs will

kick stations off in order to force a client into being the reassociation process; in the future, reassociation may be more dependent on the infrastructure with the development of better network management standards.)

After the reassociation is complete, the distribution system updates its location records to reflect the reachability of the mobile station through a different access point. As with the association service, a robust security network will drop network protocol traffic before the successful completion of authentication.

Disassociation

To terminate an existing association, stations may use the disassociation service. When stations invoke the disassociation service, any mobility data stored in the distribution system is removed. Once disassociation is complete, it is as if the station is no longer attached to the network. Disassociation is a polite task to do during the station shutdown process. The MAC is, however, designed to accommodate stations that leave the network without formally disassociating.

Authentication

Physical security is a major component of a wired LAN security solution. Network attachment points are limited, often to areas in offices behind perimeter access control devices. Network equipment can be secured in locked wiring closets, and data jacks in offices and cubicles can be connected to the network only when needed. Wireless networks cannot offer the same level of physical security, however, and therefore must depend on additional authentication routines to ensure that users accessing the network are authorized to do so. Authentication is a necessary prerequisite to association because only authenticated users are authorized to use the network.

Authentication may happen multiple times during the connection of a client to a wireless network. Prior to association, a station will perform a basic identity exchange with an access point consisting of its MAC address. This exchange is often referred to as "802.11" authentication, which is distinct from the robust cryptographic user authentication that often follows.

Deauthentication

Deauthentication terminates an authenticated relationship. Because authentication is needed before network use is authorized, a side effect of deauthentication is termination of any current association. In a robust security network, deauthentication also clears keying information.

Confidentiality

Strong physical controls can prevent a great number of attacks on the privacy of data in a wired LAN. Attackers must obtain physical access to the network medium before attempting to eavesdrop on traffic. On a wired network, physical access to the network cabling is a subset of physical access to other computing resources. By design, physical access to wireless networks is a comparatively simpler matter of using the correct antenna and modulation methods.

In the initial revision of 802.11, the confidentiality service was called *privacy*, and provided by the now-discredited Wired Equivalent Privacy (WEP) protocol. In addition to new encryption schemes, 802.11i augments the confidentiality service by providing user-based authentication and key management services, two critical issues that WEP failed to address.

MSDU delivery

Networks are not much use without the ability to get the data to the recipient. Stations provide the MAC Service Data Unit (MSDU) delivery service, which is responsible for getting the data to the actual endpoint.

Transmit Power Control (TPC)

TPC is a new service that was defined by 802.11h. European standards for the 5 GHz band require that stations control the power of radio transmissions to avoid interfering with other users of the 5 GHz band. Transmit power control also helps avoid interference with other wireless LANs. Range is a function of power; high transmit power settings make it more likely that a client's greater range will interfere with a neighboring network. By controlling power to a level that is "just right," it is less likely that a station will interfere with neighboring stations.

Dynamic Frequency Selection (DFS)

Some radar systems operate in the 5 GHz range. As a result, some regulatory authorities have mandated that wireless LANs must detect radar systems and move to frequencies that are not in use by radar. Some regulatory authorities also require uniform use of the 5 GHz band for wireless LANs, so networks must have the ability to re-map channels so that usage is equalized.

Table 2-1. Network services

Service	Station or distribution service?	Description
Distribution	Distribution	Service used in frame delivery to determine destination address in infrastructure networks
Integration	Distribution	Frame delivery to an IEEE 802 LAN outside the wireless network
Association	Distribution	Used to establish the AP which serves as the gateway to a particular mobile station
Reassociation	Distribution	Used to change the AP which serves as the gateway to a particular mobile station
Disassociation	Distribution	Removes the wireless station from the network
Authentication	Station	Establishes station identity (MAC address) prior to establishing association
Deauthentication	Station	Used to terminate authentication, and by extension, association
Confidentiality	Station	Provides protection against eavesdropping
MSDU delivery	Station	Delivers data to the recipient
Transmit Power Control (TPC)	Station/spectrum management	Reduces interference by minimizing station transmit power
Dynamic Frequency Selection (DFS)	Station/spectrum management	Avoids interfering with radar operation in the 5 GHz band

Station services

Station services are part of every 802.11-compliant station and must be incorporated by any product claiming 802.11 compliance. Station services are provided by both mobile stations and the wireless interface on access points. Stations provide frame delivery services to allow message delivery, and, in support of this task, they may need to use the authentication services to establish associations. Stations may also wish to take advantage of confidentiality functions to protect messages as they traverse the vulnerable wireless link.

Distribution system services

Distribution system services connect access points to the distribution system. The major role of access points is to extend the services on the wired network to the wireless network; this is done by providing the distribution and integration services to the wireless side. Managing mobile station associations is the other major role of the distribution system. To maintain association data and station location information, the distribution system provides the association, reassociation, and disassociation services.

Confidentiality and access control

Confidentiality and access control services are intertwined. In addition to secrecy of the data in transit, the confidentiality service also proves the integrity of frame contents. Both secrecy and integrity depend on shared cryptographic keying, so the confidentiality service necessarily depends on other services to provide authentication and key management.

Authentication and key management (AKM)
> Cryptographic integrity is worthless if it does not prevent unauthorized users from attaching to the network. The confidentiality service depends on the authentication and key management suite to establish user identity and encryption keys. Authentication may be accomplished through an external protocol, such as 802.1X, or with pre-shared keys.

Cryptographic algorithms
> Frames may be protected by the traditional WEP algorithm, using 40- or 104-bit secret keys, the Temporal Key Integrity Protocol (TKIP), or the Counter Mode CBC-MAC Protocol (CCMP). All of these algorithms are discussed in detail in Chapters 5 and 7.

Origin authenticity
> TKIP and CCMP allow the receiver to validate the sender's MAC address to prevent spoofing attacks. Origin authenticity protection is only available for unicast data.

Replay detection
> TKIP and CCMP protect against replay attacks by incorporating a sequence counter that is validated upon receipt. Frames which are "too old" to be valid are discarded.

External protocols and systems

The confidentiality service depends heavily on external protocols to run. Key management is provided by 802.1X, which together with EAP carries authentication data. 802.11 places no constraint on the protocols used, but the most common choices are EAP for authentication, and RADIUS to interface with the authentication server.

Spectrum management services

Spectrum management services are a special subset of station services. They are designed to allow the wireless network to react to conditions and change radio settings dynamically. Two services were defined in 802.11h to help meet regulatory requirements.

The first service, transmit power control (TPC), can dynamically adjust the transmission power of a station. Access points will be able to use the TPC operations to advertise the maximum permissible power, and reject associations from clients that do not comply with the local radio regulations. Clients can use TPC to adjust power so that range is "just right" to get to the access point. Digital cellular systems have a simliar feature designed to extend the battery life of mobile phones.* Lower transmit power also will have some benefit in the form of increased battery life, though the extent of the improvement will depend on how much the transmit power can be reduced from what the client would otherwise have used.

The second service, dynamic frequency selection (DFS), was developed mainly to avoid interfering with some 5 GHz radar systems in use in Europe. Although originally developed to satisfy European regulators, the underlying principles have been required by other regulators as well. DFS was key to the U.S. decision to open up more spectrum in the 5 GHz band in 2004.† DFS includes a way for the access point to quiet the channel so that it can search for radar without interference, but the most significant part of DFS is the way that it can reassign the channel on an access point on the fly. Clients are informed of the new channel just before the channel is switched.

Mobility Support

Mobility is the usually the primary motivation for deploying an 802.11 network. Transmitting data frames while the station is moving will do for data communications what mobile telephony did for voice.

---

* Power control also helps to simplify the electronics in the base station because all signals will be received at roughly the same signal.

† The decision was made in November 2003, and released as FCC 03-287. The text of the decision is available at *http://hraunfoss.fcc.gov/edocs_public/attachmatch/FCC-03-287A1.pdf*. Although the spectrum has been allocated, test procedures were still in development as of this writing, so no FCC-certified devices are yet able to use the new spectrum.

802.11 provides mobility between basic service areas at the link layer. However, it is not aware of anything that happens above the link layer. When designing deploying 802.11, networks engineers must take care so that the seamless transition at the radio layer is also supported at the network protocol layer that the station IP address can be preserved. As far as 802.11 is concerned, there are three types of transitions between access points:

No transition

> When stations do not move out of their current access point's service area, no transition is necessary. This state occurs because the station is not moving or it is moving within the basic service area of its current access point.* (Arguably, this isn't a transition so much as the absence of a transition, but it is defined in the specification.)

BSS transition

> Stations continuously monitor the signal strength and quality from all access points administratively assigned to cover an extended service area. Within an extended service area, 802.11 provides MAC layer mobility. Stations attached to the distribution system can send out frames addressed to the MAC address of a mobile station and let the access points handle the final hop to the mobile station. Distribution system stations do not need to be aware of a mobile station's location as long as it is within the same extended service area.

> Figure 2-9 illustrates a BSS transition. The three access points in the picture are all assigned to the same ESS. At the outset, denoted by *t=1*, the laptop with an 802.11 network card is sitting within AP1's basic service area and is associated with AP1. When the laptop moves out of AP1's basic service area and into AP2's at *t=2*, a BSS transition occurs. The mobile station uses the reassociation service to associate with AP2, which then starts sending frames to the mobile station.

> BSS transitions require the cooperation of access points. In this scenario, AP2 needs to inform AP1 that the mobile station is now associated with AP2. 802.11 does not specify the details of the communications between access points during BSS transitions.

> Note that even though two access points are members of the same extended set, they may nonetheless be connected by a router, which is a layer 3 boundary. In such a scenario, there is no way to guarantee seamless connectivity using 802.11 protocols only.

---

* Although my explanation makes it sound as if the "no motion" and "local motion" substates are easily distinguishable, they are not. The underlying physics of RF propagation can make it impossible to tell whether a station is moving because the signal strength can vary with the placement of objects in the room, which, of course, includes the people who may be walking around.

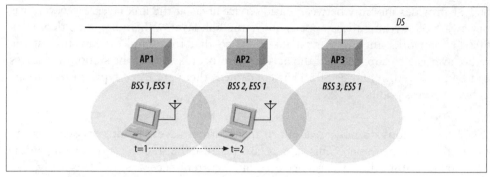

Figure 2-9. BSS transition

ESS transition

An ESS transition refers to the movement from one ESS to a second distinct ESS. 802.11 does not support this type of transition, except to allow the station to associate with an access point in the second ESS once it leaves the first. Higher-layer connections are almost guaranteed to be interrupted. It would be fair to say that 802.11 supports ESS transitions only to the extent that it is relatively easy to attempt associating with an access point in the new extended service area. Maintaining higher-level connections requires support from the protocol suites in question. In the case of TCP/ IP, Mobile IP is required to seamlessly support an ESS transition.

Figure 2-10 illustrates an ESS transition. Four basic service areas are organized into two extended service areas. Seamless transitions from the lefthand ESS to the righthand ESS are not supported. ESS transitions are supported only because the mobile station will quickly associate with an access point in the second ESS. Any active network connections are likely to be dropped when the mobile station leaves the first ESS.

Designing Networks for Mobility

Most networks are designed so that a group of access points provides access to a group of resources. All the access points under control of the networking organization are assigned to the same SSID, and clients are configured to use that SSID when connecting to the wireless network.

As client systems move around, they continuously monitor network connectivity, and shift between access points in the same SSID. 802.11 ensures that clients will be able to move associations between the access points in the same SSID, but network architects must build the network to support mobile clients. Small networks are often built on a single VLAN with a single subnet, in which case there is no need to worry about mobility. Larger networks that span subnet boundaries must apply some additional technology to provide mobility support. Many products can work

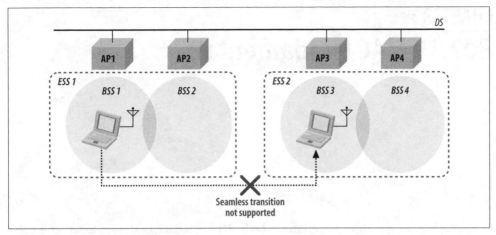

Figure 2-10. ESS transition

with a VLAN core, which allows clients to always attach to the same VLAN through-out an organization. New products even allow dynamic VLAN assignment based on authentication data. When users connect to the network, they are attached to the same VLAN everywhere; the switched network simply requires that the wireless LAN device tag frames appropriately. Some products support the Mobile IP stan-dard, or use VPN technology creatively. Trade-offs between all the different mobility strategies are discussed in Chapter 21.

In practice, ESS transitions are quite rare. They usually only occur when users leave one administrative domain for another (say, the corporate network for a hot spot), in which case the two networks in question would have different IP addresses and no trust relationship to transparently attach a client without interrupting network-layer connectivity.

Proprietary mobility systems

Many vendors, especially those who have designed products to build large-scale net-work environments, have designed their own protocols and procedures for mobility. When I started revising this book, one of the big problems with 802.11 was that it generally required a single IP subnet across an entire roaming area. As a result, wire-less LAN deployment often required substantial architecture work as well as major backbone re-engineering efforts. Several vendors rushed to fill the gap by implement-ing proprietary protocols that enabled sessions to move quickly between access points over arbitrary network topologies. Basic concepts for these solutions will be discussed in the deployment section of this book.

CHAPTER 3
802.11 MAC Fundamentals

This chapter begins our exploration of the 802.11 standard in depth. Chapter 2 provided a high-level overview of the standard and discussed some of its fundamental attributes. You are now at a fork in the book. Straight ahead lies a great deal of information on the 802.11 specification and the various related standards that it uses liberally. It is possible, however, to build a wired network without a thorough and detailed understanding of the protocols, and the same is true for wireless networks. However, there are a number of situations in which you may need a deeper knowledge of the machinery under the hood:

- Although 802.11 has been widely and rapidly adopted, security issues have continued to grab headlines. Network managers will undoubtedly be asked to comment on security issues, especially in any wireless LAN proposals. To understand and participate in these discussions, read Chapters 5 and 6. WEP with static keys should be considered fully broken. Solutions based on 802.1X and dynamic WEP keying are significantly stronger, with the full complement of protocols in 802.11i described in Chapter 7 stronger still.

- Troubleshooting wireless networks is similar to troubleshooting wired networks but can be much more complex. As always, a trusty packet sniffer can be an invaluable aid. To take full advantage of a packet sniffer, though, you need to understand what the packets mean to interpret your network's behavior.

- Tuning a wireless network is tied intimately to a number of parameters in the specification, as well as the behavior of the underlying radio technology. To understand the behavior of your network and what effect the optimizations will have requires a knowledge of what those parameters really do and how radio waves travel throughout your environment.

- Device drivers may expose low-level knobs and dials for you to play with. Most drivers provide good defaults for all of the parameters, but some give you freedom to experiment. Open source software users have the source code and are free to experiment with any and all settings.

- Wireless LAN technology is developing rapidly, and new protocol features are constantly being added. A solid understanding of the base protocol allows you to understand how new features will function and what they will mean for your network.

As with many other things in life, the more you know, the better off you are. Ethernet is usually trouble-free, but serious network administrators have long known that when you do run into trouble, there is no substitute for thorough knowledge of how the network is working. When the first edition of this book was out, wireless LANs had been given a "free ride." Because they were cool, users were forgiving when they failed; wireless connectivity was a privilege, not a right. And since there were relatively few networks and relatively few users on those networks, the networks were rarely subjected to severe stresses. An Ethernet that has only a half dozen nodes is not likely to be a source of problems; problems occur when you add a few high-capacity servers, a few hundred users, and the associated bridges and routers to glue everything together. As the typical 802.11 network grew up from an access point or two serving a dozen users into a much larger network designed to provide seamless coverage throughout a building, the stresses on the equipment and protocols has become much more apparent.

That is why you should read this chapter. Now on to the details. The key to the 802.11 specification is the MAC. It rides on every physical layer and controls the transmission of user data into the air. It provides the core framing operations and the interaction with a wired network backbone. Different physical layers may provide different transmission speeds, all of which are supposed to interoperate.

802.11 does not depart from the previous IEEE 802 standards in any radical way. The standard successfully adapts Ethernet-style networking to radio links. Like Ethernet, 802.11 uses a carrier sense multiple access (CSMA) scheme to control access to the transmission medium. However, collisions waste valuable transmission capacity, so rather than the collision detection (CSMA/CD) employed by Ethernet, 802.11 uses collision avoidance (CSMA/CA). Also like Ethernet, 802.11 uses a distributed access scheme with no centralized controller. Each 802.11 station uses the same method to gain access to the medium. The major differences between 802.11 and Ethernet stem from the differences in the underlying medium.

This chapter provides some insight into the motivations of the MAC designers by describing some challenges they needed to overcome and describes the rules used for access to the medium, as well as the basic frame structure. If you simply want to understand the basic frame sequences that you will see on an 802.11 network, skip ahead to the end of this chapter. For further information on the MAC, consult its formal specification in Clause 9 of the 802.11 standard; detailed MAC state diagrams are in Annex C.

Challenges for the MAC

Differences between the wireless network environment and the traditional wired environment create challenges for network protocol designers. This section examines a number of the hurdles that the 802.11 designers faced.

RF Link Quality

On a wired Ethernet, it is reasonable to transmit a frame and assume that the destination receives it correctly. Radio links are different, especially when the frequencies used are unlicensed ISM bands. Even narrowband transmissions are subject to noise and interference, but unlicensed devices must assume that interference will exist and work around it. The designers of 802.11 considered ways to work around the radiation from microwave ovens and other RF sources. In addition to the noise, multipath fading may also lead to situations in which frames cannot be transmitted because a node moves into a dead spot.

Unlike many other link layer protocols, 802.11 incorporates positive acknowledgments. All transmitted frames must be acknowledged, as shown in Figure 3-1. If any part of the transfer fails, the frame is considered lost.

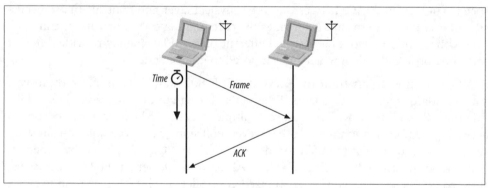

Figure 3-1. Positive acknowledgment of data transmissions

The sequence in Figure 3-1 is an *atomic* operation, which means it is a single transactional unit. Although there are multiple steps in the transaction, it is considered a single indivisible operation. Atomic operations are "all or nothing." Either every step in the sequence must complete successfully, or the entire operation is considered a failure. The sender of the data frame must receive an acknowledgment, or the frame is considered lost. It does not matter from the sender's perspective whether the initial data frame was lost in transit, or the corresponding acknowledgment was lost in transit. In either case, the data frame must be retransmitted.

One of the additional complexities of treating the frame transmission of Figure 3-1 as atomic is that the transaction occurs in two pieces, subject to control by two different stations. Both stations must work together to jointly take control of the network medium for transmissions during the entire transaction. 802.11 allows stations to lock out contention during atomic operations so that atomic sequences are not interrupted by other stations attempting to use the transmission medium.

Radio link quality also influences the speed at which a network can operate. Good quality signals can carry data at a higher speed. Signal quality degrades with range, which means that the data transmission speed of an 802.11 station depends on its location relative to the access point. Stations must implement a method for determining when to change the data rate in response to changing conditions. Furthermore, the complete collection of stations in a network must manage transmissions at multiple speeds. Rules for multirate support are discussed later in this chapter.

The Hidden Node Problem

In Ethernet networks, stations depend on the reception of transmissions to perform the carrier sensing functions of CSMA/CD. Wires in the physical medium contain the signals and distribute them to network nodes. Wireless networks have fuzzier boundaries, sometimes to the point where each node may not be able to directly communicate with every other node in the wireless network, as in Figure 3-2.

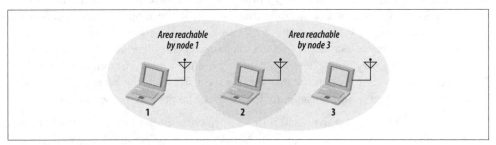

Figure 3-2. Nodes 1 and 3 are "hidden"

In the Figure 3-2, node 2 can communicate with both nodes 1 and 3, but something prevents nodes 1 and 3 from communicating directly. (The obstacle itself is not relevant; it could be as simple as nodes 1 and 3 being as far away from 2 as possible, so the radio waves cannot reach the full distance from 1 to 3.) From the perspective of node 1, node 3 is a "hidden" node. If a simple transmit-and-pray protocol was used, it would be easy for node 1 and node 3 to transmit simultaneously, thus rendering node 2 unable to make sense of anything. Furthermore, nodes 1 and 3 would not have any indication of the error because the collision was local to node 2.

Collisions resulting from hidden nodes may be hard to detect in wireless networks because wireless transceivers are generally *half-duplex*; they don't transmit and receive at the same time. To prevent collisions, 802.11 allows stations to use Request to Send (RTS) and Clear to Send (CTS) signals to clear out an area. Both the RTS and CTS frames extend the frame transaction, so that the RTS frame, CTS frame, the data frame, and the final acknowledgment are all considered part of the same atomic operation. Figure 3-3 illustrates the procedure.

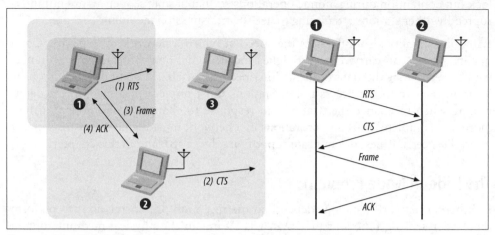

Figure 3-3. RTS/CTS clearing

In Figure 3-3, node 1 has a frame to send; it initiates the process by sending an RTS frame. The RTS frame serves several purposes: in addition to reserving the radio link for transmission, it silences any stations that hear it. If the target station receives an RTS, it responds with a CTS. Like the RTS frame, the CTS frame silences stations in the immediate vicinity. Once the RTS/CTS exchange is complete, node 1 can transmit its frames without worry of interference from any hidden nodes. Hidden nodes beyond the range of the sending station are silenced by the CTS from the receiver. When the RTS/CTS clearing procedure is used, any frames must be positively acknowledged.

The multiframe RTS/CTS transmission procedure consumes a fair amount of capacity, especially because of the additional latency incurred before transmission can commence. As a result, it is used only in high-capacity environments and environments with significant contention on transmission. For lower-capacity environments, it is not necessary.

Hidden nodes have also become less of a problem as 802.11 has grown up. In small, quiescent networks with only a few stations associated to an access point, there is very little risk of simultaneous transmission, and plenty of spare capacity to be used for retransmission. In many larger environments, the coverage is dense enough that the clients are located physically close enough to an access point that they are all within range of each other. (In fact, the range of many client systems is probably too large for most networks, which will be explored in the planning phase of this book.)

You can control the RTS/CTS procedure by setting the *RTS threshold* if the device driver for your 802.11 card allows you to adjust it. The RTS/CTS exchange is performed for frames larger than the threshold. Frames shorter than the threshold are simply sent.

MAC Access Modes and Timing

Access to the wireless medium is controlled by coordination functions. Ethernet-like CSMA/CA access is provided by the *distributed coordination function* (DCF). If contention-free service is required, it can be provided by the *point coordination function* (PCF), which is built on top of the DCF. Between the free-for-all of the DCF and the precision of the PCF, networks can use the *hybrid coordination function* (HCF), a middle ground for quality of service between the two extremes. Contention-free services are provided only in infrastructure networks, but quality of service may be provided in any network that has HCF support in the stations. The coordination functions are described in the following list and illustrated in Figure 3-4:

DCF

> The DCF is the basis of the standard CSMA/CA access mechanism. Like Ethernet, it first checks to see that the radio link is clear before transmitting. To avoid collisions, stations use a random backoff after each frame, with the first transmitter seizing the channel. In some circumstances, the DCF may use the CTS/RTS clearing technique to further reduce the possibility of collisions.

PCF

> The point coordination function provides contention-free services. Special stations called *point coordinators* are used to ensure that the medium is provided without contention. Point coordinators reside in access points, so the PCF is restricted to infrastructure networks. To gain priority over standard contention-based services, the PCF allows stations to transmit frames after a shorter interval. The PCF is not widely implemented and is described in Chapter 9.

HCF

> Some applications need to have service quality that is a step above best-effort delivery, but the rigorous timing of the PCF is not required. The HCF allows stations to maintain multiple service queues and balance access to the wireless medium in favor of applications that require better service quality. The HCF is not fully standardized yet, but is being produced as part of the eventual 802.11e specification.

Adding quality of service to the 802.11 MAC was a significant undertaking. Due to the added complexity in terms of framing, queue management, and signaling, the quality of service specifications were still subject to standards committee wrangling as this book was written, and discussion of them must be postponed to a future edition.

Carrier-Sensing Functions and the Network Allocation Vector

Carrier sensing is used to determine if the medium is available. Two types of carrier-sensing functions in 802.11 manage this process: the physical carrier-sensing and virtual carrier-sensing functions. If either carrier-sensing function indicates that the medium is busy, the MAC reports this to higher layers.

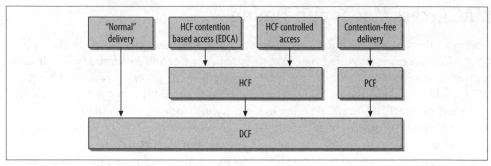

Figure 3-4. MAC coordination functions

Physical carrier-sensing functions are provided by the physical layer in question and depend on the medium and modulation used. It is difficult (or, more to the point, expensive) to build physical carrier-sensing hardware for RF-based media, because transceivers can transmit and receive simultaneously only if they incorporate expensive electronics. Furthermore, with hidden nodes potentially lurking everywhere, physical carrier-sensing cannot provide all the necessary information.

Virtual carrier-sensing is provided by the Network Allocation Vector (NAV). Most 802.11 frames carry a duration field, which can be used to reserve the medium for a fixed time period. The NAV is a timer that indicates the amount of time the medium will be reserved, in microseconds. Stations set the NAV to the time for which they expect to use the medium, including any frames necessary to complete the current operation. Other stations count down from the NAV to 0. When the NAV is non-zero, the virtual carrier-sensing function indicates that the medium is busy; when the NAV reaches 0, the virtual carrier-sensing function indicates that the medium is idle.

By using the NAV, stations can ensure that atomic operations are not interrupted. For example, the RTS/CTS sequence in Figure 3-3 is atomic. Figure 3-5 shows how the NAV protects the sequence from interruption. (This is a standard format for a number of diagrams in this book that illustrate the interaction of multiple stations with the corresponding timers.) Activity on the medium by stations is represented by the shaded bars, and each bar is labeled with the frame type. Interframe spacing is depicted by the lack of any activity. Finally, the NAV timer is represented by the bars on the NAV line at the bottom of the figure. The NAV is carried in the frame headers on the RTS and CTS frames; it is depicted on its own line to show how the NAV relates to actual transmissions in the air. When a NAV bar is present on the NAV line, stations should defer access to the medium because the virtual carrier-sensing mechanism will indicate a busy medium.

To ensure that the sequence is not interrupted, node 1 sets the NAV in its RTS to block access to the medium while the RTS is being transmitted. All stations that hear the RTS defer access to the medium until the NAV elapses.

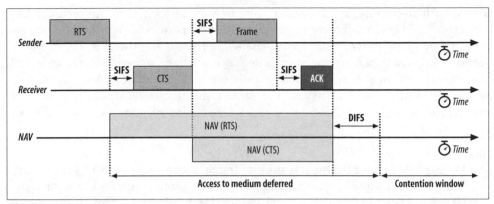

Figure 3-5. Using the NAV for virtual carrier sensing

RTS frames are not necessarily heard by every station in the network. Therefore, the recipient of the intended transmission responds with a CTS that includes a shorter NAV. This NAV prevents other stations from accessing the medium until the transmission completes. After the sequence completes, the medium can be used by any station after distributed interframe space (DIFS), which is depicted by the contention window beginning at the right side of the figure.

RTS/CTS exchanges may be useful in crowded areas with multiple overlapping networks. Every station on the same physical channel receives the NAV and defers access appropriately, even if the stations are configured to be on different networks.

Interframe Spacing

As with traditional Ethernet, the interframe spacing plays a large role in coordinating access to the transmission medium. 802.11 uses four different interframe spaces. Three are used to determine medium access; the relationship between them is shown in Figure 3-6.

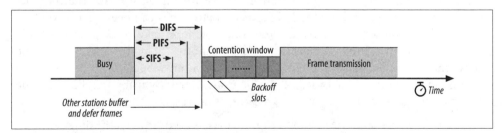

Figure 3-6. Interframe spacing relationships

We've already seen that as part of the collision avoidance built into the 802.11 MAC, stations delay transmission until the medium becomes idle. Varying interframe spacings create different priority levels for different types of traffic. The logic behind this is simple: high-priority traffic doesn't have to wait as long after the medium has become idle. Therefore, if there is any high-priority traffic waiting, it grabs the network before low-priority frames have a chance to try. To assist with interoperability between different data rates, the interframe space is a fixed amount of time, independent of the transmission speed. (This is only one of the many problems caused by having different physical layers use the same radio resources, which are different modulation techniques.) Different physical layers, however, can specify different interframe space times.

Short interframe space (SIFS)
> The SIFS is used for the highest-priority transmissions, such as RTS/CTS frames and positive acknowledgments. High-priority transmissions can begin once the SIFS has elapsed. Once these high-priority transmissions begin, the medium becomes busy, so frames transmitted after the SIFS has elapsed have priority over frames that can be transmitted only after longer intervals.

PCF interframe space (PIFS)
> The PIFS, sometimes erroneously called the priority interframe space, is used by the PCF during contention-free operation. Stations with data to transmit in the contention-free period can transmit after the PIFS has elapsed and preempt any contention-based traffic.

DCF interframe space (DIFS)
> The DIFS is the minimum medium idle time for contention-based services. Stations may have immediate access to the medium if it has been free for a period longer than the DIFS.

Extended interframe space (EIFS)
> The EIFS is not illustrated in Figure 3-6 because it is not a fixed interval. It is used only when there is an error in frame transmission.

Interframe spacing and priority

Atomic operations start like regular transmissions: they must wait for the the relevant interframe space, typically the DIFS, to end before they can begin. However, the second and any subsequent steps in an atomic operation take place after the SIFS, rather than after the DIFS. Because the SIFS is shorter than the other interframe spaces, the second (and subsequent) parts of an atomic operation will grab the medium before another type of frame can be transmitted. By using the SIFS and the NAV, stations can seize the medium for as long as necessary.

In Figure 3-5, for example, the short interframe space is used between the different units of the atomic exchange. After the sender gains access to the medium, the receiver replies with a CTS after the SIFS. Any stations that might attempt to access the medium at the conclusion of the RTS would wait for one DIFS interval. Partway through the DIFS interval, though, the SIFS interval elapses, and the CTS is transmitted.

Contention-Based Access Using the DCF

Most traffic uses the DCF, which provides a standard Ethernet-like contention-based service. The DCF allows multiple independent stations to interact without central control, and thus may be used in either IBSS networks or in infrastructure networks.

Before attempting to transmit, each station checks whether the medium is idle. If the medium is not idle, stations defer to each other and employ an orderly exponential backoff algorithm to avoid collisions.

In distilling the 802.11 MAC rules, there is a basic set of rules that are always used, and additional rules may be applied depending on the circumstances. Two basic rules apply to all transmissions using the DCF:

1. If the medium has been idle for longer than the DIFS, transmission can begin immediately. Carrier sensing is performed using both a physical medium-dependent method and the virtual (NAV) method.

   a. If the previous frame was received without errors, the medium must be free for at least the DIFS.

   b. If the previous transmission contained errors, the medium must be free for the amount of the EIFS.

2. If the medium is busy, the station must wait for the channel to become idle. 802.11 refers to the wait as *access deferral*. If access is deferred, the station waits for the medium to be idle for the DIFS and prepares for the exponential backoff procedure.

Additional rules may apply in certain situations. Many of these rules depend on the particular situation "on the wire" and are specific to the results of previous transmissions.

1. Error recovery is the responsibility of the station sending a frame. Senders expect acknowledgments for each transmitted frame and are responsible for retrying the transmission until it is successful.

   a. Positive acknowledgments are the only indication of success. Atomic exchanges must complete in their entirety to be successful. If an acknowledgment is expected and does not arrive, the sender considers the transmission lost and must retry.

   b. All unicast data must be acknowledged. Broadcast data is not acknowledged. (As a result, unicast data has an inherently higher service quality than broadcast data, even though the radio link is inherently a broadcast medium.)

   c. Any failure increments a retry counter, and the transmission is retried. A failure can be due to a failure to gain access to the medium or a lack of an acknowledgment. However, there is a longer congestion window when transmissions are retried (see next section).

2. Multiframe sequences may update the NAV with each step in the transmission procedure. When a station receives a medium reservation that is longer than the current NAV, it updates the NAV. Setting the NAV is done on a frame-by-frame basis and is discussed in much more detail in the next chapter.

3. The following types of frames can be transmitted after the SIFS and thus receive maximum priority: acknowledgments, the CTS in an RTS/CTS exchange sequence, and fragments in fragment sequences.

    a. Once a station has transmitted the first frame in a sequence, it has gained control of the channel. Any additional frames and their acknowledgments can be sent using the short interframe space, which locks out any other stations.

    b. Additional frames in the sequence update the NAV for the expected additional time the medium will be used.

4. Extended frame sequences are required for higher-level packets that are larger than configured thresholds.

    a. Packets larger than the RTS threshold must have RTS/CTS exchange.

    b. Packets larger than the fragmentation threshold must be fragmented.

Error Recovery with the DCF

Error detection and correction is up to the station that begins an atomic frame exchange. When an error is detected, the station with data must resend the frame. Errors must be detected by the sending station. In some cases, the sender can infer frame loss by the lack of a positive acknowledgment from the receiver. Retry counters are incremented when frames are retransmitted.

Each frame or fragment has a single retry counter associated with it. Stations have two retry counters: the *short retry count* and the *long retry count*. Frames that are shorter than the RTS threshold are considered to be short; frames longer than the threshold are long. Depending on the length of the frame, it is associated with either a short or long retry counter. Frame retry counts begin at 0 and are incremented when a frame transmission fails.

The short retry count is reset to 0 when:

- A CTS frame is received in response to a transmitted RTS
- A MAC-layer acknowledgment is received after a nonfragmented transmission
- A broadcast or multicast frame is received

The long retry count is reset to 0 when:

- A MAC-layer acknowledgment is received for a frame longer than the RTS threshold
- A broadcast or multicast frame is received

In addition to the associated retry count, fragments are given a maximum "lifetime" by the MAC. When the first fragment is transmitted, the lifetime counter is started. When the lifetime limit is reached, the frame is discarded and no attempt is made to transmit any remaining fragments. Naturally, higher-layer protocols may detect any loss and retransmit the data; when a higher-level protocol such as TCP retransmits data, though, it would be a new frame to the 802.11 MAC and all the retry counters will be restarted.

Using the retry counters

Like most other network protocols, 802.11 provides reliability through retransmission. Data transmission happens within the confines of an atomic sequence, and the entire sequence must complete for a transmission to be successful. When a station transmits a frame, it must receive an acknowledgment from the receiver or it will consider the transmission to have failed. Failed transmissions increment the retry counter associated with the frame (or fragment). If the retry limit is reached, the frame is discarded, and its loss is reported to higher-layer protocols.

One of the reasons for having short frames and long frames is to allow network administrators to customize the robustness of the network for different frame lengths. Large frames require more buffer space, so one potential application of having two separate retry limits is to decrease the long retry limit to decrease the amount of buffer space required.

Backoff with the DCF

After frame transmission has completed and the DIFS has elapsed, stations may attempt to transmit congestion-based data. A period called the *contention window* or *backoff window* follows the DIFS. This window is divided into slots. Slot length is medium-dependent; higher-speed physical layers use shorter slot times. Stations pick a random slot and wait for that slot before attempting to access the medium; all slots are equally likely selections. When several stations are attempting to transmit, the station that picks the first slot (the station with the lowest random number) wins. According to the standard, all slot numbers should be equally likely; see the sidebar on Spectralink Voice Priority later in this chapter for one notable exception.

As in Ethernet, the backoff time is selected from a larger range each time a transmission fails. Figure 3-7 illustrates the growth of the contention window as the number of transmissions increases, using the numbers from the 802.11b direct-sequence spread-spectrum (DSSS) physical layer. Other physical layers use different sizes, but the principle is identical. Contention window sizes are always 1 less than a power of 2 (e.g., 31, 63, 127, 255). Each time the retry counter increases, the contention window moves to the next greatest power of two. The size of the contention window is limited by the physical layer. For example, the DS physical layer limits the contention window to 1,023 transmission slots.

When the contention window reaches its maximum size, it remains there until it can be reset. Allowing long contention windows when several competing stations are attempting to gain access to the medium keeps the MAC algorithms stable even under maximum load. The contention window is reset to its minimum size when frames are transmitted successfully, or the associated retry counter is reached, and the frame is discarded.

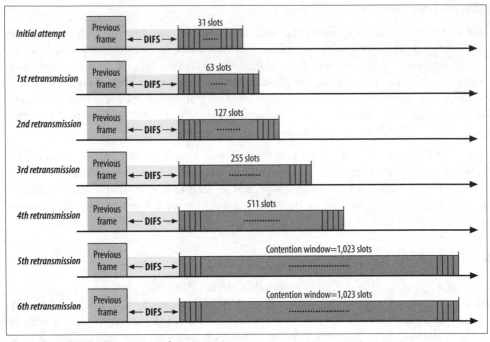

Figure 3-7. DSSS contention window size

Fragmentation and Reassembly

Higher-level packets and some large management frames may need to be broken into smaller pieces to fit through the wireless channel. Fragmentation may also help improve reliability in the presence of interference. Wireless LAN stations may attempt to fragment transmissions so that interference affects only small fragments, not large frames. By immediately reducing the amount of data that can be corrupted by interference, fragmentation may result in a higher effective throughput. Interference may come from a variety of sources. Some, but by no means all, microwave ovens cause interference with 2.4 GHz networks.* Electromagnetic radiation is generated by the magnetron tube during its ramp-up and ramp-down, so microwaves emit interference half the time. Many newer cordless phones also cause interference.†
Outdoor networks are subject to a much wider variety of interference.

Wireless LAN stations may attempt to fragment transmissions so that interference affects only small fragments, not large frames. By immediately reducing the amount

---

* In the U.S., appliances are powered by 60-Hz alternating current, so microwaves interfere for about 8 milliseconds (ms) out of every 16-ms cycle. Much of the rest of the world uses 50-Hz current, and interference takes place for 10 ms out of the 20-ms cycle.

† If you need to use a cordless phone in the same area as a wireless LAN, I suggest purchasing a 900 MHz cordless phone on eBay.

Spectralink Voice Priority

One of the challenges in supporting voice on wireless networks is that voice is far more sensitive to poor network service than data applications. If a 1,500 byte fragment of a graphics file is a tenth of a second late, the typical user will not even notice. If a delay of a tenth of a second is introduced into a phone conversation, though, it will be too much.

Providing high-quality service over an IP network is hard enough. Doing so over a wireless LAN is doubly challenging. One of the major problems that network engineers face in designing wireless LAN voice networks is that all data is treated equally. If there is a short voice frame and a long data frame, there is no inherent preference for one or the other.

Spectralink, a manufacturer of handheld 802.11 phones, has devised a special set of protocol extensions, called Spectralink Voice Priority (SVP), to assist in making the network more useful for voice transport. SVP consists of components implemented in both access points and in handsets to prioritze voice over data and coordinate several voice calls on a single AP. SVP assists with both the downlink from the AP and the uplink from handsets.

To support SVP, an access point must transmit voice frames with zero backoff. Rather than selecting a backoff slot number as required by the 802.11 standard, access points with SVP enabled will always choose zero. In the presence of contention for the wireless medium, the voice frames with zero backoff will have *de facto* priority boost because data frames are likely to have a positive backoff slot. Strictly speaking, stations implementing zero backoff are no longer compliant with 802.11 because it mandates selection of a backoff slot in accordance with defined rules. (To preserve stability under load, however, retransmitted voice frames are subject to the backoff rules.)

By selecting zero backoff, access points implementing SVP ensure that voice frames have preferential access to the air. Access points that implement SVP must also keep track of voice frames and provide preferential queuing treatment as well. SVP requires that voice frames be pushed to the head of the queue for transmission. APs implement transmit queues in many different ways; the important point is the functional result, which is that voice frames move to the head of the line. Some APs may move voice frames up to the head of a single transmit queue, while other APs may maintain multiple transmit queues and serve the high-priority voice queue first.

of data that can be corrupted by interference, fragmentation may result in a higher effective throughput. Fragmentation takes place when the length of a higher-level packet exceeds the fragmentation threshold configured by the network administrator. Fragments all have the same frame sequence number but have ascending fragment numbers to aid in reassembly. Frame control information also indicates whether more fragments are coming. All of the fragments that comprise a frame are normally sent in a *fragmentation burst*, which is shown in Figure 3-8. This figure also incorporates an RTS/CTS exchange, because it is common for the fragmentation and RTS/CTS thresholds to be set to the same value. The figure also shows how the NAV and SIFS are used in combination to control access to the medium.

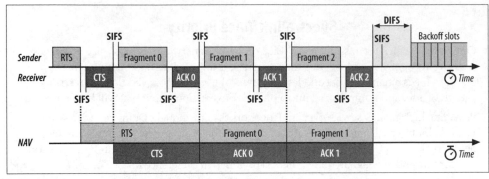

Figure 3-8. Fragmentation burst

Fragments and their acknowledgments are separated by the SIFS, so a station retains control of the channel during a fragmentation burst. The NAV is also used to ensure that other stations do not use the channel during the fragmentation burst. As with any RTS/CTS exchange, the RTS and CTS both set the NAV from the expected time to the end of the first fragments in the air. Subsequent fragments then form a chain. Each fragment sets the NAV to hold the medium until the end of the acknowledgment for the next frame. Fragment 0 sets the NAV to hold the medium until ACK 1, fragment 1 sets the NAV to hold the medium until ACK 2, and so on. After the last fragment and its acknowledgment have been sent, the NAV is set to 0, indicating that the medium will be released after the fragmentation burst completes.

Frame Format

To meet the challenges posed by a wireless data link, the MAC was forced to adopt several unique features, not the least of which was the use of four address fields. Not all frames use all the address fields, and the values assigned to the address fields may change depending on the type of MAC frame being transmitted. Details on the use of address fields in different frame types are presented in Chapter 4. Figure 3-9 shows the generic 802.11 MAC frame. All diagrams in this section follow the IEEE conventions in 802.11. Fields are transmitted from left to right.

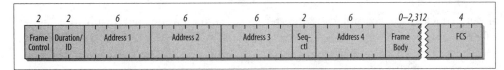

Figure 3-9. Generic 802.11 MAC frame

802.11 MAC frames do not include some of the classic Ethernet frame features, most notably the type/length field and the preamble. The preamble is part of the physical layer, and encapsulation details such as type and length are present in the header on the data carried in the 802.11 frame.

Frame Control

Each frame starts with a two-byte Frame Control subfield, shown in Figure 3-10. The components of the Frame Control subfield are:

Protocol version

Two bits indicate which version of the 802.11 MAC is contained in the rest of the frame. At present, only one version of the 802.11 MAC has been developed; it is assigned the protocol number 0. Other values will appear when the IEEE standardizes changes to the MAC that render it incompatible with the initial specification. So far, none of the revisions to 802.11 have required incrementing the protocol number.

Type and subtype fields

Type and subtype fields identify the type of frame used. To cope with noise and unreliability, a number of management functions are incorporated into the 802.11 MAC. Some, such as the RTS/CTS operations and the acknowledgments, have already been discussed. Table 3-1 shows how the type and subtype identifiers are used to create the different classes of frames.

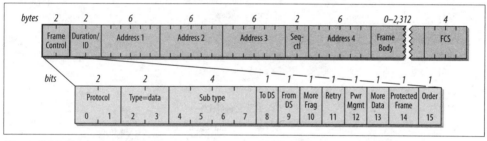

Figure 3-10. Frame control field

In Table 3-1, bit strings are written most-significant bit first, which is the reverse of the order used in Figure 3-10. Therefore, the frame type is the third bit in the frame control field followed by the second bit (b3 b2), and the subtype is the seventh bit, followed by the sixth, fifth, and fourth bits (b7 b6 b5 b4).

Table 3-1. Type and subtype identifiers

Subtype value	Subtype name
Management frames (type=00)[a]	
0000	Association request
0001	Association response
0010	Reassociation request
0011	Reassociation response
0100	Probe request
0101	Probe response

Table 3-1. Type and subtype identifiers (continued)

Subtype value	Subtype name
1000	Beacon
1001	Announcement traffic indication message (ATIM)
1010	Disassociation
1011	Authentication
1100	Deauthentication
1101	Action (for spectrum management with 802.11h, also for QoS)
Control frames (type=01)[b]	
1000	Block Acknowledgment Request (QoS)
1001	Block Acknowledgment (QoS)
1010	Power Save (PS)-Poll
1011	RTS
1100	CTS
1101	Acknowledgment (ACK)
1110	Contention-Free (CF)-End
1111	CF-End+CF-Ack
Data frames (type=10)	
0000	Data
0001	Data+CF-Ack
0010	Data+CF-Poll
0011	Data+CF-Ack+CF-Poll
0100	Null data (no data transmitted)
0101	CF-Ack (no data transmitted)
0110	CF-Poll (no data transmitted)
0111	CF-Ack+CF-Poll (no data transmitted)
1000	QoS Data [c]
1001	QoS Data + CF-Ack [c]
1010	QoS Data + CF-Poll [c]
1011	QoS Data + CF-Ack + CF-Poll[c]
1100	QoS Null (no data transmitted) [c]
1101	QoS CF-Ack (no data transmitted) [c]
1110	QoS CF-Poll (no data transmitted) [c]
1111	QoS CF-Ack+CF-Poll (no data transmitted) [c]
(Frame type 11 is reserved)	

[a] Management subtypes 0110–0111 and 1110–1111 are reserved and not currently used.

[b] Control subtypes 0000–0111 are reserved and not currently used.

[c] Proposed by the 802.11e task group, but not yet standardized. Note that these frames all have a leading one, which has caused some to refer to the first bit as the QoS bit.

ToDS and FromDS bits

These bits indicate whether a frame is destined for the distribution system. All frames on infrastructure networks will have one of the distribution system bits set. Table 3-2 shows how these bits are interpreted. As Chapter 4 will explain, the interpretation of the address fields depends on the setting of these bits.

Table 3-2. Interpreting the ToDS and FromDS bits

	To DS=0	To DS=1
From DS=0	All management and control frames Data frames within an IBSS (never infrastructure data frames)	Data frames transmitted from a wireless station in an infrastructure network.
From DS=1	Data frames received for a wireless station in an infrastructure network	Data frames on a "wireless bridge"

More fragments bit

This bit functions much like the "more fragments" bit in IP. When a higher-level packet has been fragmented by the MAC, the initial fragment and any following nonfinal fragments set this bit to 1. Large data frames and some management frames may be large enough to require fragmentation; all other frames set this bit to 0. In practice, most data frames are transmitted at the maximum Ethernet size and fragmentation is not often used.

Retry bit

From time to time, frames may be retransmitted. Any retransmitted frames set this bit to 1 to aid the receiving station in eliminating duplicate frames.

Power management bit

Network adapters built on 802.11 are often built to the PC Card form factor and used in battery-powered laptop or handheld computers. To conserve battery life, many small devices have the ability to power down parts of the network interface. This bit indicates whether the sender will be in a powersaving mode after the completion of the current atomic frame exchange. 1 indicates that the station will be in powersave mode, and 0 indicates that the station will be active. Access points perform a number of important management functions and are not allowed to save power, so this bit is always 0 in frames transmitted by an access point.

More data bit

To accommodate stations in a powersaving mode, access points may buffer frames received from the distribution system. An access point sets this bit to indicate that at least one frame is available and is addressed to a dozing station.

Protected Frame bit

Wireless transmissions are inherently easier to intercept than transmissions on a fixed network. If the frame is protected by link layer security protocols, this bit is set to 1, and the frame changes slightly. The Protected Frame bit was previously called the WEP bit.

Order bit

Frames and fragments can be transmitted in order at the cost of additional processing by both the sending and receiving MACs. When the "strict ordering" delivery is employed, this bit is set to 1.

Duration/ID Field

The Duration/ID field follows the frame control field. This field has several uses and takes one of the three forms shown in Figure 3-11.

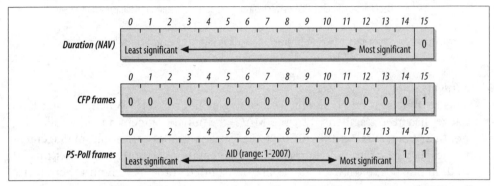

Figure 3-11. Duration/ID field

Duration: setting the NAV

When bit 15 is 0, the duration/ID field is used to set the NAV. The value represents the number of microseconds that the medium is expected to remain busy for the transmission currently in progress. All stations must monitor the headers of all frames they receive and update the NAV accordingly. Any value that extends the amount of time the medium is busy updates the NAV and blocks access to the medium for additional time.

Frames transmitted during contention-free periods

During the contention-free periods, bit 14 is 0 and bit 15 is 1. All other bits are 0, so the duration/ID field takes a value of 32,768. This value is interpreted as a NAV. It allows any stations that did not receive the Beacon* announcing the contention-free period to update the NAV with a suitably large value to avoid interfering with contention-free transmissions.

PS-Poll frames

Bits 14 and 15 are both set to 1 in PS-Poll frames. Mobile stations may elect to save battery power by turning off antennas. Dozing stations must wake up periodically. To

---

* Beacon frames are a subtype of management frames, which is why "Beacon" is capitalized.

ensure that no frames are lost, stations awaking from their slumber transmit a PS-Poll frame to retrieve any buffered frames from the access point. Along with this request, waking stations incorporate the association ID (AID) that indicates which BSS they belong to. The AID is included in the PS-Poll frame and may range from 1–2,007. Values from 2,008–16,383 are reserved and not used.

Address Fields

An 802.11 frame may contain up to four address fields. The address fields are numbered because different fields are used for different purposes depending on the frame type (details are found in Chapter 4). The general rule of thumb is that Address 1 is used for the receiver, Address 2 for the transmitter, and Address 3 field for filtering by the receiver. In an infrastructure network, for example, the third address field is used by the receiver to determine whether the frame is part of the network it is associated to.*

Addressing in 802.11 follows the conventions used for the other IEEE 802 networks, including Ethernet. Addresses are 48 bits long. If the first bit sent to the physical medium is a 0, the address represents a single station (unicast). When the first bit is a 1, the address represents a group of physical stations and is called a *multicast* (or *group*) address. If all bits are 1s, then the frame is a *broadcast* and is delivered to all stations connected to the wireless medium.

48-bit addresses are used for a variety of purposes:

Destination address
    As in Ethernet, the destination address is the 48-bit IEEE MAC identifier that corresponds to the final recipient: the station that will hand the frame to higher protocol layers for processing.

Source address
    This is the 48-bit IEEE MAC identifier that identifies the source of the transmission. Only one station can be the source of a frame, so the Individual/Group bit is always 0 to indicate an individual station.

Receiver address
    This is a 48-bit IEEE MAC identifier that indicates which wireless station should process the frame. If it is a wireless station, the receiver address is the destination address. For frames destined to a node on an Ethernet connected to an access point, the receiver is the wireless interface in the access point, and the destination address may be a router attached to the Ethernet.

---

* 802.11 specifies that stations should ignore frames that do not have the same BSSID, but most products do not correctly implement BSSID filtering and will pass any received frame up to higher protocol layers.

Transmitter address

This is a 48-bit IEEE MAC address to identify the wireless interface that transmitted the frame onto the wireless medium. The transmitter address is used only in wireless bridging.

Basic Service Set ID (BSSID)

To identify different wireless LANs in the same area, stations may be assigned to a BSS. In infrastructure networks, the BSSID is the MAC address used by the wireless interface in the access point. Ad hoc networks generate a random BSSID with the Universal/Local bit set to 1 to prevent conflicts with officially assigned MAC addresses.

The number of address fields used depends on the type of frame. Most data frames use three fields for source, destination, and BSSID. The number and arrangement of address fields in a data frame depends on how the frame is traveling relative to the distribution system. Most transmissions use three addresses, which is why only three of the four addresses are contiguous in the frame format.

Sequence Control Field

This 16-bit field is used for both defragmentation and discarding duplicate frames. It is composed of a 4-bit fragment number field and a 12-bit sequence number field, as shown in Figure 3-12. Sequence numbers are not used in control frames, so the Sequence Control field is not present.

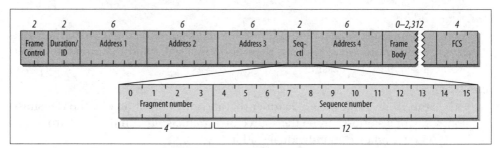

Figure 3-12. Sequence Control field

Higher-level frames are each given a sequence number as they are passed to the MAC for transmission. The sequence number subfield operates as a modulo-4096 counter of the frames transmitted. It begins at 0 and increments by 1 for each higher-level packet handled by the MAC. If higher-level packets are fragmented, all fragments will have the same sequence number. When frames are retransmitted, the sequence number is not changed.

What differs between fragments is the fragment number. The first fragment is given a fragment number of 0. Each successive fragment increments the fragment number by 1. Retransmitted fragments keep their original sequence numbers to assist in reassembly.

Stations that implement the QoS extensions use a slightly different interpretation of the sequence control field because multiple transmit queues need to be maintained.

Frame Body

The frame body, also called the Data field, moves the higher-layer payload from station to station. As originally specified, 802.11 can transmit frames with a maximum payload of 2,304 bytes of higher-level data. Implementations must support larger frame bodies to accommodate additional headers for security and QoS. 802.2 LLC headers use 8 bytes for a maximum network protocol payload of 2,296 bytes. Preventing fragmentation must be done at the protocol layer. On IP networks, Path MTU Discovery (RFC 1191) will prevent the transmission of frames with Data fields larger than 1,500 bytes.

802.11 differs from other link layer technologies in two notable ways. First, there is no higher-level protocol tag in the 802.11 frame to distinguish between higher-layer protocol types. Higher-level protocols are tagged with a type field by an additional header, which is used as the start of the 802.11 payload. Second, 802.11 does not generally pad frames to a minimum length. Many frames used by 802.11 are short, and the chips and electronics used in network interfaces has progressed to the point where a pad is no longer necessary.

Frame Check Sequence

As with Ethernet, the 802.11 frame closes with a frame check sequence (FCS). The FCS is often referred to as the cyclic redundancy check (CRC) because of the underlying mathematical operations. The FCS allows stations to check the integrity of received frames. All fields in the MAC header and the body of the frame are included in the FCS. Although 802.3 and 802.11 use the same method to calculate the FCS, the MAC header used in 802.11 is different from the header used in 802.3, so the FCS must be recalculated by access points.

When frames are sent to the wireless interface, the FCS is calculated before those frames are sent out over the wireless link. Receivers can then calculate the FCS from the received frame and compare it to the received FCS. If the two match, there is a high probability that the frame was not damaged in transit.

On Ethernets, frames with a bad FCS are simply discarded, and frames with a good FCS are passed up the protocol stack. On 802.11 networks, frames that pass the integrity check may also require the receiver to send an acknowledgment. For example, data frames that are received correctly must be positively acknowledged, or they are retransmitted. 802.11 does not have a negative acknowledgment for frames that fail the FCS; stations must wait for the acknowledgment timeout before retransmitting.

Encapsulation of Higher-Layer Protocols Within 802.11

Like all other 802 link layers, 802.11 can transport any network-layer protocol. Unlike Ethernet, 802.11 relies on 802.2 logical link control (LLC) encapsulation to carry higher-level protocols. Figure 3-13 shows how 802.2 LLC encapsulation is used to carry an IP packet. In the figure, the "MAC headers" for 802.1H and RFC 1042 might be the 12 bytes of source and destination MAC address information on Ethernet or the long 802.11 MAC header from the previous section.

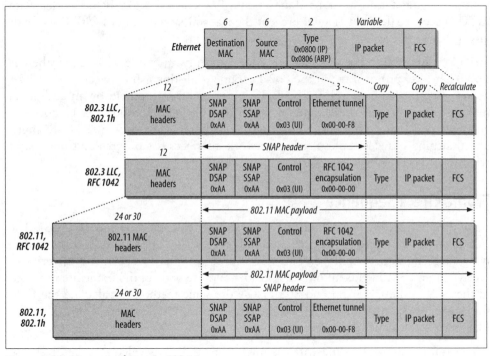

Figure 3-13. IP encapsulation in 802.11

Two different methods can be used to encapsulate LLC data for transmission. One is described in RFC 1042, and the other in 802.1H. Both standards may go by other names. RFC 1042 is sometimes referred to as *IETF* encapsulation, while 802.1H is sometimes called *tunnel* encapsulation.

As you can see in Figure 3-13, though, the two methods are quite similar. An Ethernet frame is shown in the top line of Figure 3-13. It has a MAC header composed of source and destination MAC addresses, a type code, the embedded packet, and a frame check field. In the IP world, the Type code is either 0x0800 (2048 decimal) for IP itself, or 0x0806 (2054 decimal) for the Address Resolution Protocol (ARP).

Both RFC 1042 and 802.1H are derivatives of 802.2's *sub-network access protocol* (SNAP). The MAC addresses are copied into the beginning of the encapsulation frame, and then a SNAP header is inserted. SNAP headers begin with a *destination service access point* (DSAP) and a *source service access point* (SSAP). After the addresses, SNAP includes a Control header. Like high-level data link control (HDLC) and its progeny, the Control field is set to 0x03 to denote unnumbered information (UI), a category that maps well to the best-effort delivery of IP datagrams. The last field inserted by SNAP is an organizationally unique identifier (OUI). Initially, the IEEE hoped that the 1-byte service access points would be adequate to handle the number of network protocols, but this proved to be an overly optimistic assessment of the state of the world. As a result, SNAP copies the type code from the original Ethernet frame. The only difference between 802.1H and RFC 1042 is the OUI used.

At one point, many products offered the option to switch between the two encapsulation standards, though this option is much less common. Microsoft operating systems default to using 802.1H for the AppleTalk protocol suite and IPX, and use RFC 1042 for all other protocols. Most access points now conform to the Microsoft behavior, and no longer have an option to switch encapsulation type. In fact, the Microsoft encapsulation selection is so widely supported that it was part of the Wi-Fi Alliance's certification test suite at one point.

Contention-Based Data Service

The additional features incorporated into 802.11 to add reliability lead to a confusing tangle of rules about which types of frames are permitted at any point. They also make it more difficult for network administrators to know which frame exchanges they can expect to see on networks. This section clarifies the atomic exchanges that move data on an 802.11 LAN. (Most management frames are announcements to interested parties in the area and transfer information in only one direction.)

The exchanges presented in this section are atomic, which means that they should be viewed as a single unit. Two distinct sets of atomic exchanges are defined by 802.11. One is used by the DCF for contention-based service; those exchanges are described in this chapter. A second set of exchanges is specified for use with the PCF for contention-free services. Frame exchanges used with contention-free services are intricate and harder to understand. Since very few (if any) commercial products implement contention-free service, these exchanges are not described.

Frame exchanges under the DCF dominate the 802.11 MAC. According to the rules of the DCF, all products are required to provide best-effort delivery. To implement the contention-based MAC, stations process MAC headers for every frame while they are active. Exchanges begin with a station seizing an idle medium after the DIFS.

Broadcast and Multicast Data or Management Frames

Broadcast and multicast frames, which can also be referred to as *group frames* because they are destined for more than one receiving station, have the simplest frame exchanges because there is no acknowledgment. Framing and addressing are somewhat more complex in 802.11, so the types of frames that match this rule are the following:

- Broadcast data frames with a broadcast address in the Address 1 field
- Multicast data frames with a multicast address in the Address 1 field
- Broadcast management frames with a broadcast address in the Address 1 field (Beacon, Probe Request, and IBSS ATIM frames)

Frames destined for group addresses cannot be fragmented and are not acknowledged. The entire atomic sequence is a single frame, sent according to the rules of the contention-based access control. After the previous transmission concludes, all stations wait for the DIFS and begin counting down the random delay intervals in the contention window.

Because the frame exchange is a single-frame sequence, the NAV is set to 0. With no further frames to follow, there is no need to use the virtual carrier-sense mechanism to lock other stations out of using the medium. After the frame is transmitted, all stations wait through the DIFS and begin counting down through the contention window for any deferred frames. See Figure 3-14.

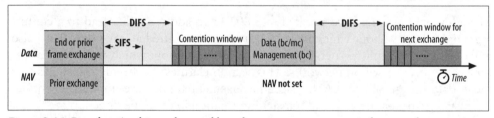

Figure 3-14. Broadcast/multicast data and broadcast management atomic frame exchange

Depending on the environment, frames sent to group addresses may have lower service quality because the frames are not acknowledged. Some stations may therefore miss broadcast or multicast traffic, but there is no facility built into the MAC for retransmitting broadcast or multicast frames.

Unicast Frames

Frames that are destined for a single station are called *directed* data by the 802.11 standard. This book uses the more common term *unicast*. Unicast frames must be acknowledged to ensure reliability, which means that a variety of mechanisms can be used to improve efficiency. All the sequences in this section apply to any unicast frame and thus can apply to management frames and data frames. In practice, these operations are usually observed only with data frames.

Basic positive acknowledgment (final fragment)

Reliable transmission between two stations is based on simple positive acknowledgments. Unicast data frames must be acknowledged, or the frame is assumed to be lost. The most basic case is a single frame and its accompanying acknowledgment, as shown in Figure 3-15.

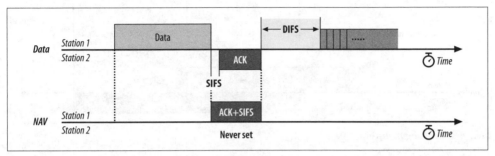

Figure 3-15. Basic positive acknowledgment of data

The frame uses the NAV to reserve the medium for the frame, its acknowledgment, and the intervening SIFS. By setting a long NAV, the sender locks the virtual carrier for the entire sequence, guaranteeing that the recipient of the frame can send the acknowledgment. Because the sequence concludes with the ACK, no further virtual carrier locking is necessary, and the NAV in the ACK is set to 0.

Fragmentation

Many higher-layer network protocols, including IP, incorporate fragmentation. The disadvantage of network-layer fragmentation is that reassembly is performed by the final destination; if any of the fragments are lost, the entire packet must be retransmitted. Link layers may incorporate fragmentation to boost speed over a single hop with a small MTU.* 802.11 can also use fragmentation to help avoid interference. Radio interference is often in the form of short, high-energy bursts and is frequently synchronized with the AC power line. Breaking a large frame into small frames allows a larger percentage of the frames to arrive undamaged. The basic fragmentation scheme is shown in Figure 3-16.

The last two frames exchanged are the same as in the previous sequence, and the NAV is set identically. However, all frames prior to the penultimate frame use the NAV to lock the medium for the next frame. The first data frame sets the NAV for a long enough period to accommodate its ACK, the next fragment, and the acknowledgment following the next fragment. To indicate that it is a fragment, the MAC sets the More Fragments bit in the frame control field to 1. All nonfinal ACKs continue to extend the lock for the next data fragment and its ACK. Subsequent data frames then

---

* This is the approach used by Multi-link PPP (RFC 1990).

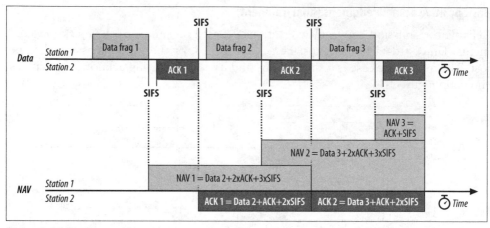

Figure 3-16. Fragmentation

continue to lengthen the NAV to include successive acknowledgments until the final data frame, which sets the More Fragments bit to 0, and the final ACK, which sets the NAV to 0. No limit is placed on the number of fragments, but the total frame length must be shorter than any constraint placed on the exchange by the PHY.

Fragmentation is controlled by the fragmentation threshold parameter in the MAC. Most network card drivers allow you to configure this parameter. Any frames larger than the fragmentation threshold are fragmented in an implementation-dependent way. Network administrators can change the fragmentation threshold to tune network behavior. Higher fragmentation thresholds mean that frames are delivered with less overhead, but the cost to a lost or damaged frame is much higher because more data must be discarded and retransmitted. Low fragmentation thresholds have much higher overhead, but they offer increased robustness in the face of hostile conditions.

RTS/CTS

To guarantee reservation of the medium and uninterrupted data transmission, a station can use the RTS/CTS exchange. Figure 3-17 shows this process. The RTS/CTS exchange acts exactly like the initial exchange in the fragmentation case, except that the RTS frame does not carry data. The NAV in the RTS allows the CTS to complete, and the CTS is used to reserve access for the data frame.

RTS/CTS can be used for all frame exchanges, none of them, or something in between. Like fragmentation, RTS/CTS behavior is controlled by a threshold set in the driver software. Frames larger than the threshold are preceded by an RTS/CTS exchange to clear the medium, while smaller frames are simply transmitted.

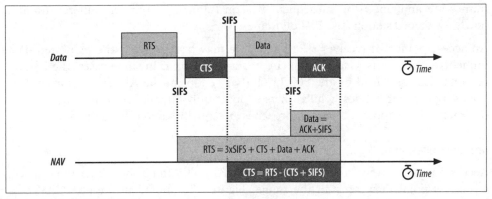

Figure 3-17. RTS/CTS lockout

RTS/CTS with fragmentation

In practice, the RTS/CTS exchange is often combined with fragmentation (Figure 3-18). Fragmented frames are usually quite long and thus benefit from the use of the RTS/CTS procedure to ensure exclusive access to the medium, free from contention from hidden nodes. Some vendors set the default fragmentation threshold to be identical to the default RTS/CTS threshold.

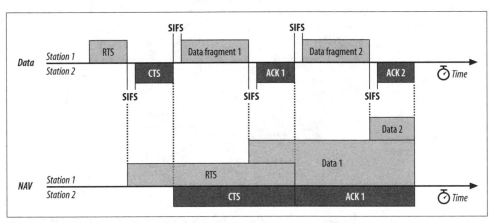

Figure 3-18. RTS/CTS with fragmentation

Powersaving Sequences

The most power-hungry components in RF systems are the amplifiers used to boost a signal immediately prior to transmission and to boost the received signal to an intelligible level immediately after its reception. 802.11 stations can maximize battery life by shutting down the radio transceiver and sleeping periodically. During sleeping periods, access points buffer any unicast frames for sleeping stations. These frames are announced by subsequent Beacon frames. To retrieve buffered frames, newly awakened stations use PS-Poll frames.

An access point that receives a PS-Poll frame may respond with the requested data immediately, or at its leisure when circumstances permit. In some cases, the PS-Poll response is determined by the 802.11 chipset vendor in the AP. Some chipset vendors support both modes, while others support only one. 802.11 only requires that one method be supported; both approaches are equally standards-compliant.

Immediate response

Access points can respond immediately to the PS-Poll. After a short interframe space, an access point may transmit the frame. Figure 3-19 shows an implied NAV as a result of the PS-Poll frame. The PS-Poll frame contains an Association ID in the Duration/ID field so that the access point can determine which frames were buffered for the mobile station. However, the MAC specification requires all stations receiving a PS-Poll to update the NAV with an implied value equal to a short interframe space and one ACK. Although the NAV is too short for the data frame, the access point acquires that the medium and all stations defer access for the entire data frame. At the conclusion of the data frame, the NAV is updated to reflect the value in the header of the data frame.

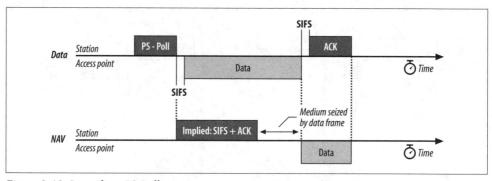

Figure 3-19. Immediate PS-Poll response

If the buffered frame is large, it may require fragmentation. Figure 3-20 illustrates an immediate PS-Poll response requiring fragmentation. Like all other stations, access points typically have a configurable fragmentation threshold.

Deferred response

Instead of an immediate response, access points can also respond with a simple acknowledgment. This is called a *deferred response* because the access point acknowledges the request for the buffered frame but does not act on it immediately. One of the advantages of using deferred response is that the software on the access point is somewhat easier to implement because the acknowledgment can be

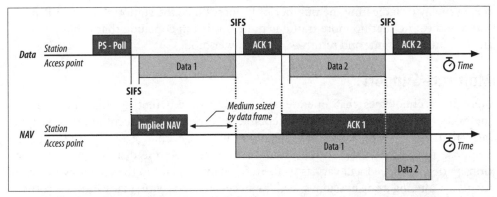

Figure 3-20. Immediate PS-Poll response with fragmentation

transmitted immediately by the chipset firmware, and the buffered data may be queued for transmission normally.

A station requesting a frame with a PS-Poll must stay awake until it is delivered. Under contention-based service, however, the access point can deliver a frame at any point. A station cannot return to a low-power mode until it receives a Beacon frame in which its bit in the traffic indication map (TIM) is clear.

Figure 3-21 illustrates this process. In this figure, the station has recently changed from a low-power mode to an active mode, and it notes that the access point has buffered frames for it. It transmits a PS-Poll to the access point to retrieve the buffered frames. However, the access point may choose to defer its response by transmitting only an ACK. At this point, the access point has acknowledged the station's request for buffered frames and promised to deliver them at some point in the future. The station must wait in active mode, perhaps through several atomic frame exchanges, before the access point delivers the data. A buffered frame may be subject to fragmentation, although Figure 3-21 does not illustrate this case.

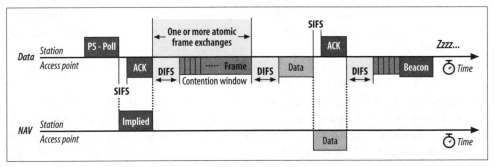

Figure 3-21. Deferred PS-Poll response example

After receiving a data frame, the station must remain awake until the next Beacon is transmitted. Beacon frames only note whether frames are buffered for a station and have no way of indicating the number of frames. Once the station receives a Beacon frame indicating that no more traffic is buffered, it can conclude that it has received the last buffered frame and return to a low-power mode.

Multirate Support

Network technologies that operate at a variety of different speeds must have a method of negotiating a mutually acceptable data rate. Speed negotiation is particularly that are available to stations. Stations may also change speed frequently in response to rapid changes in the radio environment. As the distance between stations varies, the speed will vary as well. Stations must adapt to the changing environment by altering transmission speed as necessary. As with many other protocol features, the 802.11 standards do not specify how a rate is selected. General rules are laid down by the standard, and vendors have a great deal of freedom in implementing the details. There are a few general rules that are required of all stations:

1. Every station maintains a list of *operational rates*, which is the list of rates that are supported by both the station and the BSS serving it. (A BSS typically corresponds to an access point, but newer products may offer the ability to customize operational rates on a "virtual AP" basis.) No frames may be transmitted at a rate that is higher than any rate in the operational rate set.

2. Every BSS must also maintain a *basic rate set*, which is a list of data rates that must be supported by every station joining the BSS. Any frame sent to a group receiver address must be transmitted at a basic rate, ensuring that all stations can demodulate it correctly.

3. Control frames that start a frame exchange, such as RTS and CTS frames, must also be transmitted at one of the rates in the basic rate set. This rule ensures that a station which must transmit a CTS frame in response to an RTS frame can do so at the same rate.

   — Control frames may be used in a backwards-compatiblity mode called *protection* (see Chapter 14). Protection mode is intended to prevent interference between a station supporting only an older, slower radio modulation and a newer station that supports faster radio modulations. Protection frames must be transmitted using older modulations if there are stations incapable of using newer modulations in the area.

4. Frames destined for a single station will have a unicast destination address in the Address 1 field of the frame. Unicast frames can be transmitted at any rate which is known to be supported by the destination. Selection of the data rate is not specified by any 802.11 standard.

   — Frames used in the contention-free period (see Chapter 9) may serve multiple purposes. If a frame includes an ACK, it is intended for the previous transmitter rather than the frame recipient. The transmitter must ensure that the frame is transmitted at a rate supported by both the receiver and the station the ACK is intended for.

5. Response frames, such as acknowledgments or CTS frames, must be transmitted at a rate in the basic rate set, but no faster than the initial frame in the sequence was transmitted. Response frames must use the same modulation as the initial frame (DSSS, CCK, or OFDM).*

Rate selection and fallback

Every 802.11 interface on the market supports some sort of rate fallback mechanism, which steps down the data rate in response to adverse network conditions. Rate selection behavior also determines when a card determines that it should upgrade its data rate due to improved link quality. Exactly how an 802.11 station determines it should go to a lower rate (or a higher rate) is not specified, so the implementation of rate selection is left to chipset vendors. Nearly every chipset has its own rate selection mechanism, and as a result, most 802.11 interfaces behave differently. Rate selection behavior is programmable, and is controlled by the code that runs the interface. It may be altered by driver version changes or firmware changes to an interface.

The most common algorithms used to determine when to change the data rate depend on some loose measurement of signal quality. Signal quality may be measured directly by the signal-to-noise ratio, or indirectly by observing how many frames require retransmission. Direct measurements of signal-to-noise ratios may be an instantaneous measurement of the last frame, or they may be averaged over some recent period or number of recently received frames. Some chipsets use a direct measurement of signal-to-noise ratio, but will convert it into a "signal quality" measurement first. As the signal quality drops, the chip reduces the data rate to compensate.†

Indirect measurements may monitor instantaneous or average frame loss, and compensate appropriately. A simple algorithm using indirect measurement is "if the frame is lost and the frame retry counter is exhausted, step down to the next data rate and try again; repeat until the frame is delivered or the slowest data rate is unable to successfully deliver." Chipsets that perform indirect signal quality measurements may make some modifications to avoid a time-consuming step down through all the rates supported by the PHY, especially since recent chipsets support a great number of rates, and the time to retry at the slower rates is extremely time-consuming.

Frame Processing and Bridging

At the core, a wireless access point is a glorified bridge that translates frames between a wireless medium and a wired medium. Although 802.11 does not place

---

* This is not always strictly obeyed. One chipset vendor always tries to transmit ACK frames at 24 Mbps because it is usually the highest mandatory data rate.

† The signal quality measurement is often used to make roaming decisions when stations move between APs, though no standard specifies how or even whether signal quality is an input to the algorithm.

any constraint on the wired medium's technology, I am not aware of an access point that does not use Ethernet. Most access points are designed as 802.11-to-Ethernet bridges, so it is important to understand the way that frames are transferred between the two media. See Figure 3-22.

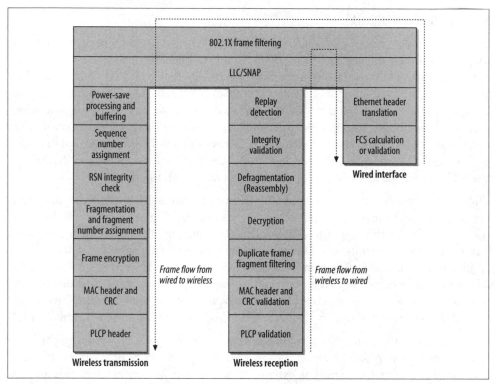

Figure 3-22. Translating frames between a wireless and a wired medium

Wireless Medium to Wired Medium (802.11 to Ethernet)

When a frame is received on the wireless interface of an access point bound for the wired network, the access point must bridge the frame between the two media. Informally, this is the series of tasks performed by the access point:

1. When a frame is received at the access point, it first checks for basic integrity. Physical layer headers that are discussed in the chapters for their respective physical layers are checked, and the FCS on the 802.11 frame is validated.

2. After verifying that the frame was likely received without error, the access point checks whether it should process the frame further.

    a. Frames sent to an access point have the MAC address of the AP (the BSSID) in the Address 1 field of the 802.11 MAC header. Frames that do not match the BSSID of the AP should be discarded. (This step is not implemented by many products.)

    b. The 802.11 MAC detects and removes duplicate frames. Frames may be duplicated for a variety of reasons, but one of the most common is that the 802.11 acknowledgment is lost or corrupted in transit. To simplify higher-level processing, the 802.11 MAC is responsible for filtering out duplicate frames.

3. Once the access point determines the frame should be processed further, it must decrypt frames protected by a link layer security algorithm. Details of the decryption can be found in subsequent chapters on security.

4. Once the frame is successfully decrypted, it is checked to see if it is a constituent fragment of a larger frame that requires reassembly. Reassembled frames are subject to integrity protection on the whole reassembled unit, rather than the individual components.

5. If the AP should bridge the frame, as determined by the BSSID check in step 2a, the relatively complex wireless MAC header is translated into the simple Ethernet MAC header.

    a. The destination address, which is found in the Address 3 field of the 802.11 MAC header, is copied to the Ethernet destination address.

    b. The source address, which is found in the Address 2 field of the 802.11 MAC header, is copied to the Ethernet source address.

    c. The Ethernet type code is copied from the SNAP header in the 802.11 Data field to the Type code in the Ethernet frame. If the Ethernet frame uses SNAP as well, the entire SNAP header can be copied.

    d. Sequence information is used in fragmentation reassembly, but is discarded when the frame is bridged.

    e. When quality of service processing is standardized, the QoS mapping from the wireless interface to the wired interface will occur here. For the moment, though, it suffices to say that it may take the form of an 802.1p prioritization bit on the wired frame, or some other form of control.

6. The FCS is recalculated. Both Ethernet and 802.11 use the same algorithm to calculate the FCS, but the 802.11 frame has several extra fields that are protected by the FCS.

7. The new frame is transmitted on the Ethernet interface.

Wired Medium to Wireless Medium (Ethernet to 802.11)

Bridging frames from the wired side of an access point to the wireless medium is quite similar to the reverse process:

1. After validating the Ethernet FCS, the access point first checks that a received frame should be processed further by checking that the destination address belongs to a station currently associated with the access point.

2. The SNAP header is prepended to the data in the Ethernet frame. The higher-level packet is encapsulated within a SNAP header whose Type code is copied from the Ethernet type code. If the Ethernet frame uses SNAP as well, the entire SNAP header can be copied.

3. The frame is scheduled for transmission. 802.11 includes complex powersaving operations that may cause an access point to hold the frame in a buffer before placing it on the transmit queue. Powersaving operations are described in Chapter 8.

4. Once a frame has been queued for transmission, it is assigned a sequence number. The resulting data is protected by an integrity check, if required. If fragmentation is required, the frame will be split according to the configured fragmentation threshold. If the frame is fragmented, fragment numbers in the Sequence Control field will also be assigned.

5. If frame protection is required, the body of the frame (or each fragment) is encrypted.

6. The 802.11 MAC header is constructed from the Ethernet MAC header.

    a. The Ethernet destination address is copied to the Address 1 field of the 802.11 MAC header.

    b. The BSSID is placed in the Address 2 field of the MAC header, as the sender of the frame on the wireless medium.

    c. The source address of the frame is copied to the Address 3 field of the MAC header.

    d. Other fields in the 802.11 MAC header are filled in. The expected transmission time will be placed in the Duration field and the appropriate flags are filled in in the Frame Control field.

7. The FCS is recalculated. Both Ethernet and 802.11 use the same algorithm to calculate the FCS, but the 802.11 frame has several extra fields that are protected by the FCS.

8. The new frame is transmitted on the 802.11 interface.

Quality of Service Extensions

Quality of service extensions may affect the order in which frames are transmitted, but it does not alter the basic path that a frame takes through the 802.11 MAC. Rather than using a single transmit queue, the 802.11e quality of service extensions will have multiple transmit queues operating at steps 4, 5, and 7 of the wired-to-wireless bridging procedure described above. At each of those steps, frames are processed in a priority order that can be affected by the contents of the frame and locally configured prioritization rules.

## CHAPTER 4

802.11 Framing in Detail

Chapter 3 presented the basic frame structure and the fields that comprise it, but it did not go into detail about the different frame types. Ethernet framing is a simple matter: add a preamble, some addressing information, and tack on a frame check at the end. 802.11 framing is much more involved because the wireless medium requires several management features and corresponding frame types not found in wired networks.

Three major frame types exist. *Data frames* are the pack horses of 802.11, hauling data from station to station. Several different data frame flavors can occur, depending on the network. *Control frames* are used in conjunction with data frames to perform area-clearing operations, channel acquisition and carrier-sensing maintenance functions, and positive acknowledgment of received data. Control and data frames work in conjunction to deliver data reliably from station to station. *Management frames* perform supervisory functions; they are used to join and leave wireless networks and move associations from access point to access point.

This chapter is intended to be a reference. There is only so much life any author can breathe into framing details, no matter how much effort is expended to make the details interesting. Please feel free to skip this chapter in its entirety and flip back when you need in-depth information about frame structure. With rare exception, detailed framing relationships generally do not fall into the category of "something a network administrator needs to know." This chapter tends to be a bit acronym-heavy as well, so refer to the glossary at the back of the book if you do not recognize an acronym.

Data Frames

Data frames carry higher-level protocol data in the frame body. Figure 4-1 shows a generic data frame. Depending on the particular type of data frame, some of the fields in the figure may not be used.

2	2	6	6	6	2	6	0–2,312	4
Frame Control	Duration ID	Address 1 (receiver)	Address 2 (sender)	Address 3 (filtering)	Seq-ctl	Address 4 (optional)	Frame Body	FCS

Figure 4-1. Generic data frame

The different data frame types can be categorized according to function. One such distinction is between data frames used for contention-based service and those used for contention-free service. Any frames that appear only in the contention-free period can never be used in an IBSS. Another possible division is between frames that carry data and frames that perform management functions. Table 4-1 shows how frames may be divided along these lines. Frames used in contention-free service are discussed in detail in Chapter 9.

Table 4-1. Categorization of data frame types

Frame type	Contention-based service	Contention-free service	Carries data	Does not carry data
Data	✓		✓	
Data+CF-Ack		✓	✓	
Data+CF-Poll		AP only	✓	
Data+CF-Ack+CF-Poll		AP only	✓	
Null	✓	✓		✓
CF-Ack		✓		✓
CF-Poll		AP only		✓
CF-Ack+CF-Poll		AP only		✓

Frame Control

All the bits in the Frame Control field are used according to the rules described in Chapter 3. Frame Control bits may affect the interpretation of other fields in the MAC header, though. Most notable are the address fields, which depend on the value of the ToDS and FromDS bits.

Duration

The Duration field carries the value of the Network Allocation Vector (NAV). Access to the medium is restricted for the time specified by the NAV. Four rules specify the setting for the Duration field in data frames:

1. Any frames transmitted during the contention-free period set the Duration field to 32,768. Naturally, this applies to any data frames transmitted during this period.

2. Frames transmitted to a broadcast or multicast destination (Address 1 has the group bit set) have a duration of 0. Such frames are not part of an atomic

exchange and are not acknowledged by receivers, so contention-based access to the medium can begin after the conclusion of a broadcast or multicast data frame. The NAV is used to protect access to the transmission medium for a frame exchange sequence. With no link-layer acknowledgment following the transmission of a broadcast or multicast frame, there is no need to lock access to the medium for subsequent frames.

3. If the More Fragments bit in the Frame Control field is 0, no more fragments remain in the frame. The final fragment need only reserve the medium for its own ACK, at which point contention-based access resumes. The Duration field is set to the amount of time required for one short interframe space and the fragment acknowledgment. Figure 4-2 illustrates this process. The penultimate fragment's Duration field locks access to the medium for the transmission of the last fragment.

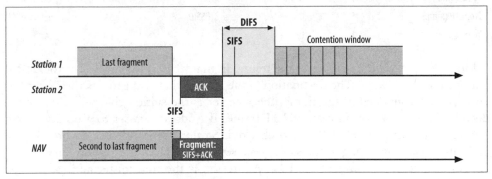

Figure 4-2. Duration setting on final fragment

4. If the More Fragments bit in the Frame Control field is set to 1, more fragments remain. The Duration field is set to the amount of time required for transmission of two acknowledgments, plus three short interframe spaces, plus the time required for the next fragment. In essence, nonfinal fragments set the NAV just like an RTS would (Figure 4-3); for this reason, they are referred to as a *virtual RTS*.

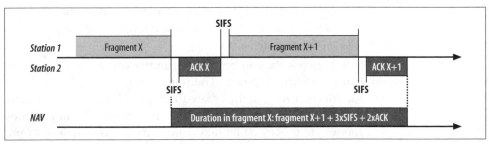

Figure 4-3. Duration settings on nonfinal fragment

Addressing and DS Bits

The number and function of the address fields depends on which of the distribution system bits are set, so the use of the address fields indirectly depends on the type of network deployed. Table 4-2 summarizes the use of the address fields in data frames. The fourth address field is only used by wireless bridges, and is therefore relatively uncommon.

Table 4-2. Use of the address fields in data frames

Function	ToDS	FromDS	Address 1 (receiver)	Address 2 (transmitter)	Address 3	Address 4
IBSS	0	0	DA	SA	BSSID	Not used
To AP (infra.)	1	0	BSSID	SA	DA	Not used
From AP (infra.)	0	1	DA	BSSID	SA	Not used
WDS (bridge)	1	1	RA	TA	DA	SA

Address 1 indicates the receiver of the frame. In many cases, the receiver is the destination, but not always. The destination is the station that will process the network-layer packet contained in the frame; the receiver is the station that will attempt to decode the radio waves into an 802.11 frame. If Address 1 is set to a broadcast or multicast address, the BSSID is also checked. Stations respond only to broadcasts and multicasts originating in the same basic service set (BSS); they ignore broadcasts and multicasts from different BSSIDs.* Address 2 is the transmitter address and is used to send acknowledgments. Transmitters are not necessarily senders. The sender is the frame that generated the network-layer protocol packet in the frame; the transmitter put the frame on to the radio link. The Address 3 field is used for filtering by access points and the distribution system, but the use of the field depends on the particular type of network used.

In the case of an IBSS, no access points are used, and no distribution system is present. The transmitter is the source, and the receiver is the destination. All frames carry the BSSID so that stations may check broadcasts and multicasts; only stations that belong to the same BSS will process broadcasts and multicasts. In an IBSS, the BSSID is created by a random-number generator.

802.11 draws a distinction between the source and transmitter and a parallel distinction between the destination and the receiver. The transmitter sends a frame on to the wireless medium but does not necessarily create the frame. A similar distinction holds for destination addresses and receiver addresses. A receiver may be an intermediate destination, but frames are processed by higher protocol levels only when they reach the destination.

---

* Not all cards perform this BSSID filtering correctly. Many products will pass all broadcasts up to higher protocol layers without validating the BSSID first.

The BSSID

Each BSS is assigned a BSSID, a 48-bit binary identifier that distinguishes it from other BSSs throughout the network. The major advantage of the BSSID is filtering. Several distinct 802.11 networks may overlap physically, and there is no reason for one network to receive link-layer broadcasts from a physically overlapping network.

In an infrastructure BSS, the BSSID is the MAC address of the wireless interface in the access point creating the BSS. IBSSs must create BSSIDs for networks brought into existence. To maximize the probability of creating a unique address, 46 random bits are generated for the BSSID. The Universal/Local bit for the new BSSID is set to 1, indicating a local address, and the Individual/Group bit is set to 0. For two distinct IBSSs to create the same BSSID, they would need to generate an identical random 46 bits.

One BSSID is reserved. The all-1s BSSID is the *broadcast BSSID*. Frames that use the broadcast BSSID pass through any BSSID filtering in the MAC. BSSID broadcasts are used only when mobile stations try to locate a network by sending probe requests. In order for probe frames to detect the existence of a network, they must not be filtered by the BSSID filter. Probe frames are the only frames allowed to use the broadcast BSSID.

To expand on these distinctions, consider the use of the address fields in infrastructure networks. Figure 4-4 shows a simple network in which a wireless client is connected to a server through an 802.11 network. Frames sent by the client to the server use the address fields as specified in the second line of Table 4-2.

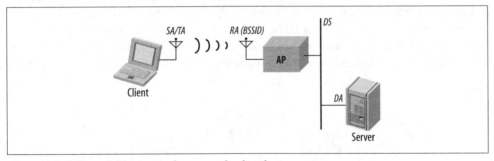

Figure 4-4. Address field usage in frames to the distribution system

In the case of frames bound for a destination on the distribution system, the client is both source and transmitter. The receiver of the wireless frame is the access point, but the access point is only an intermediate destination. When the frame reaches the access point, it is relayed to the distribution system to reach the server. Thus, the access point is the receiver, and the (ultimate) destination is the server. In infrastructure networks, access points create associated BSSs with the address of their wireless interfaces, which is why the receiver address (Address 1) is set to the BSSID.

When the server replies to the client, frames are transmitted to the client through the access point, as in Figure 4-5. This scenario corresponds to the third line in Table 4-2.

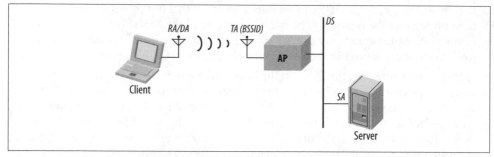

Figure 4-5. Address field usage in frames from the distribution system

Frames are created by the server, so the server's MAC address is the source address for frames. When frames are relayed through the access point, the access point uses its wireless interface as the transmitter address. As in the previous case, the access point's interface address is also the BSSID. Frames are ultimately sent to the client, which is both the destination and receiver.

The fourth line in Table 4-2 shows the use of the address fields in a *wireless distribution system* (WDS), which is sometimes called a *wireless bridge*. In Figure 4-6, two wired networks are joined by access points acting as wireless bridges. Frames bound from the client to the server traverse the 802.11 WDS. The source and destination addresses of the wireless frames remain the client and server addresses. These frames, however, also identify the transmitter and receiver of the frame on the wireless medium. For frames bound from the client to the server, the transmitter is the client-side access point, and the receiver is the server-side access point. Separating the source from the transmitter allows the server-side access point to send required 802.11 acknowledgments to its peer access point without interfering with the wired link layer.

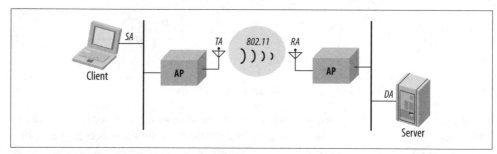

Figure 4-6. Wireless distribution system

Variations on the Data Frame Theme

802.11 uses several different data frame types. Variations depend on whether the service is contention-based or contention-free. Contention-free frames can incorporate several functions for the sake of efficiency. Data may be transmitted, but by changing the frame subtype, data frames in the contention-free period may be used to acknowledge other frames, saving the overhead of interframe spaces and separate acknowledgments. Here are the different data frame types that are commonly used:

Data

Frames of the Data subtype are transmitted only during the contention-based access periods. They are simple frames with the sole purpose of moving the frame body from one station to another.

Null

Null frames* are a bit of an oddity. They consist of a MAC header followed by the FCS trailer. In a traditional Ethernet, empty frames would be extraneous overhead; in 802.11 networks, they are used by mobile stations to inform the access point of changes in power-saving status. When stations sleep, the access point must begin buffering frames for the sleeping station. If the mobile station has no data to send through the distribution system, it can use a Null frame with the Power Management bit in the Frame Control field set. Access points never enter power-saving mode and do not transmit Null frames. Usage of Null frames is shown in Figure 4-7.

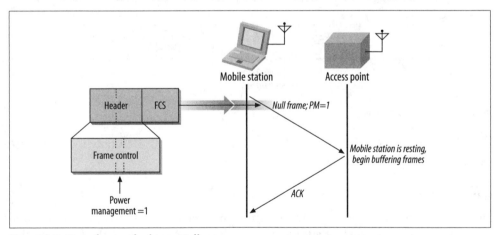

Figure 4-7. Data frame of subtype Null

---

* To indicate that Null is used as the frame type from the specification rather than the English word, it is capitalized. This convention will be followed throughout the chapter.

Several other frame types exist for use within the contention-free period. However, contention-free service is not widely implemented; the discussion of the contention-free frames (Data+CF-Ack, Data+CF-Poll, Data+CF-Ack+CF-Poll, CF-Ack, CF-Poll, and CF-Ack+CF-Poll) can be found in Chapter 9.

Applied Data Framing

The form of a data frame can depend on the type of network. The actual subtype of the frame is determined solely by the subtype field, not by the presence or absence of other fields in the frame.

IBSS frames

In an IBSS, three address fields are used, as shown in Figure 4-8. The first address identifies the receiver, which is also the destination address in an IBSS. The second address is the source address. After the source and destination addresses, data frames in an IBSS are labeled with the BSSID. When the wireless MAC receives a frame, it checks the BSSID and passes only frames in the station's current BSSID to higher protocol layers.

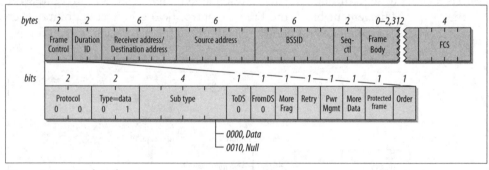

Figure 4-8. IBSS data frame

IBSS data frames have the subtype data or Null; the latter is used only to communicate power management state.

Frames from the AP

Figure 4-9 shows the format of a frame sent from an access point to a mobile station. As in all data frames, the first address field indicates the receiver of the frame on the wireless network, which is the frame's destination. The second address holds the transmitter address. On infrastructure networks, the transmitter address is the address of the station in the access point, which is also the BSSID. Finally, the frame indicates the source MAC address of the frame. The split between source and transmitter is necessary because the 802.11 MAC sends acknowledgments to the frame's transmitter (the access point), but higher layers send replies to the frame's source.

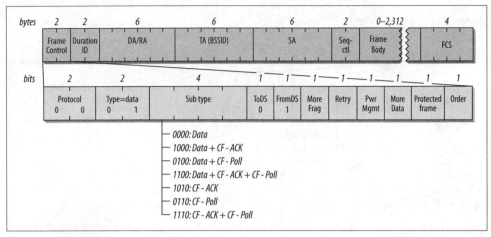

Figure 4-9. Data frames from the AP

Nothing in the 802.11 specification forbids an access point from transmitting Null frames, but there is no reason to transmit them. Access points are forbidden from using the power-saving routines, and they can acknowledge Null frames from stations without using Null frames in response. In practice, access points send Data frames during the contention-based access period, and they send frames incorporating the CF-Poll feature during the contention-free period.

Frames to the AP

Figure 4-10 shows the format of a frame sent from a mobile station in an infrastructure network to the access point currently serving it. The receiver address is the BSSID. In infrastructure networks, the BSSID is taken from the MAC address of the network station in the access point. Frames destined for an access point take their source/transmitter address from the network interface in the wireless station. Access points do not perform filtering, but instead use the third address to forward data to the appropriate location in the distribution system.

Frames from the distribution system have the ToDS bit set, but the FromDS bit is 0. Mobile stations in an infrastructure network cannot become the point coordinator, and thus never send frames that incorporate the contention-free polling (CF-Poll) functions.

Frames in a WDS

When access points are deployed in a wireless bridge (or WDS) topology, all four address fields are used, as shown in Figure 4-11. Like all other data frames, WDS frames use the first address for the receiver of the frame and the second address for the transmitter. The MAC uses these two addresses for acknowledgments and control traffic, such as RTS, CTS, and ACK frames. Two more address fields are necessary to indicate the source and destination of the frame and distinguish them from the addresses used on the wireless link.

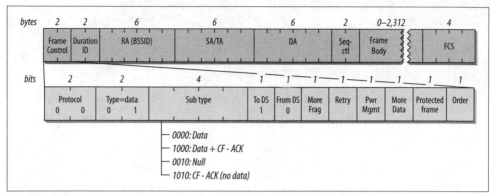

Figure 4-10. Data frames to the AP

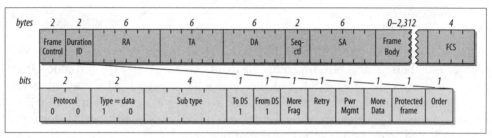

Figure 4-11. WDS frames

On a wireless bridging link, there are no mobile stations, and the contention-free period is not used. Access points are forbidden to enter power-saving modes, so the power management bit is always set to 0.

Encrypted frames

Frames protected by link layer security protocols are not new frame types. When a frame is handled by encryption, the Protected Frame bit in the Frame Control field is set to 1, and the Frame Body field begins with the appropriate cryptographic header described in Chapters 5 or 7, depending on the protocol.

Control Frames

Control frames assist in the delivery of data frames. They administer access to the wireless medium (but not the medium itself) and provide MAC-layer reliability functions.

Common Frame Control Field

All control frames use the same Frame Control field, which is shown in Figure 4-12.

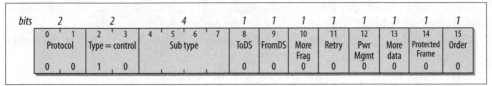

bits	2		2		4			1	1	1	1	1	1	1	1
	0	1	2	3	4	5 6	7	8	9	10	11	12	13	14	15
	Protocol		Type = control			Sub type		ToDS	FromDS	More Frag	Retry	Pwr Mgmt	More data	Protected Frame	Order
	0	0	1	0				0	0	0	0	0	0	0	0

Figure 4-12. Frame Control field in control frames

Protocol version
> The protocol version is shown as 0 in Figure 4-12 because that is currently the only version. Other versions may exist in the future.

Type
> Control frames are assigned the Type identifier 01. By definition, all control frames use this identifier.

Subtype
> This field indicates the subtype of the control frame that is being transmitted.

ToDS and FromDS bits
> Control frames arbitrate access to the wireless medium and thus can only originate from wireless stations. The distribution system does not send or receive control frames, so these bits are always 0.

More Fragments bit
> Control frames are not fragmented, so this bit is always 0.

Retry bit
> Control frames are not queued for retransmission like management or data frames, so this bit is always 0.

Power Management bit
> This bit is set to indicate the power management state of the sender after conclusion of the current frame exchange.

More Data bit
> The More Data bit is used only in management and data frames, so this bit is set to 0 in control frames.

Protected Frame bit
> Control frames may not be encrypted. Thus, for control frames, the Protected Frame bit is always 0.

Order bit
> Control frames are used as components of atomic frame exchange operations and thus cannot be transmitted out of order. Therefore, this bit is set to 0.

Request to Send (RTS)

RTS frames are used to gain control of the medium for the transmission of "large" frames, in which "large" is defined by the RTS threshold in the network card driver.

Access to the medium can be reserved only for unicast frames; broadcast and multi-cast frames are simply transmitted. The format of the RTS frame is shown in Figure 4-13. Like all control frames, the RTS frame is all header. No data is transmitted in the body, and the FCS immediately follows the header.

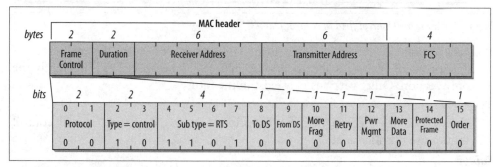

Figure 4-13. RTS frame

Four fields make up the MAC header of an RTS:

Frame Control
There is nothing special about the Frame Control field. The frame subtype is set to 1011 to indicate an RTS frame, but otherwise, it has all the same fields as other control frames. (The most significant bits in the 802.11 specification come at the end of fields, so bit 7 is the most significant bit in the subtype field.)

Duration
An RTS frame attempts to reserve the medium for an entire frame exchange, so the sender of an RTS frame calculates the time needed for the frame exchange sequence after the RTS frame ends. The entire exchange, which is depicted in Figure 4-14, requires three SIFS periods, the duration of one CTS, the final ACK, plus the time needed to transmit the frame or first fragment. (Fragmentation bursts use subsequent fragments to update the Duration field.) The number of microseconds required for the transmission is calculated and placed in the Duration field. If the result is fractional, it is rounded up to the next microsecond.

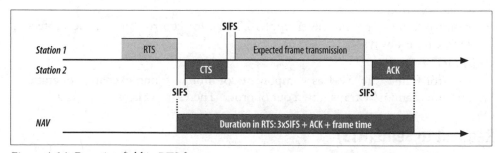

Figure 4-14. Duration field in RTS frame

Address 1: Receiver Address
The address of the station that is the intended recipient of the large frame.

Address 2: Transmitter Address
The address of the sender of the RTS frame.

Clear to Send (CTS)

The CTS frame, whose format is shown in Figure 4-15, has two purposes. Initially, CTS frames were used only to answer RTS frames, and were never generated without a preceding RTS. CTS frames were later adopted for use by the 802.11g protection mechanism to avoid interfering with older stations. The protection mechanism is described with the rest of 802.11g in Chapter 14.

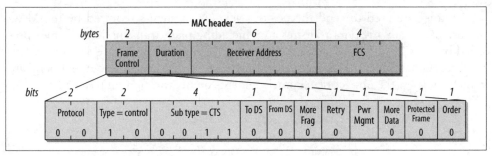

Figure 4-15. CTS frame

Three fields make up the MAC header of a CTS frame:

Frame Control
The frame subtype is set to 1100 to indicate a CTS frame.

Duration
When used in response to an RTS, the sender of a CTS frame uses the duration from the RTS frame as the basis for its duration calculation. RTS frames reserve the medium for the entire RTS-CTS-frame-ACK exchange. By the time the CTS frame is transmitted, though, only the pending frame or fragment and its acknowledgment remain. The sender of a CTS frame subtracts the time required for the CTS frame and the short interframe space that preceded the CTS from the duration in the RTS frame, and places the result of that calculation in the Duration field. Figure 4-16 illustrates the relationship between the CTS duration and the RTS duration. Rules for CTS frames used in protection exchanges are described with the protection mechanism.

Address 1: Receiver Address
The receiver of a CTS frame is the transmitter of the previous RTS frame, so the MAC copies the transmitter address of the RTS frame into the receiver address of the CTS frame. CTS frames used in 802.11g protection are sent to the sending station, and are used only to set the NAV.

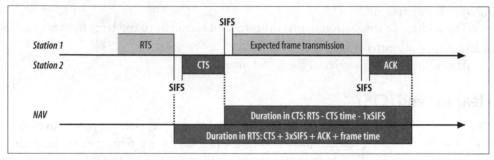

Figure 4-16. CTS duration

Acknowledgment (ACK)

ACK frames are used to send the positive acknowledgments required by the MAC and are used with any data transmission, including plain transmissions, frames preceded by an RTS/CTS handshake, and fragmented frames (see Figure 4-17). Quality-of-service enhancements relax the requirement for a single acknowledgment per Data frame. To assess the impact of acknowledgments on net throughput, see Chapter 25.

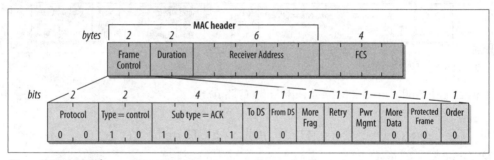

Figure 4-17. ACK frame

Three fields make up the MAC header of an ACK frame:

Frame Control
　　The frame subtype is set to 1101 to indicate an ACK frame.

Duration
　　The duration may be set in one of two ways, depending on the position of the ACK within the frame exchange. ACKs for complete data frames and final fragments in a fragment burst set the duration to 0. The data sender indicates the end of a data transmission by setting the More Fragments bit in the Frame Control header to 0. If the More Fragments bit is 0, the transmission is complete, and there is no need to extend control over the radio channel for additional transmissions. Thus, the duration is set to 0.

If the More Fragments bit is 1, a fragment burst is in progress. The Duration field is used like the Duration field in the CTS frame. The time required to transmit the ACK and its short interframe space is subtracted from the duration in the most recent fragment (Figure 4-18). The duration calculation in nonfinal ACK frames is similar to the CTS duration calculation. In fact, the 802.11 specification refers to the duration setting in the ACK frames as a *virtual CTS*.

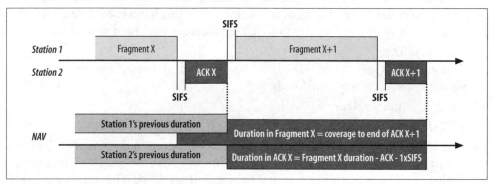

Figure 4-18. Duration in non-final ACK frames

Address 1: Receiver Address
> The receiver address is copied from the transmitter of the frame being acknowledged. Technically, it is copied from the Address 2 field of the frame being acknowledged. Acknowledgments are transmitted in response to directed data frames, management frames, and PS-Poll frames.

Power-Save Poll (PS-Poll)

When a mobile station wakes from a power-saving mode, it transmits a PS-Poll frame to the access point to retrieve any frames buffered while it was in power-saving mode. The format of the PS-Poll frame is shown in Figure 4-19. Further details on the operation of power saving modes appears in Chapter 8.

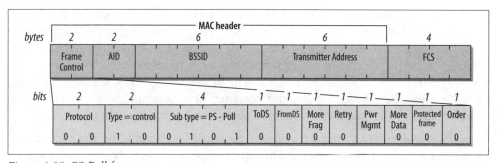

Figure 4-19. PS-Poll frame

Four fields make up the MAC header of a PS-Poll frame:

Frame Control
The frame subtype is set to 1010 to indicate a PS-Poll frame.

Association ID (AID)
Instead of a Duration field, the PS-Poll frame uses the third and fourth bytes in the MAC header for the association ID. This is a numeric value assigned by the access point to identify the association. Including this ID in the frame allows the access point to find any frames buffered for the now-awakened mobile station.

Address 1: BSSID
This field contains the BSSID of the BSS created by the access point that the sender is currently associated with.

Address 2: Transmitter Address
This is the address of the sender of the PS-Poll frame.

The PS-Poll frame does not include duration information to update the NAV. However, all stations receiving a PS-Poll frame update the NAV by the short interframe space plus the amount of time required to transmit an ACK. The automatic NAV update allows the access point to transmit an ACK with a small probability of collision with a mobile station.

Association ID (AID)

In the PS-Poll frame, the Duration/ID field is an association ID rather than a value used by the virtual carrier-sensing function. When mobile stations associate with an access point, the access point assigns a value called the Association ID (AID) from the range 1–2,007. The AID is used for a variety of purposes that appear throughout this book.

Management Frames

Management is a large component of the 802.11 specification. Several different types of management frames are used to provide services that are simple on a wired network. Establishing the identity of a network station is easy on a wired network because network connections require dragging wires from a central location to the new workstation. In many cases, patch panels in the wiring closet are used to speed up installation, but the essential point remains: new network connections can be authenticated by a personal visit when the new connection is brought up.

Wireless networks must create management features to provide similar functionality. 802.11 breaks the procedure up into three components. Mobile stations in search of connectivity must first locate a compatible wireless network to use for access. With wired networks, this step typically involves finding the appropriate data jack on the wall. Next, the network must authenticate mobile stations to establish that the authenticated identity is allowed to connect to the network. The wired-network equivalent is provided by the network itself. If signals cannot leave the wire, obtaining physical access is at least something of an authentication process. Finally, mobile stations must associate with an access point to gain access to the wired backbone, a step equivalent to plugging the cable into a wired network.

The Structure of Management Frames

802.11 management frames share the structure shown in Figure 4-20. The MAC header is the same in all management frames; it does not depend on the frame subtype. Management frames use *information elements*, little chunks of data with a numerical label, to communicate information to other systems.

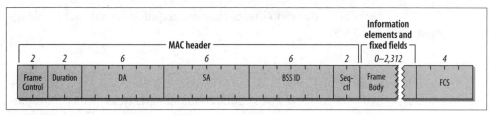

Figure 4-20. Generic management frame

Address fields

As with all other frames, the first address field is used for the frame's destination address. Some management frames are used to maintain properties within a single BSS. To limit the effect of broadcast and multicast management frames, stations are required to inspect the BSSID after receiving a mangement frame, though not all implementations perform BSSID filtering. Only broadcast and multicast frames from the BSSID that a station is currently associated with are passed to MAC management layers. The one exception to this rule is Beacon frames, which are used to announce the existence of an 802.11 network.

BSSIDs are assigned in the familiar manner. Access points use the MAC address of the wireless network interface as the BSSID. Mobile stations adopt the BSSID of the access point they are currently associated with. Stations in an IBSS use the randomly generated BSSID from the BSS creation. One exception to the rule: frames sent by the mobile station seeking a specific network may use the BSSID of the network they are seeking, or they may use the broadcast BSSID to find all networks in the vicinity.

Duration calculations

Management frames use the Duration field in the same manner that other frames do:

1. Any frames transmitted in the contention-free period set the duration to 32,768.

2. Frames transmitted during the contention-based access periods using only the DCF use the Duration field to block access to the medium to allow any atomic frame exchanges to complete.

    a. If the frame is a broadcast or multicast (the destination address is a group address), the duration is 0. Broadcast and multicast frames are not acknowledged, so the NAV is not needed to block access to the medium.

    b. If a nonfinal fragment is part of a multiframe exchange, the duration is set to the number of microseconds taken up by three SIFS intervals plus the next fragment and its acknowledgment.

    c. Final fragments use a duration that is the time required for one acknowledgment plus one SIFS.

Frame body

Management frames are quite flexible. Most of the data contained in the frame body uses fixed-length fields called *fixed fields* and variable-length fields called *information elements*. Information elements are blobs of data of varying size. Each data blob is tagged with a type number and a size, and it is understood that an information element of a certain type has its data field interpreted in a certain way. New information elements can be defined by newer revisions to the 802.11 specification; implementations that predate the revisions can ignore newer elements. Old implementations depend on backward-compatible hardware and frequently can't join networks based on the newer standards. Fortunately, new options usually can be easily turned off for compatibility.

This section presents the fixed fields and information elements as building blocks and shows how the building blocks are assembled into management frames. 802.11 mandates the order in which information elements appear, but not all elements are mandatory. This book shows all the frame building blocks in the specified order, and the discussion of each subtype notes which elements are rare and which are mutually exclusive.

Fixed-Length Management Frame Components

10 fixed-length fields may appear in management frames. Fixed-length fields are often referred to simply as *fields* to distinguish them from the variable-length information elements. Fields do not have a header to distinguish them from other parts of the frame body. Because they have a fixed length and appear in a known order, fields can be delimited without using a field header.

Authentication Algorithm Number

Two bytes are used for the Authentication Algorithm Number field, which are shown in Figure 4-21. This field identifies the type of authentication used in the initial 802.11-level authentication process before association occurs. 802.1X authentication occurs after association, and is not assigned an algorithm number. (The authentication process is discussed more thoroughly in Chapter 8.) The values permitted for this field are shown in Table 4-3. Only two values are currently defined. Other values are reserved for future standardization work.

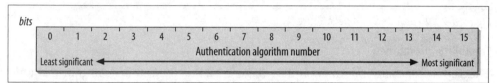

Figure 4-21. Authentication Algorithm Number field

Table 4-3. Values of the Authentication Algorithm Number field

Value	Meaning
0	Open System authentication (typically used with 802.1X authentication)
1	Shared Key authentication (deprecated by 802.11i)
2–65,535	Reserved

Authentication Transaction Sequence Number

Authentication is a multistep process that consists of a challenge from the access point and a response from the mobile station attempting to associate. The Authentication Transaction Sequence Number, shown in Figure 4-22, is a two-byte field used to track progress through the authentication exchange. It takes values from 1 to 65,535; it is never set to 0. Use of this field is discussed in Chapter 8.

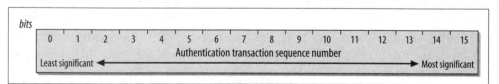

Figure 4-22. Authentication Transaction Sequence Number field

Beacon interval

Beacon transmissions announce the existence of an 802.11 network at regular intervals. Beacon frames carry information about the BSS parameters and the frames buffered by access points, so mobile stations must listen to Beacons. The Beacon Interval, shown in Figure 4-23, is a 16-bit field set to the number of *time units* between Beacon transmissions. One time unit, which is often abbreviated TU, is

1,024 microseconds (ms), which is about 1 millisecond.* Time units may also be called kilo-microseconds in various documentation (Kms or kms). It is common for the Beacon interval to be set to 100 time units, which corresponds to an interval between Beacon transmissions of approximately 100 milliseconds or 0.1 seconds.

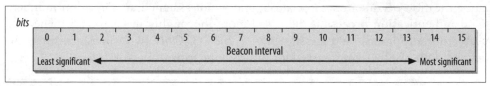

Figure 4-23. Beacon Interval field

Capability Information

The 16-bit Capability Information field (Figure 4-24) is used in Beacon transmissions to advertise the network's capabilities. Capability Information is also used in Probe Request and Probe Response frames. In this field, each bit is used as a flag to advertise a particular function of the network. Stations use the capability advertisement to determine whether they can support all the features in the BSS. Stations that do not implement all the features in the capability advertisement are not allowed to join.

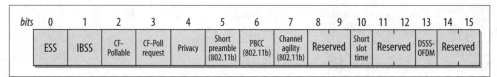

Figure 4-24. Capability Information field

ESS/IBSS
> These two bits are mutually exclusive. Access points set the ESS field to 1 and the IBSS field to 0 to indicate that the access point is part of an infrastructure network. Stations in an IBSS set the ESS field to 0 and the IBSS field to 1.

Privacy
> Setting the Privacy bit to 1 requires the use of WEP for confidentiality. In infrastructure networks, the transmitter is an access point. In IBSSs, Beacon transmission must be handled by a station in the IBSS.

Short Preamble
> This field was added to 802.11b to support the high-rate DSSS PHY. Setting it to 1 indicates that the network is using the short preamble as described in Chapter 12. Zero means the option is not in use and is forbidden in the BSS.

---

* Kilo-microseconds are an odd blend of the powers-of-2 used in computing for the kilo, and the more common 1/1,000 for micro. Presumably, the International Bureau of Weights and Measures would protest the mangling of the traditional form of the prefixes.

802.11g requires use of the short preamble, so this field is always set to 1 in a network built on the 802.11g standard.

PBCC

This field was added to 802.11b to support the high-rate DSSS PHY. When it is set to 1, it indicates that the network is using the packet binary convolution coding modulation scheme described in Chapter 12, or the higher-speed 802.11g PBCC modulation described in Chapter 14. Zero means that the option is not in use and is forbidden in the BSS.

Channel Agility

This field was added to 802.11b to support the high rate DSSS PHY. When it is set to one, it indicates that the network is using the Channel Agility option described in Chapter 12. Zero means the option is not in use and is forbidden in the BSS.

Short Slot Time (802.11g)

This bit is set to one to indicate the use of the shorter slot time supported by 802.11g, which is discussed in Chapter 14.

DSSS-OFDM (802.11g)

This bit is set to one to indicate that the optional DSSS-OFDM frame construction in 802.11g is in use.

Contention-free polling bits

Stations and access points use these two bits as a label. The meanings of the labels are shown in Table 4-4.

Table 4-4. Interpretation of polling bits in Capability Information

CF-Pollable	CF-Poll Request	Interpretation
Station usage		
0	0	Station does not support polling
0	1	Station supports polling but does not request to be put on the polling list
1	0	Station supports polling and requests a position on the polling list
1	1	Station supports polling and requests that it never be polled (results in station treated as if it does not support contention-free operation)
Access point usage		
0	0	Access point does not implement the point coordination function
0	1	Access point uses PCF for delivery but does not support polling
1	0	Access point uses PCF for delivery and polling
1	1	Reserved; unused

Current AP Address

Mobile stations use the Current AP Address field, shown in Figure 4-25, to indicate the MAC address of the access point with which they are associated. This field is used to ease associations and reassociations. Stations transmit the address of the access point that handled the last association with the network. When an association is established with a different access point, this field can be used to transfer the association and retrieve any buffered frames.

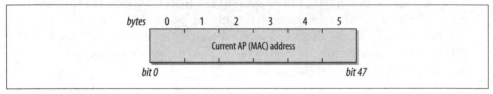

Figure 4-25. Current AP Address field

Listen interval

To save battery power, stations may shut off the antenna units in 802.11 network interfaces. While stations are sleeping, access points must buffer frames for them. Dozing stations periodically wake up to listen to traffic announcements to determine whether the access point has any buffered frames. When stations associate with an access point, part of the saved data is the *Listen Interval*, which is the number of Beacon intervals that stations wait between listening for Beacon frames. The Listen Interval, shown in Figure 4-26, allows mobile stations to indicate how long the access point must retain buffered frames. Higher listen intervals require more access point memory for frame buffering. Access points may use this feature to estimate the resources that will be required and may refuse resource-intensive associations. The Listen Interval is described in Chapter 8.

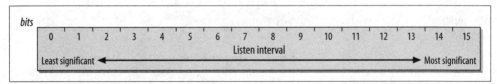

Figure 4-26. Listen Interval field

Association ID

The Association ID, shown in Figure 4-27, is a 16-bit field. When stations associate with an access point, they are assigned an Association ID to assist with control and management functions. Even though 14 bits are available for use in creating Association IDs, they range only from 1–2,007. To maintain compatibility with the Duration/ID field in the MAC header, the two most significant bits are set to 1.

Timestamp

The Timestamp field, shown in Figure 4-28, allows synchronization between the stations in a BSS. The master timekeeper for a BSS periodically transmits the number of microseconds it has been active. When the counter reaches its maximum value, it wraps around. (Counter wraps are unlikely given the length of time it takes to wrap a

Figure 4-27. *Association ID field*

64-bit counter. At over 580,000 years, I would bet on a required patch or two before the counter wrap.)

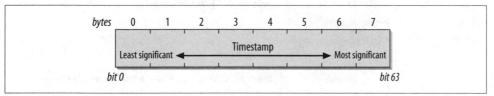

Figure 4-28. *Timestamp field*

Reason Code

Stations may send Disassociation or Deauthentication frames in response to traffic when the sender has not properly joined the network. Part of the frame is a 16-bit Reason Code field, shown in Figure 4-29, to indicate what the sender has done incorrectly. Table 4-5 shows why certain reason codes are generated. Fully understanding the use of reason codes requires an understanding of the different classes of frames and states of the 802.11 station, which is discussed in the section "Frame Transmission and Association and Authentication States."

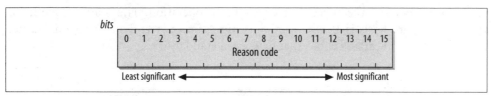

Figure 4-29. *Reason Code field*

Table 4-5. *Reason codes*

Code	Explanation
0	Reserved; unused
1	Unspecified
2	Prior authentication is not valid
3	Station has left the basic service area or extended service area and is deauthenticated
4	Inactivity timer expired and station was disassociated
5	Disassociated due to insufficient resources at the access point
6	Incorrect frame type or subtype received from unauthenticated station

Table 4-5. Reason codes (continued)

Code	Explanation
7	Incorrect frame type or subtype received from unassociated station
8	Station has left the basic service area or extended service area and is disassociated
9	Association or reassociation requested before authentication is complete
10 (802.11h)	Disassociated because of unacceptable values in Power Capability element
11 (802.11h)	Disassociated because of unacceptable values in Supported Channels element
12	Reserved
13 (802.11i)	Invalid information element (added with 802.11i, and likely one of the 802.11i information elements)
14 (802.11i)	Message integrity check failure
15 (802.11i)	4-way keying handshake timeout
16 (802.11i)	Group key handshake timeout
17 (802.11i)	4-way handshake information element has different security parameters from initial parameter set
18 (802.11i)	Invalid group cipher
19 (802.11i)	Invalid pairwise cipher
20 (802.11i)	Invalid Authentication and Key Management Protocol
21 (802.11i)	Unsupported Robust Security Network Information Element (RSN IE) version
22 (802.11i)	Invalid capabilities in RSN information element
23 (802.11i)	802.1X authentication failure
24 (802.11i)	Proposed cipher suite rejected due to configured policy
25-65,535	Reserved; unused

Status Code

Status codes indicate the success or failure of an operation. The Status Code field, shown in Figure 4-30, is 0 when an operation succeeds and nonzero on failure. Table 4-6 shows the status codes that have been standardized.

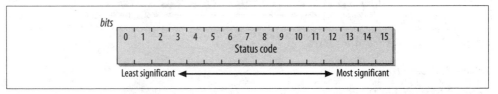

Figure 4-30. Status Code field

Table 4-6. Status codes

Code	Explanation
0	Operation completed successfully
1	Unspecified failure
2–9	Reserved; unused
10	Requested capability set is too broad and cannot be supported

Table 4-6. Status codes (continued)

Code	Explanation
11	Reassociation denied; prior association cannot be identified and transferred
12	Association denied for a reason not specified in the 802.11 standard
13	Requested authentication algorithm not supported
14	Unexpected authentication sequence number
15	Authentication rejected; the response to the challenge failed
16	Authentication rejected; the next frame in the sequence did not arrive in the expected window
17	Association denied; the access point is resource-constrained
18	Association denied; the mobile station does not support all of the data rates required by the BSS
19 (802.11b)	Association denied; the mobile station does not support the Short Preamble option
20 (802.11b)	Association denied; the mobile station does not support the PBCC modulation option
21 (802.11b)	Association denied; the mobile station does not support the Channel Agility option
22 (802.11h)	Association denied; Spectrum Management is required
23 (802.11h)	Association denied; Power Capability value is not acceptable
24 (802.11h)	Association denied; Supported Channels is not acceptable
25 (802.11g)	Association denied; the mobile station does not support the Short Slot Time
26 (802.11g)	Association denied; the mobile station does not support DSSS-OFDM
27-39	Reserved
40 (802.11i)	Information element not valid
41 (802.11i)	Group (broadcast/multicast) cipher not valid
42 (802.11i)	Pairwise (unicast) cipher not valid
43 (802.11i)	Authentication and Key Management Protocol (AKMP) not valid
44 (802.11i)	Robust Security Network information element (RSN IE) version is not supported
45 (802.11i)	RSN IE capabilites are not supported
46 (802.11i)	Cipher suite rejected due to policy
47–65,535	Reserved for future standardization work

Management Frame Information Elements

Information elements are variable-length components of management frames. A generic information element has an ID number, a length, and a variable-length component, as shown in Figure 4-31. Standardized values for the element ID number are shown in Table 4-7.

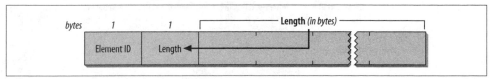

Figure 4-31. Generic management frame information element

Table 4-7. Information elements

Element ID	Name
0	Service Set Identity (SSID)
1	Supported Rates
2	FH Parameter Set
3	DS Parameter Set
4	CF Parameter Set
5	Traffic Indication Map (TIM)
6	IBSS Parameter Set
7 (802.11d)	Country
8 (802.11d)	Hopping Pattern Parameters
9 (802.11d)	Hopping Pattern Table
10 (802.11d)	Request
11–15	Reserved; unused
16	Challenge text
17–31	Reserved[a] (formerly for challenge text extension, before 802.11 shared key authentication was discontinued)
32 (802.11h)	Power Constraint
33 (802.11h)	Power Capability
34 (802.11h)	Transmit Power Control (TPC) Request
35 (802.11h)	TPC Report
36 (802.11h)	Supported Channels
37 (802.11h)	Channel Switch Announcement
38 (802.11h)	Measurement Request
39 (802.11h)	Measurement Report
40 (802.11h)	Quiet
41 (802.11h)	IBSS DFS
42 (802.11g)	ERP information
43-49	Reserved
48 (802.11i)	Robust Security Network
50 (802.11g)	Extended Supported Rates
32–255	Reserved; unused
221[b]	Wi-Fi Protected Access

[a] 802.11 shared key authentication is no longer recommended, so it is unlikely that these fields will ever be used.
[b] This is used by WPA, and is not an official part of 802.11. However, it is widely implemented, so I include it in the table.

Service Set Identity (SSID)

Network managers are only human, and they usually prefer to work with letters, numbers, and names rather than 48-bit identifiers. 802.11 networks, in the broadest sense, are either extended service sets or independent BSSs. The SSID, shown in Figure 4-32, allows network managers to assign an identifier to the service set. Stations attempting to join a network may scan an area for available networks and join the network with a specified SSID. The SSID is the same for all the basic service areas composing an extended service area.

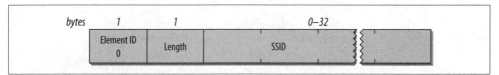

Figure 4-32. Service Set Identity information element

Some documentation refers to the SSID as the *network name* because network administrators frequently assign a character string to it. However, the SSID is just a string of bytes that labels the BSSID as belonging to a larger agglomeration. Some products require that the string be a garden variety ASCII string, though the standard has no requirement on the content of the string.

In all cases, the length of the SSID ranges between 0 and 32 bytes. The zero-byte case is a special case called the *broadcast SSID*; it is used only in Probe Request frames when a station attempts to discover all the 802.11 networks in its area.

Supported Rates

Several data rates have been standardized for wireless LANs. The Supported Rates information element allows an 802.11 network to specify the data rates it supports. When mobile stations attempt to join the network, they check the data rates used in the network. Some rates are mandatory and must be supported by the mobile station, while others are optional.

The Supported Rates information element is shown in Figure 4-33. It consists of a string of bytes. Each byte uses the seven low-order bits for the data rate; the most significant bit indicates whether the data rate is mandatory. Mandatory rates are encoded with the most significant bit set to 1 and optional rates have a 0. Up to eight rates may be encoded in the information element. As the number of data rates has proliferated, the Extended Supported Rates element was standardized to handle more than eight data rates.

In the initial revision of the 802.11 specification, the seven bits encoded the data rate as a multiple of 500 kbps. New technology, especially ETSI's HIPERLAN efforts, required a change to the interpretation. When 7 bits are used to have a multiple of

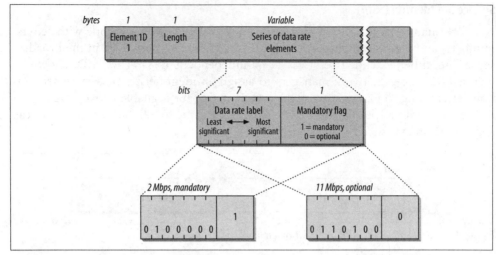

Figure 4-33. Supported Rates information element

500 kbps, the maximum data rate that can be encoded is 63.5 Mbps. Research and development on wireless LAN technology has made this rate achievable in the near future. As a result, the IEEE changed the interpretation from a multiple of 500 kbps to a simple label in 802.11b. Previously standardized rates were given labels corresponding to the multiple of 500 kbps, but future standards may use any value. Current standardized values are shown in Table 4-8.

Table 4-8. Supported Rate labels

Binary value	Corresponding rate (Mbps)
2	1
4	2
11 (802.11b)	5.5
12 (802.11g)	6
18 (802.11g)	9
22 (802.11b)	11
24 (802.11g)	12
36 (802.11g)	18
44 (802.11g)	22 (optional 802.11g PBCC)
48 (802.11g)	24
66 (802.11g)	33 (optional 802.11g PBCC)
72 (802.11g)	36
96 (802.11g)	48
108 (802.11g)	54

As an example, Figure 4-33 shows the encoding of two data rates. 2-Mbps service is mandatory and 11-Mbps service is supported. This is encoded as a mandatory 2-Mbps rate and an optional 11-Mbps rate.

FH Parameter Set

The FH Parameter Set information element, shown in Figure 4-34, contains all parameters necessary to join a frequency-hopping 802.11 network.

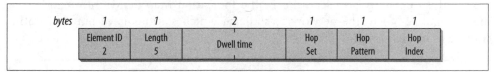

Figure 4-34. FH Parameter Set information element

The FH Parameter Set has four fields that uniquely specify an 802.11 network based on frequency hopping. Chapter 12 describes these identifiers in depth.

Dwell Time
    802.11 FH networks hop from channel to channel. The amount of time spent on each channel in the hopping sequence is called the *dwell time*. It is expressed in time units (TUs).

Hop Set
    Several hopping patterns are defined by the 802.11 frequency-hopping PHY. This field, a single byte, identifies the set of hop patterns in use.

Hop Pattern
    Stations select one of the hopping patterns from the set. This field, also a single byte, identifies the hopping pattern in use.

Hop Index
    Each pattern consists of a long sequence of channel hops. This field, a single byte, identifies the current point in the hop sequence.

DS Parameter Set

Direct-sequence 802.11 networks have only one parameter: the channel number used by the network. High-rate direct sequence networks use the same channels and thus can use the same parameter set. The channel number is encoded as a single byte, as shown in Figure 4-35.

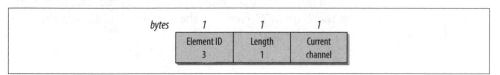

Figure 4-35. DS Parameter Set information element

Traffic Indication Map (TIM)

Access points buffer frames for mobile stations sleeping in low-power mode. Periodically, the access point attempts to deliver buffered frames to sleeping stations. A practical reason for this arrangement is that much more power is required to power up a transmitter than to simply turn on a receiver. The designers of 802.11 envisioned battery-powered mobile stations; the decision to have buffered frames delivered to stations periodically was a way to extend battery life for low-power devices.

Part of this operation is to send the Traffic Indication Map (TIM) information element (Figure 4-36) to the network to indicate which stations have buffered traffic waiting to be picked up.

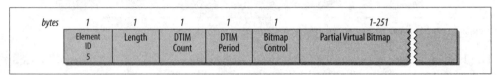

Figure 4-36. Traffic Indication Map information element

The meat of the traffic indication map is the *virtual bitmap*, a logical structure composed of 2,008 bits. Each bit is tied to the Association ID. When traffic is buffered for that Association ID, the bit is 1. If no traffic is buffered, the bit tied to the Association ID is 0.

DTIM Count
> This one-byte field is the number of Beacons that will be transmitted before the next DTIM frame. DTIM frames indicate that buffered broadcast and multicast frames will be delivered shortly. Not all Beacon frames are DTIM frames.

DTIM Period
> This one-byte field indicates the number of Beacon intervals between DTIM frames. Zero is reserved and is not used. The DTIM count cycles through from the period down to 0.

Bitmap Control and Partial Virtual Bitmap
> The Bitmap Control field is divided into two subfields. Bit 0 is used for the traffic indication status of Association ID 0, which is reserved for multicast traffic. The remaining seven bits of the Bitmap Control field are used for the Bitmap Offset field.

> To save transmission capacity, the Bitmap Offset field can be used to transmit a portion of the virtual bitmap. The Bitmap Offset is related to the start of the virtual bitmap. By using the Bitmap Offset and the Length, 802.11 stations can infer which part of the virtual bitmap is included.

CF Parameter Set

The CF Parameter Set information element is transmitted in Beacons by access points that support contention-free operation. Contention-free service is discussed in Chapter 9 because of its optional nature.

IBSS Parameter Set

IBSSs currently have only one parameter, the announcement traffic indication map (ATIM) window, shown in Figure 4-37. This field is used only in IBSS Beacon frames. It indicates the number of time units (TUs) between ATIM frames in an IBSS.

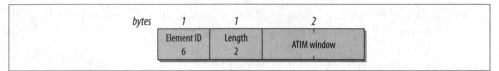

Figure 4-37. IBSS Parameter Set information element

Country

The initial 802.11 specifications were designed around the existing regulatory constraints in place in the major industrialized countries. Rather than continue to revise the specification each time a new country was added, a new specification was added that provides a way for networks to describe regulatory constraints to new stations. The main pillar of this is the Country information element, shown in Figure 4-38.

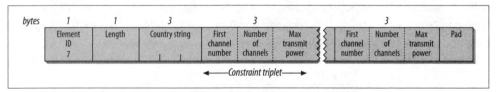

Figure 4-38. Country information element

After the initial type/length information element header, there is a country identifier, followed by a series of three-byte descriptors for regulatory constraints. Each constraint descriptor specifies a unique band, and they may not overlap, since a given frequency has only one maximum allowed power.

Country String (3 bytes)
> A three-character ASCII string of where the station is operating. The first two letters are the ISO country code (e.g., "US" for the United States). Many countries have different indoor and outdoor regulations, and the third character distinguishes between the two. When a single set of omnibus regulations covers all environments, the third character is a space. To designate indoor or outdoor regulations only, the third character may be set to "I" or "O", respectively.

First Channel Number (1 byte)

The first channel number is the lowest channel subject to the power constraint. Channel number assignment for each PHY is discussed in the appropriate chapter.

Number of Channels (1 byte)

The size of the band subject to the power constraint is indicated by the number of channels. The size of a channel is PHY-dependent.

Maximum Transmit Power (1 byte)

The maximum transmit power, expressed in dBm.

Pad (1 byte; optional)

The size of the information element must be an even number of bytes. If the length of the information element is an odd number of bytes, a single byte of zeroes is appended as a pad.

Hopping Pattern Parameters and Hopping Pattern Table

The initial 802.11 frequency hopping specification, described in Chapter 11, was built around the regulatory constraints in effect during its design. These two elements can be used to build a hopping pattern that complies with regulatory constraints in additional countries, which allows further adoption of the frequency-hopping PHY without requiring additional revision to the specification.

Request

In Probe Request frames, the Request information element is used to ask the network for certain information elements. The Request information element has the type/length header, and is followed by a list of integers with the numbers of the information elements being requested (Figure 4-39).

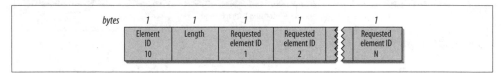

Figure 4-39. Request information element

Challenge Text

The shared-key authentication system defined by 802.11 requires that the mobile station successfully decrypt an encrypted challenge. The challenge is sent using the Challenge Text information element, which is shown in Figure 4-40.

Power Constraint

The Power Constraint information element is used to allow a network to describe the maximum transmit power to stations. In addition to a regulatory maximum, there may be another maximum in effect. The only field, a one-byte integer, is the number

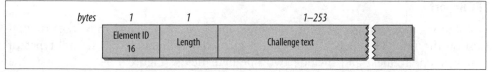

Figure 4-40. Challenge Text information element

of decibels by which any local constraint reduces the regulatory maximum. If, for example, the regulatory maximum power were 10 dBm, but this information element contained the value 2, then the station would set its maximum transmit power to 8 dBm (Figure 4-41).

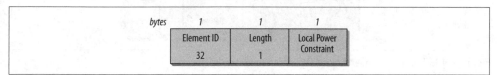

Figure 4-41. Power Constraint information element

Power Capability

802.11 stations are battery powered, and often have radios that are not as capable as access points, in part because there is not usually the need for mobile client devices to transmit at high power. The Power Capability information element allows a station to report its minimum and maximum transmit power, in integer units of dBm (Figure 4-42).

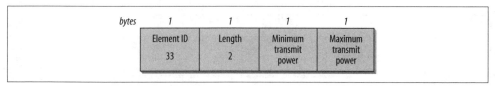

Figure 4-42. Power Capability information element

TPC Request

The Transmit Power Control (TPC) Request information element is used to request radio link management information. It has no associated data, so the length field is always zero (Figure 4-43).

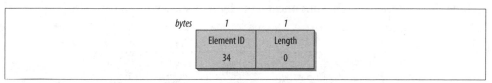

Figure 4-43. Transmit Power Request information element

TPC Report

For stations to know how to tune transmission power, it helps to know the attenuation on the link. TPC Report information elements are included in several types of management frames, and include two one-byte fields (Figure 4-44). The first, the transmit power, is the transmit power of the frame containing the information element, in units of dBm. The second, the *link margin*, represents the number of decibels of safety that the station requires. Both are used by the station to adapt its transmission power, as described in Chapter 8.

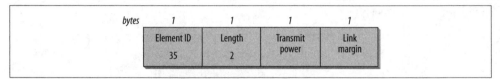

Figure 4-44. Transmit Power Report information element

Supported Channels

The Supported Channels information element is similar to the Country information element, in that it describes sub-bands that are supported. After the header, there is a series of sub-band descriptors. Each sub-band descriptor consists of a first channel number, which is the lowest channel in a supported sub-band, followed by the number of channels in the sub-band (Figure 4-45). For example, a device that only supported channels 40 through 52 would set the first channel number to 40, and the number of channels to 12.

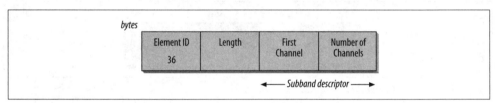

Figure 4-45. Supported Channels information element

Channel Switch Announcement

802.11h added the ability of networks to dynamically switch channels. To warn stations in the network about the impending channel change, management frames may include the Channel Switch Announcement element shown in Figure 4-46.

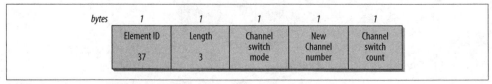

Figure 4-46. Channel Switch Announcement information element

Channel Switch Mode
When the operating channel is changed, it disrupts communication. If this field is set to 1, associated stations should stop transmitting frames until the channel switch has occurred. If it is set to zero, there is no restriction on frame transmission.

New Channel Number
The new channel number after the switch. At present, there is no need for this field to exceed a value of 255.

Channel Switch Count
Channel switching can be scheduled. This field is the number of Beacon frame transmission intervals that it will take to change the channel. Channel switch occurs just before the Beacon transmission is to begin. A non-zero value indicates the number of Beacon intervals to wait; a zero indicates that the channel switch may occur without any further warning.

Measurement Request and Measurement Report

Regular channel measurements are important to monitoring the channel and power settings. Two information elements are defined to allow stations to request measurements and receive reports. Reports are a key component of 802.11h, and will be discussed in detail in the "Spectrum Management" section of Chapter 8.

Quiet

One of the reasons for the development of dynamic frequency selection was the need to avoid certain military radar technologies. To find the presence of radar or other interference, an AP can use the Quiet element, shown in Figure 4-47, to temporarily shut down the channel to improve the quality of measurements.

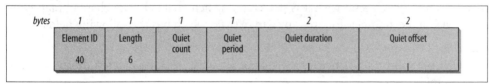

Figure 4-47. Quiet information element

Following the header, there are four fields:

Quiet Count
Quiet periods are scheduled. The count is the number of Beacon transmission intervals until the quiet period begins. It works in a similar fashion to the Channel Switch Count field.

Quiet Period
Quiet periods may also be periodically scheduled. If this field is zero, it indicates there are no scheduled quiet periods. A non-zero value indicates the number of beacon intervals between quiet periods.

Quiet Duration
> Quiet periods do not need to last for an entire Beacon interval. This field specifies the number of time units the quiet period lasts.

Quiet Offset
> Quiet periods do not necessarily have to begin with a Beacon interval. The Offset field is the number of time units after a Beacon interval that the next quiet period will begin. Naturally, it must be less than one Beacon interval.

IBSS DFS

In an infrastructure network, the access point is responsible for dynamic frequency selection. Independent networks must have a designated owner of the dynamic frequency selection (DFS) algorithm. Management frames from the designated station in an IBSS may transmit the IBSS DFS information element, shown in Figure 4-48.

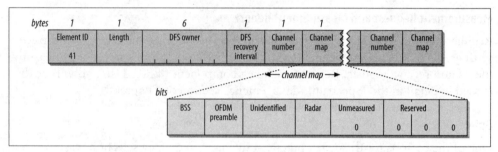

Figure 4-48. IBSS Dynamic Frequency Selection (DFS) information element

After the header, it has the MAC address of the station responsible for maintaining DFS information, as well as a measurement interval. The bulk of the frame is a series of *channel maps*, which report what is detected on each channel. The channel map consists of a channel number, followed by a map byte, which has the following fields:

BSS (1 bit)
> This bit will be set if frames from another network are detected during a measurement period.

OFDM Preamble (1 bit)
> This bit is set if the 802.11a short training sequence is detected, but without being followed by the rest of the frame. HIPERLAN/2 networks use the same preamble, but obviously not the same frame construction.

Unidentified Signal (1 bit)
> This bit is set when the received power is high, but the signal cannot be classified as either another 802.11 network (and hence, set the BSS bit), another OFDM network (and hence, set the OFDM Preamble bit), or a radar signal (and hence, set the Radar bit). The standard does not specify what power level is high enough to trigger this bit being set.

Radar (1 bit)

If a radar signal is detected during a measurement period, this bit will be set. Radar systems which must be detected are defined by regulators, not the 802.11 task group.

Unmeasured (1 bit)

If the channel was not measured, this bit will be set. Naturally, when there was no measurement taken, nothing can be detected in the band and the previous four bits will be set to zero.

ERP Information

802.11g defined the extended rate PHY (ERP). To provide backwards compatibility, the ERP information element, shown in Figure 4-49, was defined. In its first iteration, it is three bit flags in a single byte.

Non-ERP present

This bit will be set when an older, non-802.11g station associates to a network. It may also be set when overlapping networks that are not capable of using 802.11g are detected.

Use Protection

When stations incapable of operating at 802.11g data rates are present, the protection bit is set to 1. This enables backwards compatibility with older stations, as described in Chapter 14.

Barker Preamble Mode

This bit will be set if the stations which have associated to the network are not capable of the short preamble mode described in Chapter 12.

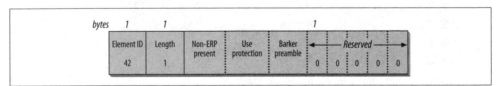

Figure 4-49. ERP information element

Robust Security Network

With the significant security enhancements in 802.11i, it was necessary to develop a way to communicate security information between stations. The main tool for this is the Robust Security Network (RSN) information element, shown in Figure 4-50. There are several variable components, and in some cases, the RSN information element might run into the limits of the information element size of 255 bytes past the header.

Version

The version field must be present. 802.11i defined version 1. Zero is reserved, and versions of two or greater are not yet defined.

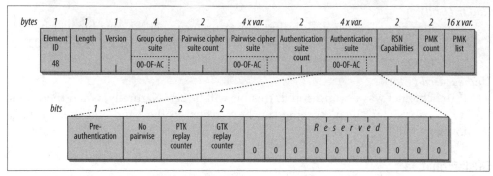

Figure 4-50. Robust Security Network (RSN) information element

Group cipher suite

Following the version number is the group cipher suite descriptor. Access points must select a single group cipher compatible with all associated stations to protect broadcast and multicast frames. Only one group cipher is allowed.

A cipher suite selector is four bytes long. It starts with an OUI for the vendor, and a number to identify the cipher. Table 4-9 shows the standardized cipher suites. (Values not shown in the table are reserved.) The OUI used by 802.11i is 00-0F-AC, which is used by the 802.11 working group.

Table 4-9. Cipher suites

OUI	Suite Type	Definition
00-0F-AC (802.11)	0	Use the group cipher suite (only valid for pairwise ciphers)
00-0F-AC	1	WEP-40
00-0F-AC	2	TKIP
00-0F-AC	3	Reserved
00-0F-AC	4	CCMP[a]
00-0F-AC	5	WEP-104
Vendor OUI	Any value	Defined by vendor

[a] This is the default value for an 802.11i network.

Pairwise Cipher Suites (count + list)

Following the group cipher suite may be several pairwise cipher suites to protect unicast frames. There is a two-byte count, followed by a series of supported cipher descriptors. The suite selector may be set to zero to indicate support for only the group cipher suite. There is no limit, other than the size of the information element, on the number of supported pairwise ciphers.

Authentication and Key Management (AKM) suites (count + list)

Like the pairwise cipher suite selector, there may be multiple authentication types defined. Following a count, there is a series of four-byte suite identifiers.

As with the cipher suites, the four-byte identifier consists of an OUI and a suite type number. Table 4-10 shows the standard authentication types.

Table 4-10. Authentication and key management suites

OUI	Suite type	Authentication	Key management
00-0F-AC	1	802.1X or PMK caching	Key derivation from preshared master key, as described in Chapter 7
00-0F-AC	2	Pre-shared key	Key derivation from pre-shared key, as described in Chapter 7
Vendor OUI	Any	Vendor-specific	Vendor-specific

RSN Capabilties
This two-byte field consists of four flags used to describe what the transmitter is capable of, followed by reserved bits that must be set to zero.

Pre-authentication
An AP may set this bit to indicate it can perform pre-authentication with other APs on the network to move security sessions around. Otherwise, this bit is set to zero. Preauthentication is discussed in Chapter 8.

No Pairwise
This bit is set when a station can support a manual WEP key for broadcast data in conjunction with a stronger unicast key. Although supported by the standard, this configuration should not be used unless absolutely necessary.

Pairwise Replay Counter and Group Replay Counter
Separate replay counters may be maintained for each priority level defined in emerging quality of service extensions. These bits describe the number of replay counters supported by the station.

PMK list (count + list)
Faster hand-offs between access points are possible when the pairwise master key is cached by the AP. Stations may provide a list of master keys to an AP on association in an attempt to bypass the time-consuming authentication. PMK caching is discussed in more detail in Chapter 8.

Extended Supported Rates

The Extended Supported Rates information element acts identically to the Supported Rates element in Figure 4-33, but it allows an information element body of up to 255 bytes to be supported.

Wi-Fi Protected Access (WPA)

Wi-Fi Protected Access is a slight modification of a subset of 802.11i, designed to bring TKIP to the market more quickly. It is identical to the Robust Security Network information element in Figure 4-50, but with the following changes:

- The element ID is 221, not 48.
- A WPA-specific tag of 00:50:F2:01 is inserted before the version field.
- Microsoft's OUI (00:50:F2) is used instead of the 802.11 working group's OUI.
- Only one cipher suite and one authentication suite are supported in the information element. However, many WPA implementations do not follow this restriction.
- TKIP is the default cipher, rather than CCMP.
- Preauthentication is not supported in WPA, so the preauthentication capabilities bit is always zero.

Types of Management Frames

The fixed fields and information elements are used in the body of management frames to convey information. Several types of management frames exist and are used for various link-layer maintenance functions.

Beacon

Beacon frames announce the existence of a network and are an important part of many network maintenance tasks. They are transmitted at regular intervals to allow mobile stations to find and identify a network, as well as match parameters for joining the network. In an infrastructure network, the access point is responsible for transmitting Beacon frames. The area in which Beacon frames appear defines the basic service area. All communication in an infrastructure network is done through an access point, so stations on the network must be close enough to hear the Beacons.

Figure 4-51 shows most the fields that can be used in a Beacon frame in the order in which they appear. Not all of the elements are present in all Beacons. Optional fields are present only when there is a reason for them to be used. The FH and DS Parameter Sets are used only when the underlying physical layer is based on frequency hopping or direct-sequence techniques. Only one physical layer can be in use at any point, so the FH and DS Parameter Sets are mutually exclusive.

The CF Parameter Set is used only in frames generated by access points that support the PCF, which is optional. The TIM element is used only in Beacons generated by access points, because only access points perform frame buffering. If the Country-specific frequency hopping extensions were to be present, they would follow the Country information element. Frequency hopping networks are much less common now, though, so I omit the frequency hopping extensions for simplicity. Likewise, the IBSS DFS element occur between the Quiet and TPC Report elements, were it to appear.

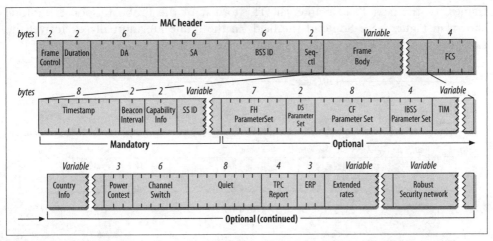

Figure 4-51. Beacon frame

Probe Request

Mobile stations use Probe Request frames to scan an area for existing 802.11 networks. The format of the Probe Request frame is shown in Figure 4-52. All fields are mandatory.

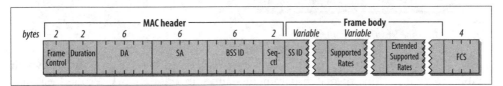

Figure 4-52. Probe Request frame

A Probe Request frame contains two fields: the SSID and the rates supported by the mobile station. Stations that receive Probe Requests use the information to determine whether the mobile station can join the network. To make a happy union, the mobile station must support all the data rates required by the network and must want to join the network identified by the SSID. This may be set to the SSID of a specific network or set to join any compatible network. Drivers that allow cards to join any network use the broadcast SSID in Probe Requests.

Probe Response

If a Probe Request encounters a network with compatible parameters, the network sends a Probe Response frame. The station that sent the last Beacon is responsible for responding to incoming probes. In infrastructure networks, this station is the access point. In an IBSS, responsibility for Beacon transmission is distributed. After a station transmits a Beacon, it assumes responsibility for sending Probe Response frames for the next Beacon interval. The format of the Probe Response frame is shown in Figure 4-53. Some of the fields in the frame are mutually exclusive; the same rules apply to Probe Response frames as to Beacon frames.

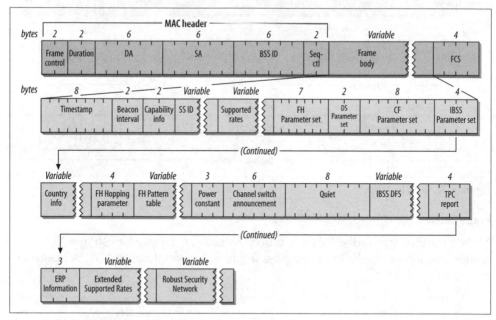

Figure 4-53. Probe Response frame

The Probe Response frame carries all the parameters in a Beacon frame, which enables mobile stations to match parameters and join the network. Probe Response frames can safely leave out the TIM element because stations sending probes are not yet associated and thus would not need to know which associations have buffered frames waiting at the access point.

IBSS announcement traffic indication map (ATIM)

IBSSs have no access points and therefore cannot rely on access points for buffering. When a station in an IBSS has buffered frames for a receiver in low-power mode, it sends an ATIM frame during the delivery period to notify the recipient it has buffered data. See Figure 4-54.

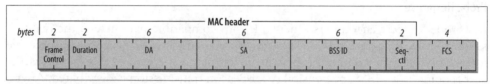

Figure 4-54. ATIM frame

Disassociation and Deauthentication

Disassociation frames are used to end an association relationship, and Deauthentication frames are used to end an authentication relationship. Both frames include a single fixed field, the Reason Code, as shown in Figure 4-55. Of course, the Frame Control fields differ because the subtype distinguishes between the different types of management frames. 802.11 revisions did not need to change the format, but many have added new reason codes.

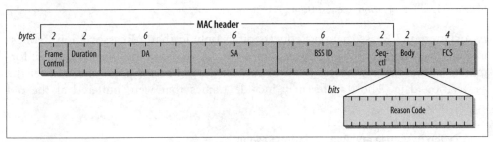

Figure 4-55. Disassociation and Deauthentication frames

Association Request

Once mobile stations identify a compatible network and authenticate to it, they may attempt to join the network by sending an Association Request frame. The format of the Association Request frame is shown in Figure 4-56.

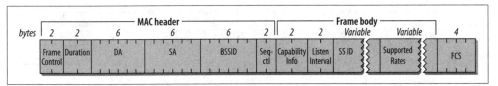

Figure 4-56. Association Request frame

The Capability Information field is used to indicate the type of network the mobile station wants to join. Before an access point accepts an association request, it verifies that the Capability Information, SSID, and (Extended) Supported Rates all match the parameters of the network. Access points also note the Listen Interval, which describes how often a mobile station listens to Beacon frames to monitor the TIM. Stations that support spectrum management will have the power and channel capability information elements, and stations supporting security will have the RSN information element.

Reassociation Request

Mobile stations moving between basic service areas within the same extended service area need to reassociate with the network before using the distribution system again. Stations may also need to reassociate if they leave the coverage area of an access point temporarily and rejoin it later. See Figure 4-57.

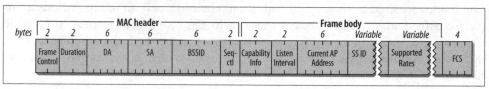

Figure 4-57. Reassociation Request frame

Association and Reassociation Requests differ only in that a Reassociation Request includes the address of the mobile station's current access point. Including this information allows the new access point to contact the old access point and transfer the association data. The transfer may include frames that were buffered at the old access point.

Association Response and Reassociation Response

When mobile stations attempt to associate with an access point, the access point replies with an Association Response or Reassociation Response frame, shown in Figure 4-58. The two differ only in the subtype field in the Frame Control field. All fields are mandatory. As part of the response, the access point assigns an Association ID. How an access point assigns the association ID is implementation-dependent.

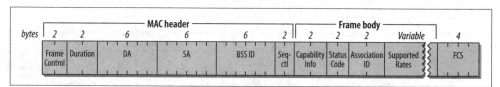

Figure 4-58. (Re)Association Response frame

Authentication

At the beginning of 802.11 networking, stations authenticated using a shared key, and exchanged Authentication frames, which are shown in Figure 4-59. With 802.11i, shared key authentication was kept in the standard, but made incompatible with the new security mechanisms. If a station uses shared key authentication, it will not be allowed to use the strong security protocols described in Chapter 8.

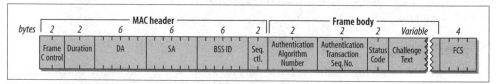

Figure 4-59. Authentication frames

Different authentication algorithms may co-exist. The Authentication Algorithm Number field is used for algorithm selection. The authentication process may involve a number of steps (depending on the algorithm), so there is a sequence number for each frame in the authentication exchange. The Status Code and Challenge Text are used in different ways by different algorithms; details are discussed in Chapter 8.

Action frame

802.11h added support for Action frames, which trigger measurements. These frames will be described in detail in the "Spectrum Management" section of Chapter 8.

Frame Transmission and Association and Authentication States

Allowed frame types vary with the association and authentication states. Stations are either authenticated or unauthenticated and can be associated or unassociated. These two variables can be combined into three allowed states, resulting in the 802.11 Hierarchy of Network Development:

1. Initial state; not authenticated and not associated
2. Authenticated but not yet associated
3. Authenticated and associated

Each state is a successively higher point in the development of an 802.11 connection. All mobile stations start in State 1, and data can be transmitted through a distribution system only in State 3. (IBSSs do not have access points or associations and thus only reach Stage 2.) Figure 4-60 is the overall state diagram for frame transmission in 802.11.

Frame Classes

Frames are also divided into different classes. Class 1 frames can be transmitted in State 1; Class 1 and 2 frames in State 2; and Class 1, 2, and 3 frames in State 3.

Class 1 frames

Class 1 frames may be transmitted in any state and are used to provide the basic operations used by 802.11 stations. Control frames are received and processed to provide basic respect for the CSMA/CA "rules of the road" and to transmit frames in an IBSS. Class 1 frames also allow stations to find an infrastructure network and authenticate to it. Table 4-11 shows a list of the frames that belong to the Class 1 group.

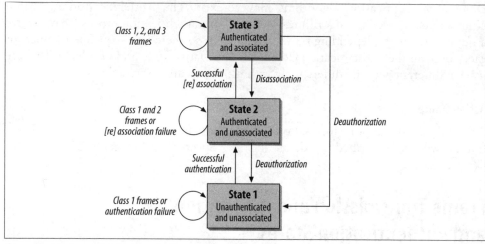

Figure 4-60. Overall 802.11 state diagram

Table 4-11. Class 1 frames

Control	Management	Data
Request to Send (RTS)	Probe Request	Any frame with ToDS and FromDS false (0)
Clear to Send (CTS)	Probe Response	
Acknowledgment (ACK)	Beacon	
CF-End	Authentication	
CF-End+CF-Ack	Deauthentication	
	Announcement Traffic Indication Message (ATIM)	

Class 2 frames

Class 2 frames can be transmitted only after a station has successfully authenticated to the network, and they can be used only in States 2 and 3. Class 2 frames manage associations. Successful association or reassociation requests move a station to State 3; unsuccessful association attempts cause the station to stay in State 2. When a station receives a Class 2 frame from a nonauthenticated peer, it responds with a Deauthentication frame, dropping the peer back to State 1.* Table 4-12 shows the Class 2 frames.

Table 4-12. Class 2 frames

Control	Management	Data
None	Association Request/Response	None
	Reassociation Request/Response	
	Disassociation	

---

* This rejection action takes place only for frames that are not filtered. Filtering prevents frames from a different BSS from triggering a rejection.

Class 3 frames

Class 3 frames are used when a station has been successfully authenticated and associated with an access point. Once a station has reached State 3, it is allowed to use distribution system services and reach destinations beyond its access point. Stations may also use the power-saving services provided by access points in State 3 by using the PS-Poll frame. Table 4-13 lists the different types of Class 3 frames.

Table 4-13. Class 3 frames

Control	Management	Data
PS-Poll	Deauthentication	Any frames, including those with either the ToDS or FromDS bits set

If an access point receives frames from a mobile station that is authenticated but not associated, the access point responds with a Disassociation frame to bump the mobile station back to State 2. If the mobile station is not even authenticated, the access point responds with a Deauthentication frame to force the mobile station back into State 1.

## CHAPTER 5

Wired Equivalent Privacy (WEP)

Anyone who is not shocked by quantum theory
has not understood it.
—Niels Bohr

In wireless networks, the word "broadcast" takes on an entirely new meaning. Wireless networks rely on an open medium, and the risk of using them is greatly increased if no cryptographic protection can be applied on the air link. With an open network medium, unprotected traffic can be seen by anybody with the right equipment. In the case of wireless LANs, the "right equipment" is a radio capable of receiving and decoding 802.11, which is hardly an expensive purchase. For extra eavesdropping power, a high-gain external antenna may be used. Antennas are inexpensive enough that you must assume that a determined attacher has purchased one.

Guarding against traffic interception is the domain of cryptographic protocols. As frames fly through the air, they must be protected against harm. Protection takes many forms, but the two most commonly cited informal objectives are maintaining the secrecy of network data and ensuring it has not been tampered with. Initially, the Wired Equivalent Privacy (WEP) standard was the answer for wireless security. In the first four years of 802.11's life, researchers built a strong case for the insecurity of WEP.

If WEP is so bad, why bother with it? In many cases, it is the only security protocol available on a particular device. WEP's design is easy to implement. Though it lacks the sophistication of later cryptographic protocols, it does not require the computational power, either. Older devices, especially handheld application-specific devices, may lack the processing punch necessary to run anything better, and WEP is the best that you can do. It is also important to learn about WEP because the WEP frame-handling operations underlie newer technology such as TKIP.

Cryptographic Background to WEP

Before discussing the design of WEP, it's necessary to cover some basic cryptographic concepts. I am not a cryptographer, and a detailed discussion of the cryptography involved would not be appropriate in this book, so this chapter is necessarily brief.*

To protect data, WEP requires the use of the RC4 cipher, which is a symmetric (secret-key) stream cipher. RC4 shares a number of properties with all stream ciphers. Generally speaking, a stream cipher uses a stream of bits, called the *keystream*. The keystream is then combined with the message to produce the *ciphertext*. To recover the original message, the receiver processes the ciphertext with an identical keystream. RC4 uses the exclusive OR (XOR) operation to combine the keystream and the ciphertext. Figure 5-1 illustrates the process.

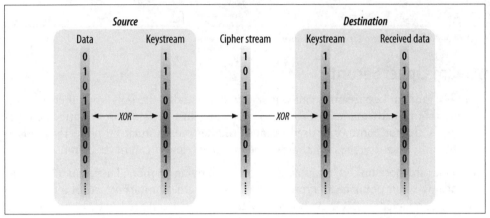

Figure 5-1. Generic stream cipher operation

Most stream ciphers operate by taking a relatively short secret key and expanding it into a pseudorandom keystream the same length as the message. This process is illustrated in Figure 5-2. The pseudorandom number generator (PRNG) is a set of rules used to expand the key into a keystream. To recover the data, both sides must share the same secret key and use the same algorithm to expand the key into a pseudorandom sequence.

Because the security of a stream cipher rests entirely on the randomness of the keystream, the design of the key-to-keystream expansion is of the utmost importance. When RC4 was selected by the 802.11 working group, it appeared to be quite secure. But once RC4 was selected as the ciphering engine of WEP, it spurred research that ultimately found an exploitable flaw in the RC4 cipher that will be discussed later.

---

* Readers interested in more detailed explanations of the cryptographic algorithms involved should consult *Applied Cryptography* by Bruce Schneier (Wiley, 1996).

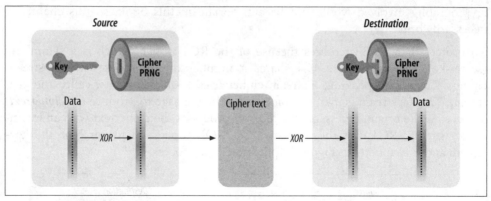

Figure 5-2. Keyed stream cipher operation

Stream Cipher Security

A totally random keystream is called a *one-time pad* and is the only known encryption scheme that is mathematically proven to protect against certain types of attacks. One-time pads are not commonly used because the keystream must be perfectly random and the same length as the data that will be protected, and it can never be reused.

Attackers are not limited to attacking the underlying cipher. They can choose to exploit any weak point in a cryptographic system. One famous Western intelligence effort, code-named VENONA, broke Soviet messages encrypted with one-time pads that were reused.[*] It is easy to understand the temptation to reuse the one-time pads. Huge volumes of keying material are necessary to protect even a small amount of data, and those keying pads must be securely distributed, which in practice proves to be a major challenge. One data bit must have a corresponding one-time pad bit. A 54 Mbps network can move about 25 Mbps of user data. If the network operates at just 10% of that capacity, the data transfer in an 8-hour workday is still 9 gigabytes. Distributing multiple gigabytes of keying material to every access point is totally impractical.

Stream ciphers are a compromise between security and practicality. The perfect randomness (and perfect security) of a one-time pad is attractive, but the practical difficulties and cost incurred in generating and distributing the keying material is worthwhile only for short messages that require the utmost security. Stream ciphers use a less random keystream but one that is random enough for most applications.

Cryptographic Politics

No discussion of cryptography would be complete without a passing reference to some of the many legal and regulatory concerns surrounding its use. Three major

---

[*] The United States National Security Agency has made some information on the project public at *http://www.nsa.gov/docs/venona*.

issues impinge upon the use of WEP, though the effect of these issues has diminished over time.

WEP requires the use of the RC4 cipher to encrypt the frame. When the first edition of this book was written, WEP was optional and not incorporated into all products. Host software could incorporate RC4 code, but open source projects had concerns about including code that infringed on the intellectual property of RSA Security, Inc. In the time since the first edition was published, this concern has faded into the background. All the major chipset vendors have licensed RC4 encryption and incorporated hardware support for RC4 into 802.11 chipsets. Device drivers are responsible for pushing WEP keys down to the hardware. Performing encryption in hardware on the card means that software no longer needs to risk infringing on RSA's intellectual property.

WEP was initially designed with short keys to satisfy the U.S. export regulations regarding cryptographic products. Initially, the standard required short 40-bit keys, but every product on the market supports at least 104-bit keys now. For a brief time, long keys looked like an important extension to the standard, though the additional security proved illusory.

Finally, some governments strictly regulate the use of any cryptographic system, WEP included. In addition to United States export regulations, many countries have import regulations that restrict importing cryptographic equipment. Other governments are also free to require additional cryptographic measures. The government of China has developed an alternative security system called WLAN Authentication and Privacy Infrastructure (WAPI), and has made it optional for wireless LAN equipment sold in China.

WEP Cryptographic Operations

Communications security has three major objectives. Any protocol that attempts to secure data as it travels across a network must help network managers to achieve these goals. *Confidentiality* is the term used to describe data that is protected against interception by unauthorized parties. *Integrity* means that the data has not been modified. *Authentication* underpins any security strategy because part of the reliability of data is based on its origin. Users must ensure that data comes from the source it purports to come from. Systems must use authentication to protect data appropriately. Authorization and access control are both implemented on top of authentication. Before granting access to a piece of data, systems must find out who the user is (authentication) and whether the access operation is allowed (authorization).

WEP provides operations that attempt to meet these objectives, though they often fail under serious scrutiny or attack. Frame body encryption supports confidentiality. An integrity check sequence protects data in transit and allows receivers to validate that the received data was not altered in transit. In practice, the operations offered by WEP are not strong and require additional strengthening measures, as discussed in the next two chapters.

WEP Data Processing

Confidentiality and integrity are handled simultaneously, as illustrated in Figure 5-3. Before encryption, the frame is run through an integrity check algorithm, generating a hash called an integrity check value (ICV). The ICV protects the contents against tampering by ensuring that the frame has not changed in transit. The frame and the ICV are both encrypted, so the ICV is not available to casual attackers.

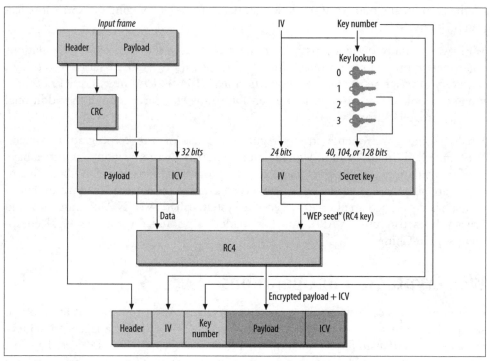

Figure 5-3. WEP operations

As input, WEP requires three items:

- The payload to be protected, which comes from the upper layer protocol stack.
- A secret key, used in frame encryption. Depending on implementation, keys may be specified as a string of key bits, or by key number. WEP allows four keys to be stored simultaneously.
- An initialization vector, used along with the secret key in frame transmission.

After processing, WEP has a single output:

- An encrypted frame, ready for transmission over an untrusted network with enough information to enable decryption at the remote end.

WEP data transmission

Driver software and the interface hardware are responsible for processing the data and sending out the encrypted packet, using the following sequence:

1. The 802.11 frame is queued for transmission. It consists of a frame header and the payload. WEP protects only the payload of the 802.11 MAC, and leaves the 802.11 frame header, as well as any lower-layer headers, intact.

2. An integrity check value (ICV) is calculated over the payload of the 802.11 MAC frame. It is calculated over the frame payload, so it starts at the first bit of the SNAP header, and goes up to the last data bit in the body. The 802.11 frame check sequence has not yet been calculated, so it is not included in the ICV calculation. The ICV used by WEP is a Cyclic Redundancy Check (CRC), a point that will be expanded on later.

3. The frame encryption key, or *WEP seed*, is assembled. WEP keys come in two parts: the *secret key*, and the *initialization vector* (IV). Stream ciphers will produce the same key stream from the same key, so an initialization vector is used to produce different stream ciphers for each transmitted frame. To reduce the occurrence of encryption with the same key stream, the sending station prepends the IV to the secret key. 802.11 does not place any constraints on the algorithm used to choose IVs; some products assign IVs sequentially, while others use a pseudorandom hashing algorithm. IV selection has some security implications because poor IV selection can compromise keys.

4. The frame encryption key is used as the RC4 key to encrypt the 802.11 MAC payload from step 1 and the ICV from step 2. The encryption process is often assisted with dedicated RC4 circuitry on the card.

5. With the encrypted payload in hand, the station assembles the final frame for transmission. The 802.11 header is retained intact. Between the 802.11 MAC header and the encrypted payload, a WEP header is inserted. In addition to the IV, the WEP header includes a *key number*. WEP allows up to four keys to be defined, so the sender must identify which key is in use. Once the final header is assembled, the 802.11 FCS value can be calculated over the entire MAC frame from the start of the header to the end of the (encrypted) ICV.

Decryption happens in the reverse order. As with any other transmission on the wireless network, the FCS is validated to ensure that the frame received was not corrupted in transit. To decrypt the protected part of the frame, the receiver will take its secret key, prepend the IV, and generate the key stream. With the decrypted data, it can then validate the ICV. Once the ICV is successfully validated, the packet data can be passed to the appropriate upper-layer protocol depending on the content of the SNAP header.

WEP key length

In theory, WEP can be used with keys of any length because RC4 does not require the use of any particular key size. Most products implement one of two key lengths, though. The only key length present in the standard is a 64-bit WEP seed, of which 40 bits are shared as a secret between the two communicating stations. Vendors have used a variety of names for the standard WEP mode: "standard WEP," "802.11-compliant WEP," "40-bit WEP," "40+24-bit WEP," or even "64-bit WEP." I personally feel that the last term is a stretch, based on hoodwinking the consumer with the length of the shared key and not the size of the shared secret, but it has become somewhat standard throughout the industry.

It is also common to implement a longer key length, typically with a 128-bit WEP seed, of which 104 bits are a kept secret. This is referred to as "WEP-104" by many documents, though it is almost always called "128-bit WEP" by sales literature. It is rare, though not unheard of, to use a third key length of 128 secret bits, which results in a 152-bit WEP seed. Confusingly, this rare implementation is often also called "128-bit WEP," although the differing key lengths makes it incompatible with WEP-104. One vendor even offers the option of using 256-bit secret keys with WEP, although the incremental security from such a long key is dubious.

In a well-designed cryptographic system, additional security can be obtained by using a longer key. Each additional bit doubles the number of potential keys and, in theory, doubles the amount of time required for a successful attack. WEP, however, is not a well-designed cryptographic system, and the extra bits in the key buy you very little. The best publicly disclosed attack against static WEP can recover the key in seconds, no matter what its length is.

Types of WEP keys

WEP can employ two different types of keys. *Mapped keys* protect traffic between a particular source and receiver. Mapped keys are sometimes referred to as *unicast keys* or *station keys* because they are well-suited to protect unicast traffic. In an infrastructure network, data is always transferred between a station and the access point serving it. 802.11 frames have both a receiver address and a destination address. Unicast traffic may have many different destination addresses, but every unicast frame transmitted in an infrastructure network will use the MAC address of the AP as its receiver address. All unicast traffic to or from a particular station can be encrypted by a single mapping key. *Default* keys, which are also referred to as *broadcast* keys, are used when no mapping relationship exists between two 802.11 stations. Default keys are a natural fit for broadcast and multicast frames because group addresses represent multiple stations and therefore cannot support key mapping relationships.

Manual (static) versus automatic (dynamic) WEP

802.11 does not specify any particular key distribution mechanism for use with WEP. As far as WEP is concerned, keys magically appear. Early WEP implementations relied on manual key distribution. Administrators were responsible for distributing a single default key to all stations in the network, usually manually. Key updates were also manual. In practice, most network deployments wound up using the same key for a very long time due to the high management overhead in changing the key. For this reason, WEP without any key distribution mechanism is often called *manual WEP* or *static WEP*.

Manual keys are an awful idea. Managing key distribution across a whole network of access points is very difficult. Keys protect data, and should therefore be changed whenever somebody with knowledge of the key leaves the organization. In theory, a well designed cryptographic system tries to limit the use of a key to as narrow a purpose as possible just in case a key is compromised. Static WEP used the same key for all frames transmitted by every station, which worsens the consequences of a key compromise.

Static WEP should not be used without a clear reason to do so. Static WEP is better than nothing, but little more can be said in its favor. It is effective for deterring casual attacks, but will not withstand determined assault. Many low-power devices such as 802.11 phones, handheld bar code scanners, and even some PDAs may not support anything better than static WEP. Until they can be replaced, static WEP offers the only possible link layer security for these devices.

Better solutions are based on *dynamic WEP*. Rather than a single key distributed to all stations, each station uses two keys. One is a key mapping key, shared between the station and access point, used to protect unicast frames. The second key is a default key, shared by all stations in the same service set, that protects broadcast and multicast frames. The encryption keys used by the clients are distributed using key encryption keys derived from strong authentication protocols that will be discussed in the next chapter.

Dynamic WEP offers significant advantages over static WEP solutions. At the highest level, the scope of each key is limited. Keys are used less often, and the result of compromising a key is lessened by using it to protect less traffic. Attackers can still mount assaults on the keys, but they have much less data to work for each key, making attacks more time-consuming. Nearly as important, dynamic keys can, as the name implies, change. At periodic intervals, the keys can be refreshed by the access point, which requires attackers to throw out accumulated data and start the assault on a key over again. By configuring short rekeying intervals, significant mitigation against attacks on keys is possible. Dynamic WEP solutions will be discussed later in this chapter.

WEP key numbering and storage

WEP keys have an associated number so that up to four keys may be defined on an 802.11 station. In the beginning, the WEP key number was meant to help facilitate changing the key across the network. Rather than switch every station to a new key simultaneously, the new key could be defined across the network and stations could be gradually switched. If, for example, an organization used key number 0 and wished to change it, key number 1 could be defined on the network. Rather than change all stations at the same time to the new key, stations could be configured to start using key number 1 during a defined transition period. At the end of the transition period, key number 0 would be disabled.

Key numbering takes on a slightly different role in dynamic WEP solutions. Each station receives two keys from the access point: a mapping key, typically stored as key number 0, and a default key, typically stored as key number 1. Stations use key 0 for protection of unicast traffic, and key 1 for protection of broadcast traffic. When frames are queued by the driver for transmission, the driver software will label unicast frames as requiring encryption with key 0, and broadcast frames as requiring encryption with key 1.

When 802.11 was new, many cards did not support WEP, or performed the RC4 encryption on the host CPU, limiting performance. RC4 is very easy to implement in hardware, and virtually every wireless LAN interface sold since 1999 has provided hardware-based RC4 encryption in the interface card itself to reduce the performance hit from encryption. (This includes most 802.11b cards and everything that has come later.) Some older cards also used firmware to limit key length to 40-bit keys rather than 104-bit keys, such as the Orinoco Silver and Gold cards. Key length restrictions were lifted in later firmware releases.

To efficiently encrypt frames, many 802.11 chipsets include a data structure called the *key cache*. Key caches consist of mappings between tuples of the destination address, the key identifier number, and the bits of the key itself. Most chipsets intended for use in station interface cards have four key slots. Static WEP uses one key slot; dynamic WEP solutions use two. When frames are queued for transmission, the destination address is looked up in the key cache and the resulting key is used to encrypt the frame. Dynamic keying solutions function identically to static WEP solutions, except that the contents of the key cache may be overwritten by key management software.

One of the ways in which chipsets intended for use in cards differ from chipsets intended for use in access points is that the AP chipsets have much larger key caches, often capable of 256 or more key entries. Even with two entries required (one mapped key and one default key) for a station, such a data structure can handle keying for more than 100 stations. Given the limited capacity of most wireless link technologies, such a large data will handle any reasonable traffic load with room to spare. However, some early APs capable of dynamic keying were unable to maintain large key data structures, and had to share keys among multiple stations. To cut costs, some vendors used card chipsets rather than AP chipsets in the AP radio. As a result, they only had four key slots and needed to share a single unicast key among all stations attached to an AP.

WEP Encapsulation

When WEP is in use, the frame body expands by eight bytes. Four bytes are used for a frame body IV header, and four are used for the ICV trailer. See Figure 5-4.

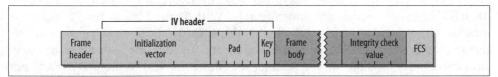

Figure 5-4. WEP frame extensions

The IV header uses 3 bytes for the 24-bit IV, with the fourth byte used for padding and key identification. When a default key is used, the Key ID subfield identifies the default key that was used to encrypt the frame. If a key mapping relationship is used, the Key ID subfield is 0. The 6 padding bits of the last byte must be 0. The integrity check is a 32-bit CRC of the data frame; it is appended to the frame body and protected by RC4. The frame check sequence protects the encrypted data.

Problems with WEP

Cryptographers have identified many flaws in WEP. The designers specified the use of RC4, which is widely accepted as a strong cryptographic cipher. Attackers, however, are not limited to a full-frontal assault on the cryptographic algorithms—they can attack any weak point in the cryptographic system. Methods of defeating WEP have come from every angle. One notable slip was a vendor who shipped access points that exposed the secret WEP keys through SNMP, allowing an attacker to ask for just the key. Most of the press, though, has been devoted to flaws beyond implementation errors, which are much harder to correct.

Cryptographic Properties of RC4

Reuse of the keystream is the major weakness in any stream cipher–based cryptosystem. When frames are encrypted with the same RC4 keystream, the XOR of the two encrypted packets is equivalent to the XOR of the two plaintext packets. By analyzing differences between the two streams in conjunction with the structure of the frame body, attackers can learn about the contents of the plaintext frames themselves. To help prevent the reuse of the keystream, WEP uses the IV to encrypt different packets with different RC4 keys. However, the IV is part of the packet header and is not encrypted, so eavesdroppers are tipped off to packets that are encrypted with the same RC4 key.

Implementation problems can contribute to the lack of security. 802.11 admits that using the same IV for a large number of frames is insecure and should be avoided. The standard allows for using a different IV for each frame, but it is not required.

WEP incorporates an integrity check, but the algorithm used is a cyclic redundancy check (CRC). CRCs can catch single-bit alterations with high probability, but they are not *cryptographically secure*. Cryptographically secure integrity checks are based on hash functions, which are unpredictable. With unpredictable functions, if the attacker changes even one bit of the frame, the integrity check will change in unpredictable ways. The odds of an attacker finding an altered frame with the same integrity check are so slim that it cannot be done in real time. CRCs are not cryptographically secure. CRC calculations are straightforward mathematics, and it is easy to predict how changing a single bit will affect the result of the CRC calculation. (This property is often used by compressed data files for repair! If just a few bits are bad, they can sometimes be identified and corrected based on a CRC value.)

Design Flaws of the WEP System

WEP's design flaws initially gained prominence when the Internet Security, Applications, Authentication, and Cryptography (ISAAC) group at the University of California, Berkeley, published preliminary results based on their analysis of the WEP standard.[*] None of the problems identified by researchers depend on breaking RC4. Here's a summary of the problems they found; I've already touched on some of them:

1. Manual key management is a minefield of problems. Setting aside the operational issues with distributing identical shared secrets to the user population, the security concerns are nightmarish. New keying material must be distributed on a "flag day" to all systems simultaneously, and prudent security practices would lean strongly toward rekeying whenever anybody using WEP leaves the company (the administrative burden may, however, preclude doing this). Widely distributed secrets tend to become public over time. Passive sniffing attacks require obtaining only the WEP keys, which are likely to be changed infrequently. Once a user has obtained the WEP keys, sniffing attacks are easy, especially since 802.11 analyzers incorporate decryption capabilities.

2. As standardized, static WEP offers a shared secret of only 40 bits. Security experts have long questioned the adequacy of 40-bit private keys, and many

[*] The report is available on the Web at *http://www.isaac.cs.berkeley.edu/isaac/wep-faq.html*. Items 3–6 on the following list are summarized from that report.

recommend that sensitive data be protected by at least 128-bit keys.[*] In the years since the initial flaws in WEP were published, the industry-standard extended key length is only 104 bits.

3. Stream ciphers are vulnerable to analysis when the keystream is reused. WEP's use of the IV tips off an attacker to the reuse of a keystream. Two frames that share the same IV almost certainly use the same secret key and keystream. This problem is made worse by poor implementations, which may not pick random IVs. The Berkeley team identified one implementation that started with an IV of 0 when the card was inserted and simply incremented the IV for each frame. Furthermore, the IV space is quite small (less than 17 million), so repetitions are guaranteed on busy networks.

4. Infrequent rekeying allows attackers to assemble what the Berkeley team calls *decryption dictionaries*—large collections of frames encrypted with the same keystreams. As more frames with the same IV pile up, more information is available about the unencrypted frames even if the secret key is not recovered. Given how overworked the typical system and network administration staff is, infrequent rekeying is the rule.

5. WEP uses a CRC for the integrity check. Although the value of the integrity check is encrypted by the RC4 keystream, CRCs are not cryptographically secure. Use of a weak integrity check does not prevent determined attackers from transparently modifying frames.[†]

6. The access point is in a privileged position to decrypt frames. Conceptually, this feature can be attacked by tricking the access point into retransmitting frames that were encrypted by WEP. Frames received by the access point would be decrypted and then retransmitted to the attacker's station. If the attacker is using WEP, the access point would helpfully encrypt the frame using the attacker's key.

Key Recovery Attacks Against WEP

In August 2001, Scott Fluhrer, Itsik Mantin, and Adi Shamir published a paper titled "Weaknesses in the Key Scheduling Algorithm of RC4." At the end of the paper, the authors describe a theoretical attack on WEP. At the heart of the attack is a weakness in the way that RC4 expands the key into the key stream, a process called the *key scheduling algorithm*.

The Fluhrer-Mantin-Shamir attack, or FMS attack for short, assumes the ability to recover the first byte of the encrypted payload. In many cryptographic systems, that

---

[*] To be fair, WEP was originally developed with the goal of being exportable under the then-current U.S. regulations for export of cryptographic systems. A longer key could not have been used without jeopardizing the commercial viability of U.S.-built 802.11 products.

[†] 802.11 requires frame retransmissions in the case of loss, so it may be possible for an attacker to retransmit a frame and cause a replacement injected frame to be accepted as legitimate.

would be a big assumption. WEP, however, is used to protect 802.11 frames, and the 802.11 frame body begins with a SNAP header. Therefore, the cleartext value of the first byte is known to be 0xAA. Because the first cleartext byte is known, the first byte of the keystream can be easily deduced from a trivial XOR operation with the first encrypted byte.

The paper's attacks are focused on a class of weak keys written in the form (B+3):FF:N. Each weak IV is used to attack a particular byte of the secret portion of the RC4 key. Key bytes are numbered from zero. Therefore, the weak IV corresponding to byte zero of the secret key has the form 3:FF:N. The second byte must be 0xFF; knowledge of the third byte in the key is required, but it need not be any specific value.

A standard WEP key is 40 secret bits, or 5 bytes numbered consecutively from 0 to 4. Weak IVs on a network protected by standard WEP must have a first byte that ranges from 3 (B=0) to 7 (B=4) and a second byte of 255. The third byte must be noted but is not constrained to any specific value. There are $5 \times 1 \times 256 = 1,280$ weak IVs of this type in a static WEP network. Additional classes of weak IVs have been exploited since the publication of the paper, bringing the total number of weak IVs to about 9,000; this is approximately 5% of the total number of IVs. These new classes depend on the relationships between IV bytes. Readers who are interested in the other classes of weak IVs should refer to the source code of WEP cracking tools.[*]

Each weak IV leaks information about a key byte. By applying probability theory, Fluhrer, Mantin, and Shamir estimated that about 60 weak IVs need to be collected for each key byte. Furthermore, and perhaps worst of all, the attack gains speed as more key bytes are determined. Guessing the first key byte helps you get the second, and so on. Success cascades through the attack, and it works in linear time. Doubling the key length only doubles the computational time for the attack to succeed.

With such a tantalizing result, it was only a matter of time before it was used to attack a real system. In early August 2001, Adam Stubblefield, John Ioannidis, and Avi Rubin applied the FMS attack to an experimental, but real, network with devastating effect.[†] In their testing, 60 resolved cases usually determined a key byte, and 256 resolved cases always yielded a full key. It took less than a week to implement the attack, from the ordering of the wireless card to the recovery of the first full key. Coding the attack took only a few hours. Key recovery was accomplished between five and six million packets, which is a small number for even a moderately busy network.

Reporting on a successful attack, however, is nothing compared to having a public code base available to use at will. The hard part of the Fluhrer-Mantin-Shamir attack was finding the RC4 weakness. Implementing their recommendations is not too

[*] For example, see the *classify()* function in Airsnort's *crack.c*.
[†] This work is described more fully in AT&T Labs Technical Report TD-4ZCPZZ.

difficult. In late August 2001, AirSnort, an open source WEP key recovery program, was released. Many tools have followed AirSnort.

Key recovery defenses

Longer keys are no defense against key recovery attacks. The time required to recover a key can be broken up into the gathering time required to collect enough frames for the attack, plus the computational time required to run the program and get the key. Computational time is only a few seconds; gathering time generally dominates the attack. Longer keys require slightly more computational time, but do not require different gathering time. As the key length increases, more weak IVs are caught in the dragnet.

One defense adopted by many vendors is to avoid using weak IVs. Most vendors have now changed products so that each IV to be used is first checked against a classifier, and any weak IVs are replaced by non-weak IVs. Unfortunately, reducing the size of the IV space may cause IV re-use to happen earlier.

Network administrators have responded to key recovery attacks by using stronger protocols, such as the 802.11i protocols discussed in Chapter 7. For many organizations, this is a solution. However, newer protocols may not be as compatible as dynamic WEP with existing equipment. To mitigate the use of WEP, most network administrators set a re-key time of between 5 and 15 minutes, depending on the acceptable overhead on the network.

Dynamic WEP

With the attention devoted to security, it was not long before the industry started to develop wireless LAN technologies with significantly improved security. The first step along this road was to bolster WEP by refreshing the keys dynamically. Rather than a single static WEP key for all frames on the network shared by all stations, dynamic WEP solutions use a set of different keys. All stations in a network share a key to encrypt broadcast frames, and each station has its own mapping key for unicast frames.[*]

WEP did not specify a key management framework. Keys are generated and distributed through a system that is not written down in 802.11. The first, and easiest key management "framework" to be implemented was manual. Network administrators needed to come up with a string of bits used as a key, and then distribute that key to all stations participating in an 802.11 service set secured by WEP. To set a key, administrators needed to touch a machine to configure a new key.

---

[*] With appropriate key distribution protocols in place, you can even have multiple groups share the same infrastructure. Each station has its own mapping key for unicast frames, but there may be multiple independent broadcast groups, each with its own default key for group frames.

Layered Security Protocols

When the first edition of this book was written, WEP was rightly viewed as an insecure security system. Classic old-school manually-distributed static-key WEP is fundamentally broken. When it became clear that the relatively minimal protection provided by WEP was insufficient for most network environments, a task group formed to develop enhancements to the security of the MAC. That work was standardized as 802.11i in June of 2004.

During the gap between the initial research that exposed WEP's flaws and the development of more secure technologies to bolster it, network administrators turned to proven security protocols at higher layers in the stack, such as IPsec (layer 3), SSL (layer 4), and SSH (layer 7). With static WEP offering only minimal security, the additional encryption strength provided by higher-layer technology was well worth it.

With the development of stronger link layer technologies, layered security protocols are no longer the magic bullet they once appeared to be. IPsec requires client software to be installed and configured. SSL-based VPNs are much simpler to set up, though they often have shortcomings when securing applications that are not web-based. SSH is well-understood and can create arbitrary TCP tunnels, but it often requires significant modifications to user procedures. (Chances are that if you are reading this book, SSH is second nature; however, it is probably not something you want your users trying to figure out.)

With the development of the improved link layer security technologies discussed in this chapter and the next two, it is finally possible to build secure networks at the link layer. One increasingly common approach to building secure wireless networks is to consider what these new technologies can do, and then determine whether additional protection at higher layer protocols is required. Balancing the trade-offs is the subject of Chapter 22, in the deployment section of the book.

Dynamic WEP uses an improved key management framework. Rather than depend on the administrator for so much manual work, dynamic WEP uses strong cryptographic protocols to generate keys and then distribute them, in encrypted form, over untrusted networks. WEP key generation typically depends on the use of a cryptographic authentication protocol, which is discussed in the next chapter.

Dynamic WEP handles frames in an identical fashion to static WEP. The only difference is that there is a much improved mechanism to generate and distribute keys on a periodic basis. The automatic key management of dynamic WEP achieves much greater security than static WEP because it dramatically shortens the lifetime of a key. Any attacks against the key must take place within a single key lifetime. Frame initialization vectors can be re-used after a key refresh because they correspond to two different WEP seeds. Key recovery attacks using Fluhrer/Mantin/Shamir must occur within a single key lifetime as well, for obvious reasons. Dynamic WEP is by no means perfect, but it is a substantial improvement over static WEP. It is widely supported by almost every card and driver.

## CHAPTER 6

User Authentication with 802.1X

What is your name?
What is your quest?
What is your favorite color?
—The Bridgekeeper
Monty Python and the Holy Grail

Security is a common thread linking many of the wireless LAN stories in the news throughout the past several years, and polls repeatedly show that network managers consider security to be a significant obstacle to wider deployment of wireless LANs. Many of the security problems that have prevented stronger acceptance of 802.11 are caused by flaws in the design of static WEP.

Manual WEP attempts to be too many solutions to multiple problems. It was intended to be used both for authentication, by restricting access to those in possession of a key, and confidentiality, by encrypting data as it traversed wireless links. In the final analysis, it does neither particularly well. Both authentication and confidentiality are important issues for wireless LANs, and the subject of a great deal of technology development since the first edition of this book.

This chapter takes on the problem of authentication, which is provided at the link layer through the use of 802.1X.* 802.1X has matured a great deal since the first edition of this book, and is increasingly the authentication protocol of choice on wireless LANs.† Static WEP authenticates machines in possession of a cryptographic key. 802.1X allows network administrators to authenticate users rather than machines, and can be used to ensure that users connect to legitimate, authorized networks rather than credential-stealing impostor networks.

---

* 802.1X is written with a capital X. In the IEEE nomenclature, lowercase letters ("802.11a" and "802.11b") are reserved for add-on specifications that revise an existing standard. Uppercase letters are used for standalone specifications. As a full, standalone protocol specification in its own right, 802.1X gets a capital letter.

† One of my personal yardsticks for the maturity of a specification is the existence of an open source implementation. Open source software frequently serves a valuable role by keeping proprietary implementations honest, and providing a low-cost reality check for users. In the 802.1X world, the xsupplicant and wpa_supplicant projects have taken on this role.

Identifying users instead of machines can lead to more effective network architecture. Rather than grouping users by function and applying security controls to the physical ports in a physical location, the identity of the user and any access rights can be integrated into the network switch fabric, and follow users around the network. Wireless LANs are often the first use of identity-based policy enforcement. It is not uncommon for companies to use the capability on wireless networks, and then find it so useful that it is later integrated into the wired network. No matter where or how users attach to the network, policy follows them around.

One of the complexities in dealing with 802.1X is that it is a framework. It is an IEEE adaptation of the IETF's Extensible Authentication Protocol (EAP), originally specified in RFC 2284 and updated by RFC 3748. EAP is a framework protocol. Rather than specifying how to authenticate users, EAP allows protocol designers to build their own *EAP methods*, subprotocols that perform the authentication transaction. EAP methods can have different goals, and therefore, often use many different methods for authenticating users depending on the requirements of a particular situation. Before a detailed discussion of how the different methods work, though, a detailed understanding of how EAP works is necessary.

The Extensible Authentication Protocol

802.1X is based on EAP. Recent work in wireless networking required an update to the standard, which is now found in RFC 3748. Back in the early 1990s, when PPP was first introduced, there were two protocols available to authenticate users, each of which required the use of a PPP protocol number. Authentication is not a "one size fits all" problem, and it was an active area of research at the time. Rather than burn up PPP protocol numbers for authentication protocols that might become obsolete, the IETF standardized EAP. EAP used a single PPP protocol number while supporting a wide variety of authentication mechanisms. EAP is a simple encapsulation that can run over any link layer, but it has been most widely deployed on PPP links. Figure 6-1 shows the basic EAP architecture, which is designed to run over any link layer and use any number of authentication methods.

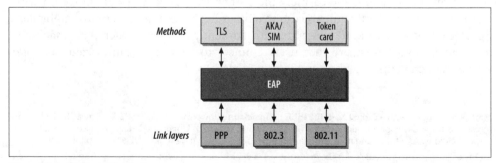

Figure 6-1. EAP architecture

EAP Packet Format

Figure 6-2 shows the format of an EAP packet. When used on PPP links, EAP is carried in PPP frames with a protocol number of 0xC227. There is no strict requirement that EAP run on PPP; the packet shown in Figure 6-2 can be carried in any type of frame. The fields in an EAP packet are:

Code

The Code field, the first field in the packet, is one byte long and identifies the type of EAP packet. It is used to interpret the Data field of the packet.

Identifier

The Identifier field is one byte long. It contains an unsigned integer used to match requests with responses to them. Retransmissions reuse the same identifier numbers, but new transmissions use new identifier numbers.

Length

The Length field is two bytes long. It is the number of bytes in the entire packet, which includes the Code, Identifier, Length, and Data fields. On some link layer protocols, padding may be required. EAP assumes that any data in excess of the Length field is link-layer padding and can be ignored.

Data

The last field is the variable-length Data field. Depending on the type of packet, the Data field may be zero bytes long. Interpretation of the Data field is based on the value of the Code field.

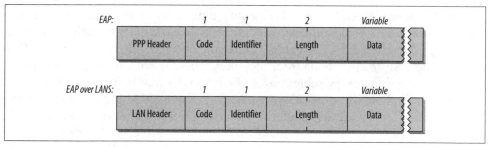

Figure 6-2. EAP packet format

EAP Requests and Responses

EAP exchanges are composed of requests and responses. The authenticator sends requests to the system seeking access, and based on the responses, access may be granted or denied. Client systems only send response packets when there is an outstanding request to send. There is no such thing as an unsolicited packet from the system seeking authentication. The format of request and response packets is shown in Figure 6-3.

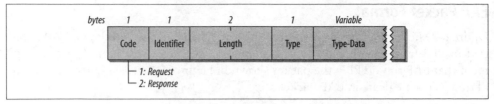

Figure 6-3. EAP Request and EAP Response packets

The Code field is set to 1 for requests and 2 for responses. The Identifier and Length fields are used as described in the previous section on the generic format. The Data field carries the data used in requests and responses. Each Data field carries one type of data, broken down into a type identifier code and the associated data:

Type
> The Type field is a one-byte field that indicates the type of request or response. Only one type is used in each packet. With one exception, the Type field of the response matches the corresponding request. That exception is that when a request is unacceptable, the peer may send a NAK to suggest an alternative type. Types greater than or equal to 4 indicate authentication methods.

Type-Data
> The Type-Data field is a variable field that must be interpreted according to the rules for each type, as described in the following sections.

Type code 1: Identity

The authenticator generally uses the Identity type as the initial request, which is often written as *EAP-Request/Identity*, or simply *Request/Identity* to indicate that the authenticator is attempting to establish some sort of username to authenticate. Frequently, the EAP Identity is the user identifier, possibly with routing information. Some technologies work by submitting an EAP Identity that may correspond to the machine. In the initial Request/Identity packet, if any information is present in the Type-Data field, it is used to prompt the user, though this is relatively uncommon. If the Type-Data field is present and contains a prompt string, its length is inferred from the length of the EAP packet, rather than having a separate delimiter.

Many EAP implementations are capable of prompting the (human) user for input to determine the user identity, though it is not required. For greater usability, most EAP implementations also allow the identity to be statically configured. Once the user name has been determined, the EAP client will respond with a *Response/Identity* packet. In Response/Identity packets, the Type-Data field contains the username. It may be a "bare" username, such as *mgast*, or it may be qualified with an Internet-style domain (*mgast@domain.com*), or a Windows-style domain name (*DOMAIN\mgast*).

Some EAP implementations may attempt to look up the user identity in a Response even before issuing the authentication challenge. If the user does not exist, the authentication can fail without further processing. Most implementations automatically reissue the identity request to give the user an opportunity to correct typos.

Type code 2: Notification

The authenticator can use the Notification type to send a message to the user. The user's system can then display the message in the *Request/Notification* for the user's benefit. Notification messages are used to provide messages to the user from the authentication system, such as a password about to expire, or the reason for an account lockout. Notification messages are not commonly used with 802.1X; only a few vendors implement them. Responses must be sent in reply to Notification requests. However, *Response/Notification* packets serve as simple acknowledgments, and the Type-Data field has a zero length.

Type code 3: NAK

Null acknowledgments (NAKs) are used to suggest a new authentication method. The authenticator issues a challenge, encoded by a type code. Authentication types are numbered 4 and above. If the end user system does not support the authentication type of the challenge, it can issue a NAK. The Type-Data field of a NAK message includes a single byte corresponding to the suggested authentication type. Most 802.1X implementations do not actively negotiate, and will simply log an error message if the client attempts to use an unsupported type.

EAP Authentication Methods

In addition to flow-control messages and negotiation messages, EAP assigns type codes to authentication methods. EAP delegates the work of proving a user identity to a subsidary protocol, the *EAP method*, which is a set of rules for authenticating a user.

The advantage of using the method construction is that it frees EAP from any particular set of assumptions about what is necessary to authenticate a user. When requirements change, as they did with the popularity of wireless networks, new EAP methods can be developed to meet the challenge. Table 6-1 lists several EAP methods with their type codes. A more detailed description of the EAP methods commonly used on wireless LANs will follow later in this chapter.

Table 6-1. Common EAP methods for 802.1X authentication

Type code	Authentication protocol	Description
4	MD5 Challenge	CHAP-like authentication in EAP
6	GTC	Originally intended for use with token cards such as RSA SecurID
13	EAP-TLS	Mutual authentication with digital certificates
21	TTLS	Tunneled TLS; protects weaker authentication methods with TLS encryption

Table 6-1. Common EAP methods for 802.1X authentication (continued)

Type code	Authentication protocol	Description
25	PEAP	Protected EAP; protects weaker EAP methods with TLS encryption
18	EAP-SIM	Authentication by mobile phone Subscriber Identity Module (SIM)
29	MS-CHAP-V2	Microsoft encrypted password authentication; compatible with Windows domains

EAP Success and Failure

At the conclusion of an EAP exchange, the user has either authenticated successfully or has failed to authenticate (Figure 6-4). Once the authenticator determines that the exchange is complete, it can issue an EAP-Success (code 3) or EAP-Failure (code 4) frame to end the EAP exchange. Implementations are allowed to send multiple requests before failing the authentication to allow a user to get the correct authentication data.

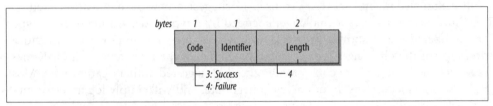

Figure 6-4. EAP Success and Failure frames

Success and Failure frames are not authenticated in any way. In the dial-up world, the telephone network provides a modicum of security that the sender is at the other end of the circuit. In wireless LANs, the lack of authentication on Success and Failure frames may require extra protocol design.

A Sample EAP Exchange

A sample EAP exchange is shown in Figure 6-5. It is not a "real" exchange that would be seen on a wireless network because it uses protocols that are not in wide deployment. It is intended only to give you a basic idea of how the protocol is supposed to work. The EAP exchange is a series of steps beginning with a request for identity and ending with a success or failure message. As a matter of notation, packets transmitted as part of an EAP method exchange are written *Request/Method* when they come from the authenticator, and *Response/Method* when they are sent in response.

1. The authenticator issues a Request/Identity packet to identify the user. Request/Identity packets serve two purposes. In addition to starting the exchange, they also serve notice to the client that the network is likely to drop any data traffic before authentication completes.

2. The end user system prompts for input, collects the user identifier, and sends the user identifier in a Response/Identity message.

3. With the user identified, the authenticator can issue authentication challenges. In step 3 in the figure, the authenticator issues an MD-5 Challenge to the user with a Request/MD-5 Challenge packet.

4. The user system is configured to use a token card for authentication, so it replies with a Response/NAK, suggesting the use of Generic Token Card authentication.

5. The authenticator issues a Request/Generic Token Card challenge, prompting for the numerical sequence on the card.

6. The user types a response, which is passed along in a Response/Generic Token Card.

7. If the user response is not correct, authentication is not possible. However, the authenticator EAP implementation allows for multiple authentication Requests, so a second Request/Generic Token Card is issued.

8. Once again, the user types a response, which is passed along in a Response/Generic Token Card.

9. On the second try, the response is correct, so the authenticator issues a Success message.

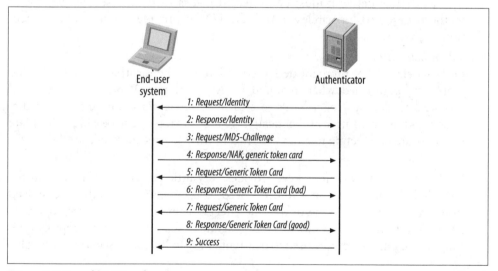

Figure 6-5. Sample EAP exchange

EAP Methods

The E in EAP is both its greatest strength and greatest weakness. Extensibility allows a protocol to develop new features as new requirements present themselves. EAP has gone from a way to preserve PPP protocol numbers into the cornerstone of wireless

LAN security because of its extensibility. Correctly deploying EAP can be difficult, however, since there can be a great number of questions to sort through to select the right protocol options. The key to EAP's flexibility is its status as a framework. New methods can be designed as new requirements arise, which enable the development of new methods for use in wireless LANs.

The topic of wireless LAN security protocols is a broad one, and this chapter draws the line at the detailed mechanics of how the protocols work on a bit-by-bit basis. A great deal of complexity will be described qualitatively, without the use of detailed packet diagrams.

Cryptographic Methods

Selecting an EAP method is usually driven by the type of back-end authentication system in use. Early EAP methods focused mainly on providing a channel to communicate with the authentication server. Newer methods designed for wireless networks enable communication with the authentication server, but also meet three major goals that are unique to wireless LANs:

Strong cryptographic protection of user credentials
> By definition, wireless LAN media should be regarded as open. Any data sent over a wireless network must be protected if it is to remain secure. Most EAP methods designed for wireless LANs use TLS to provide cryptographic protection of credentials.

Mutual authentication
> Early wireless LAN protocol design considered authentication to be something that users performed when required by APs. Falling AP prices have enabled attackers to deploy "rogue" APs to steal user credentials. Common sense dictates in addition to user authentication, client devices must be able to validate that they are connecting to a network that is what it appears to be.

Key derivation
> WEP with manually-defined keys provides very little protection of frames on the radio link. Stronger security protocols need to use dynamic keys that are derived from an entropy pool. One of the side effects of providing strong cryptographic protection is that such protocols also generate a shared stream of cryptographically secure bits that can be used to distribute keys to link-layer security protocols.

LEAP

The first widely-used method for authenticating wireless networks was Cisco's proprietary Lightweight EAP (LEAP).[*] LEAP was a huge step forward from manual-key

---

[*] Some standards may refer to LEAP as "EAP-CiscoWireless."

WEP, though it leaves a great deal to be desired. In essence, LEAP is two MS-CHAP version 1 exchanges. One authenticates the network to the user, and the second authenticates the user to the network. Dynamic keys are derived from the MS-CHAP exchanges.

Many of the worst security problems stem from the use of MS-CHAP version 1, which has numerous security problems, and is subject to dictionary attacks. Code to exploit LEAP's weaknesses is now widely available.

LEAP was an interim solution that had significant security benefits when compared to manually keyed WEP, but the use of the antiquated MS-CHAP at its core limited its useful life. Once other protocols became available, LEAP's purpose was extinguished. Cisco now recommends using PEAP or EAP-FAST.

Code 13: EAP-TLS

Transport Layer Security (TLS) was designed for use on links subject to eavesdropping. TLS is the standards-based successor to the Secure Socket Layer (SSL), the protocol that enabled secure web transactions. In many respects, the use case for wireless LANs is similar to the Internet. Data must be transmitted over a totally untrusted network with all manner of attackers. Establishing a trusted communication channel over an untrusted network is the purpose of TLS.

TLS provides mutual authentication through certificate exchange. The user is required to submit a digital certificate to the authentication server for validation, but the authentication server must also supply a certificate. By validating the server certificate against a list of trusted certificate authorities, the client can be assured that it is connecting to an network authorized by the certificate authority.

EAP-TLS was the first authentication method to meet all three goals for wireless networks. Certificates provide strong authentication of both the users to the network, and the network to users. Mutual authentication provides a strong guard against so-called "rogue" access points by enabling clients to determine that an AP has been configured by the right department, rather than an attacker who is intent only on stealing passwords. TLS also establishes a master secret that can be used to derive keys for link layer security protocols.

Though secure, EAP-TLS has seen only limited use. Any potential user of the wireless network must possess a digital certificate. Generating and distributing certificates while following processes to verify trust is a major challenge. Organizations that already had a public key infrastructure were able to use EAP-TLS easily; many organizations have shied away from building a PKI, and use an alternative method.

Code 21: EAP-TTLS and Code 25: EAP-PEAP

Practically speaking, the requirement for PKI was a major bar to the use of strong authentication on wireless LANs. PKIs are a significant undertaking in both technology and process. Most organizations found it desirable to re-use existing authentication systems, such as a Windows domain or Active Directory, LDAP directory, or Kerberos realm. Re-using existing accounts is much easier than creating a parallel authentication system. The two EAP methods intended to enable the use of so-called "legacy authentication methods" are Tunneled TLS (TTLS) and Protected EAP (PEAP).

Both TTLS and PEAP work in a similar fashion. In the first step of the protocol, they establish a TLS tunnel using routines similar to EAP-TLS. Digital certificates on the authentication server are used to validate that the network should be trusted before proceeding to the second step. In the second step, the TLS tunnel is used to encrypt an older authentication protocol that authenticates the user to the network. The first step is sometimes referred to as the "outer" authentication, since it is a tunnel that protects the second or "inner" authentication.

Certificates are still required, but only for the outer authentication. Reducing the number of certificates from hundreds or thousands down to a handful for authentication servers has made both TTLS and PEAP much more popular than EAP-TLS. Within an organization, the small number of certificates can be generated by a small certificate authority, rather than relying on expensive certificates signed by an external certificate authority.

The slight difference between TTLS and PEAP is in the way the inner authentication is handled. TTLS uses the encrypted channel to exchange attribute-value pairs (AVPs), while PEAP uses the encrypted channel to start a second EAP exchange inside of the tunnel. The use of AVPs makes TTLS much more flexible because AVPs can be used to run authentication methods that do not have corresponding EAP methods.

One minor advantage to the use of TTLS and PEAP is that the inner and outer authentications can use distinct usernames. Rather than revealing the username in unencrypted frames, both protocols can submit an anonymous username for the outer authentication, and only reveal the user's true identity through the encrypted channel. Not all client software supports the use of identity hiding.

Noncryptographic EAP Methods

Several EAP methods are not suitable for use directly on wireless networks without strong cryptographic protection. However, they may be useful as inner authentication methods with PEAP or TTLS.

Code 4: MD-5 Challenge

The MD-5 Challenge is used to implement the EAP analog of the CHAP protocol, specified in RFC 1994. Requests contain a challenge to the end user. For successful authentication, CHAP requires that the challenge be successfully encoded with a shared secret. All EAP implementations must support the MD-5 Challenge. It is not, however, widely supported on wireless networks because it does not provide dynamic keys on wireless networks.

Code 6: Generic Token Card

Token cards such as RSA's SecurID and Secure Computing's Safeword are popular with many institutions because they offer the security of "random" one-time passwords without the hassle of a one-time password (OTP) rollout. The Request contains the Generic Token Card information necessary for authentication. The Type-Data field of the request must be greater than zero bytes in length. In the Response, the Type-Data field is used to carry the information copied from the token card by the user. In both Request and Response packets, the Length field of the EAP packet is used to compute the length of the Type-Data request.

EAP-GTC was standardized along with EAP in RFC 2284. It allows the exchange of cleartext authentication credentials across the network. In addition to use with token cards, EAP-GTC is often used in practice as an EAP method for "username+password" authentication. If the existing user accounts are in a database that has one-way encrypted passwords (or compare-only passwords), EAP-GTC provides an EAP method that can validate users. Naturally, if EAP-GTC is used to transport reusable passwords, it must be used inside a tunnel for protection and server authentication.

Code 29: EAP-MSCHAP-V2

Microsoft CHAP version 2 (MS-CHAP-V2) was initially introduced with Windows 2000 and is documented in RFC 2759. It was designed to address the shortcomings of MS-CHAP by eliminating the weak encoding of passwords for older clients, providing mutual authentication, and improving keying and key generation.

MS-CHAP-V2 is widely supported by Microsoft clients, and is commonly supported and used as an inner authentication method with PEAP. MS-CHAP-V2 is the most common inner method used with Windows domains. When used as an EAP method, EAP-MSCHAP-V2 can be used with either TTLS or PEAP.

Code 18: EAP-SIM and Code 23: EAP-AKA

Two notable EAP methods working through the standards process are EAP-SIM and EAP-AKA, which can be used for authentication against mobile telephone databases. EAP-SIM provides an interface to the Subscriber Identity Module (SIM) database on GSM telephone networks. EAP-AKA is based on the authentication system in third-generation mobile telephone networks, called Authentication and Key Agreement (AKA).

EAP-SIM and EAP-AKA are useful for telecommunications companies that are interested in providing integrated billing with mobile telephone accounts. Rather than require that users generate new passwords to authenticate to data networks, they can use an existing smart chip and user account.

Other Inner Authentication Methods

TTLS is not restricted to using an EAP method for inner authentication. As a result, some older methods may be used with TTLS. For some networks, the user database is stored in such a way that there is no EAP method that provides a usable interface.

Password Authentication Protocol (PAP)

PAP was originally specified for use with PPP in RFC 1334. PAP transmits the username and password across the network unencrypted. When used with wireless networks, PAP should not be used directly, but only as an inner method inside of TTLS to ensure that the password is not revealed.

PAP can be used with any type of authentication system. Network logons can be validated against a network operating systems. Token card servers can validate cleartext token codes. PAP is also useful for one-way encrypted passwords that can be compared, but not read. One-way encrypted passwords are used in Unix */etc/passwd* files, as well as most LDAP directories. Kerberos systems also store passwords with one-way encryption.

Challenge Handshake Authentication Protocol (CHAP)

Like PAP, CHAP was originally designed for use with PPP, and is specified in RFC 1994. In CHAP, the authentication server challenges the client, and the client proves that it is in possession of the shared secret by successfully responding to the challenge.

CHAP was originally designed to avoid sending secrets, such as passwords, in the clear. The downside of CHAP is that it requires the password in cleartext at both ends of the link. On the server end, the password must either be stored in the clear, or *reversibly encrypted* to enable server software to recover the cleartext.

CHAP is not typically used in wireless environments unless a large user database already exists and is using CHAP.

MS-CHAP, version 1

MS-CHAP was designed by Microsoft to offer similar functionality to CHAP, but with enhanced functionality for Windows systems. It is proprietary to Microsoft, but documented in RFC 2433. Unlike CHAP, MS-CHAP does not require that the shared secret be stored in cleartext at both ends of the link. Instead of using the cleartext password as the shared secret, MS-CHAP uses the MD4 hash of the user password.

MS-CHAP is useful in environments where Microsoft authentication databases are used. However, there are particular issues with MS-CHAP that make it undesirable from a security point of view; it should only be used by network managers who must support very old Microsoft clients, such as Windows 95/98. MS-CHAP is not an EAP method, and is only supported by TTLS.

EAP Method Filtering

Some EAP methods are stronger than others. In the interests of "security," some equipment vendors filter EAP methods in the authenticator. EAP-MD5 is often selected as a target for EAP type filtering because it is much weaker than TLS-based methods.

EAP method filtering is not necessary, and has the potential to get in the way of good security practice. Many filters only allow TLS-based tunnel methods (types 13, 21, and 25). If a new EAP method is defined, many EAP method filter implementations will block it by default. Allowing configurable EAP method filters would be one potential solution, but I do not know of any such implementations.

In practice, EAP method filters are not that valuable from a security perspective. Authentication servers can enforce the use of strong authentication by refusing any requests using weak methods. In any case, the lack of keying material may prevent network connection. If no keys can be derived from the authentication, many APs will void the authentication, kick the client off, and start over. EAP-MD5 authentications will start, succeed, fail to key, and be restarted when the AP dissassociates the client.

Due in part to these problems, EAP method filtering is not allowed by the EAP specification. Section 2.3 of RFC 3748 mandates that authenticators must forward any EAP methods to the authentication server for processing.

802.1X: Network Port Authentication

As LAN acceptance mushroomed in the 1990s, LAN ports popped up everywhere. Some types of organizations, such as universities, were further hampered by a need for openness. Network resources must be made available to a user community, but that community is fluid. Students are not like many network users. They frequently move from computer to computer and do not have a fixed network address; they may also graduate, transfer, enroll, leave campus, work on staff, or undergo any number of changes that may require changes in access privileges. Although network access must be extended to this fluid community, academic budgets are frequently tight, so it is important to prevent unauthorized use by outsiders.

In short, a generic network sign-on was required. Academic environments would not be the sole beneficiaries, however. Authentication to access network resources is common among Internet service providers, and corporations found the idea attractive because of the increasing flexibility of staffing plans.

Authentication to network devices at the link layer is not new. Network port authentication has been required by dial-up access servers for years. Most institutions already have a wide range of deployed infrastructure to support user authentication, such as RADIUS servers and LDAP directories. PPP over Ethernet (PPPoE) could conceivably be used to require user authentication to access an Ethernet, but it would add an unacceptable level of encapsulation overhead and complexity. Instead, the IEEE took the PPP authentication protocols and developed LAN-based versions. The resulting standard was 802.1X, "Port-Based Network Access Control."

802.1X Architecture and Nomenclature

802.1X defines three components to the authentication conversation, which are all shown in Figure 6-6 (a). The *supplicant* is the end user machine that seeks access to network resources. Network access is controlled by the *authenticator*; it serves the same role as the access server in a traditional dial-up network. Both the supplicant and the authenticator are referred to as *Port Authentication Entities* (PAEs) in the specification. The authenticator terminates only the link-layer authentication exchange. It does not maintain any user information. Any incoming requests are passed to an *authentication server*, such as a RADIUS server, for actual processing.

Ports on an 802.1X-capable device are in an *authorized* state, in which the port is enabled, or an *unauthorized* state, in which it is disabled. Even while in the unauthorized state, however, the specification allows DHCP and other initialization traffic if permitted by a network manager.

The authentication exchange is logically carried out between the supplicant and the authentication server, with the authenticator acting only as a bridge. Figure 6-6 (b) shows the logical protocol architecture. From the supplicant to the authenticator (the "front end"), the protocol is EAP over LANs (EAPOL), as defined by 802.1X. On the "back end," EAP is carried in RADIUS packets. Some documentation may refer to it as "EAP over RADIUS." The supplicant is carrying on an EAP exchange with a RADIUS server, even though the port is unauthorized and the supplicant is not using an IP address.

Figure 6-6 can be read as two different scenarios. In the enterprise scenario, the supplicant is a corporate host on the edge of the enterprise network, and the RADIUS server is located in the enterprise core. The figure also depicts an ISP using 802.1X to authenticate users, in which case the lefthand side of the figure is an ISP access area, and the righthand side is the ISP backbone.

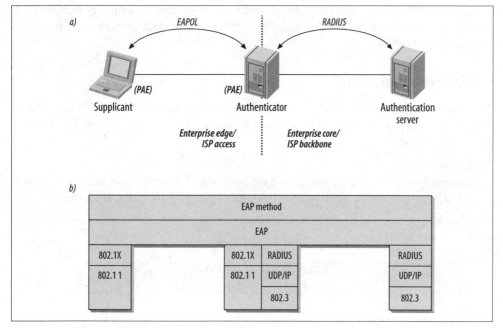

Figure 6-6. 802.1X architecture

One of the advantages of using RADIUS is that it has a great deal of support for many different user databases. In addition to local databases, a RADIUS server can be used as a gateway to LDAP directories, Unix authentication such as NIS or PAM, Kerberos realms, Microsoft Windows user accounts, or even other RADIUS servers. RADIUS is quite flexible, and can be designed to accommodate a wide range of user databases, and can even serve to integrate several disparate user databases into a unified form. There are some restrictions when using RADIUS to provide authentication based on Windows domains or Active Directory that will be discussed in Chapter 22.

802.1X is a framework, not a complete specification in and of itself. The actual authentication mechanism is implemented by the authentication server. 802.1X supplies a mechanism for issuing challenges and confirming or denying access, but it does not pass judgment on the offered credentials. Changes to the authentication method do not require complex changes to the end user devices or the network infrastructure. The authentication server can be reconfigured to "plug in" a new authentication service without changes to the end user driver software or switch firmware.

802.1X frame filtering

802.1X prevents network access by unauthorized users by requiring authentication before allowing traffic to pass. Ports in the unauthorized state are usually restricted to sending authentication frames only, while traffic is dropped. The 802.1X standard has a formal discussion of how to accomplish this process. For the purposes of this book, however, it suffices to say that unauthorized ports will drop any non-EAPOL frames. Once the station has successfully authenticated, data frames are sent to the appropriate network.

EAPOL Encapsulation

The basic format of an EAPOL frame is shown in Figure 6-7. EAPOL encapsulation is now analyzed by many popular network analyzers, including Ethereal. The frame's components are:

MAC header
> Figure 6-7 shows the encapsulation on both wired Ethernet and 802.11. The two MAC headers differ, although the payload of the 802.1X frame is identical.

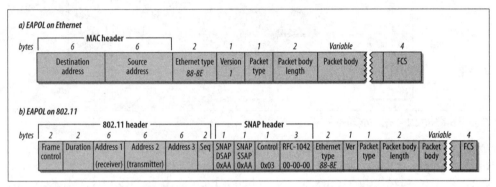

Figure 6-7. EAPOL frame format

Ethernet Type
> As with any other Ethernet frame, the Ethernet Type field contains the two-byte type code assigned to EAPOL: 88-8e.

Version
> Version 1 was standardized in the 2001 version of 802.1X; version 2 was specified in 802.1X-2004. This chapter describes the 2001 version, which is much more commonly implemented.

Packet Type
> EAPOL is an extension of EAP. In addition to the EAP messages that are described in the previous section, EAPOL adds some messages to adapt EAP to the port-based LAN environment. Table 6-2 lists the packet types and their descriptions.

Table 6-2. EAPOL message types

Packet type	Name	Description
0000 0000	EAP-Packet	Contains an encapsulated EAP frame. Most frames are EAP-Packet frames.
0000 0001	EAPOL-Start	Instead of waiting for a challenge from the authenticator, the supplicant can issue an EAPOL-Start frame. In response, the authenticator sends an EAP-Request/Identity frame.
0000 0010	EAPOL-Logoff	When a system is done using the network, it can issue an EAPOL-Logoff frame to return the port to an unauthorized state.
0000 0011	EAPOL-Key	EAPOL can be used to exchange cryptographic keying information.
0000 0100	EAPOL-Encapsulated-ASF-Alert	The Alerting Standards Forum (ASF) has defined a way of allowing alerts, such as SNMP traps, to be sent to an unauthorized port using this frame type.

Packet Body Length

This two-byte field is the length of the Packet Body field in bytes. It is set to 0 when no packet body is present.

Packet Body

This variable-length field is present in all EAPOL frames except the EAPOL-Start and EAPOL-Logoff messages. It encapsulates one EAP packet in EAP-Packet frames, one key descriptor in EAPOL-Key frames, and one alert in EAPOL-Encapsulated-ASF-Alert frames.

Addressing

In shared-media LANs such as Ethernet, supplicants send EAPOL messages to the group address of 01:80:C2:00:00:03. On 802.11 networks, ports do not exist as such, and EAPOL can proceed only after the association process has allowed both the supplicant (mobile wireless station) and the authenticator (access point) to exchange MAC addresses. In environments such as 802.11, EAPOL requests use station addresses.

802.1X on Wireless LANs

802.1X provides a framework for user authentication over any LANs, including wireless. For the purposes of this book, the "port" in 802.1X on wireless is an association between a wireless device and its access point. The successful exchange of Association Request and Association Response frames is reported to the 802.1X state engine as the link layer becoming active. Once associated, a station can exchange 802.1X frames in an attempt to become authorized. The completion of the 802.1X authentication exchange, including key distribution, is reported to the user as the interface coming up.

Sample 802.1X Exchange on 802.11

EAPOL exchanges look almost exactly like EAP exchanges. The main difference is that supplicants can issue EAPOL-Start frames to trigger the EAP exchange, and they can use EAPOL-Logoff messages to deauthorize the port when the station is done using the network. The examples in this section assume that a RADIUS server is used as the back-end authentication server, and therefore they show the authenticator performing translation from EAP on the front end to RADIUS on the back end. EAP authentication in RADIUS packets is specified in RFC 2869.

This example exchange also shows the use of EAPOL-Key frames to distribute key information for link layer security protocols. Figure 6-8 shows a sample EAPOL exchange on an 802.11 network. The figure shows a successful authentication, whose steps are:

1. The supplicant associates with the 802.11 network. Association is a simple two-frame exchange which nearly always succeeds.

2. The supplicant starts the 802.1X exchange with an EAPOL-Start message. This step is optional. Not all supplicants send EAPOL-Start messages, so this step may not be present.

3. The "normal" EAP exchange begins. The authenticator (access point) issues an EAP-Request/Identity frame. Request/Identity frames may be sent without first having an EAPOL-Start if the access point only forwards frames for authenticated sessions. Unsolicited Request/Identity frames indicate to the supplicant that 802.1X authentication is required.

4. The supplicant replies with an EAP-Response/Identity frame, which is passed on to the RADIUS server as a Radius-Access-Request packet.

5. The RADIUS server determines the type of authentication that is required, and sends an EAP-Request for the method type. The EAP-Request is encapsulated in a Radius-Access-Challenge packet to the AP. When it reaches the AP, the EAP-Request is passed on to the supplicant. EAP Requests are are often denoted *EAP-Request/Method*, where the Method refers to the EAP method in use. If PEAP is in use, the return packet will be written as EAP-Request/PEAP.

6. The supplicant gathers the reply from the user and sends an EAP-Response in return. The response is translated by the authenticator into a Radius-Access-Request with the response to the challenge as a data field.

   — Steps five and six repeat as many times as is necessary to complete the authentication. If it is an EAP method that requires certificate exchange, multiple steps are almost certainly required. Many EAP exchanges can require 10–20 round trips between the client and RADIUS server.

7. The RADIUS server grants access with a Radius-Access-Accept packet, so the authenticator issues an EAP-Success frame and authorizes the port. Authorization may depend on parameters passed back from the RADIUS server.

8. Immediately following receipt of the Access-Accept packet, the access point distributes keys to the supplicant using EAPOL-Key messages. Key distribution is discussed in the next chapter.

9. Once keys are installed in the supplicant, it can begin sending data frames to access the network. It is quite common at this point for DHCP configuration to take place.

10. When the supplicant is done accessing the network, it sends an EAPOL-Logoff message to put the port back into an unauthorized state.

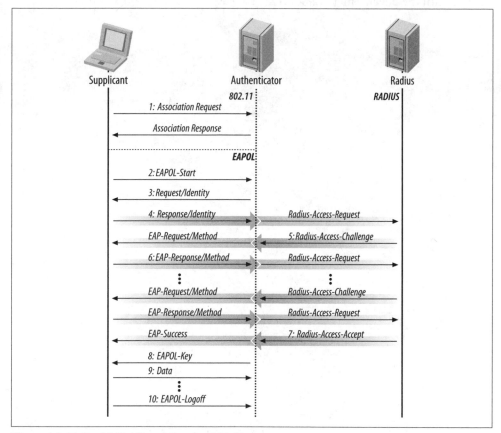

Figure 6-8. Typical 802.1X exchange on 802.11

Exchanges similar to Figure 6-8 may be used at any point. It is not necessary for the user to begin an EAPOL exchange with the EAPOL-Start message. At any point, the authenticator can begin an EAPOL exchange by issuing an EAP-Request/Identity frame to refresh the authentication data. Re-authentications are often triggered by session timeout values to refresh keys.

Dynamic keying

The EAPOL-Key frame allows keys to be sent from the access point to the client and vice versa. Key exchange frames are sent only if the authentication succeeds; this prevents the compromise of key information. EAPOL-Key frames can be used periodically to update keys dynamically as well. Several of the weaknesses in WEP stem from the long lifetime of the keys. When it is difficult to rekey every station on the network, keys tend to be used for long periods of time. Several experts have recommended changing WEP keys on a regular basis, but no practical mechanism to do so existed until the development of 802.1X.

## CHAPTER 7

802.11i: Robust Security Networks, TKIP, and CCMP

802.1X provides a framework for authentication and key management, which addresses two of the major flaws in the design of WEP. The major remaining flaw to be addressed is the lack of confidentiality provided by WEP encryption. Fixing link layer encryption was taken on by Task Group I of the 802.11 working group. In June 2004, their work was finally complete when the standard was ratified, after several delays.

802.11i takes a two-track approach to addressing the weaknesses in link-layer encryption. Its major components are two new link-layer encryption protocols. The first, the Temporal Key Integrity Protocol (TKIP) was designed to bolster security to the greatest extent possible on pre-802.11i hardware. The second, Counter Mode with CBC-MAC Protocol (CCMP), is a new encryption protocol designed from the ground up to offer the highest level of security possible.

The Temporal Key Integrity Protocol (TKIP)

The first new link layer encryption protocol to be widely implemented was the Temporal Key Integrity Protocol (TKIP).* The major motivation for the development of TKIP was to upgrade the security of WEP-based hardware. Typically, chipsets capable of WEP offered hardware support for RC4 encryption. With the heavy lifting of encryption implemented in hardware, software and firmware upgrades make the rest possible. TKIP retains the basic architecture and operations of WEP because it was designed to be a software upgrade to WEP-based solutions.

---

* TKIP was initially called "WEP2" as it worked through the standards organizations. When WEP was shown to be fundamentally flawed, the protocol was renamed to try to distinguish it from WEP.

TKIP Differences from WEP

TKIP incorporates several new protocol features to defend WEP's weak points against attack. TKIP retains WEP's basic architecture and operation, but adds "safety belts" around WEP's most vulnerable points:

Key hierarchy and automatic key management
> Rather than take the WEP approach of only a single master key that is used directly, TKIP uses *master keys*. The keys that are ultimately used to encrypt frames are derived from master keys. TKIP was also developed with key management operations so that master keys can be refreshed in a secure manner.

Per-frame keying
> Although TKIP retains the RC4-based frame encryption of WEP, it derives a unique RC4 key for each frame (from the master key) to mitigate attacks against weak WEP keys. The process by which a unique key is derived for each key is called *key mixing*.

Sequence counter
> By numbering each frame with a sequence number, out-of-order frames can be flagged, mitigating against *reply attacks*, in which attackers capture valid traffic and re-transmit it at a later time.

New message integrity check (MIC)
> TKIP replaces WEP's linear hash with a more robust cryptographic integrity check hashing algorithm called *Michael*. More robust hashing makes it easier to detect frame forgeries. Additionally, the source address is among the items protected by the integrity check, which makes it possible to detect forged frames that claim to be from a particular source.

Countermeasures on message integrity check failures
> TKIP was designed to be implemented on existing hardware, and suffers from a number of limitations. Michael can be compromised in an active attack with relative ease, so TKIP includes *countermeasures* to limit the damage from an active attack.

TKIP is also commonly used in tandem with key management protocols based on 802.1X, which enables the TKIP master keys to be derived from authentication transactions.

TKIP initialization vector use and key mixing

WEP's construction of WEP seeds from the initialization vector (IV) and the WEP key introduces major weaknesses. By simply concatenating the IV and the key to build the seed, the IV itself reveals a significant amount of key structure. Attackers can notice that IV re-use, and note that therefore, the key stream used to encrypt the frame is identical. With a 24-bit IV, the IV space lasts for 16 million frames. On a

---

busy network, 16 million frames is not very many. To make matters worse, the IV space is specific to the scope of the key in use. On a network that uses static WEP, the IV space is shared by all stations on the network. Finally, and most famously, the IV is the initial 24 bits of the key, and makes WEP keys vulnerable to recovery with the Fluher/Mantin/Shamir attack discussed in Chapter 5.

To mitigate the attacks against initialization vectors, TKIP doubles the length of the IV from 24 to 48 bits. This increases the size of the initialization vector space from 16 million to 281 trillion, which effectively prevents exhausting the IV space during the limited lifetime of a key.

TKIP also performs *key mixing* to counter attacks against WEP. Key mixing changes the RC4 key used to encrypt each frame. Every frame in TKIP is encrypted with an RC4 key unique to that frame. Key mixing, which will be discussed in more detail later, further extends the initialization vector space. By incorporating the sender's MAC address into the mixing calculation, two stations can use the same initialization vector, yet still derive different RC4 keys to encrypt frames. Key mixing also helps to counter the Fluhrer/Mantin/Shamir attack. Successful application of the principles of the attack require a collection of "weak keys" with the same secret bits. By changing the key for every frame, TKIP prevents an attacker from gathering enough data to attack any of the per-frame keys.

TKIP sequence counter and replay protection

In addition to its larger size, the TKIP initialization vector serves as a sequence counter. When a new master key is installed, the initialization vector/sequence counter is set to one. Each frame transmitted increments the sequence counter by one.

To defend against replay attacks, TKIP maintains the most recent sequence counter value received from each station. When a frame is successfully received, the sequence counter is checked against the most recently received sequence counter. If it is larger than any previous value, the frame is accepted. If it is smaller than the most recently received sequence counter value, it is rejected.

Task group E is developing quality of service extensions. Current 802.11e drafts contain a block acknowledgment protocol feature that uses a single frame to acknowledge multiple transmissions. In the January 2005 draft of 802.11e, re-ordering due to block acknowledgments must complete before applying replay detection.

802.11 unicast frames must be acknowledged. If either the original frame or its acknowledgment is lost, the frame will be retransmitted. At the receiver, this may result in the same sequence counter being received twice. Duplicate sequence numbers may simply represent evidence of an error on the link and do not necessarily indicate an active attack in progress.

The Michael integrity check and countermeasures

WEP's integrity check is a linear hash value, which is totally unsuitable for cryptographic applications. One of the major design challenges faced by TKIP was strengthening the integrity check while retaining reasonable performance. Most 802.11 chipsets in use at the time TKIP was designed used a relatively low-power processor, and were thus not capable of performing mathematical operations fast enough to do integrity checks at "air-speed." *Michael* is implemented entirely with bitwise operations such as swaps, shifts, or even discarding bits. As a result, it can run without deleterious performance effects, even on the tiny microprocessors found in most 802.11 interfaces. (Michael is discussed in detail later in this chapter.)

The corollary to Michael's design is that it does not provide a great deal of security. It is significantly better than a cyclic redundancy check, but it does not offer security against a sustained and determined attack. TKIP incorporates *countermeasures* to detect and respond to an active attack by shutting down the network and refreshing the keys in use.

Michael's countermeasures are an admission of the weakness of the underlying cryptographic fundamentals. Design of Michael was constrained by the need to be backwards-compatible with most of the existing RC4-based hardware on the market. Michael's design is elegant and accomplishes a great deal within its severe design constraints, but it is still built on a foundation of sand. Time will tell whether Michael is sufficiently secure; I would not be surprised to see a major attack against it in the next year. However, the improved protocol design of TKIP limits the negative consequences of an attack. I expect that a compromise of Michael would result in denial-of-service attacks, but would not lead to wholesale network compromise.

TKIP Data Processing and Operation

Like WEP, TKIP provides support for encryption and integrity protection as part of the same process, as shown in Figure 7-1. TKIP's design as a set of safety features around WEP is quite clear from the diagram.

As input, TKIP takes the following items:

- The frame, naturally.
- A *temporal key* used to encrypt the frame.
- A *MIC key* used with Michael to protect the frame contents. TKIP derives a pair of keys so that the station-to-AP MIC key is different from the AP-to-station MIC key. One of the ways that TKIP differs from WEP is that the MIC uses a key.
- The transmitter address is used as an input to TKIP because it is required to perform origin authentication. The transmitter address is supplied with the frame and does not need to be supplied by higher level software.
- A sequence counter, maintained by the driver or the firmware.

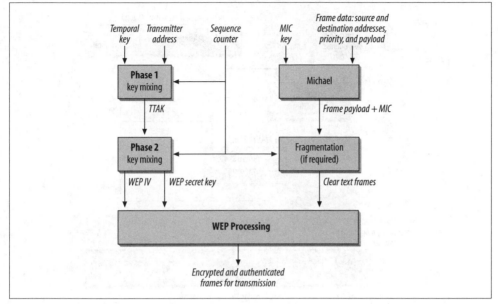

Figure 7-1. TKIP frame processing—encryption

TKIP key mixing and key construction

TKIP derives a unique key for each frame transmitted. The key is derived from the initialization vector/sequence counter, the address of the transmitter of the frame (which may not be the source of the frame), and the temporal key. Key mixing ensures that the key used varies significantly from one frame to the next, and prevents any attacks which assume that the secret component of the WEP key are constant from frame to frame. By including the transmitter address in the mixing computation, two stations can use the same initialization vector yet derive different two RC4 keys.

Limited processing power of the 802.11 controllers dictated the design of the key mixing function, which is shown in Figure 7-2. TKIP splits the computation of the mixed key into two phases. Phase one takes, as input, the transmitter address, the high-order 32 bits of the sequence counter, and the 128-bit temporal key. As output, it gives an 80-bit value. Although the computation is somewhat involved, it consists entirely of "easy" operations such as addition, shifts, and exclusive ORs, to reduce the computational load. The phase one value is constant as long as the 32 high-order bits of the sequence counter are constant, so it only needs to be computed once every 65,536 frames.

Phase two of the key mixing function must be computed for every frame. As input, phase two takes the phase one result, the temporal key, and the 16 low-order bits of the sequence counter. The only input that changes from frame to frame is the sequence counter. It changes in a well-defined way, so implementations can and do pre-compute values based on the next set of sequence counter values that will be needed as frames are queued for transmission.

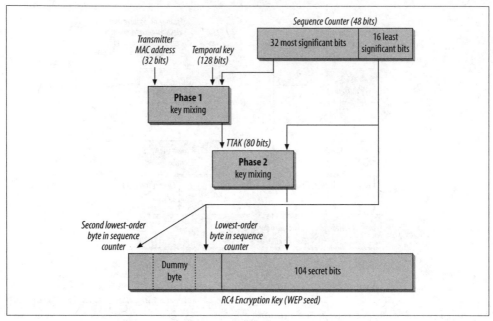

Figure 7-2. TKIP key mixing

The output of the phase two of the key mixing process is a 128-bit RC4 key that can be used as a WEP seed. The 16 low-order bytes are used to generate a WEP IV. The middle byte of the WEP IV is constructed so that it avoids generating weak RC4 keys. Many 802.11 interfaces incorporate hardware assistance that can take an RC4 key as input and generate and apply the resulting keystream to encrypt the frame. The output of the phase two mixing process can be given directly to an 802.11 interface that supports this type of hardware assistance.

TKI P data transmission

When a frame is generated and sent to TKIP for transmission, the following sequence of events occur.

1. The 802.11 frame is queued for transmission. It consists of a frame header and the payload. Like WEP, TKIP protects only the payload of the 802.11 MAC, and leaves the 802.11 frame header, as well as any lower-layer headers, intact.

2. The Message Integrity Check (MIC) is computed. Unlike WEP, TKIP's MIC is a more robust cryptographic hash. It uses a secret key as part of its validation process, and protects much more than just the 802.11 frame payload. In addition to the frame data, the MIC incorporates the source and destination address as well as the addition of *priority* bits that will be used by the future 802.11e standard.

3. Sequence numbers are assigned to fragments. Unlike WEP initialization vectors, TKIP's sequence counter increases by one with each fragment. If no fragmentation

is necessary, only one sequence counter increment will be necessary. In the case of multiple fragments, the counter will increment multiple times.

4. Each frame is encrypted with a unique per-frame WEP key. By carrying out the key mixing functions, TKIP derives the WEP key used for the frame. The per-frame key is passed to WEP as an IV plus a secret key; both components will change for every frame.

5. The frame plus Michael message integrity check value from step 2 and the RC4 key from step 4 are passed to WEP, which encapsulates the frame as described in Chapter 5. Note that this means that a TKIP-protected frame will include WEP components as well.

TKIP frames have WEP-like encapsulation. Figure 7-3 shows the encapsulation of a frame that has been protected by TKIP. The IV/KeyID is retained from WEP, but has a different interpretation. The first three bytes carry part of the TKIP sequence counter, and identify the key number in use. Although TKIP can support multiple keys, in practice, only KeyID 0 is distributed. An Extended IV (EIV) field is used to carry the remainder of the sequence counter. Following the data payload, TKIP appends the MIC. WEP adds its own integrity check value, to retain WEP in as unchanged a form as possible.

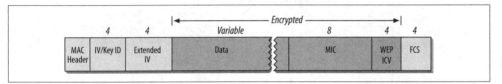

Figure 7-3. TKIP encapsulation

TKIP reception

When TKIP receives a frame, the encryption and transmission process must be reversed. TKIP's design as an expanded version of WEP adds several new checkpoints in the decryption process, and therefore it is worth treating in more detail. Figure 7-4 shows a block diagram, with all of the ways that frames may be discarded before passing up to higher protocol layers.

1. When a frame is received by the wireless interface and passes the frame check sequence to ensure it has not been corrupted, it is passed to TKIP for validation.

2. The first step TKIP takes is to check the sequence number to prevent replay attacks. TKIP's replay protection requires that frames be received in strict order. Frames that have a sequence number equal to or lower than the last received valid frame are discarded as a replay attempt. This is stricter than some other technologies, which maintain a replay window and allow "recent" arrivals to be somewhat out of order. For a link layer technology, however, it makes sense to insist on strict ordering because there is only a small possibility of out-of-order delivery on a single hop.

3. The WEP seed used to encrypt the packet is recovered. With the transmitter address, temporal key, and sequence counter, the receiver can unmix the key to recover the WEP seed.

4. With the WEP seed in hand, the outer WEP layer around the frame can be removed and the contents recovered. As part of this process, the WEP ICV is checked. Although it is a weak integrity check, it can be used to protect against applying countermeasures unnecessarily.

5. If fragmentation was applied, it may be necessary to wait for further frames to arrive before reassembling a complete payload. Fragmentation is not used often on 802.11, however.

6. Once the frame is reassembled, Michael is calculated over the contents of the frame. If the calculated MIC matches the MIC on the packet, the frame is passed to higher layers, and the sequence counter is set to the value of the sequence counter on the frame. If the MIC check fails, countermeasures are triggered.

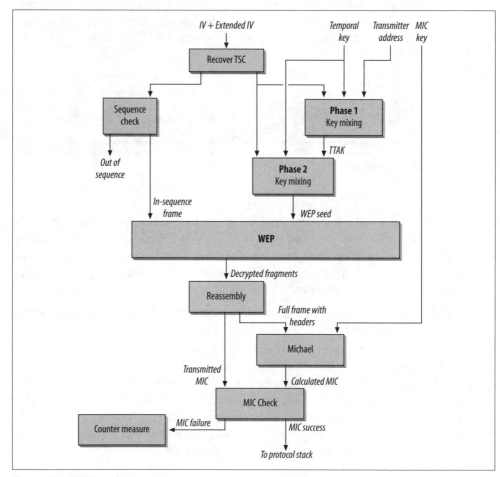

Figure 7-4. TKIP reception process

One of the reasons for retaining the WEP encapsulation is that it enables greater backwards-compatibility with existing hardware. It also prevents unnecessary triggers of MIC failures. Frames that are corrupted due to noise on the radio link will likely fail either the 802.11 frame check sequence or the WEP integrity check value, and will be discarded before triggering a MIC failure.

The Michael Integrity Check

One of WEP's weakest points was the integrity check, which was supposed to ensure that the frame was not tampered with as it traversed the wireless medium. WEP adopted the cyclic redundancy check (CRC), which proved woefully inadequate. One of the major goals of TKIP was to design a message integrity check (MIC) with much more solid cryptographic underpinnings. The resulting algorithm, called *Michael*, is a compromise in many ways. Michael is stronger than a simple linear hash, but the desire of the standards committee to make it easy to implement with low overhead placed severe constraints on its design.

From an architectural point of view, Michael plugs in to the MAC service layer. That is, Michael operates on frames passed down to it from higher-layer protocols. Michael does not protect individual 802.11 frames; it protects the reassembled data unit given to 802.11 for transmission.* Part of the reason for implementing Michael above the MAC layer as opposed to within it is that it leaves products the flexibility to implement Michael in dedicated hardware or in driver software running on the device. Older chipsets and 802.11 interfaces did not build in specialized hardware assistance for Michael because it had not been developed; these products can implement Michael with updated drivers or host software. Newer devices designed with emerging standards in mind are able to build Michael support into the chipset if desired, and will not need driver support that is as extensive.

Several attacks discussed previously served as the motivation for Michael. Two of the most notable are the bit flipping attack and a whole class of header modification. The former attack depends on the weak cryptographic properties of the CRC. As a linear hash algorithm, it is well known how changing the CRC input bits will change the output. Attackers could potentially flip bits in the frame to change its content, and change a bit in the WEP integrity check to compensate. In header modification attacks, malicious attackers may forge the source or transmitter address, or attempt to redirect frames by modifying the destination address.

Make no mistake, Michael is not a particularly secure cryptographic protocol. It was designed to offer breathing room to users who have an extensive installed base while

---

* In practice, the distinction between the MAC service layer and the MAC protocol layer is not particularly necessary. Although 802.11 can accommodate frames over 2,000 bytes, most commercial implementations limit frame size to be compatible with Ethernet to avoid higher-layer fragmentation.

they upgrade the security of their networks. It is only a short-term fix while the long-term solution is developed.

Michael data processing

Michael operates on higher-level frames passed down to the MAC. When a higher-level frame is queued for transmission, one of the first transmission steps is to compute the message integrity check (MIC) value. Michael operates on the input shown in Figure 7-5 (a). In addition to the destination address (DA) and source address (SA), Michael adds four zero bytes before the unencrypted data. The last three bytes are reserved; the first is a priority field that is reserved for future standardization work.

Michael operates on 32-bit blocks of data. Data is padded out with zeros so that it will be a multiple of 32-bit blocks. Padding is used only for the computation of the MIC. It is not transmitted. Michael computes the MIC value by working on successive 32-bit blocks of data.

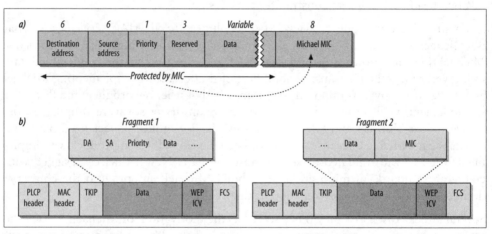

Figure 7-5. Michael input

When complete, the MIC is added on to the tail of the data frame, and the data-plus-MIC is given to 802.11 for transmission. If it needs to be fragmented, it will be. During the fragmentation process, the MIC value may be split across multiple 802.11 fragments, which is acceptable. In Figure 7-5, the data-plus-MIC unit from higher layers requires fragmentation and is split across the frame boundary. This is a perfectly acceptable occurrence because the two fragments will be reassembled before validating the MIC. Figure 7-5 (b) illustrates this process. The input from Figure 7-5 (a) has been split into two frames for transmission. Each layer will get its own MAC and PLCP headers, and will be processed by the WEP layer in TKIP.

Michael countermeasures

Michael is not very resistant to attack, although it appears to be as good as one could hope, given the constraints of a great deal of legacy hardware on the market. Michael is not able to withstand a determined active attack, so it incorporates *countermeasures* against such attacks.

Countermeasures happen at the MIC check. To make it to that point, a frame must have passed through the replay protection and the WEP integrity check value validation. Forging a frame to pass the replay protection and the WEP integrity check is not a trivial matter, especially since the latter value depends on the value of the mixed per-frame key.

If an attacker were able to bypass replay protection and the WEP integrity check, it would be possible to mount a brute-force attack on the Michael integrity check. To guard against brute-force attempts to pass Michael, Michael's countermeasures shut down communications to limit the number of active attacks that can be made against any particular key. If an attack is sustained, countermeasures call for refreshing the key and shutting down communications.

When a station detects a MIC failure, it executes the following procedure:

1. The MIC failure is noted and logged. Before the MIC is validated, the frame must pass through the replay protection hurdle as well as the legacy WEP integrity check. Getting a frame to Michael for validation is not a trivial undertaking. Therefore, any MIC validation error is likely to be an extremely security-relevant matter that should be investigated by system administrators.

2. If the failure is the second one within a 60-second window, countermeasures dictate shutting down communications for a further 60 seconds. When the second MIC failure within 60 seconds is detected, all TKIP communication is disabled for 60 seconds. Instituting a communication blackout makes it impossible for an attacker to mount a sustained attack quickly.

3. Keys are refreshed. Stations delete their copies of the master keys and request new keys from the authenticator; authenticators are responsible for generating and distributing new keys.

Although 802.11i sets the Michael countermeasures time at 60 seconds, some vendors allow configuration of the Michael countermeasures window to other values.

Counter Mode with CBC-MAC (CCMP)

TKIP is better than WEP, but that is the only statement that can be made with certainty. WEP's basis in a stream cipher will always leave lingering doubts about the security of anything built using a similar set of operations. To address the concerns of the 802.11 user community, the IEEE working group began developing a security protocol based on the Advanced Encryption Standard (AES) block cipher. AES is a flexible

What Is WPA?

Wi-Fi Protected Access (WPA) is a marketing standard put together by the Wi-Fi Alliance. The Wi-Fi Alliance leaves the details of hammering out standards to other bodies like the IEEE. As a trade association, however, they react to ensure that the perception of the industry remains positive.

When the first cracks appeared in the foundation of WEP, the IEEE launched a working group to develop improved security standards. Building secure cryptographic protocols is difficult work, however, and 802.11i has been delayed repeatedly past its expected due date. 802.11i specifies two new security protocols: TKIP and CCMP. TKIP was designed to be backwards compatible with existing hardware at the time it was developed, whereas CCMP was designed essentially from the ground up. As a result, TKIP was finished well before CCMP was ready.

To address security concerns in the market, the Wi-Fi Alliance worked to speed up deployment of TKIP by coming up with an interim marketing standard called WPA. WPA version 1 is based on the third draft of 802.11i (from mid-2003); WPA version 2 is the final standardized version of 802.11i from mid-2004.

WPA includes both authentication through 802.1X and encryption. It comes in two flavors: *WPA Personal*, which is equivalent to pre-shared key authentication in 802.11i, and *WPA Enterprise*, which uses the authenticated key mode that derives keys from TLS entropy.

cipher that can operate at many key lengths and block sizes; to prevent user confusion, 802.11i mandates the use of AES with both 128-bit keys and 128-bit blocks.

There has been some concern over the key size used with 802.11i. AES can operate with a variety of key lengths. The U.S. National Security Agency has approved AES for use with "secret" data with 128-bit and longer keys, but more sensitive "top secret" data requires the use of 192- or 256-bit keys.[*] Some observers have therefore concluded that 128-bit keys do not offer adequate security. Regardless of the merits in the debate over key size, 128-bit AES is much better suited to 802.11 frame encryption RC4 at any key length.

The link-layer security protocol based on AES is called the *Counter Mode with CBC-MAC Protocol* (CCMP).[†] The name comes from the underlying use of the block cipher, in the Counter Mode with CBC-MAC (CCM) mode, which is specified in

---

[*] See the Committee on National Security Systems (CNSS) Policy No. 15, Fact Sheet No. 1, "National Policy on the Use of the Advanced Encryption Standard (AES) to Protection National Security Systems and National Security Information" at *http://www.nstissc.gov/Assets/pdf/fact%20sheet.pdf*.

[†] One of the delays in finishing 802.11i was that the AES algorithm was initially based on a different mode of operation, AES-OCB. Intellectual property concerns required that it be dropped from the final specification in favor of CCMP.

RFC 3610. CCM is a "combined" mode of operation, in which the same key is used in encryption for confidentiality as well as creating a cryptographically secure integrity check value.

In September 2003, the National Institute of Standards and Technology (NIST) began a study of CCM. In May 2004, NIST gave its approval to CCM, which will allow 802.11i to serve as the basis for secure wireless LANs in demanding applications.

CCMP Data Processing

Like other link-layer encryption methods, CCMP provides support for encryption and integrity protection as part of the same process, as shown in Figure 7-6.

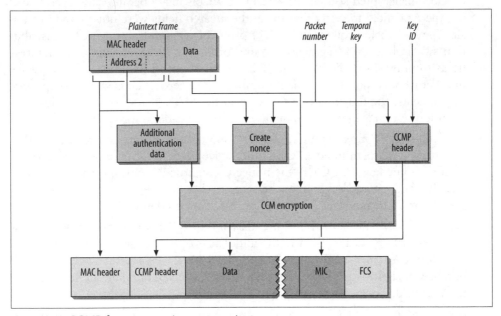

Figure 7-6. CCMP frame processing—encryption

As input, CCMP takes the following items:

- The frame, naturally.
- A *temporal key* used to encrypt and authenticate the frame. One key is used for both frame encryption and frame authentication.
- A *key identifier* to support the use of multiple keys over the air. Only one key, however, will be used for any given frame.
- A *packet number*, used to uniquely identify the frame being transmitted. The packet number is incremented for each frame transmission, but it remains the same for each attempt to transmit the frame. That is, retransmissions do not cause the PN to increment.

CCMP data transmission

When a frame is generated and sent to TKIP for transmission, this procedure occurs:

1. The 802.11 frame is queued for transmission. It consists of a frame header and the payload. Like WEP, TKIP protects only the payload of the 802.11 MAC, and leaves the 802.11 frame header, as well as any lower-layer headers, intact.

2. A 48-bit *Packet Number* (PN) is assigned. As with the TKIP sequence number, packet numbers are never re-used for the same temporal key. Packet numbers are increased by one for every transmission, and are used for replay detection.

3. The *Additional Authentication Data* (AAD) field is constructed. It consists of the fields in the frame header which must be authenticated for security but must also remain unencrypted so that the 802.11 protocols may operate. The receiver will use the AAD field to verify that the authenticated fields were not altered in transit. The AAD field protects the 802.11 protocol version, frame type, the distribution system bits, and fragmentation and order bits. It also protects the address fields from the MAC header, and the sequence control field, with the sequence number (though not the fragment number) set to zero. It ends with two optional components: the fourth address field from the MAC header (if the wireless distribution system is in use), and quality of service header information.

4. Next, the *CCMP nonce* is built. Nonces are little bits of data that guarantee that the encryption operation occurs on unique data. Nonces should never be re-used with the same key. In CCMP, the nonce is constructed with the packet number and the sender's address so that the same packet number can be used by multiple stations. The nonce also includes priority data used in QoS.

5. Next, the *CCMP header* is built. It consists of the packet number, broken across six bytes, with a key identifier in the middle. As in WEP, there are four potential key slots used in CCMP. The Extended IV bit is always set to 1 in CCMP because an eight-byte header is always needed to accommodate the large packet number field. The header is shown in Figure 7-7.

6. All the inputs to the CCM encryption engine are available at this point. As input, it takes the 128-bit temporal key, the nonce from step 4, the additional authentication data from step 3, and the frame body. All the data is authenticated with a 8-byte MIC, and the frame body and MIC are encrypted. Figure 7-6 illustrates the encryption process.

7. The encrypted frame is prepared for transmission by taking the original MAC header and appending the CCMP header and the encrypted data from step 6. The resulting frame is pushed down to the radio interface for transmission, and looks like Figure 7-10.

The encapsulation of a CCMP-protected frame is quite straightforward, and is shown in Figure 7-7. Following the MAC header, a CCMP header holds the packet number and key ID. The higher-layer protocol frame and its MIC are encrypted before the FCS.

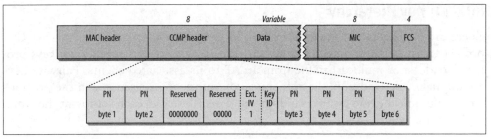

Figure 7-7. CCMP encapsulation

CCMP reception

When CCMP receives a frame, the encryption and transmission process must be reversed. With no backwards compatibility baggage requiring the use of the WEP engine, the CCMP decryption process is a straightforward reversal of Figure 7-6:

1. When a frame is received by the wireless interface and passes the frame check sequence to ensure it has not been corrupted, it is passed to CCMP for validation.

2. The additional authentication data (AAD) is recovered from the received frame. It consists only of frame headers, which are transmitted in the clear.

3. The CCMP nonce is also recovered from the frame. It consists of the packet number, the sender's address, and contents of the quality of service field, all of which are available in the frame header in the clear.

4. The receiver decrypts the ciphertext. It requires the temporal key, the nonce recovered from step 3, the authentication data from step 2, and of course, the encrypted frame body. When the process completes, the receiver has a copy of the decrypted frame plus the decrypted integrity code.

5. The integrity check is calculated over the plaintext data and the additional authentication data. If the calculated integrity check value matches the integrity check value extracted in step 4, then processing proceeds. Otherwise, processing ends.

6. A plaintext frame is constructed from the MAC header and the data recovered in step 4. To pass through the replay detection check, the packet number must be greater than or equal to the last received packet number that passed through the integrity check process.

Robust Security Network (RSN) Operations

In addition to defining TKIP and CCMP, 802.11i also defines a set of procedures that build what the standard calls *Robust Security Networks* (RSNs). These operations define how keys are derived and distributed.

802.11i Key Hierarchy

There are two types of keys used by link layer encryption protocols. *Pairwise keys* protect traffic between a station and the AP it is currently serving. *Group keys* protect broadcast or multicast traffic from an AP to its associated clients. Pairwise keys are ultimately derived from the authentication information discussed in the previous chapter; group keys are created randomly and distributed to each station at the whim of the access point.

Pairwise key hierarchy

Both TKIP and CCMP take a single master key and expand it into the different keys required for frame protection operations. By using key derivation, stations can refresh encryption keys without re-running the whole authentication process. The master key is the root secret that must be carefully protected because all keying material is derived from it. Part of the key hierarchy's purpose is to derive keys used to protect transmission of the temporal keys.

Keying starts with the master key. In the pairwise key hierarchy, which is shown in Figure 7-8, the master key is unsurprisingly called the *pairwise master key* (PMK), which is 256 bits long. The PMK must come from somewhere. In WPA-PSK, the pairwise master key is configured. In configurations using an authentication server, the master key is computed by the RADIUS server and sent to the access point in a Microsoft Point-to-Point Encryption (MPPE) vendor-specific RADIUS attribute.

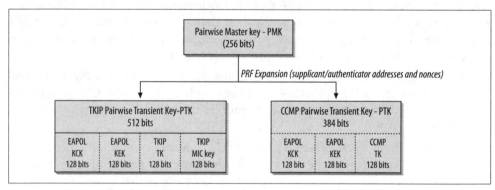

Figure 7-8. Pairwise key hierarchies

To obtain the temporal keys described earlier in this chapter, the PMK is expanded through the use of a defined pseudorandom function.[*] To further randomize data, the expansion is based on the pre-master key, the MAC addresses of both the

---

[*] Many encryption protocols use pseudorandom functions to expand a small seed into a large amount of random data. TLS is perhaps the best known example.

supplicant and authenticator, and two random nonce values transmitted as part of the four-way key exchange handshake.

Both TKIP and CCMP use the pseudorandom function expansion to expand the 256 bits into the *pairwise transient key* (PTK). In both the TKIP and CCMP hierarchy, the two chunks of 128 bits of the transient key are used for keys that protect the temporal keys during distribution.

Both key hierarchies start with two EAPOL keys, used to secure transmission of keying material using the EAPOL-Key message discussed in the previous chapter. Two 128-bit keys are used. The first, the *EAPOL Key Confirmation Key* (KCK), is used to compute message integrity checks on keying messages. The second, the *EAPOL Key Encryption Key* (KEK), is used to encrypt keying messages. Both will be discussed in the section on the four-way handshake.

TKIP's transient key consists of a total of 512 bits, with the additional 256 bits used as the 128-bit temporal key that is used in TKIP data processing, and the 128-bit key for the Michael integrity check. TKIP requires two additional keys because it uses traditional encryption and authentication schemes that strictly separate encryption from authentication. CCMP's transient key is only 384 bits because only a single 128-bit temporal key is used for authentication and encryption.

Group key hierarchy

Link layer security protocols use a different set of keys for broadcast and multicast transmissions. Every associated station will have a different pre-master key, and thus, there is no way to derive a key for use with multiple destinations from the disparate authentication exchanges. Instead, the authenticator maintains a *group master key* (GMK) as the basis for temporal keys. The group master key is expanded into the group key hierarchy shown in Figure 7-9 by the use of a pseudorandom function. No key encryption or key confirmation keys are generated because the key exchange uses the pairwise EAPOL keys for key distribution.

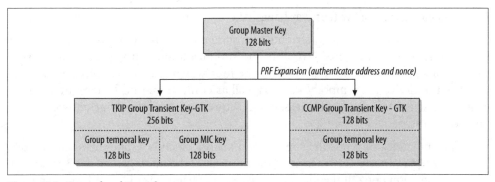

Figure 7-9. Group key hierarchy

Networks may update the group keys when stations leave the network, either because they are finished or are deauthenticated. In TKIP, countermeasures may also trigger the regeneration of the group keys.

802.11i Key Derivation and Distribution

Rather than simply taking the master secret and using it as the input to a cryptographic protocol, 802.11i specifies a mechanism to derive keys. To prevent replay attacks, the exchange makes use of random numbers, and requires a handshake. Pairwise and group keys are updated through separate handshakes, which are both shown in Figure 7-10.

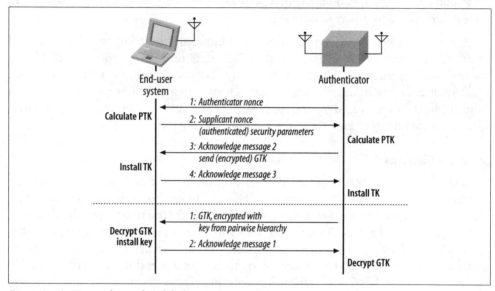

Figure 7-10. Key exchange handshakes

Updating pairwise keys: the four-way handshake

Pairwise, or unicast, keys are distributed through a procedure known as the *four-way handshake*, shown in Figure 7-10. Both the supplicant and authenticator are in possession of a shared pairwise master key. The four-way handshake exchanges parameters used to derive the temporal keys, as well as confirm that both sides are ready to begin encrypted transmission. Messages in sequence are implicitly acknowledged by the next message.

1. The authenticator sends the supplicant a *nonce*, which is a random value that prevents replay attacks. There is no authentication of the message, but there is no danger from tampering. If the message is altered, the handshake fails and will be rerun.

At this point, the supplicant can expand the pairwise master key into the full pairwise key hierarchy. Expansion requires the MAC addresses of the supplicant and authenticator, the pairwise master key, and the two nonces.

2. The supplicant sends a message that has the supplicant nonce and a copy of the security parameters from the initial association with the network. The whole message is authenticated by an integrity check code calculated using the EAPOL Key Confirmation Key.

The authenticator receives the message and extracts the supplicant nonce, which allows the authenticator to derive the full pairwise key hierarchy. Part of the key hierarchy is the key used to "sign" the message. If the authenticator cannot validate the message, the handshake fails.

3. Keys are now in place on both sides of the handshake, but need to be confirmed. The Authenticator sends the supplicant a message indicating the sequence number for which the pairwise key will be added. It also includes the current group transient key to enable update of the group key. The group transient key is encrypted using the EAPOL Key Encryption Key, and the entire message is authenticated using the Key Confirmation Key.

4. The supplicant sends a final confirmation message to the authenticator to indicate that it has received the keying messages and the authenticator may start using the keys. The message is authenticated using the Key Confirmation Key.

Updating group keys: the group key handshake

The group key handshake is considerably simpler than the four-way handshake, in part because it uses part of the results from the four-way handshake. Because the group transient key is encrypted with the Key Encryption Key from the pairwise hierarchy, the group key handshake requires that a successful four-way handshake has already occurred. It consists of only two steps:

1. The authenticator sends the group transient key (GTK), encrypted with the Key Encryption Key from the pairwise key hierarchy. The message is also authenticated with a code calculated with the Key Confirmation Key.

2. The supplicant sends an acknowledgment message, indicating the authenticator should begin to use the new key for group frames. This message is also authenticated using the Key Confirmation Key.

Even though the group key handshake is updating a key used by several stations, the use of the Key Encryption Key to protect data means that the handshake is inherently pairwise. When the group key is updated, the group key exchange must be run once for each station.

Although group key updates are generally controlled by the authenticator, stations may request a group key update by sending an unsolicited confirmation message.

Mixing Encryption Types

To allow for migration between different encryption protocols, as well as to accommodate older devices incapable of anything stronger than WEP, 802.11i defines a trust hierarchy for encryption protocols. WEP with 40-bit keys is the weakest protocol, followed by WEP with 104-bit keys, TKIP, and CCMP.

As part of the initial association to the network, each station can negotiate the encryption protocols it uses for both unicast and group data. The only restriction is that the group key must use either the same strength or a weaker encryption protocol. Access points use the "lowest common denominator" for the group key. In a network where the least capable associated station is only able to run dynamic WEP, the group key will be dynamic WEP. Other stations may, however, use stronger unicast protection mechanisms. Many access points provide policy controls to set a minimum acceptable encryption strength, and may prevent stations from associating with weaker protocols than desired by the network administrators.

The standard allows for nearly any mixture of encryption methods, with the exception that a station using CCMP for group frames must only support CCMP for unicast frames. However, many drivers do not support every allowed mode. Most notably, drivers usually do not support the combination of CCMP for unicast data in combination with older RC4-based frame encryption for the group key.

Key Caching

Pairwise master keys are the foundation of 802.11i security. Generating them is quite an expensive operation if the pairwise master key is the result of an 802.1X exchange. Most EAP methods require multiple messages and a significant amount of computation per step. The 802.1X authentication process may take several seconds, during which the user is unable to send or receive data. Client systems located on the boundary between two access points may be particularly affected if the wireless interface bounces back and forth between two (or more) access points with equivalent signal strength.

Reducing the authentication overhead is the motivation for *PMK caching*, which is shown in Figure 7-11. Rather than require a station to perform the full 802.1X exchange every time it connects to an access point, it references an existing session by the pairwise master key security association identifier. If the access point has an existing association, it accepts the association and proceeds immediately to the four-way handshake. In the four-way handshake, both the supplicant and authenticator will prove to each other possession of the cached PMK.

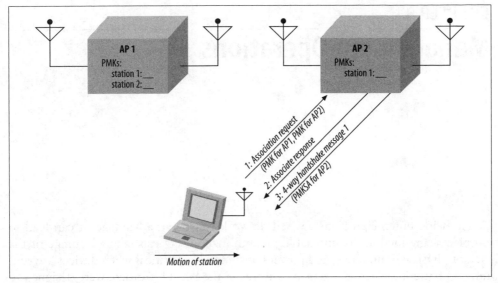

Figure 7-11. PMK caching

Stations that do not have cached master keys must perform a full 802.1X authentication to generate them. One of the motivations for preauthentication, which is discussed in the next chapter, is that can be used to establish master keys on access points before the handoff occurs, so that a master key is waiting.

CHAPTER 8
Management Operations

While being untethered from a wired network can be an advantage, it can lead to problems: the medium is unreliable, unauthorized users can take advantage of the lack of physical boundaries, and power consumption is critical when devices are running on batteries. The management features of the 802.11 protocol were designed to reduce the effect of these problems. In essence, management operations are all the behind-the-scenes tasks that wireless network devices perform so that the wireless link looks much like other types of network connections.

802.11 management is a cooperative affair, shared between client devices and the network infrastructure. Unfortunately, this leaves a great deal of the protocol operation in the hands of devices that may vary greatly. Some device drivers allow you to customize the management features discussed in this chapter. Keep in mind, though, that the capabilities of the device driver vary from one product to another, and the state of wireless networking is such that some vendors are trying to produce the most feature-rich products possible, while others are aiming at a lower-cost market and trying to produce the simplest products. The only way to know what is possible is to understand the capabilities that have been built into the protocol. Then you'll be in a good position to work with whatever hardware drops in your lap.

Management Architecture

Conceptually, the 802.11 management architecture is composed of three components: the MAC layer management entity (MLME), a physical-layer management entity (PLME), and a system management entity (SME). The relation between the different management entities and the related parts of 802.11 is shown in Figure 8-1.

802.11 does not formally specify the SME. It is the method by which users and device drivers interact with the 802.11 network interface and gather information about its status. Both the MAC and PHY layers have access to a management information base (MIB). The MIB has objects that can be queried to gain status information, as well as objects that can cause certain actions to take place.

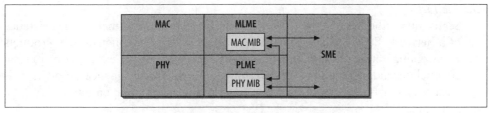

Figure 8-1. Relationship between management entities and components of the 802.11 specification

There are three defined interfaces between the management components. The station management entity may alter both the MAC and PHY MIBs through the MLME and PLME service interfaces. Additionally, changes to the MAC may require corresponding changes in the PHY, so an additional interface between the MLME and PLME allows the MAC to make changes to the PHY.

Scanning

Before using any network, you must first find it. With wired networks, finding the network is easy: look for the cable or a jack on the wall. In the wireless world, stations must identify a compatible network before joining it. The process of identifying existing networks in the area is called *scanning*.

Several parameters are used in the scanning procedure. These parameters may be specified by the user; many implementations have default values for these parameters in the driver.

BSSType (independent, infrastructure, or both)
> Scanning can specify whether to seek out independent ad hoc networks, infrastructure networks, or all networks.

BSSID (individual or broadcast)
> The device can scan for a specific network to join (individual) or for any network that is willing to allow it to join (broadcast). When 802.11 devices are moving, setting the BSSID to broadcast is a good idea because the scan results will include all BSSs in the area.

SSID ("network name")
> The SSID assigns a string of bits to an extended service set. Most products refer to the SSID as the network name because the string of bits is commonly set to a human-readable string. Clients wishing to find any network should set this to the broadcast SSID.

ScanType (active or passive)
> Active scanning uses the transmission of Probe Request frames to identify networks in the area. Passive scanning saves battery power by listening for Beacon frames.

ChannelList

Scans must either transmit a Probe Request or listen on a channel for the existence of a network. 802.11 allows stations to specify a list of channels to try. Products allow configuration of the channel list in different ways. What exactly constitutes a channel depends on the physical layer in use. With direct-sequence products, it is a list of channels. With frequency-hopping products, it is a hop pattern.

ProbeDelay

This is the delay, in microseconds, before the procedure to probe a channel in active scanning begins. This delay ensures that an empty or lightly loaded channel does not completely block the scan.

MinChannelTime and MaxChannelTime

These values, specified in time units (TUs), specify the minimum and maximum amount of time that the scan works with any particular channel.

Passive Scanning

Passive scanning saves battery power because it does not require transmitting. In passive scanning, a station moves to each channel on the channel list and waits for Beacon frames. Any Beacons received are buffered to extract information about the BSS that sent them.

In the passive scanning procedure, the station sweeps from channel to channel and records information from any Beacons it receives. Beacons are designed to allow a station to find out everything it needs to match parameters with the basic service set (BSS) and begin communications. In Figure 8-2, the mobile station uses a passive scan to find BSSs in its area; it hears Beacon frames from the first three access points. If it does not hear Beacons from the fourth access point, it reports that only three BSSs were found.

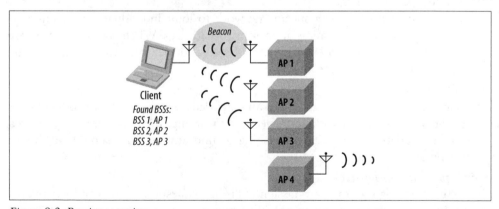

Figure 8-2. Passive scanning

Active Scanning

In active scanning, a station takes a more assertive role. On each channel, Probe Request frames are used to solicit responses from a network with a given name. Rather than listening for that network to announce itself, an active scan attempts to find the network. Stations using active scanning employ the following procedure for each channel in the channel list:

1. Move to the channel and wait for either an indication of an incoming frame or for the ProbeDelay timer to expire. If an incoming frame is detected, the channel is in use and can be probed. The timer prevents an empty channel from blocking the entire procedure; the station won't wait indefinitely for incoming frames.

2. Gain access to the medium using the basic DCF access procedure and send a Probe Request frame.

3. Wait for the minimum channel time, MinChannelTime, to elapse.
   a. If the medium was never busy, there is no network. Move to the next channel.
   b. If the medium was busy during the MinChannelTime interval, wait until the maximum time, MaxChannelTime, and process any Probe Response frames.

Probe Response frames are generated by networks when they hear a Probe Request that is searching for the extended service set to which the network belongs. At a party, you might look for a friend by wandering around the dance floor shouting out her name. (It's not polite, but if you really want to find your friend, you may not have much choice.) If your friend hears you, she will respond—others will (you hope) ignore you. Probe Request frames function similarly, but they can also use a broadcast SSID, which triggers a Probe Response from all 802.11 networks in the area. (It's like shouting "Fire!" at the party—that's sure to result in a response from everybody!)

One station in each BSS is responsible for responding to Probe Requests. The station that transmitted the last Beacon frame is also responsible for transmitting any necessary Probe Response frames. In infrastructure networks, the access points transmit Beacons and thus are also responsible for responding to itinerant stations searching the area with Probe Requests. IBSSs may pass around the responsibility of sending Beacon frames, so the station that transmits Probe Response frames may vary. Probe Responses are unicast management frames and are therefore subject to the positive acknowledgment requirement of the MAC.

It is common for multiple Probe Responses to be transmitted as a result of a single Probe Request. The purpose of the scanning procedure is to find every basic service area that the scanning station can join, so a broadcast Probe Request results in a response from every access point within range. Any overlapping independent BSSs may also respond.

Figure 8-3 shows the relationship between the transmission of Probe frames and the various timing intervals that can be configured as part of a scan.

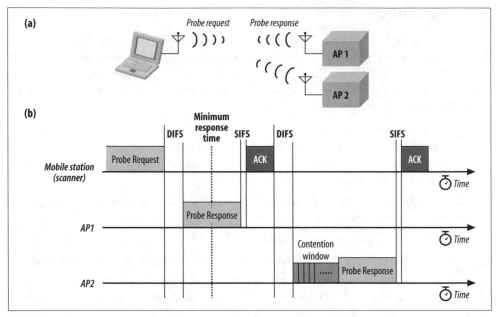

Figure 8-3. Active scanning procedure and medium access

In Figure 8-3 (a), a mobile station transmits a probe request to which two access points respond. The activity on the medium is shown in Figure 8-3 (b). The scanning station transmits the Probe Request after gaining access to the medium. Both access points respond with a Probe Response that reports their network's parameters. Note that the second Probe Response is subject to the rules of the distributed coordination function and must wait for the contention window to elapse before transmitting. The first response is transmitted before the minimum response time elapses, so the station waits until the maximum response time has elapsed before collating the results. In areas with a large number of networks, it may be necessary to adjust the maximum channel time so the responses from all the access points in the area can be processed.

Scan Report

A scan report is generated at the conclusion of a scan. The report lists all the BSSs that the scan discovered and their parameters. The complete parameter list enables the scanning station to join any of the networks that it discovered. In addition to the BSSID, SSID, and BSSType, the parameters also include:[*]

Beacon interval (integer)
    Each BSS can transmit Beacon frames at its own specific interval, measured in TUs.

DTIM period (integer)
    DTIM frames are used as part of the powersaving mechanism.

---

[*] The items actually exposed by any particular software vary.

Timing parameters

Two fields assist in synchronizing the station's timer to the timer used by a BSS. The Timestamp field indicates the value of the timer received by the scanning station; the other field is an offset to enable a station to match timing information to join a particular BSS.

PHY parameters, CF parameters, and IBSS parameters

These three facets of the network have their own parameter sets, each of which was discussed in detail in Chapter 4. Channel information is included in the physical-layer parameters.

BSSBasicRateSet

The basic rate set is the list of data rates that must be supported by any station wishing to join the network. Stations must be able to receive data at all the rates listed in the set. The basic rate set is composed of the mandatory rates in the Supported Rates information element of management frames, as in Chapter 4.

What's in a Name? (or, the Security Fallacy of Hidden SSIDs)

The SSID is an important scanning parameter. Stations search for an SSID when scanning, and may build a list of SSIDs for presentation to the user. As a unique identifier for a network, the SSID is often given mythic security properties it does not actually possess.

At the dawn of 802.11, the SSID was broadcast in the clear in Beacon frames, right there for the listening. All that was necessary was an 802.11 interface tuned to the right radio channel. When the stone age of 802.11 began, one vendor began to treat the SSID as a valuable security token. By enabling the "closed network" option on that vendor's equipment, the SSID was no longer put in Beacon frames, thus "protecting" the network from attackers. To further "protect" the SSID from prying eyes, access points operating a closed network would not respond to Probe Requests with the broadcast SSID.

Closed networks break passive scanning because the SSID is no longer available for easy collection. In order to prevent a closed network from being completely closed to clients, however, access points must respond to Probe Requests containing the correct SSID. Management frames have no encryption, and the SSID value is right there for the taking in the Probe Request. To be scrupulously correct, the closed network may offer a vanishingly small incremental amount of security because the SSID is only available when stations search for the network, rather than several times per second in Beacon frames.

Hiding an SSID can cause problems with 802.11 management. Although most 802.11 interfaces and their associated drivers can handle hidden SSIDs, not all can. Hiding an SSID is a nonstandard procedure that can cause problems, and does not provide any real security. Leave the SSID in the Beacon frames for interoperability, and use a real security solution like 802.1X if you need it.

Joining

After compiling the scan results, a station can elect to join one of the BSSs. Joining is a precursor to association; it is analogous to aiming a weapon. It does not enable network access. Before this can happen, both authentication and association are required.

Choosing which BSS to join is an implementation-specific decision and may even involve user intervention. BSSs that are part of the same ESS are allowed to make the decision in any way they choose; common criteria used in the decision are power level and signal strength. Observers cannot tell when a station has joined a network because the joining process is internal to a node; it involves matching local parameters to the parameters required by the selected BSS. One of the most important tasks is to synchronize timing information between the mobile station and the rest of the network, a process discussed in much more detail in the section "Timer Synchronization," later in this chapter.

The station must also match the PHY parameters, which guarantees that any transmissions with the BSS are on the right channel. (Timer synchronization also guarantees that frequency-hopping stations hop at the correct time, too.) Using the BSSID ensures that transmissions are directed to the correct set of stations and ignored by stations in another BSS.* Capability information is also taken from the scan result, which matches the use of WEP and any high-rate capabilities. Stations must also adopt the Beacon interval and DTIM period of the BSS, though these parameters are not as important as the others for enabling communication.

Authentication

Wireless network media of any sort are open to all sorts of malicious tampering because attackers can literally immerse themselves in the network medium. Gaining a foothold is trivial if you are standing in it. Prepare now to enter the authentication twilight zone. There are multiple forms of "authentication" offered by 802.11, many of which would not pass the laugh test from serious security experts.

When most network administrators refer to authentication, the implication is that only strong authentication is worth considering as authentication. Anything that is not based on cryptography does not prove identity. With the right EAP method, 802.1X authentication can be quite strong, but 802.1X messages can only be exchanged once a system has performed a lower-level 802.11 "authentication" prior to association.

---

* Technically, this is true only for stations obeying the filtering rules for received frames. Malicious attackers intent on compromising network security can easily choose to disobey these rules and capture frames, and most existing product implementations do not correctly implement the filtering rules.

802.11 "Authentication"

802.11 requires that a station establish its identity before sending frames. This initial 802.11 "authentication" occurs every time a station attaches to a network. It should be stressed, however, that they provide no meaningful network security. There are no cryptographic secrets that are passed around or validated, and the authentication process is not mutual. It is far more accurate to think of 802.11's low-level authentication as an initial step in the handshake process that a station uses to attach to the network, and one that identifies the station to the network.

802.11 authentication is a one-way street. Stations wishing to join a network must perform 802.11 authentication to it, but networks are under no obligation to authenticate themselves to a station. The designers of 802.11 probably felt that access points were part of the network infrastructure and thus in a more privileged position.

Open-system authentication

Open-system authentication is the only method required by 802.11. Calling it authentication is stretching the meaning of the term a great deal. In open-system authentication, the access point accepts the mobile station at face value without verifying its identity. (Imagine a world where similar authentication applied to bank withdrawals!) Providing network security requires building something on top of the resulting network session. An open-system authentication exchange consists of two frames, shown in Figure 8-4.

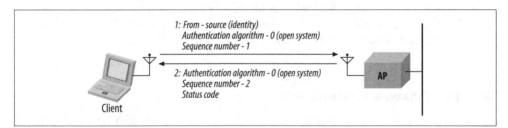

Figure 8-4. Open-system authentication exchange

The first frame from the mobile station is a management frame of subtype authentication. 802.11 does not formally refer to this frame as an authentication request, but that is its practical purpose. In 802.11, the identity of any station is its MAC address. Like Ethernet networks, MAC addresses must be unique throughout the network and can readily double as station identifiers. Access points use the source address of frames as the identity of the sender; no fields within the frame are used to further identify the sender.

There are two information elements in the body of the authentication request. First, the Authentication Algorithm Identification is set to 0 to indicate that the open-system method is in use. Second, the Authentication Transaction Sequence number is set to 1 to indicate that the first frame is in fact the first frame in the sequence.

The access point then processes the authentication request and returns its response. Like the first frame, the response frame is a management frame of subtype authentication. Three information elements are present: the Authentication Algorithm Identification field is set to 0 to indicate open-system authentication, the Sequence Number is 2, and a Status Code indicates the outcome of the authentication request. Values for the Status Code are shown in Table 4-6.

Address Filtering (MAC "Authentication")

WEP is not required by 802.11, and a number of earlier products implement only open-system authentication. To provide more security than straight open-system authentication allows, many products offer an "authorized MAC address list." Network administrators can enter a list of authorized client addresses, and only clients with those addresses are allowed to connect.

While address filtering is better than nothing, it leaves a great deal to be desired. MAC addresses are generally software- or firmware-programmable and can easily be overridden by an attacker wishing to gain network access. Distribution of lists of authorized devices can be painful because it typically must be done for each device in the network. Furthermore, there is a fair amount of churn on the list. New cards are purchased, old cards break down, employees leave the organization and take cards with them, and so on.

Authorized address filtering may be part of a security solution, but it should not be the linchpin. Rather than depend on MAC address, use 802.1X-based user authentication if possible. Once network administrators have made the effort to authenticate users, authentication will be as secure as standards provide for, and address filtering will only add complexity without any substantial additional security benefit.

The legacy of shared-key authentication

Shared-key authentication makes use of WEP and therefore can be used only on products that implement WEP, though non-WEP products are now nearly impossible to find. Shared-key authentication, as its name implies, requires that a shared key be distributed to stations before attempting authentication. The fundamental theoretical underpinning of shared-key authentication is that a challenge can be sent to the client, and a response proves possession of the shared key. A shared-key authentication exchange consists of four management frames of subtype authentication, shown in Figure 8-5.

The first frame is nearly identical to the first frame in the open-system authentication exchange. Like the open-system frame, it has information elements to identify the authentication algorithm and the sequence number; the Authentication Algorithm Identification is set to 1 to indicate shared-key authentication.

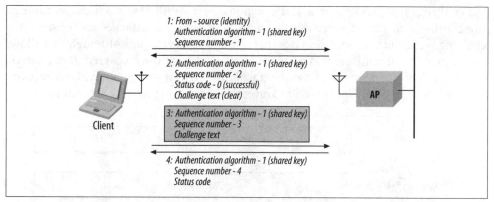

1: From - source (identity)
Authentication algorithm - 1 (shared key)
Sequence number - 1

2: Authentication algorithm - 1 (shared key)
Sequence number - 2
Status code - 0 (successful)
Challenge text (clear)

3: Authentication algorithm - 1 (shared key)
Sequence number - 3
Challenge text

4: Authentication algorithm - 1 (shared key)
Sequence number - 4
Status code

Client

AP

Figure 8-5. Shared-key authentication exchange

Instead of blindly allowing admission to the network, the second frame in a shared-key exchange serves as a challenge. Up to four information elements may be present in the second frame. Naturally, the Authentication Algorithm Identification, Sequence Number, and Status Code are present. The access point may deny an authentication request in the second frame, ending the transaction. To proceed, however, the Status Code should be set to 0 (success), as shown in Figure 8-5. When the Status Code is successful, the frame also includes a fourth information element, the Challenge Text. The Challenge Text is composed of 128 bytes generated using the WEP keystream generator with a random key and initialization vector.

The third frame is the mobile station's response to the challenge. To prove that it is allowed on the network, the mobile station constructs a management frame with three information elements: the Authentication Algorithm Identifier, a Sequence Number of 3, and the Challenge Text. Before transmitting the frame, the mobile station processes the frame with WEP. The header identifying the frame as an authentication frame is preserved, but the information elements are hidden by WEP.

After receiving the third frame, the access point attempts to decrypt it and verify the WEP integrity check. If the frame decrypts to the Challenge Text, and the integrity check is verified, the access point will respond with a status code of successful. Successful decryption of the challenge text proves that the mobile station has been configured with the WEP key for the network and should be granted access. If any problems occur, the access point returns an unsuccessful status code.

Defeating shared-key authentication

Shared key authentication is subject to a trivial attack. At the heart of the shared-key authentication procedure is the encryption of the challenge text. Upon receipt of the random challenge, a station in posession of the WEP key is able to generate a keystream from the WEP key, then perform an exclusive-OR operation between the keystream and the data. However, the exclusive-OR is a reversible operation that relates the challenge text, keystream, and the response text. With any two items, recovering the third is a matter of reversing the right operation. An attacker can observe the challenge text and response, and use that to derive a keystream. Although this allows an attacker to authenticate to a network by playing back the recovered keystream on a new challenge, it does not allow an attacker to send arbitrary data without recovering the WEP key first. Figure 8-6 illustrates the keystream recovery procedure.

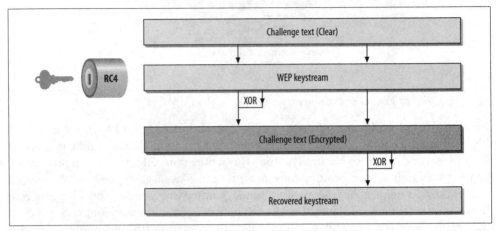

Figure 8-6. Defeating shared-key authentication

Nevertheless, attacks against shared key authentication are effective enough that it is generally not recommended. 802.11i does not allow a station that performed 802.11 authentication via shared keys to become associated to a Robust Security Network.

Preauthentication

Preauthentication is used to speed up association transfer. Authentication can often cause a lag between the time a station decides to move to a new AP and the time that the frames start flowing through that AP. Preauthentication attempts to reduce the time by getting the time-consuming authentication relationship established before it is needed. Due to the overloading of the term "authentication" by both the low-level 802.11 authentication and the 802.1X authentication, there are two different types of preauthentication. As it is commonly used by network engineers, though, it usually refers to the 802.1X authentication.

802.11 Preauthentication

Stations must authenticate with an access point before associating with it, but nothing in 802.11 requires that low-level authentication take place immediately before association. Stations can 802.11-authenticate with several access points during the scanning process so that when association is required, the station is already authenticated. As a result of preauthentication, stations can reassociate with access points immediately upon moving into their coverage area, rather than having to wait for the authentication exchange.

In both parts of Figure 8-7, there is an extended service set composed of two access points. Only one mobile station is shown for simplicity. Assume the mobile station starts off associated with AP1 at the left side of the diagram because it was powered on in AP1's coverage area. As the mobile station moves towards the right, it must eventually associate with AP2 as it leaves AP1's coverage area.

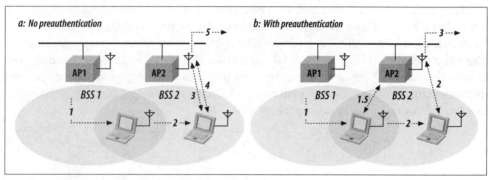

Figure 8-7. Time savings of preauthentication

Preauthentication is not used in the most literal interpretation of 802.11, shown in Figure 8-7 (a). As the mobile station moves to the right, the signal from AP1 weakens. The station continues monitoring Beacon frames corresponding to its ESS, and will eventually note the existence of AP2. At some point, the station may choose to disassociate from AP1, and then authenticate and reassociate with AP2. These steps are identified in the figure, in which the numbers are the time values from Table 8-1.

Table 8-1. Chronology for Figure 8-7

Step	Action without preauthentication: Figure 8-7 (a)	Action with preauthentication: Figure 8-7 (b)
0	Station is associated with AP1	Station is associated with AP1
1	Station moves right into the overlap between BSS1 and BSS2	Station moves right into the overlap between BSS1 and BSS2 and detects the presence of AP2
1.5		Station preauthenticates to AP2
2	AP2's signal is stronger, so station decides to move association to AP2	AP2's signal is stronger, so station decides to move association to AP2
3	Station authenticates to AP2	Station begins using the network
4	Station reassociates with AP2	
5	Station begins using the network	

Figure 8-7 (b) shows what happens when the station is capable of preauthentication. With this minor software modification, the station can authenticate to AP2 as soon as it is detected. As the station is leaving AP1's coverage area, it is authenticated with both AP1 and AP2. The time savings become apparent when the station leaves the coverage area of AP1: it can immediately reassociate with AP2 because it is already authenticated. Preauthentication makes roaming a smoother operation because authentication can take place before it is needed to support an association. All the steps in Figure 8-7 (b) are identified by time values from Table 8-1.

802.11i Preauthentication and Key Caching

When a network is authenticated with 802.1X, the most time-consuming step in getting from the 802.11 join to the ability to send network protocol packets is the 802.1X authentication, especially if it uses an EAP method with several frame round-trips. Preauthentication, shown in Figure 8-8, allows a station to establish a security context with a new AP before associating to it. In essence, preauthentication decouples the association and security procedures, and allows them to be performed independently. WPA explicitly excluded preauthentication.

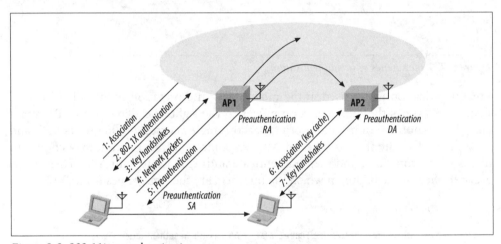

Figure 8-8. 802.11i preauthentication

Figure 8-8 shows the following sequence of steps.

1. The station associates to the first access point it finds on the network. It selects this AP based on the criteria in its firmware.

2. Once associated, the station can perform an 802.1X authentication. This step uses EAPOL frames as described in Chapter 6, with an Ethertype of (hexadecimal) 88-8E. EAPOL frames are converted into RADIUS packets by the AP, and the session is authenticated.

3. Dynamic keys for the radio link are derived on both sides through the four-way handshake for pairwise keys and the group key handshake for the group keys.

---

4. With keys configured, the station is "on the air" and can send and receive network protocol packets.

   Station software is in control of roaming behavior, and can use that to its advantage. As the station moves in such a way that AP2 appears to be a better choice, it can perform preauthentication to speed up the process of moving over to AP2. Rather than move everything all at once, though, it performs preauthentication to cut down on the interruption between sending network packets.

5. Preauthentication commences with an EAPOL-Start message sent from the station to the new AP. A station can only be associated with a single AP, so the preauthentication frames are channeled through the old AP. Preauthentication is a complete 802.1X exchange.

   a. Preauthentication frames use the Ethertype of (hexadecimal) 88-C7 because most APs apply special processing to the regular authentication Ethertype. The source address of the frames is the station, the receiver address is the BSSID of its current AP (in this case, the MAC address of AP1's wireless interface), and the destination address is the BSSID of the new AP (in this case, AP2's wireless interface).

   b. When received by AP1, the frames are sent over the distribution system to AP2. The AP only has a MAC address. If the two APs are not connected directly to the same Ethernet broadcast domain, they must have an alternative method of shuttling preauthentication frames between devices.

   c. During this entire step, the station remains associated to AP1, and can send and receive network packets through its existing encrypted connection. Because the station is still on the air, there is no apparent authentication occuring.

   d. The result of the preauthentication is that a security context with AP2 is established. The station and AP2 have derived a pairwise master key, which can be further processed to create keys between the station and AP2. Both the station and the AP store the pairwise master key in a key cache.

6. When the station pulls the trigger, the association is moved to AP2. As part of the initial association, the station includes a copy of its key cache to tell AP2 that it was already authenticated.

7. AP2 receives the authentication request and searches its key cache. Finding an entry, it starts the fourway pairwise key handshake immediately. By proceeding to key derivation, the station is unable to send and receive packets for only a short time.

802.11 preauthentication moves the time-consuming 802.1X EAP method to occur in parallel with sending and receiving network frames on an authenticated connection. The first association will be slow because the full EAP exchange is required. On subsequent associations, however, preauthentication can dramatically reduce handoff times.

Association

Once authentication has completed, stations can associate with an access point (or reassociate with a new access point) to gain full access to the network. Association is a recordkeeping procedure that allows the distribution system to track the location of each mobile station, so frames destined for the mobile station can be forwarded to the correct access point. After association completes, an access point must register the mobile station on the network so frames for the mobile station are delivered to the access point. One method of registering is to send a gratuitous ARP so the station's MAC address is associated with the switch port connected to the access point.

Association is restricted to infrastructure networks and is logically equivalent to plugging into a wired network. Once the procedure is complete, a wireless station can use the distribution system to reach out to the world, and the world can respond through the distribution system. 802.11 explicitly forbids associating with more than one access point.

Association Procedure

The basic association procedure is shown in Figure 8-9.

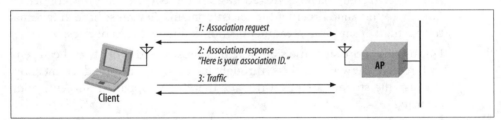

Figure 8-9. Association procedure

Like authentication, association is initiated by the mobile station. No sequence numbers are needed because the association process is a three-step exchange. The two frames are management frame subtypes defined by the specification. As unicast management frames, both steps in the association procedure are composed of an association frame and the required link-layer acknowledgment:

1. Once a mobile station has authenticated to an access point, it can issue an Association Request frame. Stations that have not yet authenticated receive a Deauthentication frame from the access point in response.

2. The access point then processes the association request. 802.11 does not specify how to determine whether an association should be granted; it is specific to the access point implementation. One common consideration is the amount of space required for frame buffering. Rough estimates are possible based on the Listen Interval in the Association Request frame.

a. When the association request is granted, the access point responds with a status code of 0 (successful) and the Association ID (AID). The AID is a numerical identifier used to logically identify the mobile station to which buffered frames need to be delivered. More detail on the process can be found in the "Power Conservation" section of this chapter.

b. Unsuccessful association requests include only a status code, and the procedure ends.

3. The access point begins processing frames for the mobile station. In all commonly used products, the distribution system medium is Ethernet. When an access point receives a frame destined for an associated mobile station, that frame can be bridged from the Ethernet to the wireless medium or buffered if the mobile station is in a powersaving state. In shared Ethernets, the frame will be sent to all the access points and will be bridged by the correct one. In switched Ethernets, the station's MAC address will be associated with a particular switch port. That switch port is, of course, connected to the access point currently providing service for the station.

Reassociation Procedure

Reassociation is the process of moving an association from an old access point to a new one. Over the air, it is almost the same as an association; on the backbone network, however, access points may interact with each other to move frames. When a station moves from the coverage area of one access point to another, it uses the reassociation process to inform the 802.11 network of its new location. The procedure is shown in Figure 8-10.

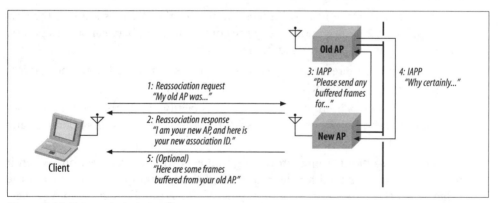

Figure 8-10. Reassociation procedure

The mobile station begins the procedure associated with an access point. The station monitors the quality of the signal it receives from that access point, as well as the signal quality from other access points in the same ESS. When the mobile station detects that another access point would be a better choice, it initiates the reassociation procedure. The factors used to make that decision are product-dependent. Received signal strength can be used on a frame-by-frame basis, and the constant Beacon transmissions provide a good baseline for signal strength from an access point. Before the first step, the mobile station must authenticate to the new access point if it has not done so already.

Figure 8-10 depicts the following steps:

1. The mobile station issues a Reassociation Request to the new access point. Reassociation Requests have content similar to Association Requests. The only difference is that Reassociation Request frames contain a field with the address of the old access point. The new access point must communicate with the old access point to determine that a previous association did exist. Although a standard inter-access point protocol was defined by the IEEE, many implementations remain proprietary. If the new access point cannot verify that the old access point authenticated the station, the new access point responds with a Deauthentication frame and ends the procedure.

2. The access point processes the Reassociation Request. Processing Reassociation Requests is similar to processing Association Requests; the same factors may be used in deciding whether to allow the reassociation:

    a. If the Reassociation Request is granted, the access point responds with a Status Code of 0 (successful) and the AID.

    b. Unsuccessful Reassociation Requests include just a Status Code, and the procedure ends.

3. The new access point contacts the old access point to finish the reassociation procedure. This communication is part of the IAPP.

4. The old access point sends any buffered frames for the mobile station to the new access point. 802.11 does not specify the communication between access points. At the conclusion of the buffered frame transfer:

    a. Any frames buffered at the old access point are transferred to the new access point so they can be delivered to the mobile station.

    b. The old access point terminates its association with the mobile station. Mobile stations are allowed to associate with only one access point at any given time.

5. The new access point begins processing frames for the mobile station. When it receives a frame destined for the mobile station, that frame is bridged from the Ethernet to the wireless medium or buffered for a mobile station in a power-saving mode.

Reassociation is also used to rejoin a network if the station leaves the coverage area and returns later to the same access point. Figure 8-11 illustrates this scenario.

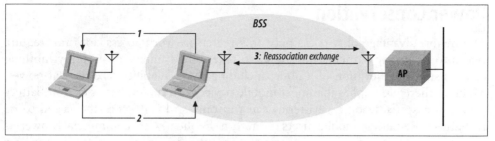

Figure 8-11. Reassociation with the same access point

What Is Roaming?

Roaming is not a word used in the 802.11 standard at all. (A task group recently formed to address roaming issues, but it is far from completing its work.) However, people use the word roaming informally a great deal when talking about 802.11. Generally speaking, most people are referring to the process of moving from one access point to another.

Roaming has suffered a bit from "buzzword overload" in the past few years, and now means different things to different speakers. At the most basic level, roaming is the process of moving a station between APs. How does a station decide to move between APs? The 802.11 standard has nothing to say on the matter. Decisions to move between APs are based entirely on the hardware and software, and up to each manufacturer. Some client devices will pick up on the strongest signal available when the interface is initialized, and hang on for dear life, only moving when the initial AP is no longer reachable. Some devices will always head for the strongest available signal, which may result in flip-flops between APs when two signals are evenly balanced. Still other devices will incorporate recent history into roaming decisions to avoid excessive movements between two nearby APs. How stations decide if and when to move between APs is entirely up to the manufacturer. With apologies to Milton Friedman, roaming is always and everywhere a client phenomenon.

Digging deeper into a second level of meaning, "roaming" is also used to discuss how a station can change APs while keeping active network connections open. If IP subnet boundaries are involved, this is an added level of complexity that needs to be addressed outside any standards. Chapter 21 discusses how to build a wireless LAN, and discusses how to achieve seamless roaming across arbitrary network topologies.

Roaming is sometimes given yet another meaning, referring to the process of moving a network session from one network (say, an 802.11 wireless LAN) to another disparate network (say, a 3G mobile telephone network). The IEEE has started another working group to define roaming operations to move network sessions and state between different types of IEEE 802 networks.

Power Conservation

The major advantage of wireless networks is that network access does not require nodes to be in any particular location. To take full advantage of mobility, nothing can constrain the location of a node, including the availability of electrical power. Mobility therefore implies that most mobile devices can run on batteries. But battery power is a scarce resource; batteries can run only so long before they need to be recharged. Requiring mobile users to return frequently to commercial power is inconvenient, to say the least. Many wireless applications require long battery life without sacrificing network connectivity.

As with any other network interface, powering down the transceiver can lead to great power savings in wireless networks. When the transceiver is off, it is said to be *sleeping*, *dozing*, or in *powersaving mode* (PS). When the transceiver is on, it is said to be *awake*, *active*, or simply *on*. Power conservation in 802.11 is achieved by minimizing the time spent in the latter stage and maximizing the time in the former. 802.11 accomplishes this without sacrificing connectivity.

Power Management in Infrastructure Networks

Power management can achieve the greatest savings in infrastructure networks. All traffic for mobile stations must go through access points, so they are an ideal location to buffer traffic. Most traffic can be buffered. The standard forbids buffering frames that require in-order delivery and have Order bit set because buffer implementations could possibly re-order frames. There is no need to work on a distributed buffer system that must be implemented on every station; the bulk of the work is left to the access point. By definition, access points are aware of the location of mobile stations, and a mobile station can communicate its power management state to its access point. Furthermore, access points must remain active at all times; it is assumed that they have access to continuous power. Combining these two facts allows access points to play a key role in power management on infrastructure networks.

Access points have two power management–related tasks. First, because an access point knows the power management state of every station that has associated with it, it can determine whether a frame should be delivered to the wireless network because the station is active or buffered because the station is asleep. But buffering frames alone does not enable mobile stations to pick up the data waiting for them. An access point's second task is to announce periodically which stations have frames waiting for them. The periodic announcement of buffer status also helps to contribute to the power savings in infrastructure networks. Powering up a receiver to listen to the buffer status requires far less power than periodically transmitting polling frames. Stations only need to power up the transmitter to transmit polling frames after being informed that there is a reason to expend the energy.

Power management is designed around the needs of the battery-powered mobile stations. Mobile stations can sleep for extended periods to avoid using the wireless network interface. Part of the association request is the Listen Interval parameter, the number of Beacon periods for which the mobile station may choose to sleep. Longer listen intervals require more buffer space on the access point; therefore, the Listen Interval is one of the key parameters used in estimating the resources required to support an association. The Listen Interval is a contract with the access point. In agreeing to buffer any frames while the mobile station is sleeping, the access point agrees to wait for at least the listen interval before discarding frames. If a mobile station fails to check for waiting frames after each listen interval, they may be discarded without notification.

Unicast frame buffering and delivery using the Traffic Indication Map (TIM)

When frames are buffered, the destination node's Association ID (AID) provides the logical link between the frame and its destination. Each AID is logically connected to frames buffered for the mobile station that is assigned that AID. Multicast and broadcast frames are buffered and linked to an AID of zero. Delivery of buffered multicast and broadcast frames is treated in the next section.

Buffering is only half the battle. If stations never pick up their buffered frames, saving the frames is a rather pointless exercise. To inform stations that frames are buffered, access points periodically assemble a traffic indication map (TIM) and transmit it in Beacon frames. The TIM is a virtual bitmap composed of 2,008 bits; offsets are used so that the access point needs to transmit only a small portion of the virtual bitmap. This conserves network capacity when only a few stations have buffered data. Each bit in the TIM corresponds to a particular AID; setting the bit indicates that the access point has buffered unicast frames for the station with the AID corresponding to the bit position.

Mobile stations must wake up and enter the active mode to listen for Beacon frames to receive the TIM. By examining the TIM, a station can determine if the access point has buffered traffic on its behalf. To retrieve buffered frames, mobile stations use PS-Poll Control frames. When multiple stations have buffered frames, all stations with buffered data must use the random backoff algorithm before transmitting the PS-Poll.

Each PS-Poll frame is used to retrieve one buffered frame. That frame must be positively acknowledged before it is removed from the buffer. Positive acknowledgment is required to keep a second, retried PS-Poll from acting as an implicit acknowledgment. Figure 8-12 illustrates the process.

If multiple frames are buffered for a mobile station, then the More Data bit in the Frame Control field is set to 1. Mobile stations can then issue additional PS-Poll requests to the access point until the More Data bit is set to 0, though no time constraint is imposed by the standard.

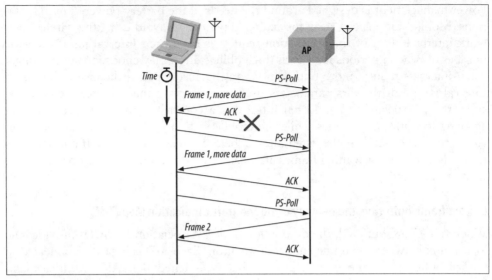

Figure 8-12. PS-Poll frame retrieval

After transmitting the PS-Poll, a mobile station must remain awake until either the polling transaction has concluded or the bit corresponding to its AID is no longer set in the TIM. The reason for the first case is obvious: the mobile station has success-fully polled the access point; part of that transaction was a notification that the mobile station will be returning to a sleeping mode. The second case allows the mobile station to return to a power conservation mode if the access point discards the buffered frame. Once all the traffic buffered for a station is delivered or dis-carded, the station can resume sleeping.

The buffering and delivery process is illustrated in Figure 8-13, which shows the medium as it appears to an access point and two associated powersaving stations. The hash marks on the timeline represent the beacon interval. Every beacon interval, the access point transmits a Beacon frame with a TIM information element. (This fig-ure is somewhat simplified. A special kind of TIM is used to deliver multicast traffic; it will be described in the next section.) Station 1 has a listen interval of 2, so it must wake up to receive every other TIM, while station 2 has a listen interval of 3, so it wakes up to process every third TIM. The lines above the station base lines indicate the ramp-up process of the receiver to listen for the TIM.

At the first beacon interval, there are frames buffered for station 1. No frames are buffered for station 2, though, so it can immediately return to sleep. At the second beacon interval, the TIM indicates that there are buffered frames for stations 1 and 2, although only station 1 woke up to listen to the TIM. Station 1 issues a PS-Poll and receives the frame in response. At the conclusion of the exchange, station 1 returns to sleep. Both stations are asleep during the third beacon. At the fourth beacon, both wake up to listen to the TIM, which indicates that there are frames buffered for both.

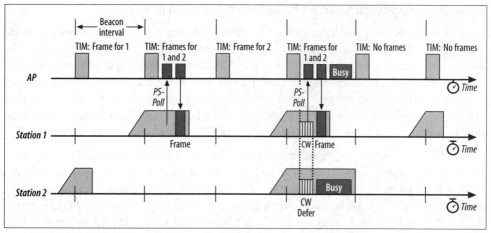

Figure 8-13. Buffered frame retrieval process

Both station 1 and station 2 prepare to transmit PS-Poll frames after the expiration of a contention window countdown, as described in Chapter 3. Station 1 wins because its random delay was shorter. Station 1 issues a PS-Poll and receives its buffered frame in response. During the transmission, station 2 defers. If, at the end of that frame transmission, a third station, which is not illustrated, seizes the medium for transmission, station 2 must continue to stay awake until the next TIM. If the access point has run out of buffer space and has discarded the buffered frame for station 2, the TIM at the fifth beacon indicates that no frames are buffered, and station 2 can finally return to a low-power mode.

Stations may switch from a power conservation mode to active mode at any time. It is common for laptop computers to operate with full power to all peripherals when connected to AC power and conserve power only when using the battery. If a mobile station switches to the active mode from a sleeping mode, frames can be transmitted without waiting for a PS-Poll. PS-Poll frames indicate that a powersaving mobile station has temporarily switched to an active mode and is ready to receive a buffered frame. By definition, active stations have transceivers operating continuously. After a switch to active mode, the access point can assume that the receiver is operational, even without receiving explicit notification to that effect.

Access points must retain frames long enough for mobile stations to pick them up, but buffer memory is a finite resource. 802.11 mandates that access points use an *aging function* to determine when buffered frames are old enough to be discarded. The standard leaves a great deal to the discretion of the developer because it specifies only one constraint. Mobile stations depend on access points to buffer traffic for at least the listen interval specified with the association, and the standard forbids the aging function from discarding frames before the listen interval has elapsed. Beyond that, however, there is a great deal of latitude for vendors to develop different buffer management routines.

Delivering multicast and broadcast frames: the Delivery TIM (DTIM)

Frames with a group address cannot be delivered using a polling algorithm because they are, by definition, addressed to a group. Therefore, 802.11 incorporates a mechanism for buffering and delivering broadcast and multicast frames. Buffering is identical to the unicast case, except that frames are buffered whenever any station associated with the access point is sleeping. Buffered broadcast and multicast frames are saved using AID 0. Access points indicate whether any broadcast or multicast frames are buffered by setting the first bit in the TIM; this bit corresponds to AID 0.

Each BSS has a parameter called the DTIM Period. TIMs are transmitted with every Beacon. At a fixed number of Beacon intervals, a special type of TIM, a Delivery Traffic Indication Map (DTIM), is sent. The TIM element in Beacon frames contains a counter that counts down to the next DTIM; this counter is zero in a DTIM frame. Buffered broadcast and multicast traffic is transmitted after a DTIM Beacon. Multiple buffered frames are transmitted in sequence; the More Data bit in the Frame Control field indicates that more frames must be transmitted. Normal channel acquisition rules apply to the transmission of buffered frames. The access point may choose to defer the processing of incoming PS-Poll frames until the frames in the broadcast and multicast transmission buffers have been transmitted.

Figure 8-14 shows an access point and one associated station. The DTIM interval of the access point is set to 3, so every third TIM is a DTIM. Station 1 is operating in a sleep mode with a listen interval of 3. It will wake up on every third beacon to receive buffered broadcast and multicast frames. After a DTIM frame is transmitted, the buffered broadcast and multicast frames are transmitted, followed by any PS-Poll exchanges with associated stations. At the second beacon interval, only broadcast and multicast frames are present in the buffer, and they are transmitted to the BSS. At the fifth beacon interval, a frame has also been buffered for station 1. It can monitor the map in the DTIM and send a PS-Poll after the transmission of buffered broadcast and multicast frames has concluded.

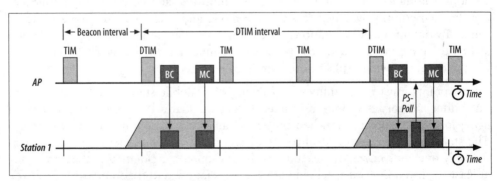

Figure 8-14. Multicast and broadcast buffer transmission after DTIMs

To receive broadcast and multicast frames, a mobile station must be awake for DTIM transmissions. Nothing in the specification, however, keeps powersaving stations in infrastructure networks from waking up to listen to DTIM frames. Some products that implement powersaving modes will attempt to align their awakenings with DTIM transmissions. If the system administrator determines that battery life is more important than receiving broadcast and multicast frames, a station can be configured to sleep for its listen period without regard to DTIM transmissions. Some documentation may refer to this as *extremely low power*, *ultra powersaving mode*, *deep sleep*, or something similar.

Several products allow configuration of the DTIM interval. Lengthening the DTIM interval allows mobile stations to sleep for longer periods and maximizes battery life at the expense of timely delivery. Shorter DTIM intervals emphasize quick delivery at the expense of more frequent power-up and power-down cycles. You can use a longer DTIM when battery life is at a premium and delivery of broadcast and multicast frames is not important. Whether this is appropriate depends on the applications you are using and how they react to long link-layer delays.

IBSS Power Management

Power management in an IBSS is not as efficient as power management in an infrastructure network. In an IBSS, far more of the burden is placed on the sender to ensure that the receiver is active. Receivers must also be more available and cannot sleep for the same lengths of time as in infrastructure networks.

As in infrastructure networks, power management in independent networks is based on traffic indication messages. Independent networks must use a distributed system because there is no logical central coordinator. Stations in an independent network use *announcement traffic indication messages* (ATIMs), which are sometimes called *ad hoc traffic indication messages*, to preempt other stations from sleeping. All stations in an IBSS listen for ATIM frames during specified periods after Beacon transmissions.

If a station has buffered data for another station, it can send an ATIM frame as notification. In effect, the ATIM frame is a message to keep the transceiver on because there is pending data. Stations that do not receive ATIM frames are free to conserve power. In Figure 8-15 (a), station A has buffered a frame for station C, so it sends a unicast ATIM frame to station C during the ATIM transmission window, which has the effect of notifying station C that it should not enter powersaving mode. Station B, however, is free to power down its wireless interface. Figure 8-15 (b) shows a multicast ATIM frame in use. This frame can be used to notify an entire group of stations to avoid entering low-power modes.

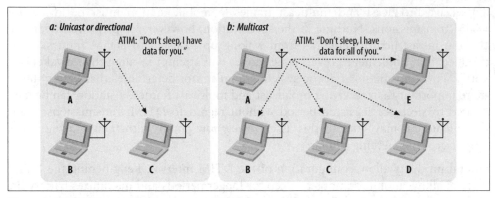

Figure 8-15. ATIM usage

A time window called the *ATIM window* follows the Beacon transmission. This window is the period during which nodes must remain active. No stations are permitted to power down their wireless interfaces during the ATIM window. It starts at the time when the beacon is expected and ends after a period specified when the IBSS is created. If the beacon is delayed due to a traffic overrun, the usable portion of the ATIM window shrinks by the same amount.

The ATIM window is the only IBSS-specific parameter required to create an IBSS. Setting it to 0 avoids using any power management. Figure 8-16 illustrates the ATIM window and its relation to the beacon interval. In the figure, the fourth beacon is delayed due to a busy medium. The ATIM window remains constant, starting at the target beacon interval and extending the length of the ATIM window. The usable period of the ATIM window shrinks by the length of the delay in beacon transmission.

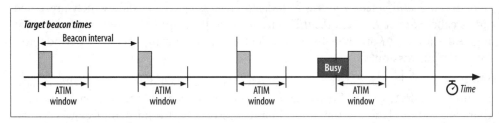

Figure 8-16. ATIM window

To monitor the entire ATIM window, stations must wake up before the target beacon transmission. Four situations are possible: the station has transmitted an ATIM, received an ATIM, neither transmitted nor received, or both transmitted and received. Stations that transmit ATIM frames must not sleep. Transmitting an ATIM indicates an intent to transmit buffered traffic and thus an intent to stay active. Stations to which ATIM frames are addressed must also avoid sleeping so they can receive any frames transmitted by the ATIM's sender. If a station both transmits and receives ATIM frames, it stays up. A station is permitted to sleep only if it neither transmits nor receives an ATIM. When a station stays up due to ATIM traffic, it remains active until the conclusion of the *next* ATIM window, as shown in Figure 8-17. In the figure, the station goes active for the first ATIM window. If it does not send or receive any ATIM frames, it sleeps at the end of the ATIM window. If it sends or receives an ATIM frame, as in the second ATIM window, the station stays active until the conclusion of the third ATIM window.

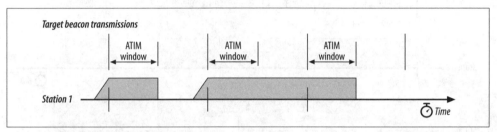

Figure 8-17. ATIM effects on powersaving modes

Only certain control and management frames can be transmitted during the ATIM window: Beacons, RTS, CTS, ACK, and, of course, ATIM frames. Transmission takes place according to the rules of the DCF. ATIM frames may be transmitted only during the ATIM window because stations may be sleeping outside the ATIM window. Sending an ATIM frame is useless if other stations in the IBSS are sleeping. In the same vein, acknowledgments are required for unicast ATIM frames because that is the only guarantee that the ATIM was received and that the frame destination will be active for the remainder of the beacon interval. Acknowledgments are not required for multicast ATIM frames because multicast frames cannot be efficiently acknowledged by a large group of stations. If all potential recipients of an ATIM frame were required to acknowledge it, the mass of acknowledgments could potentially interrupt network service.

Buffered broadcast and multicast frames are transmitted after the conclusion of the ATIM window, subject to DCF constraints. Following the transmission of broadcast and multicast frames, a station may attempt to transmit unicast frames that were announced with an ATIM and for which an acknowledgment was received. Following all transmissions announced with an ATIM, stations may transmit unbuffered frames to other stations that are known to be active. Stations are active if they have transmitted the Beacon, an ATIM, or are not capable of sleeping. If contention is severe enough to prevent a station from sending the buffered frame it announced with an ATIM, the station must reannounce the transmission with an ATIM at the start of the next ATIM window.

Figure 8-18 illustrates several of these rules. In the first beacon interval, the first station transmits a multicast ATIM to stations 2, 3, and 4. Multicast ATIM frames need not be acknowledged, but the transmission of the ATIM means that all stations must remain active for the duration of the first beacon window to receive multicast frames from station 1. When the ATIM window ends, station 1 can transmit its multicast frame to the other three stations. After doing so, station 4 can take advantage of the remaining time before the beacon to transmit a frame to station 1. It was not cleared with an ATIM, but it is known to be active.

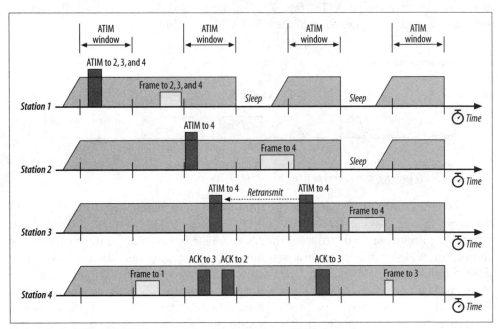

Figure 8-18. Effect of ATIM on powersaving modes in an IBSS network

In the second beacon interval, stations 2 and 3 have both buffered a frame for station 4, so each transmits an ATIM. Station 4 acknowledges both. At the conclusion of the ATIM window, station 1 has neither transmitted nor received an ATIM and can enter a low-power state until the next beacon interval. However, station 2's frame is extremely long and robs station 3 of the opportunity to transmit its frame.

Station 3 still has a buffered frame for station 4 when the third beacon interval opens. It therefore retransmits its ATIM frame to station 4, which is acknowledged. Station 2 is not involved in any ATIM exchanges and can enter a low-power state when the ATIM window ends. At that time, no broadcast or multicast frames have been buffered, and the ATIM-cleared frame from station 3 to station 4 can be transmitted. After the frame from 3 to 4 is transmitted, station 4 can again take advantage of the remaining time before the beacon frame to transmit a frame of its own to station 3, which is known to be active because of the ATIM exchange.

Stations are responsible for maintaining sufficient memory to buffer frames, but the buffer size must be traded off against the use of that memory for other purposes. The standard allows a station in an independent network to discard frames that have been buffered for an "excessive" amount of time, but the algorithm used to make that determination is beyond the scope of the standard. The only requirement placed on any buffer management function is that it retain frames for at least one beacon period.

Timer Synchronization

Like other wireless network technologies, 802.11 depends a great deal on the distribution of timing information to all the nodes. It is especially important in frequency-hopping networks because all stations on the network must change frequency channels in a coordinated pattern. Timing information is also used by the medium reservation mechanisms.

In addition to local station timing, each station in a basic service area maintains a copy of the *timing synchronization function* (TSF), which is a local timer synchronized with the TSF of every other station in the basic service area. The TSF is based on a 1-MHz clock and "ticks" in microseconds. Beacon frames are used to periodically announce the value of the TSF to other stations in the network. The "now" in a timestamp is when the first bit of the timestamp hits the PHY for transmission.

Infrastructure Timing Synchronization

The ease of power management in an infrastructure network is based on the use of access points as central coordinators for data distribution and power management functions. Timing in infrastructure networks is quite similar. Access points are responsible for maintaining the TSF time, and any stations associated with an access point must simply accept the access point's TSF as valid.

When access points prepare to transmit a Beacon frame, the access point timer is copied into the Beacon's timestamp field. Stations associated with an access point accept the timing value in any received Beacons, but they may add a small offset to the received timing value to account for local processing by the antenna and transceiver. Associated stations maintain local TSF timers so they can miss a Beacon frame and still remain roughly synchronized with the global TSF. The wireless medium is expected to be noisy, and Beacon frames are unacknowledged. Therefore, missing a Beacon here and there is to be expected, and the local TSF timer mitigates against the occasional loss of Beacon frames.

To assist active scanning stations in matching parameters with the BSS, timing values are also distributed in Probe Response frames. When a station finds a network by scanning, it saves the timestamp from the Beacon or Probe Response and the value of the local timer when it was received. To match the local timer to the network timer, a station then takes the timestamp in the received network advertisement and adds the number of microseconds since it was received. Figure 8-19 illustrates this process.

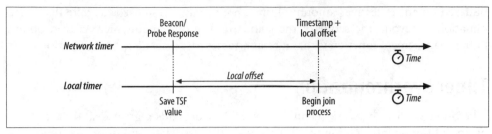

Figure 8-19. Matching the local timer to a network timer

IBSS Timing Synchronization

IBSSs lack a central coordination point, so the Beacon process is distributed. TSF maintenance is a subset of the Beacon generation process. Time is divided into segments equivalent to the interbeacon timing period. Beacon frames are supposed to be transmitted exactly as the beacon interval ends, at the so-called target Beacon transmission time (TBTT). Independent networks take the TBTT as a guideline.

All stations in the IBSS prepare to transmit a Beacon frame at the target time. As it approaches, all other traffic is suspended. Timers for the transmission of frames other than Beacon frames or ATIM frames are stopped and held to clear the medium for the important management traffic. All stations in the IBSS generate a *backoff timer* for Beacon transmission; the backoff timer is a random delay between zero and twice the minimum contention window for the medium. After the target beacon interval, all stations begin to count the Beacon backoff timer down to zero. If a Beacon is received before the station's transmission time, the pending Beacon transmission is canceled.

In Figure 8-20, each station selects a random delay; station 2 has randomly generated the shortest delay. When station 2's timer expires, it transmits a Beacon, which is received by stations 1 and 3. Both stations 1 and 3 cancel their Beacon transmissions as a result. Because timer synchronization ensures that all stations have synchronized timers, multiple Beacon frames do not pose a problem. Receivers simply process multiple Beacon frames and perform multiple updates to the TSF timer.

Beacon generation interacts closely with power management. Beacon frames must be generated during the active period around each Beacon interval so that all stations are available to process the Beacon. Furthermore, the Beacon sender is not allowed to enter a low-power state until the end of the next active period. The latter rule ensures that at least one station is awake and can respond to probes from new stations scanning to discover networks.

Rules for adopting the received timestamp are more complex in an independent network. No centralized timer exists, so the goal of the standard is to synchronize all timers to the timer of the fastest-running clock in the BSS. When a Beacon is received, the

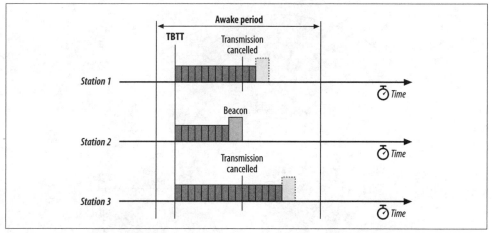

Figure 8-20. Distributed Beacon generation

timestamp is adjusted for processing delays and compared to the local TSF. The received timestamp updates the local timer only if it is later than the local timer.

Spectrum Management

802.11a was originally developed as a standard for the United States only. European radio regulations for the 5 GHz frequency band are stricter, which necessitated the development of special procedures to adapt the 802.11 MAC for use in Europe, which were eventually standardized as 802.11h in 2003.

Transmit Power Control (TPC)

Transmit power control is required by European regulations[*] to ensure that 5 GHz radio transmitters stay within regulatory power limits and avoid interfering with certain satellite services. Developing better control over transmission power brings many other benefits, some of which have been long known in the world of mobile telephony. High-powered client transmissions may cover very large areas. In a densely-deployed network of APs, a single client at high power may have much higher range than is necessary. Long range is not always a plus. Running a radio transmitter at high power decreases battery life. If the range of a transmission is longer than necessary, the extra reach represents "wasted" power. Higher power may also lead to a reduction in network throughput as client devices interfere with each other unnecessarily.

---

[*] ERC/DEC/(99)23, available at *http://www.ero.dk/doc98/Official/Pdf/DEC9923E.PDF*.

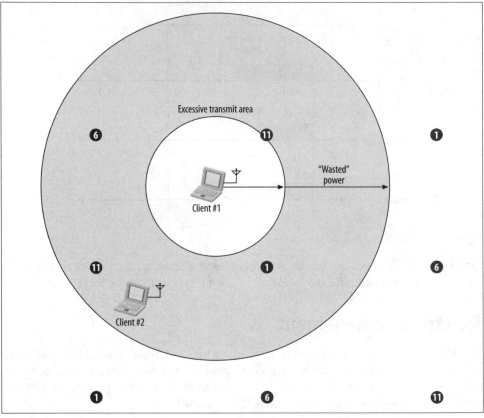

Figure 8-21. High client power interference with multiple APs

For an illustration of problems caused by high client power, consider Figure 8-21. In the figure, nine APs are shown in a network.* Client #1 is associated with the center AP in the top row. If the client computer is configured to transmit at maximum power, the range of the transmission will reach out to the outer circle. However, the transmission to the AP requires power to only the inner circle. The difference between the two circles is the excess range caused by transmitting too high. Running the radio transmitter higher than necessary will drain the battery on a portable device faster than is strictly necessary. (To extend the battery life of phones, mobile telephone networks have incorporated transmit power limitation techniques for many years.)

Controlling the range of transmission also makes the network function more smoothly. All transmissions must gain exclusive access to the radio medium. When excessive power is used, the area covered by a transmission is much larger than it should be. Any

---

* Note that laying out a nine-AP network using only three non-overlapping channels is not possible, which is a strong argument for using 802.11a in high-density environments.

station operating on channel 11 within the outer circle must defer to a frame in progress from Client #1. The shaded area between the optimum transmit power and the excessive power represents the area which is blocked because Client #1 is transmitting at power that is too high. For example, Client #2 is blocked from communicating with its nearby AP because it must share the radio medium. Reducing transmission power to the level required to reach only the serving AP may improve communications throughout the network by limiting overlap between nearby APs.

Basic operation of transmit power control

Transmit power control (TPC) is an 802.11 service that attempts to hold transmit power to the lowest possible productive level. It takes into account the maximum power allowed by regulators, as well as further constraints. Although designed to satisfy regulatory requirements, transmit power control may have additional benefits.

The absolute cap on any radio transmission is set by regulatory authorities, and is found in the relevant documents and rules published by the authority. Regulatory maximum power may be configured into an AP or station, or it may be learned from Beacon frames containing Country elements. Radio transmissions may be subject to additional constraints that further reduce the maximum power. European regulations specify a further *mitigation requirement* of at least 3 dB to reduce interference with satellite services.

Maximum transmission power is specified using the Country element in Beacon frames, and is available to any station wishing to associate to a network. The Country element specifies the regulatory maximum power, and the Power Constraint element can be used to specify a lower maximum transmission power specific to the network.

Before beginning operation, stations must calculate the maximum transmission power that may be used. Typically, this is calculated by taking the regulatory maximum power and subtracting any constraints for mitigation or additional local constraints. For example, network administrators may wish to specify a restrictive local maximum transmission power to reduce range and therefore interference.

Changes to the association process

When a spectrum management-capable station associates (or reassociates) to an access point, it must supply the minimum and maximum transmission power in a Power Capability information element. Access points may incorporate the information supplied by a client into the association process, and are free to use it any manner. How, or even whether, an access point uses the power capability information is not specified by 802.11 standards. Stations that have high power and may violate regulations may be rejected to preserve regulatory compliance. Access points may also reject clients with low transmit power capability; the standard suggests that it may increase the possibility of hidden nodes, although that seems unlikely.

Changing the transmission power

Both access points and client stations may dynamically adjust the transmission power on a frame-by-frame basis. For each frame, the receiver may compute the *link margin*, the amount by which the received power exceeds the minimum acceptable value. Link margin is the margin of safety. If a station's transmissions were received at the minimum acceptable value, the link margin would be zero, indicating that any detrimental change to the link would interrupt communication. Most stations aim for a small link margin, but the specific calculation of link margin and the determination of a particular desired value are not specified by the standard.

To make informed changes to transmission power, stations may request a radio link measurement. Stations send an Action frame requesting a transmission report. The Action frame sent in response contains a TPC Report element with two descriptive statistics. First, it contains the transmit power of the report frame. Based on the transmission power, the receiver of the report can estimate the path loss of the radio link. Second, the report frame contains a value for the link margin, which informs the receiver of the ratio between the received power and the minimum acceptable power. If the minimum acceptable power were, say, –70 dBm and the signal was received at –60 dBm, the link margin would be reported as 10 dB. If the link margin is "too high," transmit power can be reduced. If the link margin is "too low," the transmit power can be increased. Like many other components of the 802.11 standard, "too high" and "too low" are left to the discretion of the software.

The standard is designed to ensure that the maximum transmission power is not exceeded, but it does not restrict power selection in any way. There is no requirement for advanced functionality. That said, it is conceivable that advanced access points supporting transmit power control may attempt to keep track of the power required to reach each associated station, so that close-in stations require less power than far-away stations.

Dynamic Frequency Selection (DFS)

In addition to the requirement for transmit power control, European regulations require that stations avoid interfering with 5 GHz radar systems, as well as spread the power load across all available channels. Accomplishing this is the task of 802.11's Dynamic Frequency Selection (DFS) mechanism.

Basic operation of DFS

Dynamic frequency selection consists of a number of procedures to enable 802.11 devices to change the radio channel based on measurements and regulatory requirements. It can affect the initial association procedure and ongoing network operation.

When stations first associate to the network, the Association Request frame includes a Supported Channels information element, which communicates the channels supported by the station. Access points may reject the association based on the content of the information element, though such behavior is not specified by the standard. One approach would be to reject stations that support "too few" channels, on the theory that it limits the ability of the access point to switch operation on to different channels because it must move to a channel supported by all associated stations.

Once used on an operational network, DFS will periodically test the channel for potential interference from other radio systems, most notably 5 GHz European radar systems. Testing the channel is accomplished by stopping transmissions on the network, measuring for potential interference, and, if necessary, advertising that the channel will change.

Quieting the channel

To perform tests on the radio channel, *quiet periods* or *quiet intervals* are used. Quiet intervals are a time when all stations in the BSS do not transmit, which is helpful when making measurements for potential interference from radar systems. Quiet periods are scheduled by the inclusion of the Quiet information element in Beacon and Probe Response frames, and describe when and how long all stations should cease transmissions. Only the most recently transmitted Quiet information is effective. When multiple Quiet information elements are transmitted, the most recent one supercedes all prior scheduled quiet periods. During the quiet period, all stations set the network allocation vector (NAV) to the length of the quiet period to ensure that the virtual carrier sensing algorithm will defer transmissions.

When an upcoming quiet interval is scheduled, the radio channel still operates under normal rules for access to the radio medium, with the additional rule that any frame exchange must complete before the start of the quiet period. If a scheduled frame exchange cannot be completed, the station relinquishes control of the channel and defers transmission until after the conclusion of the quiet period. Failure to transmit a frame due to an impending quiet period does not, however, increase the transmission count. When the quiet period resumes, all stations must contend for access to the radio channel again. There is no preservation of channel access across a quiet period.

In an infrastructure network, channel quiet scheduling is completely under the control of the access point. Access points are allowed to change the duration of quiet periods, the time between quiet periods, or even to stop scheduling quiet periods altogether. Independent networks choose the quiet period scheduling when the network is created. When new stations take over responsibility for sending Beacon and Probe Response frames, they have no discretion to alter the quiet period parameters, and simply copy the previously used parameters.

Measuring

At any point, measurements of the radio channel can be taken. Stations may request other stations to measure the radio channel. Access points may find measurements from stations to be particularly useful in learning about the state of the radio channel because the reports from stations are likely to come from a variety of different geographical locations. Measurements may be taken in a quiet period or while the radio is in service.

Any station may ask other stations to make a measurement. Inquiries for radio information are sent in Measurement Request frames, described in Figure 8-23. In an infrastructure network, all frames must go through the access point. Associated client stations may only ask the AP for radio information. Access points in an infrastructure network may ask either a single station or a group of stations for a measurement, simply by addressing the request frame appropriately. In independent networks, there is no centralized point of control, and any station may issue a request to any other single station or group of stations. Although requests to a group address field are allowed, receiving stations are also allowed to disregard them.

After sending a measurement request, the standard assumes that the receiver needs time to gather the data for its reply. Following the transmission of a measurement request, a station refrains from sending any further frames.

Upon receipt of a Measurement Request frame, a station must determine how to respond. The Measurement Request frame must always be answered, even if the response is a refusal to perform the requested measurement. To be processed, a request must be received in enough time to set up and take the measurement. Measurement requests specify a time at which the measurement is to occur. If a request is held in a long transmission queue, it is conceivable that it could be arrive at the destination after the requested measurement should begin. Stations are allowed to ignore such "late" requests. The receiver of a measurement request must also be able to collect the data supported in the request. Depending on the receiver's hardware, it may not be possible to support all requests. Although increasingly rare, not all 802.11 hardware is capable of supporting every allowed channel.[*] Many cards on the market today do not support multichannel operation, either, so a request to measure a different channel from the current operating channel cannot be supported. Stations may refuse to perform a measurement for any nonspecified reason, provided the requester has not marked the request as mandatory.

In addition to the polled operation, in which stations ask for measurements, it is possible for stations to spontaneously report statistics by sending unsolicited Measurement Report frames.

---

[*] For example, the Cisco CB-20 card, based on the Radiata chipset, could only support the eight lowest 802.11a channels. It would be appropriate for such a card to refuse a measurement request in the high U-NII band.

Radar scan

One of the major reasons to quiet the channel is to search for the presence of 5 GHz radar systems in use in Europe. The regulations* do not require any particular search method for these radar systems. It only requires that radar be detected when its signal strength rises above a defined interference threshold.

When a radio interface is started, it must search for a radar signal on the channel. No transmissions are allowed until the "coast is clear" and it has been established that there is no radar to interfere with. Radar detection must be carried out periodically throughout operation. Whenever radar signals are detected, the network must switch to another channel to avoid interference.

Spectrum management services enable a network to move to another channel. The decision to move to another channel may be caused by the presence of radar interference, but the generic mechanism to switch channels may be useful for a variety of purposes beyond compliance with European radio regulations. Networks capable of altering their operational channel may do so to minimize interference with other 802.11 devices and optimize the radio plan. Channel switching is designed to move as many of the associated stations to the new channel as possible, but it is always possible that communications with some or all of the associated stations may be disrupted. The standards do not place any constraints on how to select the new channel, but simply say that an access point should attempt to choose a channel supported by as many of its stations as possible. Some regulators have drafted rules that mandate energy spreading across the entire band, so it may be that regulatory requirements force a switch to channels that are not supported by all stations.

In an infrastructure network, the selection of the operating channel is under the sole control of the access point. As part of the association process, access points collect information about which channels can be supported by the associated stations. Access points inform associated stations of the impending switch by using the Channel Switch Announcement information element in management frames, as well as Action frames. To improve the ability of an access point to send an channel switch announcement, the appropriate action frame may be sent after the PCF Interframe Space (PIFS), which gives it a higher priority than any new atomic exchange on the medium. The standard suggests, but does not require, that the channel switch be scheduled far enough in advance that any powersaving stations have the opportunity to become active and receive the channel switch announcement.

IBSS operation

Changing the operating channel in an independent network is significantly more complicated than in an infrastructure network because there is no single logical

---

* ETSI EN 301 893, available from *http://www.etsi.org*.

controller for frequency selection operation. Instead of having the function reside in the access point, independent networks have the *DFS owner service*, which coordinates multiple stations to run the frequency selection service.

One station in a network is designated the DFS owner, and is responsible for collecting measurement reports and monitoring the channel for radar signals. If any station in the independent network observes a radar signal, it will be reported in the channel map subfield. Upon notification that radar has been detected, the DFS owner takes charge of changing the channel.

The DFS owner is responsible for deciding on the new channel, and sending the channel switch announcement frame. It may not be possible to select a channel that complies with regulatory requirements and is supported by all stations. Independent networks do not have a central point of data collection, so even if there is a channel supported by all stations, there is no guarantee that the DFS owner will be aware of it.

In an independent network, the DFS owner may change. Just like Beacon generation, stations may join or leave the network, including the DFS owner. To cope with the DFS owner going away, stations may enter *DFS owner recovery mode*. In this mode, multiple stations can become DFS owners, and will schedule the channel switch announcement frames required by the standard. However, the first station to transmit the channel switch frame becomes the only DFS owner, and other stations will drop the role. DFS owner recover is similar in concept to the distributed Beacon generation discussed in Figure 8-20.

Action Frames

Action frames are used to request a station to take action on behalf of another. Spectrum management services use Action frames to request that measurements be taken, gather the results of those measurements, and announce any required channel switches. Figure 8-22 shows the format of the Action frame, which is essentially a category plus details that depend on the category. The action details may vary depending on the category field.

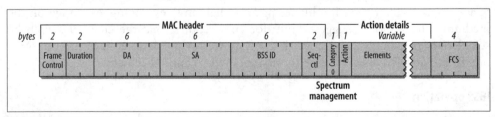

Figure 8-22. Action frame

Category

The category field is set to zero for spectrum management.

Action

All spectrum management frames use the first byte of the action details to specify the type of action being undertaken. Table 8-2 shows the possible values for the Action subfield. Values not shown are reserved.

Elements

Spectrum management action frames carry information in information elements. The details for many information elements can be found in Chapter 4. Several additional information elements were defined in 802.11h and are described in this section.

Table 8-2. Types of spectrum management action frames

Value	Type of spectrum management action frame
0	Measurement Request
1	Measurement Report
2	TPC Request
3	TPC Report
4	Channel Switch Announcement

Measurement Request frame

The Measurement Request frame is used to request that a station make measurements and send the results to the sender. Its format is shown in Figure 8-23. The frame consists of a series of measurement request information elements. The number of potential measurements is limited by the size of the frame, rather than any aspect of the frame construction.

Periodic measurements are allowed by the standard. Periodic reports are enabled or disabled by sending a measurement request to a station with instructions to turn the periodic measurement on or off. Stations cannot disable measurements on access points in infrastructure networks.

Category

Set to zero to indicate spectrum management action frames.

Action

Set to zero to indicate that it is a measurement request.

Dialog Token

This field acts like a sequence number. It is set to a non-zero value to assist in matching measurement responses to outstanding requests.

A single Measurement Request frame may request multiple measurements by using multiple Measurement Request information elements within the body of the frame.

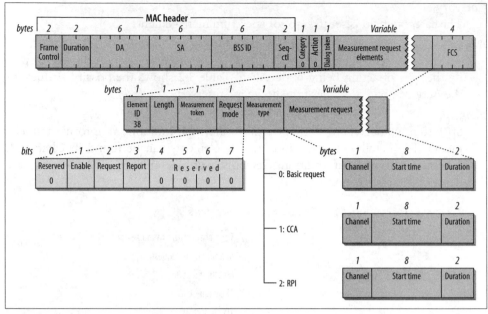

Figure 8-23. Measurement Request frame

A single information element is shown in exploded view, consisting of the following fields:

Element ID
Measurement Request elements are type 38.

Length
The length, in bytes, of the information element following this field.

Measurement Token
Each Measurement Request frame may make several requests by including several Measurement Request elements within the frame body. Each request is given its own value for the Measurement Token so that the different requests can be distinguished.

Measurement Request Mode bitmap
There are three bits in the Measurement Request Mode bitmap that are used to indicate what types of spectrum management frames are supported. Bit number 2 (numbered starting from 0) is the Request bit, and is set to one to signify that the transmitter will process incoming measurement requests. Bit number 3 is the Report bit, which is set to one to signify that the transmitter will accept unsolicited reports. The Enable bit is set to one when the other two bits are valid.

Measurement Type
The type of measurement being requested by the information element, as shown in Table 8-3.

Measurement Request

If a measurement is requested, there may be an additional field to give timing parameters. As it turns out, the three types of measurements that are currently standardized all have the same format, consisting of a channel number, the value of the timer function at which the measurement should start, and the duration of the measurement in time units. A timer start value of zero indicates the measurement should be taken immediately. This field is not present when the frame is used to turn measurements on or off.

Table 8-3. Measurement Type values

Measurement Type value	Name
0	Basic measurement
1	Clear channel assessment
2	Receive power indication (RPI) histogram

Measurement Report

The Measurement Report frame is used to send the results of a measurement to the requester. Its format is shown in Figure 8-24. The frame consists of a series of measurement report information elements. The number of potential reports is limited by the size of the frame, rather than any aspect of the frame construction.

Category

Set to zero to indicate spectrum management action frames.

Action

Set to one to indicate that it is a measurement report.

Dialog Token

If the measurements were taken as the result of a measurement request from another station, the Dialog Token field from that request is copied into the response. If the frame is sent as an unsolicited report, the Dialog Token is zero.

A single Measurement Report frame may contain the results for several measurements, each transmitted in its own information element. For clarity, a single information element is shown in the information element header, and the three possible report elements are shown below.

Element ID

Measurement Request elements are type 39.

Length

The length, in bytes, of the information element following this field.

Measurement Token

Each Measurement Request frame may make several requests by including several Measurement Request elements within the frame body. Each request is

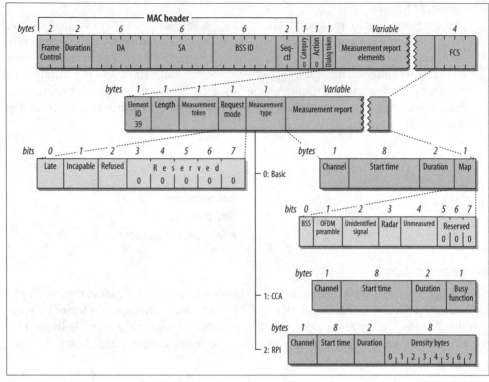

Figure 8-24. Measurement Report frame

given its own value for the Measurement Token so that the different requests can be distinguished.

Measurement Report Mode bitmap

There are three bits in the Measurement Report Mode bitmap that are used to indicate why a measurement is being refused, if the report frame is being used to deny a measurement. The Late bit is set to one when the measurement request arrives after the start time specified in the measurement. The Incapable bit is set to one when a station is unable to perform the requested measurement. The Refused bit is set to one when the station is capable of performing the measurement, but does not wish to do so.

Measurement Type

The type of measurement being requested by the information element, as shown in Table 8-3.

Measurement Report

The Measurement Report frame contains the requested measurement data. Unlike the Measurement Request, the contents are different for each type of report. All three reports are shown underneath the information element header. All share a common header that reports the channel number that the request is

---

for, the time the measurement started, and the duration of the measurement. However, the data is reported in different ways for each type of measurement.

In a *basic report*, the data reported are a series of bit flags for the channel:

BSS (1 bit)
This bit will be set if frames from another network are detected during a measurement period.

OFDM Preamble (1 bit)
This bit is set if the 802.11a short training sequence is detected, but without being followed by the rest of the frame. HIPERLAN/2 networks use the same preamble, but not the same frame construction.

Unidentified Signal (1 bit)
This bit is set when the received power is high, but the signal cannot be classified as either another 802.11 network (and hence, set the BSS bit), another OFDM network (and hence, set the OFDM Preamble bit), or a radar signal (and hence, set the Radar bit). The standard does not specify what power level is high enough to trigger this bit being set.

Radar (1 bit)
If a radar signal is detected during a measurement period, this bit will be set. Radar systems that must be detected are defined by regulators, not the 802.11 task group.

Unmeasured (1 bit)
If the channel was not measured, this bit will be set. Naturally, if there was no measurement taken, nothing can be detected in the band and the previous four bits will be set to zero.

In a *CCA report*, the main field is the CCA Busy Fraction, which describes the fraction of time on which the clear channel assessment function was set to busy. It is a single byte, so the fraction is multiplied by 255 to convert to an integer ranging from 0 to 255, where higher values indicate the channel was busy more often.

RPI histogram reports are used to report the spread of received power on an interface. Stations can request an RPI histogram to determine how well another station is able to see signals from the current network, or it may use the report to scout out other channels when it is time to change the operating channel. An RPI histogram report contains information on the strength of received signals. However, unlike a one-frame measurement, it can report the spread of power received over the measurement duration to give the receiver an indication of the overall level of transmissions. The histogram contains eight bytes, each of which represents a range of received power, as shown in Table 8-4. Each byte has a value representing the fraction of power signals that fall into its range. The time fraction over which the received signal falls into the power range for the byte is scaled so that each byte ranges from 0 to 255, with its value depending on the fraction of time signals were received at that power level.[*]

Table 8-4. RPI power mapping

RPI number	Corresponding power (dBm)
0	Less than −87
1	−87 to −82
2	−81 to −77
3	−78 to −72
4	−71 to −67
5	−66 to −62
6	−61 to −57
7	−56 and higher

TPC Request and Report

TPC Request and TPC Report frames are both shown in Figure 8-25. They are both straightforward, consisting of Action frames with the spectrum management type. Each frame contains its corresponding information element, as described in Chapter 4. As with other frames, the Dialog Token field is used to match up requests with responses.

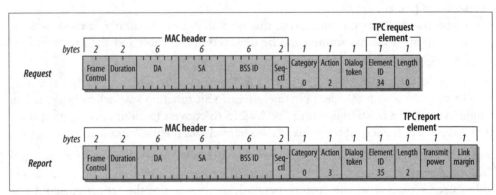

Figure 8-25. TPC Request and Report frames

Channel Switch Announcement

When the channel must be changed, stations that are part of the network must be informed of the impending change so that they may prepare to switch to the specified new channel. Channel Switch Announcement frames, shown in Figure 8-26, are

---

[*] Although the values of all 8 bytes theoretically add to 255, the standard notes that they may add up to 262 due to rounding effects.

essentially Action frame wrappers around the Channel Switch Announcement element that was described in Chapter 4. As such, they have all the functions of a channel switch announcement element, and are used to specify the time at which the network will switch to a new channel.

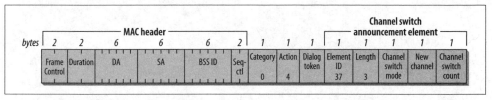

Figure 8-26. Channel Switch Announcement frame

## CHAPTER 9

Contention-Free Service with the PCF

To support applications that require near real-time service, the 802.11 standard includes a second coordination function to provide a different way of accessing the wireless medium. The point coordination function (PCF) allows an 802.11 network to provide an enforced "fair" access to the medium. In some ways, access to the medium under the PCF resembles token-based medium access control schemes, with the access point holding the token. This chapter describes medium access under the PCF, detailed frame diagrams for the PCF frames, and how power management operations interact with the PCF.

The PCF has not been widely implemented. A media server product for the home implemented the PCF, though it was not commercially successful. Some enterprise-class products have implemented the PCF because it gives the access points more control over access to the wireless medium, and helps the network to to wrest control away from the anarchy of a herd of individual stations. For many readers, this chapter may not be necessary. If you are not using a product that implements the PCF, there is no need to read this chapter unless you have an interest in the standard itself.

Contention-Free Access Using the PCF

If contention-free delivery is required, the PCF may be used. The PCF is an optional part of the 802.11 specification; products are not required to implement it. However, the IEEE designed the PCF so stations that implement only the distributed coordination function (DCF) will interoperate with point coordinators.

Contention-free service is not provided full-time. Periods of contention-free service arbitrated by the point coordinator alternate with the standard DCF-based service. The relative size of the contention-free period can be configured. 802.11 describes the contention-free periods as providing "near isochronous" services because the contention-free periods will not always start at the expected time, as described in the "Contention-Free Period Duration" section later in this chapter.

Contention-free service uses a centralized access control method. Access to the medium is restricted by the point coordinator, a specialized function implemented in access points. Associated stations can transmit data only when they are allowed to do so by the point coordinator. In some ways, contention-free access under the PCF resembles token-based networking protocols, with the point coordinator's polling taking the place of a token. Fundamentals of the 802.11 model remain in place, however. Although access is under the control of a central entity, all transmissions must be acknowledged.

PCF Operation

Figure 9-1 shows a transfer using the PCF. When the PCF is used, time on the medium is divided into the contention-free period (CFP) and the contention period. Access to the medium in the former case is controlled by the PCF, while access to the medium in the latter case is controlled by the DCF and the rules from Chapter 8. The contention period must be long enough for the transfer of at least one maximum-size frame and its associated acknowledgment. Alternating periods of contention-free service and contention-based service repeat at regular intervals, which are called the contention-free repetition interval.

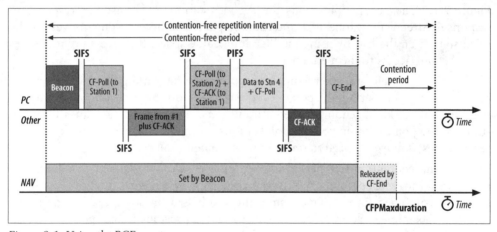

Figure 9-1. Using the PCF

Reserving the medium during the contention-free period

At the beginning of the contention-free period, the access point transmits a Beacon frame. One component of the beacon announcement is the maximum duration of the contention-free period, *CFPMaxDuration*. All stations receiving the Beacon set the NAV to the maximum duration to lock out DCF-based access to the wireless medium.

As an additional safeguard to prevent interference, all contention-free transmissions are separated only by the short interframe space and the PCF interframe space. Both are shorter than the DCF interframe space, so no DCF-based stations can gain access to the medium using the DCF.

The polling list

After the access point has gained control of the wireless medium, it polls any associated stations on a *polling list* for data transmissions. During the contention-free period, stations may transmit only if the access point solicits the transmission with a polling frame. Contention-free polling frames are often abbreviated CF-Poll. Each CF-Poll is a license to transmit one frame. Multiple frames can be transmitted only if the access point sends multiple poll requests.

The polling list is the list of privileged stations solicited for frames during the contention-free period. Stations get on the polling list when they associate with the access point. The Association Request includes a field that indicates whether the station is capable of responding to polls during the contention-free period.

Transmissions from the Access Point

Generally, all transmissions during the contention-free period are separated by only the short interframe space. To ensure that the point coordinator retains control of the medium, it may send to the next station on its polling list if no response is received after an elapsed PCF interframe space. (Such a situation is illustrated in Figure 9-1.) The access point polls the second station on its list but receives no response. After waiting one PCF interframe space, the access point moves to the third station on the list. By using the PCF interframe space, the access point ensures that it retains access to the medium.

The access point may use several different types of frames during the contention-free period. During this period, the point coordinator has four major tasks. In addition to the "normal" tasks of sending buffered frames and acknowledging frames from the stations, the point coordinator can poll stations on the polling list to enable them to send frames; it may also need to transmit management frames.

Time in the contention-free period is precious, so acknowledgments, polling, and data transfer may be combined to improve efficiency. When any subset of these functions are combined into a single frame, the result is a bit strange. A single frame could, for example, acknowledge the receipt of the previous frame, poll a different station for buffered data, and send its own data to the station on the polling list.

Several different frame types can be used in the contention-free period:

Data
> The standard vanilla Data frame is used when the access point is sending a frame to a station and does not need to acknowledge a previous transmission. The standard Data frame does not poll the recipient and thus does not allow the recipient to transmit any data in return. The data only frame used in the contention-free period is identical to the Data frame used in contention-based periods.

CF-Ack
> This frame is used by stations to acknowledge the receipt of a frame when no data needs to be transmitted. Contention-free acknowledgments are longer than

the standard control frame acknowledgment, so this frame may not be used in actual implementations.

CF-Poll

CF-Poll frames are sent by the access point to a mobile station to give the mobile station the right to transmit a single buffered frame. It is used when the access point does not have any data for the mobile station. When a frame for the mobile station is available, the access point uses the Data+CF-Poll frame type.

Data+CF-Ack

This frame combines data transmission with an acknowledgment. Data is directed to the frame recipient; the acknowledgment is for the previous frame transmitted and usually is not for the recipient of the data.

Data+CF-Poll

This frame is used by access points to transmit data to a mobile station and request one pending frame from the mobile station. The Data+CF-Poll can only be sent by the access point during the contention-free period.

CF-ACK+CF-Poll

This frame acknowledges the last frame from one of the access point's clients and requests a buffered frame from the next station on the polling list. It is directed to the next station on the polling list, although the acknowledgment may be intended for any mobile station associated with the access point.

Data+CF-ACK+CF-Poll

This frame brings together the data transmission, polling feature, and acknowledgment into one frame for maximum efficiency.

CF-End

This frame ends the contention-free period and returns control of the medium to the contention-based mechanisms of the DCF.

CF-End+CF-Ack

This is the same as the CF-End frame but also acknowledges the previously transmitted Data frame.

Any Management

No restriction is placed by the standard on which management frames can be transmitted during the contention-free period. If the rules applying to a particular frame type allow its transmission, the access point may transmit it.

Contention-Free Period Duration

The minimum length of the contention period is the time required to transmit and acknowledge one maximum-size frame. It is possible for contention-based service to overrun the end of the contention period, however. When contention-based service runs past the expected beginning of the contention-free period, the contention-free period is *foreshortened*, as in Figure 9-2.

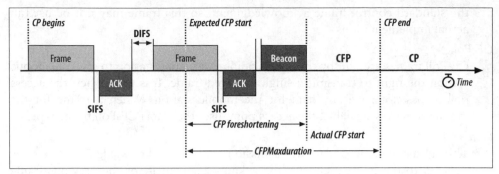

Figure 9-2. Data+CF-Ack and Data+CF-Poll usage

When the contention-free period is foreshortened, the existing frame exchange is allowed to complete before the beacon announcing the start of contention-free operation is transmitted. The contention-free period is shortened by the amount of the delay. Contention-free service ends no later than the maximum duration from the expected beginning point, which is referred to as the Target Beacon Transmission Time (TBTT).

The point coordinator may also terminate the contention-free period prior to its maximum duration by transmitting a CF-End frame. It can base this decision on the size of the polling list, the traffic load, or any other factor that the access point considers important. Products will sometimes selectively use the PCF for a particular frame exchange by starting contention-free service, performing the desired frame transmission, and then ending it.

Detailed PCF Framing

Several frame types are used exclusively within the contention-free period. They combine, in various states, data transmission, acknowledgment, and polling. This section describes when various frames are used and how the different functions interact during frame exchanges. Contention-free frames combine several functions into a single frame.

Data+CF-Ack

The Data+CF-Ack frame combines two different functions for transmission efficiency. Data is transmitted in the frame payload, and the frame implicitly acknowledges the receipt of data received one short interframe space previously. Generally, the data and the acknowledgment are intended for two separate stations. In Figure 9-3, the contention-free acknowledgment is coupled with the data for transmission to the access point in the previous frame, but the data may be intended for any station on the 802.11 network.

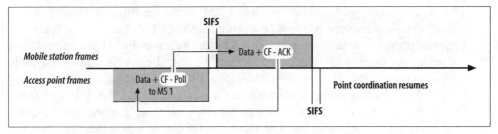

Figure 9-3. Data+CF-Ack usage

This frame is used only in infrastructure networks because it is transmitted during the contention-free period. It may be transmitted by either the access point or a mobile station. During the contention-free period, however, the access point is responsible for polling, and it is unlikely that it would transmit this frame subtype because it does not include a poll.

Data+CF-Poll

The Data+CF-Poll frame is used by access points in infrastructure networks during the contention-free period. When the access point does not need to acknowledge any outstanding frames, it sends a Data+CF-Poll to transmit data to the recipient and allows the recipient to send one buffered frame in response. The data in the frame body must be intended for the recipient of the poll; the two operations cannot be "split" across two different receivers. In Figure 9-3, the access point uses a Data+CF-Poll frame to send one frame to the mobile station and to solicit the response.

Data+CF-Ack+CF-Poll

The Data+CF-Ack+CF-Poll frame is used by access points in infrastructure networks during the contention-free period. When the access point has data to transmit, must acknowledge a frame, and needs to poll a station on the polling list, all the functions can be combined into one frame. Figure 9-4 illustrates the usage of Data+CF-Ack+CF-Poll. As with Data+CF-Ack, the components of the Data+CF-Ack+CF-Poll frame are generally intended for different stations. The data transmission and polling must be intended for the same station, but the acknowledgment is for the previous transmission.

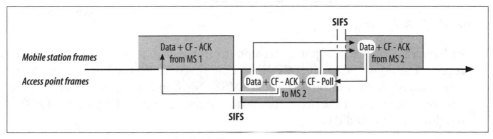

Figure 9-4. Usage of Data+CF-Ack+CF-Poll

The figure begins with mobile station 1 (MS1) transmitting a Data+CF-Ack frame. The Data must go to the access point, but the CF-Ack is used to acknowledge the previous Data frame transmitted by the access point. (That frame is not shown in the figure.) Moving down the polling list, the access point then polls mobile station 2 (MS2). However, the access point must acknowledge the data from MS1, which it does by transmitting a frame with a CF-Ack component. When the access point also has data to transmit, all three features can be combined into one omnibus frame. The Data and CF-Poll components are intended for the recipient of the frame, but the CF-Ack is intended for the transmitter of the *previous* frame. MS1 must listen to the access point frames to note the acknowledgment.

CF-Ack (no data)

When only an acknowledgment is required, a header-only frame with just the CF-Ack function can be transmitted. In Figure 9-4, if MS2 had no data to transmit, it would have responded with a CF-Ack frame.

CF-Poll (no data)

CF-Poll can also be transmitted by itself. Naturally, only access points perform this function, so the CF-Poll frame is transmitted only by access points in infrastructure networks during the contention-free period.

"Naked" CF-Polls are transmitted when the access point has no buffered data for the recipient and does not need to acknowledge the receipt of previous frames. One common situation in which no acknowledgment is necessary is when the access point transmits a CF-Poll and the polled station has no data and does not respond. If the access point has no data for the next station on the polling list, it transmits a CF-Poll, as in Figure 9-5.

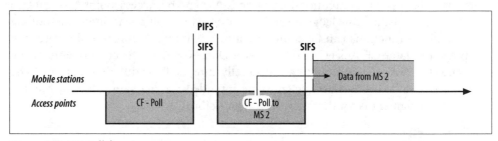

Figure 9-5. CF-Poll framing usage

In Figure 9-5, the access point attempts to transmit data to MS1 but does not receive a response. After the PCF interframe space has elapsed, the access point can proceed down the polling list to MS2. No frame from MS1 needs to be acknowledged, and if the access point has no data for MS2, it can use a CF-Poll to allow MS2 to send data.

CF-Ack+CF-Poll (no data)

The final subtype of Data frame is the CF-Ack+CF-Poll, which is also transmitted by access points. Like all CF-Poll frames, it is used only during the contention-free period and only by access points. It incorporates the acknowledgment function and the polling function into a frame with no data. Figure 9-6 illustrates its usage.

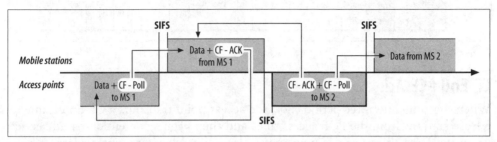

Figure 9-6. CF-Ack+CF-Poll usage

The scenario is a slight variation on the previous setting. Instead of a timeout waiting for MS1 to respond, MS1 returns a frame. When the access point takes control of the medium, it uses a CF-Ack+CF-Poll to acknowledge receipt of the frame from MS1 and notifies MS2 that it is allowed to send a frame.

Contention-Free End (CF-End)

When the contention-free period ends, the access point transmits a CF-End frame to release stations from the PCF access rules and begin contention-based service. The format of the CF-End frame is shown in Figure 9-7. Four fields make up the MAC header of the CF-End frame:

Frame Control

The frame subtype is set to 1110 to indicate a CF-End frame.

Duration

CF-End announces the end of the contention-free period and thus does not need to extend the virtual carrier sense. Duration is set to 0. Stations that receive the CF-End frame cut the virtual carrier sense short to resume contention-based access.

Address 1: Receiver Address

CF-End is relevant to the operation of all mobile stations, so the receiver address is the broadcast address.

Address 2: BSSID

CF-End is announced by the access point to all the stations associated with its BSS, so the second address field is the BSSID. In infrastructure networks, the BSSID is the address of the wireless interface in the access point, so the BSSID is also the transmitter address.

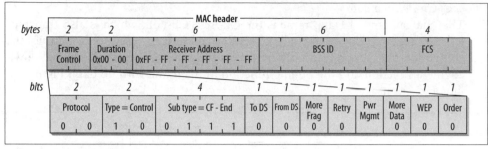

Figure 9-7. CF-End frame

CF-End+CF-Ack

When the contention-free period ends, the access point transmits a CF-End frame to release stations from the PCF access rules and then begins contention-based service using the DCF. If the access point must also acknowledge receipt of data, it may simultaneously end the contention-free period and acknowledge the previous frame by using the CF-End+CF-Ack frame, which combines both functions. The format of the CF-End+CF-Ack frame is shown in Figure 9-8. Four fields make up the MAC header of the CF-End+CF-Ack frame:

Frame Control
> The frame subtype is set to 1111 to indicate a CF-End+CF-Ack frame.

Duration
> CF-End+CF-Ack announces the end of the contention-free period and thus does not need to extend the virtual carrier sense. Duration is set to 0.

Address 1: Receiver Address
> CF-End+CF-Ack is relevant to the operation of all mobile stations, so the receiver address is the broadcast address.

Address 2: BSSID
> CF-End+CF-Ack is announced by the access point to all the stations associated with its BSS, so the second address field is the BSSID. In infrastructure networks, the BSSID is the address of the wireless interface in the access point, so the BSSID is also the transmitter address.

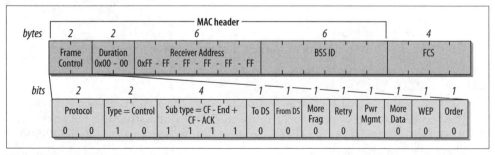

Figure 9-8. CF-End+CF-Ack frame

CF Parameter Set

Access points that support contention-free operation may include the CF Parameter Set information element, which is shown in Figure 9-9. CF Parameter Set elements are included in Beacon frames to keep all mobile stations apprised of contention-free operations. They are also included in Probe Response frames to allow stations to learn about contention-free options supported by a BSS. Four fields make up the CF Parameter Set information element:

CFP Count
> This field, which is one byte in length, tells how many DTIM frames will be transmitted before the start of the next contention-free period. Zero indicates that the current frame is the start of contention-free service.

CFP Period
> This one-byte field indicates the number of DTIM intervals between the start of contention-free periods.

CFP MaxDuration
> This value is the maximum duration of the contention-free period as measured in time units (TUs). Mobile stations use this value to set the NAV to busy for the entire contention-free period.

CFP DurRemaining
> This value is the number of TUs remaining in the current contention-free period. Mobile stations use it to update the NAV throughout the contention-free period. When DCF-based contention-free service is provided, it is set to 0.

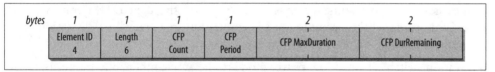

Figure 9-9. CF Parameter Set information element

Power Management and the PCF

Power conservation during the contention-free period is similar to power conservation during the contention-based period, with a few minor exceptions. The basic distinction between the two is that frame delivery must obey the PCF rules, so buffered frames can be delivered only to CF-Pollable stations. Stations that do not support PCF operations must wait until contention-based service resumes before retrieving buffered frames.

Stations on the polling list are not allowed to sleep during the contention-free period. When the access point is performing its point coordination functions, it may poll any station on the polling list at any time. Frames destined for stations on the polling list do not need to be buffered during the contention-free period because those stations do not sleep.

Frame buffering is identical under contention-free and contention-based service. By maintaining power-saving status for each station, the access point can buffer frames for any station in a low-power mode. Broadcast and multicast frames are buffered whenever an associated station is in a low-power mode.

In addition to the buffer status associated with contention-free service, the access point also sets bits in the TIM for any station it intends to poll. The reason for setting these bits is related to how buffered frames are delivered. Like contention-based service, DTIM frames trigger the transmission of broadcast and multicast frames. If the total time required to transmit multicast and broadcast frames exceeds the Beacon interval, the access point will transmit one Beacon interval's worth of buffered frames and stop. Remaining frames will, however, cause the access point to keep the bit corresponding to AID 0 set.

After transmitting the buffered broadcast and multicast frames, the access point goes through the list of AIDs whose TIM bits are set in increasing order and transmits any pending data. Transmissions are conducted according to the rules of the PCF, so it is not necessary to include a delay before beginning transmission. Stations on the polling list are added to the TIM, so they will be included in this process. Multiple buffered frames can be transmitted, but this is entirely up to the access point implementation—in contention-free service, mobile stations can transmit only when given permission by the access point. A station is not allowed to resume sleeping until all frames have been delivered to it, as indicated by a 0 More Data bit. When a station is cleared to resume sleeping, it sleeps until the next DTIM transmission. DTIM frames signal the beginning of the contention-free period, so all stations that implement the PCF are required to wake up for every DTIM.

If a station switches from a low-power mode to the active mode, any frames buffered for it are transferred to the point coordination function for delivery during the contention-free period. The transfer does not result in immediate delivery, but the access point can place the frames into a queue for transmission as soon as the point coordination function permits.

## CHAPTER 10

Physical Layer Overview

*Any girl can be glamorous.
All you have to do is stand still and look stupid.*
—Hedy Lamarr

Protocol layering allows for research, experimentation, and improvement on different parts of the protocol stack. The second major component of the 802.11 architecture is the physical layer, which is often abbreviated PHY. This chapter introduces the common themes and techniques that appear in each of the radio-based physical layers and describes the problems common to all radio-based physical layers; it is followed by more detailed explanations of each of the physical layers that are standardized for 802.11.

Physical-Layer Architecture

The physical layer is divided into two sublayers: the Physical Layer Convergence Procedure (PLCP) sublayer and the Physical Medium Dependent (PMD) sublayer. The PLCP (Figure 10-1) is the glue between the frames of the MAC and the radio transmissions in the air. It adds its own header. Normally, frames include a preamble to help synchronize incoming transmissions. The requirements of the preamble may depend on the modulation method, however, so the PLCP adds its own header to any transmitted frames. The PMD is responsible for transmitting any bits it receives from the PLCP into the air using the antenna. The physical layer also incorporates a clear channel assessment (CCA) function to indicate to the MAC when a signal is detected.

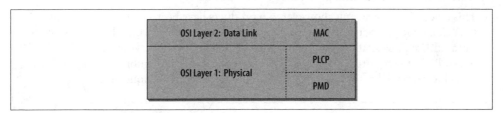

Figure 10-1. Physical layer logical architecture

The Radio Link

Three physical layers were standardized in the initial revision of 802.11, which was published in 1997:

- Frequency-hopping (FH) spread-spectrum radio PHY
- Direct-sequence (DS) spread-spectrum radio PHY
- Infrared light (IR) PHY

Later, three further physical layers based on radio technology were developed:

- 802.11a: Orthogonal Frequency Division Multiplexing (OFDM) PHY
- 802.11b: High-Rate Direct Sequence (HR/DS or HR/DSSS) PHY
- 802.11g: Extended Rate PHY (ERP)
- The future 802.11n, which is colloquially called the MIMO PHY or the High-Throughput PHY

This book discusses the physical layers based on radio waves in detail; it does not discuss the infrared physical layer, which to my knowledge has never been implemented in a commercial product.

The IR PHY

802.11 also includes a specification for a physical layer based on infrared (IR) light. Using infrared light instead of radio waves seems to have several advantages. IR ports are less expensive than radio transceivers—in fact, the cost is low enough that IR ports are standard on practically every laptop.

IR is extremely tolerant of radio frequency (RF) interference because radio waves operate at a totally different frequency. This leads to a second advantage: IR is unregulated. Product developers do not need to investigate and comply with directives from several regulatory organizations throughout the world.

Security concerns regarding 802.11 are largely based on the threat of unauthorized users connecting to a network. Light can be confined to a conference room or office by simply closing the door. IR-based LANs can offer some of the advantages of flexibility and mobility but with fewer security concerns. This comes at a price. IR LANs rely on scattering light off the ceiling, so range is much shorter.

This discussion is academic, however. No products have been created based on the IR PHY. The infrared ports on laptops comply with a set of standards developed by the Infrared Data Association (IrDA), not 802.11. Even if products were created around the IR PHY, the big drivers to adopt 802.11 are flexibility and mobility, which are better achieved by radio's longer range and ability to penetrate opaque objects.

Licensing and Regulation

The classic approach to radio communications is to confine an information-carrying signal to a narrow frequency band and pump as much power as possible (or legally allowed) into the signal. Noise is simply the naturally present distortion in the frequency band. Transmitting a signal in the face of noise relies on brute force—you simply ensure that the power of the transmitted signal is much greater than the noise.

In the classic transmission model, avoiding interference is a matter of law, not physics. With high power output in narrow bands, a legal authority must impose rules on how the RF spectrum is used. In the United States, the Federal Communications Commission (FCC) is responsible for regulating the use of the RF spectrum. Many FCC rules are adopted by other countries throughout the Americas. European allocation is performed by the European Radiocommunications Office (ERO) and the European Telecommunications Standards Institute (ETSI). In Japan, the Ministry of Internal Communications (MIC) regulates radio usage. Worldwide "harmonization" work is often done under the auspices of the International Telecommunications Union (ITU). Many national regulators will adopt ITU recommendations.

For the most part, an institution must have a license to transmit at a given frequency. Licenses can restrict the frequencies and transmission power used, as well as the area over which radio signals can be transmitted. For example, radio broadcast stations must have a license from the FCC. Likewise, mobile telephone networks must obtain licenses to use the radio spectrum in a given market. Licensing guarantees the exclusive use of a particular set of frequencies. When licensed signals are interfered with, the license holder can demand that a regulatory authority step in and resolve the problem, usually by shutting down the source of interference. Intentional interference is equivalent to trespassing, and may be subject to criminal or civil penalties.

Frequency allocation and unlicensed frequency bands

Radio spectrum is allocated in bands dedicated to a particular purpose. A band defines the frequencies that a particular application may use. It often includes guard bands, which are unused portions of the overall allocation that prevent extraneous leakage from the licensed transmission from affecting another allocated band.

Several bands have been reserved for unlicensed use. For example, microwave ovens operate at 2.45 GHz, but there is little sense in requiring homeowners to obtain permission from the FCC to operate microwave ovens in the home. To allow consumer markets to develop around devices built for home use, the FCC (and its counterparts in other countries) designated certain bands for the use of "industrial, scientific, and medical" equipment. These frequency bands are commonly referred to as the *ISM bands*. The 2.4-GHz band is available worldwide for unlicensed use.* Unlicensed use,

---

* The 2.4-GHz ISM band is reserved by the FCC rules (Title 47 of the Code of Federal Regulations), part 15.247. ETSI reserved the same spectrum in ETSI Technical Specifications (ETS) 300-328.

however, is not the same as unlicensed sale. Building, manufacturing, and designing 802.11 equipment does require a license; every 802.11 card legally sold in the U.S. carries an FCC identification number. The licensing process requires the manufacturer to file a fair amount of information with the FCC. Much this information is a matter of public record and can be looked up online by using the FCC identification number.

The Nonexistent Microwave Absorption Peak of Water

It is often said that microwave ovens operate at 2.45 GHz because it corresponds to a particular excitation mode of water molecules. This is sometimes even offered as a reason why 802. 11 cannot be used over long distances. If atmospheric water vapor would severely attenuate any microwave signals in rain or in humid climates, then 802.11 is not suitable for use over long distances.

The existence of a water excitation mode in the microwave range is a myth. If there was an excitation mode, water would absorb a significant amount of the microwave energy. And if that energy was absorbed effectively by water, microwave ovens would be unable to heat anything other than the water near the surface of food, which would absorb all the energy, leaving the center cold and raw. An absorption peak would also mean that atmospheric water vapor would disrupt satellite communications, which is not an observed phenomenon. NASA Reference Publication 1108(02), *Propagation Effects on Satellite Systems at Frequencies Below 10 GHz*, discusses the expected signal loss due to atmospheric effects, and the loss is much more pronounced at frequencies above 10 GHz. The absorption peak for water, for example, is at 22.2 GHz.

Microwave ovens do not work by moving water molecules into an excited state. Instead, they exploit the unusually strong dipole moment of water. Although electrically neutral, the dipole moment allows a water molecule to behave as if it were composed of small positive and negative charges at either end of a rod. In the cavity of a microwave oven, the changing electric and magnetic fields twist the water molecules back and forth. Twisting excites the water molecules by adding kinetic energy to the entire molecule but does not change the excitation state of the molecule or any of its components.

Use of equipment in the ISM bands is generally license-free, provided that devices operating in them do not emit significant amounts of radiation. Microwave ovens are high-powered devices, but they have extensive shielding to restrict radio emissions. Unlicensed bands have seen a great deal of activity in the past three years as new communications technologies have been developed to exploit the unlicensed band. Users can deploy new devices that operate in the ISM bands without going through any licensing procedure, and manufacturers do not need to be familiar with the licensing procedures and requirements. At the time this book was written, a number of new communications systems were being developed for the 2.4-GHz ISM band:

- The variants of 802.11 that operate in the band (the frequency-hopping layer, both direct sequence layers, and the OFDM layer)
- Bluetooth, a short-range wireless communications protocol developed by an industry consortium led by Ericsson
- Spread-spectrum cordless phones introduced by several cordless phone manufacturers
- X10, a protocol used in home automation equipment that can use the ISM band for video transmission

Unfortunately, "unlicensed" does not necessarily mean "plays well with others." All that unlicensed devices must do is obey limitations on transmitted power. No regulations specify coding or modulation, so it is not difficult for different vendors to use the spectrum in incompatible ways. As a user, the only way to resolve this problem is to stop using one of the devices; because the devices are unlicensed, regulatory authorities will not step in.

Other unlicensed bands

Additional spectrum is available in the 5 GHz range. The United States was the first country to allow unlicensed device use in the 5 GHz range, though both Japan and Europe followed.* There is a large swath of spectrum available in various countries around the world:

- 4.92–4.98 GHz (Japan)
- 5.04–5.08 GHz (Japan)
- 5.15–5.25 GHz (United States, Japan)
- 5.25–5.35 GHz (United States)
- 5.47–5.725 GHz (United States, Europe)
- 5.725–5.825 GHz (United States)

Devices operating in 5 GHz range must obey limitations on channel width and radiated power, but no further constraints are imposed. Japanese regulations specify narrower channels than either the U.S. or Europe.

Spread Spectrum

Spread-spectrum technology is the foundation used to reclaim the ISM bands for data use. Traditional radio communications focus on cramming as much signal as possible into as narrow a band as possible. Spread spectrum works by using mathematical functions to diffuse signal power over a large range of frequencies. When the

---

* Europe is obviously not a single country, but there is a European-wide spectrum regulator.

receiver performs the inverse operation, the smeared-out signal is reconstituted as a narrow-band signal, and, more importantly, any narrow-band noise is smeared out so the signal shines through clearly.

Use of spread-spectrum technologies is a requirement for unlicensed devices. In some cases, it is a requirement imposed by the regulatory authorities; in other cases, it is the only practical way to meet regulatory requirements. As an example, the FCC requires that devices in the ISM band use spread-spectrum transmission and impose acceptable ranges on several parameters.

Spreading the transmission over a wide band makes transmissions look like noise to a traditional narrowband receiver. Some vendors of spread-spectrum devices claim that the spreading adds security because narrowband receivers cannot be used to pick up the full signal. Any standardized spread-spectrum receiver can easily be used, though, so additional security measures are mandatory in nearly all environments.

This does not mean that spread spectrum is a "magic bullet" that eliminates interference problems. Spread-spectrum devices can interfere with other communications systems, as well as with each other; and traditional narrow-spectrum RF devices can interfere with spread spectrum. Although spread spectrum does a better job of dealing with interference within other modulation techniques, it doesn't make the problem go away. As more RF devices (spread-spectrum or otherwise) occupy the area that your wireless network covers, you'll see the noise level go up, the signal-to-noise ratio decrease, and the range over which you can reliably communicate drop.

To minimize interference between unlicenced devices, the FCC imposes limitations on the power of spread-spectrum transmissions. The legal limits are one watt of transmitter output power and four watts of effective radiated power (ERP). Four watts of ERP are equivalent to 1 watt with an antenna system that has 6-dB gain, or 500 milliwatts with an antenna of 10-dB gain, etc.* The transmitters and antennas in PC Cards are obviously well within those limits—and you're not getting close even if you use a commercial antenna. But it is possible to cover larger areas by using an external amplifier and a higher-gain antenna. There's no fundamental problem with doing this, but you must make sure that you stay within the FCC's power regulations.

---

* Remember that the transmission line is part of the antenna system, and the system gain includes transmission line losses. So an antenna with 7.5-dB gain and a transmission line with 1.5-dB loss has an overall system gain of 6 dB. It's worth noting that transmission line losses at UHF freqencies are often very high; as a result, you should keep your amplifier as close to the antenna as possible.

The Unlikely Invention of Spread Spectrum

Spread spectrum was patented in the early 1940s by Austrian-born actress Hedy Lamarr. She was certainly better known for other reasons: appearing in the first nude scene on film in the Czech film *Ecstasy*, her later billing as "the most beautiful woman in the world" by Hollywood magnate Louis Mayer, and as the model for Catwoman in the Batman comics.

Before fleeing the advance of Nazi Germany, she was married to an Austrian arms merchant. While occupying the only socially acceptable role available to her as a hostess and entertainer of her husband's business clients, she learned that radio remote control of torpedoes was a major area of research for armaments vendors. Unfortunately, narrowband radio communications were subject to jamming, which neutralized the advantage of radio-guided weapons. From these discussions, she first hit on the idea of using a complex but predetermined hopping pattern to move the frequency of the control signal around. Even if short bursts on a single frequency could be jammed, they would move around quickly enough to prevent total blockage. Lamarr worked out everything except how to precisely control the frequency hops.

After arriving in the United States, she met George Antheil, an avant-garde American composer known as the "bad boy of music" for his dissonant style. His famous *Ballet mécanique* used (among many outrageous noisemakers) 16 player pianos controlled from a single location. Performing the piece required precisely controlled timing between distributed elements, which was Lamarr's only remaining challenge in controlling the hopping pattern. Together, they were granted U.S. patent number 2,292,387 in 1942. The patent expired in 1959 without earning a cent for either of them, and Lamarr's contributions went unacknowledged for many years because the name on the patent was Hedy Kiesler Markey, her married name at the time. The emerging wireless LAN market in the late 1990s led to the rediscovery of her invention and widespread recognition for the pioneering work that laid the foundation for modern telecommunications.

Frequency-hopping techniques were first used by U.S. ships blockading Cuba during the Cuban Missile Crisis. It took many years for the electronics underpinning spread-spectrum technology to become commercially viable. Now that they have, spread-spectrum technologies are used in cordless and mobile phones, high-bandwidth wireless LAN equipment, and every device that operates in the unlicensed ISM bands. Unfortunately, Hedy Lamarr died in early 2000, just as the wireless LAN market was gaining mainstream attention.

Types of spread spectrum

The radio-based physical layers in 802.11 use three different spread-spectrum techniques:

Frequency hopping (FH or FHSS)
> Frequency-hopping systems jump from one frequency to another in a random pattern, transmitting a short burst at each subchannel. The 2-Mbps FH PHY is specified in clause 14.

Direct sequence (DS or DSSS)
> Direct-sequence systems spread the power out over a wider frequency band using mathematical coding functions. Two direct-sequence layers were specified. The initial specification in clause 15 standardized a 2-Mbps PHY, and 802.11b added clause 18 for the HR/DSSS PHY.

Orthogonal Frequency Division Multiplexing (OFDM)
> OFDM divides an available channel into several subchannels and encodes a portion of the signal across each subchannel in parallel. The technique is similar to the Discrete Multi-Tone (DMT) technique used by some DSL modems. Clause 17, added with 802.11a, specifies the OFDM PHY. Clause 18, added in 802.11g, specifies the ERP PHY, which is essentially the same but operating at a lower frequency.

Frequency-hopping systems are the cheapest to make. Precise timing is needed to control the frequency hops, but sophisticated signal processing is not required to extract the bit stream from the radio signal. Direct-sequence systems require more sophisticated signal processing, which translates into more specialized hardware and higher electrical power consumption. Direct-sequence techniques also allow a higher data rate than frequency-hopping systems.

RF Propagation with 802.11

In fixed networks, signals are confined to wire pathways, so network engineers do not need to know anything about the physics of electrical signal propagation. Instead, there are a few rules used to calculate maximum cable length, and as long as the rules are obeyed, problems are rare. RF propagation is not anywhere near as simple.

Signal Reception and Performance

Space is full of random electromagnetic waves, which can easily be heard by tuning a radio to an unused frequency. Radio communication depends on making a *signal* intelligible over the background *noise*. As conditions for reception degrade, the signal gets closer to the noise floor. Performance is determined largely by the the most important factor, the *signal-to-noise ratio* (SNR). In Figure 10-2, the SNR is illustrated by the height of the peak of the signal above the noise floor.

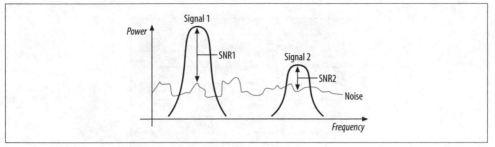

Figure 10-2. Signal-to-noise ratio and the noise floor

Having a strong signal is important, but not the whole story. Strong signals can be hard to pick out of noisy environments. In some situations, it may be possible to raise the power to compensate for a high noise floor. Unlicensed networks have only limited ability to raise power because of tight regulatory constraints. As a result, more effort is placed on introducing as little additional noise as possible before attempting to decode the radio signal.

The Shannon limit

Interestingly enough, there is no theoretical maximum to the amount of data that can be carried by a radio channel. The capacity of a communications channel is given by the Shannon-Hartley theorem, which was proved by Bell Labs researcher Claude Shannon in 1948. The theorem expresses the mathematical limit of the capacity of a communications channel, which is named after the theorem and is often called the *Shannon limit* or the *Shannon capacity*. The original Shannon theorem expressed the maximum capacity C bits per second as a function of the bandwidth W in Hertz, and the absolute ratio of signal power to noise. If the gain is measured in decibels, simply solve the equation that defines a decibel for the power ratio for the second form.

$$C <= W \log_2 (1 + S/N) \qquad \text{(S/N as power ratio)}$$
$$C <= W \log_2 (1 + 10^{\wedge}(0.1 * SNR)) \qquad \text{(SNR in decibels)}$$

Figure 10-3 shows the Shannon limit as a function of the signal-to-noise ratio. Shannon's theorem reflects a theoretical reality of an unlimited bit rate. To get to an unlimited bit rate, the code designer can require an arbitrarily large number of signal levels to distinguish between bits, but the fine distinctions between the arbitrarily close signal rates will be swamped by the noise. One of the major goals for 802.11 PHY designers is to design encoding rates as close to the Shannon limit as possible.

Alternatively, the Shannon theorem can be used to prescribe the minimum theoretical signal to noise ratio to attain a given data rate. Solve the previous equations for the signal to noise ratio:

$$S/N = 2 ^{\wedge} (C/W) - 1 \qquad \text{(S/N as power ratio)}$$
$$SNR = 10 * \log_{10} (2 ^{\wedge} (C/W) - 1) \qquad \text{(SNR as dB)}$$

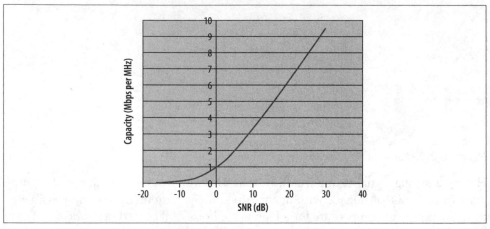

Figure 10-3. Shannon limit as a function of SNR

Take 802.11a as an example. A single 20 MHz channel can carry a signal at a data rate up to 54 Mbps. Solving for the required signal-to-noise ratio yields 7.4 dB, which is much lower than what is required by most real products on the market, reflecting the need of products to work in the real-world with much worse than ideal performance.[*]

Decibels and Signal Strength

Amplifiers may boost signals by orders of magnitude. Rather than keep track of all those zeroes, amplifier power is measured in decibels (dB).

$$dB = 10 \times \log^{10} \text{(power out/power in)}$$

Decibel ratings are positive when the output is larger than the input and negative when the output is smaller than the input. Each 10-dB change corresponds to a factor of 10, and 3-dB changes are a factor of 2. Thus, a 33-dB change corresponds to a factor of 2000:

$$33 \text{ dB} = 10 \text{ dB} + 10 \text{ dB} + 10 \text{ dB} + 3 \text{ dB} = 10 \times 10 \times 10 \times 2 = 2000$$

Power is sometimes measured in dBm, which stands for dB above one milliwatt. To find the dBm ratio, simply use 1 mW as the input power in the first equation.

It is helpful to remember that doubling the power is a 3-dB increase. A 1-dB increase is roughly equivalent to a power increase of 25%. With these numbers in mind, you can quickly perform most gain calculations in your head.

---

[*] Or, as another example, the telephone network makes channels with a frequency band of 180 Hz to 3.2 kHz, at a signal-to-noise ratio of 45 dB. That makes the maximum theoretical speed of an analog signal about 45 kbps. The trick behind the 56 kbps modem is that the downstream path is all digital, and as a result has a higher signal-to-noise ratio.

Path Loss, Range, and Throughput

In 802.11, the speed of the network depends on range. Several modulation types are defined by the various 802.11 standards, ranging in speed from 1 Mbps to 54 Mbps. Receiver circuits must distinguish between states to extract bits from radio waves. Higher speed modulations pack more bits into a given time interval, and require a cleaner signal (and thus higher signal-to-noise ratio) to successfully decode.

As radio signals travel through space, they degrade. For the most part, the noise floor will be relatively constant over the limited range of an 802.11 network. Over distance, the degradation of the signal will limit the signal-to-noise ratio at the receiver. As a station strays farther from an access point, the signal level drops; with a constant noise floor, the degraded signal will result in a degraded signal to noise ratio. Figure 10-4 illustrates this concept. As range from the access point increases, the received signal gets closer to the noise floor. Stations that are closer have higher signal to noise ratios. As a matter of network engineering, when the signal-to-noise ratio gets too small to support a high data rate, the station will fall back to a lower data rate with less demanding signal-to-noise ratio requirements.

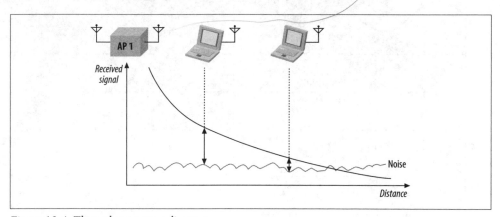

Figure 10-4. Throughput versus distance

When there are no obstacles to obstruct the radio wave, the signal degradation can be calculated with the following equation. The loss in free-space is sometimes called the *path loss* because it is the minimum loss that would be expected along a path with a given length. Path loss depends on the distance and the frequency of the radio wave. Higher distances and higher frequencies lead to higher path loss. One reason why 802.11a has shorter range than 802.11b and 802.11g is that the path loss is much higher at the 5 GHz used by 802.11a. The equation for free-space path loss is:

Path loss (dB) = 32.5 + 20 log F + log d

where the frequency F is expressed in GHz, and the distance d is expressed in meters. Path loss is not, however, the only determinant of range. Obstacles such as walls and windows will reduce the signal, and antennas and amplifiers may be used to boost the signal, which compensates for transmission losses. Range calculations often include a fudge factor called the *link margin* to account for unforeseen losses.

Total loss = TX power + TX antenna gain – path loss – obstacle loss – link margin + RX antenna gain

Multipath Interference

Although there is a relatively simple equation for predicting radio propagation, it is only an estimate for 802.11 networks. In addition to straight-line path losses, there are other phenomena that can inhibit signal reception with 802.11. One of the major problems that plague radio networks is *multipath fading*. Waves are added by superposition. When multiple waves converge on a point, the total wave is simply the sum of any component waves. Figure 10-5 shows a few examples of superposition.

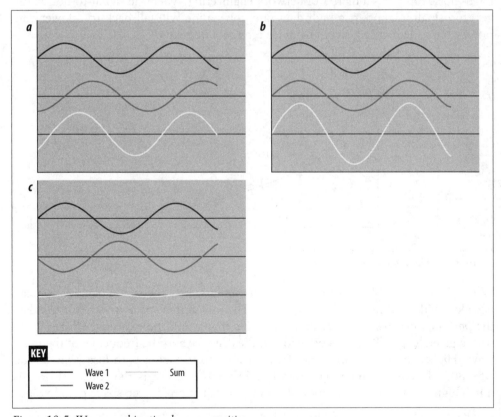

Figure 10-5. Wave combination by superposition

In Figure 10-5 (c), the two waves are almost exactly the opposite of each other, so the net result is almost nothing. Unfortunately, this result is more common than you might expect in wireless networks. Most 802.11 equipment uses omnidirectional antennas, so RF energy is radiated in every direction. Waves spread outward from the transmitting antenna in all directions and are reflected by surfaces in the area. Figure 10-6 shows a highly simplified example of two stations in a rectangular area with no obstructions.

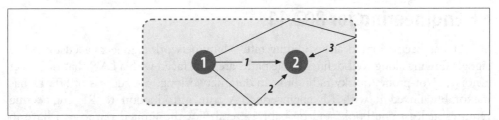

Figure 10-6. Multiple paths

This figure shows three paths from the transmitter to the receiver. The wave at the receiver is the sum of all the different components. It is certainly possible that the paths shown in Figure 10-6 will all combine to give a net wave of 0, in which case the receiver will not understand the transmission because there is no transmission to be received.

Because the interference is a delayed copy of the same transmission on a different path, the phenomenon is called *multipath fading* or *multipath interference*. In many cases, multipath interference can be resolved by changing the orientation or position of the receiver.

Inter-Symbol Interference (ISI)

Multipath fading is a special case of inter-symbol interference. Waves that take different paths from the transmitter to the receiver will travel different distances and be delayed with respect to each other, as in Figure 10-7. Once again, the two waves combine by superposition, but the effect is that the total waveform is garbled. In real-world situations, wavefronts from multiple paths may be added. The time between the arrival of the first wavefront and the last multipath echo is called the delay spread. Longer delay spreads require more conservative coding mechanisms. 802.11b networks can handle delay spreads of up to 500 ns, but performance is much better when the delay spread is lower. When the delay spread is large, many cards will reduce the transmission rate; several vendors claim that a 65-ns delay spread is required for full-speed 11-Mbps performance at a reasonable frame error rate. (Discussion of reading the specification sheets is found in Chapter 16.) Analysis tools can be used to measure the delay spread.

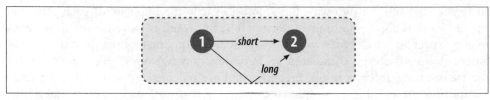

Figure 10-7. Inter-symbol interference

RF Engineering for 802.11

802.11 has been adopted at a stunning rate. Many network engineers accustomed to signals flowing along well-defined cable paths are now faced with a LAN that runs over a noisy, error-prone, quirky radio link. In data networking, the success of 802.11 has inexorably linked it with RF engineering. A true introduction to RF engineering requires at least one book, and probably several. For the limited purposes I have in mind, the massive topic of RF engineering can be divided into two parts: how to make radio waves and how radio waves move.

RF Components

RF systems complement wired networks by extending them. Different components may be used depending on the frequency and the distance that signals are required to reach, but all systems are fundamentally the same and made from a relatively small number of distinct pieces. Two RF components are of particular interest to 802.11 users: *antennas* and *amplifiers*. Antennas are of general interest since they are the most tangible feature of an RF system. Amplifiers complement antennas by allowing the antennas to pump out more power, which may be of interest depending on the type of 802.11 network you are building.

Antennas

Antennas are the most critical component of any RF system because they convert electrical signals on wires into radio waves and vice versa. In block diagrams, antennas are usually represented by a triangular shape, as shown in Figure 10-8.

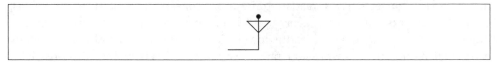

Figure 10-8. Antenna representations in diagrams

To function at all, an antenna must be made of conducting material. Radio waves hitting an antenna cause electrons to flow in the conductor and create a current. Likewise, applying a current to an antenna creates an electric field around the antenna. As the current to the antenna changes, so does the electric field. A changing electric field causes a magnetic field, and the wave is off.

The size of the antenna you need depends on the frequency: the higher the frequency, the smaller the antenna. The shortest simple antenna you can make at any frequency is 1/2 wavelength long (although antenna engineers can play tricks to reduce antenna size further). This rule of thumb accounts for the huge size of radio broadcast antennas and the small size of mobile phones. An AM station broadcasting at 830 kHz has a wavelength of about 360 meters and a correspondingly large antenna, but an 802.11b network interface operating in the 2.4-GHz band has a wavelength of just 12.5 centimeters. With some engineering tricks, an antenna can be incorporated into a PC Card or around the laptop LCD screen, and a more effective external antenna can easily be carried in a backpack or computer bag.

Antennas can also be designed with directional preference. Many antennas are omnidirectional, which means they send and receive signals from any direction. Some applications may benefit from directional antennas, which radiate and receive on a narrower portion of the field. Figure 10-9 compares the radiated power of omnidirectional and directional antennas.

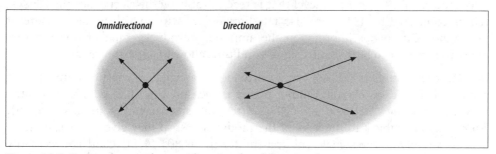

Figure 10-9. Radiated power for omnidirectional and directional antennas

For a given amount of input power, a directional antenna can reach farther with a clearer signal. They also have much higher sensitivity to radio signals in the dominant direction. When wireless links are used to replace wireline networks, directional antennas are often used. Mobile telephone network operators also use directional antennas when cells are subdivided. 802.11 networks typically use omnidirectional antennas for both ends of the connection, although there are exceptions— particularly if you want the network to span a longer distance. Also, keep in mind that there is no such thing as a truly omnidirectional antenna. We're accustomed to thinking of vertically mounted antennas as omnidirectional because the signal doesn't vary significantly as you travel around the antenna in a horizontal plane. But if you look at the signal radiated vertically (i.e., up or down) from the antenna, you'll find that it's a different story. And that part of the story can become important if you're building a network for a college or corporate campus and want to locate antennas on the top floors of your buildings.

Of all the components presented in this section, antennas are the most likely to be separated from the rest of the electronics. In this case, you need a transmission line (some kind of cable) between the antenna and the transceiver. Transmission lines usually have an impedance of 50 ohms.

In terms of practical antennas for 802.11 devices in the 2.4-GHz band, the typical wireless PC Card has an antenna built in. Built-in antennas work, but they will never be anything to write home about. At best, the built in antenna in a PC card is mediocre. Larger antennas perform better. Some PC Card 802.11 interfaces have external antenna jacks. With an optional external antenna, the card has better performance, at the cost of aesthetic quality. In response to the need for improved antenna performance without ugly space-consuming external antennas, many laptops now use an antenna built into the frame around the laptop screen.

Amplifiers

Amplifiers make signals bigger. Signal boost, or gain, is measured in decibels (dB). Amplifiers can be broadly classified into three categories: low-noise, high-power, and everything else. Low-noise amplifiers (LNAs) are usually connected to an antenna to boost the received signal to a level that is recognizable by the electronics the RF system is connected to. LNAs are also rated for noise factor, which is the measure of how much extraneous information the amplifier introduces. Smaller noise factors allow the receiver to hear smaller signals and thus allow for a greater range.

High-power amplifiers (HPAs) are used to boost a signal to the maximum power possible before transmission. Output power is measured in dBm, which are related to watts (see the "Decibels and Signal Strength" sidebar earlier in this chapter). Amplifiers are subject to the laws of thermodynamics, so they give off heat in addition to amplifying the signal. The transmitter in an 802.11 PC Card is necessarily low-power because it needs to run off a battery if it's installed in a laptop, but it's possible to install an external amplifier at fixed access points, which can be connected to the power grid where power is more plentiful.

This is where things can get tricky with respect to compliance with regulations. 802.11 devices are limited to one watt of power output and four watts effective radiated power (ERP). ERP multiplies the transmitter's power output by the gain of the antenna minus the loss in the transmission line. So if you have a 1-watt amplifier, an antenna that gives you 8 dB of gain, and 2 dB of transmission line loss, you have an ERP of 4 watts; the total system gain is 6 dB, which multiplies the transmitter's power by a factor of 4.

## CHAPTER 11

The Frequency-Hopping (FH) PHY

Of all the physical layers standardized in the first draft of 802.11 in 1997, the frequency-hopping spread spectrum (FH or FHSS) layer was the first layer to see widespread deployment. The electronics used to support FH modulation are relatively cheap and do not have high power requirements. Initially, the main advantage to using frequency-hopping networks was that a greater number of networks could coexist, and the aggregate throughput of all the networks in a given area was high. At this point, however, FH networks are largely a footnote in the history of 802.11. Although it is a standard, only one vendor still manufactures and sells frequency-hopping systems, and they are being phased out. Higher-throughput specifications have demolished the advantage of aggregate throughput, and newer chipsets are less power-hungry.

This chapter describes the basic concepts used by the frequency-hopping PHY and the modulation techniques used. It also shows how the physical layer convergence procedure prepares frames for transmission on the radio link and touches briefly on a few details of the physical medium itself. At this point, the FH PHY is largely a footnote in the history of 802.11, so you may want to skip this chapter and move ahead to the next section on the direct-sequence PHY. However, understanding how 802.11 technology developed will give you a better feeling for how all the pieces fit together.

Frequency-Hopping Transmission

Frequency hopping depends on rapidly changing the transmission frequency in a predetermined, pseudorandom pattern, as illustrated in Figure 11-1. The vertical axis of the graph divides the available frequency into a number of slots. Likewise, time is divided into a series of slots. A hopping pattern controls how the slots are used. In the figure, the hopping pattern is {2,8,4,6}. Timing the hops accurately is the key to success; both the transmitter and receiver must be synchronized so the receiver is always listening on the transmitter's frequency.

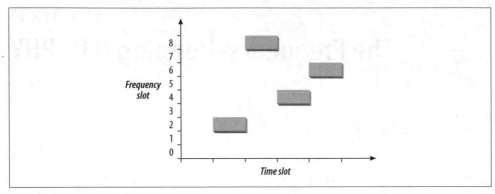

Figure 11-1. Frequency hopping

Frequency hopping is similar to frequency division multiple access (FDMA) but with an important twist. In FDMA systems, each device is allocated a fixed frequency. Multiple devices share the available radio spectrum by using different frequencies. In frequency-hopping systems, the frequency is time-dependent rather than fixed. Each frequency is used for a small amount of time, called the *dwell time*.

Among other things, frequency hopping allows devices to avoid interfering with primary users assigned to the same frequency band. It works because primary users are assigned narrow frequency bands and the right to transmit at a power high enough to override the wireless LAN. Any interference caused by the secondary user that affects the primary user is transient because the hopping sequence spreads the energy out over a wide band.[*] Likewise, the primary user only knocks out one of the spread-spectrum device's slots and looks like transient noise. Figure 11-2 shows the result when frequency slot 7 is given to a primary user. Although the transmission in the fourth time slot is corrupted, the other three transmissions succeed.

If two frequency-hopping systems need to share the same band, they can be configured with different hopping sequences so they do not interfere with each other. During each time slot, the two hopping sequences must be on different frequency slots. As long as the systems stay on different frequency slots, they do not interfere with each other, as shown in Figure 11-3. The gray rectangles have a hopping sequence of {2,8,4,7}, as in the previous figures. A second system with a hopping sequence of {6,3,7,2} is added. Hopping sequences that do not overlap are called *orthogonal*. When multiple 802.11 networks are configured in a single area, orthogonal hopping sequences maximizes throughput.

---

[*] If the primary user of a frequency band notices interference from secondary users, regulators can (and will) step in to shut down the secondary user, hence the low power used by spread-spectrum modulation techniques.

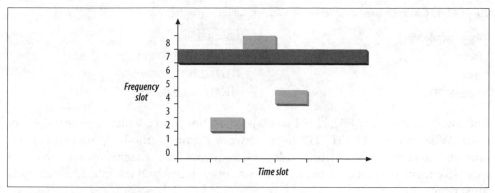

Figure 11-2. Avoiding interference with frequency hopping

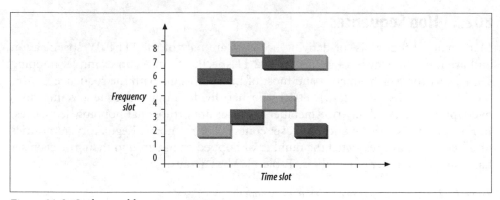

Figure 11-3. Orthogonal hopping sequences

802.11 FH Details

802.11 divides the microwave ISM band into a series of 1-MHz channels. Approximately 99% of the radio energy is confined to the channel. The modulation method used by 802.11 encodes data bits as shifts in the transmission frequency from the channel center. Channels are defined by their center frequencies, which begin at 2.400 GHz for channel 0. Successive channels are derived by adding 1-MHz steps: channel 1 has a center frequency of 2.401 GHz, channel 2 has a center frequency of 2.402 GHz, and so on up to channel 95 at 2.495 GHz. Different regulatory authorities allow use of different parts of the ISM band; the major regulatory domains and the available channels are shown in Table 11-1.

Table 11-1. Channels used in different regulatory domains

Regulatory domain	Allowed channels
U.S. (FCC)	2 to 79 (2.402–2.479 GHz)
Canada (IC)	2 to 79 (2.402–2.479 GHz)
Europe (excluding France and Spain) (ETSI)	2 to 79 (2.402–2.479 GHz)

Regulatory domain	Allowed channels
France	48 to 82 (2.448–2.482 GHz)
Spain	47 to 73 (2.447–2.473 GHz)
Japan (MKK)	73 to 95 (2.473–2.495 GHz)

The dwell time used by 802.11 FH systems is 390 time units, which is almost 0.4 seconds. When an 802.11 FH PHY hops between channels, the hopping process can take no longer than 224 microseconds. The frequency hops themselves are subject to extensive regulation, both in terms of the size of each hop and the rate at which hops must occur.

802.11 Hop Sequences

Mathematical functions for deriving hop sets are part of the FH PHY specification and are found in clause 14.6.8 of the 802.11 specification. As an example, hopping sequence 1 for North America and most of Europe begins with the sequence {3, 26, 65, 11, 46, 19, 74, 50, 22, ...}. 802.11 further divides hopping sequences into non-overlapping sets, and any two members of a set are orthogonal hopping sequences. In Europe and North America, each set contains 26 members. Regulatory authorities in other areas have restricted the number of hopped channels, and therefore each set has a smaller number of members. Table 11-2 has details.

Table 11-2. Size of hop sets in each regulatory domain

Regulatory domain	Hop set size
U.S. (FCC)	26
Canada (IC)	26
Europe (excluding France and Spain) (ETSI)	26
France	27
Spain	35
Japan (MIC)	23

Joining an 802.11 Frequency-Hopping Network

Joining a frequency-hopping network is made possible by the standardization of hop sequences. Beacon frames on FH networks include a timestamp and the FH Parameter Set element. The FH Parameter Set element includes the hop pattern number and a hop index. By receiving a Beacon frame, a station knows everything it needs to synchronize its hopping pattern.

Based on the hop sequence number, the station knows the channel-hopping order. As an example, say that a station has received a Beacon frame that indicates that the BSS is using the North America/Europe hop sequence number 1 and is at hop index 2. By looking up the hop sequence, the station can determine that the next channel is 65. Hop times are also well-defined. Each Beacon frame includes a Timestamp field, and the hop occurs when the timestamp modulo dwell time included in the Beacon is 0.

ISM Emission Rules and Maximum Throughput

Spectrum allocation policies are the limiting factor of frequency-hopping 802.11 systems. As an example, consider the three major rules imposed by the FCC in the U.S.:*

1. There must be at least 75 hopping channels in the band, which is 83.5-MHz wide.

2. Hopping channels can be no wider than 1 MHz.

3. Devices must use all available channels equally. In a 30-second period, no more than 0.4 seconds may be spent using any one channel.

Of these rules, the most important is the second one. No matter what fancy encoding schemes are available, only 1 MHz of bandwidth is available at any time. The frequency at which it is available shifts continuously because of the other two rules, but the second rule limits the number of signal transitions that can be used to encode data.

With a straightforward, two-level encoding, each cycle can encode one bit. At 1 bit per cycle, 1 MHz yields a data rate of 1 Mbps. More sophisticated modulation and demodulation schemes can improve the data rate. Four-level coding can pack 2 bits into a cycle, and 2 Mbps can be squeezed from the 1-MHz bandwidth.

The European Telecommunications Standards Institute (ETSI) also has a set of rules for spread-spectrum devices in the ISM band, published in European Telecommunications Standard (ETS) 300-328. The ETSI rules allow far fewer hopping channels; only 20 are required. Radiated power, however, is controlled much more strictly. In practice, to meet both the FCC and ETSI requirements, devices use the high number of hopping channels required by the FCC with the low radiated power requirements of ETSI.

Effect of Interference

802.11 is a secondary use of the 2.4-GHz ISM band and must accept any interference from a higher-priority transmission. Catastrophic interference on a channel may prevent that channel from being used but leave other channels unaffected. With approximately 80 usable channels in the U.S. and Europe, interference on one channel reduces the raw bit rate of the medium by approximately 1.25%. (The cost at the IP layer will be somewhat higher because of the interframe gaps, 802.11 acknowledgments, and framing and physical-layer covergence headers.) As more channels are affected by interference, the throughput continues to drop. See Figure 11-4.

* These rules are in rule 247 of part 15 of the FCC rules (47 CFR 15.247).

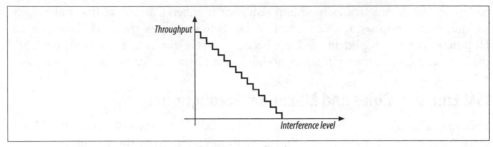

Figure 11-4. Throughput response to interference in FHSS systems

Gaussian Frequency Shift Keying (GFSK)

The FH PHY uses Gaussian frequency shift keying (GFSK).[*] Frequency shift keying encodes data as a series of frequency changes in a carrier. One advantage of using frequency to encode data is that noise usually changes the amplitude of a signal; modulation systems that ignore amplitude (broadcast FM radio, for example) tend to be relatively immune to noise. The *Gaussian* in GFSK refers to the shape of radio pulses; GFSK confines emissions to a relatively narrow spectral band and is thus appropriate for secondary uses. Signal processing techniques that prevent widespread leakage of RF energy are a good thing, particularly for secondary users of a frequency band. By reducing the potential for interference, GFSK makes it more likely that 802.11 wireless LANs can be built in an area where another user has priority.

2-Level GFSK

The most basic GFSK implementation is called 2-level GFSK (2GFSK). Two different frequencies are used, depending on whether the data that will be transmitted is a 1 or a 0. To transmit a 1, the carrier frequency is increased by a certain deviation. Zero is encoded by decreasing the frequency by the same deviation. Figure 11-5 illustrates the general procedure. In real-world systems, the frequency deviations from the carrier are much smaller; the figure is deliberately exaggerated to show how the encoding works.

The rate at which data is sent through the system is scalled the *symbol rate*. Because it takes several cycles to determine the frequency of the underlying carrier and whether 1 or 0 was transmitted, the symbol rate is a very small fraction of the carrier frequency. Although the carrier frequency is roughly 2.4 billion cycles per second, the symbol rate is only 1 or 2 million symbols per second.

---

[*] The term *keying* is a vestige of telegraphy. Transmission of data across telegraph lines required the use of a key. Sending data through a modern digital system employs modulation techniques instead, but the word keying persists.

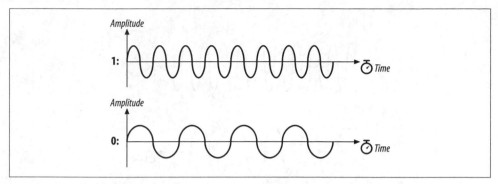

Figure 11-5. 2-level GFSK

Frequency changes with GFSK are not sharp changes. Instantaneous frequency changes require more expensive electronic components and higher power. Gradual frequency changes allow lower-cost equipment with lower RF leakage. Figure 11-6 shows how frequency varies as a result of encoding the letter M (1001101 binary) using 2GFSK. Note that the vertical axis is the frequency of the transmission. When a 1 is transmitted, the frequency rises to the center frequency plus an offset, and when a 0 is transmitted, the frequency drops by the same offset. The horizontal axis, which represents time, is divided into symbol periods. Around the middle of each period, the receiver measures the frequency of the transmission and translates that frequency into a symbol. (In 802.11 frequency-hopping systems, the higher-level data is scrambled before transmission, so the bit sequence transmitted to the peer station is not the same as the bit sequence over the air. The figure illustrates how the principles of 2GFSK work and doesn't step through an actual encoding.)

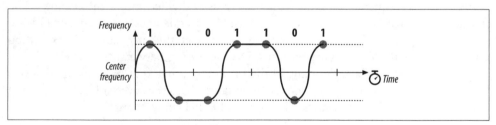

Figure 11-6. GFSK encoding of the letter M

4-Level GFSK

Using a scheme such as this, there are two ways to send more data: use a higher symbol rate or encode more bits of information into each symbol. 4-level GFSK (4GFSK) uses the same basic approach as 2GFSK but with four symbols instead of two. The four symbols (00, 01, 10, and 11) each correspond to a discrete frequency, and therefore 4GFSK transmits twice as much data at the same symbol rate. Obviously, this increase comes at a cost: 4GFSK requires more complex transmitters and receivers. Mapping of the four symbols onto bits is shown in Figure 11-7.

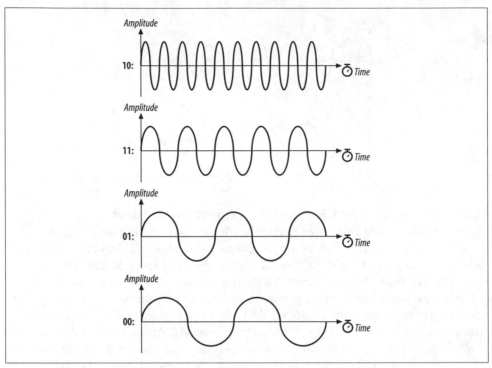

Figure 11-7. Mapping of symbols to frequencies in 4GFSK

With its more sophisticated signal processing, 4GFSK packs multiple bits into a single symbol. Figure 11-8 shows how the letter M might be encoded. Once again, the vertical axis is frequency, and the horizontal axis is divided into symbol times. The frequency changes to transmit the symbols; the frequencies for each symbol are shown by the dashed lines. The figure also hints at the problem with extending GFSK-based methods to higher bit rates. Distinguishing between two levels is fairly easy. Four is harder. Each doubling of the bit rate requires that twice as many levels be present, and the RF components distinguish between ever-smaller frequency changes. These limitations practically limit the FH PHY to 2 Mbps.

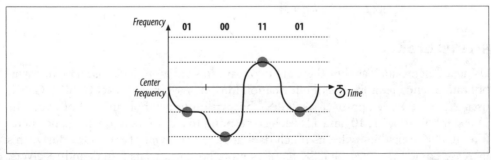

Figure 11-8. 4GFSK encoding of the letter M

FH PHY Convergence Procedure (PLCP)

Before any frames can be modulated onto the RF carrier, the frames from the MAC must be prepared by the Physical Layer Convergence Procedure (PLCP). Different underlying physical layers may have different requirements, so 802.11 allows each physical layer some latitude in preparing MAC frames for transmission over the air.

Framing and Whitening

The PLCP for the FH PHY adds a five-field header to the frame it receives from the MAC. The PLCP is a relay between the MAC and the physical medium dependent (PMD) radio interface. In keeping with ISO reference model terminology, frames passed from the MAC are PLCP service data units (PSDUs). The PLCP framing is shown in Figure 11-9.

Preamble

As in a wired Ethernet, the preamble synchronizes the transmitter and receiver and derives common timing relationships. In the 802.11 FH PHY, the Preamble is composed of the Sync field and the Start Frame Delimiter field.

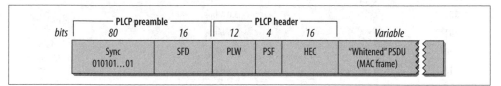

Figure 11-9. PLCP framing in the FH PHY

Sync

The sync field is 80 bits in length and is composed of an alternating zero-one sequence (010101...01). Stations search for the sync pattern to prepare to receive data. In addition to synchronizing the sender and receiver, the Sync field serves three purposes. First of all, the presence of a sync signal indicates that a frame is imminent. Second, stations that have multiple antennas to combat multipath fading or other environmental reception problems can select the antenna with the strongest signal. Finally, the receiver can measure the frequency of the incoming signal relative to its nominal values and perform any corrections needed to the received signal.

Start Frame Delimiter (SFD)

As in Ethernet, the SFD signals the end of the preamble and marks the beginning of the frame. The FH PHY uses a 16-bit SFD: 0000 1100 1011 1101.

Header

The PLCP header follows the preamble. The header has PHY-specific parameters used by the PLCP. Three fields comprise the header: a length field, a speed field, and a frame check sequence.

PSDU Length Word (PLW)

The first field in the PLCP header is the PLW. The payload of the PLCP frame is a MAC frame that may be up to 4,095 bytes long. The 12-bit length field informs the receiver of the length of the MAC frame that follows the PLCP header.

PLCP Signaling (PSF)

Bit 0, the first bit transmitted, is reserved and set to 0. Bits 1–3 encode the speed at which the payload MAC frame is transmitted. Several speeds are available, so this field allows the receiver to adjust to the appropriate demodulation scheme. Although the standard allows for data rates in increments of 500 kbps from 1.0 Mbps to 4.5 Mbps, the modulation scheme has been defined only for 1.0 Mbps and 2.0 Mbps.[*] See Table 11-3.

Table 11-3. PSF meaning

Bits (1-2-3)	Data rate
000	1.0 Mbps
001	1.5 Mbps
010	2.0 Mbps
011	2.5 Mbps
100	3.0 Mbps
101	3.5 Mbps
110	4.0 Mbps
111	4.5 Mbps

Header Error Check (HEC)

To protect against errors in the PLCP header, a 16-bit CRC is calculated over the contents of the header and placed in this field. The header does not protect against errors in other parts of the frame.

No restrictions are placed on the content of the Data field. Arbitrary data may contain long strings of consecutive 0s or 1s, which makes the data much less random. To make the transmitted data more like random white noise, the FH PHYs apply a *whitening* algorithm to the MAC frame. This algorithm scrambles the data before radio transmission. Receivers invert the process to recover the data.

Frequency-Hopping PMD Sublayer

Although the PLCP header has a field for the speed at which the MAC frame is transmitted, only two of these rates have corresponding standardized PMD layers. Several

---

[*] It is unlikely that significant further work will be done on high-rate, frequency-hopping systems. For high data rates, direct sequence is a more cost-effective choice.

features are shared between both PMDs: antenna diversity support, allowances for the ramp up and ramp down of the power amplifiers in the antennas, and the use of a Gaussian pulse shaper to keep as much RF power as possible in the narrow frequency-hopping band. Figure 11-10 shows the general design of the transceiver used in 802.11 frequency-hopping networks. It is required that the transceiver have a sensitivity of −80 dBm for both 1 Mbps and 2 Mbps transmission.

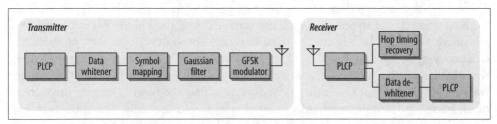

Figure 11-10. Frequency-hopping transceiver

PMD for 1.0-Mbps FH PHY

The basic frequency-hopping PMD enables data transmission at 1.0 Mbps. Frames from the MAC have the PLCP header appended, and the resulting sequence of bits is transmitted out of the radio interface. In keeping with the common regulatory restriction of a 1-MHz bandwidth, 1 million symbols are transmitted per second. 2GFSK is used as the modulation scheme, so each symbol can be used to encode a single bit. 802.11 specifies a minimum power of 10 milliwatts (mW) and requires the use of a power control function to cap the radiated power at 100 mW, if necessary.

PMD for 2.0-Mbps FH PHY

A second, higher-speed PMD is available for the FH PHY. As with the 1.0-Mbps PMD, the PLCP header is appended and is transmitted at 1.0 Mbps using 2GFSK. In the PLCP header, the PSF field indicates the speed at which the frame body is transmitted. At the higher data rate, the frame body is transmitted using a different encoding method than the physical-layer header. Regulatory requirements restrict all PMDs to a symbol rate of 1 MHz, so 4GFSK must be used for the frame body. Two bits per symbol yields a rate of 2.0 Mbps at 1 million symbols per second. Firmware that supports the 2.0-Mbps PMD can fall back to the 1.0-Mbps PMD if signal quality is too poor to sustain the higher rate.

Carrier sense/clear channel assessment (CS/CCA)

To implement the CSMA/CA foundation of 802.11, the PCLP includes a function to determine whether the wireless medium is currently in use. The MAC uses both a virtual carrier-sense mechanism and a physical carrier-sense mechanism; the physical layer implements the physical carrier sense. 802.11 does not specify how to determine whether a signal is present; vendors are free to innovate within the required performance constraints of the standard. 802.11 requires that 802.11-compliant signals with certain power levels must be detected with a corresponding minimum probability.

Characteristics of the FH PHY

Table 11-4 shows the values of a number of parameters in the FH PHY. In addition to the parameters in the table, which are standardized, the FH PHY has a number of parameters that can be adjusted to balance delays through various parts of an 802.11 frequency-hopping system. It includes variables for the latency through the MAC, the PLCP, and the transceiver, as well as variables to account for variations in the transceiver electronics. One other item of note is that the total aggregate throughput of all frequency-hopping networks in an area can be quite high. The total aggregate throughput is a function of the hop set size. All sequences in a hop set are orthogonal and noninterfering. In North America and most of Europe, 26 frequency-hopping networks can be deployed in an area at once. If each network is run at the optional 2 Mbps rate and half the airtime is able to carry user payload data, the area can have a total of 26 Mbps throughput provided that the ISM band is relatively free of interference.

Table 11-4. FH PHY parameters

Parameter	Value	Notes
Slot time	50 μs	
SIFS time	28 μs	The SIFS is used to derive the value of the other interframe spaces (DIFS, PIFS, and EIFS).
Contention window size	15–1,023 slots	
Preamble duration	96 μs	Preamble symbols are transmitted at 1 MHz, so a symbol takes 1 μs to transmit; 96 bits require 96 symbol times.
PLCP header duration	32 μs	The PLCP header is 32 bits, so it requires 32 symbol times.
Maximum MAC frame	4,095 bytes	802.11 recommends a maximum of 400 symbols (400 bytes at 1 Mbps, 800 bytes at 2 Mbps) to retain performance across different types of environments.
Minimum sensitivity	−80 dBm	

## CHAPTER 12

The Direct Sequence PHYs: DSSS and HR/DSSS (802.11b)

The intial revision of the 802.11 specification in 1997 had a second physical layer based on direct sequence spread spectrum (DSSS) technology. The DSSS PHY in 802.11 had data rates of 1 Mbps and 2 Mbps. Although it operated at the same speed as the frequency hopping PHY, it quickly became clear that direct sequence technologies had the potential for higher speeds than frequency hopping technologies. As a result, even though the two had equivalent speeds, direct sequence became the PHY of choice. In 1999, a PHY with data rates of 5.5 Mbps and 11 Mbps was specified in 802.11b. The older 1 and 2 Mbps PHYs and the newer 5.5 and 11 Mbps PHYs are often combined into a single interface, even though they are described by different specifications. (It is usually referred to as "802.11b" support, even though the two lower rates are not part of 802.11b.) This chapter describes the basic concepts and modulation techniques used by the direct sequence physical layers. It also shows how the PLCP prepares frames for transmission on the radio link and touches briefly on a few details of the physical medium itself.

Direct Sequence Transmission

Direct sequence transmission is an alternative spread-spectrum technique that can be used to transmit a signal over a much wider frequency band. The basic approach of direct-sequence techniques is to smear the RF energy over a wide band in a carefully controlled way. Changes in the radio carrier are present across a wide band, and receivers can perform correlation processes to look for changes. The basic high-level approach is shown in Figure 12-1.

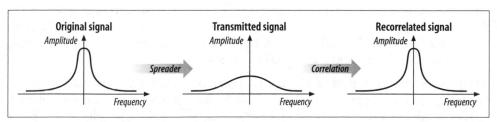

Figure 12-1. Basic DSSS technique

At the left is a traditional narrowband radio signal. It is processed by a *spreader*, which applies a mathematical transform to take a narrowband input and flatten the amplitude across a relatively wide frequency band. To a narrowband receiver, the transmitted signal looks like low-level noise because its RF energy is spread across a very wide band. The key to direct-sequence transmission is that any modulation of the RF carrier is also spread across the frequency band. Receivers can monitor a wide frequency band and look for changes that occur across the entire band. The original signal can be recovered with a *correlator*, which inverts the spreading process.

At a high level, a correlator simply looks for changes to the RF signal that occur across the entire frequency band. Correlation gives direct-sequence transmissions a great deal of protection against interference. Noise tends to take the form of relatively narrow pulses that, by definition, do not produce coherent effects across the entire frequency band. Therefore, the correlation function spreads out noise across the band, and the correlated signal shines through, as illustrated in Figure 12-2.

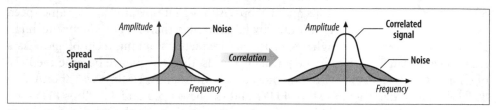

Figure 12-2. Spreading of noise by the correlation process

Direct-sequence modulation works by applying a chipping sequence to the data stream. A *chip* is a binary digit used by the spreading process. Bits are higher-level data, while chips are binary numbers used in the encoding process. There is no mathematical difference between a bit and a chip, but spread-spectrum developers have adopted this terminology to indicate that chips are only a part of the encoding and transmission process and do not carry any data. Chipping streams, which are also called *pseudorandom noise codes* (PN codes), must run at a much higher rate than the underlying data. (The requirement for high-speed oscillators to generate chip streams and recover data from chip streams is one of the major power drains in direct sequence PHYs.) Figure 12-3 illustrates how chipping sequences are used in the transmission of data using direct-sequence modulation. At the left-hand side is a single data bit, which is either a one or a zero. For each data bit, several chips are used. In the figure, the chip stream consists of an 11-bit code. It is combined with the single data bit, to produce 11 chips that carry the single data bit. The 11-chip/single-data-bit sequence is transmitted over the radio link and received at the other end. Every chunk of 11 chips is the compared to an identical chip stream. If it matches the spreading code, a single zero data bit is recovered; if not, a single one data bit is recovered.

The process of encoding a low bit-rate signal at a high chip rate has the side effect of spreading the signal's power over a much wider bandwidth. One of the most important quantities in a direct-sequence system is its *spreading ratio*, which is the number

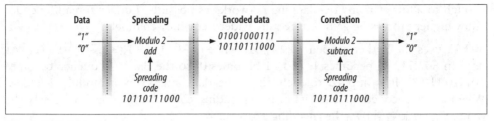

Figure 12-3. Chipping

of chips used to transmit a single bit.[*] Higher spreading ratios improve the ability to recover the transmitted signal but require a higher chipping rate and a larger frequency band. Doubling the spreading ratio requires doubling the chipping rate and doubles the required bandwidth as well. There are two costs to increased chipping ratios. One is the direct cost of more expensive RF components operating at the higher frequency, and the other is an indirect cost in the amount of bandwidth required. Therefore, in designing direct-sequence systems for the real world, the spreading ratio should be as low as possible to meet design requirements and to avoid wasting bandwidth.

Direct-sequence modulation trades bandwidth for throughput. Compared to traditional narrowband transmission, direct-sequence modulation requires significantly more radio spectrum and is much slower. However, it can often coexist with other interference sources because the receiver's correlation function effectively ignores narrowband noise. It is easier to achieve high throughput using direct-sequence techniques than with frequency hopping. Regulatory authorities do not impose a limit on the amount of spectrum that can be used; they generally set a minimum lower bound on the processing gain. Higher rates can be achieved with a wider band, though wider bands require a higher chip rate.

Encoding in 802.11 Direct Sequence Networks

For the PN code, 802.11 adopted an 11-bit Barker word. Each bit is encoded using the entire Barker word as a chipping sequence. Detailed discussion of Barker words and their properties are well beyond the scope of this book. The key attribute for 802.11 networks is that Barker words have good *autocorrelation* properties, which means that the correlation function at the receiver operates as expected in a wide range of environments and is relatively tolerant to multipath delay spreads. 11 bits are in the word because regulatory authorities often require a 10-dB processing gain in direct sequence systems. Using an 11-bit spreading code for each bit allows 802.11 to meet the regulatory requirements with some margin of safety, but it is small

---

[*] The spreading ratio is related to a figure known as the *processing gain*. The two are sometimes used interchangeably, but the processing gain is slightly lower because it takes into account the effects of using real-world systems as opposed to perfect ideal systems with no losses.

enough to allow as many overlapping networks as possible. Longer spreading codes allow higher processing gains but require wider frequency channels.

802.11 uses the Barker sequence {+1, −1, +1, +1, −1, +1, +1, +1, −1, −1, −1}. As used in 802.11, +1 becomes 1, and −1 becomes 0, so the Barker sequence becomes 10110111000. It is applied to each bit in the data stream by a modulo-2 adder.* When a 1 is encoded, all the bits in the spreading code change; for 0, they stay the same. Figure 12-4 shows the encoding process.

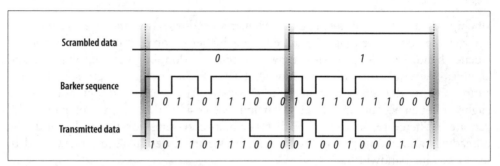

Figure 12-4. Encoding with the Barker word

Receivers can look at the number of 1s in a received bit time. The Barker sequence has six 1s and five 0s. An 11-bit sequence with six 1s must therefore correspond to a transmitted 0, and an 11-bit sequence with six 0s must correspond to a transmitted 1. In addition to counting the numbers of 1s and 0s, the receiver can analyze the pattern of received bits to infer the value of the transmitted bit.

Radio Spectrum Usage in 802.11 Direct Sequence Networks

Channels for the DS PHY are much larger than the channels for the FH PHY. The DS PHY has 14 channels in the 2.4-GHz band, each 5 MHz wide. Channel 1 is placed at 2.412 GHz, channel 2 at 2.417 GHz, and so on up to channel 13 at 2.472 GHz. Channel 14 was defined especially for operation in Japan, and has a center frequency that is 12 MHz from the center frequency of channel 13. Table 12-1 shows which channels are allowed by each regulatory authority. Channel 10 is available throughout North America and Europe, which is why many products use channel 10 as the default operating channel.

---

* Encoding with the Barker sequence is similar to a number of other techniques. Some cellular systems, most notably in North America, use code division multiple access (CDMA) to allow several stations to access the radio medium. CDMA exploits some extremely complex mathematics to ensure that transmissions from each mobile phone look like random noise to every other mobile phone in the cell. The underlying mathematics are far more complicated than a simple, fixed pseudorandom noise code.

Table 12-1. Channels used in different regulatory domains

Regulatory domain	Allowed channels
U.S. (FCC)/Canada (IC)	1 to 11 (2.412–2.462 GHz)
Europe, excluding Spain (ETSI)	1 to 13 (2.412–2.472 GHz)
Spain	10 to 11 (2.457–2.462 GHz)
Japan (MIC)	1 to 13 (2.412–2.462 GHz) and 14 (2.484 GHz)

Channel energy spread

Within a channel, most of the energy is spread across a 22-MHz band. Because the DS PHY uses an 11-MHz chip clock, energy spreads out from the channel center in multiples of 11 MHz, as shown in Figure 12-5. To prevent interference to adjacent channels, the first side lobe is filtered to 30 dB below the power at the channel center frequency, and additional lobes are filtered to 50 dB below the power at the channel center. This corresponds to reducing the power by a factor of 1,000 and 100,000, respectively. These limits are noted in Figure 12-5 by the use of dBr, which means dB relative to the power at the channel center. Figure 12-5 uses a logarithmic scale: –30 dBr is only one thousandth, and –50 dBr is one hundred thousandth.

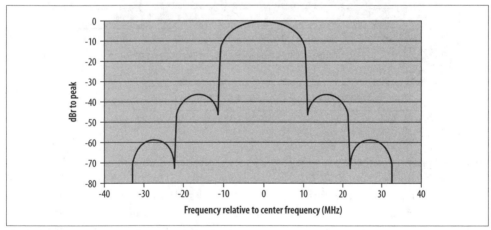

Figure 12-5. Energy spread in a single 802.11 DS transmission channel

With the transmit filters in place, RF power is confined mostly to 22-MHz frequency bands. European regulators cap the maximum radiated power at 100 mW; the FCC in the U.S. allows a substantially higher transmission power of 1,000 mW. If directional antennas are used, the power can be concentrated into an even higher radiated power.

Adjacent channel rejection and channel separation

To avoid interference, 802.11 equipment must be separated in the frequency domain. The initial specification called for 35 dB rejection when two signals were 30 MHz apart, but the spectral separation was tightened up to 25 MHz in 802.11b. To measure adjacent channel rejection, input a maximum-speed signal at the center frequency of a channel, shown by the left curve in Figure 12-6. Its power is 6 dB above the specified minimum sensitivity; for an 802.11b receiver, that is −70 dBm. A second 802.11b signal at 11 Mbps is sent in, 35 dB stronger, but at least 25 MHz away. The right curve depicts the interference test signal. As long as the frame error rate is less than 8%, the receiver passes the test. Note that there is reasonably significant overlap between the first lobe of the interfering signal and the main center lobe of the on-channel signal.

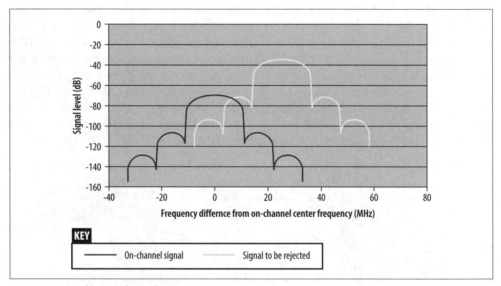

Figure 12-6. Adjacent channel rejection

Adjacent channel rejection also influences the number of channels that can be used simultaneously. Although 802.11 networks operating in the ISM band have 14 defined channels, they are closely packed. Real signals must be spaced out to prevent interference. 802.11b specifies that a 25 MHz (5 channel number) spacing is sufficient. Figure 12-7 shows the spectral mask of transmissions on the so-called non-overlapping channels (1, 6, and 11). By comparing Figure 12-7 to the previous figure, it is easy to see that using the nonoverlapping channel set requires all components in the system to run at maximum effectiveness. Many real-world radios, however, are incapable of rejecting strong adjacent-channel transmissions near the limit.

Although it is possible to have channels overlap more closely by using a four-channel layout (say, 1, 4, 7, and 11), it is not a generally useful deployment strategy. Greater overlap of the channels will result in more interference between radios operating on adjacent frequencies. Greater interference may trigger the carrier sensing mechanisms to report that the medium is busy or cause frames to be mangled in flight. In either case, the peak throughput of each channel is less. It may be that trading some amount of peak throughput for total area capacity is a good trade, but that is not generally true.

 Whether you call them 1, 6, and 11; A, B, and C; or Tom, Dick, and Harry, you only have three mostly nonoverlapping channels with 2.4 GHz wireless LANs.

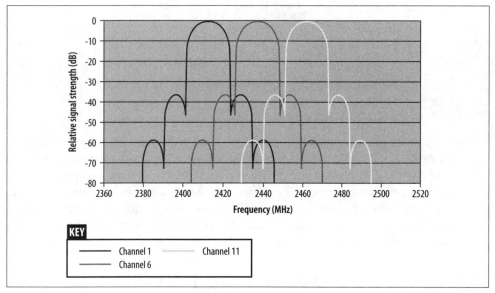

Figure 12-7. Channel separation in 802.11 DS networks

Maximum theoretical throughput

If the signal processing techniques used by the DS PHY are used, then the maximum throughput would be a function of the frequency space used. Roughly speaking, the ISM band is 80-MHz wide. Using the same spreading factor of 11 would lead to a maximum bit rate of slightly more than 7 Mbps. However, only one channel would be available, and products would need to have an oscillator running at 77 MHz to generate the chipping sequence. High-frequency devices are a tremendous drain on batteries, and the hypothetical high-rate encoding that uses the entire band makes terrible use of the available spectrum. To achieve higher throughput, more sophisticated techniques must be used. 802.11b increases the symbol rate slightly, but it gets far more mileage from more sophisticated encoding techniques.

Interference response

Direct-sequence–modulated signals are more resistant to interference than frequency-hopping signals. The correlation process enables direct-sequence systems to work around narrowband interference much more effectively. With 11 chips per bit, several chips can be lost or damaged before a single data bit is lost. The disadvantage is that the response of direct-sequence systems to noise is not incremental. Up to a certain level, the correlator can remove noise, but once interference obscures a certain amount of the frequency band, nothing can be recovered. Figure 12-8 shows how direct-sequence systems degrade in response to noise.

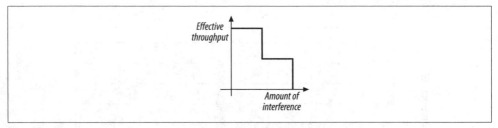

Figure 12-8. Throughput response to interference in DSSS systems

Direct-sequence systems also avoid interfering with a primary user more effectively than frequency-hopping systems. After direct-sequence processing, signals are much wider and have lower amplitudes, so they appear to be random background noise to traditional narrowband receivers. Two direct-sequence users in the same area can cause problems for each other quite easily if the two direct-sequence channels are not separated by an adequate amount. Generally speaking, interference between two direct-sequence devices is a problem long before a primary band user notices anything.

Differential Phase Shift Keying (DPSK)

Differential phase shift keying (DPSK) is the basis for 802.11 direct-sequence systems. As the name implies, phase shift keying (PSK) encodes data in phase changes of the transmitted signal. The absolute phase of a waveform is not relevant in PSK; only changes in the phase encode data. Like frequency shift keying, PSK resists interference because most interference causes changes in amplitude. Figure 12-8 shows two identical sine waves shifted by a small amount along the time axis. The offset between the same point on two waves is the phase difference.

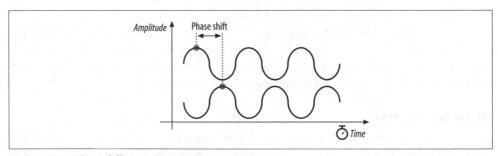

Figure 12-9. Phase difference between two sine waves

Differential Binary Phase Shift Keying (DBPSK)

The simplest form of PSK uses two carrier waves, shifted by a half cycle relative to each other. One wave, the reference wave, is used to encode a 0; the half-cycle shifted wave is used to encode a 1. Table 12-2 summarizes the phase shifts.

Table 12-2. DBPSK phase shifts

Symbol	Phase shift
0	0
1	180˚ (π radians)

Figure 12-10 illustrates the encoding as a phase difference from a preceding sine wave.

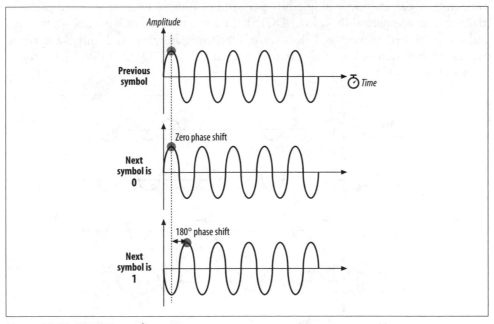

Figure 12-10. DBPSK encoding

To stick with the same example, encoding the letter M (1001101 in binary) is a matter of dividing up the time into seven symbol times then transmitting the wave with appropriate phase shift at each symbol boundary. Figure 12-11 illustrates the encoding. Time is divided into a series of symbol periods, each of which is several times the period of the carrier wave. When the symbol is a 0, there is no change from the phase of the previous symbol, and when the symbol is a 1, there is a change of half a cycle. These changes result in "pinches" of the carrier when 1 is transmitted and a smooth transition across the symbol time boundary for 0.

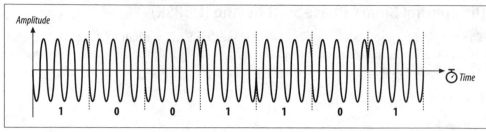

Figure 12-11. The letter M encoded in DBPSK

Differential Quadrature Phase Shift Keying (DQPSK)

Like 2GFSK, DBPSK is limited to one bit per symbol. More advanced receivers and transmitters can encode multiple bits per symbol using a technique called differential quadrature phase shift keying (DQPSK). Rather than a fundamental wave and a half-cycle shifted wave, DQPSK uses a fundamental wave and three additional waves, each shifted by a quarter cycle, as shown in Figure 12-12. Table 12-3 summarizes the phase shifts.

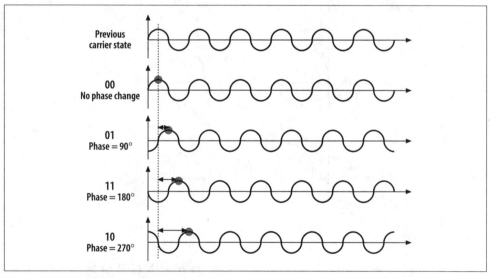

Figure 12-12. DQPSK encoding

Table 12-3. DQPSK phase shifts

Symbol	Phase shift
00	0
01	90° ($\pi/2$ radians)
11	180° (π radians)
10	270° ($3\pi/2$ or $-\pi/2$ radians)

Now encode M in DQPSK (Figure 12-13). In the UTF-8 character set, M is represented by the binary string 01001101 or, as the sequence of four two-bit symbols, 01-00-11-01. In the first symbol period, there is a phase shift of 90 degrees; for clarity, the figure shows the phase shift from a pure sine wave. The second symbol results in no phase shift, so the wave continues without a change. The third symbol causes a phase shift of 180 degrees, as shown by the sharp change from the highest amplitude to the lowest amplitude. The final symbol causes a phase shift of 90 degrees.

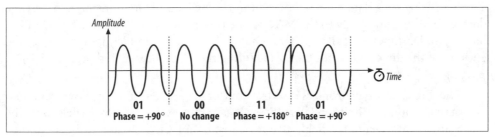

Figure 12-13. The letter M encoded in DQPSK

The obvious advantage of DQPSK relative to DBPSK is that the four-level encoding mechanism can have a higher throughput. The cost of using DQPSK is that it cannot be used in some environments because of severe multipath interference. Multipath interference occurs when the signal takes several paths from the transmitter to the receiver. Each path has a different length; therefore, the received signal from each path has a different delay relative to the other paths. This delay is the enemy of an encoding scheme based on phase shifts. Wavefronts are not labeled or painted different colors, so a wavefront could arrive later than expected because of a long path or it could simply have been transmitted late and phase-shifted. In environments where multipath interference is severe, DQPSK will break down much quicker than DBPSK.

The "Original" Direct Sequence PHY

The physical layer itself consists of two components. The Physical Layer Convergence Procedure (PLCP) performs some additional PHY-dependent framing before transmission, while the Physical Medium Dependent (PMD) layer is responsible for the actual transmission of frames.

PLCP Framing and Processing

The PLCP for the DS PHY adds a six-field header to the frames it receives from the MAC. In keeping with ISO reference model terminology, frames passed from the MAC are PLCP service data units (PSDUs). The PLCP framing is shown in Figure 12-14.

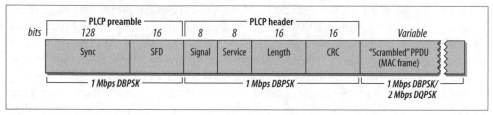

Figure 12-14. DS PLCP framing

The FH PHY uses a data whitener to randomize the data before transmission, but the data whitener applies only to the MAC frame trailing the PLCP header. The DS PHY has a similar function called the *scrambler*, but the scrambler is applied to the entirety of the direct-sequence frame, including the PLCP header and preamble.

Preamble

>The Preamble synchronizes the transmitter and receiver and allows them to derive common timing relationships. It is composed of the Sync field and the Start Frame Delimiter field. Before transmission, the preamble is scrambled using the direct-sequence scrambling function.

Sync

>The Sync field is a 128-bit field composed entirely of 1s. Unlike the FH PHY, the Sync field is scrambled before transmission.

Start Frame Delimiter (SFD)

>The SFD allows the receiver to find the start of the frame, even if some of the sync bits were lost in transit. This field is set to 0000 0101 1100 1111, which is different from the SFD used by the FH PHY.

Header

>The PLCP header follows the preamble. The header has PHY-specific parameters used by the PLCP. Five fields comprise the header: a signaling field, a service identification field, a Length field, a Signal field used to encode the speed, and a frame-check sequence.

Signal

>The Signal field is used by the receiver to identify the transmission rate of the encapsulated MAC frame. It is set to either 0000 1010 (0x0A) for 1-Mbps operation or 0001 0100 (0x14) for 2-Mbps operation.

Service

>This field is reserved for future use and must be set to all 0s.

Length

>This field is set to the number of microseconds required to transmit the frame as an unsigned 16-bit integer, transmitted least-significant bit to most-significant bit.

CRC

>To protect the header against corruption on the radio link, the sender calculates a 16-bit CRC over the contents of the four header fields. Receivers verify the CRC before further frame processing.

No restrictions are placed on the content of the Data field. Arbitrary data may contain long strings of consecutive 0s or 1s, which makes the data much less random. To make the data more like random background noise, the DS PHY uses a polynomial scrambling mechanism to remove long strings of 1s or 0s from the transmitted data stream.

DS Physical Medium Dependent Sublayer

The PMD is a complex and lengthy specification that incorporates provisions for two data rates (1.0 and 2.0 Mbps). Figure 12-15 shows the general design of a transceiver for 802.11 direct-sequence networks.

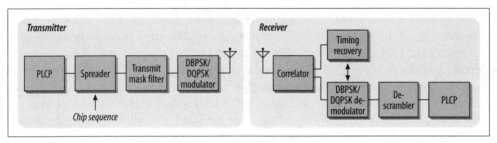

Figure 12-15. Direct-sequence transceiver

Transmission at 1.0 Mbps

At the low data rate, the direct-sequence PMD enables data transmission at 1.0 Mbps. The PLCP header is appended to frames arriving from the MAC, and the entire unit is scrambled. The resulting sequence of bits is transmitted from the physical interface using DBPSK at a rate of 1 million symbols per second. The resulting throughput is 1.0 Mbps because one bit is encoded per symbol. Like the FH PMD, the DS PMD has a minimum power requirement and can cap the power at 100 mW if necessary to meet regulatory requirements.

Transmission at 2.0 Mbps

Like the FH PHY, transmission at 2.0 Mbps uses two encoding schemes. The PLCP preamble and header are transmitted at 1.0 Mbps using DBPSK. Although using a slower method for the header transmission reduces the effective throughput, DBPSK is far more tolerant of noise and multipath interference. After the preamble and header are finished, the PMD switches to DQPSK modulation to provide 2.0-Mbps service. As with the FH PHY, most products that implement the 2.0-Mbps rate can detect interference and fall back to lower-speed 1.0-Mbps service.

CS/CCA for the DS PHY

802.11 allows the carrier sense/clear channel assessment function to operate in one of three modes:

Mode 1

> When the energy exceeds the energy detection (ED) threshold, it reports that the medium is busy. The ED threshold depends on the transmit power.

Mode 2

> Implementations using Mode 2 must look for an actual DSSS signal and report the channel busy when one is detected, even if the signal is below the ED threshold.

Mode 3

> Mode 3 combines Mode 1 and Mode 2. A signal must be detected with sufficient energy before the channel is reported busy to higher layers.

Once a channel is reported busy, it stays busy for the duration of the intended transmission, even if the signal is lost. The transmission's duration is taken from the time interval in the Length field. Busy medium reports must be very fast. When a signal is detected at the beginning of a contention window slot, the CCA mechanism must report a busy medium by the time the slot has ended. This relatively high performance requirement must be set because once a station has begun transmission at the end of its contention delay, it should seize the medium, and all other stations should defer access until its frame has concluded.

Characteristics of the DS PHY

Table 12-4 shows the values of a number of parameters in the DS PHY. In addition to the parameters in the table, which are standardized, the DS PHY has a number of parameters that can be adjusted to balance delays through various parts of an 802.11 direct-sequence system. It includes variables for the latency through the MAC, the PLCP, and the transceiver, as well as variables to account for variations in the transceiver electronics. One other item of note is that the total aggregate throughput of all direct-sequence networks in an area is much lower than the total aggregate throughput of all nonoverlapping frequency-hopping networks in an area. The total aggregate throughput is a function of the number of nonoverlapping channels. In North America and most of Europe, three direct-sequence networks can be deployed in an area at once. If each network is run at the optional 2 Mbps rate and the efficiency of the protocol allows 50% of the headline rate to become user data throughput, the total throughput is 3 Mbps, which is dramatically less than the frequency-hopping total aggregate throughput.

Table 12-4. DS PHY parameters

Parameter	Value	Notes
Slot time	20 μs	
SIFS time	10 μs	The SIFS is used to derive the value of the other interframe spaces (DIFS, PIFS, and EIFS).
Contention window size	31 to 1,023 slots	

Table 12-4. DS PHY parameters (continued)

Parameter	Value	Notes
Preamble duration	144 µs	Preamble symbols are transmitted at 1 MHz, so a symbol takes 1 µs to transmit; 144 bits require 144 symbol times.
PLCP header duration	48 µs	The PLCP header is 48 bits, so it requires 48 symbol times.
Maximum MAC frame	4–8,191 bytes	
Minimum receiver sensitivity	−80 dBm	
Adjacent channel rejection	35 dB	See text for measurement details.

Like the FH PHY, the DS PHY has a number of attributes that can be adjusted by a vendor to balance delays in various parts of the system. It includes variables for the latency through the MAC, the PLCP, and the transceiver, as well as variables to account for variations in the transceiver electronics.

Complementary Code Keying

802.11 direct-sequence systems use a rate of 11 million chips per second. The original DS PHYs divided the chip stream up into a series of 11-bit Barker words and transmitted 1 million Barker words per second. Each word encoded either one bit or two bits for a corresponding data rate of 1.0 Mbps or 2.0 Mbps, respectively. Achieving higher data rates and commercial utility requires that each code symbol carry more information than a bit or two.

Straight phase shift encoding cannot hope to carry more than a few bits per code word. DQPSK requires that receivers distinguish quarter-cycle phase differences. Further increasing the number of bits per symbol would require processing even finer phase shifts, such as an eighth-cycle or sixteenth-cycle shift. Detecting smaller phase shifts is more difficult in the presence of multipath interference and requires more sophisticated (and thus expensive) electronics.

Instead of continuing with straight phase-shift keying, the IEEE 802.11 working group turned to an alternate encoding method. Complementary code keying (CCK) divides the chip stream into a series of 8-bit code symbols, so the underlying transmission is based on a series of 1.375 million code symbols per second. CCK is based on sophisticated mathematical transforms that allow the use of a few 8-bit sequences to encode 4 or even 8 bits per code word, for a data throughput of 5.5 Mbps or 11 Mbps. In addition, the mathematics underlying CCK transforms allow receivers to distinguish between different codes easily, even in the presence of interference and multipath fading. Figure 12-16 illustrates the use of code symbols in CCK. It is quite similar to the chipping process used by the slower direct-sequence layers; the difference is that the code words are derived partially from the data. A static repeating code word such as the Barker word is not used.

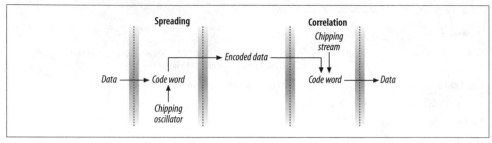

Figure 12-16. Code symbols in CCK

Barker spreading, as used in the lower-rate, direct-sequence layers, uses a static code to spread the signal over the available frequency band. CCK uses the code word to carry information, as well as simply to spread the signal. Several phase angles are used to prepare a complex code word of eight bits.

High Rate Direct Sequence PHY

To distinguish it from the original direct sequence PHY, the high rate PHY that runs at 11 Mbps is abbreviated as HR/DSSS. Like its predecessor, it is split into a convergence procedure that prepares frames for radio transmission, and a medium-dependent layer that turns the bits into radio waves in the air.

PLCP Framing and Scrambling

The long headers required by the original PHY greatly reduce performance. The 802.11 MAC requires an acknowledgment for every data frame, and the 192 microsecond preamble is much, much longer than the MAC acknowledgment. At the 11 Mbps data rate, the preamble and PLCP framing header sucks up 25% of the time used to transmit a 1,500 byte frame and its corresponding MAC acknowledgment. As long as a new PHY was being developed, the designers of 802.11b came up with a new "short" framing format that improves protocol efficiency and, hence, throughput. Using the short headers cuts the preamble and PLCP framing overhead cuts the preamble and framing overhead to 14%. While still substantial, it is a dramatic improvement. Figure 12-17 shows the PLCP framing specified in 802.11b. When 802.11b was first released, short headers were not supported by all devices because of the large installed base of 2 Mbps direct sequence equipment. At this point, almost every card can safely support the short preamble, and most access point vendors use it by default.

Naturally, the optional short format may be used only if all stations support it. To prevent networks configured for the short format from disappearing, 802.11b requires that stations answering Probe Requests from an active scan return a response using the same PLCP header that was received. If a station that supports

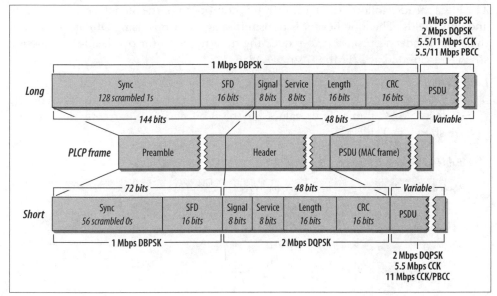

Figure 12-17. HR/DSSS PLCP framing

only the long PLCP header sends a Probe Response, an access point returns a response using the long header, even if the BSS is configured for the short header.

Preamble
> Frames begin with the preamble, which is composed of the Sync field and the SFD field. The preamble is transmitted at 1.0 Mbps using DBPSK.

Long Sync
> The Long Sync field is composed of 128 one bits. It is processed by the scrambler before transmission, though, so the data content varies. High-rate systems use a specified seed for the scrambling function but support backwards compatibility with older systems that do not specify a seed.

Short Sync
> The Short Sync field is composed of 56 zero bits. Like the Long Sync, it is also processed by the scrambler.

Long SFD
> To indicate the end of the Sync field, the long preamble concludes with a Start of Frame Delimiter (SFD). In the long PLCP, the SFD is the sequence 1111 0011 1010 0000. As with all IEEE specifications, the order of transmission from the physical interface is least-significant bit first, so the string is transmitted right to left.

Short SFD
> To avoid confusion with the Long SFD, the Short SFD is the reverse value, 0000 0101 1100 1111.

The PLCP header follows the preamble. It is composed of the Signal, Service, Length, and CRC fields. The long header is transmitted at 1.0 Mbps using DBPSK. However, the short header's purpose is to reduce the time required for overhead transmission so it is transmitted at 2.0 Mbps using DQPSK.

Long Signal

The Long Signal field indicates the speed and transmission method of the enclosed MAC frame. Four values for the 8-bit code are currently defined and are shown in Table 12-5.

Table 12-5. Signal field values

Speed	Value (msb to lsb)	Hex value
1 Mbps	0000 1010	0x0A
2 Mbps	0001 0100	0x14
5.5 Mbps	0011 0111	0x37
11 Mbps	0110 1110	0x6E

Short Signal

The Short Signal field indicates the speed and transmission method of the enclosed frame, but only three values are defined. Short preambles can be used only with 2 Mbps, 5.5 Mbps, and 11 Mbps networks.

Service

The Service field, which is shown in Figure 12-18, was reserved for future use by the first version of 802.11, and bits were promptly used for the high-rate extensions in 802.11b. First of all, the Length field describes the amount of time used for the enclosed frame in microseconds. Above 8 Mbps, the value becomes ambiguous. Therefore, the eighth bit of the service field is used to extend the Length field to 17 bits. The third bit indicates whether the 802.11b implementation uses locked clocks; clock locking means that transmit frequency and symbol clock use the same oscillator. The fourth bit indicates the type of coding used for the packet, which is either 0 for CCK or 1 for PBCC. All reserved bits must be set to 0. The Service field is transmitted from left to right (b0 to b7), which is the same in both the short and long PLCP frame formats. (Further changes are made by 802.11g, which will be discussed in Chapter 14.)

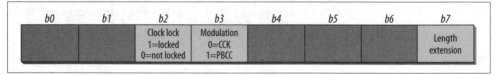

Figure 12-18. Service field in the HR/DSSS PLCP header

Length

The Length field is the same in both the short and long PLCP frame formats and is the number of microseconds required to transmit the enclosed MAC frame. Approximately two pages of the 802.11b standard are devoted to calculating the value of the Length frame, but the details are beyond the scope of this book.

CRC

The CRC field is the same in both the short and the long PLCP frames. Senders calculate a CRC checksum using the Signal, Service, and Length fields. Receivers can use the CRC value to ensure that the header was received intact and was not damaged during transmission. CRC calculations take place before data scrambling.

The data scrambling procedure for the HR/DSSS PHY is nearly identical to the data scrambling procedure used with the original DS PHY. The only difference is that the scrambling function is seeded to specified values in the HR/DSSS PHY. Different seeds are used for short and long PLCP frames.

HR/DSSS PMD

Like the DS PHY, the 802.11b PHY uses a single PMD specification. The general transceiver design is shown in Figure 12-19.

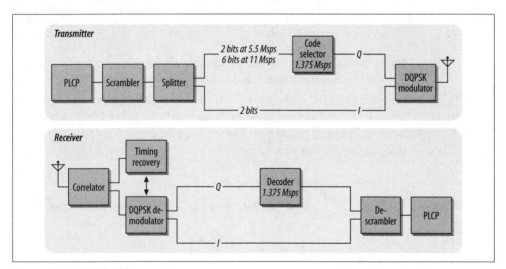

Figure 12-19. HR/DSSS transceiver

Transmission at 1.0 Mbps or 2.0 Mbps

To ensure backwards compatibility with the installed base of 802.11-based, direct-sequence hardware, the HR/DSSS PHY can transmit and receive at 1.0 Mbps or 2.0

Mbps. Slower transmissions are supported in the same manner as the lower-rate, direct-sequence layers described in previously in this chapter. Any transmissions at the slower rates must use long headers.

Transmission at 5.5 Mbps with CCK

Higher-rate transmission is accomplished by building on the DQPSK-based phase shift keying techniques. DQPSK transmits two bits per symbol period, encoded as one of four different phase shifts. By using CCK, the symbol words themselves carry additional information. 5.5-Mbps transmission encodes four data bits into a symbol. Two bits are carried using conventional DQPSK, and the other two are carried through the content of the code words. Figure 12-20 illustrates the overall process.

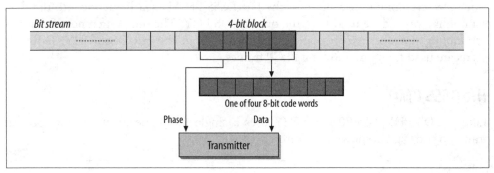

Figure 12-20. 802.11b transmission at 5.5 Mbps

1. The MAC frame embedded in the PCLP frame is divided into a string of 4-bit blocks. Each 4-bit block is further divided into two 2-bit segments.

2. The first 2-bit segment is encoded by means of a DQPSK-type phase shift between the current symbol and the previous symbol (Table 12-6). Even and odd symbols use a different phase shift for technical reasons. Symbol numbering starts with 0 for the first 4- bit block.

Table 12-6. Inter-symbol DQPSK phase shifts

Bit pattern	Phase angle (even symbols)	Phase angle (odd symbols)
00	0	P
01	$\pi/2$	$3\pi/2$
11	π	0
10	$3\pi/2$	$\pi/2$

3. The second 2-bit segment is used to select one of four code words for the current symbol (Table 12-7). The four code words can be derived using the mathematics laid out in clause 18.4.6.5 of the 802.11 standard.

Table 12-7. Mbps code words

Bit sequence	Code word
00	i,1,i,−1,i,1,−1,1
01	−i,−1,−i,1,1,1,−i,1
10	−i,1,−i,−1,−i,1,1,1
11	i,−1,i,1,−i,1,1,1

Transmission at 11 Mbps with CCK

To move to a full 11 Mbps, 8 bits must be encoded with each symbol. As with other techniques, the first two bits are encoded by the phase shift of the transmitted symbol relative to the previous symbol. Six bits are encoded using CCK. Figure 12-21 illustrates the process.

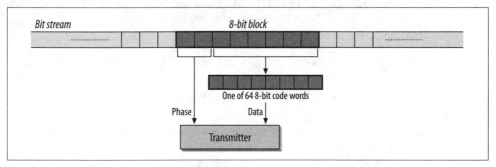

Figure 12-21. 802.11b transmission at 11 Mbps

1. The MAC frame embedded in the PCLP frame is divided into a string of 8-bit blocks. Each 8-bit block is further divided into four 2-bit segments.

2. The first 2-bit segment is encoded by means of a DQPSK-type phase shift between the current symbol and the previous symbol. As with the 5.5-Mbps rate, even and odd symbols use a different phase shift for technical reasons. Symbol numbering starts with 0 for the first 8-bit block. The phase shifts are identical to the phase shifts used in 5.5-Mbps transmission.

3. The remaining six bits are grouped into three successive pairs. Each pair is associated with the phase angle in Table 12-8 and is used to derive a code word.

Table 12-8. Phase angle encoding for 11-Mbps transmission

Bit pattern	Phase angle
00	0
01	$\pi/2$
10	π
11	$3\pi/2$

As an example, consider the conversion of the bit sequence 0100 1101 into a complex code for transmission on an 802.11b network. The first two bits, 01, encode a phase shift from the previous symbol. If the symbol is an even symbol in the MAC frame, the phase shift is $\pi/2$; otherwise, the shift is $3\pi/2$. (Symbols in the MAC frame are numbered starting from 0, so the first symbol in a frame is even.) The last six bits are divided into three 2-bit groups: 00, 11, and 01. Each of these is used to encode an angle in the code word equation. The next step in transmission is to convert the phase angles into the complex code word for transmission.

Clear channel assessment

Like the original DS PHY, high-rate implementers have three choices for the CS/CCA operation mode. All the direct-sequence CCA modes are considered to be part of the same list. Mode 1 is identical to the DS PHY's CCA Mode 1, and Modes 2 and 3 are used exclusively by the original DS PHY. Modes 4 and 5 are the HR/DSSS-specific CCA modes.

Mode 1

> When the energy exceeds the energy detection (ED) threshold, the medium is reported busy. The ED threshold depends on the transmit power used. This mode is also available for classic direct-sequence systems.

Mode 4

> Implementations using Mode 4 look for an actual signal. When triggered, a Mode 4 CCA implementation starts a 3.65 ms timer and begins counting down. If no valid HR/DSSS signal is received by the expiration of the timer, the medium is reported idle. 3.65 ms corresponds to the transmission time required for the largest possible frame at 5.5 Mbps.

Mode 5

> Mode 5 combines Mode 1 and Mode 4. A signal must be detected with sufficient energy before the channel is reported busy to higher layers.

Once a channel is reported busy, it stays busy for the duration of the intended transmission, even if the signal is lost. The channel is considered busy until the time interval in the Length field has elapsed. Implementations that look for a valid signal may override this requirement if a second PLCP header is detected.

Optional Features of the 802.11b PHY

802.11b includes two optional physical-layer features, neither of which is widely used. Packet Binary Convolutional Coding (PBCC) was proposed as a method of reaching the 11 Mbps data rate, but it was never widely implemented. Proposals for further revisions to wireless LAN technology in the ISM band specified PBCC, but those proposals were rejected in the summer of 2001.

A second optional feature, *channel agility*, was designed to assist networks in avoiding interference. Channel agility causes the center channel to shift periodically in the hope that interference can be avoided. Channel agility was never widely used because it was not particularly helpful. In the presence of interference, some throughput would be recovered as receivers hopped to another channel, but the additional spectrum required made it much more effective to hunt down and fix the interference, or remap channels around it.

Characteristics of the HR/DSSS PHY

Table 12-9 shows the values of a number of parameters in the HR/DSSS PHY. Like the DS PHY, the HR/DSSS PHY has a number of parameters that can be adjusted to compensate for delays in any part of a real system.

Table 12-9. HR/DSSS PHY parameters

Parameter	Value	Notes
Maximum MAC frame length	4,095 bytes	
Slot time	20 μs	
SIFS time	10 μs	The SIFS is used to derive the value of the other interframe spaces (DIFS, PIFS, and EIFS).
Contention window size	31 to 1,023 slots	
Preamble duration	144 μs	Preamble symbols are transmitted at 1 MHz, so a symbol takes 1 μs to transmit; 96 bits require 96 symbol times.
PLCP header duration	48 bits	The PLCP header transmission time depends on whether the short preamble is used.
Minimum sensitivity	−76 dBm	
Adjacent channel rejection	35 dB	See text for measurement notes.

One other item of note is that the total aggregate throughput of all HR/DSSS networks in an area is still lower than the total aggregate throughput of all nonoverlapping frequency-hopping networks in an area. The total aggregate throughput is a function of the number of nonoverlapping channels. In North America and most of Europe, three HR/DSSS networks can be deployed in an area at once. Running each network at the top speed of 11 Mbps, and assuming user payload data throughput of 50%, the total aggregate throughput will be 16.5 Mbps.

## CHAPTER 13

802.11a and 802.11j:
5-GHz OFDM PHY

Go West, young man, and grow up with the country!
—John B.L. Soule[*]

The 2.4 GHz ISM bands are crowded, and often choked with non-802.11 traffic. In an attempt to develop higher data rates, the 802.11 working group standardized a physical layer using unlicensed spectrum around 5 GHz. Large tracts of undeveloped spectrum were available for unlicensed use, and far fewer devices have used the spectrum.

802.11a was standardized in 1999, but it took a significant amount of time to bring products to market. 802.11a hardware finally hit the market in late 2001. Today, the best known manufacturer of 802.11a chipsets is Atheros Communications. In form and function, they look similar to any other wireless LAN card. Most are CardBus cards, although some additional form factors are used more widely now. The range of very high data rates is quite short, but generally, 802.11a has a comparable data rate to 802.11b at comparable distance.

Initially, 802.11a was designed for the 5-GHz Unlicensed National Information Infrastructure (U-NII) bands in the United States. With the success of 802.11a in the American market, other regulators developed rules to allow 802.11a. The 802.11 working group supported these efforts through 802.11h for Europe, which was discussed in Chapter 8, and 802.11j for Japan.

This chapter begins with a qualitative introduction to the basis of OFDM. When all the mathematical formalism is stripped away, OFDM is a method for chopping a large frequency channel into a number of subchannels. The subchannels are then used in parallel for higher throughput. I anticipate that many readers will skip the first section, either because they are already familiar with OFDM or are interested only in how the frequency bands are used and how the PCLP wraps up frames for transmission.

---

[*] This is often attributed to Horace Greeley, who did much to popularize it.

Orthogonal Frequency Division Multiplexing (OFDM)

802.11a is based on orthogonal frequency division multiplexing (OFDM). OFDM is not a new technique. Most of the fundamental work was done in the late 1960s, and U.S. patent number 3,488,445 was issued in January 1970. Recent DSL work (HDSL, VDSL, and ADSL) and wireless data applications have rekindled interest in OFDM, especially now that better signal-processing techniques make it more practical.[*] OFDM does, however, differ from other emerging encoding techniques such as code division multiple access (CDMA) in its approach. CDMA uses complex mathematical transforms to put multiple transmissions onto a single carrier; OFDM encodes a single transmission into multiple subcarriers. The mathematics underlying the code division in CDMA is far more complicated than in OFDM.

OFDM devices use one wide-frequency channel by breaking it up into several component subchannels. Each subchannel is used to transmit data. All the "slow" subchannels are then multiplexed into one "fast" combined channel.

Carrier Multiplexing

When network managers solicit user input on network build-outs, one of the most common demands is for more speed. The hunger for increased data transmissions has driven a host of technologies to increase speed. OFDM takes a qualitatively similar approach to Multilink PPP: when one link isn't enough, use several in parallel.

OFDM is closely related to plain old frequency division multiplexing (FDM). Both divide the available bandwidth into slices called *carriers* or *subcarriers* and make those carriers available as distinct channels for data transmission. OFDM boosts throughput by using several subcarriers in parallel and multiplexing data over the set of subcarriers.

Traditional FDM was widely used by first-generation mobile telephones as a method for radio channel allocation. Each user was given an exclusive channel, and guard bands were used to ensure that spectral leakage from one user did not cause problems for users of adjacent channels. Figure 13-1 illustrates the traditional FDM approach.

The trouble with traditional FDM is that the guard bands waste bandwidth and thus reduce capacity. To avoid wasting transmission capacity with unused guard bands, OFDM selects channels that overlap but do not interfere with each other. Figure 13-2 illustrates the contrast between traditional FDM and OFDM.

---

[*] The lack of interest in OFDM means that references on it are sparse. Readers interested in the mathematical background that is omitted in this chapter should consult *OFDM for Wireless Multimedia Applications* by Richard van Nee and Ramjee Prasad (Artech House, 2000).

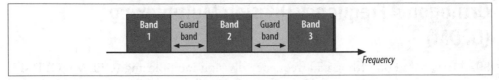

Figure 13-1. Traditional FDM

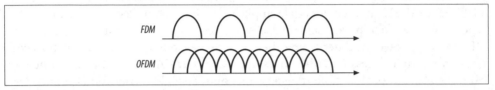

Figure 13-2. FDM versus OFDM

Overlapping carriers are allowed because the subcarriers are defined so that they are easily distinguished from one another. The ability to separate the subcarriers hinges on a complex mathematical relationship called *orthogonality*.

Orthogonality Explained (Without Calculus)

Orthogonal is a mathematical term derived from the Greek word *orthos*, meaning straight, right, or true. In mathematics, the word "orthogonal" is used to describe independent items. Orthogonality is best seen in the frequency domain, looking at a spectral breakdown of a signal. OFDM works because the frequencies of the subcarriers are selected so that at each subcarrier frequency, all other subcarriers do not contribute to the overall waveform. One common way of looking at orthogonality is shown in Figure 13-3. The signal has been divided into its three subcarriers. The peak of each subcarrier, shown by the heavy dot at the top, encodes data. The subcarrier set is carefully designed to be orthogonal; note that at the peak of each of the subcarriers, the other two subcarriers have zero amplitude.

OFDM takes the coded signal for each subchannel and uses the inverse fast Fourier transform (IFFT) to create a composite waveform from the strength of each subchannel. OFDM receivers can then apply the FFT to a received waveform to extract the amplitude of each component subcarrier.

Guard Time

With the physical layers discussed in Chapter 12, the main problem for receivers was inter-symbol interference (ISI) (Figure 13-4). ISI occurs when the delay spread between different paths is large and causes a delayed copy of the transmitted bits to shift onto a previously arrived copy.

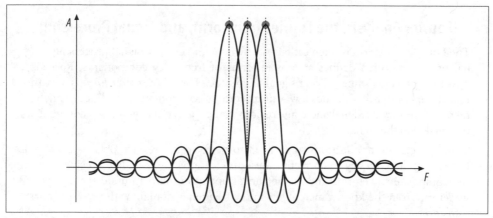

Figure 13-3. Orthogonality in the frequency domain

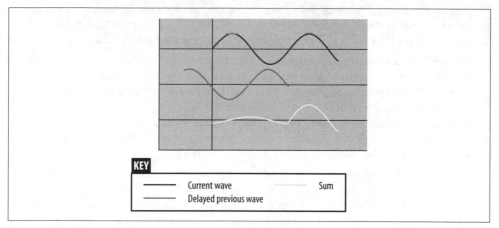

Figure 13-4. ISI reviewed

With OFDM, inter-symbol interference does not pose the same kind of problem. The Fourier transform used by OFDM distills the received waveform into the strengths of the subcarriers, so time shifts do not cause dramatic problems. In Figure 13-4, there would be a strong peak for the fundamental low-frequency carrier, and the late-arriving high-frequency component could be ignored.

As with all benefits, however, there is a price to pay. OFDM systems use multiple subcarriers of different frequencies. The subcarriers are packed tightly into an operating channel, and small shifts in subcarrier frequencies may cause interference between carriers, a phenomenon called *inter-carrier interference* (ICI). Frequency shifts may occur because of the Doppler effect or because there is a slight difference between the transmitter and receiver clock frequencies.

Fourier Analysis, the Fourier Transform, and Signal Processing

The Fourier transform is often called "the Swiss Army knife of signal processing." Signal processing often defines actions in terms of frequency components. Receivers, however, process a time-varying signal amplitude. The *Fourier transform* is a mathematical operation that divides a waveform into its component parts. Fourier analysis takes a time-varying signal and converts it to the set of frequency-domain components that make up the signal.

Signal-processing applications often need to perform the reverse operation as well. Given a set of frequency components, these applications use them like a recipe to build the composite waveform. The mathematical operation used to build the composite waveform from the known ingredients in the frequency domain is the *inverse Fourier transform*.

Strictly speaking, Fourier analysis is applied to smooth curves of the sort found in physics textbooks. To work with a set of discrete data points, a relative of Fourier transform called the *discrete Fourier transform* (DFT) must be used. Like the Fourier transform, the DFT has its inverted partner, the inverse DFT (IDFT).

The DFT is a computationally intensive process of order N^2, which means that its running time is proportional to the square of the size of the number of data points. If the number of data points is an even power of two, however, several computational shortcuts can be taken to cut the complexity to order $N \log N$. On large data sets, the reduced complexity boosts the speed of the algorithm. As a result, the "short" DFT applied to 2^n data points is called the *fast Fourier transform* (FFT). It also has an inverted relative, the *inverse fast Fourier transform* (IFFT).

Fast Fourier transforms used to be the domain of supercomputers or special-purpose, signal-processing hardware. But with the microprocessor speeds available today, sophisticated signal processing is well within the capabilities of a PC. Specialized digital signal processors (DSPs) are now cheap enough to be used in almost anything—including the chip sets on commodity 802.11 cards.

To address both ISI and ICI, OFDM transceivers reserve the beginning portion of the symbol time as the *guard time* and perform the Fourier transform only on the non–guard time portion of the symbol time. The non–guard time portion of the symbol is often called the *FFT integration time* because the Fourier transform is performed only on that portion of the symbol.

Delays shorter than the guard time do not cause ICI because they do not allow frequency components to leak into successive symbol times. Selecting the guard time is a major task for designers of OFDM systems. The guard time obviously reduces the overall throughput of the system because it reduces the time during which data transmission is allowed. A guard time that is too short does not prevent interference but does reduce throughput, and a guard time that is too long reduces throughput unnecessarily.

Cyclic Extensions (Cyclic Prefixes)

The most straightforward method of implementing the guard time would be simply to transmit nothing during the guard time, as shown in Figure 13-5.

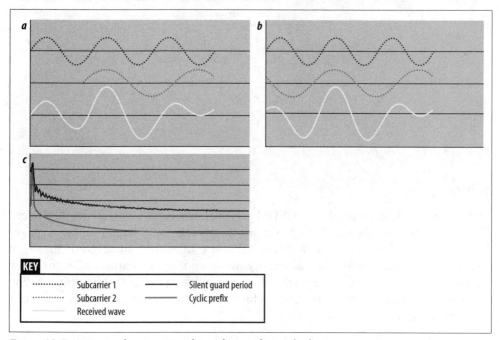

Figure 13-5. Naive implementation of guard time (do not do this!)

Simplistic implementations of the guard time can destroy orthogonality in the presence of common delay spreads. OFDM depends on having an integer number of wavelengths between each of the carriers. When the guard time is perfectly quiet, it is easy to see how a delay can destroy this necessary precondition, as in Figure 13-5. When the two subcarriers are added together, the spectral analysis shows subcarrier 1 (two cycles/symbol) as a strong opdpresence and a relatively smaller amount of subcarrier 2 (three cycles/symbol). In addition, the spectral analysis shows a large number of high-frequency components, muddying the waters further. These components are the consequence of suddenly turning a signal "on."

Solving the problems associated with a quiet guard time is quite simple. Each subcarrier is extended through the FFT integration period back through the preceding guard time. Extending each subcarrier (and hence the entire OFDM symbol) yields a Fourier transform that shows only the amplitudes of the subcarrier frequencies. This technique is commonly called *cyclic extension*, and it may be referred to as the "cyclic prefix extension." The guard time with the extended prefix is called the *cyclic prefix*.

In Figure 13-6, the cyclic prefix preserves the spectral analysis. Subcarrier 1 was not shifted and is not a problem. Subcarrier 2 is delayed, but the previous symbol appears only in the guard time and is not processed by the Fourier transform. Thanks to the cyclic prefix extension, when subcarrier 2 is processed by the Fourier transform, it is a pure wave at three cycles per integration time.

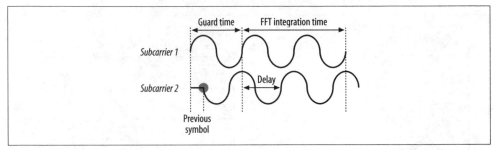

Figure 13-6. Cyclic prefix extension

Windowing

One further enhancement helps OFDM transceivers cope with real-world effects. Transitions can be abrupt at symbol boundaries, causing a large number of high-frequency components (noise). To make OFDM transmitters good radio citizens, it is common to add padding bits at the beginning and end of transmissions to allow transmitters to "ramp up" and "ramp down" from full power. Padding bits are frequently needed when error correction coding is used. Some documentation may refer to the padding as "training sequences."

Windowing is a technique used to bring the signal for a new symbol gradually up to full strength while allowing the old symbol to fade away. Figure 13-7 shows a common windowing function based on a cosine curve. At the start of the symbol period, the new function is brought up to full strength according to the cosine function. When the symbol ends, the cosine curve is used to fade out the bits at the end of the symbol.

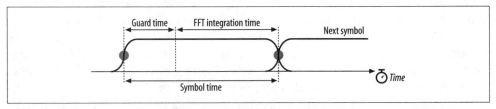

Figure 13-7. Cosine windowing technique

OFDM as Applied by 802.11a

802.11a is not a radical application of OFDM. The task group responsible for standardizing OFDM took the middle ground to apply OFDM to wireless LAN.

OFDM Parameter Choice for 802.11a

When choosing OFDM parameters, there are usually three given items of information. Bandwidth is fixed, often by regulatory authorities. Delay is determined by the environment in which the OFDM system will operate; most office buildings generally show a delay spread of 40–70 ns, though in some environments, the delay spread can approach 200 ns. Finally, the bit rate is usually a design goal, although the goal is usually "make the bit rate as high as possible, given the constraints of the other parameters."

One common guideline is that the guard time should be two to four times the average delay spread. As a result, the 802.11a designers selected a guard time of 800 ns. Symbol duration should be much larger than the guard time, but within reason. Larger symbol times mean that more subcarriers can fit within the symbol time. More subcarriers increase the signal-processing load at both the sender and receiver, increasing the cost and complexity of the resulting device. A practical choice is to select a symbol time at least five times the guard time; 802.11a matches the 800-ns guard time with a 4-μs symbol time. Subcarrier spacing is inversely related to the FFT integration time. 802.11a has a 3.2-μs integration time and a subcarrier spacing of 0.3125 MHz (1/3.2 μs).

Operating channels in 802.11a are specified as 20 MHz–wide. The bandwidth of an operating channel is a design decision. Wider operating channels have higher throughput, but fewer operating channels fit into the assigned frequency spectrum. The use of a 20-MHz operating channel allows for reasonable speeds on each channel (up to 54 Mbps), as well as a reasonable number of operating channels in the assigned spectrum. 802.11a offers a wide variety of choices in modulation and coding to allow for a trade-off between robust modulation and conservative coding, which yields low, reliable throughput, finer-grained modulation, and aggressive coding, resulting in higher, yet somewhat more fragile, throughput.

Structure of an Operating Channel

Like the DS PHYs, the OFDM physical layer organizes the spectrum into operating channels. Each 20-MHz channel is composed of 52 subcarriers. 4 of the subcarriers are used as *pilot carriers* for monitoring path shifts and ICI, while the other 48 subcarriers are used to transmit data. Subcarriers are spaced 0.3125 MHz apart. As shown in Figure 13-8, channels are numbered from −26 to 26. Subcarrier 0 is not used for signal-processing reasons.

Pilot subcarriers are assigned to subcarriers −21, −7, 7, and 21. To avoid strong spectral lines in the Fourier transform, the pilot subcarriers transmit a fixed bit sequence specified in 802.11a using a conservative modulation technique.

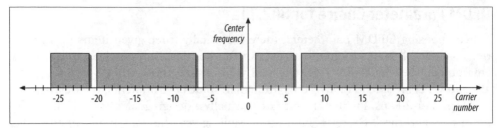

Figure 13-8. Structure of an OFDM channel

Subchannel modulation techniques

802.11a uses a technique called *quadrature amplitude modulation* (QAM) on each of the subcarriers to transmit data. QAM encodes data on a single carrier wave, but that carrier wave is composed of two components, called the *in-phase* and *quadrature* components. QAM performs amplitude modulation on both components; that is, it varies the size of the carrier wave based on the input. The main carrier wave is called in the in-phase component, abbreviated I. Lagging behind a quarter-cycle out of phase is the quadrature component, abbreviated Q. (Alternatively, QAM can be modeled mathematically as a single wave by using complex numbers.) Essentially, the amplitude of the composite signal and phase shifts within it both encode information.[*]

QAM is widely used in radio transmission systems. In North American television transmission, the in-phase component carries luminance, or brightness information, while the quadrature component carries the color information. AM radio is capable of stereo reception as well; a QAM system system called C-QUAM encodes the stereo information on the quadrature component.

Both television and radio are analog systems. In digital systems, the in-phase and quadrature components are restricted to particular levels, or *quantized.* With both components restricted to a particular set of levels, the result is that a *constellation* is formed. Constellations are usually displayed by plotting allowed values of the in-phase signal and quadrature signal against each other on a two-dimensional plot. Each point in the constellation is assigned to a symbol, and each symbol is assigned to a specific bit value. QAM is described in writing with the number of bits in the constellation, such as 64-QAM. Because the number of quantized values should always be a multiple of two in each direction, the number preceding QAM is always a power of two. 802.11a uses square constellations, and many of the proposals for faster codes use square constellations as well, which means that both directions must be an even power of two, and the number is also a perfect square (16-QAM, 64-QAM, 256-QAM).

To transmit data at higher rates, define a constellation with more points. However, as the data rate increases, the received signal quality must be good enough to distinguish

---

[*] The phase shift modulation used by direct-sequence 802.11 PHYs is a special case of QAM, where the amplitude does not change but the phase does.

between adjacent points in the constellation. As they are packed closer together, the acceptable error range around a point shrinks. 802.11a specifies the maximum acceptable errors from a constellation point as part of the PHY. Figure 13-10 shows the constellations used by 802.11a. At the lowest bit rates are BPSK and QPSK, the two phase-shift keying modulations used by the direct sequence PHYs.

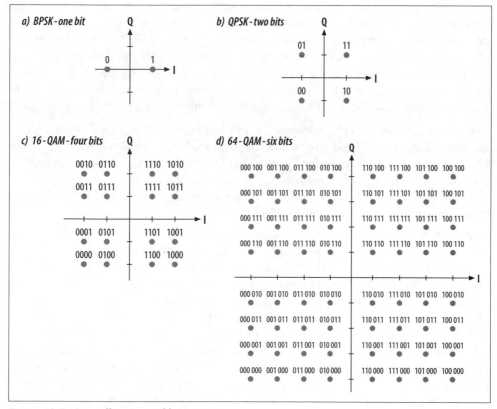

Figure 13-9. Constellations used by 802.11a

The total capacity of the radio channel is obtained by multiplying the number of subchannels by the number of bits per channel. A radio channel using 64-QAM on each subchannel can carry six bits per subchannel. In 802.11a, there are 48 subchannels, which gives a capacity of 288 bits per channel. However, there is a second attribute to account for. Most radio channels are not capable of error-free operation, and incorporate an error correction code.

Forward error correction with convolutional coding

Strictly speaking, forward error correction is not part of OFDM. However, OFDM is used in applications for which the signal is subject to narrowband interference or frequency-specific narrowband fading, also known as deep fading. When fading occurs, a channel's ability to carry data may go to zero because the received amplitude is so small. To keep a few faded channels from driving the bit error rate to the sky, OFDM implementations often apply an error correction code across all the subchannels. Implementations that use an error correction code in conjunction with OFDM are sometimes called coded OFDM (COFDM).

Coded OFDM uses a *forward error correction* (FEC) code on each channel. Forward error correction is a system that allows a receiver to detect corrupted bits and repair the transmission, provided that the fraction of lost or damaged bits is small enough. To provide the error-correction capability, redundant bits are added to the data stream. FEC codes work by creating a state engine that depends on the data bits currently being transmitted and encoding them across several symbols. By smearing noise out through several transmitted symbols, transient noise may be reduced to the point where resulting errors do not affect the receiver's ability to reconstruct the bit stream.

Two classes of forward error correction codes can be used. *Block codes* work by taking input blocks of a fixed size, while *convolutional codes* work on streams of any length. Block codes are used for applications in which the data is naturally stored, transmitted, or processed in chunks. DVDs, CDs, and hard disks use a block code. Convolutional codes, however, are the easy choice for wireless LANs because the frames being transmitted may be a variety of sizes.[*]

Convolutional codes have two main parameters. The *constraint length* determines how long a data bit is averaged into successive transmissions. Longer constraint lengths average data bits (and hence, any noise) over a longer time period, improving the reliability of the transmission at the cost of more complexity in the decoder. For relatively short constraint lengths, the Viterbi algorithm is used; it is recommended by the 802.11a standard itself. One of the reasons for the recommendation is that the Viterbi decoder is a *maximum likelihood* decoder. The results from a Viterbi decoder are the most likely data bits that were transmitted. Not all decoders are maximum likelihood, though it is obviously an important property for digital transmission systems. 802.11a uses a constraint length of 7, which is the limit of where a Viterbi decoder can practically be used. (Complexity of Viterbi decoding grows exponentially with constraint length.)

The second parameter, the *coding rate* (R), determines how many redundant bits are added. It is expressed as the number of data bits transmitted as a ratio of the total number of coded bits. A convolutional code with R=1/2 transmits one data bit for every two code bits. More aggressive codes may have less redundant information, such as R=3/4, where only 25% of the bits are redundant. Selecting a coding rate is a

---

[*] In 1993, it was discovered that two convolutional codes can be combined into a *turbo code*. Turbo codes are extremely powerful, though at the cost of additional latency over convolutional codes. They are used in applications where the additional latency is not a major factor, such as space and satellite communications. For further information about turbo codes, see the Jet Propulsion Laboratory's site at *http://www331.jpl.nasa.gov/public/JPLtcodes.html*, which features overview comparing the performance of turbo codes to the error correction codes used on the Voyager and Cassini probes. Turbo codes also underpin 1xEV-DO, Qualcomm's 3G Internet access system.

matter of engineering. As the code rate decreases, more code bits are available to correct errors, and the code becomes more robust. However, the price of robustness is decreased throughput. 802.11a specifies three code rates ranging from 1/2 at the most conservative end to 3/4 at the most aggressive end.[*]

Convolutional code rates may be transformed by *puncturing*. A punctured code changes a lower-rate convolutional code into a higher-rate code by discarding some of the coded bits. When data is coded, the lower-rate code is run. In the case of 802.11a, the lowest code rate is 1/2, which doubles the size of the data. To puncture to a 3/4 rate, one third of the coded data is discarded, or "punctured." To puncture to a 2/3 rate, 30% of the coded data is discarded. The coded data, minus the dropped bits, are transmitted. At the receiver, dummy bits are stuffed into the decoder to stand in for the punctured bits. Figure 13-10 illustrates the process to puncture a rate 1/2 code to a rate 3/4 code. One of the advantages of using a punctured code is that it can be implemented as single convolutional coder under software control, and different puncturing patterns can be used to alter the rate in software.

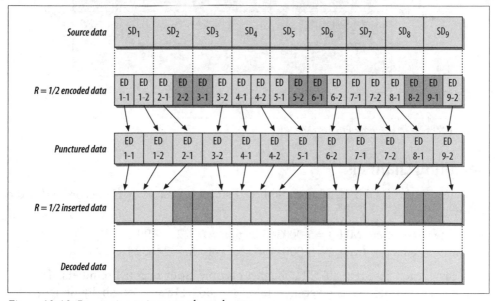

Figure 13-10. Puncturing to increase the code rate

Subchannel interleaving

Each operating channel has 48 constituent subcarriers. In essence, each operating channel is a multiplexed sum of 48 separate data streams. The incoming stream of

---

[*] The basic convolutional code specified by 802.11a uses a constraint length of 7 and a code rate of 1/2. This code was used on the Voyager deep-space probe.

coded bits must be mapped on to the correct subcarrier. Rather than use a simple round-robin algorithm that maps the first bit on to the first subcarrier, the second bit on to the second subcarrier, and so on, 802.11a uses a pair of interleaving rules. The first rule ensures that bits in sequence are transmitted on widely separated subcarriers, and the second ensures that bits in sequence are mapped on to different constellation points. As an example, Figure 13-11 illustrates the interleaver in operation with 16-QAM, which has 192 bits. Each of the 192 bits must be mapped on to one of the 48 data-carrying subcarriers. The figure plots the bit position against the subcarrier, clearly showing how each subcarrier is responsible for four coded bits.

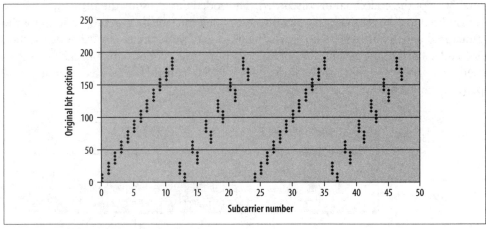

Figure 13-11. Interleaving with 16-QAM

Operating Channels

Channels in the 5-GHz band are numbered starting every 5 MHz according to the following formulas:

$$\text{center frequency (MHz)} = 5,000 + 5 \times n, n = 0,1,2, .. 199$$
$$\text{center frequency (MHz)} = 5,000 - 5 * (256 - n), n = 240, 241, .. 255$$

Obviously, each 20-MHz 802.11a channel occupies four channel numbers. The recommended channel use is given in Table 13-1. 802.11a was originally designed for the United States. European channelization was added as part of 802.11h in late 2003, and Japanese operation was added with 802.11j in late 2004.[*]

---

[*] European radio regulations are standardized by the European Conference of Postal and Telecommunications Administrations (CEPT). The European Radiocommunications Office develops regulations for CEPT; the 5 GHz radio LAN regulations are ERC/DEC/(99)23 (available at *http://www.ero.dk/doc98/Official/ Pdf/DEC9923E.PDF*). Japanese operation was approved by the Ministry of Internal Communications (*http:// www.soumu.go.jp/*), in Articles 49.20 and 49.21 (*http://www.soumu.go.jp/joho_tsusin/eng/Resources/ Legislation/MRA/020226_00.html*).

Table 13-1. Operating channels for 802.11a/j

Frequency	Allowed in?	Allowed power[a]	Channel numbers	Center frequency (GHz)
4.920–4.980 GHz	Japan	250 mW EIRP and < 1 W, or 10 mW EIRP	240	4.920
			244	4.940
			248	4.960
			252	4.980
5.040–5.080 GHz	Japan	250 mW EIRP and < 1 W, or 10 mW EIRP	8	5.040
			12	5.060
			16	5.080
5.15–5.25 GHz	Japan	200 mW (< 10 mW/MHz)	34	5.170
			38	5.190
			42	5.210
			46	5.230
U-NII lower band (5.15–5.25 GHz)	United States	40 mW (2.5 mW/MHz)	36	5.180
			40	5.200
			44	5.220
			48	5.240
U-NII mid-band (5.25–5.35 GHz)	United States	200 mW (12.5 mW/MHz)	52	5.260
			56	5.280
			60	5.300
			64	5.320
5.470–5.725	Europe (CEPT) (allowed in United States as of 11/2003, subject to U-NII rules[b])	1 W EIRP	100	5.500
			104	5.520
			108	5.540
			112	5.560
			116	5.580
			120	5.600
			124	5.620
			128	5.640
			132	5.660
			136	5.680
			140	5.700
U-NII upper band (5.725–5.825 GHz)		800 mW (50 mW/MHz)	149	5.745
			153	5.765
			157	5.785
			161	5.805

[a] In the United States, the allowed power is the maximum output power using a 6-dBi antenna gain.

[b] The additional spectrum was opened in FCC 03-287 (*http://hraunfoss.fcc.gov/edocs_public/attachmatch/FCC-03-287A1.pdf*), but test procedures were still in development as this book went to press. Without testing, no devices were able to be certified to operate in this spectrum in the United States.

There is one other feature of note about the operating bands. As with the DS PHYs, a transmit mask limits power leakage into the side bands. The mask is shown in Figure 13-12.

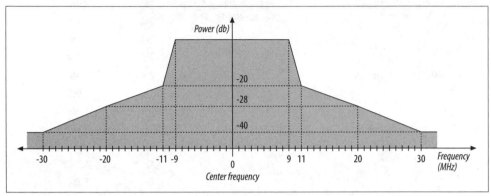

Figure 13-12. Transmit spectrum mask for 802.11a

Figure 13-13 gives an overall view of the 802.11a channels available in the U.S. Four channels are available in each of the U-NII bands in the U.S. In the two lower U-NII bands, channels are allowed to overlap, and a 30-MHz guard band is present at both the lower end of the low U-NII band and the upper end of the mid U-NII band.

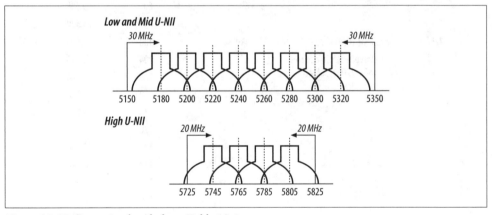

Figure 13-13. Operating bands from Table 13-1

OFDM PLCP

Like all the other physical layers, the OFDM PHY includes its own PLCP, which adds physical layer–specific framing parameters.

Framing

The OFDM PHY adds a preamble and a PLCP header. It also adds trailing bits to assist the encoding schemes used. This section divides the PLCP frame logically, but some components span different fields in the protocol unit. Figure 13-14 is the jumping-off point for discussion of the OFDM frame.

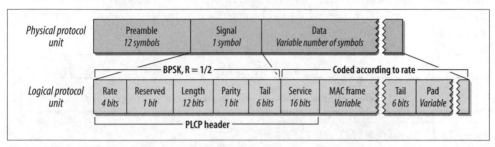

Figure 13-14. OFDM PLCP framing format

Figure 13-15 shows the start of a frame, but includes the guard intervals and windowing used by the transmitter. The preamble lasts 16 μs, which is evenly divided between short and long training sequences; the difference between the two is described in the next section. After the preamble, one OFDM symbol carries the Signal field, then a variable number of data symbols carry the end of the PLCP header, the MAC payload, and the trailer. All symbols use a modified cosine window to ensure smooth transitions. After the short preamble, which is used to synchronize frequencies, a guard time protects against multipath fading.

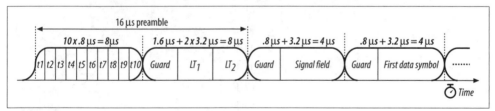

Figure 13-15. Preamble and frame start

Preamble

As with all other common IEEE 802 networks, and certainly all 802.11 physical layers, the OFDM physical protocol unit begins with a preamble. It is composed of 12 OFDM symbols that synchronize various timers between the transmitter and the receiver. The first 10 symbols are a short training sequence, which the receiver uses to lock on to the signal, select an appropriate antenna if the receiver is using multiple antennas, and synchronize the large-scale timing relationships required to begin decoding the following symbols. The short training sequences are transmitted without a guard period. Two long training sequences follow the short training sequences.

Long training sequences fine-tune the timing acquisition and are protected by a guard interval.

Header

The PLCP header is transmitted in the Signal field of the physical protocol unit; it incorporates the Service field from the Data field of the physical protocol unit. As shown in Figure 13-16, the Signal field incorporates the Rate field, a Length field, and a Tail field.

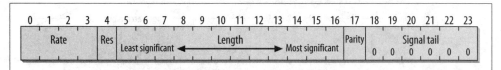

Figure 13-16. Signal field of OFDM PLCP frame

Rate (4 bits)
Four bits encode the data rate. Table 13-2 shows the bits used to encode each of the data rates. See the section "OFDM PMD" later in this chapter for details on the encoding and modulation scheme used for each data rate.

Table 13-2. Rate bits

Data rate (Mbps)	Bits (transmission order)
6	1101
9	1111
12	0101
18	0111
24	1001
36	1011
48	0001
54	0011

Length (12 bits)
12 bits encode the number of bytes in the embedded MAC frame. Like most fields, it is transmitted least-significant bit to most-significant bit. The length is processed by a convolutional code to protect against bit errors.

Parity (1 bit) and Reserved (1 bit)
Bit 4 is reserved for future use and must be set to 0. Bit 17 is an even parity bit for the first 16 Signal bits to protect against data corruption.

Tail (6 bits)
The Signal field ends with six 0 tail bits used to unwind the convolutional code. As such, they must by definition be processed by the convolutional code.

Service (16 bits)

The final field in the PLCP header is the 16-bit Service field. Unlike the other components of the PLCP header, it is transmitted in the Data field of the physical protocol unit at the data rate of the embedded MAC frame. The first eight bits are set to 0. As with the other physical layers, MAC frames are scrambled before transmission; the first six bits are set to 0 to initialize the scrambler. The remaining nine bits are reserved and must set to 0 until they are adopted for future use.

Data

The encoding scheme used for the data depends on the data rate. Before transmission, data is scrambled, as it is with the other physical layers. The Service field of the header is included in the Data field of the physical protocol unit because it initializes the scrambler.

Trailer

The Data field of the physical protocol unit ends with a trailer. (The 802.11a specification does not call the ending fields a trailer, but it is a descriptive term.) It is composed of two fields:

Tail (6 bits)

Like the tail bits in the PLCP header, the tail bits appended to the end of the MAC frame bring the convolutional code smoothly to an end. Six bits are required because the convolutional code has a constraint length of seven.

Pad (variable)

As used by 802.11a, OFDM requires that fixed-size blocks of data bits be transferred. The Data field is padded so that its length is an integer multiple of the block size. The block size depends on the modulation and coding used by the data rate; it is discussed in the next section.

OFDM PMD

The OFDM PHY uses a cocktail of different modulation schemes to achieve data rates ranging from 6 Mbps to 54 Mbps. In all cases, the physical layer uses a symbol rate of 250,000 symbols per second across 48 subchannels; the number of data bits per symbol varies. An OFDM symbol spans all 48 subchannels.

Encoding and Modulation

There are four rate tiers with the OFDM PHY: 6 and 9 Mbps, 12 and 18 Mbps, 24 and 36 Mbps, and 48 and 54 Mbps. Support is required for 6, 12, and 24 Mbps, which are lowest speeds in each of the first three tiers, and therefore the most robust in the presence of interference. The lowest tier uses binary phase shift keying (BPSK) to encode 1 bit per subchannel, or 48 bits per symbol. The convolutional coding means that either half or one quarter of the bits are redundant bits used for error correction, so there are only 24 or 36 data bits per symbol. The next tier uses quadrature phase shift keying (QPSK) to encode 2 bits per subchannel, for a total of 96 bits per symbol. After subtracting overhead from the convolutional code, the receiver is left with 48 or 72 data bits. The third and fourth tiers use generalized forms of BPSK and QPSK known as quadrature amplitude modulation (QAM). 16-QAM encodes 4 bits using 16 symbols, and 64-QAM encodes 6 bits using 64 symbols. The third tier uses 16-QAM along with the standard R=1/2 and R=3/4 convolutional codes. To achieve higher rates with 64-QAM, however, the convolutional codes use R=2/3 and R=3/4. Table 13-3 summarizes the coding methods used by each data rate in the OFDM PHY.

Table 13-3. Encoding details for different OFDM data rates

Speed (Mbps)	Modulation and coding rate (R)	Coded bits per carrier[a]	Coded bits per symbol	Data bits per symbol[b]
6	BPSK, R=1/2	1	48	24
9	BPSK, R=3/4	1	48	36
12	QPSK, R=1/2	2	96	48
18	QPSK, R=3/4	2	96	72
24	16-QAM, R=1/2	4	192	96
36	16-QAM, R=3/4	4	192	144
48	64-QAM, R=2/3	6	288	192
54	64-QAM, R=3/4	6	288	216
72[c]	64-QAM	6	288	288

[a] Coded bits per subchannel is a function of the modulation (BPSK, QPSK, 16-QAM, or 64-QAM).
[b] The data bits per symbol is a function of the rate of the convolutional code.
[c] Although no rate has been standardized without a convolutional code, many products offer a mode where it is dropped for additional throughput.

Radio Performance: Sensitivity and Channel Rejection

Like other physical layers, 802.11a specifies minimum performance requirements for the receiver, which are shown in Table 13-4. Minimum sensitivity has been discussed for the other physical layers. The only feature of note in 802.11a is that the wide range in data speeds means that a minimum performance requirement is quoted for each data speed. In comparison with the requirements laid down by the direct-sequence layers, 802.11a is just as stringent. 802.11a requires a −76 dBm sensitivity, which is comparable to the 18 Mbps and 24 Mbps data rates in 802.11a.[*]

---

[*] Note, however, that path loss is worse at the 802.11a frequencies.

More interesting is the specification of channel rejection. As with the other physical layers, begin by injecting a signal slightly (3 dB) above the minimum sensitivity on a given channel. On either rejection test, bring up a second signal on either an adjacent or nonadjacent channel. When the channel under test suffers a 10% frame error rate, note the difference in power between the two channels.

What the table says is that as the data rate increases, the more easily a signal is disrupted at the receiver. If an 802.11a network is built too dense, so that 54 Mbps signals from adjacent APs are regularly received in the middle of the two, it is possible that the client radio chipsets will not be able to decode the transmissions. However, this scenario is unlikely due to the relatively short range of 54 Mbps transmissions. Furthermore, many chipsets will perform better than the standard requires, but most vendors do not quote rejection in the data sheets for their cards.

Table 13-4. Receiver performance requirements

Data rate (Mbps)	Minimum sensitivity (dBm)	Adjacent channel rejection (dB)	Nonadjacent channel rejection (dB)
6	−82	16	32
9	−81	15	31
12	−79	13	29
18	−77	11	27
24	−74	8	24
36	−70	4	20
48	−66	0	16
54	−65	−1	15

Clear Channel Assessment

The OFDM PHY specification leaves implementers a great deal of latitude in selecting techniques for noting a busy channel. Received signal strength thresholds determine whether the channel is in use, but the main guideline for 802.11a equipment is that it must meet certain performance standards. Implementations are free to use the Packet Length field from the PLCP header to augment clear channel assessment, but this is not required.

Transmission and Reception

The block diagram for an 802.11a receiver is shown in Figure 13-17. When a frame is ready for transmission, the 802.11a interface runs the following procedure:

1. Select a transmission rate. Algorithms for selecting a data rate are implementation-dependent, so products sold by different vendors may select different rates under identical circumstances. The rate dictates the modulation and convolutional code, as well as the number of data bits per subcarrier. See Table 13-3.

2. Transmit the PLCP preamble, which consists of long and short training sequences.

3. Begin transmission of the PLCP header with the SIGNAL field, which is not scrambled. It is coded with the convolutional coder.

4. Create the data field of the packet.

   a. Create the SERVICE field, which is currently set to all zeros. It has seven zeros for scrambler initialization, and nine reserved bits set to zero.

   b. Append the data.

   c. Put on the six zero tail bits.

   d. Pad with zeros to a multiple of the data bit per subcarrier block size.

5. Scramble the data, which helps avoid long strings of zeros or ones.

6. Encode the data with the convolutional coder. If necessary, puncture the output of the convolutional code to generate an encoded string at a higher rate than 1/2.

7. Divide the coded data into blocks for processing. The block size depends on the modulation rate for the data symbols.

   a. Perform the interleaving process and map bits from the block on to the 48 subcarriers.

   b. Insert the four pilot subcarriers at the designated locations.in the channel.

   c. Use the inverse Fourier transform to convert the frequency-domain data into time-domain data for transmission.

8. Repeat step 5 for each data block until there are no more.

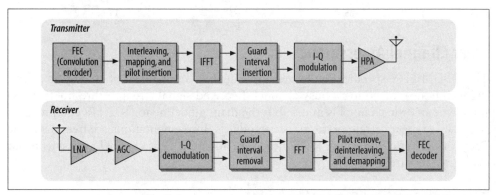

Figure 13-17. A transceiver block diagram

Acknowledgment

Support of the 6, 12, and 24 Mbps data rates is required by 802.11a. Upon receipt of a frame, the 802.11 MAC requires an acknowledgment. Acknowledgments must be sent at a supported data rate for all associated stations. Most devices send acknowledgments at 24 Mbps because it minimizes the overhead while obeying the stricture to transmit at a mandatory rate.

An example of OFDM encoding

OFDM encoding, as you can no doubt see by now, is an intense, multistep process. One of the additions that 802.11a made to the original specification was Annex G, an encoding of Schiller's *Ode to Joy* for transmission over an 802.11a network. Shortly after 802.11a was published, the IEEE 802.11 working group discovered several errors in the example and published a correction. If you are interested in learning about OFDM encoding in detail, you can refer to this example.

Characteristics of the OFDM PHY

Parameters specific to the OFDM PHY are listed in Table 13-5. Like the physical layers presented in Chapters 11 and 12, the OFDM PHY also incorporates a number of parameters to adjust for the delay in various processing stages in the electronics. As a final note, the extra radio bandwidth provided offers a great deal of throughput. In the United States, there are currently 12 channels, with the additional space for eight channels recently cleared. 20 co-located channels operating with 50% of the transmission time devoted to user traffic can move over 500 Mbps. This number is far greater than any other physical layer yet standardized.

Table 13-5. OFDM PHY parameters

Parameter	Value	Notes
Maximum MAC frame length	4,095 bytes	
Slot time	9 μs	
SIFS time	16 μs	The SIFS is used to derive the value of the other interframe spaces (DIFS, PIFS, and EIFS).
Contention window size	15 to 1,023 slots	
Preamble duration	20 μs	
PLCP header duration	4 μs	
Receiver sensitivity	−65 to −82 dBm	Depends on speed of data transmission.

Like the other physical layers, the OFDM PHY has a number of attributes that can be adjusted by a vendor to balance delays in various parts of the system. It includes variables for the latency through the MAC, the PLCP, and the transceiver, as well as variables to account for variations in the transceiver electronics.

## CHAPTER 14

802.11g: The Extended-Rate PHY (ERP)

When wireless LANs first entered the mainstream computing consciousness, there was one practical choice. 802.11b had recently been standardized, and offered the prospect of near-Ethernet speed, which, to be fair, by that point was not very fast at all. As 802.11a emerged from the laboratory into commercially-available chipsets, users had a desire to obtain higher speeds than 802.11b, while retaining backwards compatibility with the installed base of 802.11b hardware. The result is 802.11g, which offers a headline bit rate comparable to 802.11a while still operating in the microwave band. By working at slightly less than half the frequency, 802.11g devices have better range than the 5 GHz 802.11a devices.

802.11g is not a revolutionary specification. In fact, if you read the new clauses added by the specification, it is clear that it uses much of the existing work done elsewhere. The new physical layers it specifies are built on existing work, and there are only slight modifications. Most of 802.11g is occupied with providing backwards compatibility.

802.11g Components

802.11g is really several physical layer specifications in one. It adds one umbrella clause for the Extended Rate PHY (ERP). However, there are several different "flavors" of ERP:

ERP-DSSS and ERP-CCK

> These modes are backwards compatible with the original direct sequence specification (1 Mbps and 2 Mbps) described in Chapter 11, as well as the 802.11b enhancements (5.5 Mbps and 11 Mbps) described in Chapter 12. To retain backwards compatibility, a few minor changes are required.

ERP-OFDM

> This is the major mode of 802.11g. It is essentially running 802.11a in the ISM frequency band (2.4 GHz), with a few minor changes to provide backwards

compatibility. It supports the same speeds as 802.11a: 6, 9, 12, 18, 24, 36, 48, and 54 Mbps. Speeds of 6, 12, and 24 Mbps are mandatory.

ERP-PBCC

This is an optional extension to the PBCC standard provided in 802.11b, and provides data rates of 22 Mbps and 33 Mbps. Although it is part of the standard, it is not implemented by most major chipsets in the market, and is not widely used.

DSSS-OFDM

This a hybrid scheme, which encodes packet data using the DSSS headers, and OFDM encoding of the payload. Part of the reason for developing this implementation was for backwards compatibility. Although the body is OFDM-modulated and unintelligible to 802.11b, information in the headers is able to provide information on the duration of the packet. It is optional, and not widely implemented.

Any device that implements 802.11g is required to support a few mandatory modes. For backwards compatibility, 802.11g devices must support DSSS modulation (802.11) at 1 and 2 Mbps, and CCK modulation (802.11b) at 5.5 and 11 Mbps. Basic OFDM support is required, and all 802.11g stations are further required to support OFDM modulation at 6, 12, and 24 Mbps.

Compatibility Changes

The mandatory modes in 802.11g are slight modifications of existing physical layers, with a few minor alterations made for backwards compatibility. The modifications required of 802.11g stations assist coexistence with older implementations. They are not changes to the existing specifications. An 802.11b card will work as it always has. The only difference is that an 802.11g card will have a few features not present in 802.11b.

802.11b devices implement two different specifications: the original, slow direct sequence (DSSS) from the initial 802.11 standard, and the high-rate complementary code keying (CCK) PHY from 802.11b. 802.11g adopts both of those standards, and makes only a few minor changes. Naturally, any 802.11g station must be able to hear not only older stations but other 802.11g stations, so any 802.11g-compliant station must support all the preambles and synchronization found in 802.11g. More significantly, 802.11g stations must support the short preamble because it helps a great deal in maintaining high throughput. 802.11g radios are required to be more sensitive to signals as well.

802.11g devices must also implement ERP-OFDM, which is based heavily on 802.11a. In fact, it looks almost exactly like 802.11a, with a few obvious changes. Most notably, 802.11g adopts the frequency plan of 802.11b, so there are still only three ostensibly nonoverlapping channels for use. (See Chapter 13 for the adjacent-channel overlap map; the same note about three mostly nonoverlapping channels applies to 802.11g as well.) It also uses interframe spacing and slot times that are compatible with older ISM-band 802.11 stations. Regulatory structures may be different around 802.11g and 802.11b, however. Japan allows 802.11b operation in channels 1–14, but 802.11g is only allowed on channels 1–13.

Protection

One of the major differences between 802.11b and 802.11g is *protection*, which is required because of an asymmetry between the chipsets that implement the specifications. One of the problems faced by the designers of 802.11g is that it uses a different modulation scheme than 802.11b. 802.11g chips are built with backwards compatibility, and have no problem receiving and decoding an 802.11b signal. As is normally the case in technology, the converse is not true. 802.11b chipsets have no way of making sense of the higher-speed 802.11g transmissions. Part of the solution is to require that 802.11g stations transmit at a rate supported by all stations in basic service set. If an AP is to serve both 802.11b and 802.11g stations, it will need to send Beacon frames at a frame data rate of no higher than 11 Mbps.

The second part of the solution is to avoid interference between 802.11g and 802.11b networks. To ensure that 802.11b stations are aware of 802.11g transmissions, 802.11g specifies a protection mechanism to "protect" 802.11b stations from interference. The basic operation of the protection mechanism is shown in Figure 14-1. To avoid interference during the transmission of the OFDM frame and its acknowledgment, a slower frame is sent to update the NAV. There are two main protection modes. More commonly, 802.11g stations will use *CTS-to-self protection*, as shown in Figure 14-1 (a). When a station has a frame for transmission that needs protection, it will transmit a CTS frame with a receiver address of its own MAC address; that is, the destination of the CTS frame is the station itself. In the CTS, it will update the Network Allocation Vector (NAV) to tell other stations using the physical medium that it will be using the radio link for the time necessary to transmit the CTS, the OFDM-modulated frame, and an OFDM-modulated acknowledgment. Although the station sends the CTS to itself, all stations on the network are required to listen to CTS frames and update the NAV accordingly. The CTS frame is sent at the maximum speed it can be, using a modulation that can be received by all stations. Throughput may suffer a significant hit as a result of this exchange. A maximum Ethernet-size data frame and its acknowledgment require 294 microseconds at the highest speed, but the CTS to clear out the network requires at least 107 microseconds, and possibly more than 200 microseconds if long preambles are in use.

Figure 14-1 (b) shows the second mechanism, which is a full RTS/CTS exchange. Full RTS/CTS exchanges are more robust against hidden nodes, but come with a cost in network capacity. As in the CTS-to-self case, the compatibility frames used to reserve the medium may be have a transmission time comparable to or longer than the data.

Both the RTS and CTS frames will take 100 microseconds, while a maximum-size data frame and its ACK only require 300 microseconds. Based on calculations of the time required for the extra RTS, I estimate that the use of full RTS/CTS exchanges versus CTS-to-self to be a reduction of approximately one third in overall data throughput.*

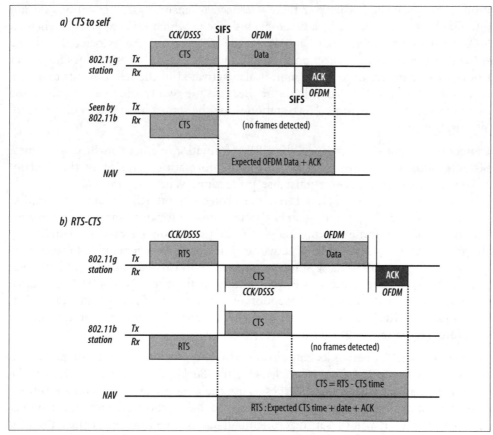

Figure 14-1. Basic overview of protection mechanism

To ensure that the protection frames are received and processed by all stations on the network, protection frames are transmitted using 802.11b rules. They may be transmitted using phase shift keying at 1 Mbps or 2 Mbps, or CCK at 5.5 Mbps or 11 Mbps. Any 802.11b station will be able to understand these modulations, and can update its virtual carrier sense accordingly. Figure 14-1 shows this by labeling the transmission modulation, and only showing the compatible modulations as received by an 802.11b station.

---

* See "When is 54 Not Equal to 54: An Analysis of 802.11g Throughput" at *http://www.oreillynet.com/pub/a/wireless/2003/08/08/wireless_throughput.html*.

Only the protection frames are required to be transmitted at the 802.11b-compatible data rates. Protection does not require 802.11g stations to use a slower data rate for the payload data, as is commonly asserted.

Protection is activated whenever there is a need to ensure 802.11g stations do not interfere with 802.11b stations. One obvious case in which this happens is when an 802.11b station associates with an AP. All the 802.11g stations associated with the AP will then start using protection to ensure that the 802.11b station does not suffer from or cause interference. Protection is also activated in the less obvious case of a co-channel AP with 802.11b-only traffic. Because the two co-channel APs share the same physical medium, an 802.11b station using the same channel on a different AP also triggers protection.

Protection is controlled through the ERP information element in Beacon frames. 802.11g adds a *Use Protection* bit in to an information element in the Beacon. When the bit is set, stations must use protection. When a non–802.11g-capable station associates to a wireless LAN, the protection bit will be set. The station responsible for sending the Beacon is also responsible for deciding whether to activate protection. In infrastructure networks, the protection activation is handled by the access points; in independent networks, it is the Beacon generator. Protection is activated when a non-802.11g station associates with the network, as well as when non–802.11g-capable stations are transmitting in the area. Non–802.11g-capable stations may be deduced by the reception of a management frames, including Beacons and Probe Responses, from an overlapping network that does not indicate the data rates supported by 802.11g.

Beacons in 802.11g networks can also control the preamble length for protection purposes. In the ERP information element, the *Barker Preamble Mode* bit can be used to tell associated stations whether to use the long preamble or short preamble. If all the stations associated to a network are capable of short preambles, the Barker Preamble Mode bit will be set to zero, and all stations will use short preambles for efficiency. Once a station that is not capable of short preambles associates with the network, however, the bit will be set to one, and all protection frames will use long preambles.

As with most other technology that is required to be backwards compatible, 802.11g can suffer for it. If protection is not enabled, 802.11a and 802.11g throughput is identical. Once protection is activated, however, my calculations showed it to be very roughly 50%, depending on the ratio of TCP data segments to TCP ACKs. Transmitting a full-size 1,500 byte Ethernet frame over 802.11 requires 428 microseconds for both the frame and the 802.11 acknowledgment. When CTS-to-self protection is used, the transmission time jumps to 557 microseconds; RTS/CTS adds further bloat, and requires 774 microseconds for the same transmission. Avoiding the need for protection is one of the reasons that many 802.11g access points offer the ability to accept associations from 802.11g-capable stations only. By shunning stations that are not capable of 802.11g speeds, there is an increased probability that protection can remain disabled. Of course, a station that is shunned may very well find a different network that can accommodate it on the same channel, which would still trigger the activation of protection.

 Although 802.11a and 802.11g are capable of the same speed, the extra transmission time required for protection may cut payload data throughput by half.

Protection is not required for the ERP-PBCC and DSSS-OFDM physical layers. As shown in Figure 14-2, both of them begin with an 802.11b-compatible header, and therefore the virtual carrier sense and NAV are updated without needing to send extra frames. An 802.11b station will receive the header and update the virtual carrier sensing mechanism based on the contents of the header. No transmissions will be allowed until the medium lock expires. Although the 802.11b station cannot detect the body of the frame, it is prevented from interference by the header. There is a cost to using ERP-PBCC or DSSS-OFDM. In a sense, they are always using protection because they use a much slower header. Both ERP-PBCC and DSSS-OFDM have, at minimum, 96 microsecond headers that can never be dropped. In contrast, the common ERP-OFDM mode must use the same header on a CTS frame that takes 107 microseconds to transmit, plus a 10 microsecond SIFS gap. However, ERP-OFDM needs to pay the penalty only when protection is required, while the optional modes always need to suffer the hit.

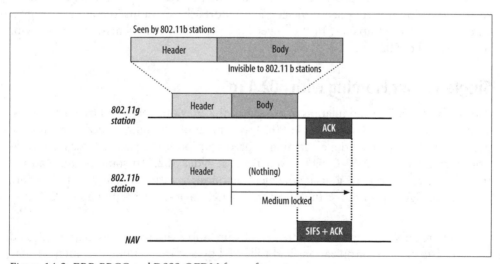

Figure 14-2. ERP-PBCC and DSSS-OFDM frame format

ERP Physical Layer Convergence (PLCP)

The ERP PHY's convergence layer is quite complicated. Due to the plethora of operational modes, there are a number of different ways that frames will be bundled up for transmission by the radio interface. Each of the modes described at the start of the chapter has its own physical layer framing.

ERP-OFDM Framing

This mode is the meat of the specification. All stations are required to implement it, and it is what is colloquially meant by "802.11g support" because most stations default to using it. In practice, understanding ERP-OFDM physical framing will provide you with the understanding of most 802.11g transmissions in the air.

The format of the ERP-OFDM frame at the physical layer, shown in Figure 14-3, is nearly identical to 802.11a. ERP-OFDM uses an identical logical protocol data unit, shown as the top line of the figure. In fact, the only major difference from 802.11a is that the frame is followed by a six microsecond idle time called the *signal extension*, which is shown in the second line of the figure, where the logical construction is assembled for transmission. The reason for the extra 6 μs is to make timing calculations and frame rates identical to 802.11a. 802.11a uses a 16 μs SIFS time, which is used in part to finish decoding the previous frame. For backwards compatibility, 802.11g uses the 10 μs idle time used by 802.11b. To provide enough time for the decoding process to finish, 802.11g adds 6 μs idle time to the end of the frame, leaving a 16 μs gap for the hardware to run its decode process. Of course, the NAV is set so that the virtual carrier sense mechanism reports the medium idle after the signal extension period completes. In the lower line, the OFDM transmissions are shown. It is identical to 802.11a.

Single-Carrier Framing with 802.11g

Although the OFDM modulation discussed in the previous section is by far the most common, it is also possible to use 802.11b-compatible framing directly around the higher speed body. Traditional framing is used with both the packet binary convolution coding and the DSSS-OFDM layer. Because older 802.11b stations can read the frame header, they can avoid using the medium during transmission and do not require protection. Figure 14-4 shows the use of traditional single-carrier framing in 802.11g.

Preamble
> The Preamble is identical to the 802.11b preamble discussed in Chapter 12, and consists of a synchronization field followed by a start of frame delimiter. It may be either the long preamble of 144 bits or the short preamble of 72 bits. In either case, the Preamble is transmitted at 1 Mbps using DBPSK modulation. Before modulation, the data is scrambled just as it is in 802.11b.

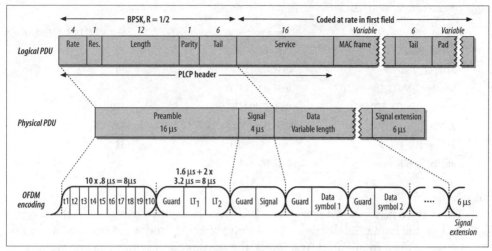

Figure 14-3. ERP-OFDM PLCP frame format

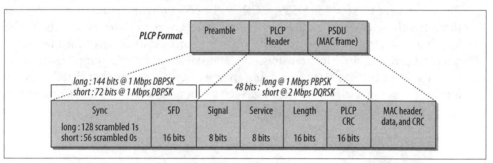

Figure 14-4. Long preamble ERP PLCP frame format

PLCP Header

The PLCP header is identical to the PLCP header discussed in Chapter 12. It consists of the Signal field, Service field, a Length field, and a PLCP-layer CRC check. The Length and CRC fields are identical to the 802.11b interpretation.

Signal field

This field is used to show the rate at which the PLCP payload (the MAC frame) is modulated. Initially, it was defined as the multiplier of 100 kbps that would result in the encoding rate. With the field defined as only eight bits, it would limit the encoding speed to 25.5 Mbps. To accommodate increased speeds, the Signal field consists of a label that describes the speed, as shown in Table 14-1. The signal field is not needed to tell the receiver what the encoding rate of a DSSS-OFDM frame is because there is a separate OFDM header to perform that task.

Table 14-1. Value of the SIGNAL field in the single-carrier frame header

Speed	Signal field value (hex/binary)	Signal field value, decimal
1 Mbps (ERP-DSSS)	0x0A (0000 1010)	10
2 Mbps (ERP-DSSS)	0x14 (0001 0100)	20
5.5 Mbps (ERP-CCK, ERP-PBCC)	0x37 (0011 0111)	55
11 Mbps (ERP-CCK, ERP-PBCC)	0x6E (0110 1110)	110
22 Mbps (ERP-PBCC)	0xDC (1101 1100)	220
33 Mbps (ERP-PBCC)	0x21 (0010 0001)	33
Any DSSS-OFDM speed	0x1E (0001 1110)	30

Service field

The service field, shown in Figure 14-5, contains control bits to help the receiver decode the frame. As discussed previously, bits 0, 1, and 4 are reserved and must be set to zero. In all 802.11g stations, the transmit and symbol clocks are locked, so bit 2 is always set to 1. Bit 3 is set when the frame body is modulated with PBCC, and set to zero for DSSS, CCK, and DSSS-OFDM modulations. The last three length extension bits are used to assist receivers in determining the frame length in bytes from the Length field, which is expressed in terms of the number of microseconds required for transmission. The standards have a complicated set of rules for when the bits must be set, but they are beyond the level of detail required for this book, especially since the single-carrier framing technique is uncommon.

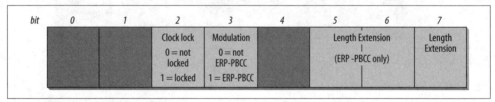

Figure 14-5. 802.11g SERVICE field

Frame Body

The final component of the PLCP frame is its payload, which is the MAC frame, modulated either by PBCC or OFDM. Details of the frame body modulation will be discussed in subsequent sections.

PBCC coding

To transmit a frame using PBCC, the frame data is first run through a convolutional code. The frame is broken into 2-bit elements, and are used as input into a convolutional code that outputs three bits. Each 3-bit block is mapped on to a symbol using 8PSK. Receivers will reverse the process, translating a single phase shift into one of eight symbols. After translating the symbol to a three-bit sequence, the convolutional code is used to remove the redundant bit and recover the original data. See Figure 14-6.

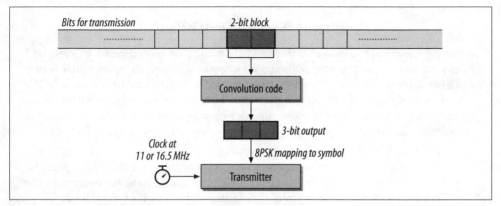

Figure 14-6. PBCC processing

Achieving a 22 Mbps data rate with this physical encoding is straightforward. The symbol clock continues to run at 11 MHz, just as in 802.11b, but each symbol is now capable of transmitting two bits. To run at 33 Mbps, the symbol rate for the data portion of the frame must be increased to 16.5 MHz. At two bits per symbol, the overall data rate is 33 Mbps. Clock speed switching must occur between the PLCP preamble and its payload.

DSSS-OFDM framing

DSSS-OFDM is a hybrid framing technique. The higher-layer packet is encoded with OFDM, and the OFDM-modulated packet is framed with a traditional-single carrier header, as shown in Figure 14-7. Headers are transmitted in accord with 802.11b (including the data scrambler used by 802.11b), but the frame body is modulated using OFDM, in a process identical to the encoding used in 802.11 and described in Chapter 13. Although similar to the encoding in 802.11a, the DSSS-OFDM framing eliminates the initial short training sequences. It also adds a 6 μs signal extension field to allow the convolution decode extra time to finish. The transition from direct sequence modulation to OFDM that occurs at the end of the PLCP header is somewhat complex from a radio engineering point of view, but is beyond the scope of this book.

ERP Physical Medium Dependent (PMD) Layer

Once the PLCP frame is ready for transmission, it is dispatched to the Physical Medium Dependent (PMD) layer. The PMD is responsible for taking the data and sending it out the antenna. Due to the wide variety of modulation schemes that might be used, an 802.11g transceiver must implement several different transmission modes, either wholly or partially, and switch between them as needed. Some functions, however, are shared by all transceivers regardless of operating mode.

Atheros "Super G" Extensions

Although the speed has increased dramatically in the past several years, wireless networks are still not fast. Under optimum conditions, a standards-based wireless network can achieve about 30 Mbps. In the race to get the highest number possible on the side of the box, nearly all chipset manufacturers have implemented extended functions to increase speed. By far, the most notable (or notorious) was Atheros' Super G enhancements, with three good features, and one that has drawn a great deal of fire.

Block acknowledgment (also called frame bursting)
> In the standard 802.11 radio link management scheme, every data frame must be followed by an acknowledgment, after which the station must re-contend for the medium. Block acknowledgments allow a station to transmit several frames, separated only by the short interframe space so there is no contention for the medium. The sequence is then followed by a single block acknowledgment. Block acknowledgment developed according to the current 802.11e drafts is generally interoperable between vendors.

Packet clustering
> The 802.11 frame can hold much more data than a standard 1,500 byte Ethernet-size frame. Using the full payload size improves the payload-to-overhead ratio, and increases speed.

Hardware data compression
> By compressing data prior to transmission, it requires less time to transmit and gives an effective throughput increase to the link. Hardware compression is most effective when there is redundant data, such as uncompressed text. It is not as effective when transmitting compressed images.

Channel bonding (also called "turbo mode")
> Instead of using a single 22 MHz channel, the bonding feature doubles the bandwidth. With more spectrum to spread the signal over, a higher number of bits can be pushed through the now-wider channel. To ensure that the wider bandwidth stays within regulatory limits, channel bonding is restricted in some products to operate in the middle of the band on channel 6.

By far the most controversial feature of the Super G feature set is the channel bonding. In late 2003, Broadcom accused Super G of interfering with regular 802.11g transmissions, and had a private demonstration at Comdex. (I was barred from observing.) Later tests revealed some interference, but found that Broadcom's chipsets were more susceptible to degredation than those of other vendors. Atheros has implemented a mode which monitors for standard 802.11g transmissions, and refrains from using channel bonding if other networks are present.

The main lesson is that any channel bonding feature is likely to increase interference by sucking up more of the available scarce spectrum. Spectrum-hungry transmissions modes are unsuitable for use in a large area requiring multiple access points because they cut the number of available channels from an already-too-low three to one. Deploy a channel bonding device in your home, but keep it off your company's network.

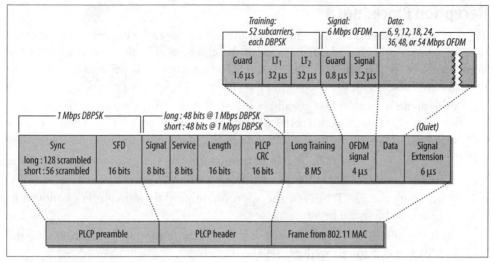

Figure 14-7. DSSS-OFDM frame format

Clear Channel Assessment (CCA)

Only one CCA mode is defined for 802.11g, which combines a minimum energy threshold with the ability to decode a signal. Energy detection is based on receiving a valid signal at the start of a transmission slot with a signal power of –76 dBm or greater. As a performance requirement, within a specified window, the PHY should have a high probability of correctly reporting the medium busy. Both the time window and the probability are shown in Table 14-2.

Table 14-2. 802.11g CCA performance requirements

	Long slot (20 μs)	Short slot (9 μs)
CCA time	15 μs	4 μs
Detection probability	>99%	>90%

CCA is integrated with a PLCP-level virtual carrier sense. When a PLCP header is received, it will include a length field that indicates the amount of time the medium will be busy. The physical layer will continue to report the medium busy for that time period, even if the physical signal is lost. (Note that this is similar in concept and operation to the Network Allocation Vector at the MAC layer.) Part of the reason for doing this is that not all implementations will support all the transmission modes, so it is important that the physical layer correctly avoids interfering with transmissions it cannot demodulate.

Reception Procedure

802.11g stations have a more complicated procedure for receiving frames than chips that implement other standards because of the choice and backwards compatibility. When an incoming frame is detected, an 802.11g station will need to detect it and then demodulate it with the correct physical layer.

1. Is the preamble an OFDM preamble (like 802.11a), or the traditional single-carrier preamble used by 802.11b? Frames modulated with OFDM will be processed exactly the same as 802.11a frames, just received on a different frequency.

2. If the frame is not an OFDM frame, it must decode the preamble, and find the end of the preamble to see the PCLP SIGNAL and SERVICE fields.

3. By decoding the PLCP header, the appropriate modulation can be employed to demodulate the frame body.

   a. If the SERVICE field indicates that the frame is modulated with PBCC, the PBCC reception procedures will be triggered.

   b. If the SERVICE field doesn't indicate the presence of PBCC, the data rate is checked. Data rates of 1 and 2 Mbps are processed with the DSSS reception algorithm, and data rates of 5.5 Mbps and 11 Mbps are processed according to the CCK reception algorithm; both are described in Chapter 12.

   c. If the SIGNAL field indicates a speed of 3 Mbps, DSSS-OFDM reception is used. It will switch the demodulator to receiving OFDM at the end of the PCLP header.

Characteristics of the ERP PHY

802.11g has very similar characteristics to 802.11a, with one notable exception. Although each channel has similar performance to an 802.11a channel, there are only three channels. If each channel is run at the highest data rate and 50% efficiency, the total aggregate throughput is only 81 Mbps. It is a high number, but does not begin to approach 802.11a.

Table 14-3. ERP PHY parameters

Parameter	Value	Notes
Maximum MAC frame length	4,095 bytes	
Slot time	20 μs 9 μs	If the network consists only of 802.11g stations, the slot time may be shortened from the 802.11b-compatible value to the shorter value used in 802.11a.
SIFS time	10 μs	The SIFS is used to derive the value of the other interframe spaces (DIFS, PIFS, and EIFS).
Signal extension time	6 μs	Every 802.11g packet is followed by the signal extension time.
Contention window size	15 or 31 to 1,023 slots	If the station supports only 802.11b rates, it will be 31 slots for compatibility. Otherwise, the contention window may be shorter.
Preamble duration	20 μs	

## CHAPTER 15

A Peek Ahead at 802.11n: MIMO-OFDM

802.11 task group N (TGn) has an interesting goal. Most IEEE task groups focus on increasing the peak throughput, making data fly as fast as possible during the time it is being transmitted. TGn's goal is to achieve 100 Mbps net throughput, after subtracting all the overhead for protocol management features like preambles, interframe spacing, and acknowledgments. Although the goal is 100 Mbps net throughput, the final proposal seems certain to blow past that number, and offer many times that throughput in maximum configurations. There are two roads to 100 Mbps: improve the efficiency of the MAC, increase the peak data rate well beyond 100 Mbps—or both.

Six complete proposals were made to the group creating the eventual 802.11n, but support has coalesced around two main proposals, from groups named TGnSync and WWiSE (short for "World-Wide Spectrum Efficiency"). Both camps have chipmakers. Atheros, Agere, Marvell, and Intel are part of TGnSync; Airgo, Broadcom, Conexant, and Texas Instruments are the core of WWiSE. However, quite a few manufacturers of electronic devices that might use 802.11 (Cisco, Nokia, Nortel, Philips, Samsung, Sanyo, Sony, and Toshiba) have also become part of the effort, and they are disproportionately represented in TGnSync.

At a very high level, both proposals are similar, though they differ in the emphasis on increasing peak data rates versus improving efficiency. Each of them makes use of multiple-input/multiple-output (MIMO) technology in several configurations and provides for backwards compatibility with installed systems in the same frequency band. Both support operation in the current 20 MHz channels, with provisions to use double-width 40 MHz channels for extra throughput.

As the standards war is fought across the globe at IEEE meetings, a "pre-N" access point has already hit the streets, based on Airgo's chipset. Purchasing it well before the standards process is underway is a roll of the dice. When most "pre-G" products were brought to market, the task group had begun to work in earnest on a single proposal. TGn is currently in the "dueling proposal" stage right now, and there is no guarantee that an early device will be firmware upgradeable to the final 802.11n standard. 802.11n is likely to be the last chance to standardize a PHY this decade. Developing a standard is as much political engineering as technical engineering. IEEE rules require that a proposal get a 75% supermajority vote before becoming the basis for a standard. As this book went to press, TGnSync was garnering a clear majority of support, but was still falling short of the necessary 75%. I expect that features from competing proposals will be incorporated into the working document to bring the vote count to the necessary level. As a result, this chapter describes both of the main competing proposals. Although TGnSync will probably be the basis for the 802.11n specification, some horse trading will likely result in a few WWiSE features being incorporated.

This chapter describes both the WWiSE and TGnSync proposals. The final standard will have some resemblance to both of them, and will likely pick and choose features from each. Fortunately, many basic concepts are shared between the two. As you read this, keep in mind that the proposals themselves may have changed quite a bit since the drafts upon which this chapter was based were written.

Common Features

Although the two proposals are different, there is a great deal of similarity between the two. Practically speaking, some features are required to reach the goal of 100 Mbps throughput.

Multiple-Input/Multiple-Output (MIMO)

Up until 2004, 802.11 interfaces had a single antenna. To be sure, some interfaces had two antennas in a diversity configuration, but the basis of diversity is that the "best" antenna is selected. In diversity configurations, only a single antenna is used at any point. Although there may be two or more antennas, there is only one set of components to process the signal, or *RF chain*. The receiver has a single input chain, and the transmitter has a single output chain.

The next step beyond diversity is to attach an RF chain to each antenna in the system. This is the basis of Multiple-Input/Multiple-Output (MIMO) operation.* Each RF chain is capable of simultaneous reception or transmission, which can dramatically improve throughput. Furthermore, simultaneous receiver processing has benefits in resolving multipath interference, and may improve the quality of the received signal far beyond simple diversity. Each RF chain and its corresponding antenna are responsible for transmitting a *spatial stream*. A single frame can be broken up and multiplexed across multiple spatial streams, which are reassembled at the receiver. Both the WWiSE and TGnSync proposals employ MIMO technology to boost the data rate, though their applications differ.

---

* MIMO is pronounced "MyMoe." I attended a symposium in which a standards committee attendee described the standardization vote on the acronym's pronunciation.

MIMO antenna configurations are often described with the shorthand "YxZ," where Y and Z are integers, used to refer to the number of transmitter antennas and the number of receiver antennas. For example, both WWiSE and TGnSync require 2x2 operation, which has two transmit chains, two receive chains, and two spatial streams multiplexed across the radio link. Both proposals also have additional required and optional modes. I expect that the common hardware configurations will have two RF chains on the client side to save cost and battery power, while at least three RF chains will be used on most access points. This configuration would use 2x3 MIMO for its uplink, and 3x2 MIMO on the downlink.

Channel Width

802.11a currently uses 20 MHz channels because that is the channel bandwidth allowed by all regulators worldwide. Doubling the channel bandwidth to 40 MHz doubles the theoretical information capacity of the channel. Although promising for the future, some regulators do not currently allow 40 MHz operation. Japan is the most notable exception.

MAC Efficiency Enhancements

As this book has repeatedly pointed out, the efficiency of the 802.11 MAC is often poor. In most usage scenarios, it is very difficult to exceed 50–60% of the nominal bit rate of the underlying physical layer. Every frame to be transmitted requires a physical-layer frame header, as well as the pure overhead of preamble transmission. The 802.11 MAC adds further overhead by requiring that each frame be acknowledged. Overhead is particular bad for small frames, when the overhead takes more time than the frame data itself. Figure 15-1 shows the efficiency, defined as the percentage of the nominal bit rate devoted to MAC payload data, for a variety of frame sizes. The values in the figure are exclusively for MAC payload data. Any network measurement would require additional LLC data, and networks that are encrypted would have additional overhead bytes. Furthermore, most network protocols provide their own acknowledgment facilities, which further reduces real-world efficiency. The point of Figure 15-1 is that small frames have particularly poor efficiency.

Both TGnSync and WWiSE adopt techniques to improve the efficiency of the radio channel. Concepts are similar, but the details differ. Both offer some form of *block ACKs* (sometimes called *frame bursting*). By removing the need for one acknowledgment frame for every data frame, the amount of overhead required for the ACK frames, as well as preamble and framing, is reduced. Block acknowledgments are helpful, but only if all the frames in a burst can be delivered without a problem. Missing one frame in the block or losing the acknowledgment itself carries a steep penalty in protocol operations because the entire block must be retransmitted.

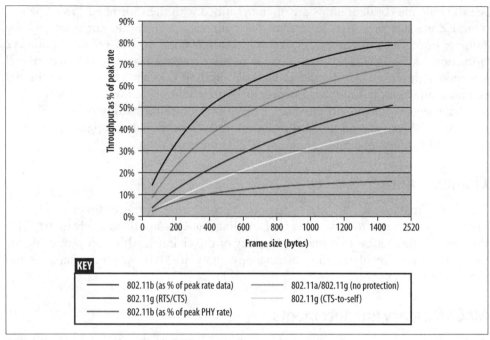

Figure 15-1. MAC Efficiency

Frame aggregation is also part of both proposals. Many of the packets carried by 802.11 are small. Interactive network sessions, such as telnet and SSH, make heavy use of rapid-fire small packets. Small packets become small frames, each of which requires physical-layer framing and overhead. Combining several small packets into a single relatively large frame improves the data-to-overhead ratio. Frame aggregation is often used with *MAC header compression*, since the MAC header on multiple frames to the same destination is quite similar.

WWiSE

The WWiSE consortium includes several well-known chipmakers: Airgo (the manufacturer of the first "pre-N" devices on the market), Broadcom, Conexant, and Texas Instruments. Motorola joined the consortium in February 2005, just as this book headed to press.

MAC Enhancements

As would be expected from a name touting spectral efficiency, WWiSE is more the more heavily weighted towards improving the MAC efficiency of the two proposals. To get to 100 Mbps net payload throughput, 12,000 bytes (960,000 bits) need to be transmitted in 960 microseconds. WWiSE's PHY specification has a 135 Mbps data rate in a basic two-antenna configuration with two data streams, which can move the data in 711 microseconds. The remaining 249 microseconds are used for preambles, framing, interframe spacing, and the single block acknowledgment.

Channels and radio modes

WWiSE uses both 20 MHz and 40 MHz channels. 40 MHz operation may be through a single 40 MHz channel, or through a 20 MHz *channel pair* in which both channels are used simultaneously for data transmission. One channel is designated as the primary channel, and operates normally. The secondary channel is used only for channel aggregation, and does not have stations associated on it. The secondary channel is used for "overflow" from the primary; carrier sensing functions are performed only on the primary channel.

Although the use of two channels is really a physical layer operation, there are some housekeeping functions performed by the MAC. A new information element, the Channel Set element, is sent in the primary channel Beacon frames so that stations are informed of the secondary channel in the pair. Access points also send Beacon frames on the secondary channel; unlike most Beacon operations, though, the purpose is to discourage clients from associating, or other devices from choosing that channel for operation. A secondary channel Beacon frame is very similar to the primary channel Beacon, but the only supported rate is a mandatory MIMO PHY rate. To further discourage use of the channel, it may also include the contention-free information element.

Protection

Like 802.11g, the new PHYs require enhanced protection mechanisms to avoid interfering with existing stations. Naturally, the protection mechanisms specified in 802.11g are adopted for operation of 2.4 GHz stations that may have to avoid interfering with older direct sequence or 802.11b equipment. When access points detect the presence of older equipment, it will trigger the use of RTS-CTS or CTS-to-self protection as described in Chapter 14.

However, additional protection may be required to avoid having a MIMO station transmit at a rate not understood by 802.11a or 802.11g equipment. The WWiSE proposal contains an OFDM protection scheme to allow MIMO stations to appropriately set the NAV on older OFDM stations. The protection mechanism is identical to the one described in Chapter 14, but it takes place using OFDM data rates.

Finally, the WWiSE proposal uses two bits in the ERP information element in Beacon frames to indicate whether OFDM protection is needed. In some cases, OFDM protection may be needed to assist an older 802.11g network, but no protection is needed for 802.11b stations. Access points monitor the radio link to determine if OFDM protection is needed. To assist stations using channel pairs, they also report on whether a secondary channel is in use.

Aggregation, bursting, and acknowledgment

The WWiSE proposal increases the maximum payload size from 2,304 bytes to over 8,000 bytes. Increasing the payload increases the payload-to-overhead and the ratio can increase efficiency if the larger frames or bursts can be delivered successfully.

Aggregation bundles multiple higher-level network protocol packets into a single frame. Each packet gets a subframe header with source and destination addresses, and a length to delimit the packet, as shown in Figure 15-2. Aggregation can only be used when the frames bundled together have the same value for the Address 1 field, which is the receiver of the frame. Frames from an access point in an infrastructure network use Address 1 as the destination, so access points can only aggregate frames bound for a single station. A station in an infrastructure network can, however, aggregate frames to multiple destinations. Station transmissions use the Address 1 field for the AP, since all frames must be processed by the AP prior to reaching the backbone network. Upon aggregation, the destination address is the "next hop" processing station, and the source is the creator of the frame. Upon deaggregation, the individual subframes will be processed according to the sub-frame headers. Due to the requirement that the receiver address must be the same, it is not possible to aggregate a mixture of unicast, broadcast, and multicast data. The proposal contains no rules about when to use aggregation.

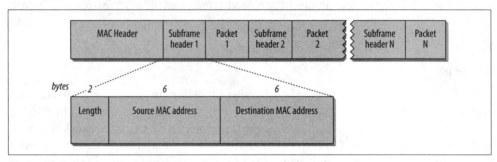

Figure 15-2. Aggregation in WWiSE

Bursting is a related, but slightly different concept. Frame aggregation glues higher-layer protocol packets together for transmission in larger lumps. Bursting does the same at the physical layer. Once a station has invested a significant amount of protocol overhead to obtain control of the channel, it can just keep on transmitting. One of the advantages of using multiple physical frames, as opposed to higher-layer frames, is that each physical frame has its own source and destination. A frame burst can consist of traffic intended for a variety of different destination addresses. In a frame burst, there are two additional interframe spaces defined, the Zero Interframe Space (ZIFS) and the Reduced Interframe Space (RIFS). Successive frames that use the same transmit power may use the ZIFS for immediate transmission. If the transmit power is changed between frames, the RIFS may be used. The RIFS is shorter than other interframe spaces, though, so it allows a station to retain control of the channel. In Figure 15-3, the first frame cannot be aggregated, and is transmitted after the transmitter gains control of the channel. Once it has gained control, it can hold on as long as allowed. The second and third frames use the same transmission power, and so are transmitted after the zero interframe space. Additionally, they share the Address 1 field and are therefore bundled into an aggregate frame. For transmission of the next frame, power needs to be changed, requiring the use of the reduced interframe space. The fourth and fifth frames can be aggregated, and are transmitted as a single aggregate frame. When the queued data has been transmitted, the station relinquishes control of the channel.

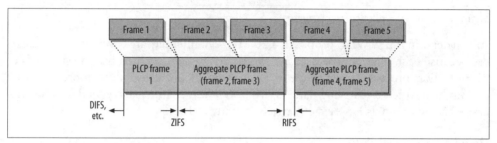

Figure 15-3. Bursting in WWiSE

In the initial version of the 802.11 MAC, a positive acknowledgment was required for every unicast data frame. WWiSE lifts this restriction, and allows for a more flexible acknowledgment policy. In addition to the "normal" policy, frames can be transmitted without an acknowledgment requirement, or with block acknowledgments instead.

The WWiSE MIMO PHY

The WWiSE proposal is a slight evolution of 802.11a, using MIMO technology. The basic channel access mechanisms are retained, as is the OFDM encoding. At a high level, the WWiSE PHY is mainly devoted to assigning bits to different antennas.

Structure of an operating channel

Like 802.11a, the radio channel is divided into 0.3125 MHz subcarriers. As in the 802.11a channel subdivisions, a 20 MHz channel in the WWiSE proposal is divided into 56 subcarriers. 40 MHz channels, which are optional, are divided into 112 subcarriers. In addition to being optional, 40 MHz channels are only supported in the 5 GHz band because it is not possible to squeeze multiple 40 MHz channels into the ISM band. (And if you thought network layout was hard with three channels, wait until you try with two!) Figure 15-4 shows the structure of both the 20 MHz and 40 MHz operating channels in the WWiSE proposal.

As in 802.11a, subcarriers are set aside as pilots to monitor the performance of the radio link. Fewer pilot carriers are needed in a MIMO system because the pilot carriers run through as many receiver chains. A 20 MHz 802.11a channel uses four pilot

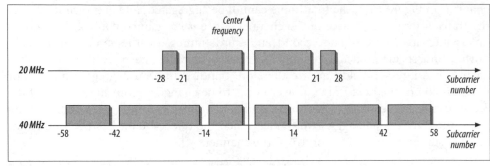

Figure 15-4. WWiSE pilot carrier structure

subcarriers. In the WWiSE proposal, a 20 MHz channel requires only two pilot carriers because each pilot is processed by two receiver chains, which has the same effect as four pilots processed by a single receiver chain. With fewer pilots, more subcarriers can be devoted to carrying data. 20 MHz WWiSE channels have 54 data subcarriers; 40 MHz channels have exactly twice as many at 108.

Modulation and encoding

The WWiSE proposal does not require new modulation rates. It uses 16-QAM (4 bit) and 64-QAM (6 bit) modulation extensively, but does not require finer-grained modulation constellations.

Coding is enhanced, however. A new convolutional code rate of 5/6 is added. Like the 2/3 and 3/4 code rates defined by 802.11a, the 5/6 code is defined by puncturing the output to obtain a higher code rate. WWiSE also defines the use of a low density parity check (LDPC) code.

Interleaver

In 802.11a, the interleaver is responsible for assigning bits to subcarriers. MIMO interleavers are more complex because they must assign bits to a spatial stream in addition to assigning bits to positions on the channel itself. The WWiSE interleaver takes bits from the forward error coder and cycles through each spatial stream. The first bit is assigned to the first spatial stream, the second bit is assigned to the second spatial stream, and so on. The interleaver is also responsible for scrambling the encoded bits within each spatial stream.

Space-time block coding

In most cases, an antenna will be used for each spatial stream. However, there may be cases when the number of antennas is greater than the number of spatial streams. If, for example, most APs wind up using three antennas while clients only use two, there is an "extra" transmit antenna, and the two spatial data streams need to be assigned to the three antennas. Transmitting a single spatial stream across multiple antennas is called *space-time block coding* (STBC).

The basic rule for splitting a spatial stream across multiple antennas is to transmit two related streams on different antennas. As discussed in Chapter 13 on 802.11a, the radio wave is composed of in-phase and quadrature components, where the quadrature wave is a quarter-cycle out of phase with the in-phase component. Phase shifts are represented mathematically by the imaginary part of the complex number in the constellation. The complex conjugate of a complex number has the same real part, but flips the sign on the imaginary part. Physically, the radio wave from the complex conjugate will have the same in-phase component, but the quadrature component will have the oppose phase shift. When there are extra antennas, the WWiSE proposal mandates that a spatial stream and its complex conjugate are transmitted on an antenna pair. Table 15-1 reviews the rules. The rules for splitting spatial streams are independent of the channel bandwidth, although 40 MHz spatial streams will carry more bits.

Table 15-1. WWiSE encoding rules when antennas outnumber spatial streams

Transmit antennas	Spatial streams	First spatial stream	Second spatial stream	Third spatial stream
2	1	Coded across antennas 1 and 2	N/A	N/A
3	2	Coded across antennas 1 and 2	Transmitted normally on third antenna	N/A
4	2	Coded across antennas 1 and 2	Coded across antennas 3 and 4	N/A
4	3	Coded across antennas 1 and 2	Third antenna	Fourth antenna

Modulation rates

There are 24 data rates defined by the WWiSE PHY, with 49 different modulation options. Rather than take up a great deal of space in a table, here is a basic formula for the data rates:

Data rate (Mbps) = 0.0675 × channel bandwidth × number of spatial streams × coded bits per subcarrier × code rate

Channel bandwidth
Either 20 for 20 MHz channels, or 40 for 40 MHz channels or channel pairs.

Number of spatial streams
The number of spatial streams can be equal to 1, 2, 3, or 4. It must be less than or equal to the number of transmission antennas. Support for at least two spatial streams is mandatory.

Coded bits per subcarrier
In most cases, this will either be 6 for 64-QAM or 4 for 16-QAM. BPSK (1 coded bit per subcarrier) and QPSK (2 coded bits per subcarrier) are only supported in the 20 MHz channel mode with one spatial stream.

Code rate
The code rate may be 1/2 or 3/4 when used with 16-QAM, and 2/3, 3/4, or 5/6 when used with 64-QAM.

There may be multiple ways to get to the same data rate. As an example, there are four ways to get 108 Mbps:

- Four spatial streams in 20 MHz channels, using 16-QAM with R=1/2.
- Two spatial streams in 20 MHz channels, using 64-QAM with R=2/3.
- One spatial stream in a 40 MHz channel, using 64-QAM with R=2/3.
- Two spatial streams in 40 MHz channels, using 16-QAM with R=1/2.

In a basic mode with a single spatial stream, channel capacity is slightly higher than with 802.11a because fewer pilot carriers are used. Single-channel modulation tops out at 60.75 Mbps, rather than the 54 Mbps in 802.11a. By using all the highest throughput parameters (four 40 MHz spatial streams, with 64-QAM and a 5/6 code), the WWiSE proposal has a maximum throughput of 540 Mbps.

MIMO and transmission modes

Previous 802.11 PHY specifications had fairly simple transmission modes. The WWiSE proposal has 14 transmission modes, depending on 3 items:

- The number of transmit antennas, noted by xTX, where x is the number of transmit antennas. It ranges from 1 to 4, although a single antenna is only supported for 40 MHz channels. All 20 MHz channels must use at least two transmit antennas, though they may have only one spatial stream.
- Whether the frame is used in a greenfield (GF) or mixed mode (MM) environment. Mixed mode transmissions use physical headers that are backwards-compatible with other OFDM PHYs, while greenfield transmissions use a faster physical header.
- The channel bandwidth, which may be 20 MHz or 40 MHz.

Table 15-2 shows the resulting 14 transmission modes. There are several physical layer encodings defined for each of these modes, and they will be discussed in the PLCP section. The number of active antennas is only loosely related to the number of spatial streams. A system operating in the 4TX40MM mode has four transmit antennas, but it may have two or three spatial streams.

Table 15-2. WWiSE transmission modes

	20 MHx channels	40 MHz channels
Greenfield	2TX20GF 3TX20GF 4TX20GF	1TX40GF 2TX40GF 3TX40GF 4TX40GF
Mixed mode	2TX20MM 3TX20MM 4TX20MM	1TX40MM 2TX40MM 3TX40MM 4TX40MM

WWiSE PLCP

The PLCP must operate in two modes. In Greenfield mode, it operates without using backwards-compatible physical headers. Greenfield access is simpler: it can operate without backwards compatibility. As a starting point, consider Figure 15-5; it shows the PLCP encapsulation in the 1TX40GF, 2TX20GF, and 2TX40GF modes.

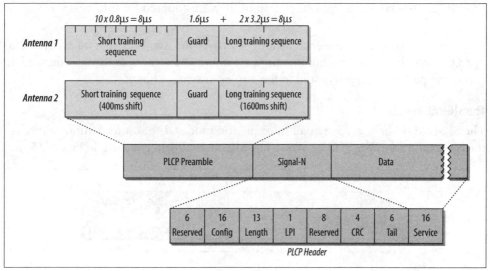

Figure 15-5. Greenfield 1TX40 and 2TX20/2TX40 modes

The fields in the frame are similar in name and purpose to all of the other PLCP frames discussed in this book.

MIMO-OFDM PLCP Preamble
> The preamble consists of well-known bit sequences to help receivers lock on to the signal. Depending on the transmission mode, the preamble may be split into multiple parts. It generally consists of both short and long training sequences. In the WWiSE proposal, the same preamble is transmitted on all the antennas, but with small time shifts relative to the others. Figure 15-5 shows the training sequences used by two-antenna transmission modes. Although the training sequences consist of different bits, the shift is the same. Naturally, the single antenna 40 MHz mode would only have one active antenna transmitting a preamble.

SIGNAL-N
> The SIGNAL-N field contains information that helps to decode the data stream. It is always sent using QPSK, R=1/2, and is not scrambled. It contains information on the number of spatial streams, channel bandwidth, modulation, and coding, and a CRC. More detail on the SIGNAL-N field follows this section.

SERVICE

The SERVICE field is identical to its usage in 802.11a. Unlike the other components of the PLCP header, it is transmitted in the Data field of the physical protocol unit at the data rate of the embedded MAC frame. The first eight bits are set to 0. As with the other physical layers, MAC frames are scrambled before transmission; the first six bits are set to 0 to initialize the scrambler. The remaining nine bits are reserved and must set to 0 until they are adopted for future use.

Data

The final field is a sequence of four microsecond symbols that carry the data. Data bits have six zero tail bits to ramp down the error correcting code, and as many pad bits as are required to have an even symbol block size.

The SIGNAL-N field

The SIGNAL-N field is used in all transmission modes. It has information to recover the bit stream from the data symbols. The SIGNAL-N field is shown in Figure 15-6.

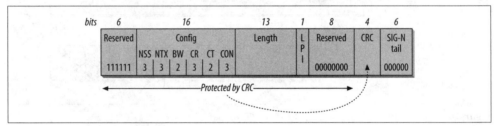

Figure 15-6. WWiSE SIGNAL-N field

CONFIG

Six fields are grouped into the Configuration subfield.

NSS (number of spatial streams)

Three bits are used to indicate how many spatial streams are used. The value is zero-based, so it ranges from zero to three.

NTX (number of transmission antennas)

Three bits are used to indicate how many antennas are used to carry the number of spatial streams. The value is zero-based, so it ranges from zero to three.

BW (bandwidth)

Two bits carry the channel bandwidth. 20 MHz is represented by zero, and 40 MHz is represented by one.

CR (code rate)

Three bits indicate the code rate. 1/2 is zero, 2/3 is one, 3/4 is two, and 5/6 is three.

CT (code type)

Two bits indicate the type of code. Zero is a convolutional code, and one is the optional LDPC.

CON (constellation type)
> Three bits indicate the type of constellation: zero for BPSK, one for QPSK, two for 16-QAM, and three for 64-QAM.

LENGTH
> A 13-bit identifier for the number of bytes in the payload of the physical frame. It ranges from zero to 8,191.

LPI (Last PSDU indicator)
> When multiple physical frames are sent in a burst, the LPI bit is set on the last one to notify other stations that the burst is coming to an end.

CRC
> The CRC is calculated over all the fields except for the CRC and the tail bits.

Tail
> Six bits are used as tail bits to ramp down the convolutional coder.

In the other transfer modes, shown in Figure 15-7, the preamble is split into chunks. In between the chunks, there may be Signal fields. SIGNAL-N fields are defined by the 802.11n proposal and are only decoded by 802.11n stations; the SIGNAL-MM field is used to retain backwards compatibility in a mixed mode with older OFDM stations. It is identical to the Signal field used by 802.11a, and is shown in Figure 13-16.

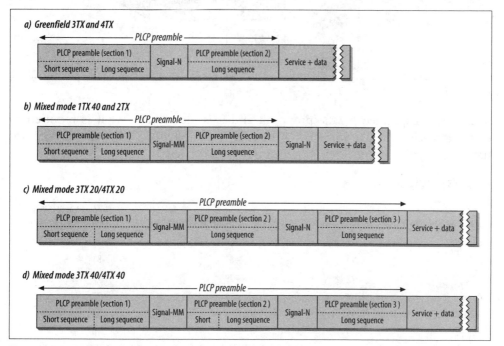

Figure 15-7. PLCP frame format for other transfer modes

WWiSE PMD

Figure 15-8 shows the basic layout of the WWiSE transmitter. It is essentially the same as the 802.11a transceiver, but it has multiple transmit chains. The interleaver is responsible for dividing coded bits among the different transmit chains and spatial streams.

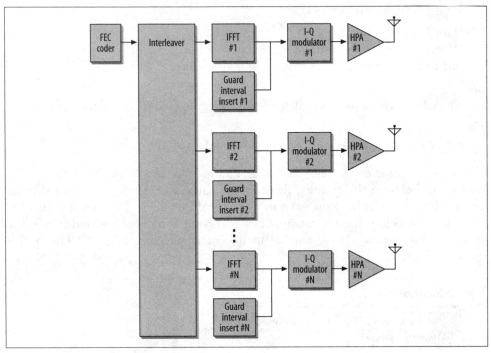

Figure 15-8. WWiSE transceiver

Sensitivity is specified by the proposal, and it is identical to what is required of 802.11a receivers. Table 15-3 shows the required sensitivity. The proposal does not have any adjacent channel rejection requirements.

Table 15-3. WWiSE receiver sensitivity

Constellation	Rate	Sensitivity (dBm)	802.11a Sensitivity (dBm), for reference
BPSK	1/2	−82	−82
BPSK	3/4	−81	−81
QPSK	1/2	−79	−79
QPSK	3/4	−77	−77
16-QAM	1/2	−74	−74
16-QAM	3/4	−70	−70
64-QAM	2/3	−66	−66

Table 15-3. WWiSE receiver sensitivity (continued)

Constellation	Rate	Sensitivity (dBm)	802.11a Sensitivity (dBm), for reference
64-QAM	3/4	−65	−65
64-QAM	5/6	−64	N/A

Characteristics of the WWiSE PHY

Parameters specific to the WWiSE PHY are listed in Table 15-4. Like the other physical layers, it also incorporates a number of parameters to adjust for the delay in various processing stages in the electronics.

Table 15-4. WWiSE MIMO PHY parameters

Parameter	Value	Notes
Maximum MAC frame length	8,191 bytes	
Slot time	9 µs	
SIFS time	16 µs	The SIFS is used to derive the value of the other interframe spaces (DIFS, PIFS, and EIFS).
RIFS time	2 µs	
Contention window size	15 to 1,023 slots	
Preamble duration	16 µs	
PLCP header duration	4 µs	
Receiver sensitivity	-64 to -82 dBm	Depends on speed of data transmission

TGnSync

The TGnSync consortium is composed of a wider array of companies. In addition to the chipmakers that one would expect to find (Atheros, Agere, and Intel, and Qualcomm), TGnSync notably includes manufacturers of other electronic devices. Network equipment manufacturers and even consumer electronics companies are represented. One of the goals of TGnSync is to support new networked devices in the home; promotional materials refer to sending HDTV or DVD video streams across wireless networks. The goal of streaming video probably accounts for some of the emphasis placed on high peak data rates.

TGnSync MAC Enhancements

Although the TGnSync proposal has a higher peak data rate, the group did not completely neglect the development of MAC enhancements to improve efficiency and operation. Efficiency is improved through the development of frame aggregation and bursting, as well as changes to acknowledgment policies. Some protection of older transmissions is performed at the MAC layer. Notably, several MAC enhancements are designed to save battery power, which is likely a reflection of the group's membership.

Channels, radio modes, and coexistence

Although some regulators do not allow them, the TGnSync proposal makes 40 MHz channel support mandatory. If it were adopted without change, a TGnSync chipset would support both 20 MHz and 40 MHz channels, even in regulatory domains that did not allow the latter channel bandwidth. The TGnSync proposal also has MAC features that enable the use of networks with both 20 MHz- and 40 MHz-capable stations. When stations have large amounts of data to transmit, it is possible to negotiate a temporary use of a wider channel before falling back to 20 MHz operation.

MAC operational modes can also be classified based on the types of stations in the network. *Pure mode* networks consist only of 802.11n stations. No protection is necessary to account for older 802.11a and 802.11g stations. Alternatively, TGnSync 802.11n devices may operate in the *legacy mode* just like an 802.11a or 802.11g station. Most operation, though, will be in *mixed mode*, where a TGnSync network must co-exist with a legacy network on the same channel, and may accept associations from older 802.11a or 802.11g stations.

Association requests are handled differently in each mode. Pure mode networks stay pure by ignoring association requests from older stations, and sending Beacon frames with an information element that directs associated stations to use only the new 802.11n transmission modes. Pure mode networks also transmit Beacon frames using the TGnSync high throughput PLCP, which makes them unreadable by legacy devices. Mixed mode access points are visible to legacy devices because they transmit Beacons using the legacy format.

Mixed mode is required to coexist with older devices. (If the experience of 802.11g deployment is any guide, most 802.11n devices are likely to operate in the mixed mode for quite some time.) Mixed mode is a broad classification with several subdivisions. *Mixed capable* networks will allow association from legacy devices, but do not divide time between legacy and high-throughput transmissions. Access points in *managed mixed* networks do actively divide the time between high-throughput transmissions and legacy transmissions. Much like the division between the contention-free period and the contention period (see Chapter 9), an AP operating in managed mixed mode will allow legacy stations their timeslice, while using mechanisms similar to the protection mechanism to reserve some timeslice for MIMO stations only.

Aggregation and bursting

Initial 802.11 stations typically send frames in the order they are received. For throughput purposes, it is highly desirable to reorder frames so that they can coalesce into larger aggregated frames. Aggregation in TGnSync is a MAC-layer function that bundles several MAC frames into a single PLCP frame for transmission.

Figure 15-9 shows the basic format of a single physical-layer frame containing several MAC layer frames. Several MAC frames are put into the same PLCP frame, with an appropriate delimiter between them. The delimiter has a small reserved field, a length field for the following MAC frame, a CRC to protect the delimiter, and a unique pattern to assist in recovering individual frames from the aggregate. MAC frames are put into the aggregate without modification, and contain the full header and MAC CRC. Even if one frame out of an aggregate is lost, it may be possible to successfully receive all the remaining frames.

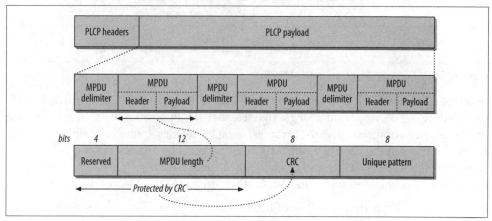

Figure 15-9. TGnSync frame aggregation

Exchanging aggregated frames is only possible once the channel has been configured for it. Figure 15-10 illustrates the process. The sender of an aggregate, called the *initiator*, must send an Initiator Aggregation Control (IAC) frame. IAC frames work much like RTS frames, but have additional fields to assist with channel control. Initiators can request channel measurements, offer different types of coding on the aggregate frame, and accept aggregates in the return direction. Upon receiving the IAC, the destination system, called the *responder*, generates a Responder Aggregation Control (RAC) frame. RAC frames work much like CTS frames: they close the loop by notifying the sender that an aggregate will be accepted, and finishing the parameter negotiation. When aggregate frames are received, an acknowledgment is required. TGnSync defines a new acknowledgment type, the BlockACK, which can be used to acknowledge all the MAC frames contained in an aggregate.

To further improve MAC efficiency, TGnSync defines a MAC header compression algorithm for use in conjunction with aggregate frames. It works in the same manner as Van Jacobsen header compression on serial dial-up lines. Frames between two destinations share most of the fields in the MAC header, most notably the MAC addresses inside the packet. Therefore, a one-byte Header ID (HID) is assigned to a unique set of the three MAC addresses inside a MAC frame. The Header ID can also save the Duration field, since the aggregate will have its own Duration, as well as the two bytes for QoS control. When frames are transmitted between the same sender

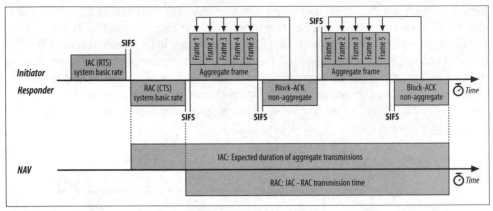

Figure 15-10. TGnSync block acknowledgment

and destination, rather than repeating the same 22 bytes of header information, it is replaced by the corresponding single byte Header ID. Figure 15-11 (a) shows the use of the header compression MAC frames. First, a header frame containing the full header is transmitted, and a header ID is assigned. The header ID can be used to reference the prior full header by sending a single byte to reference previously-transmitted information about the Duration, addressing, and QoS data.

Figure 15-11 (b) illustrates the use of header compression. Five frames for two destinations from the MAC have been aggregated into a single frame for physical transmission. Rather than transmit a complete header on each constituent MAC frame in the aggregate, the system uses header compression. There are two destinations and therefore two unique MAC headers. They are each transmitted and assigned a header ID number. The five data frames following the aggregate each refer to the appropriate header number. A header ID number is unique only within the context of a single aggregate frame. Compared to transmitting full headers on all five frames, the overhead due to MAC framing is cut by more than half.

Header compression is useful when a single aggregate contains multiple frames between the same source and destination pair. However, the benefits of aggregation in TGnSync are not confined to pairs. Single-receiver aggregation is required; an optional extension allows aggregate frames to contain MAC frames for multiple receivers, in which case they are called Multiple Receiver Aggregate (MRA) frames. Inside the single transmitted aggregate frame, there are multiple Initiator Access Control frames. Each IAC specifies an offset to transmit the response to the aggregated frames, which will usually be a block acknowledgment response. To distinguish multiple receiver aggregate frames from single-receiver aggregate frames, multiple-receiver frames start with a control item called the Multiple Receiver Aggregate Descriptor (MRAD). Figure 15-12 shows the operation of multiple-receiver aggregation. The initiator's aggregate frame starts with the aggregate descriptor, and is followed by the aggregated frames for each destination. An IAC frame is used to divide them.

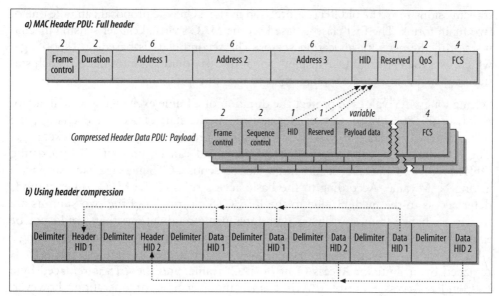

Figure 15-11. TGnSync MAC header compression

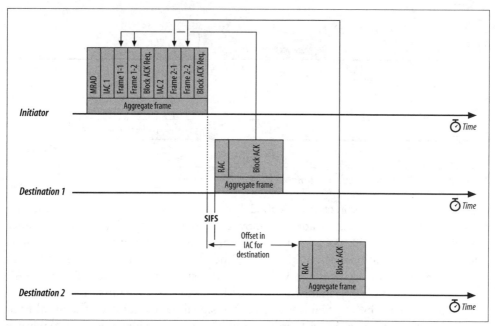

Figure 15-12. TGnSync MRA

Protection

As with all PHYs that have followed existing hardware on to the market, the TGnSync proposal implements protection to avoid having the new PHY step on transmissions from the old PHY. Protection in the TGnSync proposal can take one of two main forms. The first class is based on the MAC's virtual carrier sensing mechanism with the network allocation vector. The second class is based on "spoofing," which uses the existing PLCP header format to carry duration information. Each station may make its own determination as to the appropriate mechanism.

Setting long NAV values to protect the duration of a frame exchange is a small adaptation of the 802.11g protection mechanism. At the start of a frame exchange, the RTS frame will contain a NAV long enough to protect the entire frame exchange. The RTS frame is sent using a "legacy" rate, and can be understood by existing OFDM receivers. In response, the target station sends a CTS message back, also with a long NAV value. According to the basic access rules of the MAC, other stations defer access to the medium due to the RTS/CTS clearing, and the two stations are free to exchange frames at higher data rates using modulations that would not be understood by older stations. LongNAV intervals may be terminated early by using a CF-End frame. When this protection is used for aggregate frames, the RTS is replaced by an Initiator Access Control (IAC) frame, and the CTS is replaced by a Responder Access Control (RAC) frame; the principle of operation, however, remains identical. See Figure 15-13.

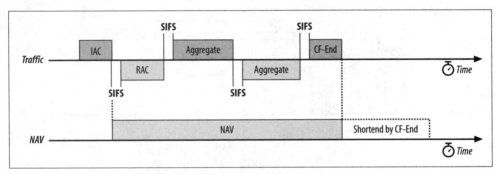

Figure 15-13. TGnSync protection: LongNAV

The second class of protection is called "spoofing," and depends on setting the length field in the PLCP header. TGnSync retains the existing OFDM header described in Chapter 13. Because it is identical to the 802.11a/g format, spoofing is effective with all stations. The OFDM PLCP header contains two numbers that are used by receivers to determine how long the transmission will take. The SIGNAL field, which is shown in Figure 13-16, encodes both the transmission rate for the body and its length in bits. Stations decode the signal field and divide the number of bits by the rate to come up with an approximate transmission time.* To maximize

---

* There are some slight offsets to account for interframe spacing, but the concept remains identical.

the amount of time that can be spoofed, the data rate in the legacy SIGNAL field is always set to the lowest possible value of six Mbps.

In *pairwise spoofing*, two stations will each send an incorrect length and rate so that older stations will be in receiving mode for the duration of the current frame and its next response. Newer TGnSync stations ignore the older SIGNAL field, and use an 802.11n SIGNAL field instead. Figure 15-14 illustrates pairwise spoofing. When Frame 1 is transmitted, pairwise spoofing is used to lengthen the receiving time of the frame through the end of Frame 2. TGnSync stations will interpret the spoofing as a longer NAV, and will therefore act as if the NAV were set for the duration of Frame 2. Naturally, a station within range of the responder will be set to the receiving state; if, however, there is a hidden node, the NAV will protect transmission over Frame 2. 802.11a/g stations will interpret the spoofed time as receiving time, even if they are out of range of the second frame. When Frame 2 is transmitted, it also employs pairwise spoofing to protect Frame 2 and Frame 3.

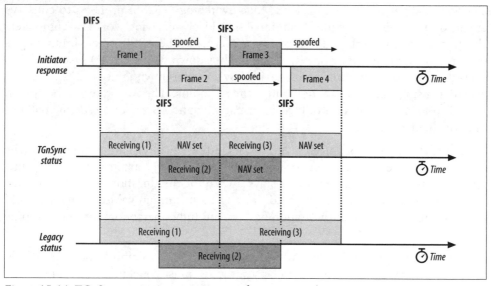

Figure 15-14. TGnSync protection: pairwise spoofing

If a long lock-out period is needed for multiple responses to a single frame, *single-ended spoofing* may also be used. With single-ended spoofing, the first frame in the exchange uses spoofing to protect the entire exchange, allowing all the responses to come in during the protected period. Figure 15-15 illustrates single-ended spoofing with frame aggregation. The first aggregate frame is a multiple-receiver aggregate, allowing responses from two other stations. It sets spoofed duration equal to the time expected for the entire exchange. TGnSync stations will go into receiving mode for the duration of the first frame, and then act as if the NAV were set for the spoofed duration. Legacy devices go into receiving mode for the entire spoofed duration.

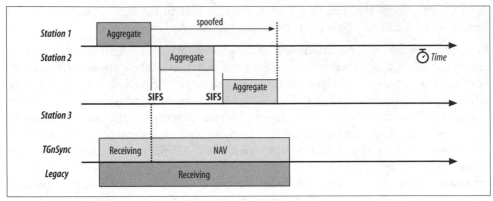

Figure 15-15. TGnSync protection: single-ended spoofing

Powersaving

TGnSync defines the Timed Receive Mode Switching (TRMS) protocol to conserve energy and extend battery life. Traditional 802.11 powersaving works by completely shutting down an interface and requiring buffering at the AP. In single-input/single-output radios, there is only one RF chain to shut down. With MIMO systems, however, there can be significant power savings by shutting down unused RF chains, but retaining a single active chain to monitor the radio link. The two states of the system are called *MIMO enabled* for full receive capability, and *MIMO disabled* when all but one RF chain is shut down.

Stations activate TRMS power saving by including an information element in the association request. The basic parameter in TRMS powersaving is the hold time. After a station transmits a frame, it stays awake for the duration of the hold time. Any transmitted frame resets the hold timer to its maximum value. Setting the hold time to zero indicates that the station will remain fully operational for one slot time before sleeping.

In infrastructure networks, the AP is responsible for maintaining the TRMS hold timer for every station. If the timer elapses, the AP must conclude it has entered the MIMO disabled state, and trigger it to power on sleeping receive chains. In an independent BSS, each station must maintain a hold timer for all the other stations.

The timer is a tunable parameter. If it is set to a larger value, stations will use more power to keep the receiver fully operational. Throughput is likely to be better, but at the cost of some battery life. In some cases, network capacity may not be affected much at all. Networks that use the NAV lengthening procedure for protection must transmit the initial RTS/CTS exchange in single-antenna mode manner compatible with all OFDM stations, and will cause stations to enable MIMO operation without additional frames. Advanced transmission modes may suffer, however, because many of them require multiantenna frame exchanges to become fully operational.

TGnSync PHY Enhancements

To develop a higher peak data rate, the TGnSync proposal depends on technology similar to WWiSE. Frames are divided into spatial streams that can be multiplexed across antennas in a MIMO configuration. More aggressive coding, including a larger constellation, higher convolutional code rate, and a reduced guard interval are present to improve the data rate. Wider channels are also required by TGnSync where supported. Support for 40 MHz channels must be built in to TGnSync-compliant devices, whereas it is optional in WWiSE.

Structure of a channel

Both 20 MHz and 40 MHz channels are divided into 0.3125 MHz subcarriers, just as in 802.11a. The 20 MHz channel is identical to an 802.11a channel, and is shown in Figure 15-16 (a). The 40 MHz channel proposed in TGn Figure 15-16 (b) is a modification of the 20 MHz structure. Two 20 MHz channels are bonded together, and the resulting spectral band is divided into 128 subchannels. The center frequencies of the old 20 MHz channels are located at +/−32. The legacy channels apply a spectral mask from −6 to +6 and roll off the amplitude of transmissions at the end of the bands. With a single continuous channel, however, there is no need to use a spectral mask, and the middle of the band can be used at full strength. Full-strength transmissions in the middle of the band allow for eight new subcarriers. Using a single contiguous 40 MHz block of spectrum reclaims subcarriers that would have otherwise been wasted. Thus, in TGnSync, a 40 MHz channel provides throughput equal to 2.25 times the 20 MHz channel, rather than simply doubling the throughput. To further boost throughput, one of the pilot carriers from the 20 MHz channel is removed, so a 40 MHz channel has 6 pilot carriers instead of 8.

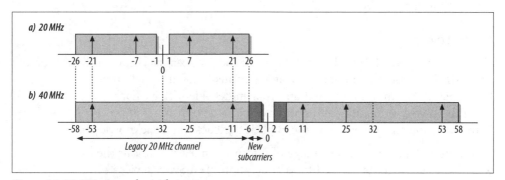

Figure 15-16. TGnSync channel structure

Basic MIMO rates

There are 32 modulation and coding pairs defined by the TGnSync PHY. In the basic MIMO mode, every spatial stream must use an identical modulation technique, so the data rate is simply a multiple of the single spatial stream data rate. Rather than take up a great deal of space in a table, here is a basic formula for the data rates:

Data rate (Mbps) = 12 × channel bandwidth factor × number of spatial streams × coded bits per subcarrier × code rate × guard interval factor

Channel bandwidth factor
20 MHz channels are the baseline, and are assigned a channel bandwidth factor of 1. 40 MHz channels carry more than twice the data, and are assigned a channel bandwidth factor of 2.25.

Number of spatial streams
The number of spatial streams can be equal to 1, 2, 3, or 4. It must be less than or equal to the number of transmission antennas. Support for at least two spatial streams is mandatory.

Coded bits per subcarrier
This is either 6 for 64-QAM, 4 for 16-QAM, 2 for QPSK, or 1 for BPSK.

Code rate
The code rate may be 1/2 when used with BPSK; 1/2 or 3/4 when used with QPSK or 16-QAM; or 2/3, 3/4, or 7/8 when used with 64-QAM.

Guard interval factor
The basic guard interval is 800 ns, and is assigned the factor 1. 400 ns guard intervals increase throughput slightly, and are assigned a factor of 1.11.

In a basic mode with a single spatial stream, channel capacity is identical to 802.11a, with the exception that a 7/8 rate code may be used for a 63 Mbps data rate. By using the highest capacity parameters (four 40 MHz channels, 64-QAM with a 7/8 code rate, and the short guard interval), the TGnSync proposal has a maximum throughput of 630 Mbps.

Transmit modes

There are three MIMO modes that the TGnSync proposal calls for. In the mandatory *basic MIMO* mode, the number of spatial streams is equal to the number of antennas. Each spatial stream is modulated and transmitted identically. Each channel is coded using the same modulation, and sent with the same transmission power. Any changes in transmission rate are based on the implicit feedback of lost acknowledgments.

Two optional modes take advantage of information learned about the radio channel, which is referred to as "closed-loop" operation. TGnSync devices send "sounding" frames to each other to measure the performance of the link. Based on the information gleaned from sounding and calibration, *beamforming* can be used to boost signal quality. Higher signal quality means that a given data rate can be used at longer range. For a given signal-to-noise ratio, a beamformed transmission can carry more data. Beamforming is an optional protocol feature. It is unlikely that most client devices will be unable to send beamformed transmissions. However, client devices must be able to receive beamformed frames to receive the benefits.

In the *basic MIMO with beamforming* mode, every channel must be coded the same way. Before beginning transmission, a sounding exchange is required to calibrate the radio channel. Based on the information from the sounding exchange, the power and coding for the spatial streams is selected. Basic beamforming mode requires that all spatial streams be transmitted at the same power with the same coding. Basic beamforming can be used whenever the number of spatial streams is less than or equal to the number of transmission antennas, but its signal processing advantages are most evident when the number of antennas transmitting a signal is greater than the number of receiving antennas. If the number of spatial streams is less than the number of transmit antennas, a *spatial steering* matrix is used to assign bits to transmission antennas.

An optional *advanced beamforming MIMO (ABF-MIMO) mode* is also defined. It works in a manner similar to the basic beamforming mode, but with the additional capability of using different transmission power on each transmit stream, as well as the possibility of using a different modulation and code on each spatial stream. Like the basic beamforming mode, it requires the gathering of radio status information to calibrate the channel. An optional mode in the advanced beamforming mode allows beamforming to occur in both directions if it is supported in both directions. The advanced beamforming MIMO mode also includes one new constellation: 256-QAM, which transmits 8 coded bits per subcarrier.

To obtain the throughput for the advanced beamforming mode, use the equation in the previous section for each spatial stream, and add the spatial streams together. For 256-QAM, use 8 coded bits per subcarrier. 256-QAM is only used with a rate R=3/4 code rate.

Optional coding

In addition to the convolutional code supported by the original OFDM specification, the TGnSync proposal also includes two optional additional error correction codes. The first technique uses the Reed-Solomon block code, which was developed in 1960. It is widely used in many digital applications, most notably as the error-correction code on CDs and DVDs. The TGnSync proposal combines the Reed-Solomon code with the existing convolutional code in a conventional manner. First, the data stream is encoded with the Reed-Solomon code, and then the output of that encoding process is handed to a convolutional code.* Both codes have complementary properties. Convolutional codes work by spreading errors out over time, and can deal with relatively isolated

---

* The combination of a block encoder followed by a convolutional encoder is especially popular, and has been used extensively by deep-space probes. Galileo, Cassini, the Mars Pathfinder, and the Mars Rover all used Reed-Solomon/convolutional code combinations.

errors; the Reed-Solomon code works well at correcting error bursts. An alternative to the Reed-Solomon/convolutional combination is a low-density parity check (LDPC) code.

Optional short guard interval

To further improve MAC efficiency, the TGnSync proposal allows the use of a short guard interval. In the 802.11a and 802.11g standards as well as the WWiSE proposal, the guard interval is 800 ns. In Chapter 13, it was discussed that that the guard interval should be two to four times the delay spread. An 800 ns guard interval allows a 200 ns delay spread, which is much higher than was observed in many environments. Most offices and homes have a much smaller delay spread, on the order of 50–100 ns. In that case, using a 400 ns guard interval can boost throughput by approximately 10%.

TGnSync Physical Transmission (PLCP and PMD)

The basic frame format of the PLCP in the TGnSync proposal is shown in Figure 15-17. It uses the same header as the existing OFDM, and therefore does not require the use of high-overhead protection to avoid interfering with 802.11a or 802.11g networks. Fields prefaced with "L-" in the figure are legacy fields common to 802.11a and 802.11g; see Chapters 13 and 14 for details.

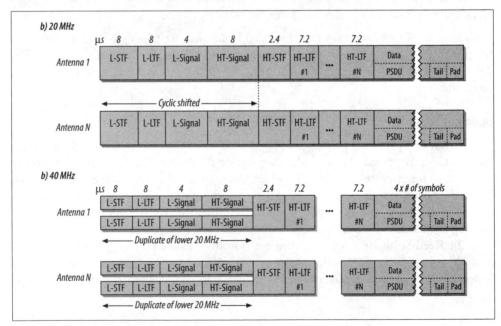

Figure 15-17. TGnSync PLCP frame format

Legacy header

The first three fields in the TGnSync PLCP frame are identical to the 802.11a/g PLCP header.

L-STF (Legacy Short Training Field)
> The legacy short training field is identical to its definition in 802.11a. It lasts eight microseconds.

L-LTF (Legacy Long Training Field)
> The legacy long training field is identical to its definition in 802.11a. It also lasts eight microseconds.

L-SIG (Legacy Signal)
> These three fields are identical to the corresponding fields used by 802.11a and adopted by 802.11g. For details, see Figure 13-16. The L-SIG field is transmitted using BPSK, R=1/2 modulation and coding.

The contents of the L-SIG field is ignored by TGnSync stations. When spoofing protection is employed, the contents of the legacy signal field are not descriptive. TGnSync stations will look in the high-throughput headers following the legacy headers for the actual length and coding rate of the enclosed MAC frame.

To take advantage of the spatial diversity that is the result of having multiple antennas transmitting the same legacy header, TGnSync offers an optional cyclic delay. Each antenna transmits its legacy frame with a slight alteration in its cyclic prefix length, such that the total delay shift is 50 ns.

When 40 MHz channels are used, as in Figure 15-17 (b), the legacy header is transmitted on each 20 MHz subchannel. That is, subcarriers −58 to −6 in the lower 20 MHz subchannel and subcarriers +6 to +58 in the upper 20 MHz subchannel both transmit the older 802.11a-style header.

High Throughput header

Immediately following the legacy preamble is a "high throughput" header specific to the TGnSync proposal. The main component of the high throughput header is the high throughput signal (HT-SIG) field, which is shown in Figure 15-18. The HT-SIG field is used to detect whether a frame carries TGnSync-encoded data at high data rates, or if it is merely a legacy data frame. The HT-SIG field is modulated conservatively, using Q-BPSK, R=1/2 modulation and coding. Q-BPSK uses two data points in its constellation, but they are present on the in the quadrature component. The Q-BPSK constellation is compared to the BPSK constellation in Figure 15-18 (b).

The three-byte high-throughput header is composed of several fields, and is transmitted in the order shown. Least significant bits in each field are transmitted first.

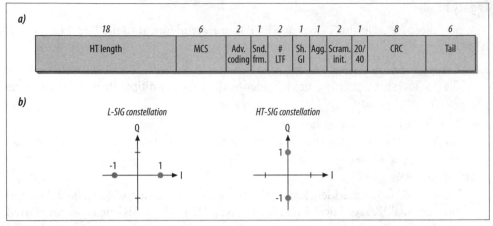

Figure 15-18. TGnSync HT-SIG field

HT-Length (18 bits)

This field is the number of bytes in the payload of the PLCP frame. When aggregation is used, it may be quite large if several full-size MAC frames are included in the payload.

Modulation and Coding Set (MCS) (6 bits)

One of the disadvantages to using MIMO is that there are myriad options when you account for different modulation schemes, differing numbers of spatial streams, and different code rates. The MCS field selects the modulation and coding scheme, along with the number of spatial streams. Values of 0–31 are used for basic MIMO modes, and values of 33–63 are used for advanced MIMO modes.

Advanced Coding (2 bits)

This two-bit field is used to indicate whether the optional advanced coding is used. No advanced coding is indicated by zero. LDPC is indicated by 1. Reed-Solomon coding is indicated by 2. The value 3 is not used.

Sounding packet (1 bit)

Requests and responses used to measure channel performance set this bit. When set, it indicates that every antenna is transmitting its own spatial stream. If it is not set, then the frame should not be used to measure channel information.

Number of HT-LTFs (2 bits)

Following the HT-Signal field are high-throughput training fields. Each spatial stream requires a training field.

Short Guard Interval (1 bit)

When set to one, this bit flag indicates that the short 400 ns guard interval is used on MIMO symbols in the Data field of the frame.

Aggregation (1 bit)
  If this bit is set to one, it indicates that the PLCP frame carries several MAC frames in an aggregate burst.

Scrambler initialization (2 bits)
  These two bits are used to seed the scrambler.

20/40 BW (1 bit)
  If set to one, this bit indicates that a 40 MHz channel is used. When set to zero, it indicates a 20 MHz channel.

CRC (8 bits)
  The CRC is used to protect the legacy signal field, and all the fields in the HT-SIG field before the CRC.

Tail (6 bits)
  The HT-SIG field is protected by a convolutional code, and as always, six bits are needed to ramp down the convolutional coder.

High-Throughput training fields

Following the high-throughput headers are high-throughput short and long training fields. A single short training field spans the entire operating channel. In 20 MHz channels, the bandwidth of the high-throughput short training field (HT-STF) is 20 MHz. When the wider 40 MHz channels are used, the HT-STF has a bandwidth of 40 MHz. The short training field fine-tunes the receivers in MIMO operation.

When several spatial streams are transmitted over several chains, finer control of the amplification applied to the incoming signal is important. Long training fields (HT-LTFs) are used to further tune each receiver chains. One HT-LTF is used for each spatial stream. In basic MIMO mode, there is one receiver chain for each spatial stream; in the advanced mode, there may be more receiver chains than spatial streams.

Data, tail, and padding

Data bits are encoded according to modulation and coding methods that are defined by the high-throughput header. Like other OFDM physical layers, data is scrambled before transmission, using the scrambler initialization bits in the high-throughput header. Following the data, there is a six-bit tail that ramps down the convolutional code, and enough padding bits to make the data to be transmitted equal to the symbol block size.

TGnSync PMD

The basic design of a TGnSync transceiver is shown in Figure 15-19, which depicts the design of a beamforming transmitter, rather than a basic MIMO transmitter. An incoming scrambled frame is handed to the forward-error correction coder, which is usually a convolutional coder. Coded bits from the FEC coder are then sent to different spatial streams by the spatial parser, which is responsible for dividing the unified bit stream into subsidiary streams for transmission. Each spatial stream is punctured up to the desired rate. In the beamforming mode, the puncturing occurs for each spatial stream and may occur at different rates. Basic transmitters must puncture every stream to the same rate. (Logically, the puncturing in the basic MIMO transmitter can occur before the spatial parser.) Each spatial stream now consists of a sequence of coded bits, ready for mapping on to OFDM carriers by the interleaver. After the interleaver, each block of bits can be mapped on to a single symbol by the constellation mapper. In the basic MIMO mode, each interleaved spatial stream is processed by a single transmission chain; the advanced mode uses a spatial steering matrix to assign symbols to any transmit chain. The spatial steering matrix shown in the figure could be replaced by a one-to-one interface between the spatial stream processors and the transmit antennas for basic MIMO operation. Each transmit chain takes its symbol sequence and modulates it on to the airwaves. There is no mention in the specification of required channel rejection or sensitivity performance.

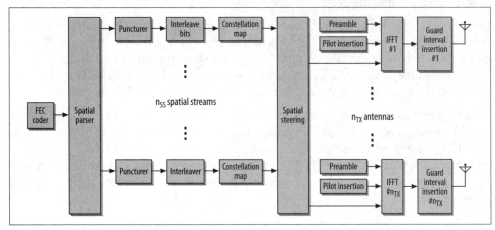

Figure 15-19. 2x2 TGnSync MIMO transceiver

Comparison and Conclusions

Both proposals are essentially MIMO evolutions of the 802.11a PHY. Both require support for a 2x2 mode, where both the sender and receiver have two transceivers active. However, it is likely that most products that are based on the eventual 802.11n standard (which may or may not resemble either of the proposals) will support at least some of the optional modes. It is likely that cost constraints on client devices will restrict them to operating in a two-transceiver mode, while APs will have more transceivers. Basic APs may have only two, while the most expensive enterprise-class APs have three or four transceivers.

Table 15-5 shows the data rates for the two spatial stream modes for each proposal. Higher data rates are possible with additional spatial streams, albeit at the extra cost of silicon. TGnSync's proposed peak rates are higher, although at the cost of more aggressive coding. WWiSE's 135 Mbps data rate is accomplished by using 64-QAM at R=5/6; TGnSync gets to 140 Mbps by using a 7/8 rate code and cutting the guard interval to half. (Without the short guard interval, TGnSync's data rate is only 126 Mbps.) The advanced beamforming mode uses the much larger 256-QAM constellation. Though TGnSync's data rates are higher, I expect that the more aggressive coding will lead to shorter range.

Table 15-5. Top speed for major 802.11n proposals (two spatial streams)

	20MHz channels	40 MHz channels
WWISE	135 Mbps	270 Mbps
TGnSync		
Basic mode	140 Mbps (+3.7%)	315 Mbps (+16.7%)
Advanced beamforming mode	160 Mbps (+18.5%)	360 Mbps (+33.3%)

Spectral usage is a major point of contention between the two groups. WWiSE has focused much more heavily on improving MAC efficiency than on the data rate, even going so far as to argue that using 40 MHz channels to improve the data rate before improving efficiency is a waste of scarce unlicensed spectrum. While there may be merit to that point, the 40 MHz channelization approach used by TGnSync has the advantage of being able to reclaim spectrum in the middle of a wider channel. WWiSE merely doubles throughput in their 40 MHz mode, while TGnSync squeezes more than double the capacity out of the wider channel. Both approaches have their drawbacks. TGnSync's proposal would probably lead to chipsets that are always capable of 40 MHz operation, adding extra cost and complexity, even though regulators may not allow them. In countries where 40 MHz channels are allowed, the extra speed would be welcome. In areas where 40 MHz channels are only a pipe dream of chipset manufacturers, the extra cost may not be welcome. On the other hand, WWiSE's denial of the need for high-speed channels seems to be denying the five-fold leap in data rates that occurs with every new 802.11 PHY.

For maximum speed, TGnSync requires closed-loop operation, which would be a major undertaking to implement in silicon. Sounding frames must be used to measure the channel, and responses must be collected to calibrate the radio channel. WWiSE uses only open loop operation, which is simpler to implement. The WWiSE proposal also offers the ability to spread a single encoded stream across multiple antennas without using closed-loop operation. If closed-loop operation were to be problematic to implement in silicon, 802.11n could be delayed unacceptably.

Frame aggregation is an important part of meeting the larger goal set for the eventual 802.11n standard. However, taking full advantage of aggregation opportunities requires more intelligent queuing than is currently implemented. Whether 802.11n offers a huge increase in speed is likely to depend a great deal on how well improved queuing algorithms are able to coalesce collections of small packets into large aggregates. Neither proposal specifies queueing, so the performance boost may vary between vendors.

Aggregation as designed by the protocol is a bit more intelligent in TGnSync, although this is only a minor advantage. WWiSE's proposal only allows aggregation when the Address 1 field in the MAC header is the same. In an infrastructure network, the Address 1 field is the BSSID. All frames from a station to an AP can be aggregated, so the two proposals are identical in the upstream direction. In the downstream direction, WWiSE must use a physical-layer frame burst to change directions. Each new direction must have a new PLCP header. TGnSync can reduce overhead by using a multiple-receiver aggregate frame, and collecting responses from each receiver in the aggregate.

Powersaving modes in 802.11 have been neglected, and are not very sophisticated. TGnSync attempts to come up with extended powersaving operations for some of the new MAC structures, while WWiSE does not. This is likely due to the presence of equipment vendors that use chips in the TGnSync consortium, while WWiSE is comprised only of chip vendors. While the trade-off between high speed and battery life is application-specific and may not always make sense, it is always good to see the standards bodies thinking ahead about problems that may occur.

## CHAPTER 16

802.11 Hardware

When writing a specification, it is important to leave some room for interpretation to allow innovation. A standard which is too rigid will drain the life out of implementation, while a standard that is too loose does not foster interoperability. This chapter is about what the standard does not exactly specify. How does hardware implement the standard? Where does the standard allow discretion in protocol implementation, and what does that mean for the administrator?

General Structure of an 802.11 Interface

Figure 16-1 shows a block diagram of a generic wireless LAN interface. It is not representative of any particular manufacturer's product, but is intended to serve as a general guide to the discussion of how cards are put together. Cards must implement the physical interface and the link-layer control expected by the operating system.

Like any other system based on radio technology, wireless LAN interfaces have antennas. Most 802.11 interfaces have two antennas for *antenna diversity* to improve reception in the presence of multipath interference. When a radio signal is received, the radio system selects the antenna with the strongest signal, and runs with it. Antenna diversity alleviates multipath because one of the two antennas should receive a signal if the weak signal is caused by self-interference of multiple signals. Diversity cannot help if the signal weakness is caused by distance because both antennas will receive equally weak signals. Many types of diversity are possible, but by far the most common implementation is to perform diversity reception on received frames only. Most, if not all, products on the market do not have any diversity for transmitted frames, and will always use a "primary" antenna for transmissions.

Early antenna diversity implementations were helpful, but limited by lack of sophistication. Multiple-input/multiple-output (MIMO) technology promises higher data rates and better performance. Detailed descriptions of MIMO are beyond this book. In essence, it improves the receiver's performance by using both antennas rather than choosing one exclusively.

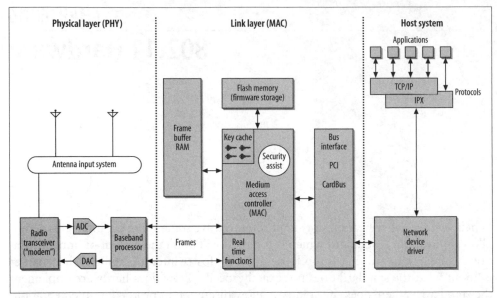

Figure 16-1. Generic wireless card structure

Antennas deliver the radio signal to a *transceiver*. The transceiver is sometimes called a radio "modem" by analogy with the modems commonly used for telecommunications. Transceivers will use amplifiers to boost the outgoing signal for distance, or the incoming signal for further processing. Radio transceivers also downconvert the high-frequency signals into much more manageable signals by extracting the data bits from the high-frequency carrier waves. Transceiver systems are usually shielded to prevent the high frequencies in use from interfering with other system components, which is why radio interfaces typically have a metal shield covering a good chunk of the interface card's area.

After the transceiver, the next step in the chain is the *baseband processor*, which is the interface between the digital and analog parts of the wireless LAN system. Bits come from the computer, and are turned into radio waves for the antennas. Turning bits into radio waves is called *modulation*; the reverse process is called *demodulation*. The baseband processor is responsible for handling the complex spread-spectrum modulations, as well as physical carrier sensing. Generally speaking, physical carrier sensing is integrated with demodulation. When radio energy is received in excess of a threshold, the baseband processor attempts to demodulate it. Many different modulation techniques exist for use with wireless LANs. One of the reasons why older 802.11b stations are blind to the existence of 802.11g transmissions is that the older baseband processors used in 802.11b stations are not capable of demodulating OFDM transmissions.

At the heart of the interface is the *medium access controller* (MAC), which is responsible for taking incoming frames from the host operating system's network stack and deciding when to squirt the frames out the antenna into the air. The MAC accepts frames from the operating system for delivery through a system bus interface. Most wireless LAN interfaces are based on the CardBus standard; some interfaces use Mini-PCI. On the other side of the MAC, it ties into the baseband processor to send frames to the radio system.

MACs may work with several frames at once, and can use a small RAM buffer to store frames being worked on. One of the most common reasons to work on a frame is to offload security functions from the host operating system. Rather than requiring frames to have been encrypted by the main system CPU before transmission, a MAC with security functions can accept frames from the driver that are to be encrypted with a specified key. Frequently, such MACs implement a *key cache*, which can store multiple keys. Drivers queue frames with a notation to encrypt with key 1 before transmission, and the MAC offloads the encryption from the host system. Older MAC chips could perform RC4 encryption offload for WEP and could be retrofitted for TKIP, while the newest MAC chips are able to perform AES encryption in hardware.

In addition to the RAM buffer for frames in process, most interfaces also have a small flash memory to store firmware for the MAC. When the MAC is powered up, it retrieves and runs code from flash. To implement a new security protocol like TKIP, put new firmware in the flash and reboot the MAC. Firmware allows the use of relatively generic processors rather than hard-to-change application-specific integrated circuits (ASICs), which is a great help when working with protocols like 802.11 that may change quickly. Most 802.11 MAC chips are actually fairly generic microprocessors.

Some MACs implement a "real-time" section of the 802.11 MAC for items that require immediate response. Rather than requiring the host operating system to respond to power-save polling operations or send acknowledgments, these frames are often automatically generated by the MAC. In other systems, the real-time functions are handled by the baseband processor. (Most modern systems implement both the MAC and baseband in a single chip, so the distinction is no longer of burning relevance.)

The block diagram of Figure 16-1 is a general guide only. To reduce cost and complexity, many systems use a single chip for both the MAC and the baseband processor. Some solutions even implement the radio transceiver on the same chip as the MAC and baseband controller. Interfaces based on Atheros chipsets do not have flash memory for firmware because Atheros chips are given code when the MAC is started by the driver. Firmware generally refers to code stored with the hardware; Atheros devices can be programmed by system software.

Software-Defined Radios: A Digression

Two significant problems with 802.11 are the inefficiency of the MAC, which limits throughput, and the rapid change in physical layer technology, which makes devices obsolete quickly. A natural reaction to the inefficiency, especially from technically adept engineers, is to want to implement specific optimizations or new protocol features on the hardware they already own.

With wireless LANs, customizing the behavior of the interface is generally not possible. The baseband processor, or the functions of the baseband processor, are implemented directly in the integrated circuit for speed, and cannot be changed. So-called application specific integrated circuits (ASICs) have particular logic laid out in their circuitry, and cannot be used for anything other than what they were designed for. Furthermore, wireless LAN interfaces use radio components optimized to run with the frequencies allocated to wireless LAN usage by regulators.

However, future radios may be reprogrammable. Instead of using dedicated hardware for the baseband processor, designers can use "programmable logic" devices, such as Field Programmable Gate Arrays (FPGAs). Radio waves are analog waves that carry digital data. In many cases, radios only need programmable signal processing, and can use digital signal processor (DSP) chips. No matter what type of programmable logic is used, the end goal is the same. Rather than having a modulation fixed in place during the design phase, radios based on programmable logic can change modulation, coding, and bit rate on the fly with new software. The price of the flexibility is that programmable logic devices are bigger, run slower, and consume more power (and therefore generate more heat) than nonprogrammable devices.* By using programmable devices, the behavior of the radio can be changed at will, simply by loading new software. New modulation types, bit rates, or even new frequency bands can be implemented without changing hardware.†

Radio interfaces controlled completely by software (or programmable logic) are called *software-defined radios* or *universal radios*. In environments where the modulation and coding change rapidly or frequently, they are extremely useful. One of the first major software-defined radios was the SPEAKEasy project, launched by the U.S. military to replace 10 radio systems using different modulations with a single software radio that could perform the same work as all 10 radio systems, but in a much smaller package. Software-defined radios are subject to certification rules in the United States that couple the radio software with the hardware, and require manufacturers to take steps to avoid alteration of the software to operate outside the approved range.‡

---

* Programmable logic devices are often used in the design of application-specific devices. After the logic is designed and thoroughly tested, the FPGA will be redesigned as an application-specific device. The resulting fixed-logic device is sometimes called a "hard copy" of its programmable ancestor.

† It's intereting to note that the open source process has started to adopt programmable logic. OpenCores (*http://www.opencores.org*) is the repository of hardware designs in the same pattern that SourceForge (*http://www.sourceforge.net*) is for software.

‡ The FCC rules regarding the certification of software-defined radios are in Appendix B of FCC 01-264, which is available at *http://www.fcc.gov/Bureaus/Engineering_Technology/Orders/2001/fcc01264.pdf*. The first software-defined radio, a GSM base station developed by Vanu, was certified in November 2004.

Although software defined radios are an interesting development worth watching, the full programmability will probably not be implemented in 802.11 devices. (Limited programmability is used by both Broadcom and Atheros in their current chipsets.) Programmable logic is much more expensive, and would price the resulting 802.11 devices out of the market. It may find a foothold for use with 802.11 in a radio that implements several types of radio link, of which 802.11 is one.

A Few Words on 802.11 Hardware Implementations

At the time this book was written, there were four major chipsets used to build 802.11 vendors. In alphabetical order, the established vendors are:

Atheros
> Most interfaces that include 802.11a are based on Atheros chipsets. Many 802.11g devices are based on Atheros chipsets as well.

Broadcom
> Most of the non-Centrino built-in 802.11g interfaces available at the time this book was written were based on the Broadcom 802.11g chipset. Apple's AirPort Extreme is based on Broadcom silicon.

Conexant (Prism)
> The Prism chipset line went through several corporate transitions before it wound up at Conexant.

Intel (Centrino)
> Many built-in wireless LAN interfaces in laptops are based on Intel's "Centrino" brand. Technically, Centrino is a marketing term that refers to a whole set of Intel silicon, including the system CPU. For example, the Intel/PRO 2200 card is the the Centrino 802.11g interface.

One of the more notable new chipset vendors is Airgo Networks, which is building a MIMO chipset that underlies prestandard 802.11n products on the market.

It is often useful to know the chipset vendor behind the card. Most of the chipset vendors make *reference designs* available to their customers. Reference designs typically include both hardware and software. 802.11 card vendors can take a reference design, modify it slightly (or not at all), arrange for a new label to be put on the manufactured device, and start selling it. Very few card vendors make significant enhancements to the driver, and will simply repackage reference drivers. Naturally, the track record of different vendors varies. Some make updated drivers available quickly, others may not. Knowing who supplied the chipset in the card can make it easier to obtain either the reference driver, or a more recent driver for another similar card using the same chipset. Naturally, knowing the chipset is vital for picking out the correct driver for open souce operating systems.

Learning more about cards: FCC filings

802.11 interfaces are, in the language of regulatory agencies, *intentional radiators*. Rather than simply complying with a standard that limits the amount of radio frequency energy given off, 802.11 interfaces are designed to spew radio waves into the air. Intentional radiators are tested for compliance with every country's regulatory requirements, which generates a great deal of paperwork.

In the United States, radio devices are regulated by the Federal Communications Commission (FCC), and radio transmission devices are tested for compliance with FCC rules. Before a device can legally be sold, it must be assigned an identification number. Take a look at your favorite card and look for the FCC ID.

An FCC ID is composed of two parts: the *grantee code*, which is the first three letters, and the product code, which may be up to 14 letters and numbers. Grantee codes are unique to an organization. (The grantee code may be separated by a space, dash, or not at all.) For example, the FCC ID for a Lucent Gold card is IMR-WLPCE24H. IMR is Lucent's grantee code, while WLPCE24H is specific to the Gold card.

As part of the testing process, manufacturers must submit test reports, product photographs, and other documentation, which becomes part of the public record. To look up information on your favorite card, go to the search engine maintained by the FCC's Office of Engineering Technology at *http://www.fcc.gov/oet/fccid/*.

FCC identifiers can be useful if you are trying to figure out what driver to use with a particular card. Most products have internal photographs available, which may enable you to determine whose chipset is in use. Say, for example, you had a Proxim Gold a/b/g combo card and wanted to know what chipset it used. By searching the FCC database on its ID (HZB-8460), you could obtain internal photographs of the device, which clearly show the presence of Atheros chips on the system board.

Implementation-Specific Behavior

802.11 is not a rigorous standard. Several components of the standard are relatively loose and leave a great deal up to the particular implementation. Most implementations are also relatively young, and may behave in a nondeterministic fashion. I have participated in tests that made use of several identical computers, all imaged from the same software distribution and using the exact same wireles LAN hardware and driver revision. Even though there were several computers in the same location with identical configuration, behavior was significantly different.

Rebooting Interface Cards

802.11 is a complex protocol with many options, and running the newest protocols exposes the newest bugs. 802.11 interfaces use relatively general-purpose microprocessors running software. As with a great deal of software, cards that are in a strange state may be helped by "rebooting" to clear any protocol state stored in the MAC processor. External cards can be rebooted by removing and re-inserting them; internal cards must be rebooted by power cycling them through the system software. It is not sufficient to unload and reload drivers, since the object is to clear all state in the wireless LAN interface.

Restarting a card may be required to clear state that is preventing successful operation. As a first step, restart the card when:

- The client system is associated, but cannot send or receive traffic. If the network is encrypted, the problem is often a lack of synchronization of cryptographic keys. This problem is often exacerbated by roaming because every change between APs results in the transmission of new keys.

- No scan list can be built. If you are sure that there is a network within range but it will not show up in the client utility, the card may be in a state where it is unable to supply a scan list.

- Authentication/association failures occur in rapid succession. If the state of the client system software prevents a successful connection but the network is on a "preferred" list for connection, the attempt will be retried.

Scanning and Roaming

Every card behaves differently when searching for a network to attach to, and in how it decides to move between APs. 802.11 places no constraints on how a client device makes its decision on how to move between APs, and does not allow for any straightforward way for the AP to influence the decision. Most client systems use signal strength or quality as the primary metric, and will attempt to communicate with the strongest AP signal.

Most cards monitor the signal-to-noise ratio of received frames, as well as the data rate in use, to determine when to roam to a new AP. When the signal-to-noise ratio is low at a slow data rate, the client system begins to look for another AP. Many clients put off moving as long as possible, in part because the process of looking for a new AP requires tuning to other channels and may interrupt communications in process. Client stickiness is sometimes referred to as the *bug light* syndrome. Once a client has attached to an AP, it hangs on for dear life, like a bug drawn to a bug zapper. Even if the client moves a great distance from the AP with a consequent drop in signal strength, most clients do not begin the roaming process until the signal is almost lost.

Roaming in 802.11 is entirely driven by client decisions. Where to send the Association Request frames is entirely in the hands of the client system's driver and firmware, and is not constrained by the 802.11 specification in any way. It would be 802.11-compliant, though awful, to connect to the AP with the weakest signal! (An unfortunate corollary is that driver updates to fix bugs may alter the roaming behavior of client systems in undesirable ways.) Access points do not have protocol operations that can influence where clients attach to, and whether they will move or not. Implementing better roaming technology is a major task for 802.11 as time-critical streaming applications begin to use 802.11.

 To borrow a phrase from Milton Friedman, roaming is always and everywhere a client phenomenon.

Rate Selection

802.11 lays out basic ground rules for how multirate support needs to work, but it leaves the rate selection algorithm up to the software running on the interface. Generally speaking, an interface tries to transmit at higher speeds several times before downgrading to lower speeds. Part of that is simply common sense. In the time it takes to transmit a frame with a 1,500-byte payload at 1 Mbps, it would be possible to transmit the same frame 8 times at 11 Mbps, or over 20 times on an 802.11g network running at 54 Mbps with protection enabled. (Without protection, the multiplier is 40!) If the frame was corrupted by a one-time event, it makes sense to retry a few times before accepting the more drastic penalty of lowering the data rate.

Step-down algorithms are generally similar. After trying some number of times to transmit a frame, it falls to a lower data rate. Most cards step down one rate at a time until an acknowledgment is received, though there is no requirement for them to do so. It would be a valid rate selection algorithm to slow down to the minimum data rate at the first sign of trouble. Step-up algorithms work the same way in reverse. When "several" frames are received with a much higher signal-to-noise ratio than is required for the current rate, the interface may consider stepping up to the next highest rate.

Reading the Specification Sheet

Early testing of 802.11 devices focused on range and throughput because there was little else that could be tested. In some environments, range may be an important factor, and one that can be determined in part by reading the specification sheet for a card.

Range is largely a function of receiver sensitivity, which is a measurement of the weakest signal that a receiver can correctly translate into data. Better sensitivity measurements result in improved range. (Improving sensitivity can also help other performance factors, too, but range is the easiest one to discuss.) Most vendors have focused on improving performance, and the resulting improvements (Atheros' XR, and Broadcom's BroadRange) have been announced with great fanfare.

Not all vendors publish complete specification sheets. Cisco discloses a great deal of information, with receiver sensitivities disclosed at each data rate in all frequency bands supported. (The card's 5 GHz performance has a slight dependence on the frequency.) Many vendors simply report the supported data rates without any indication of sensitivity.

Sensitivity Comparison

As an example, compare the sensitivity of some common 802.11b cards. Sensitivity is defined by each 802.11 PHY. For the direct sequence rates, it is defined as the received power at which the input frame error rate is 8%, for 1024 byte frames. The standards require that the sensitivity be −76 dBm or better for 11 Mbps, and −80 dBm for 2 Mbps.* Lower sensitivity is better because it means the card can receive weaker signals than required.

The sensitivities reported in Table 16-1 were taken from data sheets and user manuals for four well-known 802.11b cards and a new a/b/g card. The Cisco Aironet 350 had a reputation for pulling in weak signals well, which is entirely justified by the data. At 11 Mbps, it was sensitive to a signal half as strong as the Orinoco Gold card, and nearly a quarter of the signal required by the Microsoft card. However, the march of technology has improved sensitivities at higher bit rates. All the older-generation cards are less sensitive than the Atheros-based Cisco tri-mode card currently on the market.

Table 16-1. Sensitivity (in dBm) for various cards

Card	11 Mbps	5.5 Mbps	2 Mbps	1 Mbps
Cisco 350	−85	−89	−91	−94
Orinoco Gold (Hermes)	−82	−87	−91	−94
Linksys WPC11 (Prism)	−82	−85	−89	−91
Microsoft MN-520	−80	−83	−83	−83
Cisco CB-21 (a/b/g); 802.11b performance only	−90	−92	−93	−94

Delay Spread

When radio waves bounce off objects, several echos of the wave will converge on the receiver. The difference between the first wave's arrival and the last arrival is the *delay spread*. Receivers can pick through the noise to find the signal, but only if

---

* This corresponds roughly to a bit error rate of .001% (10^{-5}).

the delay spread is not excessive. Some vendors also quote the maximum delay spread on their data sheets. Table 16-2 reports the delay spread for three of the cards listed above.

Table 16-2. Delay spread (in ns) for various cards

Card	11 Mbps	5.5 Mbps	2 Mbps	1 Mbps
Cisco 350	140	300	400	500
Orinoco Gold (Hermes)	65	225	400	500
Cisco CB-21 (a/b/g); 802.11b performance only	130	200	300	350

Cards rated for higher delay spreads are capable of dealing with worse multipath interference. Again, the Cisco Aironet 350 was an extremely capable card for its day, capable of dealing with over twice the time-smearing as the Hermes-based card.

## CHAPTER 17

Using 802.11 on Windows

Whether you've made it to this point by skipping Chapters 3–16, or whether you've read all the theory, we're now going to get our hands dirty and start installing equipment.

Development of 802.11 management interfaces has followed the familiar progression of Windows applications. In the beginning, there was a great deal of variation between individual vendors. As popularity grew, Microsoft integrated 802.11 configuration into the operating system, subsuming vendor-specific management tools into an overall framework.

From the standpoint of practical system and network administration, working with 802.11 is similar to working with Ethernet. Installing 802.11 drivers is nearly identical to installing Ethernet drivers, and the network interfaces behave almost exactly like Ethernet interfaces. 802.11 interfaces cause an ARP cache to be brought into existence, and other software may even perceive the wireless interface as an Ethernet interface. Unlike many Ethernet drivers, however, 802.11 drivers can have a number of advanced knobs and features that reflect the additional management features presented in Chapter 8.

This chapter discusses Windows configuration of wireless cards on both Windows XP and Windows 2000. I strongly advise using Windows XP for wireless-enabled machines because it is generally easier to use and has substantial additional support for new protocols. Third-party supplicants generally disable the built-in supplicant. Occasionally, however, a driver will refuse to work with a security system other than Microsoft security stack.

Windows XP

Windows XP continues the long-time Windows practice of incorporating functionality that was previously only supplied by third parties into the operating system itself. Rather than relying on each 802.11 card manufacturer to supply a configuration utility, Microsoft has built a standard configuration utility, called Windows Zero Configuration (also called ZeroConfig, ZeroConf, or WZC), which works with most cards. Card manufacturers must still provide driver software, but the configuration can be handled through Windows screens rather than card-specific programs. This section discusses ZeroConfig because it presents a card-independent view of configuration, which makes it popular with network administrators and help desks.

Card Installation

Before starting the process, it generally pays to get the latest drivers for your card from the manufacturer's web site. Other network technologies are far more mature than 802.11, and do not require frequent driver updates. Unfortunately, rapid innovation in wireless is accompanied by rapid driver changes.

For major vendors, this is usually found in a "support" or "downloads" section. Many smaller vendors are rebadging reference designs, and may not have drivers available. In such cases, it is often possible to use the reference driver from the chipset vendor.

Many drivers ship with an installer, which I generally prefer not to run. Several cards have licensed third-party 802.1X stacks, which can interfere with the operation of ZeroConf. It is usually best to obtain the latest drivers from the card vendor's web site before installing the card.

Third-party 802.1X stacks and the driver update process

Several third-party 802.1X stacks exist. On Windows, they are generally implemented as a shim in the network stack that intercepts EAPOL frames between the hardware and the network protocol. Many card vendors, frustrated with the progress of the built-in Microsoft supplicant, have turned to third-party stacks to enable 802.1X. Many third-party stacks are incompatible with ZeroConfig. Rather than use the ZeroConfig screens to set parameters, third-party stacks often require an additional software configuration tool. They may also require additional supplicant software to support advanced protocols.

To avoid using the bundled 802.1X stack, update the driver without running the installer from the vendor. The best practice is to get the driver from the vendor web site, unzip it, and then use the update driver panel of the device manager to roll the new version of the driver into your operating system configuration. Figure 17-1 illustrates how to upgrade only the driver. By going to the Driver tab of the hardware properties, you can access the Update Driver button.

Two tricks may be used to avoid installing the third-party 802.1X stacks. Many executable driver installation files are self-extracting ZIP packages, and can be opened by an *unzip* program. Extract the drivers to a temporary location, and update from a

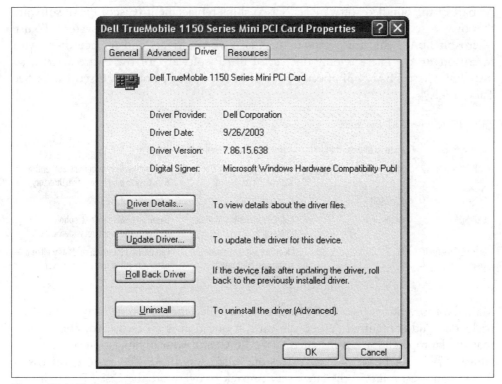

Figure 17-1. Updating the driver without the baggage

file. An alternative is to run the software installer, and immediately run the uninstaller. Most uninstallers will remove configuration tools and third-party shims while leaving the new driver in place.

Cisco client software

Cisco cards have one additional pitfall. Protected EAP (PEAP) is still a developing standard. Although written by representatives from both Cisco and Microsoft, the two companies' implementations are not compatible. Most of the industry has shipped PEAP implementations that will autodetect which version is in use.* Even Cisco's authentication server, CiscoSecure ACS, has a configuration option to be compatible with the Microsoft PEAP implementation.

Microsoft's PEAP implementation supports the use of EAP-MS-CHAP-V2 and EAP-TLS as inner authentication protocols; Cisco's PEAP implementation supports EAP-SIM and EAP-GTC. Most Windows shops will be seeking to use an existing user database, such as an Active Directory, which is possible only with EAP-MS-CHAP-V2.

---

* Both the Funk and Meetinghouse clients do this, as does the Radiator RADIUS server.

As part of the bundled software set, Cisco ships replacement (Cisco) PEAP software that overwrites the standard (Microsoft) PEAP implementation on the system. To use Microsoft PEAP, you must remove the Cisco PEAP drivers and replace them with Microsoft PEAP. There is only one set of PEAP software for the entire system, so installing Cisco PEAP will affect all cards on the system, not just Cisco cards. See Table 17-1.

Table 17-1. Inner EAP methods

EAP method	Cisco or Microsoft PEAP?	Authentication credentials	Notes
EAP-MS-CHAP-V2	Microsoft	Shared password (or MD4 hash of the password)	Used with Windows domain authentication; easy to plug in to Active Directory
EAP-TLS	Microsoft	User certificate	Generally not used
EAP-SIM	Cisco	Subscriber Identity Module (SIM) card	Based on GSM mobile telephone authentication; not yet widely used
EAP-GTC (Generic Token Card)	Cisco	Cleartext authentication string passed through encrypted tunnels	Can be used for token cards as well as a generic method for static passwords

Many laptop vendors offer 802.11 cards preinstalled into the system, with software preloaded and configured. When the card in question is a Cisco card, chances are that the laptop vendor has installed Cisco PEAP and your organization will need to adjust its system build process to restore Microsoft PEAP. To restore Microsoft PEAP, you must reinstall the latest service pack to overwrite the Cisco PEAP drivers with the Microsoft PEAP drivers.

Choosing a Network

When Windows starts up, the ZeroConfig system will attempt to find any networks in the area. ZeroConfig may automatically connect to networks which it already has a configuration for. If no networks have yet been configured, the wireless interface will produce the bubble shown in Figure 17-2.

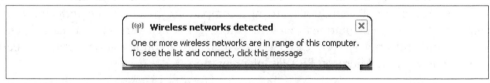

Figure 17-2. Prompt that WLANs are in the neighborhood

By clicking on the box, or by right clicking on the wireless interface and choosing "View Available Wireless Networks", you can get to the list of detected networks (Figure 17-3). By choosing to Connect to any one of them, Windows will attempt to automatically configure the appropriate settings. However, it has no way of selecting

the appropriate EAP method, and therefore is often unable to automatically configure encrypted networks. Attaching to an unencrypted network is easy, but you will
be prompted to confirm connecting to a network that provides no security.

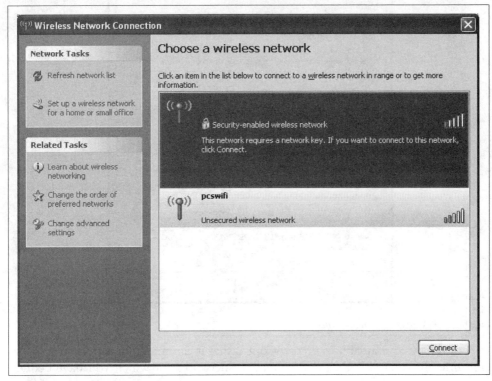

Figure 17-3. Viewing available wireless LANs

Configuring Security Parameters and 802.1X

In many cases, it is necessary to manually configure the security properties of a network. Windows can automatically default settings for encryption and authentication
type, but may still be wrong. 802.1X settings are always defaulted to using EAP-TLS,
even though EAP-TLS is not commonly used. To change security parameters, go to
"Change Advanced Setttings" to get the interface properties, and hit the Wireless
Networks tab (Figure 17-4).

To add a network, you can select it from the Preferred Networks pane and choose
Properties, or you may add it manually by specifying a network name, as in
Figure 17-5. If you are manually adding a network, you must configure the correct
properties from scratch. If Windows has automatically configured the network, it
will pick the strongest protocols available.

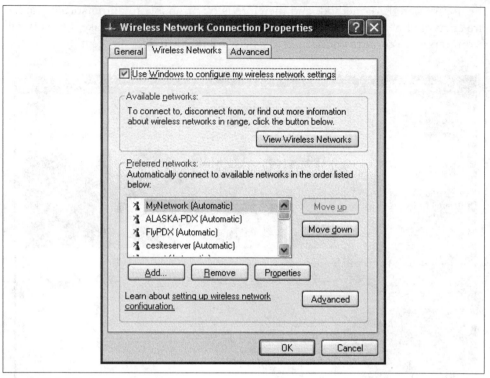

Figure 17-4. Wireless Networks tab

One of the positive attributes of ZeroConf is that it can maintain properties for several different wireless LANs, and connect to networks for which you have defined settings appropriately.

The first major choice to make is the type of network authentication you will use. In the figure, I show WPA. However, there are four options:

Open authentication.
> This is used for networks that perform no authentication, as well as networks that are using legacy dynamic WEP solutions. Selecting it means that the initial link layer authentication takes place using the open authentication method described in Chapter 8. Any network implementing open authentication may require 802.1X on top of it, though it does not have to.

Shared authentication.
> This option is used for networks that do shared-key WEP authentication. It will require you to enter a key in the "Network Key" fields. Shared-key WEP authentication is not very strong, and does not offer serious protection. The only reason to use this option is to connect to a network of APs that requires it.

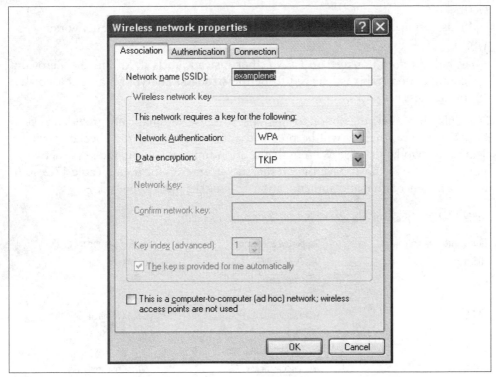

Figure 17-5. Association properties

WPA authentication.
> This is short for WPA Enterprise. It uses 802.1X for user authentication, and uses the authenticated keying mode defined in 802.11i. This option is only available if WPA software is installed and the driver has support for WPA.

WPA-PSK authentication.
> This is short for WPA Personal. Rather than derive the master secret, this method uses a preshared master key. Link encryption keys are derived from the preshared key and random values exchanged by both the client and the AP.

After choosing the authentication type, you will need to select the encryption used on the link.

Disabled.
> This is used on open networks that do not apply link layer encryption. Many 802.11 hot spots currently fall into this category, although most should offer stronger encryption in the future.

WEP.
> This includes WEP using both manual and dynamic keys. To use dynamic WEP, check the box that says "The key is provided to me automatically". Manual WEP keys can be configured by unchecking the box and entering the key.

TKIP.

This option is used for TKIP, which is the default value for WPA networks.

AES.

Windows does not refer to CCMP, but instead labels it AES in the ZeroConf configuration.* This is believed to be the strongest encryption available for use on wireless networks.

The dialog box offers the option to enter a key, or use automatically provided keys. If 802.1X is in use, the key will be provided automatically and the checkbox will be cleared. Networks that use WPA authentication must use automatic keys; networks built on WPA-PSK must have the preshared key entered for them. Table 17-2 summarizes the encryption and authentication options that are supported.

Table 17-2. Summary of encryption and authentication methods

Authentication framework	Supported encryption	Authentication methods
Open	Disabled (no WEP)	802.1X optional
	WEP (key specified)	
	WEP (automatic key)	
WPA	WEP (automatic key)	802.1X required
	TKIP	
	AES (supported cards only)	
WPA-PSK	WEP (automatic key)	802.1X not used
	TKIP	
	AES (supported cards only)	

After configuring the association properties, configure the authentication properties. The association properties tab, shown in Figure 17-6, is the screen on which the EAP method is selected. The figure shows a machine which has three options: PEAP, EAP-TLS ("Smart card or other Certificate"), and TTLS ("SecureW2"). Clicking on the properties button will configure the selected EAP method.

After the EAP method, there is a checkbox to "Authenticate as computer when computer information is available". Checking this box allows a system to authenticate to the network using machine credentials, which allows Windows domain housekeeping to occur before user authentication. Operation of this process is discussed in a later section of this chapter.

---

* This is probably due to intellectual property concerns that caused the AES-based encryption algorithm to be changed during the 802.11i draft process.

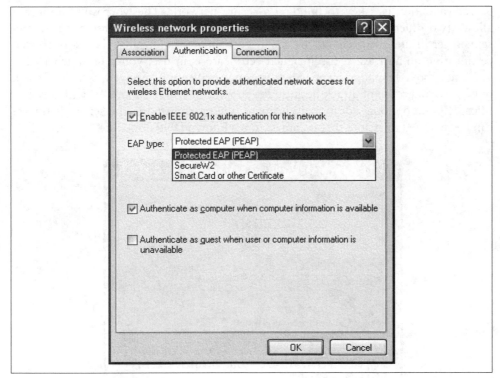

Figure 17-6. Authentication properties

Configuring EAP Methods

On the authentication tab, you select an EAP method, but configuration is handled by clicking on the Properties button. Not all the methods displayed in the authentication properties tab are supplied by Microsoft. Third-party software can add EAP types to the drop-down list. Text in the EAP method box is one of the ways that you can determine whether Microsoft or Cisco PEAP is in use. Microsoft PEAP, which is technically PEAP version 0, displays as "Protected EAP (PEAP)", while Cisco PEAP displays simply as "PEAP".

EAP-TLS

Figure 17-7 shows the configuration screen that is displayed when EAP-TLS is selected. The top box specifies whether the client certificate used to authenticate the user is stored on a smart card, or in the certificate stores that Windows maintains. Large organizations issue smart cards to employees, sometimes embedded in employee identification card. Most midsized and smaller companies will opt instead to issue certificates stored on each machine.

Server validation is a key to building a secure network. The Microsoft supplicant allows two different levels of authentication. When the authentication server presents a certificate to the client, the client can validate that against the list of trusted certification authorities. If a self-signed certificate is in use, you must uncheck the validation box. The supplicant will trust any certificate it received, which opens a huge potential route of attack because the supplicant will trust any AP with any certificate. As an optional additional safeguard, the name listed in the server certificate can be validated to ensure that it comes from a known DNS domain.

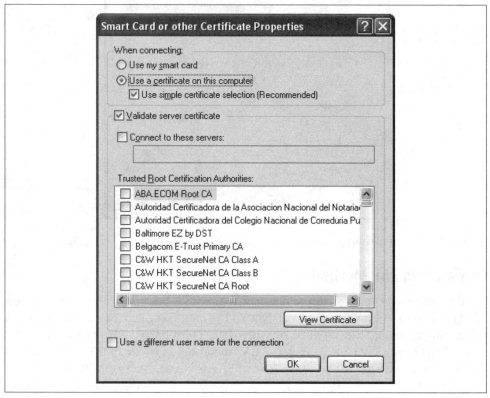

Figure 17-7. EAP-TLS configuration screen

PEAP version 0

Microsoft PEAP configuration, shown in Figure 17-8, is similar to EAP-TLS. Server validation is identical, and should be enabled. The major configuration is the inner authentication method to be used inside the protected tunnel; see Table 17-1 for a brief discussion of the various options.

Microsoft's implementation allows the list to contain any EAP authentication plug-in. By default, the list contains EAP-TLS and EAP-MSCHAP-V2. The latter is more common because it enables easy integration with Active Directory or NT Domain user accounts. Each inner authentication method can have its own subconfiguration. With

EAP-MSCHAP-V2, the inner method configuration has only one option. When the box is checked, the Windows logon credentials are automatically submitted to the network. The checkbox is sometimes called the PEAP *single sign-on* because the supplicant automatically submits logon credentials without prompting the end user.

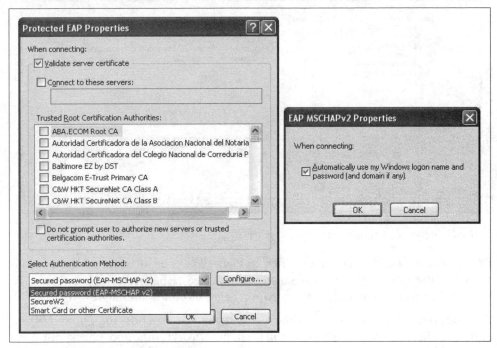

Figure 17-8. PEAP version 0 configuration

Clearing credentials from the registry

When single sign-on is not enabled, user passwords will be saved to the registry. When a user connects to a particular network name for the first time, the system will prompt the user for a username, password, and Windows domain. If authentication is successful, the credentials are saved to the Registry for future use. Whenever the user chooses to connect to the same network in the future, Windows will automatically submit the previously successful credentials.

As a user-friendly feature, credential caching leaves something to be desired, in large part because there is not a convenient way to clear out user credentials that are no longer useful. Many wireless networks plug in to existing authentication sources, and most large-scale networks enforce regular password change policies. When an enforced password change invalidates the cached credentials in the Registry, the user must clear out the registry to change the password.

User credentials are stored in the Registry under *HKCU\Software\Microsoft\EAPOL\ UserEapInfo*, as shown in Figure 17-9. Each network interface configured to do

PEAP authentication without single-sign on will be represented by a long identifier consisting of a big string of letters and numbers.

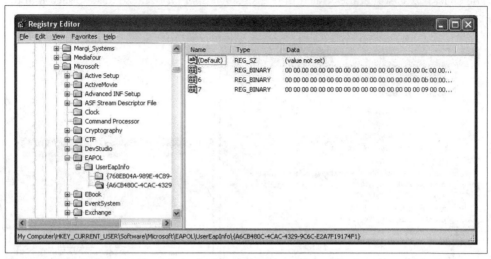

Figure 17-9. Stored user credentials in the Registry

Each network card is given an identifier. In Figure 17-9, the interface with the identifier {768EB04A-989E-4C89-9B85-93DF52F5EDE6} has three cached network passwords. To remove the cached password for the network, delete its corresponding registry key.

To find out which network interface the string corresponds to, go to *HKLM\Software\Microsoft\WindowsNT\CurrentVersion\NetworkCards* and check out keys below that value. Figure 17-10 shows the mapping of the registry string to an "ORiNOCO 802.11abg ComboCard Gold."

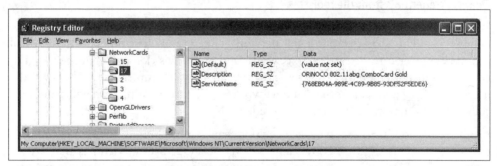

Figure 17-10. Cross-referencing the interface to the text name in the Registry

Storing the user password in the registry decreases the usability of the Windows supplicant with a user-entered password. Microsoft representatives have defended password caching as a user convenience feature that prevents the need to repeatedly re-enter the password, and pointed out the benefit of using an existing Active Directory user account with automatic use of Windows credentials. Other supplicants, however, store the user password in a more easily accessible place.

The Microsoft supplicant on Windows CE does not cache credentials. Users are prompted for credentials every time the supplicant reauthenticates. Most Windows CE devices do not have keyboards, and entering credentials quickly can be quite difficult.

SecureW2: TTLS with ZeroConfig

Third-party supplicants present network administrators with a difficult choice. Users are often comfortable with the Windows GUI for configuring wireless interfaces, but TTLS support is generally only available by using a third-party client that disables ZeroConfig. Fortunately, there is a solution. ZeroConfig has a programming interface that enables additional EAP support through "plug-ins" that implement a particular authentication method. SecureW2 is a TTLS plug-in for Windows ZeroConfig. It is an open source project, released under the GPL. Source code and binary packages are available from *http://www.securew2.com.*

As a plug-in, SecureW2 configuration is accessed through the same screens as EAP-TLS and PEAP. When the Properties button is first clicked, SecureW2 displays its main configuration screen (Figure 17-11). SecureW2 configuration data is bundled into a profile. Each wireless network stored by ZeroConfig is associated with a SecureW2 profile. Different networks may each be associated with a single SecureW2 profile. SecureW2 installers can be built with an administrative packaging tool that allows profiles to be included in the installer.

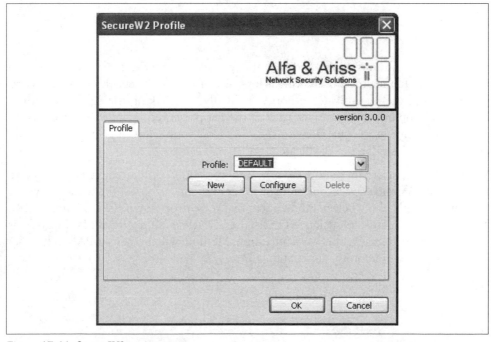

Figure 17-11. SecureW2 main screen

Four tabs are used to define the profile. The Connection tab, shown in Figure 17-12, is used to specify the first-stage identity used by TTLS. By unchecking the box, the user account specified on the fourth tab will be used in the first stage. By default, the outer identity is anonymous.

Figure 17-12. SecureW2 profile creation

Server authentication is configured with the second tab, the Certificates tab shown in Figure 17-13. Rather than presenting a long list of certificate checkboxes to accept, you must add each certificate authority manually. By clicking the Add CA button, the list will pop up. In XP Service Pack 2, the list presented is pulled from the computer's certificate store. Just as with the Microsoft supplicant, it is possible to validate the server name in the certificate.

With the outer username and network authentication configured, it is possible to finally configure the user account for the inner authentication. Authentication type is configured with the "Select Authentication" tab drop-down (see Figure 17-14). Much of the impetus for using TTLS is that cleartext password authentication is required; in such cases, the Authentication Method will be set to PAP. The user account is configured on the fourth tab.

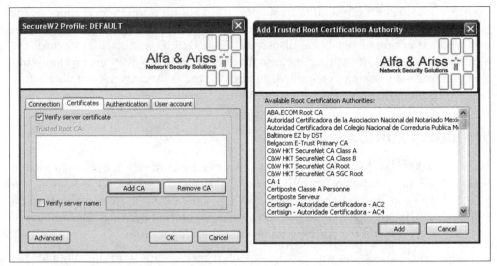

Figure 17-13. SecureW2 certificate configuration

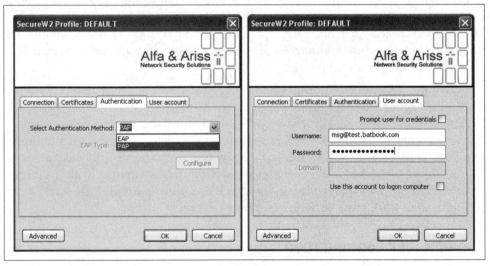

Figure 17-14. SecureW2 authentication method and user account screens

WPA Configuration and Installation

Wi-Fi Protected Access (WPA) is the typical security baseline used in most organizations. WPA is built into Windows XP Service Pack 2, and available as a patch for XP Service Pack 1. Enabling WPA is a matter of selecting either WPA or WPA-PSK as the authentication method in the association properties of the card. Microsoft does not implement WPA for other operating systems; use of WPA on other operating systems requires a third-party supplicant.

To use WPA, the entire system must support it. In addition to OS-level support, the hardware and its driver must be capable of WPA support. Drivers will prevent unsupported options from being displayed. On a Dell TrueMobile 1150 card, the option for AES does not appear because that device only has RC4 encryption built-in. If WPA is not working as expected, ensure that the latest driver is installed before contacting your vendor's support organization.

Windows 2000

Windows 2000 is still widely used. Many older machines have not been upgraded to Windows XP to save money, and Windows 2000 remains a serviceable operating system. Wireless configuration on Windows 2000 is significantly more complex than on Windows XP, in large part because it lacks solid integration between the selection of a wireless network and the corresponding security configuration.

Windows 2000 did not ship with 802.1X support from the start. It was initially added as a patch on top of Service Pack 3,* and was later integrated into Service Pack 4. Microsoft has not ported WPA functionality to Windows 2000, although a WPA client is available from the Wireless Security Corporation (*http://www.wirelesssecuritycorp.com*). Many observers feel that 802.1X support on Windows 2000 is not a priority for Microsoft, and its inclusion into recent service packs is an illustration of increased difficulty in persuading users to upgrade.

Although 802.1X configuration has been integrated into the driver layer, Windows 2000 still depends on a card utility to configure which network the system will attach to. The separation can be particularly problematic for users who travel between an encrypted networks and unencrypted networks. Although using the card utility to switch networks is straightforward, it is usually necessary to manually enable or disable security. Windows 2000 may present network administrators with a difficult choice. If the software configuration tool bundles a third-party 802.1X stack, extra administration work must be done to separate the two.

Dynamic WEP Configuration

The Wireless Configuration Service on Windows 2000 only supports dynamic WEP for encryption. TKIP support is only possible by using a third-party supplicant. To configure dynamic WEP, set up the card's utility for use with manual WEP key. As far as the card utility is concerned, a manual WEP key is in use. Frames are dispatched by the driver to the card, to be encrypted by one of the keys stored in the card's key cache. The Wireless Configuration process, however, will push new keys into the card as required by the network's security policy.

---

* See Microsoft knowledge base article 313664 for the patch.

The manual WEP key need not be configured anywhere else on the network. It must only be the correct length. For networks using 128-bit WEP, the key should be entered as 26 hexadecimal digits, such as 12345678901234567890123456. This dummy key is never used, since it is replaced by the dynamically derived key after a successful 802.1X authentication.

In my experience, the Wireless Configuration Service on Windows 2000 is not as reliable as the process on Windows XP. Several bugs have caused the service to fail after a successful authentication. Interestingly enough, the symptom of this type of failure is that the connection will be keyed succesfully, but traffic will be disrupted at the first reauthentication period. With no software running to process 802.1X frames, any attempted reauthentications or re-key operations will fail.

Windows Computer Authentication

When the Windows authentication subsystem was designed, it used a network connection to send user credentials to the domain controller for validation. When the network subsystem started, it would obtain a network address, if necessary for the protocol in use, and contact the domain controller. Besides validating user credentials, the domain offered several other services. Network administrators could define *domain policies* to control the behavior of any system in the domain, or *login scripts* to customize the user environment as part of the login process.

In the wired world, domain services are not a problem. Users attach to the network, and the system itself starts sending packets. When the Windows startup process was designed, there was no way of authenticating wired network connections. In the wireless world, though, where users must authenticate to active a wireless connection, network authentication can be a bit of a chicken and egg problem. Users can certainly authenticate to the wireless network once they supply credentials to the login box, but how can those credentials be validated without a network connection to send packets to the domain controller? Windows NT, 2000, and XP provide a partial solution in terms of credential caching. Once a user has successfully logged in to a computer that is a member of a Windows domain, credentials are cached for the future.

Credential caching is only part of the solution because it depends on logging in to the computer on a wired connection first. Microsoft has developed a much better solution called *computer authentication* or *machine authentication*. When the system first starts up, the computer authenticates to the wireless network as itself. With the wireless network up and operational, the computer can then download any required information from the domain and validate the credentials of any user against the domain controller. Users who have never logged in to the system and have no cached credentials can log in as well.

A fair amount of functionality depends on having a network connection early in the boot process. In addition to domain services, drive mappings are attempted early enough that they may fail if the computer is not authenticated. In most cases, Windows computer authentication should be considered mandatory for a smooth-functioning network.

To set up Windows computer authentication, you must have an Active Directory back end. Computers must have accounts defined in the Active Directory, and they must be granted Dial-In permission.

How It Works

Computer authentication adds an extra 802.1X authentication process to the boot process. First the computer authenticates as itself. After obtaining user credentials from the login box, a second 802.1X transaction is run to authenticate as the user. The process is shown in Figure 17-15.

The figure identifies several steps in the process. It starts when the computer comes up and starts its networking system. It begins an 802.1X authentication as the computer in parallel to other system start-up tasks.

1. The machine authentication is started. It may be started by an EAPOL-Start from the supplicant, or by a Request/Identity frame from the authenticator.

2. The network collects the identity of the machine. In the first authentication, the "user" identity is of the form host/ComputerName.ActiveDirectoryDomain, where both the ComputerName and the ActiveDirectoryDomain are available from the system properties.

3. The computer authenticates against its computer account on the RADIUS server, or in the back-end database behind the RADIUS server. This process may take several round-trips because of the need to exchange certificates, establish cryptographic keys, and so forth.

   Computer authentication uses the same EAP method as user authentication. If EAP-TLS is employed for user authentication, the computer must also have its own certificate. When PEAP is configured for user authentication, the computer uses EAP-MSCHAP-V2 as its inner method. The "password" used in the inner authentication is generated when the computer joins the domain, and is not available to any other software.

4. When the authentication succeeds, the computer is attached to the network. It receives an EAP-Success frame from the authenticator, and on wireless LANs, EAPOL-Key frames to provide keys for the connection.

   When authentication completes, the computer will be attached to the network, and can send and receive traffic. By sending a DHCP request, the computer can join the network and locate a nearby domain controller by using NetBIOS over

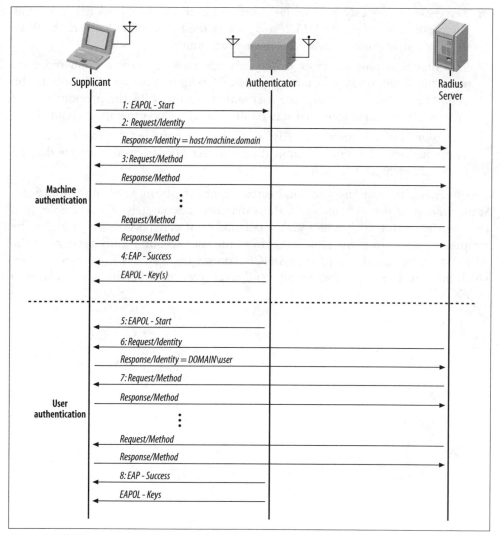

Machine authentication

1: EAPOL - Start

2: Request/Identity

Response/Identity = host/machine.domain

3: Request/Method

Response/Method

⋮

Request/Method

Response/Method

4: EAP - Success

EAPOL - Key(s)

User authentication

5: EAPOL - Start

6: Request/Identity

Response/Identity = DOMAIN\user

7: Request/Method

Response/Method

⋮

Request/Method

Response/Method

8: EAP - Success

EAPOL - Keys

Figure 17-15. Startup process with Windows computer authentication

TCP/IP. Before user authentication, the computer can establish a relationship with the domain controller. The user presses Control-Alt-Delete to begin the login process. The system uses its connection to the domain controller to load the user login script, configure Windows domain policies, and perform other login tasks.

5. When the user desktop is about to start, the second authentication starts. The end user authentication must be triggered by the operating system. Typically, the machine authentication established at the start of the session is only used for a few minutes until the user authentication begins.

6. The network requests the identity of the end user. On Windows networks, this is typically of the form *DOMAIN\user*, where the two components are the Windows NT-style domain name, and the user account.

7. The supplicant authenticates to the network with credentials from the user. With the Windows supplicant, the same EAP plug-in must be used for both the computer authentication and the user authentication. Like the previous step, it may require multiple round-trips to establish a secure cryptographic channel.

8. The user authentication succeeds, and keys are provided for the connection. These keys will be different from the computer keys because they are derived from a different TLS session.

Computer authentications can be treated separately from user authentications. Authorization of the two authentications may occur separately. For example, in a network that performs dynamic VLAN assignment, it may be possible to assign the computer account to a different VLAN from the user account. Early versions of the Microsoft supplicant did not trigger DHCP requests upon successful authentication, which prevented the user from sending and receiving traffic. Patches are available to fix this problem.

## CHAPTER 18

802.11 on the Macintosh

Apple Computer has been a key player in establishing the market for 802.11 equipment. Most companies in the 802.11 market saw their contributions in terms of standards committee activity and technology development. Apple contributed by distilling complex technology into an easy-to-use form factor and applying its mass-marketing expertise.

In 1999, 802.11 was a promising technology that had demonstrated its value in a few narrow markets. 802.11 interfaces cost around $300, and access points were around $1,000. Apple saw the promise in the technology and moved aggressively, releasing $300 access points and $99 interfaces. With a new competitor suddenly pricing the gear at a third of the prevailing price, other vendors were forced to drop prices dramatically, and the market took off. Prices have been dropping ever since.

Apple's cards are branded with the name AirPort. AirPort refers to the first-generation 802.11b network interfaces, while AirPort Extreme is used to refer to newer 802.11g-based hardware. (Due to a focus on small offices and home offices, Apple does not sell 802.11a hardware.) This chapter discusses only the AirPort Extreme hardware, although the differences in configuration and management are vanishingly small. In addition to easy configuration of the wireless interface, the Apple 802.1X supplicant is the easiest to configure. The 802.1X supplicant was included for the first time in OS X 10.3, better known to most of the world by its code name of Panther.

The AirPort Extreme Card

Apple offers tightly integrated systems because the hardware and the software are designed in tandem. Unlike the chaotic IBM-compatible world, with Apple one company is responsible for both the hardware and software, and it shows. You can install the hardware and software and connect to an existing network in only a few minutes. If an AirPort card is plugged in during system installation, this can be done as part of the initial configuration.

Software Installation

Drivers for the AirPort are included in OS 9.1 and later, so there is no need to download and install drivers. If the AirPort card is installed before the system first boots, the first-time boot configuration utility will allow you to configure the AirPort interface out of the box by selecting a network name and choosing how to configure TCP/IP. For a network that uses DHCP, the configuration instructions are only a few screens long.

AirPort cards added after the system first boots can be configured by the AirPort Setup Assistant.* After inserting the card, run the Setup Assistant. When it starts, you will see the dialog box in Figure 18-1.

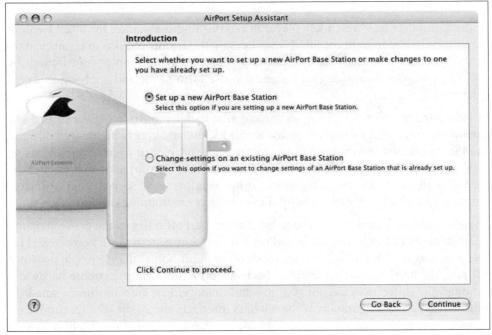

Figure 18-1. Initial AirPort Setup Assistant screen

Choose to configure the AirPort card and click Continue. The next step, shown in Figure 18-2, is to select the network you wish to join. Every network within range is displayed in the pop-up menu. Figure 18-2 shows the user selecting the *secure.utah.edu* network.

---

* Cards can also be configured with the System Preferences application. For completeness, this chapter discusses the Setup Assistant first and the System Preferences application later in terms of monitoring and changing the configuration. However, there is no reason why you cannot configure the card straight from the System Preferences application.

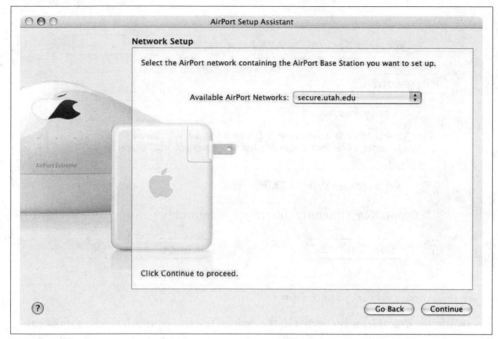

Figure 18-2. AirPort card network selection

Once the network is selected, you can move on to the third step: entering the nework password, which is only useful for networks protected by WEP or WPA. 802.1X configurations must be set up in Internet Connect, as described later in this chapter.

When connecting to a network, several different types of security can be selected. Figure 18-3 shows the dialog box. The type of security is selected with the drop-down box from WPA Personal (WPA-PSK), WPA Enterprise (WPA with RADIUS authentication), and WEP. To make matters easier for users, Apple has allowed administrators to input WEP keys as variable-length passwords. The ASCII text of the password is then hashed into a WEP key of the appropriate length. WEP keys can also be entered in hexadecimal by prefacing them with a dollar sign, such as $EB102393BF. Hex keys are either 10 hex digits (40-bit) or 26 hex digits (104-bit). Interpretation of the input string can be forced to ASCII by enclosing the key in double quotes.*

Configuring and Monitoring an AirPort Interface

You may need to change the AirPort configuration from time to time. You may move between different 802.11 networks (ESSs) or need to change the WEP keys or IP settings. Once the card is installed, you can change its configuration with the configuration tools provided with OS X. Apple's configuration programs don't allow users to change any of the more complex 802.11 parameters. All the information needed to join

---

* For more information, see article 106250 in Apple's Knowledge Base at *http://kbase.info.apple.com*.

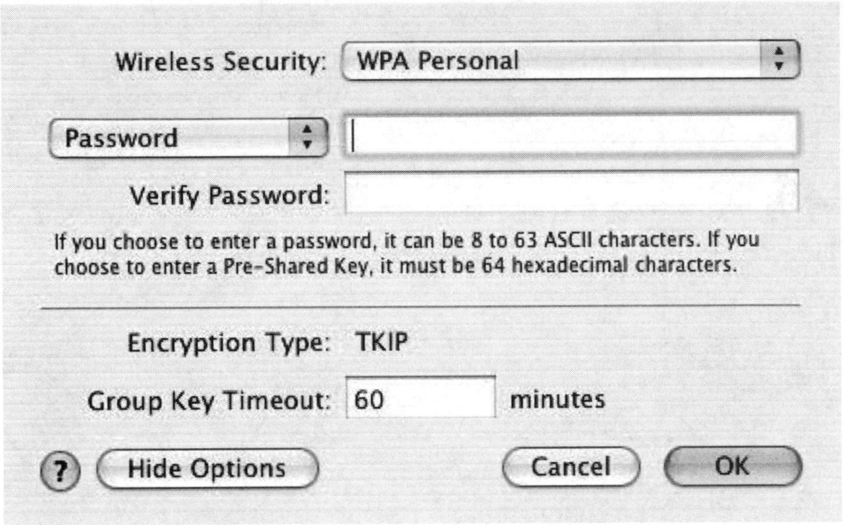

Wireless Security: WPA Personal
Password
Verify Password:
If you choose to enter a password, it can be 8 to 63 ASCII characters. If you choose to enter a Pre-Shared Key, it must be 64 hexadecimal characters.
Encryption Type: TKIP
Group Key Timeout: 60 minutes
?
Hide Options
Cancel
OK

Figure 18-3. AirPort network password entry

a network, for example, is broadcast in the Beacon frames. Apple decided in most cases, it's enough to present the user with network names and prompt for security settings.

Basic configuration with the AirPort status icon

Once configuration is complete, the AirPort status icon is displayed in the upper-right corner of the screen, next to the speaker volume, battery, and clock icons, provided you haven't turned off those icons. The AirPort icon also indicates radio strength. In Figure 18-4, there are several solid wavefronts on the icon. As you move farther from the access point and the signal degrades, the number of bars decreases. When it is clicked, a drop-down command list offers the option of turning the power to the AirPort card on or off, selecting or creating networks, and opening the Internet Connect application to monitor the radio interface. It is quite handy for users to be able to turn off the card at will. When you are out of range of a network, or just not using it, the card can easily be powered down to save battery power.

(41%) Fri 6:49 PM
AirPort: On
Turn AirPort Off
✓ Little Green Men
Luminiferous Ether
Other...
Create Network...
Open Internet Connect...

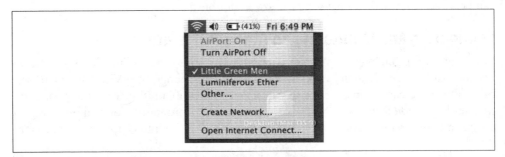

Figure 18-4. AirPort status icon

In Figure 18-4, there are two networks within range: "Little Green Men" and "Luminiferous Ether." The checkmark by "Little Green Men" indicates that it is the network to which the user is currently connected, although the user can switch between the two networks simply by selecting a preference. Any other network can be selected by using the "Other..." option and entering the name of the network.

An IBSS can be created by going to the Create Network option and selecting the basic radio parameters shown in Figure 18-5. The computer is set to create an IBSS with the network name of Very Independent BSS; the radio channel defaults to 11 but can be changed to any of the 11 channels acceptable in North America and Europe. Every computer taking part in the IBSS must use the same channel. IBSS networks can only be configured for WEP.

Figure 18-5. IBSS parameter setup

After you've set up an independent network, the system adds a new section titled "Computer to Computer Networks" to the drop-down list, as shown in Figure 18-6. The AirPort status icon also changes to a computer in the pie-wedge shape to indicate that the network is an IBSS rather than an infrastructure network.

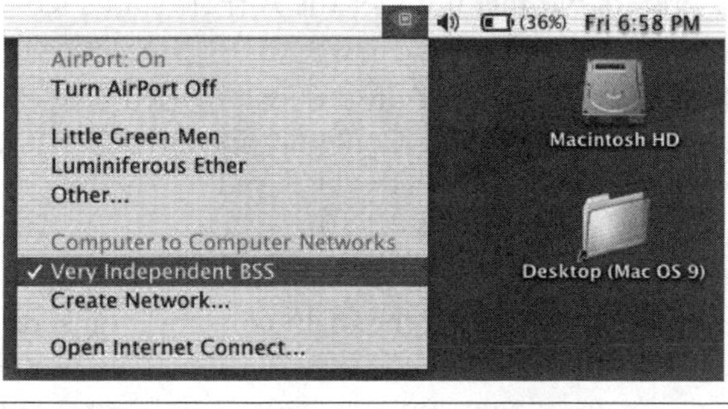

Figure 18-6. AirPort status icon while associated to an IBSS

Configuration with the System Preferences application

If you move between different ESSs, you can create a "location" for each and use this to configure the ESS/password pair, which you can then pick from a menu as you move to a different location. You can also preconfigure an ESS/password pair if you're not currently on the network for which you are setting up.

The System Preferences application allows you to configure many system attributes, including those that are network-related. Figure 18-7 shows the network panel of the System Preferences application. The Show pop-up list can be set to any of the network interfaces in the system. Naturally, when set to AirPort, it enables the fourth tab, as shown in the figure. The default tab is TCP/IP (Figure 18-7), which can be set to configure interfaces manually or with the assistance of DHCP or BootP. When set to DHCP, as in the figure, the leased address is shown. Although the DHCP server on my network provided DNS servers, the server IP addresses are not shown. (They are, however, placed in */etc/resolv.conf*, as with any other common Unix system.)

The other network panel worthy of note is the AirPort tab (Figure 18-8), which can set the network to join by default. In most cases, it should be left to Automatic, which enables the computer to search through any networks in the general vicinity for one that has already been configured. Automatic selection can reference security configurations built with Internet Connect, if necessary.

Monitoring the wireless interface

The wireless-interface status can be monitored with the Internet Connect application. The Internet Connect application can be launched from either the Applications folder on the hard disk or from the AirPort status icon. It can be used to display the signal strength of the nearest access point, as well as change the network with which the station is associated. If the network is changed, it will reference any 802.1X configuration necessary to authenticate to the network. See Figure 18-9.

802.1X on the AirPort

802.1X on Panther is set up through the Internet Connect application, which can be launched from the drop-down menu under the AirPort status icon, or directly from the hard disk.

To see the 802.1X configuration, click on the lock labeled 802.1X. If the lock does not appear, either select New 802.1X Configuration from the File menu, or press Command-Shift-X. Once 802.1X has been displayed for the first time, it will always appear as an icon across the top (Figure 18-10).

To see the full configuration, select the Configuration drop down menu and choose Edit Configuration..., which brings up the main configuration screen (Figure 18-11). The easiest task from here is to edit the configuration. This brings up a configuration screen. Put in the username and password, and select any authentication

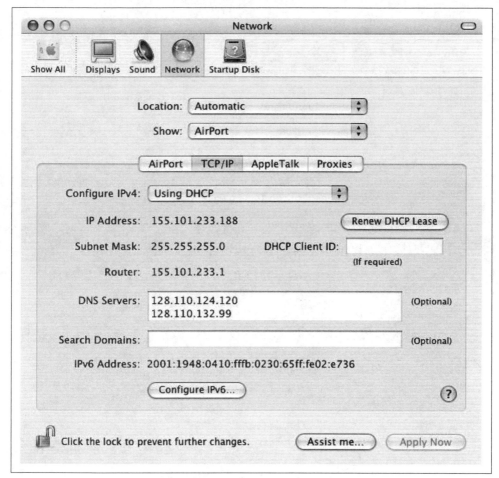

Figure 18-7. TCP/IP preferences tab of the Network Preferences settings

protocols that may be used. This screen allows selection of the network interface to which the 802.1X credentials apply. In most cases, it will remain set to the AirPort card, although wired 802.1X is gaining prominence. The username and password are straightforward, as is the wireless network. By default, the drop down for Wireless Network will display any encrypted networks detected by the AirPort, but it is possible to type in an arbitrary SSID.

After typing in credentials, it may be necessary to configure the authentication method. The supplicant has different configuration screens for each method, as discussed in subsequent sections.

After returning to the main screen of Internet Connect, you can press the Connect button to associate to the network and attempt 802.1X authentication. The status bar at the bottom will go through the following stages:

Figure 18-8. AirPort preferences tab of the Network Preferences settings

Idle

    The AirPort is not associated to any network.

Connecting

    The AirPort is associating with the selected SSID.

Authenticating

    The AirPort is trading EAPOL frames with the AP or switch as it tries to validate user credentials.

Connected via (EAP method)

    If the authentication succeeds, the status bar will note that the system is connected, and it will display the EAP method in use, as well as the time which the system has been authenticated.

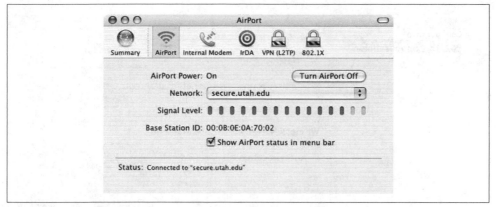

Figure 18-9. Internet Connect monitoring application

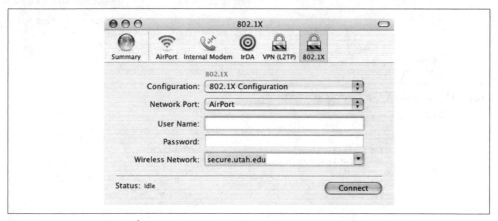

Figure 18-10. 802.1X configuration in Internet Connect

Configuring EAP Methods

Each of the EAP methods has a different method configuration. Generally speaking, the Mac supplicant hides a great deal of the complexity, unless it is required.

TTLS configuration

There are two potential TTLS configuration options, shown in Figure 18-12. The first, which is mandatory, is the inner authentication type. In most cases, I expect this will be set to PAP, though it is also possible to use CHAP, MS-CHAP, or MS-CHAP-V2. Like most supplicants, the Mac supplicant supports hiding the user identity by configuring an anonymous outer identity.

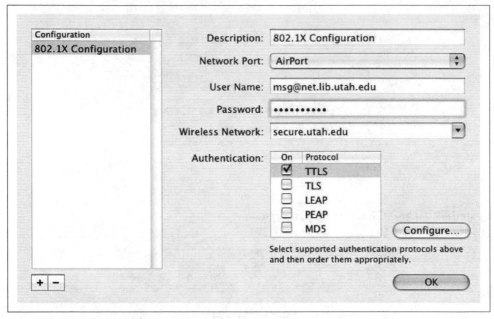

Figure 18-11. 802.1X Configuration screen

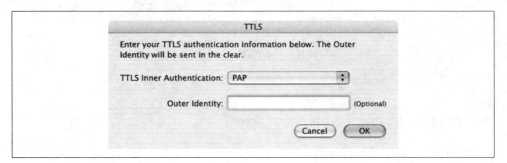

Figure 18-12. TTLS configuration screen

PEAP configuration

On the Mac supplicant, only EAP-MSCHAP-V2 is supported as an inner authentication method. This allows interoperability with user accounts stored as MD4 hashes or in cleartext. The main use for this method is to support user accounts stored in a Windows network. On the configuration screen, Figure 18-13, the only option is to configure an outer identity to hide the user identity.

The Keychain

In Mac OS, passwords and certificates are stored on a *keychain*, which holds security-relevant information in a centralized location. By logging in, the certificates and user credentials required for network authentication are available to any application

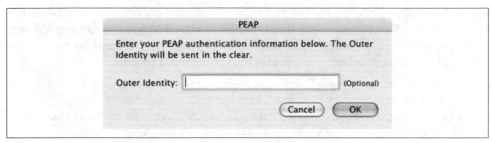

Figure 18-13. PEAP configuration screen

allowed by the user. Figure 18-14 shows a simple keychain, which contains one RADIUS server certificate, the CA that signed that certificate, and the 802.1X configuration for a network. The keychain provides access control to protect configurations.

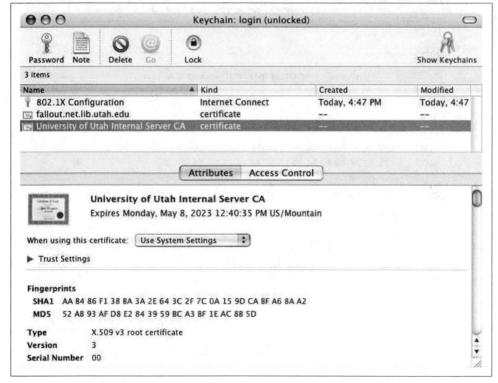

Figure 18-14. The keychain viewer

Adding to the keychain

When connecting to an 802.1X-protected network for the first time, any certificates that are not yet trusted will cause the authentication to fail. Rather than failing the authentication, the supplicant will present the certificates to the user, as shown in

Figure 18-15. By inspecting the certificates, users can make a decision about whether to trust them. More likely, a centralized information technology department will test user credentials on the wireless network before turning the system over to the end user, and can add any relevant certificates during the build process.

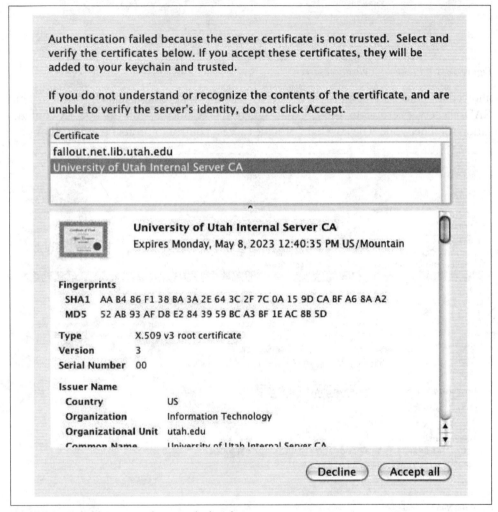

Figure 18-15. Adding a certificate to the keychain

Troubleshooting

When 802.1X authentication fails, the message that is received (Figure 18-16) does not provide a great deal of information. An error code does not provide detailed diagnostic information about why the failure has occurred.

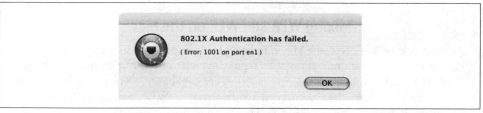

Figure 18-16. X failure dialog box

Fortunately, the supplicant is capable of producing extensive debug logging. Create the directory */var/log/eapolclient*. If the directory exists and the *NSDebugEnabled* environment variable is set when Internet Connect launches, it will log EAPOL frames from the user to */var/log/eapolclient/uid(number)-(network interface).log*. For example, if UID 501 attempts to use 802.1X on the AirPort (typically *en1*), the file will be *uid501-en1.log*. Internet Connect must be launched from the command line to pick up the environment variable in the Terminal it is launched from.

```
Mac:~$ sudo mkdir /var/log/eapolclient
Mac:~$ NSDebugEnabled=YES; export NSDebugEnabled
Mac:~$ /Applications/Internet\ Connect.app/Contents/MacOS/Internet\ Connect
```

The debug log will dump out every frame sent and received, in both ASCII and hexadecimal. It does not print decrypted frames for EAP methods that use encryption. As an example, the following two EAPOL-Key frames were received after a successful 802.1X authentication:

```
-----------------------------------------
2005/02/15 17:00:42.903841 Receive Packet Size: 75

Ether packet: dest 0:30:65:2:e7:36 source 0:b:e:a:70:2 type 0x888e
EAPOL: proto version 0x1 type Key (3) length 57
Signature: 6c 08 b3 97 b1 74 f2 ec  0e 2c 1f 66 ff 40 78 42 is valid
EAPOL Key Descriptor: type RC4 (1) length 13 Broadcast index 2
replay_counter: 42 11 48 e2 00 00 00 18
key_IV:        ca 7e d9 ff d4 47 80 ba  9e eb 33 c8 82 17 02 7c
key_signature: 6c 08 b3 97 b1 74 f2 ec  0e 2c 1f 66 ff 40 78 42
key:           fc 7a 7c 67 f6 f6 f5 7d  a5 94 cb 49 1a

-----------------------------------------
2005/02/15 17:00:42.960436 Receive Packet Size: 64

Ether packet: dest 0:30:65:2:e7:36 source 0:b:e:a:70:2 type 0x888e
EAPOL: proto version 0x1 type Key (3) length 44
Signature: ce b3 45 05 47 72 5a 98  7c 64 0c d8 52 0d 8f 78 is valid
EAPOL Key Descriptor: type RC4 (1) length 13 Unicast index 0
replay_counter: 42 11 48 e2 00 00 00 19
key_IV:        45 e5 2a ad 1c 9c ea 8f  3c 58 a4 c4 6a e0 fa 82
key_signature: ce b3 45 05 47 72 5a 98  7c 64 0c d8 52 0d 8f 78
EAPOL: 2 bytes follow body:
0000  00 00
```

Mixing WPA and WEP on the Mac

As this book went to press, the Mac supplicant had a bug related to the interoperability in environments which mix encryption types. It is relatively common to run dynamic WEP and TKIP simultaneously. Stations that are capable of TKIP run it for unicast data, while broadcast data is encrypted with dynamic WEP. Stations that are only capable of dynamic WEP use it for both unicast and broadcast data.

In a mixed WEP/TKIP environment, Macintoshes are unable to connected to the network. During the association process, the supplicant learns the network supports both WEP and TKIP, and accepts the security parameters by associating. However, during the key handshake, the supplicant insists on running only TKIP. With two different sets of security parameters in the association process and the keying process, the standards dictate that the AP should fail keying and kick the system off the network.

As a workaround, either reduce the security of the network to run only dynamic WEP, run two parallel wireless networks (one WEP and one TKIP) so that Macs can use a TKIP-only network, or force all dynamic WEP devices off the network until they can be upgraded to TKIP.

## CHAPTER 19

Using 802.11 on Linux

When the first edition of this book was written, 802.11 was only just coming to Linux. Cards had to be selected carefully because very few cards were supported with full open source drivers that evolved at the same pace as the Linux kernel. Linux support has now moved into the mainstream, with many vendors actively sponsoring driver development projects, or at the very least supporting efforts to target their hardware. Broadcom is a notable exception.

Most 802.11 devices are supported by the PCMCIA system. As with Windows drivers, installing wireless cards on Linux creates Ethernet interfaces. Many Linux drivers expose an Ethernet interface through the kernel, and most drivers even name the resulting interfaces with the *eth* prefix. Programs can use the Ethernet interface to send and receive data at the link layer, and the driver handles Ethernet-to-802.11 conversions.* Many of the things you would expect to see with an Ethernet interface remain the same. ARP works identically, and the IP configuration is done with the same utilities provided by the operating-system distribution. *ifconfig* can even be used to monitor the interface status and see the data sent and received.

PCMCIA Support on Linux

Initially, most wireless networking adapters were add-on cards that were based on the PC Card specification.† PC Cards attach to the system bus through a 16-bit controller interface that operates at 8 MHz. Even though performance was limited by the bus to be roughly comparable to the 16-bit ISA bus, it was more than capable of supporting

---

* There are two major encapsulation formats for data on 802.11. RFC 1042 is used for IP, and universally supported. Windows and MacOS support IPX and AppleTalk with 802.1H. Not all Linux drivers support 802.1H.

† The Personal Computer Memory Card International Association (PCMCIA) is the industry group that came up with the PC Card specification. Initially, the cards were known as "PCMCIA cards," but the name was later shortened to "PC Card." I use both interchangeably, especially since Linux support for these cards still goes by the longer PCMCIA. (In reference to the unwieldy nature of the acronym, one common joke expands it as "People who Can't Manage Computer Industry Acronyms.")

relatively slow 802.11b wireless LANs. Higher-performance 802.11a and 802.11g cards require the performance of the next-generation CardBus interface, which drives a 32-bit bus at 33 MHz. CardBus provides the dramatically improved performance required by higher-bandwidth network interfaces. CardBus cards look nearly identical to PC Cards, and are used in the same slots. Both CardBus and PC Cards are, not surprisingly, configured and managed through the Linux PCMCIA utilities.

Using external interfaces with antennas that protrude from the case of the laptop is not always desirable. Laptop vendors have adopted a different form factor for "built-in" wireless devices called Mini-PCI. Mini-PCI is a small version of the PCI interface that is only a few inches long. There no limit on what could be made into a Mini-PCI card, but by far the most popular use of the slot is to add wireless networking capabilties to laptops. Most Mini-PCI wireless cards consist of a PCI-to-Cardbus bridge combined with a CardBus wireless LAN interface, and are therefore configured and managed through the Linux PCMCIA system.

PCMCIA Card Services Overview

Card Services grew out of an attempt to simplify system configuration. Rather than dedicating system resources to individual devices, the host system maintained a pool of resources for PC Cards and allocated resources as necessary. Figure 19-1 shows the procedure by which cards are configured on Linux.

When a card is inserted, the *cardmgr* process orchestrates the configuration of the device, as shown in Figure 19-1. The orchestration pulls together system resources, kernel components, and kernel driver modules through the configuration files stored in */etc/pcmcia*. Roughly speaking, the host takes the following steps:

1. A card is inserted into an empty PC Card socket, and *cardmgr* is notified of this event. In addition to any hardware operations (such as supplying power to the socket), *cardmgr* queries the *card information structure* (CIS) to determine the type of card inserted and the resources it needs. For more information on the CIS, see the sidebar "Card Information Structure" later in this chapter.

2. *cardmgr* attempts to identify the card and load the appropriate kernel modules for support. The PCMCIA card database stored in */etc/pcmcia/config* is used to map the CIS database to drivers. Drivers can also be loaded automatically through a hardware identification list that is part of the module and stored in a module map (*/lib/modules/(kernel version)/module.*map*). The main task of the identification is to associate cards with a *class*. For the purposes of configuring network cards, the important point to note is that items in the *network* class have additional network configuration operations performed on them later. The card is identified by the CIS data from step 1, and the class setting is set in the main system configuration file. At this point, *cardmgr* beeps once. Successful identification results in a high-pitched beep; unsuccessful identifications are indicated by a beep of lower pitch.

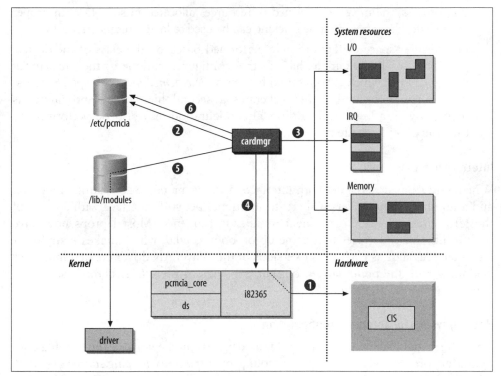

Figure 19-1. Linux PCMCIA configuration system

3. *cardmgr* determines which resources are available to allocate to the card. Blocks of system resources are reserved for PCMCIA card use in the main configuration file, and *cardmgr* doles out resources as needed to cards. The number of I/O ports needed and the size of the required memory window are obtained from the CIS.

4. Resources allocated by *cardmgr* are programmed into the PCMCIA controller, which is depicted in Figure 19-1 as interaction with the PCMCIA device driver. The Intel i82365SL PCMCIA controller is the most common chip on the market, which is why the kernel module is shown as "i82365." The new kernel-based PCMCIA system uses the *yenta_socket* driver instead of a chipset-specific driver. PCMCIA controllers implement *resource steering* to map resources required by the card onto available system resources. A card may ask for an interrupt, but the actual assigned interrupt is irrelevant. In operation, the card simply asks the PCMCIA controller to raise an interrupt, and the controller is responsible for looking up the interrupt assigned to the socket and firing the correct interrupt line.

5. Part of the configuration information obtained from the lookup in step 2 is the name of the device driver that should be loaded to use the newly inserted card. Drivers for PCMCIA cards are implemented as kernel modules. As part of the inser-

tion process, the driver is informed of resources allocated in step 4. With proper module dependencies, module stacking can be used to load multiple modules.

6. Further user-space configuration is performed based on the class of the device. Network cards, for example, have further configuration done by the */etc/pcmcia/ network* script, which is configured by editing */etc/pcmcia/network.opts*. Successful configuration in this step generates a second high beep, and failure is reported with a low beep. Additional configuration may also be performed by the Linux hotplug system.

Interface names in Linux

When a driver creates the network interface, it is given a name consisting of a prefix and a number. Many drivers will create additional network interface with a name of the form *ethX*, where *X* is the next number in sequence. Most laptops now have built-in Ethernet interfaces that come up on boot as *eth0*, which makes many wireless interfaces start as *eth1*. Older versions of the WaveLAN driver created interfaces beginning with the prefix *wvlan*, but current versions use *eth*. Atheros-based cards come up using the prefix *ath*.

Hotplug system for automatic configuration

To perform automatic configuration, Linux depends on the work of the hotplug configuration project, whose web site is found at *http://linux-hotplug.sourceforge.net/*. When a device is inserted, the hotplug system will call any needed PCI configuration commands before configuring the interface. Hotplug scripts can help to automatically configure systems with large numbers of network interfaces, or perform arbitrary configuration tasks. Many wireless devices implementing new standards are under continued development after the product is released. New firmware updates to cards can make new protocol features possible, or fix bugs in the released version. Hotplug can also be configured to automatically update firmware when particular cards are plugged in.

PCMCIA Card Services Installation

As of kernel 2.4, PCMCIA support has been integrated into the kernel, and was probably installed with your distribution. It is not necessary to upgrade the kernel PCMCIA support. It may be necessary to fetch drivers for your interface, but it is almost certain that the PCMCIA support is up-to-date enough to handle any wireless interface you throw at it. (Older distributions can update PCMCIA software through a distribution maintainer's package, or by building from the source at *http:// pcmcia-cs.sourceforge.net/*.)

Most configuration information is automatically detected from the environment without difficulty. Depending on the distribution and its installation, it may be

> ## Card Information Structure
>
> To enable automatic configuration, every PC Card has a blob of data that enables the card to describe itself to the host system. The blob is called the *card information structure* (CIS) and takes a relatively straightforward link-list format. The building blocks of the CIS are called *tuples* because they have three components: a type code to identify the type of tuple, a length field, and a series of data bytes. Tuple formats range from trivial to highly complex, which is why this book does not attempt to classify them any further. Brave, stout-hearted readers can order the specification from the PCMCIA and use the *dump_cis* tool on Linux to read the CIS of inserted cards.
>
> The CIS assists the host in automatic configuration by reporting information about itself to the host operating system. For example, network interface cards identify themselves as such, and the CIS enables the Card Services software to allocate the appropriate resources such as I/O ports and interrupt request (IRQ) lines. On Linux, the system administrator uses configuration files to match the CIS data to the driver.

necessary to inform the PCMCIA software which controller is running the PCMCIA slots by setting the PCIC variable in the system configuration file. Kernel PCMCIA software sets the value to *yenta_socket*. Systems that use the standalone PCMCIA support will set the variable to either *tcic* for Databook TCIC-2 chipsets, or *i82365* for the Intel i82365SL chipset. Slackware features a "probe" option to load modules until one successfully loads.

Monitoring the Cards

The main tool used to control the PCMCIA subsystem is the *cardctl* command. It has several subcommands that can be used to view information or configuration status. Each argument can also take a slot number. Many laptop computers have two PCMCIA slots, in which case the slots are numbered 0 and 1. An increasing number of notebooks designed for portability have only a single slot, and therefore only have slot 0.

In addition to the hardware-based eject system, *cardctl* can be used to remove drivers by sending the "card is removed" notification. Once the software has removed all the associated drivers and powered the slot down, the card can be restarted by sending a software notification of the card insertion. Having software control over the card allows the "reboot" of a card without having to physically remove and reinsert it.

```
[root@bloodhound]# cardctl eject 0
[root@bloodhound]# cardctl insert 0
```

Drivers are selected based on the CIS data. To see the contents of the card's CIS, insert it and wait for it to power up, then use the *info* or *ident* subcommands to *cardctl* to see the identification information. Here is the information from a Proxim

8480 Gold card. Like nearly all cards with 802.11a capabilities, it is based on the Atheros chipset. The card even reports itself as an Atheros reference design:

```
root@bloodhound:~# cardctl info 0
PRODID_1="Atheros Communications, Inc."
PRODID_2="AR5001-0000-0000"
PRODID_3="Wireless LAN Reference Card"
PRODID_4="00"
MANFID=0271,0012
FUNCID=6
root@bloodhound:~# cardctl ident 0
  product info: "Atheros Communications, Inc.", "AR5001-0000-0000", "Wireless LAN
Reference Card", "00"
  manfid: 0x0271, 0x0012
  function: 6 (network)
```

In addition to extracting the CIS identification with *cardctl*, the complete structure can be printed out with *cis_dump*. In addition to identification information, the CIS includes information about the supported speeds. In the case of the Proxim 8480, it reports exclusively on the 802.11a speeds, even though it is capable of 802.11b-compatible operation:

```
root@bloodhound:~# dump_cis
Socket 0:
  manfid 0x0271, 0x0012
  config_cb base 0x0000 last_index 0x01
  cftable_entry_cb 0x01 [default]
    [master] [parity] [serr] [fast back]
    Vcc Vnom 3300mV Istatic 25mA Iavg 450mA Ipeak 500mA
    irq mask 0xffff [level]
    mem_base 1
  BAR 1 size 64kb [mem]
  vers_1 7.1, "Atheros Communications, Inc.", "AR5001-0000-0000",
    "Wireless LAN Reference Card", "00"
  funcid network_adapter [post]
  lan_speed 6 mb/sec
  lan_speed 9 mb/sec
  lan_speed 12 mb/sec
  lan_speed 18 mb/sec
  lan_speed 24 mb/sec
  lan_speed 36 mb/sec
  lan_speed 48 mb/sec
  lan_speed 54 mb/sec
  lan_speed 72 mb/sec
  lan_media 5.4_GHz
  lan_node_id 20 00 4d a6 d4 0a
  lan_connector Closed connector standard

Socket 1:
  no CIS present
```

Once the card has been inserted into the system, use the *status* subcommand to check on it. The *config* subcommand will also report the system interrupt assigned by the system. In my case, the laptop uses a PCI-to-Cardbus bridge, so the card inherits the IRQ assigned to the PCI bus.

```
root@bloodhound:~# cardctl status 0
  3.3V CardBus card
  function 0: [ready]
root@bloodhound:~# cardctl config 0
  Vcc 3.3V  Vpp1 3.3V  Vpp2 3.3V
  interface type is "cardbus"
  irq 11 [exclusive] [level]
  function 0:
```

The lights are not useful

Many drivers are intended to work with several different pieces of hardware, and each manufacturer may customize the number and purpose of the lights on the card. Usually, there is one light to indicate that the card is powered up, and a second light that will blink to indicate traffic from the card. It may or may not blink in response to traffic from other stations. A few cards may have a third light to indicate association status.

Linux drivers generally do not make an attempt to control the lights on each card in a vendor-specific way, and internal cards may not have any lights at all. If your card behaves differently, don't panic. Check at the access point for an association; if an association exists, then the card is functioning normally but uses the lights in a different manner.

Troubleshooting Resource Conflicts

One of the revolutionary developments hyped by PCMCIA card vendors was that users were no longer directly responsible for maintaining low-level hardware configurations on IBM-compatible hardware. In many respects, this hype was overblown because users are still responsible for maintaining the resource pools used by PCMCIA Card Services to draw from for automatic configuration, and therefore they must still be familiar with the hardware configuration. Three major resources are managed by Card Services for users: IRQ lines, I/O ports, and direct memory access (DMA) channels. DMA channels are not required by network cards, however, and are not discussed in this section.

IRQs

IRQs are used by devices that must use the CPU periodically. Interfaces use IRQs so that when a buffer fills, the system CPU can be notified and drain the buffer. One limitation of the PC architecture is that it has only 15 available IRQs, and many are occupied by standard hardware. Table 19-1 shows common IRQ usage, which may help you determine which IRQs are available for PCMCIA cards. Disabling any extra components frees the IRQ. Table 19-1 also shows common IRQ settings on PC hardware. As a rule of thumb, IRQs 3, 5, and 10 are readily available on most machines.

Table 19-1. Common IRQ settings

IRQ number	Common usage	Purpose
0	System timer	Fires 18 times per second to maintain coarse clocking.
1	Keyboard	Allows operating system to monitor keyboard strokes by user.
2	Cascade	Two interrupt controller chips are used; the second controls IRQs 8–15 and is wired into IRQ 2 on the primary.
3	Second serial port	The second and fourth serial ports (COM2 and COM4 under Windows) both use IRQ 3. If only one serial port is present, IRQ 3 may be used by expansion devices.
4	First/third serial port	The first and third serial ports (COM1 and COM3 under Windows) both use IRQ 4. Generally, it is not a good idea to use IRQ 4 for expansion devices because loss of the serial port also means that terminal-emulation software cannot be used.
5	Second parallel port	Most systems have only one parallel port, but IRQ 5 is also commonly used for sound cards.
6	Floppy controller	All systems have floppy disks, which can be especially important on portable computers.
7	First parallel port	The first parallel port can frequently be disabled on laptops without an issue, unless the parallel port is used extensively for printing.
8	RTC	The Real-Time Clock maintains finer-grained timers
9	Video (older systems)	Older systems required an IRQ for the video controller, and it was typically assigned to IRQ 9. Most video controllers are now on the PCI bus and do not require a dedicated IRQ.
10		Usually available for expansion devices.
11	Usually PCI bus or SCSI controller	Generally not available for expansion devices.
12	Usually PS/2 mouse port	Generally not available.
13	FPU	The floating-point unit IRQ is used by the math coprocessor, even on systems with a CPU with an integrated math coprocessor such as the Pentium series.
14	Primary IDE	The first IDE channel is used by the main system hard disk, and thus IRQ 14 is almost never available on a portable system.
15	Secondary IDE	Portable systems typically place the CD-ROM on IRQ 15, making this IRQ unavailable for use.

I/O ports

I/O addresses are used for bidirectional communication between the system and a peripheral device. They tend to be somewhat poorly organized, and many devices have overlapping defaults. Each I/O port can be used to transfer a byte between the peripheral device and the CPU. Most devices require the ability to transfer multiple bytes at a time, so a block of ports is assigned to the device. The lowest port number is also called the base I/O address. A second parameter describes the size of the I/O window. Table 19-2 lists some of the common port assignments. Refer to your hardware vendor's documentation for details on additional devices such as IR ports, USB controllers, the PCMCIA controller, and any resources that may be required by motherboard components.

Table 19-2. Common I/O ports

Device name	I/O range (size)
Communication ports	
First parallel port	0x3bc–0x3bf (4)
First serial port	0x3f8–0x3ff (8)
Second serial port	0x2f8–0x2ff (8)
Disk drives	
Primary IDE	master: 0x1f00x1f7 (8)
	slave: 0x3f60x3f7 (2)
Secondary IDE	master: 0x1700x177 (8)
	slave: 0x376 (1)
Floppy controller	0x3f00x3f5 (6)
Input devices	
Keyboard	0x060 (1)
	0x064 (1)
Multimedia/gaming	
Sound card	0x2200x22f (16)
	FM Synth: 0x3880x38b (4)
	MIDI: 0x3300x331 (2)
Joystick/Game port	0x2000x207 (8)
System devices	
Interrupt controllers	0x0200x021 (2)
	0x0a00x0a1 (2)
DMA controllers	DMA channels 0-3: 0x0000x00f (16)
	Page registers: 0x0800x08f (16)
	DMA channels 4-7: 0x0c00x0df
CMOS/real time clock	0x0700x073 (4)
Speaker	0x061
Math coprocessor	0x0f00x0ff (16)

Linux Wireless Extensions and Tools

802.11 interfaces act like Ethernet interfaces once they are active, but they have many more configuration options than Ethernet interfaces because of the underlying radio technology. Rather than have each driver responsible for implementing its own configuration utility and reporting mechanisms, the Wireless Extension API was developed to allow all drivers to implement common functionality and use common configuration commands. Wireless extensions are also a great help to application developers needing to get details from the interface because they can do it in a device-independent way. For example, *xsupplicant* makes use of wireless extensions to set WEP keys on an interface without having to understand each driver's operations for setting keys. (At press time, system calls for WPA keying were not yet part of the official wireless extensions release.)

Compiling and Installing

Wireless LAN extensions are enabled with the *CONFIG_NET_RADIO* kernel configuration option. *CONFIG_NET_RADIO*-enabled kernels collect wireless statistics and expose additional data structures used by most drivers. Most distributions that include kernels with wireless extensions also include the wireless tools. If more recent versions are required, you may download them from *http://www.hpl.hp.com/ personal/Jean_Tourrilhes/Linux*, although it is probably easier to wait for your distribution's kernel source to integrate the latest version and rebuild the kernel.

Interface Configuration with Wireless Tools and iwconfig

The main command-line tool for managing a wireless-extension-enabled driver is *iwconfig*, which is designed to be a "wireless *ifconfig*." It can be used to set the radio interface parameters before using *ifconfig* to set traditional network parameters.

When run with no parameters, *iwconfig* displays a list of system interfaces. Interfaces that are not wireless will report that they have no wireless-specific data, while interfaces that do report wireless data will dump out the data that they have. Not all drivers implement all features. When *iwconfig* is run on a system with an old Orinoco card and an Atheros CardBus card, for example, the output will probably resemble this:

```
[root@bloodhound]# iwconfig
lo        no wireless extensions.

eth0      no wireless extensions.

eth1      IEEE 802.11-DS  ESSID:"11b-is-slow"  Nickname:"HERMES I"
          Mode:Managed  Frequency:2.457GHz  Access Point:00:E0:03:04:18:1C
          Bit Rate:2Mb/s   Tx-Power=15 dBm    Sensitivity:1/3
          RTS thr:off    Fragment thr:off
          Encryption key:off
          Power Management:off
          Link Quality:46/92 Signal level:-51 dBm  Noise level:-94 dBm
          Rx invalid nwid:0  invalid crypt:0  invalid misc:0
```

```
ath0     IEEE 802.11  ESSID:"11a-is-very-fast"
         Mode:Managed  Frequency:5.28GHz  Access Point: 00:0B:0E:00:F0:43
         Bit Rate:36Mb/s   Tx-Power:off   Sensitivity=0/3
         Retry:off   RTS thr:off   Fragment thr:off
         Encryption key:E452-94AC-09DB-2200-1256-6D7D-74  Security mode:open
         Power Management:off
         Link Quality:31/94  Signal level:-64 dBm  Noise level:-95 dBm
         Rx invalid nwid:0  Rx invalid crypt:0  Rx invalid frag:0
         Tx excessive retries:0  Invalid misc:0  Missed beacon:0
```

Both cards report the frequency of operation and some statistics about the quality of reception. The "nickname" reported by the Orinoco card is not reported by the Atheros card because it is a feature that is not implemented by the Atheros driver. (By default, the nickname is set to "HERMES I" after the name of the Lucent chipset used in the Orinoco card.)

Wireless Extensions reports information on the link quality in two ways. It reports a noise floor and signal level, and both are printed out by the driver. The signal to noise ratio is the difference between them. In the previous example, the SNR on *eth1* was 43 dB, and the SNR on *ath0* is 31 dB. The Link Quality statistic printed out by the driver reports the RSSI and the noise floor. In the previous example, the card is reporting an RSSI of 31 dB over a noise floor of –94 dBm.

Finding networks

Some drivers support the use of wireless extensions to build a list of networks in the area. Rather than configuration, use the *iwlist* command to get information from the card. As arguments, it takes the interface and a subcommand. *scan* will print out the list of information discovered in the area. Root privileges are required to retrieve scan data.

```
root@bloodhound:~# iwlist eth1 scan
eth1     Scan completed :
         Cell 01 - Address: 00:07:50:D5:CE:88
                   ESSID:"LuminiferousEther"
                   Mode:Master
                   Frequency:2.417GHz
                   Quality:0/10  Signal level:-70 dBm  Noise level:-256 dBm
                   Encryption key:on
                   Bit Rate:1Mb/s
                   Bit Rate:2Mb/s
                   Bit Rate:5.5Mb/s
                   Bit Rate:11Mb/s
         Cell 02 - Address: 00:09:5B:72:12:58
                   ESSID:"Mom's House"
                   Mode:Master
                   Frequency:2.467GHz
                   Quality:0/10  Signal level:-22 dBm  Noise level:-256 dBm
                   Encryption key:on
                   Bit Rate:1Mb/s
                   Bit Rate:2Mb/s
```

```
                    Bit Rate:5.5Mb/s
                    Bit Rate:11Mb/s
        Cell 03 - Address: 00:0D:72:9B:FE:69
                    ESSID:"2WIRE086"
                    Mode:Master
                    Frequency:2.442GHz
                    Quality:0/10  Signal level:-28 dBm  Noise level:-256 dBm
                    Encryption key:on
                    Bit Rate:1Mb/s
                    Bit Rate:2Mb/s
                    Bit Rate:5.5Mb/s
                    Bit Rate:11Mb/s
                    Bit Rate:22Mb/s
                    Bit Rate:6Mb/s
                    Bit Rate:9Mb/s
                    Bit Rate:12Mb/s
```

Setting the network name

To connect to a network, the first task is to select the network that will be joined. That is done by configuring the SSID with the *essid** parameter. If the network name includes a space, it must be enclosed in quotation marks. The network interface probably will not become active and start searching for the network until you use *ifconfig* to activate it. Progress of the scan can be checked by repeatedly running *iwconfig* and looking at the frequency. For example, the scan searching out an AP on channel 56 might look something like this:

```
[root@bloodhound]# iwconfig ath0 essid "Space Cadet"
[root@bloodhound]# ifconfig ath0 up
[root@bloodhound]# iwconfig ath0
. . .
Mode:Managed  Frequency:2.412GHz  Access Point: 00:00:00:00:00:00
. . .
[root@bloodhound]# iwconfig ath0
. . .
Mode:Managed  Frequency:2.447Hz  Access Point: 00:00:00:00:00:00
. . .
[root@bloodhound]# iwconfig ath0
. . .
Mode:Managed  Frequency:5.17GHz  Access Point: 00:00:00:00:00:00
. . .
[root@bloodhound]# iwconfig ath0
. . .
Mode:Managed  Frequency:5.28GHz  Access Point: 00:0B:0E:00:F0:43
. . .
```

---

* I use the term SSID in this book to refer to a network name. Some drivers, including the WaveLAN drivers, use ESSID instead. The distinction is that an ESSID is a network name assigned to an extended service set, not any old service set.

When the card discovers the network, it will associate with the AP and report the AP's MAC address in the *iwconfig* output. Associating with the network is merely the first step. Other configuration may be necessary before the logical network connection.

Some drivers have problems if the channel is automatically configured. If the channel is hard set, the driver may not search. To get a driver stuck on a channel to search, disable the card with *cardctl eject*, reset the SSID, and then reenable the interface with *ifconfig*.

Setting the network channel

Different cards support different operating frequencies. On a modern Atheros-based card, the entire ISM band is supported up to channel 14, and all three of the 5 GHz bands are supported as well. With drivers that support the operation, it is possible to get a list of supported channels by using the *iwlist* command:

```
root@bloodhound:~# iwlist ath0 channel
ath0      255 channels in total; available frequencies :
          Channel 01 : 2.412 GHz
          Channel 02 : 2.417 GHz
          Channel 03 : 2.422 GHz
          Channel 04 : 2.427 GHz
          Channel 05 : 2.432 GHz
          Channel 06 : 2.437 GHz
          Channel 07 : 2.442 GHz
          Channel 08 : 2.447 GHz
          Channel 09 : 2.452 GHz
          Channel 10 : 2.457 GHz
          Channel 11 : 2.462 GHz
          Channel 12 : 2.467 GHz
          Channel 13 : 2.472 GHz
          Channel 14 : 2.484 GHz
          Channel 34 : 5.17 GHz
          Channel 36 : 5.18 GHz
          Channel 38 : 5.19 GHz
          Channel 40 : 5.2 GHz
          Channel 42 : 5.21 GHz
          Channel 44 : 5.22 GHz
          Channel 46 : 5.23 GHz
          Channel 48 : 5.24 GHz
          Channel 50 : 5.25 GHz
          Channel 52 : 5.26 GHz
          Channel 56 : 5.28 GHz
          Channel 58 : 5.29 GHz
          Channel 60 : 5.3 GHz
          Channel 64 : 5.32 GHz
          Channel 100 : 5.5 GHz
          Channel 104 : 5.52 GHz
          Channel 108 : 5.54 GHz
          Channel 112 : 5.56 GHz
          Current Frequency:5.28GHz (channel 56)
```

The operating frequency can be selected in three ways. Most cards will hunt for an SSID if it is given to them as described previously. For cards that do not support scanning, the *freq* parameter can take an operating frequency directly, or the *channel* parameter can be used with the appropriate channel number, and the driver will derive the frequency from the channel number. The following two commands are equivalent:

```
[root@bloodhound]# iwconfig ath0 freq 2.432G
[root@bloodhound]# iwconfig ath0 channel 4
```

Setting the network mode and associating with an access point

Most 802.11 stations are in either ad hoc networks or infrastructure networks. The *iwconfig* nomenclature for these two modes is *Ad-hoc* and *Managed*. Select between them by using the *mode* parameter:

```
[root@bloodhound]# iwconfig ath0 mode Ad-hoc
[root@bloodhound]# iwconfig ath0 mode Managed
```

For stations in an infrastructure network, the *ap* parameter may be used to request an association with the specified MAC address. However, the station is not required to remain associated with the specified access point and may choose to roam to a different access point if the signal strength drops too much:

```
[root@bloodhound]# iwconfig ath0 ap 01:02:03:04:05:06
```

Setting the data rate

Most cards support multiple bit rates. *iwconfig* allows the administrator to choose between them by using the *rate* parameter. Bit rates can be specified after the *rate* parameter, or the keyword *auto* can be used to specify that the card should fall back to lower bit rates on poor-quality channels. If *auto* is combined with a bit rate, the driver may use any rate lower than the specified rate:

```
[root@bloodhound]# iwconfig ath0 rate auto
```

Configuring static WEP keys

The key parameter controls the WEP function of the driver. Keys can be entered as hexadecimal strings using the *key* subcommand. Enter the string without any delimiters, four digits at a time with dashes between the two-byte groups, or in the colon-separated byte form. The following commands are equivalent:

```
[root@bloodhound]# iwconfig ath0 key 0123456789
[root@bloodhound]# iwconfig ath0 key 0123-4567-89
[root@bloodhound]# iwconfig ath0 key 01:23:45:67:89
```

Many drivers support the use of 104-bit WEP keys as well. 104 bits is 13 bytes, or 26 hexadecimal characters:

```
[root@bloodhound]# iwconfig ath0 key 12345678901234567890123456
[root@bloodhound]# iwconfig ath0 key 1234-5678-9012-3456-7890-1234-56
[root@bloodhound]# iwconfig ath0 key 12:34:56:78:90:12:34:56:78:90:12:34:56
```

Although multiple keys can be entered using a bracketed index number, this capability is not used on many networks. Dynamic WEP key assignment through 802.1X is a much easier way to ensure the use of multiple keys, and is much more secure.

```
[root@bloodhound]# iwconfig ath0 key 0123-4567-89
[root@bloodhound]# iwconfig ath0 key 9876-5432-01 [2]
[root@bloodhound]# iwconfig ath0 key 5432-1678-90 [3]
```

Once multiple keys have been entered, select one by entering the index number without a key value:

```
[root@bloodhound]# iwconfig ath0 key [2]
```

Activate WEP processing using *key on* and disable WEP using *key off*. These can be combined with an index number to select a new WEP key:

```
[root@bloodhound]# iwconfig ath0 key [3] on
[root@bloodhound]# iwconfig ath0 key off
```

Finally, two types of WEP processing can be done. An *open* system accepts data frames sent in the clear, and a *restricted* system discards cleartext data frames. Both of these parameters can be combined with an index number:

```
[root@bloodhound]# iwconfig ath0 key [4] open
[root@bloodhound]# iwconfig ath0 key [3] restricted
```

The *key* parameter may also be accessed with the *encryption* parameter, which may be abbreviated to as few characters as *enc*. I prefer to use *key* because it seems clearer to me, but you may choose whichever you like.

Tuning 802.11 parameters

iwconfig allows you to tune the RTS and fragmentation thresholds. The RTS threshold of most drivers is 2,347, which effectively disables RTS clearing. In an environment likely to have hidden nodes, it can be set using the *rts_threshold* parameter with *iwconfig*. *rts_threshold* can be abbreviated as *rts*.

```
[root@bloodhound]# iwconfig wvlan0 rts 500
```

The default value of the fragmentation threshold is 2,346. In noisy environments, it may be worth lowering the fragmentation threshold to reduce the amount of data, which must be retransmitted when frames are lost to corruption on the wireless medium. Set the parameter by using the *fragmentation_threshold* argument to *iwconfig*. It may be set anywhere from 256 to 2,356, but it may take on only even values. *fragmentation_threshold* may be abbreviated as *frag*.

```
[root@bloodhound]# iwconfig ath0 frag 500
```

802.11 stations maintain several retry counters. When frames are retransmitted "too many" times or wait for transmission for "too long," they are discarded. Two retry counters are maintained. The long retry counter, set by the *retry* parameter, is the number of times transmission is attempted for a frame longer than the RTS threshold.

The short retry counter, set by the *retry min* parameter, is the number of times trans-mission will be attempted for a frame shorter than the RTS threshold. Unlike many drivers, *iwconfig* also allows for configuration of the maximum frame lifetime with the *retry lifetime* parameter. To specify a value in milliseconds or microseconds, append "m" or "u" to the value:

```
[root@bloodhound]# iwconfig ath0 retry 4
[root@bloodhound]# iwconfig ath0 retry min 7
[root@bloodhound]# iwconfig ath0 retry lifetime 400m
```

Agere (Lucent) Orinoco

Wireless networking is far older than the 802.11 standard. Several proprietary approaches had been released and were gaining a foothold in the market in the early 1990s. One of the first notable products was the NCR WaveLAN, released when NCR was a division at AT&T.* When Lucent was spun off from AT&T in 1996, the WaveLAN division, like most communications product manufacturing at AT&T, was made a part of Lucent.

Early WaveLAN hardware was a completely proprietary system. After 802.11 was finally standardized in 1997, new hardware that complied with the standard was sold under the WaveLAN brand. To distinguish the standards-compliant cards from the proprietary cards, the former were called "WaveLAN IEEE" cards, while the latter were simply "WaveLAN" cards.

As the market for 802.11 hardware continued to develop, Lucent decided to rename the WaveLAN division under another brand name. The new name, Orinoco, comes from the third largest river system in the world. During the rainy season in South America, the Orinoco swells with fresh rainfall flowing in from over 200 tributaries. At its peak, the river grows to over 10 miles wide and more than 300 feet deep. Nearly 1,000 miles of the Orinoco's 1,300 miles are navigable; it is no wonder that the river's name is derived from the native words for "a place to paddle."

Lucent's initial strategy for support on open source platforms was to offer a choice of drivers. A closed-source proprietary binary driver, *wavelan2_cs*, provided full func-tionality, and a second, less functional open source driver, *wvlan_cs*, was made avail-able under the GPL. *wvlan_cs* was based on a low-library provided with the closed source driver, and it was an evolutionary dead-end. Rather than continue along that path, *wvlan_cs* was rewritten with new low-level operations and became *orinoco_cs* in Linux kernel version 2.4. (*orinoco_cs* was originally known as *dldwd_cs*, which stood for David's Less Dodgy WaveLAN Driver!)

---

* NCR, which was founded in 1884 as the National Cash Register Company, was acquired by AT&T in 1991. I can only assume that a cash register company was interested in wireless networking because it would enable cash registers to be placed anywhere without wiring.

In addition to the WaveLAN cards and any OEM versions of WaveLAN cards, *orinoco_cs* contains basic support for some PRISM-2–based cards and Symbol cards that use the same MAC chipset. *orinoco_cs* has been part of the Linux kernel distribution since kernel Version 2.4.3.

Compiling and Installing

All distributions based on the 2.4 and later kernels include *orinoco_cs*. In many cases, it will be possible to use the driver that shipped with your kernel. The major exception is if you plan to run xsupplicant and need to apply the key management patch, which will be discussed later.

PCMCIA configuration

Older distributions may ship with the *wvlan_cs* driver still enabled. To change the driver used by the distribution, it is sufficient to change the module binding the PCMCIA configuration. The author of *orinoco_cs* supplies a file, *hermes.conf*, which contains card definitions for the cards supported by *orinoco_cs*. Because *hermes.conf* ends in *.conf*, it is sourced by the line at the end of */etc/pcmcia/config* that reads all *.conf* files. However, to avoid binding conflicts, you must comment out all the lines that bind the older *wvlan_cs* driver to newly inserted cards. Alternatively, it is sufficient to edit the definition of your wireless card to bind the *orinoco_cs* driver after grabbing identification information from the output of *dump_cis*:

```
# in hermes.conf
#
card "Lucent Technologies Wavelan/IEEE"
    version "Lucent Technologies", "WaveLAN/IEEE"
    bind "orinoco_cs"

# from standard /etc/pcmcia/config
#
# card "Lucent Technologies WaveLAN/IEEE"
#    version "Lucent Technologies", "WaveLAN/IEEE"
#    bind "wvlan_cs"
```

Doing it yourself

This is part of the kernel, so you generally don't need to install it unless you're looking for a particular bug fix or feature enhancement. The most common reason to recompile the driver is a requirement to support dynamic WEP with 802.1X authentication. xsupplicant distributes a patch to be applied for rekeying. Firmware updates may also be necessary to support dynamic keys. I have used firmware version 8.42. Later versions almost certainly work, but earlier versions may not.

Requirements are straightforward. The code itself is fetched from the distribution site at *http://ozlabs.org/people/dgibson/dldwd/*. Make sure that you have a copy of *patch* to apply the patches of interest (the rekey patch is not required in version 0.15rc2):

```
gast@bloodhound:~$ cd orinoco-0.13e
gast@bloodhound:~/orinoco-0.13e$ patch -p1 < ../rekey_patch_orinoco-0.13e
patching file orinoco.c
patching file orinoco.h
msg@bloodhound:~/orinoco-0.13e$ make
  (build messages snipped)
root@bloodhound:/home/msg/orinoco-0.13e# make install
if [ -d /etc/pcmcia ]; then install -m 644 -o 0 -g 0 hermes.conf /etc/pcmcia/hermes.
conf; fi
mkdir -p /lib/modules/2.4.26/kernel/drivers/net/wireless
for f in hermes.o orinoco.o orinoco_cs.o orinoco_plx.o orinoco_tmd.o orinoco_pci.o;
do \
    if test -e /lib/modules/2.4.26/pcmcia/$f; then \
        install -m 644 -o 0 -g 0 $f /lib/modules/2.4.26/pcmcia/$f; \
    else \
        install -m 644 -o 0 -g 0 $f /lib/modules/2.4.26/kernel/drivers/net/wireless/
$f; \
    fi; \
done
depmod -a
```

At the end of the build process, the system has several kernel modules: *orinoco_cs.o*, the PCMCIA interface; *orinoco.o*, the hardware driver; and *hermes.o*, the driver for the MAC chip.

Configuring the orinoco_cs Interface

Configuration of *orinoco_cs* is identical to the configuration of *wvlan_cs*. When the card is inserted, the */etc/pcmcia/wireless* script is run, using the configuration options in */etc/pcmcia/wireless.opts*. The wireless script is a frontend to the *iwconfig* program. Editing fields in *wireless.opts* sets the arguments to *iwconfig*. For details on configuring the options to *iwconfig*, see the previous section on the *wvlan_cs* driver.

Atheros-Based cards and MADwifi

802.11a is the choice for high-speed, high-density 802.11 networks, and most 802.11a devices on the market use Atheros chipsets.[*] The driver project is called the "Multiband Atheros Driver for WiFi," or *MADwifi*; the project's home page is *http://sourceforge.net/projects/madwifi/*.

---

[*] It is likely that any card with 802.11a support is based on an Atheros chipset. Rather than include a list that will quickly become outdated, I suggest you refer to the searchable list at *http://customerproducts.atheros.com/customerproducts/*.

Resetting on WEP Key Installation

When using dynamic WEP on Linux, the 802.1X supplicant derives WEP keys from the authentication exchange, and then loads them into the driver. Up until 1999, many cards did not support the dynamic provisioning of keys, and needed to reset the micro-controller in the card to make the new key take effect. Drivers were written with this assumption, and the code that updated keys would reset the hardware.

Resetting the hardware when a key is installed is undesirable behavior with dynamic WEP. Once the authentication has completed, a key must be installed. If the driver resets after key installation, the link will bounce. In many cases, the AP will note the link bounce and require a new authentication. Once the supplicant detects the link state change, it will run the authentication again to derive a new key. After the new authentication completes, the supplicant resets the card to install the new key, starting the cycle over yet again.

Most interface cards have firmware upgrades available which eliminate the need to reset the hardware after key installation. Once the right version of firmware is in place, the driver needs to be updated to a dynamic WEP-capable version that does not send reset commands.

If dynamic WEP is not working because the card resets after the authentication succeeds, check either the source code or the online forums for the driver for your card to see if an update or patch is required.

Although best known for 802.11a support, there are several Atheros chips available. There are three generations of chipset. The initial chipset, the 5210, only supported 802.11a. It was followed by the first dual-band chipset, the 5211, which added 802.11b support. Most devices now on the market use the 5212, which is a dual-band/tri-mode chipset that can support 802.11a, 802.11b, and 802.11g. In addition to the different radio support, later generations are capable of performing much more complex security operations. All chipsets are supported by MADwifi.

Driver Architecture and the Hardware Access Layer (HAL)

MADwifi is split into two parts: an open source driver, and a closed-source library called the Hardware Access Layer (HAL). Atheros chipsets are extremely flexible, and capable of tuning outside the unlicensed bands because they use a limited form of a software-defined radio.

Atheros has interpreted FCC regulations as requiring that the HAL be kept closed. (Broadcom interprets the rules in the same way, and they have a similar chipset on the market.) FCC rules require that software-defined radios must not be modifiable by the user to operate outside of their certified frequency bands. Devices that do not enforce the terms of their certification are potentially subject to sanctions. If devices sold for use in the unlicensed spectrum were suddenly able to disrupt licensed communications, vendors of such devices might also be penalized.*

For commercial products, ensuring that the software stays in the unlicensed spectrum is easy—just avoid compiling and distributing code that breaks the rules. Users cannot edit compiled code, so they are unable to break the rules. Open source software changes the game. Distributing code that follows the rules does not prevent modification that break the rules.

Atheros faced a choice: ship a driver with completely open source code and risk losing regulatory approval to sell chips, or find some way of protecting the radio spectrum. Obviously, a driver exists because they took the latter course. Rather than have the open source driver interface directly with the radio chipset, it accesses the radio through the HAL's API. The HAL is generic enough that it is used unchanged by many other operating systems developing open source drivers; there are zero dependencies on the host system software, though it does depend on the host hardware's instruction set. The HAL is available for x86 architectures (both 32- and 64-bit), ARM, MIPS, PowerPC, and XScale. Although closed-source code is often viewed with suspicion in the open source community, I consider it a sign of corporate commitment to the Linux platform that Atheros was willing to support the development of the driver.

Requirements

MADwifi makes extensive use of wireless extensions, and is consistently developed against the latest version. Either use a recent distribution with current wireless extensions support, or upgrade the kernel to a recent distribution.

Drivers often make use of other kernel functionality, and MADwifi is no different. Building MADwifi depends on having kernel headers and configuration files for the running kernel. If you have built a custom kernel for your hardware, by definition you have kernel source and configuration. Not all distributions will install the kernel source and configuration by default; you may have to find the right package.

UUCP tools will also be necessary to get the HAL. To safely transfer the binary HAL over arbitrary network paths, it is uuencoded. MADwifi's *make* script calls uudecode. Depending on your distribution, uudecode may be part of the shell archive utilities package (*sharutils*), or it may be part of a UUCP tools package.

---

* Christian Sandvig, a professor at the University of Illinois at Urbana-Champaign, takes exception to the SDR interpretation of FCC rules in a paper titled "Hidden Interfaces to 'Ownerless' Networks" (*http://www.spcomm.uiuc.edu/users/csandvig/research/Hidden_Interfaces.pdf*).

Building the Driver

MADwifi is still under active development, and it changes regularly. Rather than having periodic packaged releases, it is constantly maintained in CVS. Fetch the latest version from CVS:

```
root@bloodhound:~# cvs -z3 -d:pserver:anonymous@cvs.sourceforge.net:/cvsroot/madwifi
co madwifi
```

When the command completes, the source code and (encoded HAL files) will be downloaded into a directory *madwifi*. To build the driver, use the standard open source command set:

```
root@bloodhound:~# cd madwifi
root@bloodhound:~/bloodhound# make
  (lots of build messages)
root@bloodhound:~/bloodhound# make install
```

The main modules are *wlan.o*, *ath_pci.o*, and *ath_hal.o*. Several other cryptographic modules are loaded on demand to support particular encryption schemes. If the MADwifi build system cannot detect the right place in the filesystem to install to, you may need to manually place the required modules in the correct location and run *depmod -a* to update modules.

Using the Driver

Current versions of the MADwifi driver publish a list of supported cards to the kernel, which is revealed when module dependencies are built. The MADwifi driver supported device list includes several devices with the manufacturer ID of 0x168c, which belongs to Atheros. Provided that module dependencies are built correctly, there is no need to modify the PCMCIA configuration scripts.

Loading the driver creates an interface prefaced with *ath*. Most likely, it will be *ath0*, since you will only have one Atheros card running in your system. Older versions of MADwifi used the prefix *wlan*. If you see *wlan0*, update the driver.

MADwifi is correctly integrated with the Linux hotplug system. When the module is inserted, the hotplug system will attempt to register the interface. It is almost certain that the start-up scripts in place on your distribution will need to be edited. Open wireless networks can probably have light editing; using 802.1X requires heavier editing because the interface must be authenticated before starting DHCP.

802.1X on Linux with xsupplicant

I have been fortunate enough to volunteer at the Interop Labs wireless security initiatives for the past few years, where I get to experience interoperability close up. In 2004, developers from the Open1X project participated in the interoperability test

Using Windows Drivers Under Linux

Not all card manufacturers have committed to supporting Linux. Revealing intellectual property by giving away driver source code is usually the major concern. Finding the engineering time to write, maintain, and support drivers given to the user community is another.

Drivers written natively for Linux are preferable for a variety of reasons. However, if your card vendor does not yet have a Linux driver, you can use the Windows driver through a wrapper program. Two software packages can run the Windows NDIS driver in a sandbox and translate Windows system calls into their Linux equivalents. The NDISWrapper project (*http://ndiswrapper.sourceforge.net/*) is a completely open source implementation. A company called Linuxant provides a commercial program called DriverLoader (*http://www.linuxant.com/driverloader/*) for the same purpose. Trial licenses are free, but ongoing use does require payment.

event, bringing open source code into an event that had previously been the preserve of product manufacturers. As the popularity of wireless networks has waxed, so has interest in solutions for connecting Linux systems to secure wireless LANs. *xsupplicant* is one of the leading implementations of 802.1X for Linux.

Requirements

Before even considering working with xsupplicant, the most important task is to ensure that 802.11 is already working! Many "wireless" problems are really PC Card problems. Obviously, you will not be able to attach to an authenticated network until building and configuring xsupplicant, but you should be able to insert your wireless card and have it recognized by the system. Card Services will generally sound a high-pitched beep when a card is inserted to indicate it is recognized, resources were successfully allocated, and the driver was loaded. (A second low-pitched beep may follow indicating a configuration failure, but that is okay. Chances are that you want your ultimate configuration to run xsupplicant, so it's acceptable at the outset to not have configuration support immediately.) With the driver successfully loaded, you should be able to run *iwconfig* and obtain statistics from the driver.

Even if the driver for your chosen card is working, make sure it has support for dynamic WEP. Although there is some dispute over the absolute security level of dynamically keyed WEP systems, it is unquestionable that dynamic WEP has a significantly higher level of security than a single-key WEP system. It is a virtual certainty that any card you want to use with xsupplicant should support the use of dynamic keys. Most modern cards, those released in early 2003 and later, have driver support for dynamic WEP already, but a few older cards require patches. The popular Hermes-based Orinoco 802.11b cards fall into the latter category. Depending on the driver, you may also need to rebuild your kernel (or at least get a copy of your kernel's configuration) in order to compile a driver.

Finally, xsupplicant needs one major library. As discussed previously, most EAP methods are based on TLS in one way or another. xsupplicant uses the OpenSSL TLS implementation. Install version 0.9.7 or later. Before fetching the source from *openssl.org*, check to see if there is a package available for your distribution.

Compiling and Installing xsupplicant

Compiling and installing xsupplicant follows the same routine that any other open-source package. Released code can be fetched from *http://sourceforge.net/projects/open1x/*, and compiled in the standard Unix way:

```
root@bloodhound:~# tar -xzvf xsupplicant-1.0.1.tar.gz
root@bloodhound:~# cd xsupplicant
root@bloodhound:~/xsupplicant# ./configure
root@bloodhound:~/xsupplicant# make
root@bloodhound:~/xsupplicant# make install
```

As this book went to press, xsupplicant 1.0.1 was several months old, and massive development had occurred in the CVS version. (This section is written using a late 2004 CVS version.) Among many other improvements, the CVS version has preliminary WPA support. The CVS version can be fetched from an anonymous CVS server, and compiled in the standard Unix way:

```
root@bloodhound:~# cvs -z3 -d:pserver:anonymous@cvs.sourceforge.net:/cvsroot/
xsupplicant co xsupplicant
root@bloodhound:~# cd xsupplicant
root@bloodhound:~/xsupplicant# ./configure
root@bloodhound:~/xsupplicant# make
root@bloodhound:~/xsupplicant# make install
```

As a result of the build, you get three executables installed; the only one you are likely to use is */usr/local/sbin/xsupplicant*.

Configuring xsupplicant

When run, xsupplicant searches for its configuration file in */etc*. The config file, */etc/xsupplicant.conf*, does not get installed by default, so copy it over to the expected location.

```
root@bloodhound:~/xsupplicant# cp etc/xsupplicant.conf /etc/
```

Configuration files specify the authentication method, user identity, possibly the password, and a certificate location to validate the certificate from the network. Certificate authentication of the network may be disabled by setting the certificate location to NONE, but it is not recommended. When setting up the network, you may need to convert certificates between different forms. OpenSSL can easily convert between different formats by specifying the formats on the command line.

```
root@bloodhound:~# openssl x509 -inform DER -outform PEM -in MyCA.der -out MyCa.pem
```

Passwords are stored in the configuration file in a nonencrypted form, so you may wish to have the system prompt for the password to avoid putting sensitive information in configuration files. When no password is in the file for the network you are connecting to, xsupplicant will prompt the user.

In the configuration file, settings can be stored as part of a profile for an SSID. The following example is a simple configuration for a network using PEAP, with EAP-MSCHAP-V2 inner authentication on a network called *batnet*. xsupplicant can be configured to run a command after authentication completes, or that can be left to the configuration scripts on the operating system.

```
### GLOBAL SECTION

logfile = /var/log/xsupplicant.log
network_list = all
default_netname = batnet

first_auth_command = dhcpcd %i

###  NETWORK SECTION

batnet{
  # allow_types = eap_tls, eap_md5, eap_gtc, eap-otp
  allow_types = eap_peap

  # Phase 1 ("outer") identity
  identity = msg
  # Alternative, but common specification is to not reveal username
  # identity = anonymous

  eap-peap {
      # It is a good idea to validate the certificate and not do "none"
      # root_cert = NONE
      root_cert = rootCA.pem
      root_dir = /etc/xsupplicant.d
      chunk_size = 1398
      random_file = /dev/random

      # ** Inner method configuration
      allow_types = eap_mschapv2

      # Inner method configuration
      eap-mschapv2 {
        username = msg
        password = imnottelling
      }
  }
}
```

Pseudorandom number generation

Like many other security protocols, EAP methods require a "good" source of random numbers. Linux provides two random number devices, */dev/random* and */dev/urandom*. The former returns random bits that are within the system's entropy pool. If insufficient entropy is available, the read will block until sufficient entropy is available, while the latter will return as much data is requested, perhaps at the cost of quality.

Connecting and Authenticating to a Network

The first step in gaining access to an 802.1X-protected network is to associate to it. xsupplicant depends on the system to perform the association. The initial configuration should also configure the card to use encrypted frames, although the key configured does not matter. Configure a dummy key to indicate to the driver that it should run in encrypted mode; xsupplicant will replace the key after successful authentication with a wireless extension library call. The most common way of configuring the connection is to use *iwconfig* to plumb a key and configure the network, and then use *ifconfig* to bring the interface up and start searching for the network. Naturally, these commands may be triggered by the configuration system scripts when a wireless card is inserted.

```
root@bloodhound:~# iwconfig ath0 key 12345678901234567890123456
root@bloodhound:~# iwconfig essid essid "batnet"
root@bloodhound:~# ifconfig ath0 up
```

After the system has associated with the network, run xsupplicant. The *-i* option indicates which interface it should run on. Debugging is activated with *-d*, with the following letters determining what information is printed out. Log messages are sent to the console with *-f*. The following example has cut the raw packet dumps.

```
root@bloodhound:~# /usr/local/sbin/xsupplicant -i ath0 -dasic -f
Using default config!
network_list: all
Default network: "default"
Startup command: "echo "some command""
First_Auth command: "dhclient %i"
Reauth command: "echo "authenticated user %i""
Logfile: "/var/log/xsupplicant.log"
Allow Types: ALL
ID: "msg"
peap root_cert: "NONE"
peap chunk: 1398
peap rand: "/dev/random"
PEAP Allow Types: ALL
mschapv2 username: "msg"
mschapv2 password: "imnottelling"
Interface ath0 initalized!
```

At this point, xsupplicant has read the configuration file, and checks to see if the wireless interface is associated to an AP. If it is, the authentication process can begin.

```
[INT] Interface ath0 is wireless!
[INT] The card reported that the destination MAC address is now 00 0B 0E 00 F0 40
[INT] Working with ESSID : batnet
[CONFIG] Working from config file /etc/xsupplicant.conf.
[STATE] (global) -> DISCONNECTED
[STATE] Processing DISCONNECTED state.
[STATE] DISCONNECTED -> CONNECTING
[STATE] CONNECTING -> ACQUIRED
[STATE] Processing ACQUIRED state.
```

Once the system has associated to an AP, it begins authenticating.

```
Connection established, authenticating...
[STATE] Sending EAPOL-Response-Identification
[STATE] ACQUIRED -> AUTHENTICATING)
[STATE] Processing AUTHENTICATING state.
[STATE] Sending EAPOL-Response-Authentication
****WARNING**** Turning off certificate verification is a *VERY* bad idea!  You
should not use this mode outside of basic testing, as it will compromise the security
of your connection!
[AUTH TYPE] Packet in (1) :
20
[AUTH TYPE] Setting Key Constant for PEAP v0!
[INT] Interface eth0 is NOT wireless!
Userdata is NULL!  We will probably have problems!
[STATE] (global) -> DISCONNECTED
[STATE] Processing DISCONNECTED state.
[STATE] DISCONNECTED -> CONNECTING
[STATE] Processing AUTHENTICATING state.
[STATE] Sending EAPOL-Response-Authentication
```

At this point, a great deal of debugging output will appear as certificates are exchanged back and forth and validated by both sides of the conversation. Once the TLS tunnel is established, the debug output shows the inner authentication. In the case of EAP-MSCHAP-V2, the RADIUS server sends a challenge. Based on the challenge value and the shared secret, a response is generated.

```
[AUTH TYPE] (EAP-MSCHAPv2) Challenge
[AUTH TYPE] (EAP-MS-CHAPv2) ID : 2F
[AUTH TYPE] Authenticator Challenge : C6 02 26 BE C3 E0 44 03 13 6E 1F BA F0 B3 1D 5A
[AUTH TYPE] Generated PeerChallenge : 28 62 AA A2 8C 8E EB 82 D1 9B 2F 9A 54 67 93 2C
[AUTH TYPE] PeerChallenge : 28 62 AA A2 8C 8E EB 82
[AUTH TYPE] AuthenticatorChallenge : C6 02 26 BE C3 E0 44 03
[AUTH TYPE] Username : msg
[AUTH TYPE] Challenge : 48 E7 AA 53 54 52 98 62
[AUTH TYPE] PasswordHash : C5 A2 37 B7 E9 D8 E7 08 D8 43 6B 61 48 A2 5F A1
[AUTH TYPE] Response : 4D 96 51 8C 18 3A F7 C7 70 15 47 13 19 D8 D6 9B 36 00 AD E8 FA
9A 0F 28
[AUTH TYPE] myvars->NtResponse = 4D 96 51 8C 18 3A F7 C7 70 15 47 13 19 D8 D6 9B 36
00 AD E8 FA 9A 0F 28
```

```
[AUTH TYPE] response->NT_Response = 4D 96 51 8C 18 3A F7 C7 70 15 47 13 19 D8 D6 9B
36 00 AD E8 FA 9A 0F 28
[AUTH TYPE] (EAP-MSCHAPv2) Success!
[AUTH TYPE] Server authentication check success!  Sending phase 2 success!
```

Once the system has successfully authenticated, the AP will supply keys. Keys are both encrypted and authenticated, using keys derived from the shared cryptographic keys from the phase 1 TLS exchange. Two key messages are sent, one with the unique unicast key for the station, and one with the broadcast key shared by all stations. xsupplicant uses the wireless extensions API to set the keys in the driver, where they will be viewable with *iwconfig*.

```
Processing EAPoL-Key!
[INT] Key Descriptor    = 1
[INT] Key Length        = 13
[INT] Replay Counter    = 41 2F BB 2D 00 00 00 D5
[INT] Key IV            = 69 4C 45 D7 CF C3 DD CD 2A 3A F3 CB 04 7A F4 A3
[INT] Key Index (RAW)   = 01
[INT] Key Signature     = C2 05 6C 3A EB 25 E9 B9 8E FC 60 D6 77 44 57 22
[INT] EAPoL Key Processed: broadcast [2] 13 bytes.
[INT] Key before decryption : ED 5D 03 D2 7A DE B4 60 29 FD FD F5 42
[INT] Key after decryption : FB BB AC D3 6F 7D 0A 3F FF 2A CF 33 4E
[INT] Successfully set WEP key [2]
Processing EAPoL-Key!
[INT] Key Descriptor    = 1
[INT] Key Length        = 13
[INT] Replay Counter    = 41 2F BB 2D 00 00 00 D6
[INT] Key IV            = 66 15 69 E2 B2 8C 0E 89 7C D3 94 8C 93 25 43 1B
[INT] Key Index (RAW)   = 80
[INT] Key Signature     = 49 C1 15 B8 E9 D0 87 53 A6 FD 5D 76 CB 51 9D 65
[INT] EAPoL Key Processed: unicast [1] 13 bytes.
[INT] Using peer key!
[INT] Successfully set WEP key [1]
[INT] Successfully set the WEP transmit key [1]
```

Some drivers implement private system calls to report keys. Atheros cards using the MADwifi driver can list keys with *iwlist ath0 key*; many drivers will also report the unicast key in *iwconfig*.

Commercial 802.1X on Linux

In addition to xsupplicant, there is one commercial program available from Meetinghouse Data Communications. Meetinghouse's AEGIS client supports a wide variety of EAP methods (MD5, TLS, TTLS, PEAP, and LEAP). Due to the difficulties in keeping up with new distributions, however, it is only officially supported on RedHat versions 8 and 9. The Linux version of the Meetinghouse supplicant does not support WPA for the same reason xsupplicant does not: the lack of a standard WPA keying API.

WPA on Linux

WPA is not generally available on Linux because there is no standard way of obtaining the necessary information to perform the four-way handshake. xsupplicant runs in user space, but some of the data necessary to compute the four-way handshake must be obtained through the driver. Each driver has defined its own system calls for fetching this data, which requires supplicants to track the development of private system calls in every driver. A future release of the wireless extensions API will support the necessary system calls, and WPA will be made available in both open source and commercial products.

## CHAPTER 20

Using 802.11 Access Points

In even the simplest 802.11 network, proper configuration of the access points is essential. Without properly configured network interfaces, no traffic will be bridged on to the wired network.

In the early days of 802.11, access points were simple devices. They had a pair of interfaces, and connected wireless devices to an existing wired LAN. Early APs were bridges between the wireless and wired realms, with few additional features. When the first generation of wireless LAN products hit the market, there was a broad separation into cheaper home gateways and expensive business-class products. Products in both classes performed the same functions, although the latter typically used higher-capacity components to provide flexibility and investment protection, as well as the first crude large-scale management tools.

At the dawn of 802.11, APs were initially standalone independent devices. In the early days, wireless LANs offered the ability to have untethered access, but lacked serious security and management capabilities. Although these islands of networking occasionally communicated with each other, they were not often used as part of a large-scale network system because the protocols to enable them to do so had not been developed or tested on a large scale. As wireless networks became more popular and grew larger, flaws in the traditional standalone access point model became apparent.

Sensing a market opportunity, several vendors have built a second generation of wireless network hardware. Newer approaches concentrate management and support functions for APs into an chassis that has the basic functions of an Ethernet switch, which enables the APs themselves to be dumbed-down radio interfaces. Although there are several approaches, the broad category of "lightweight" or "thin" access points plus a control system is often labeled a *wireless switch*. A great deal of interest has surrounded the switch-based architecture since it was first popularized in late 2002, but the fundamental technology must perform the same functions as first-generation access points.

This chapter discusses, in general terms, how to use access points. It takes a look at a full-featured standalone device, the Cisco 1200 series AP. Although there is a great deal of power in the Cisco 1200, it can be formidable to configure. For a look at the lower end of the market, this chapter looks at the Apple AirPort Express.

General Functions of an Access Point

Broadly speaking, there are two price classes of access points in the marketplace. A low-cost tier consisting of home devices is sold widely through retail channels directly to the end user. These low-cost devices are often specialized computing platforms with only limited memory and storage.* The higher-cost tier incorporates additional features required to support large deployments; frequently, these devices have additional memory and storage and incorporate more general-purpose hardware. The difference between the two price tiers is that the higher-cost devices are meant to work together as a system to build a much more reliable, secure, and manageable network. To use a somewhat simplistic analogy, the small-scale wireless LANs that have proliferated in homes and small offices are like cordless phones. They extend a single network out over a limited range, and that is all. Large-scale wireless LANs are much more like cellular telephony, with a strong focus on maintaining a network connection in a much more demanding environment. Frequent user motion and and hand-off between APs is a given, as is a much higher standard of management and troubleshooting tools.

Cutting across the different market segments, however, is a set of generic features that are required to fulfill the service promises made in the 802.11 standard. Configuration of these features, of course, is vendor-specific, but many products are fairly similar to each other in purpose and design.

Most obviously, access points are bridges between the wireless world and the wired world. As bridges, then, all access points have features that one would expect to see on a network bridge. They have at least two network interfaces: a wireless interface that understands the details of 802.11 and a second interface to connect to wired networks. I am not aware of any access point that does not use Ethernet as the wired back-end, though it is certainly not required by any part of the standard. As wireless LANs have grown up, more of the high-end access points have begun to support VLANs on the network uplink. Lower-end access points may have a "WAN" port, which is usually a second Ethernet port for use with a cable modem or DSL, though I have seen a few products that have RS-232 serial ports to support dial-up modems.

All wireless interfaces must provide basic support for the 802.11 channel access rules, but the similarity ends there. Early access points implemented the entire 802.11 protocol at the edge of the network; many newer devices have moved some of the 802.11 processing away from the edge of the network and have split the 802.11 MAC across

---

* For cost savings, many of the low-cost run a stripped-down version of Linux, and have been the subject of a great deal of software hacking. See, for example, the HyperWRT (*http://www.hyperwrt.org*) and wifi-box (*http://sourceforge.net/projects/wifi-box*) projects.

multiple system components. Most access points offer the ability to use external antennas to fine-tune range and coverage area.

Bridges have some buffer memory to hold frames as they are transferred between the two interfaces, and they store MAC address associations for each port in a set of internal tables. Bridging tables are, of course, highly implementation-specific, and there is no guarantee of similarities across the industry. The most basic and inexpensive devices will usually assume that they are the only access point in the network, and bridge accordingly. When access points support roaming, it may be necessary to move sessions and user data in between access points. High-end access points may need to augment a basic bridging table with VLAN information on the wired interface, as well as information about how users authenticate their connections.

Commercial-grade devices are also designed to work cooperatively; the most common feature is a vendor-proprietary method to move association data from access point to access point without interrupting link-layer connectivity. Network management is generally much more sophisticated on commercial-grade products to enable network engineers to manage the tens or hundreds of devices used to create a large-scale coverage area.

Initially, management through a TCP/IP network interface was a standard feature. One of the big innovations in the past few years has been the development of "thin" access point solutions that move management functions from access points to central concentration devices.

Depending on the market for which an access point is developed, it may offer services to its wireless clients. The most popular service is DHCP; wireless stations may be assigned addresses automatically upon association. Larger-scale devices often rely on existing DHCP servers on the network to ensure consistence across access points. Many access points can also perform network address translation (NAT), especially the "home gateway"–type products that can connect to a modem and dial up an ISP.

Security has been a sore point for wireless network managers since before the advent of 802.11's success. Access points have a privileged position with respect to security concerns because they are the gateways to the wired network and are ideally positioned to implement security policies. In addition to first-generation security approaches such as MAC address filtering, most products now implement stronger user-based authentication. Wi-Fi Protected Access (WPA) can be run with a pre-shared key in most home products, and with an external authentication server in large corporate deployments. Many high-end devices now offer significant integration with the existing wired network. Using those features to best extend the wired network will be discussed in the next chapter.

Management interfaces often leave something to be desired. Configuration of access points tends to be challenging because access points must be manufactured cheaply, and low-cost devices tend not to have the processing power to run an easy-to-use configuration engine. Most vendors use lightweight operating systems running on low-powered hardware, but one of the trade-offs of using a lightweight operating system is that it does not provide the programming environment necessary to build rich functionality. Early access points offered both a command-line interface and a web-based management interface. The recent development of "Wi-Fi switches" offers some hope for network administrators. Rather than requiring management of individual APs as standalone network elements, stripped-down (or "thin") access points are managed through a handful of centralized control switches. With greater processing power and functionality, the switches can support more functionality and much improved management interfaces.

Debugging and troubleshooting tools are as advanced as management tools, which unfortunately means that they often leave network administrators mired in inconclusive or irrelevant information. Ideally, products should maintain detailed logs of activities, but it is common to find vague logs of results that give very little insight into failures. Counters can be helpful, but only if the right counters are accurately maintained. Tools such as *ping* and *traceroute* are common, but network analyzers and packet capture tools are not.

Types of Access Points

Broadly speaking, there are three major types of access points. Many of the best-known devices are low-cost access points sold at major consumer electronics outlets. Although these devices make up the bulk of the market, they are unsuited for use in a large-scale deployment. Just as consumer electronics-class Ethernet switches are not suitable for building a major network, cheap APs cannot offer the features needed to build a major wireless netowrk. Higher-priced devices with significant additional functionality exist for the corporate enterprise market.

For the home: residential gateways

The low-cost tier is composed of devices often called *residential gateways*. Residential gateways are designed to be as low-cost as possible, so only the basic features required for the typical small or home office are included. To further reduce cost, most of the residential products are based on "reference designs" from 802.11 chipmakers. Equipment manufacturers may (or may not) customize a reference design, the external case, and sell the resulting device under their own brands.

Residential gateways generally share the following characteristics:

- Most devices include a DHCP server to make plug-and-play configuration easier.
- They are often deployed by users with one routable IP address, so NAT implementations are common.* Many can use PPPoE or DHCP to dynamically assign the routable external address.

---

* The NAT implementation is usually restrictive. It is able to translate many internal devices to varying ports on the external IP address, and fixed ports on the external IP address to specific internal addresses (for, say, inbound web or SSH requests). Some vendors may refer to this as port address translation (PAT) instead of NAT.

- Depending on the type of customer the residential gateway is aimed at, the WAN interface is a modem, a serial port, or even DSL. (Some residential gateway products may use an Ethernet port as the "WAN" connection to a cable modem or DSL modem.)

- They are often built as a single integrated unit, complete with a built-in antenna. If suitable coverage cannot be found, it is necessary to relocate the entire unit.

- Many products now claim to have an *IPsec pass-through* feature to allow the use of IPsec through NAT, which works with varying degrees of success depending on the IPsec VPN solution chosen.

- Configuration of residential gateways usually relies on a default internal IP address. When it is plugged in and powered up for the first time, you connect with a web browser to its default address and enter the default username and password. In some cases, all of a manufacturer's devices may come up with the same address by default. A popular choice for the default web address is often 192.168.0.1, the first address in the RFC 1918 reserved address block of traditional class C address. As wireless LANs have become more popular, however, some vendors have built equipment to coexist with other gear by default, either by choosing a random value for the final number in the IP address, or by testing to ensure the address is not in use.

- They are often sold directly to the end user and are designed to be aesthetically pleasing. Unfortunately for many end users, the improved visual design sometimes prevents the stacking of residential gateways with other network equipment. Many vendors design their equipment to be stackable with their other components, however.

- Security configuration options are often limited to smaller-scale solutions. Much older residential gateways only implemented MAC filtering or static WEP, so be careful about purchasing used equipment. Nearly every device now sold uses WPA's preshared key authentication with dynamic encryption keys.

- Most residential devices do not have sophisticated radios. They typically have just a single radio interface, running either 802.11g or 802.11a. The former is more common in residential devices because the 2.4 GHz frequency used by 802.11g has greater coverage. Residential networks are typically limited by their uplink to the Internet, and do not need to be built with small coverage areas for dense, high-bandwidth coverage.

As this book was written, residential gateways typically cost $35 to $100. Common manufacturers are D-Link, Linksys, and Netgear. Apple's AirPort is sometimes placed in this category as well, although it is priced significantly higher and has more features.

For the office: enterprise access points

Enterprise gateways, which often go by many other names that imply the buyer values features over cost, provide everything residential gateways do, plus additional features useful for larger-scale environments. Enterprise gateways generally share the following characteristics:

- The area over which mobility is required is much larger and requires several access points working in concert. Enterprise products support some sort of protocol to move sessions between access points.

- Enterprise products are built around upgradeability to offer a service life as long as possible. They are typically built on relatively high-powered generic hardware, and implement a great deal of higher-layer functionality in software that can be easily upgraded. They may have radios that are easy to swap out. Early enterprise APs used PC Card radios, so a switch from 802.11b to 802.11a involved changing a card, and possibly a software upgrade. As the price of components has fallen, radio cards are typically no longer upgradeable, but the software is.

- One of the advantages to the high level of software control of an enterprise-grade AP is that new security developments can often be added in with a software update. Any serious enterprise-grade AP will support WPA, and most vendors promised easy software upgrade paths to 802.11i. As new security features are standardized, they can be added on to an existing network without changing hardware. Enterprise-grade APs often add security in layers, so new security mechanisms can be used in conjunction with older mechanisms. Hardware-based enhancements to security often appear in more expensive devices first, too. When chipsets started supporting AES acceleration in hardware, it appeared on high-end devices first. Some enterprise APs can support multiple security standards simultanously.

- Enterprise-type deployments are frequently intended to create a coverage blanket throughout a relatively large area. Power is not always convenient to the location of an access point, but it is typically abundant in the wiring closet. All enterprise-grade APs support drawing power over Ethernet using IEEE 802.3af.

- The radio side of a high-end AP is frequently much more sophisticated than a low-cost AP. Most enterprise APs have an antenna connector that allows the attachment of a variety of external antennas to tailor the coverage area and coverage quality to your needs. Some APs are beginning to incorporate highly advanced antenna technology that allows very fine control over transmission patterns, or allows a single antenna to be used by multiple MAC chips. Transmission power can usually be adjusted to enlarge or shrink the coverage area as desired. Many enterprise APs can also support multiple virtual radio networks over the antenna.

- In addition to radio tunability, enterprise APs can support some form of virtual access points. Multiple SSIDs can be configured, and each can be assigned its own authentication and encryption settings. This feature is often used to create parallel networks with different security settings to accommodate older equipment while offering maximum security for newer equipment.

- Enterprise APs are designed to integrate into an existing network. On the security side, that means that they often must integrate into an existing security architecture, usually by plugging in to an existing user database. Once users are successfully authenticated to the network, though, they must take advantage of network services. A second integration point is the way that an enterprise AP extends existing access control and user privileges that may already be present on the wired network.

- Integration with an existing network also extends to the data plane as well. Most enterprise-grade APs are designed to perform dynamic VLAN assignment based on user attributes from the authentication server.

- Frequently, site survey tools come bundled with enterprise-class products so network managers can plan large deployments by directly assessing coverage quality. These tools vary greatly in their sophistication. Some site survey tools are little more than a historical statistical readout, while extremely advanced tools can derive a network layout from the physical environment.

- Reflecting the administrative demands, configuration of enterprise-class devices is done with easily scripted command-line interfaces or SNMP, and monitoring and management capabilities are far more extensive than in residential gateways. Some products are also controlled through large-scale management frameworks that enable a single administrator to monitor and change configuration on hundreds or even thousands of access points.

- Enterprise gateways are often deployed in packs. Aesthetic requirements in typical office space may require unobtrusive mounting, so these devices offer flexibility in the way that they mount in the building. Many are designed to be mounted above ceilings, and may be *plenum rated*.* Devices installed in air ducts and air-handling spaces must meet strict smoke emission requirements for safety reasons. Plenum-rated APs can be installed nearly everywhere; devices that lack the necessary certifications may be restricted in possible mounting locations.

Naturally, these additional capabilities do not come without a price. Most enterprise-grade APs list for $500 to 1,000, though they are often available at significant discounts. Over time, the price of high-end APs does fall, but it is not subject to the same downward pressure as residential-class products. The canonical example of an enterprise-grade AP is the Cisco 1200 or Cisco 1100. Both are built on relatively generic hardware, run a full-blown version of the Internetwork Operating System, and are given new features on a regular basis. Proxim, Symbol, 3Com, and HP produce competing products with similar feature sets.

---

* For information on flame tests, see *http://www.houwire.com/catalog/technical/cable_flame.asp*.

For the large office: wireless switches

One of the biggest changes in the time since the first edition of this book was published is the emergence of the "wireless switch" or "thin AP" architecture, in which relatively lightweight access points are controlled by a centralized switch. The driver behind the thin AP or wireless switch architecture is increased efficiency over first-generation products. Part of the efficiency is based on the technology itself. Thin AP architectures remove processing from the AP and move it to an aggregation device. Eliminating processing at the AP removes components and cost from the AP, increasing service lifetime. If configuration is removed from the AP as well, there are fewer managed elements in the network.

Centralizing capabilities in the controller can also lead to increased flexibility. For the same cost, concentrated hardware in the controller can provide more processing power than distributed processing at the access point. Coordinating activity between access points allows network managers to load-balance clients between APs, monitor radio activity centrally, and extend the existing network more easily.

The cost of a wireless switch-based solution may depend a great deal on its size. Most vendors offer a variety of controllers, which may range from just a few APs up to hundreds of APs. The original switch solution was Symbol's Mobius product; solutions were later built from the ground up by Airespace, Aruba, and Trapeze.

Power over Ethernet (PoE)

If your network will be of any size at all, power over Ethernet (PoE) is extremely important. When designing a wireless network, access points should be located where it makes sense to put them for radio propagation purposes, not where it makes sense to put them for electrical power purposes.

Access points sold in the first wave of products had to be powered like most other computing devices—that is, plugged into a nearby AC power outlet. To make matters worse, many of them used large "wall wart" transformers that blocked adjacent outlets, too. Locating access points was not a matter of finding the best locations for providing service, but near nearby power outlets. Modifying access point locations can be challenging if one of the constraints is staying near electrical power.

Due to the dangers of electrical work, there are legal requirements to use licensed electricians in many locations. Some organizations may have also negotiated with unions to provide skilled electrical labor. In either case, modifying access point locations may be quite expensive. In many locations, data cable such as Ethernet can be moved or installed by network technicians, so APs can be installed or relocated by nonunion labor.*

---

* Some jurisdictions may define Ethernet as "low-voltage wiring," which requires that it be installed by an electrician. The city of Redmond, Washington, taxes low-voltage wiring as part of the building permit process.

Types of PoE

There are a number of types of power equipment on the market; many comply with the IEEE 802.3af standard. 802.3af defines a transmission standard that can supply 48 volts DC up to a maximum of approximately 15 watts at the full length-reach of an Ethernet cable. The standard itself can be downloaded from the IEEE Get802 site, and more information is available from *http://www.poweroverethernet.com/*.

The most basic distinction is which wires in the Ethernet cable supply the power. Data is always carried on the data conductors (wire pairs 1 and 2 and 3 and 6). Alternative A in the standard carries power on the data conductors, while Alternative B carries power on the unused pairs (wire pairs 4 and 5 and 7 and 8). When power is carried on the data cables, the voltage polarity may go either way, as shown in Figure 20-1. The corresponding pinout is in Table 20-1. Power carried on the unused data cables must have a specified polarity. Nearly all vendors use positive polarity on the first pair; the notable exception is early Cisco-proprietary power devices, which reversed polarity from most other devices.

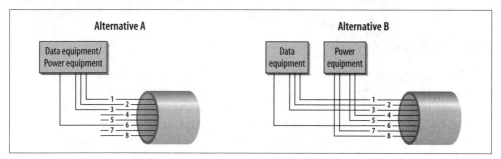

Figure 20-1. Power wire map

Table 20-1. Wire usage in 802.3af

Wire number	Pair mapping	Alternative A (MDI-X)	Alternative A (MDI)	Alternative B
1	1 - data	−	+	
2	1 - data	−	+	
3	2 - data	+	−	
4	3 (unused)			+
5	3 (unused)			+
6	2 - data	+	−	
7	4 (unused)			−
8	4 (unused)			−

A further distinction between types of power devices is where the power is supplied. Power equipment may be present in the switch, which is referred to as *endpoint* power. Alternatively, it may be added into the wiring by a *power injector*, in which case it is called *mid-span* equipment. Most 802.11 installations to date have used power injectors, and therefore mid-span equipment. As switch vendors have come out with power blades and they have been much more widely purchased, endpoint injection is become much more common. Figure 20-2 illustrates the difference between the two options. The injector shown in the mid-span case may be a stand-alone device, or it may be a "power patch panel" with multiple ports. Gigabit data links can only be endpoint powered, although this is not yet an important distinction for 802.11.

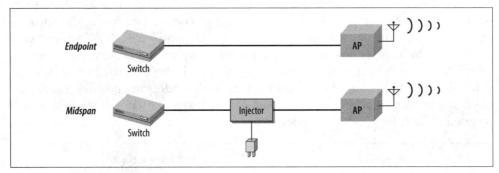

Figure 20-2. Endpoint and mid-span power injectors

802.3af incorporates detection of powered devices to avoid frying equipment plugged into a power port. Early PoE equipment would supply the full voltage all the time, and had a propensity to destroy devices that were not designed to cope with power. For safety reasons, 802.3af includes a handshake that slowly ramps up power. If there is no response to the initial probe from the power equipment, it stops providing it to protect the device at the end.

Power injectors almost always have two copper Ethernet ports and a power cord. One Ethernet port is for the network connection, and the second provides power on the network connection on the first port. A notable exception is the Cisco AIR-PWRINJ-FIB, which provides power on an Ethernet port while using a 100BASE-FX fiber for network connectivity.

Selecting Access Points

When choosing an access point, you should take a number of factors into account. With the emergence of 802.11 as the main vendor-neutral standard, standards compliance is generally not a big factor. Any serious vendor hoping to build large networks must promise compatibility with all existing standards, and will often need to commit to supporting important future landmark standards. Several organizations have launched test programs to certify interoperability. The best-known program is the Wi-Fi Alliance's Wi-Fi certification, though other organizations are seeking to capitalize on the popularity of wireless LANs by launching competing programs. The most rigorous test program in the industry is run by the University of New Hampshire's Inter-Operability Lab (IOL). The IOL test program is not as widely known as the commercial programs because it is intended to help build better products, not to provide marketing "seals of approval" to vendors. As always, when you study certification programs, ensure that the vendor has gone through the relevant tests that are of interest to you.

Security is often a prime concern when deploying a wireless network. With WEP thoroughly broken, you almost certainly want to select an access point that has security capabilities based on 802.1X and 802.11i. Small installations can use pre-shared key authentication, while more security-conscious installations should opt for full RADIUS integration. In larger environments, it may also be worthwhile to select a product that can act as multiple virtual access points as well as mix encryption and authentication types.

In some deployments, getting power to the access points can be a major headache. To blanket an area with the coverage required for a large implementation, access points often need to be placed in an area where power is not easily accessible. Long antenna runs can degrade signal quality unacceptably, so it is much better to bring power to the location. Installing new electrical conduits is often quite expensive. Work must be performed by licensed electricians, and building codes may impose additional restrictions. Many products can supply power over the Ethernet cable. Cheaper products often have proprietary power equipment, while more expensive products can use standards-based power equipment. Network wire is not subject to the same restrictions as electrical cable and can be installed by network administrators.

Some environments may require providing coverage over both indoor and outdoor areas. External antennas are often useful for creating a dense coverage blanket over an area, or for beaming the signal in a particular direction over a courtyard. Not all access points can connect to external antennas; it may be an extra-cost option. Even if an access point has an external antenna connector, there is no guarantee that you'll be able to find a wide range of antennas available for use. 802.11 only requires that any connectors for external antennas have a standard impedance of 50 ohms. If external antennas are important for your deployment plans, make sure that a wide range of antennas is available, whether through the 802.11 vendor or another source. Outdoor installations may require environmentally "hardened" access points or enclosures as well.

Environmental considerations may also play a role in certifications required for APs. Equipment installed in air-handling spaces must be plenum rated. Certified plenum-rated devices are lit on fire and the resulting smoke is tested for clarity. Opaque smoke might be forced through a ventilation system and distributed throughout a building, which would obscure emergency exit signs and would be a hazard. Plenum-rated devices are made of materials that do not release dense smoke. The smoke is often quite hazardous. Plenum-rated APs are safer because they will not obscure exits, not because the smoke is nontoxic. Devices that are installed above the ceiling do not generally need to be plenum rated unless the above-ceiling area is an air return space. Buildings with air-handling ducts do not generally need plenum-rated APs, but many building inspectors will mistakenly require them. Local building codes may also require them.

If roaming is important, you will need to sort through a variety of different technologies and approaches, with the added wrinkle that roaming may not always perform well between different vendors' products. The best way to ensure interoperability between vendors is to select a system that bases roaming and handoff on dynamic VLAN assignment. As stations authenticate, they will retain the same logical point of attachment to the network.

802.11 includes a number of powersaving functions in the standard. Most are optional. If your deployment is based heavily on battery-powered devices, it may be worth evaluating which powersaving features are included with particular devices. It may also be worth experimenting with devices to see just how much longer batteries last with the powersaving functions enabled.

Device management is an important consideration. Wireless networks are a new service, and network staff will need to plan, evaluate, purchase, deploy, and maintain the additional hardware. Large deployments may have tens or hundreds of access points, which can easily make network management a headache without good tools. Does the vendor offer an access point manager to configure large numbers of devices in parallel? Can management of the access points be incorporated into your existing network management infrastructure using tools that you already have deployed? Are the management tools secure enough? Many products can be managed only with cleartext protocols, which may be just an annoyance or a major violation of a security policy. Experience with other network devices has shown that software upgrades are a frequent occurrence. How is the software upgraded, and how much functionality can upgrades add? Can new protocol features be added with firmware updates?

Depending on the size of the deployment, it may be possible to evaluate equipment before buying. See if you can get a feel for the range of each access point and test with a variety of common cards. Capacity on an 802.11 network is ultimately limited by the radio link, but you will want to make sure that there are no other capacity restrictions. Does the access point provide the processing power to run the wireless side at maximum capacity with security protocols enabled? Not all products incorporate cryptographic acceleration for all protocols. Products that depend on a central cryptographic processor to run security systems may run out of capacity if they are upgraded to faster PHY standards, and may also suffer if the uplink is insufficient. Fast Ethernet suffices for 802.11a/g-based networks today, but it will likely limit the performance of radios built on the future 802.11n standard. Try to set up a test network and get a feel for the configuration required to integrate the access points with the rest of your network gear.

As with many other purchasing decisions, of course, there are a number of "soft" factors that may not be easily quantifiable. Warranties, a relationship with the vendor, and the quality of the technical support may all influence the purchasing decision. Soft factors are not technical nor easily quantifiable, however, so I will not discuss them.

Are Access Points Really Necessary?

Access points are not required for a wireless network. Wireless stations can be used in independent networks, which do not require an access point. Building a Unix box that routes between an Ethernet network and a wireless network is not difficult, and hardware can often be reused from the scrap pile. Why, then, would anybody use an access point?

Now that most access points have fallen well below the $100 mark, building a Unix router is no longer a cost-effective option for single–access point networks. Once you consider what your time is worth, building a Unix router is a pretty silly use of time. Access point hardware has some advantages over redeployed general-purpose platforms, too. Access points are small devices with no moving parts. As a result, they do not consume a great deal of electrical power and do not generate much heat. There is one notable exception to this rule, though. Apple offers a "software base station" that transforms any desktop machine into a bridging access point. With a few mouse clicks and very little effort, a desktop computer can become a base station.

Unix-based routers have never been effective in larger deployments because of the lack of mobility support. Effective roaming requires transparent *bridged* access, not routed access, to the link layer at different physical locations. However, roaming with 802.11 is possible only when access points can communicate with each other to track the movement of a wireless station. In the future, it is likely that an open source Unix distribution will have the features necessary for an access point: low-level access to fundamental 802.11 parameters on the card, Ethernet bridging, and an IAPP. Until then, though, there is no substitute for commercial products.

Cisco 1200 Access Point

Cisco's 1200 Series access point is the standard-bearer for standalone access points. It runs a version of Cisco's Internetwork Operating System (IOS). At first, 1200s ran a system based on VxWorks, but Cisco released an IOS upgrade to bring the 1200 in to the fold. The upgrade tool is available from Cisco's support web site. No new features or continuing development has been done on VxWorks for quite some time.

On an individual basis, the Cisco 1200 can be managed from either a web interface or an IOS command-line interface. Larger installations can be managed through the Wireless LAN Solutions Engine (WLSE). The command-line interface is available through a local console serial cable with a Cisco RJ-45 pinout, or once the network interface is configured, telnet or SSH.

Unix-Based Access Points

One of the most basic preconditions for making a Unix-based access point is enabling access point functions in the wireless interface card. One of the major hurdles is rewriting the 802.11 headers. All traffic in an infrastructure network flows through the access point. Access points must rewrite the transmitter and receiver addresses in the 802.11 headers. Other management functions may be required as well. For example, 802.11 includes a number of powersaving mechanisms for infrastructure networks in the specification, but they can be used only on networks with access points that implement them.

There is also a nontechnical hurdle. Many vendors have actively supported the development of open source Unix drivers for their cards. After all, vendors make money selling hardware, and it is a good thing for them to sell cards for all client systems, even those that run open source Unix. Access points are a different story, however. Vendors have not been as forthcoming with the interface used to put cards into the access point mode. Access points are quite lucrative, and providing a driver interface in the access point mode in the card could potentially cannibalize access point sales.

At one point, the only way to get an Intersil-based card to act as an access point interface was to purchase the reference design from Intersil. (The reference design shipped with firmware that had access point functionality, and that firmware was not sold separately.) Intersil's shipping station firmware does, however, include something called a "Host AP Mode." In the Host AP Mode, the PRISM chipset automatically takes care of "menial" tasks, such as transmitting Beacon frames and acknowledging incoming transmissions. Jouni Malinen has developed a driver to use the Host AP Mode with Linux. In conjunction with the Ethernet bridging implementation in the kernel, this driver can be used to build an access point with full 802.1X and WPA support. It is available from *http://www.epitest.fi/Prism2/*.

With the present state of driver software, it is possible to build a Unix-based router. (I mean "router" pedantically, as "layer 3 network device.") One interface would connect to a wired network as it always has, and a second wireless interface could be run in IBSS mode. Ross Finlayson has established a community network at a coffee house in Mountain View, California using a FreeBSD-based router. The project's home page is at *http://www.live.com/danastreet/*, and there is a page devoted specifically to the router itself at *http://www.live.com/ wireless/unix-base-station.html*.

Setting Up the 1200

Hardware setup on the 1200 is straightforward. It may be powered either from a local power supply or with a Cisco-specific power injector. The power circuitry is the same. The power supply puts out 48 volts, just as a power injector would.

The 1200 uses a Bridge-group Virtual Interface (BVI). BVIs are a software construct used in IOS that allows routing and bridging of protocols over the same interface.

APs need to bridge 802.11 frames to 802.3, but also need to route IP for management purposes, which makes BVIs the obvious choice. Configure the IP address on a BVI from the global configuration prompt. APs may get their IP address either from a static assignment, or from a built-in DHCP client. Both commands are shown below:

```
ap1200# configure terminal
ap1200(config)# interface BVI1
ap1200(config-if)# ip address 192.168.1.5 255.255.255.0
ap1200(config-if)# ip address dhcp client-id FastEthernet0
```

To check on the status of the interface and see what addresses have been assigned, use *show ip interface*:

```
ap1200#show ip interface brief
Interface              IP-Address      OK? Method Status    Protocol
Dot11Radio0            unassigned      YES TFTP   up        up
FastEthernet0          unassigned      YES NVRAM  up        up
Virtual-Dot11Radio0    unassigned      YES TFTP   down      down
BVI1                   192.168.5.191   YES DHCP   up        up
```

Configuring Radio Interfaces

The 1200 has two radios. Radio 0 is the 2.4 GHz radio, which is usually 802.11g, but may be 802.11b in older hardware. Radio 1 is the 5 GHz radio. Each radio can be configured independently by using the interface configuration commands. Data rates can be allowed simply by entering them with the *speed* command, or they may be labeled as required by prefacing them with *basic-*. In the following command list, the first speed command allows all data rates. The second requires 1 Mbps and 2 Mbps operation, but allows 5.5 Mbps and 11 Mbps operation. The last two are special. *speed range* allows all, but requires only the slowest speed. *speed throughput* sets all data rates to required.

```
ap1200# configure terminal
ap1200(config)# interface dot11radio 0
ap1200(config-if)# speed 1.0 2.0 5.5 11.0
ap1200(config-if)# speed basic-1.0 basic-2.0 5.5 11.0
ap1200(config-if)# speed range
ap1200(config-if)# speed throughput
```

Transmission power may be configured for each radio by setting a local maximum power in milliwatts. Like *speed*, *power* is an interface-specific configuration command. 802.11b/g radios are capable of up to 100 mW power. Due to limitations in chip design with OFDM, 802.11a radios are only capable of 40 mW transmission.

```
ap1200# configure terminal
ap1200(config)# interface dot11radio 0
ap1200(config-if)# power local 100
```

In addition to power settings, the operating channel may be configured for each radio with the *channel* command. As an argument, *channel* takes the frequency in

MHz. Alternatively, using the *least-congested* keyword will force the AP to monitor all channels and pick the clearest one.

```
ap1200# configure terminal
ap1200(config)# interface dot11radio 0
ap1200(config-if)# channel 2412
ap1200(config-if)# channel least-congested
```

Two different types of 802.11b preambles are used. Long preambles are more compatible, but short preambles give much better performance. Generally, this option should be set to short unless there is a known older device that needs to use the network. To disable short preamble, use the *no preamble-short* interface command.

```
ap1200# configure terminal
ap1200(config)# interface dot11radio 0
ap1200(config-if)# no preamble-short
```

Beacon frames are used to announce the existence of a network, as well as announce buffered with DTIM information elements. The Beacon interval can be tuned to balance delivery of buffered frames with battery consumption using the *beacon period* and *beacon dtim-period* commands.

```
ap1200# configure terminal
ap1200(config)# interface dot11radio 0
ap1200(config-if)# beacon period 100
ap1200(config-if)# beacon dtim-period 5
```

In addition to the Beacon interval, the RTS/CTS threshold can be configured. Lower values will cause RTS/CTS handshaking to occur. Depending on the environment, it might also be worth altering the number of times a frame will be retransmitted, or the threshold at which it will be fragmented using the following commands.

```
ap1200# configure terminal
ap1200(config)# interface dot11radio 0
ap1200(config-if)# rts threshold 2000
ap1200(config-if)# rts retries 2
ap1200(config-if)# packet retries 8
ap1200(config-if)# fragment-threshold 1500
```

Internetworking

Different clients will encapsulate frames in different ways. By far the most common is to use RFC 1042 SNAP encapsulation, which is the default. IOS allows configuration of 802.1H as well. The setting is global for a radio, and cannot be configured on a per-protocol basis.

```
ap1200# configure terminal
ap1200(config)# interface dot11radio 0
ap1200(config-if)# payload-encapsulation snap
ap1200(config-if)# payload-encapsulation dot1h
```

With dynamic VLAN assignment, the use of VLANs on the wired side is becoming increasingly common. IOS on the 1200 supports both native and tagged VLANs. It is important to assign VLAN 1, the native VLAN, to the same IP network as other devices on the network to ensure communication across the so-called native VLAN. The native VLAN is noted by adding the keyword *native* at the end of an encapsulation command for the subinterface.

```
ap1200# configure terminal
ap1200(config)# interface dot11radio0.1
ap1200(config-subif)# encapsulation dot1q 1 native
ap1200(config-subif)# interface fastethernet0.1
ap1200(config-subif)# encapsulation dot1q 1 native
```

Further VLANs can be configured in a similar way, omitting the native. It is common practice to keep the subinterface number equal to the VLAN tag. For example, to configure VLAN 10, the following commands would be used. To configure VLAN 20, all the references to 10 would be replaced with 20.

```
ap1200# configure terminal
ap1200(config)# interface dot11radio0.10
ap1200(config-subif)# encapsulation dot1q 10
ap1200(config-subif)# interface fastethernet0.10
ap1200(config-subif)# encapsulation dot1q 10
```

Configuring Security

Radio networks are broadcast from an AP as an SSID. Each SSID acts somewhat like its own virtual self-contained access point within the 1200. Each SSID can have its own security configuration, as well as its own VLAN mapping. Interestingly enough, the VLAN mapping is slightly spongy. A default VLAN can be assigned to an SSID. If the RADIUS server in use returns a different VLAN, the client device will be re-mapped on to the specified VLAN.* The per-SSID default will only be used when nothing is supplied by the RADIUS server. (This approach is not quite as clean as many other products on the market, which work on an either/or basis with default VLANs and RADIUS servers.)

Authentication to each SSID is configured using the *authentication* command. In general, this command will be set to "open" authentication, but may add EAP authentication as an optional method. The following commands configure an SSID of babelfish to map to VLAN 42 while requiring EAP authentication against the server group *rad_eap*.

```
ap1200# configure terminal
ap1200(config)# interface dot11radio 0
ap1200(config-if)# ssid babelfish
ap1200(config-ssid)# vlan 42
ap1200(config-ssid)# authentication open eap rad_eap
```

---

* Cisco APs require a set of RADIUS tunnel attributes to be supplied, and they must be tagged. It requires the Tunnel-Type attribute to be set to "VLAN", the Tunnel-Medium-Type attribute to be set to IEEE-802, and the Tunnel-Private-Group-ID attribute to be set to the VLAN ID.

To define the RADIUS server for EAP authentication, define each server, and associate it with a group. By default, RADIUS servers that are not assigned UDP ports are assigned to the old RADIUS ports (1645 and 1646), so they must be explicitly assigned to the new ports.

```
ap1200# configure terminal
ap1200(config)#radius-server host 192.168.200.187 auth-port 1645 acct-port 1646
key MySecret
ap1200(config)#radius-server host 192.168.200.188 auth-port 1812 acct-port 1813
key MySecret
ap1200(config)#aaa group server radius rad_eap
ap1200(config-sg-radius)#server 192.168.200.187 auth-port 1645 acct-port 1646
ap1200(config-sg-radius)#server 192.168.200.188 auth-port 1812 acct-port 1813
```

Configuring WPA-PSK

WPA preshared keys are configured through the SSID command. By setting the SSID up for WPA key management, it is possible to specify either an ASCII or hexadecimal pre-shared key for use with WPA.

```
ap1200(config)#interface dot11radio 0
ap1200(config-if)#ssid LuminiferousEther
ap1200(config-ssid)#authentication key-management wpa optional
ap1200(config-ssid)#wpa-psk ascii Thisisaverylongsecretpresharedkey!
```

Monitoring

A basic monitoring tool is the list of associated stations, which can be obtained from an unprivileged prompt:

```
ap1200> show dot11 association

802.11 Client Stations on Dot11Radio0:

SSID [LuminiferousEther] :

MAC Address     IP address      Device      Name      Parent      State
0002.2d6e.abda 192.168.200.150  -           -         self        Assoc
```

To view details on a particular association, ask for it by MAC address. The complete association record will be printed out, including the types of encryption in use. This station is associated and uses TKIP for encryption.

```
ap1200> show dot11 association 0002.2d6e.abda
Address         : 0002.2d6e.abda    Name            :
IP Address      : 192.168.200.150   Interface       : Dot11Radio 0
Device          :    -              Software Version :
CCX Version     :

State           : Assoc             Parent          : self
SSID            : LuminiferousEther VLAN            : 0
```

```
Hops to Infra      : 1              Association Id   : 120
Clients Associated: 0               Repeaters associated: 0
Tunnel Address       :0.0.0.0
Key Mgmt type      : WPA PSK        Encryption       : TKIP
Current Rate       : 11.0           Capability       :
Supported Rates    : 1.0 2.0 5.5 11.0
Signal Strength    : -39  dBm       Connected for    : 1463 seconds
Signal Quality     : 79 %           Activity Timeout : 55 seconds
Power-save         : Off            Last Activity    : 4 seconds ago

Packets Input      : 535            Packets Output   : 245
Bytes Input        : 61629          Bytes Output     : 137018
Duplicates Rcvd    : 0              Data Retries     : 18
Decrypt Failed     : 0              RTS Retries      : 0
MIC Failed         : 0
MIC Missing        : 0
```

Troubleshooting

IOS has extensive debugging facilities that can be used to troubleshoot problems. Tracing is activated by the *debug* command, which is followed by the area to perform tracing on. By default, tracing is sent to the console. If you are attached to the device over the network, you will need to send the debugging output to the current login screen with the following command:

```
ap1200# terminal monitor
```

The most troublesome part of working with secure 802.11 networks is the initial association and key distribution phase. Troubleshooting of these actions can be accomplished with *debug dot11* and its subcommands. Some common troubleshooting debugging commands are shown in Table 20-2.

Table 20-2. Cisco 1200 debugging commands

Debug area	Commands	Remarks
EAP authentication	debug radius authentication	Prints out RADIUS packets; decodes attributes; explains actions
	debug dot11 aaa authenticator process	
	debug dot11 aaa authenticator state-machine	May show servers timeout or fail
MAC filtering	debug dot11 aaa authenticator mac-authen	Shows MAC addresses and response from authentication system
WPA	debug dot11 aaa authenticator process	Shows key exchange
	debug dot11 aaa authenticator state-machine	
	debug dot11 aaa manager keys	

Turning off debugging is simple. Just enter the following command:

```
ap1200# undebug all
```

Apple AirPort

There are now two types of AirPort base stations that are on the market from Apple. Both the AirPort Express and AirPort Extreme Base Station are 802.11g devices. The AirPort Extreme is designed more as a home gateway, and it has a modem and external antenna port. Although more costly than a number of other devices on the market, it is also more functional and is a common small-office solution.

First-Time Setup

The first-time setup is done with the same AirPort Setup Assistant application that configures new wireless interfaces. AirPorts fresh out of the shrink wrap broadcast their existence to the world so that a Mac OS client can be used for configuration. After connecting to the AirPort and clicking through to the configuration screen, the network security setup screen of Figure 20-3 is presented. The configuration displayed shows a WPA pre-shared key security method. It is also possible to configure WEP from this screen.

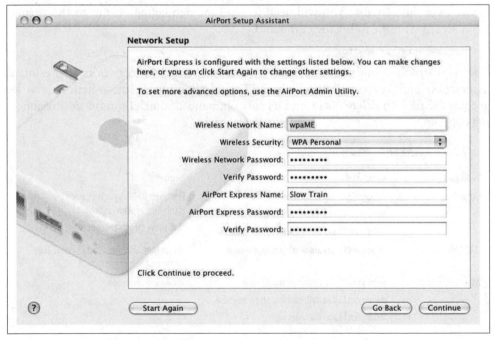

Figure 20-3. Network security settings

The Management Interface

Once the bootstrap configuration is done with the Setup Assistant, the AirPort Base Station is on the network and must be configured with the AirPort Utility (Figure 20-4). This is a separate configuration utility that will feel vaguely familiar if you have ever seen Lucent's AP Manager. When it is started, the AirPort Admin Utility searches all the AirPort base stations on the network and displays them in a list. Individual base stations can be selected for further configuration. When changes are made, the base station must be restarted for the changes to take effect. The "Other" button at the top allows configuration of any AirPort Base Station that the manager can send IP packets to. Far-away base stations may not appear on the browse list, but by clicking on "Other" and entering an IP address, the Manager can configure any base station to which it has IP connectivity.

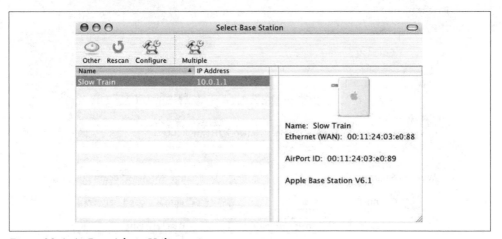

Figure 20-4. AirPort Admin Utility main screen

Configuring the wireless interface

When a base station is selected for configuration, the configuration screen will pop up. Several tabs are used to group configuration information into logical subsets, and the wireless interface configuration is available by default. Across the top, there are buttons to restart the access point, upload new firmware, return the base station to factory defaults, and change the password. (New firmware is distributed as part of the Admin Utility package, and will automatically be used to update old AirPorts as the manager discovers them.)

The AirPort configuration is shown in Figure 20-5. Security settings are similar to those shown in previously in Figure 20-3. The "closed network" option prevents the inclusion of the SSID information element in Beacon frames and requires that stations associating provide it. It is a toy security option, and does not really close the network. As dual-mode 802.11b/g devices, it is possible to configure them in a b/g compatibility mode, or attempt to keep 802.11b devices off the network to reduce the overhead of protection.

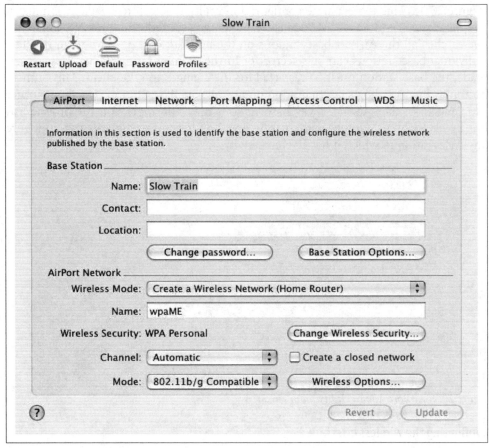

Figure 20-5. Wireless interface configuration

Configuration of the LAN interface

The AirPort may be used as a NAT device, in which case it will translate IP traffic from wireless devices on to its address on the Ethernet interface. Client computers can be statically addressed by the network administrator, or the built-in DHCP server can be turned on and assigned a range of addresses to assign to clients. When NAT is used to hide several computers behind one IP address, the address specified in the Internet properties is used as the public address. The wired LAN interface is given the private address 10.0.1.1, and DHCP is used to lease out addresses from 10.0.1.2 to 10.0.1.200 (in this case, you can't select the range of addresses for the

DHCP server to give out). The AirPort base station can be connected to wired networks by its Fast Ethernet LAN port if the DHCP server is disabled.

The Port Mapping tab, shown in Figure 20-6, can be used to add inbound static port mappings. The public port is translated to the private IP address and port number listed in the mapping. The figure illustrates an address translation for inbound web services to port 80 on host 10.0.1.201.

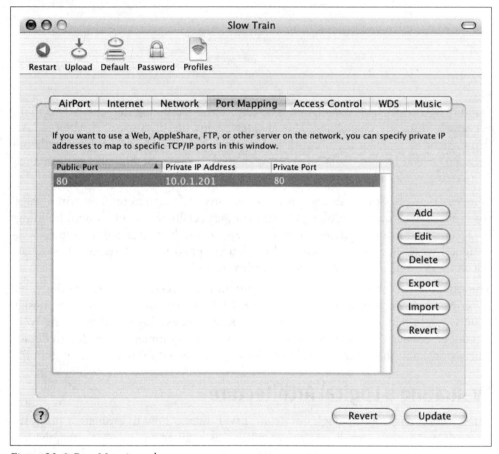

Figure 20-6. Port Mapping tab

Access control

Like most other products, the AirPort Base Station supports filtering by client MAC address. The Access Control tab lets you identify clients by their AirPort ID (MAC address) and add them to a list of allowed clients, together with a description.

## CHAPTER 21

Logical Wireless Network Architecture

Planning a wireless LAN installation is a significant undertaking that cuts across many previously disparate disciplines. This chapter begins the discussion of wireless LAN deployment by tackling the network architecture. Network design is about trade-offs between several factors, including cost, manageability, availability, and performance. Wireless networks add the additional dimension of mobility to the mix.

Wireless networks often extend an existing wired infrastructure. The wired infrastructure may be quite complex to begin with, especially if it spans several buildings in a campus setting. Wireless networks depend on having a solid, stable, well-designed wired network in place. If the existing network is not stable, chances are the wireless extension is doomed to instability as well.

This chapter discusses four approaches to building a wireless LAN. All are discussed in terms of the technical features of wireless LANs that influence how you design your wireless network. How do the features of wireless LANs influence network topology? Besides the 802.11 equipment, what other equipment is needed to deploy a network? How should the logical network be constructed for maximum mobility?

Evaluating a Logical Architecture

Before presenting any topologies in detail, I will discuss how to evaluate a proposed network. Each of the topologies presented in this chapter has its own strengths and weaknesses. Choosing a topology depends on which criteria are compelling on your network. Here are discuss several evaluation criteria that I have found to be important.

Mobility

Portability results in a productivity gain because users can access information resources wherever it is convenient to do so. At the core, however, portability removes only the physical barriers to connectivity. It is easy to carry a laptop between several locations, so people do. But portability does not change the ritual of connecting to networks at each new location. It is still necessary to physically connect to the network and reestablish network connections, and network connections cannot be used while the device is being moved.

If, for example, you have a remotely mounted filesystem and put a laptop to sleep, it may not be there when the laptop wakes up in a different location. Any open files or activity against the filesystem may need to timeout before you can regain control of the computer. DHCP clients may impose more pedestrian restrictions. Common DHCP clients attempt to renew the lease on the last address obtained, and may need to go through multiple DHCP exchanges to get an address on a new IP subnet.

Mobility, on the other hand, is a far more powerful concept: it removes further barriers, most of which are based on the logical network architecture. Network connections stay active even while the device is in motion. This is critical for tasks requiring persistent, long-lived connections, which may be found in database applications. Support personnel frequently access a tracking database that logs questions, problems, and resolutions. The same argument can be made for a number of tracking applications in a health care setting. Accessing the database through a wireless network can boost productivity because it allows people to add small amounts of information from different locations without needing to reconnect to the database each time. Inventory applications are another example and one of the reasons why retail and logistics are two of the markets that have been quicker to adopt 802.11. When taking inventory, it makes far more sense to count boxes or products where they sit and relay data over a wireless network than to record data on paper and collate the data at the end of the process.*

Traditional wired Ethernet connections provide portability. I can take my laptop computer anywhere on the campus at work and plug in. (If I'll tolerate slow speeds, I can even make a phone call and access my corporate network anywhere in the world.) Each time I access the network, though, I'm starting from scratch. I have to reestablish connections, even if I only moved a few feet. What I'd really like is to walk into the conference room and connect to the corporate network without doing anything.

Defining "mobility"

Wireless networking and mobility are intertwined concepts. Without mobility, wireless networking would not be particularly interesting. Mobility means that applications just work, no matter where the computer is. Unfortunately, building a network that provides location-independent services requires a great deal of location-based configuration and knowledge.

Translating the high-level definition of mobility into technical details can be done in several different ways. Many technologies can be used to provide mobility for network users, and not all of them are good. Providing network transport that is truly independent of the application and transparent to it has several requirements.

---

* Indeed, the early adopters of wireless LAN technology tended to be in organizations where the work was mobile—health care, logistics, and education.

1. Consistent MAC-layer attachment to the same link-layer network. Mobility requires that the existing data-link layer look the same regardless of location. Extensive engineering in 802.11 provides link-layer mobility.

   a. Transparent handoffs between access points. Users may need to perform an initial configuration operation to select a network to connect to, but they should not be involved in handoff decisions. If the signal strength gets too low, the software should attempt to locate a better signal and transfer to it without user intervention. Every wireless card I am aware of currently switches between access points that are part of the same network. 802.11 was designed around this requirement, and any piece of wireless LAN equipment you buy should have no trouble meeting it.

   b. The inter-access point handoff can break down when the access points are located in different broadcast domains. If two stations are exchanging frames and one moves to a new access point, 802.11 cannot guarantee that the two stations stay attached to the same broadcast domain. One opportunity for vendors to improve on 802.11 is to link access points with the same SSID together so they no matter where they attach to the network, stations in the wireless LAN attach the same broadcast domain everywhere, even if the access points are connected to different local broadcast domains.

   c. Moving a client system between two access points also requires either setting up a new set of security parameters for encryption and integrity protection, or transferring security parameters from the old access point to the new access point. 802.11 does not specify either procedure. Depending on the hardware in use, the process of establishing a security context with the new access point can take a fair amount of time. In bulk data transfer, the blip may not be noticeable; for voice conversations, it often is.

2. No configuration changes are required to the client network stack. For the most part, this means that clients can maintain the same network address as they move throughout the network. In most networks, the address is an IP address, although there may be some applications that require maintenance of other network protocol addresses as well. Extensive engineering has been devoted to network layer mobility, especially in the IP world, which traditionally has not provided it. Address maintenance is a major network engineering challenge, especially if it is required across what would otherwise be an IP subnet boundary.

   a. Before maintaining an address, the client must obtain one. At the initial connection to a wireless LAN, the system should somehow get an address, most likely through DHCP. That address should be used for the duration of the wireless LAN session. From the client's perspective, it keeps the IP address as it moves through the network, and does not need to alter its address or any other stack information to attach to any new access points.

   b. Wireless networks can have brief interruptions of connectivity as clients move between coverage areas or suffer from transient radio link problems.

For brief interruptions, access points should maintain enough session information so that the client can simply rejoin the network. Access points may also need to buffer frames so that clients can fetch any traffic that was received during the interruption.

c. Equally important, the client must appear to maintain its address. If the client connects to a server somewhere, the server should be able to use the same address for the duration of the connection. Furthermore, any other state the network maintains is often associated with an IP address. Many networks use NAT to reach the Internet, and the NAT records are associated with the client IP address.

d. Depending on the application, it may be necessary to have logical network path preservation. Transmitted frames must always emerge from the same egress point on the network, so they are subject to whatever controls the network requires. No matter what the location of the client throughout the network, it always appears as if it is attached to the same point at the edge of the network.

No single technology supplies all of the components of mobility. At the link layer, much is provided by 802.11, although additional functionality is often required above and beyond what the standard lays out. By and large, moving the association between access points is easy. In networks that do not use link-layer security, bridging records can be transferred between access points in a few milliseconds to tens of milliseconds. Re-establishing the link-layer security context may take a few hundred milliseconds, and depends heavily on the responsiveness of the authentication server. Some companies have devoted significant engineering resources to building products that accelerate the security context establishment. Newer "Wi-Fi switch" products may also speed up the roaming process by holding client association records in a centralized location so that there is no need to transfer it between APs.

At the network layer, several different approaches may be taken to offer network-layer mobility. Several early devices used address translation (NAT). NAT is not, never has been, and never will be a mobility protocol. By dragging the network infrastructure up into higher protocol layers, any failure of the translation breaks applications. Some applications are almost incompatible with NAT, such as H.323, while others require specific application support, such as IPsec's use of NAT Traversal. Some devices rely heavily on NAT to provide mobility. Avoid them.

Some form of tunneling is often used to provide application-independent mobility. Client devices are designated with a "home" network, and then inter-AP protocols automatically direct traffic back to the home location from any place it is not directly accessible. Tunneling protocols must be defined at the network layer so that tunnels can carry data across arbitrary network boundaries. However, the tunneling protocol itself may work at the link layer (making VLAN attachment points available throughout the network) or at the network layer (making IP addresses routable throughout the network). The only open industry standard tunneling protocol is Mobile IP (see sidebar later in this chapter).

One challenge network architects often face is the distance over which mobility must be provided. Small installations are easy because there are a number of techniques that offer comparable functionality for up to 25 access points. The real challenges come when designing mobility for larger installations, or organizations that have widely distributed locations. Part of the key to designing a successful mobility solution is to determine what users expect. What sort of tasks require that an IP address be continuously maintained? Interactive terminal sessions, such as telnet and SSH, require that the source IP address remain the same. Other applications may be able to initiate new connections upon reattaching to the network, and the process of reconnecting may be transparent to the users. Generally speaking, most users do not expect to maintain an IP address if they need to use a car, train, or plane to travel between network sites. Still, large, spread-out campuses might require higher-than-average mobility support.

 Call it the "dinosaur juice" rule for mobility: if you burn fossil fuels for transportation, it is probably acceptable for the IP address to change.

Security

As the networks of the world have united into a single, globe-spanning behemoth, security has taken on new importance. Wireless LANs were once the bane of security-conscious networking organizations, but newer tools make it easier to build networks with significant security protections. In addition to traditional security issues such as traffic separation between user groups and maintaining appropriate access privileges, wireless networks present new challenges, like rogue access points and unauthorized clients.

Many of logical architecture's security ramifications are related to the selection of encryption and authentication protocols. But the architecture may have some additional security implications based on technology available at the edge of the network.

Traditional access points are autonomous devices that act as independent network elements. Access points are placed out in user areas, and are usually not physically secured. Unfortunately, the popularity of 802.11 may make unsecured access points in public areas targets for theft. Traditional access points have local software and configuration, and may also be attractive targets to attackers who can use learn sensitive security information from the configuration, such as the RADIUS shared secret. Newer "thin" access points help address this concern by removing a great deal of functionality from the access point and pulling it back into secured controllers that can be locked away in wiring closets.

Attackers may also remove access points to obtain additional network privileges. In some architectures, access points must be connected to relatively privileged network ports. If, for example, several VLANs are made available through a wireless network, many access points require that the access point connect to a link tagged with all the available VLANs. In such a setup, an attacker may obtain direct access to the backbone by removing an access point and connecting to its port.

Mobile IP

802.11 performs a sleight-of-hand trick with MAC addresses: stations communicate with a MAC address as if it were fixed in place, just like any other Ethernet station. Instead of being fixed in a set location, however, access points note when the mobile station is nearby and relay frames from the wired network to it over the airwaves. It does not matter which access point the mobile station associates with because the appropriate access point performs the relay function. The station on the wired network can communicate with the mobile station as if it were directly attached to the wire.

Mobile IP performs a similar trick with IP addresses. The outside world uses a single IP address that appears to remain in a fixed location, called the *home location*. Rather than being serviced by a user's system, however, the IP address at the home location (the *home address*) is serviced by what is called the *home agent*. Like the access point, the home agent is responsible for keeping track of the current location of the mobile node. When the mobile node is "at home," packets can simply be delivered directly to it. If the mobile node attaches to a different network (called a *foreign network* or *visited network*), it *registers* its so-called foreign location with the home agent so that the home agent can redirect all traffic from the home address to the mobile node on the foreign network.

Consider two wireless LANs built on different IP subnets. On its home subnet, a wireless station can send and receive traffic "normally."

When the wireless station moves from its home subnet to the second ("foreign") subnet, it attaches to the network using the normal procedure. It associates with an access point and probably requests an IP address using DHCP. On a wireless station that is unable to use Mobile IP, connections are interrupted at this point because the IP address changes suddenly, invalidating the state of all open TCP connections.

Wireless stations equipped with Mobile IP software, however, can preserve connection state by registering with the home agent. The home agent can accept packets for the mobile station, check its registration tables, and then send the packets to the mobile station at its current location. The mobile station has, in effect, two addresses. It has its home address, and it can continue to use this address for connections that were established using the home address. It may also use the address it has been assigned on the foreign network. No TCP state is invalidated because the mobile station never stopped using its home address.

Naturally, system administrators (rightly) rebel at installing new software on end-user systems. An alternative is to use *proxy mobile IP*, in which the network edge incorporates the functions of the agent software. Moving Mobile IP functions into the access points eliminates the need to install client software, although it does increase the complexity of the access points.

I have omitted a great deal of the protocol operations. Designing a protocol to allow a station to attach anywhere in the world and use an address from its home network is a significant engineering endeavor. Several security problems are evident, most notably the authentication of protocol operations and the security of the redirected packets from the home network to the mobile station's current location. Maintaining accurate routing information, both the traditional forwarding tables at Internet gateways and the Mobile IP agents, is a major challenge. And, of course, the protocol must work with both IPv4 and IPv6. For a far more detailed treatment of Mobile IP, I highly recommend *Mobile IP: Design Principles and Practices* by Charles Perkins (Prentice Hall).

One additional concern is that many government networks need to be designed to comply with regulations and best practices. The National Institute of Standards and Technology (NIST) is responsible for developing many of the computing standards used by the U.S. federal government; these standards are referred to as Federal Information Processing Standards (FIPS). One particular standard, FIPS-140, lays out requirements for secure network designs. Not surprisingly, FIPS-140 specifies that certain types of data must be encrypted. Less obviously, FIPS-140 also requires that approved encryption algorithms and modes must be used. Not all security protocols and standards are created equal, and only some network designs are capable of meeting FIPS-140 criteria. FIPS requirements affect most federal agencies, but may also exert a powerful influence by requiring compliance on the part of an agency's suppliers and contractors. (FIPS requirements are discussed in more detail in Chapter 22.)

Performance

For the benefit of mobility, wireless networks impose a cost. Simply, performance is nowhere near what can be expected from a well-engineered wired LAN. Wireless networks have smaller advertised bit rates than wired LANs. To make matters worse, the big number in the glossy brochure omits a great deal of protocol overhead.[*] Table 21-1 gives rule-of-thumb estimates for the maximum throughput based on the technology.

Table 21-1. Maximum throughput for different 802.11 technologies

Technology	Advertised throughput	Estimated maximum continuous throughput	Estimated maximum perceived throughput with 5:1 multiplexing factor
Single radio systems			
802.11b	11 Mbps	6 Mbps	30 Mbps
802.11a	54 Mbps	30 Mbps	150 Mbps

---

[*] The effective throughput is actually much lower. Quantifying the exact impact of the protocol overhead is very difficult; for one straw-man calculation, see *http://www.oreillynet.com/pub/a/wireless/2003/08/08/wireless_throughput.html*.

Table 21-1. Maximum throughput for different 802.11 technologies (continued)

Technology	Advertised throughput	Estimated maximum continuous throughput	Estimated maximum perceived throughput with 5:1 multiplexing factor
802.11g, no protection	54 Mbps	30 Mbps	150 Mbps
802.11g, with protection	54 Mbps	15 Mbps	225 Mbps
Dual radio systems			
802.11a+802.11b	11+54 Mbps	36 Mbps	180 Mbps
802.11a+802.11g (without protection)	54+54 Mbps	60 Mbps	300 Mbps

Unlike wired networks, the speed at which wireless networks operate depends on the distance from the nearest network uplink. As stations move farther from the serving access point, signals become weaker and the operational speed falls. Throughput depends on distance from the access point and the position of the device in a way that is unfamiliar to users of wired networks.

Throughputs in the neighborhood of Table 21-1 require very strong signals, and by necessity, limited distances from the access point. As a practical matter, most wireless LANs have been built for coverage. At the fringes of connectivity, throughput is at the lowest rate for the technology, not the highest rate. Figure 21-1 illustrates the typical scenario. Although stations close-in connect at the maximum data rate, stations that are further away require much longer time intervals to transmit the same data. Even if the radio medium is in constant use, the maximum throughput of the stations associated to the AP in Figure 21-1 would be much less than 6 Mbps.

Even though the maximum data rates shown in Figure 21-1 are small, the magic of statistical multiplexing can make the rate seem much bigger than it is. Networks are based on the principle that user traffic is often quite bursty. Although users demand a peak data rate of a megabit per second, users are often idle. The network only needs to supply the peak data rate during email fetches and web page downloads; when the connection is idle, other users can get their megabit per second service. In my experience, a multiplexing factor of between 3:1 and 7:1 can be used to account for the burstiness of network traffic. Although an 802.11b network may only deliver 6 Mbps, it can accommodate 20–30 users demanding megabit service because very few applications require continuous service. (Voice applications are a notable exception.) The last column in Table 21-1 shows the effective throughput with a 5:1 multiplexing factor. Depending on applications and experience, you may need to use a higher or lower factor on your network.

Figure 21-1 is only a qualitative display of how the speed of a network changes with ditsance. Free-space loss calcuations can be used to get a more quantitative grasp of a network's range and propagation characteristics. *Free-space loss*, or *path loss*, is the transmission loss over space, with no obstructions. It is an "ideal" number, describing only how the electromagnetic waves diminish in strength over distance while

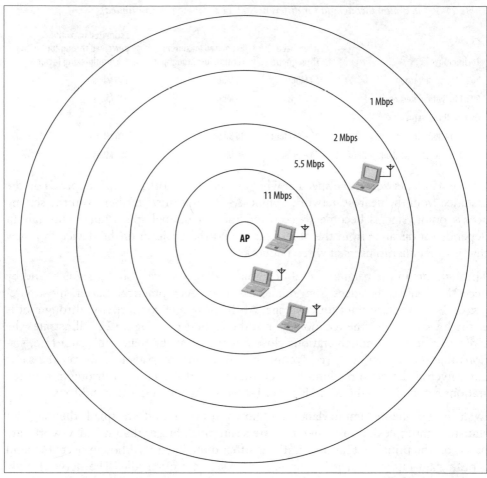

Figure 21-1. Dependence of performance on range

neglecting a number of factors that are relevant to building 802.11 networks. Indoor networks must deal with walls, windows, doors, and the fact that many signals may not be line of sight. Free-space loss calculations assume the noise floor is also sufficiently low that the receiver sensitivity is the limiting factor. In many environments, the number of unlicensed devices operating in the 2.4 GHz ISM band push up the noise floor well past the lower limits of many receivers.

Free-space loss depends only on two inputs: the frequency of the signal and the distance it must cover. Higher frequencies attenuate faster, as do longer distances.

$$\text{FSL (in dB)} = 32.5 + 20 * [\log_{10} (\text{frequency in GHz}) + \log_{10} (\text{distance in meters})]$$

Table 21-2 is based on a free-space calcuation for both 2.4 GHz and 5 GHz wireless LANs. For the ISM frequency, it uses 2.437 GHz, the center frequency of channel 6. For the 5 GHz frequency, it uses 5.250 GHz, which is the midpoint of the U-NII lower and mid-bands. (Some early 802.11 cards were only able to function in the two low bands, so some networks restrict 802.11a channel usage to the first 8.) It assumes that power is transmitted at the maximum of 20 dBm (100 mW) in the 2.4 GHz band, and at the maximum practical power of 14 dBm (25 mW) for many 802.11a devices. For a receiver cut-off, the sensitivity listed on the data sheet for the Cisco CB-21 a/b/g client card was used. By using the sensitivity directly, it is an implied assumption that the noise floor is significantly below the values listed in the sensitivity column. Do not expect to get the ranges noted in this table, since it is only a calculation of the maximum ideal range. It is, however, a useful guide to comparing different modulation rates as well as the different frequency bands in use.

Table 21-2. Free-space range for different modulation speeds

Modulation type and speed	Sensitivity (Cisco CB-21)	Maximum free-space range (meters)	Free-space range relative to maximum speed	Percentage of maximum range modulation
2.4 GHz				
1 Mbps DSSS	−94	4,850	13.9	100%
2 Mbps DSSS	−93	4,300	12.3	89%
5.5 Mbps CCK	−92	3,850	11.0	79%
11 Mbps CCK	−90	3,050	8.7	63%
6 Mbps OFDM	−86	1,930	5.5	40%
9 Mbps OFDM	−86	1,930	5.5	40%
12 Mbps OFDM	−86	1,930	5.5	40%
18 Mbps OFDM	−86	1,930	5.5	40%
24 Mbps OFDM	−84	1,530	4.4	32%
36 Mbps OFDM	−80	970	2.8	20%
48 Mbps OFDM	−75	550	1.6	11%
54 Mbps OFDM	−71	350	1.0	7%
5 GHz				
6 Mbps OFDM	−89	630	7.0	100%
9 Mbps OFDM	−89	630	7.0	100%
12 Mbps OFDM	−89	630	7.0	100%
18 Mbps OFDM	−85	400	4.4	63%
24 Mbps OFDM	−82	280	3.1	44%
36 Mbps OFDM	−79	200	2.2	32%
48 Mbps OFDM	−74	110	1.2	18%
54 Mbps OFDM	−72	90	1.0	14%

The performance of a wireless network differs from a wired network in another important way. Most wireline networks are built using switches, so multiple independent traffic flows can be switched independently. Wireless networks are inherently a shared medium. Within an access point's coverage area, only one client may transmit data. Wireless networks often are built simply to cover an area. As they become popular, network administrators must add capacity by shrinking the coverage area of individual APs to reduce bandwidth contention. Limiting bandwidth contention by making coverage areas smaller is the approach taken by most "Wi-Fi switches."

Physical characteristics of the wireless medium negatively affect performance and service quality. 802.11 uses a fully-acknowledged MAC for reliability, but the need for acknowledgments increases the transmission latency for frames. Lost packets and the potential for retransmission may also increase the variability in latency, called *jitter*. For some applications, the difference in service is imperceptible to the user. Bulk data transfers depend much more on available capacity than the service quality. However, if you plan to run voice on your wireless network, you will need to spend some time engineering acceptable service quality. Voice depends on regular delivery of small amounts of data, not high throughput. Some of the architectures discussed in this chapter are better suited to applications with demands for high quality network service.

Traditional quality of service queuing and controls are important not only because of the need to cope with the relatively low reliability of wireless signals, but also because the bandwidth is so limited. With only a few megabits per second on each access point, a single ill-behaved client can soak up all the available capacity. Some access points provide better traffic shaping and policing to engineer allocation of scarce wireless medium capacity than others, and some logical architectures are better able to cope with high-bandwidth applications.

As with many other network engineering tasks, building a wireless LAN with the necessary performance is a matter of analyzing the types of applications you intend to run on the LAN and removing as many bottlenecks as possible. In some cases, it may be possible to build enough network capacity to provide the required user experience. For other applications, it may be necessary to manage resource allocations using traffic management tools on the access points making up the network.

Backbone Engineering

Access points are the edge of the ever-expanding network. In most cases, they do not offer new network services; they just make existing services more widely available and easy to use. As edge devices, though, they must plug into a network core to interconnect users with resources. Expect to do some additional configuration of the network core when wireless is added to the edge of the LAN.

When 802.11 was a new standard and products had just emerged, there was no mobility except for what the network engineers created, and no traffic separation at all. Mobility was entirely up to the network engineer. If the access points could be placed in a single link layer network, mobility existed. If not, mobility remained elusive. Early wireless LANs required, as a matter of practice, that the network be built around a switched core so that a single subnet snaking through the entire campus could be used to connect up all the access points. Many newer networks are built around a switched core, but older networks frequently have constraints that prevents building a purely switched core.

After the first wave of products arrived, the industry produced devices that could attach users to multiple VLANs. Although these products allowed for multiple user groups over the air and the backbone wire, the backbone configuration impact was even larger. Rather than extending a single VLAN through the campus for the access points, every VLAN had to be extended to every access point throughout the campus. One of the goals of centralized Wi-Fi controllers is to further reduce backbone reengineering by allowing for simpler configurations of the access device connections.

Beacons, BSSIDs, and VLAN integration

Extending existing VLANs over the air is one of the major tasks that standards groups are working on. In the meantime, vendors have taken a variety of approaches. As you evaluate these approaches, there are a few fundamentals.

802.11 built in the concept of having multiple "service sets," but did not explicitly define what a service set was. Moreover, there are two types of service set identifiers (SSIDs) in 802.11. Extended Service Set IDs (ESSIDs) are "network names."* Multiple APs can be configured to advertise a set of connections into the air. When a client wishes to connect to a wireless network, it issues probes for the ESSID it is trying to find, and APs belonging to that SSID respond. ESSIDs can be transmitted in Beacon frames, although they do not have to be. (ESSID hiding is a security-through-obscurity practice; if you flip back to Chapter 9 you will note that the Probe Response frame includes the unencrypted SSID.) The second type of service set, the Basic Service Set ID (BSSID), is the MAC address of the AP. It is used as the transmitter or receiver address on frames that are bridged between the wireless and wired networks.

Generally speaking, each ESSID being transmitted should have its own BSSID. Although there is nothing to prevent an access point from transmitting multiple ESSIDs in a single Beacon, or even responding to ESSIDs not included in its Beacon, such behavior causes problems for many drivers. The Windows Zero Configuration software, for example, generally does not accept a configuration for a secondary, hidden ESSID. Rather than probing for the hidden ESSID, it attempts to attach to the transmitted ESSID in the Beacon.

---

* This is a bit of a simplification. ESSIDs are only network names for infrastructure networks. As always, this book generally assumes that you are running an infrastructure network, not an ad hoc network.

When APs were first able to attach users to different VLANs, a common way of providing the configuration to users was to expose each VLAN as an SSID, and allow users to choose. While such an approach allows a great deal of flexibility in the way that users are assigned to VLANs, and allows them to switch between VLANs as circumstances dictate, the flexibility is a double-edged sword that may lead to confusion for users as they select the wrong configuration. Transmitting Beacon frames for a number of extra SSIDs requires the use of scarce wireless network capacity. For many environments, it makes more sense to dynamically assign users to VLANs based on a user profile database.

IP addressing

IP addresses are often a reflection of the physical network topology, and wireless networks are no different. Assigning IP addresses is a subordinate decision to the topology that you choose. Some network designs may require new address assignments and routing configuration, while others do not. Organizations that attempt to allocate address space hierarchically, perhaps for reasons of routing table size, may find it difficult to reconcile logical address assignment with the underlying physical topology. Furthermore, organizations that make use of registered IP address space may find that it is at a premium.

Network Services

Ideally, new network devices should plug into existing infrastructure and just work with a minimum of reconfiguration. A few network services are important to the user experience, and should be considered in some detail.

DHCP

Users expect to be able to plug in to a network and just have it work. Wireless networks are no exception, and can make the problem worse. Users expect to be able to attach to *any* wireless network and have it just work. Practically speaking, the only way to have the IP stack for a wireless interface self-configure appropriately for an arbitrary number of networks is to use DHCP.

Many access points have built-in DHCP servers. Smaller networks consisting of an access point or two may choose to use the built-in DHCP service, but larger networks should have a single source of DHCP addressing information. Access point DHCP servers may not cope with the load very well, and some access points may reclaim leased addresses when an association lapses.

Any DHCP service should have a view of the total available address space, and this is best done outside the access point. Access points act like bridges, and pass DHCP requests from the wireless network through to the wired network, where a DHCP server can reply. With judicious use of DHCP helpers, a single server can support multiple IP networks, whether they are implemented as VLANs or multiple wireless subnets.

Users expect DHCP, so use it. For maximum effect, deploy as few DHCP servers as possible.

Operating system login

One of the challenges to wireless networking is that validating user credentials often depends on making a network connection to an authentication server. For example, Windows logins are validated against domain controllers. In a wired world, making that connection is trivial because the network is available whenever the cable is plugged in. In a wireless network, though, there is a bit of a chicken and egg problem. User credentials are used to authenticate the network connection, but a network connection is required to validate the user credentials. Not all operating system vendors have considered this problem. If yours has not, you may need to configure special login features or use additional client software to plug the gap.

Client Integration

Different logical architectures require different client software support. It is easy to build a network that has no client integration beyond the new drivers by leaving out security entirely. However, security is a requirement for nearly every network.

The most basic level of security is a static WEP key. Some older devices may not support anything better than static WEP, in which case you are stuck with it in the absence of a forklift upgrade. Static WEP configuration is typically built into driver software or client configuration utilities, and requires no more client integration than using the card itself. For security reasons, though, you want to run something other than static WEP if at all possible.

Link-layer solutions based on 802.1X offer significant advances in security, but require more sigificant client integration work. 802.1X supplicant software must be loaded on the client system and set up correctly. Supplicant software is incorporated into recent operating systems (Windows 2000, Windows XP, and Mac OS X 10.3). Older systems may require a client software package to implement 802.1X.

VPN solutions vary, depending on both the vendor and the type of VPN technology. SSL-based VPNs work by directing client access through a secure web site that acts as a portal for applications. Because the technology is based on a secure web site, there is no client installation beyond the web browser that probably is already installed on most systems. One downside to SSL VPN technology, however, is securing non-web applications may require additional effort and user retraining. IPsec VPNs require a much more disruptive software installation, but are much better at handling an arbitrary IP-based application. One of the reasons that VPN client software loads are more complex is that most vendors require their own VPN client for maximum functionality between the client and gateway.

Some organizations may be limited in their ability to impose client software on users. Universities, for example, often have users who must open VPN tunnels to external network sites. Professional development classes are often taken by students who have careers, and may need to connect to corporate resources from the classroom. Generally speaking, IPsec tunnels inside IPsec tunnels with multiple clients is a configuration that does not work well, if at all.

Topology Examples

After deciding what is important, you can sketch out what the wireless LAN will look like. Broadly speaking, there are two major ways of deploying a wireless LAN, and the choice depends broadly on whether you decide to use security at the link layer. This section describes and analyzes four different major architectures for wireless LANs. To a certain extent, this section presents four fairly rigid examples. As the market for wireless LAN network hardware matures, equipment may incorporate features from multiple topologies, allowing you to mix and match the features that best suit your needs.

Topology 1: The Monolithic Single-Subnet Network

In the beginning, there was one topology. Access points were simple bridges, and served only to attach wireless stations to the single wired network they were connected to. Without much networking intelligence in the access point, wireless networks needed to be designed around the trivial bridging engines in access points. Networks that supported mobility were correspondingly simple. When access points are simple bridges without any sophisticated knowledge of, say, VLANs or routing, they must all attach to the same IP subnet. As long as a station stays on the same IP subnet, it does not need to reinitialize its networking stack and can keep its TCP connections open.

Equipment limitations dictated the resulting network architecture. Every AP was attached to a single network. While the network provided mobility, it was often difficult to build, especially on large campuses. In addition to modifying backbone network configuration, administrators had to set aside new IP address ranges and route appropriately. The architecture was developed to shield wired networks from the danger of wireless networks in the time before the development of strong security protocols. These days, the high configuration overhead and management cost of building two parallel networks has driven this topology nearly to extinction on any network larger than a few access points.

Figure 21-2 shows the typical early wireless LAN deployment topology. All the APs are connected to a single monolithic network. The network is a single link-layer domain, and every station connected to the network is given an IP address on the IP subnet. For this reason, the monolithic architecture may be referred to as the *single-subnet wireless LAN*, the *walled garden architecture*, or occasionally the *VPN architecture*. (It should also be noted that most home networks take the single subnet approach, although typically with only one access point.)* The guiding principle of Figure 21-2 is that the access points in use cannot provide any services other than link-layer mobility, so they must all be connected to the same logical link layer. Other design decisions underlying this topology help augment the access control of the wireless device and lower management overhead by taking advantage of existing services, each of which will be considered in turn.

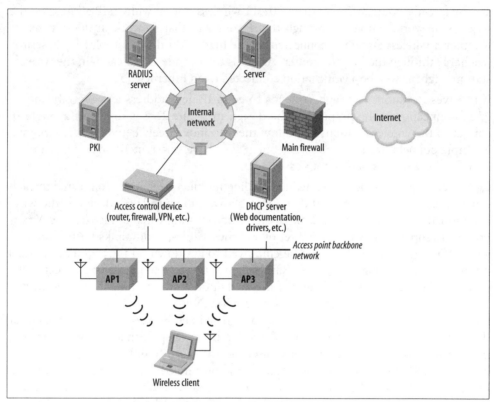

Figure 21-2. The single subnet wireless LAN deployment topology

Mobility

In Figure 21-2, the network linking all the access points, which is often called the access point backbone, is a single IP subnet. To allow users to roam between access points, the network should be a single IP subnet, even if it spans multiple locations, because IP does not allow for network-layer mobility. (Mobile IP is the exception to this rule; see the sidebar earlier in this chapter.) Network-layer mobility is supplied by the use of a

---

* Very large homes may require multiple APs. Generally speaking, an AP should be good for coverage over 3,000–5,000 square feet, which is sufficient for all but the largest homes.

switching infrastructure that supports linking all the access points together, and an IP addressing scheme that does not require anything beyond link-layer mobility.

In Figure 21-2, the backbone network may be physically large, but it is constrained by the requirement that all access points connect directly to the backbone router (and each other) at the link layer. 802.11 hosts can move within the last network freely, but IP, as it is currently deployed, provides no way to move across subnet boundaries. To the IP-based hosts of the outside world, the VPN/access control boxes of Figure 21-2 are the last-hop routers. To get to an 802.11 wireless station with an IP address on the wireless network, simply go through the IP router to that network. It doesn't matter whether a wireless station is connected to the first or third access point because it is reachable through the last-hop router. As far as the outside world can tell, the wireless station might as well be a workstation connected to an Ethernet.

If it leaves the subnet, though, it needs to get a IP new address and reestablish any open connections. The purpose of the design in Figure 21-2 is to assign a single IP subnet to the wireless stations and allow them to move freely between access points. Multiple subnets are not forbidden, but if you have different IP subnets, seamless mobility between subnets is not possible.

Older access points that cooperate in providing mobility need to be connected to each other at layer 2. One method of doing this, shown in Figure 21-3 (a), builds the wireless infrastructure of Figure 21-2 in parallel to the existing wired infrastructure. Access points are supported by a separate set of switches, cables, and uplinks in the core network. Virtual LANs (VLANs) can be employed to cut down on the required physical infrastructure, as in Figure 21-3 (b). Rather than acting as a simple layer-2 repeater, the switch in Figure 21-3 (b) can logically divide its ports into multiple layer-2 networks. The access points can be placed on a separate VLAN from the existing wired stations, and the "wireless VLAN" can be given its own IP subnet. Frames leaving the switch for the network core are tagged with the VLAN number to keep them logically distinct and may be sent to different destinations based on the tag. Multiple subnets can be run over the same uplink because the VLAN tag allows frames to be logically separated. Incoming frames for the wired networks are tagged with one VLAN identifier, and frames for the wireless VLAN are tagged with a different VLAN identifier. Frames are sent only to ports on the switch that are part of the same VLAN, so incoming frames tagged with the wireless VLAN are delivered only to the access points.

By making the access point backbone a VLAN, it can span long distances. VLAN-aware switches can be connected to each other, and the tagged link can be used to join multiple physical locations into a single logical network. In Figure 21-4, two switches are connected by a tagged link, and all four access points are assigned to the same VLAN. The four access points can be put on the same IP subnet and act as if they are connected to a single hub. The tagged link allows the two switches to be separated, and the distance can depend on the technology. By using fiber-optic links, VLANs can be made to go between buildings, so a single IP subnet can be extended across as many buildings as necessary.

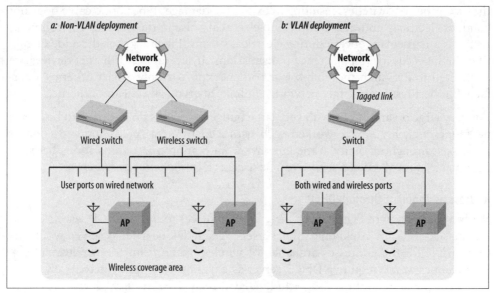

Figure 21-3. Physical topologies for 802.11 network deployment

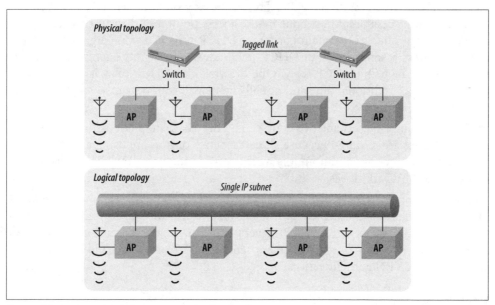

Figure 21-4. Using VLANs to span multiple switches

Tagged links can vary widely in cost and complexity. To connect different physical locations in one building, you can use a regular copper Ethernet cable. To connect two buildings together, fiber-optic cable is a must. Different buildings are usually at different voltage levels relative to each other. Connecting two buildings with a conductor such as copper would enable current to flow between (and possibly through) the two Ethernet switches, resulting in expensive damage. Fiber-optic cable does not conduct electricity and does not pick up electrical noise in the outdoor environment, which is a particular concern during electrical storms. Fiber also has the added benefit of high speeds for long-distance transmissions. If several Fast Ethernet devices are connected to a switch, the uplink is a bottleneck if it is only a Fast Ethernet interface. For best results on larger networks, uplinks are typically Gigabit Ethernet.

For very large organizations with very large budgets, uplinks do not need to be Ethernet. One company I have worked with uses a metro-area ATM cloud to connect buildings throughout a city at the link layer. With appropriate translations between Ethernet and ATM, such a service can be used as a trunk between switches.

Address assignment through DHCP

Within the context of Figure 21-2, there are two places to put a DHCP server. One is on the access point backbone subnet itself. A standalone DHCP server would be responsible for the addresses available for wireless stations on the wireless subnet. Each subnet would require a DHCP server as part of the rollout. Alternatively, most devices capable of routing also include DHCP relay. The security device shown in Figure 21-2 includes routing capabilities, and some firewalls and VPN devices include DHCP relay. With DHCP relay, requests from the wireless network are bridged to the access point backbone by the access point and then further relayed by the access controller to the main corporate DHCP server. If your organization centralizes address assignment with DHCP, take advantage of the established, reliable DHCP service by using DHCP relay. One drawback to DHCP relay is that the relay process requires additional time and not all clients will wait patiently, so DHCP relay may not be an option.

Static addressing is acceptable, of course. The drawback to static addressing is that more addresses are required because all users, active or not, are using an address. To minimize end-user configuration, it is worth considering using DHCP to assign fixed addresses to MAC addresses.

As a final point, there may be an interaction between address assignment and security. If VPN solutions are deployed, it is possible to use RFC 1918 (private) address space for the infrastructure. DHCP servers could hand out private addresses that enable nodes to reach the VPN servers, and the VPN servers hand out routable addresses once VPN authentication succeeds.

Security

This is the oldest of the architectures in this chapter, and pre-dates all the work done on link-layer security in the past several years. It is generally used on networks where link-layer security is not a priority, either because security is secondary to providing services (as in the case of an ISP) or because security is provided through higher-layer protocols with VPN technology. Security trade-offs in wireless network design are discussed in more detail in Chapter 22.

Backbone engineering

Depending on the existing backbone, using this topology may require prohibitive work on the backbone, or it may be relatively easy. For maximum mobility, every access point must be attached to the wireless VLAN that snakes throughout the campus. If a network is built on a switched core, it may be relatively easy to create a VLAN that spans multiple switches across several wiring closets. However, there may be fundamental limitations on what is possible. If buildings are separated by routers, it may not be possible to build a single VLAN that spans an entire campus, and it may be necessary to settle for disjointed islands of mobility. Even worse, many older networks are not built around switched cores that allow easy VLAN extensions everywhere.

Furthermore, there is a practical limitation on the network diameter of a VLAN. 802.1D, the bridging standard, recommends that VLANs be built with a maximum diameter of seven switch hops. Depending on the physical topology, it may be impossible to build a single VLAN that can span the desired coverage area within the recommended limit. Alternatively, it may be possible to do so, but only with extensive modifications to the network core.

Performance

Performance of this design can vary greatly because it incorporates a single choke point. One of the most important aspects of making this design perform well is limiting the effect of pushing all the traffic through a single logical path. All the backbone devices must have sufficient capacity to handle the load from the entire wireless network.

Wireless LAN protocols are based on collision avoidance, and can sustain much higher loads than the collision-detection protocols used on wired LANs. Depending on the number of users associated with a particular access point, it may be reasonable to assume that the radio link is saturated. Maximum throughput rates vary slightly from product to product, but 6 Mbps is a reasonable maximum rate for 802.11b, with 802.11a and 802.11g both weighing in at 27–30 Mbps.

Avoiding congestion is much easier with the slow speeds of 802.11b. With only a 6 Mbps potential load per access point, a full duplex Fast Ethernet links to the access point backbone should be able to handle slightly over 30 APs. While 30 APs is not a monstrous network, it is enough to provide blanket coverage over a large open space for low-bandwidth applications. Upgrading to Gigabit Ethernet on the choke point vastly increases the number of APs that can be attached. Depending on the breakdown between upstream and downstream traffic, it is possible to connect 200–300 APs without worrying about backbone network congestion. Of course, gigabit choke point devices cost significantly more than Fast Ethernet choke point devices.

802.11a and 802.11g, with their potentially higher speeds, could pose more of a problem. With several times the speed, only a few access points can saturate a Fast Ethernet choke point. Assuming a favorable breakdown between upstream and downstream transmission, full duplex Fast Ethernet can connect six APs, which is not enough to cover many midsized offices. Dual-band APs that do both 802.11a and 802.11g present a double whammy because each radio may offer a high load.

Table 21-3 summarizes the discussion of backbone technology and the number of APs required to saturate the link. It is meant only as a "back of the envelope" estimate. Each backbone technology is divided by the AP-offered load to estimate the number of APs required to saturate the link. It does not take into account any protocol overhead or realistic split between upstream and downstream traffic. It is meant as a rough guide to select an appropriate uplink technology from your wireless subnet.

Table 21-3. Estimated APs required for backbone saturation

	802.11b (~6 Mbps)	802.11a or 802.11g (~30 Mbps)	Dual-band a/b (~36 Mbps)	Dual-band a/g (~60 Mbps)
Half-duplex Fast Ethernet (100 Mbps)	16	3	2	1
Full-duplex Fast Ethernet (200 Mbps)	33	6	5	3
Full-duplex Gigabit Ethernet (2,000 Mbps)	333	66	55	33

Client integration

This is the most varied of the architectures in terms of client integration. In the case of a service provider, it is likely that little or no client work is required. No security of any sort is applied, so there is nothing to configure. If extensive higher-layer security is applied on top of this architecture, however, there is extensive desktop integration to be done.

Topology 2: "E.T. Phone Home" or "Island Paradise"

Some organizations are simply too large to build a single access point network. The classic example is a major research university with multiple buildings distributed over several square miles. Configuring a single access point network to snake through the entire campus is simply out of the question, not least because large campuses depend on routed networks for broadcast isolation.

Network administrators compromised by dividing the wireless network into several "islands" of connectivity. In the university environment, an island often corresponds to a building or department, and it takes its IP addressing and routing information from that department's address allocation. Separating wireless LANs into islands also serves a valuable political purpose. Different departments can each build their own wireless network, complete with its own security policies and network service goals. Islands can also be built more quickly because no coordination is required between them. Many islands can be built simultaneously.

Piecemeal deployments look like multiple instances of the single subnet of Figure 21-2. The topology provides seamless mobility between the access points connected to the access point backbone network. In networks that cannot support a single VLAN for the access point backbone, a frequent compromise is to limit mobility to local areas where it is most useful. For example, in a multi-building campus, a typical goal is to provide seamless mobility within individual buildings, but not roaming between buildings. Each building would have a wireless LAN that looked something like Figure 21-2, and all the access point backbone networks would ultimately connect to a campus backbone.

In Figure 21-5 (a), there are several "islands" of connectivity, and each island provides mobility within itself. Inter-island roaming cannot be provided by 802.11 itself, but requires additional technology such as Mobile IP or a special client. 802.11 allows an ESS to extend across subnet boundaries, but does not support a seamless roaming operation.

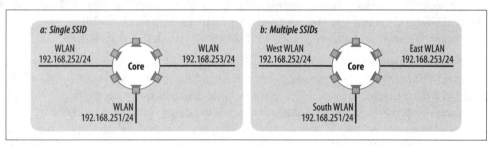

Figure 21-5. Noncontiguous deployments

If you must break the campus into disjointed coverage areas, be sure to preserve the mobility that is most important to your users. In most cases, mobility within a building is important. Most buildings are built around a switched core, and can support an island of connectivity.

Mobility

The single-subnet architecture achieved mobility by creating a single subnet for all access points, and keeping all the users on the that restricted subnet. This architecture borrows the same philosophy, but is designed to work with networks that are not able to create a single subnet.

At the most basic level, this architecture provides portability. Users can move between islands without restriction, but need to reestablish any open network connections as they move between islands. Connection reestablishment may be handled in a variety of ways, some of which may be transparent to the user. Many universities simply accept the limitations of portability, and instruct users to close any applications that use network resources before moving. If portability limitations are problematic, it may be possible to achieve mobility between IP networks by using client software or tunneling protocols.

This topology looks much like the first topology, except that it is replicated in several pieces. Most likely, the islands of connectivity connect to the network core through firewalls. Mobility between islands may be achieved by using a tunneling protocol that ensures that a user attaches to the same logical location on the network, no matter what their physical location.

Figure 21-6 shows how mobility can be grafted on to a collection of scattered networks. In Figure 21-6 (a), clients are given a local IP address that is tied to location. The local networks are represented by Net X and Net Y. Upon connection, clients are issued addresses from the IP space assigned to the X and Y networks. However, the client also initiates a connection to a central concentration point. Clients logically attach to the concentrator, and receive an address from a network logically attached to the concentrator, which is denoted by Net Z in the diagram. Packets sent from the client use its central anchor point address, Z, as the source, but they are bundled into a tunnel for transmission. Replies are routed back to Z, but the concentrator maintains a mapping of addresses on network Z to location-based addresses. Note that Figure 21-6 (a) does not specify any particular tunneling method. Mobile IP works in essentially this way, and a few specialized IPsec clients work this way as well.

Although the approach of Figure 21-6 (a) is conceptually straightforward, it requires changing the software on all wireless devices. In addition to the administrative challenge of loading new software on any wireless device and the potential instability of changing the network stack, it is likely that vendors of this software would not be able to support every operating system platform. Even if the major operating systems were supported, many embedded devices could not be. Figure 21-6 (b) offers an alternative approach where the tunneling is moved into the network. In Figure 21-6 (b), access points do not connect to a backbone network for the purpose of delivering traffic. The backbone network is used only to connect APs to the traffic concentration point. Any frames or packets from the client are delivered through the tunnel to the concentrator device, where they are sent on to the rest of the network. It does not matter where clients attach to the network because traffic is always routed to the traffic concentration point.

In both of the cases in Figure 21-6, the key is that client IP addresses become location-independent. IP addresses on local networks are used for the purpose of connectivity, but the logical point of attachment to the network is through a defined anchor point, just as in the previous topology.

Tunneling approaches work to unite disjointed coverage areas. In the first topology, mobility was all-or-nothing. Figure 21-5's disjointed coverage areas force network architects to design mobility around areas that are most important to users, subject to the constraints of the local network design. By using a tunneling approach, the network can be reunited into a single mobility cloud, but without the need to re-engineer the entire network backbone. There is, however, the difficulty of configuring any tunneling and working out the overlay topology.

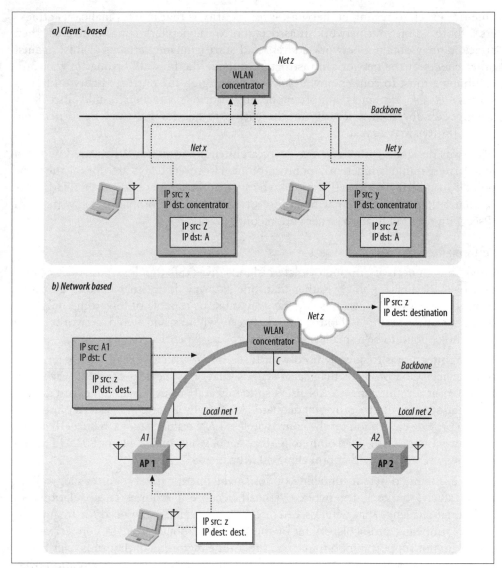

Figure 21-6. Mobility through tunneling

Security

One of the advantages of this architecture is that it is easy to use it with IPsec. IPsec is a suite of strong, trusted encryption protocols that have been widely used in hostile network environments, and that trust has allowed IPsec to be used to protect a great deal of sensitive information traversing the Internet. Many organizations that have a need to protect private personal information make extensive use of IPsec.

One drawback to relying on network-layer security is that it gives malicious attackers a foothold on your network. If association to the network is not protected, then attackers may obtain a network address and start launching attacks against against other clients or the network infrastructure outside the firewall. Strong firewall protection is a must to contain any attacks originating on the untrusted network. Host security is also extremely important because devious attackers would also likely attempt to subvert host security on the clients to hijack VPN tunnels, so personal firewall software is a must.

IPsec was designed with a point-to-point architecture in mind. When used between major sites, traffic is inherently point-to-point. However, LANs are not meant to be point to point networks. (Just ask anybody who has experience with ATM LAN Emulation!) Applications that make use of multicast will probably not work with IPsec without modification or network reconfiguration.

Performance

Providing connectivity through isolated islands gives this topology a distinct advantage over the first topology. Rather than one gateway device that handles all traffic from the wireless LAN, each island gateway must be capable of fowarding only that island's traffic. Multiple choke points between wireless and wired networks allow each choke point to be a smaller, and therefore less expensive, device.

This architecture is frequently used with IPsec, often with an existing VPN termination device. One problem that can occur is that VPN devices are often sized for remote user termination. If LAN users suddenly start using IPsec, the existing VPN termination device may prove inadequate. A centrally located VPN device must be able to provide encryption for the entire wireless LAN traffic load; each 802.11b access point may offer a traffic load of up to 6 Mbps each, while an 802.11a or 802.11g access point may serve up a load approaching 30 Mbps.

There are many different tunneling options available for this broad topology. Tunneling always imposes a network overhead because it requires encapsulation. An additional challenge that wireless LAN devices must face is the need for fragmentation in tunneling protocols. Many of the LAN backbones used to connect access points do not support jumbo frames, so any tunneling protocol that runs over Ethernet must incorporate fragmentation and reassembly. Beyond the fragmentation overhead, any tunneling protocol requires additional header information. Depending on the protocol selected, fragmentation overhead may be nontrivial.

Running user traffic across a network backbone may diminish the service quality. Large networks may not be able to provide consistent low-latency forwarding performance between the access points and the concentration device, especially if the tunneling mechanism is implemented over a best-effort protocol like IP. In the case of user data traffic, any service quality diminishment is likely to be negligable. If the wireless network must be used to support voice protocols, however, the impact of tunneling may be more substantial.

Backbone

Compared to the single-subnet architecture, this topology integrates much better with networks that cannot support a single VLAN everywhere. At worst, this architecture requires creating several miniature single-subnet backbones. If tunneling functions are moved into the network, though, it is possible to extend networks out to remote locations without any backbone work.

Client

VPN software is typically used with this approach, which requires configuring client software on any machine that will use the wireless network. In some organizations, this may not represent a large burden, especially if most of the users already have VPN software. However, many organizations limit the number of users given remote access privileges to limit the amount of client integration work necessary, or prevent remote access devices from being overwhelmed with the load. If you work for such an organization, there is a significant client software installation burden with a widespread wireless deployment. As mentioned previously, personal firewall software is mandatory to protect each client from link-layer attacks. Give preference to VPN clients that include personal firewall software, especially if the personal firewall policies can be centrally managed.

Topology 3: Dynamic VLAN Assignment

Both the single-subnet and island topologies are designed around the limitations of the first access points to hit the market. Early access points attached all users to the same network, and did very little to enforce different privileges on different groups of users. This topology was the first to embrace the wired world of VLANs and make them available to user groups. Instead of building a second parallel network, this topology extends the existing network, complete with any security systems and filters, into the wireless realm.

802.1X is the cornerstone of dynamic VLAN assignment. It plugs the wireless network neatly into an existing authentication infrastructure. Authentication servers have user profiles and privileges, and can map that privilege information on to the wireless LAN. For example, Figure 21-7 shows a RADIUS server handing out VLAN assignments to the access point. As part of the RADIUS access accept message, it includes an attribute that assigns an authenticated user to a particular VLAN. Based on that information, the access point tags any frames from the user on to the appropriate VLAN.

The advantage of doing authentication at the link layer, rather than a higher layer, is that users can be placed on a particular network with the privileges associated with that network from the start. When the access point receives the Access Accept message from the RADIUS server, it sends an 802.1X EAP Success message to the client.

Network card drivers on the client interpret the EAP Success message as the equivalent event to a "link up" message, and send their DHCP request and begin initializing the network stack. By the time the network stack has begun to initialize, the network has already automatically configured itself to restrict the user to a particular set of access rights.

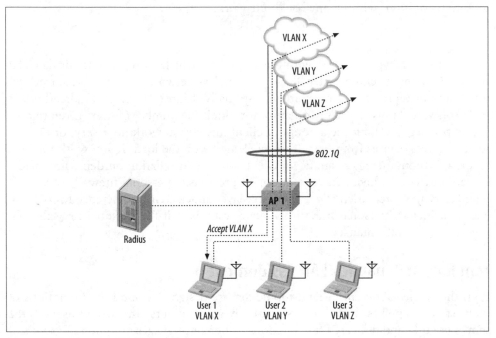

Figure 21-7. Dynamic VLAN topology

Mobility

At the highest level, mobility in this topology is identical to the first topology. Users are attached to a consistent VLAN throughout the network, and thus can maintain the same IP address regardless of location. With the same IP address, any transport-layer state or application state remains valid throughout the life of the connection.

However, the underlying implementation of mobility offers several advantages over the single-subnet architecture. The first set of advantages have to do with the use of authentication services. Attributes from the RADIUS server ensure that users are always attached to the same VLAN, and hence, they stay attached to the same logical point on the network.

In addition to aiding mobility, providing consistent VLAN attachment can make other services work better. Providing mobility at the link layer reduces the apparent mobility to higher-layer protocols, and hence, the amount of work required of them.

IPsec tunnels stay up consistently because the IP address does not change. Likewise, Mobile IP location updates are not necessary because the IP address is maintained.

Security

Because the VLAN assignment is based on 802.1X and RADIUS, security in this topology is based on dynamically generated keys at the link layer, either through dynamic WEP, WPA, or CCMP. Dynamic key generation enables the second benefit of using authentication services. Once users have been identified, they can be separated into groups for different security treatment.

To separate traffic in the air between user groups, access points use multiple key sets. Upon authentication, every user is given a default (broadcast) key, and a key mapping (unicast) key. Broadcast domains are defined by the stations in possession of the same broadcast key. In Figure 21-8, the two users on the left are part of the same user group, and share the same broadcast key. When one sends, say, an ARP request, the other responds. Users who are part of a different broadcast domain are not able to decrypt and process the frame because they have a different broadcast key. Although user groups share the same radio capacity, they are not members of the same user group and remain separated over the radio network.

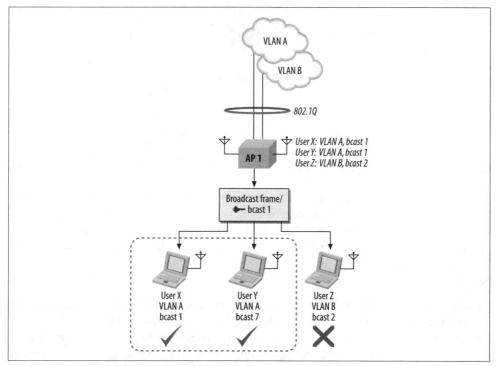

Figure 21-8. Broadcast separation by keys

Furthermore, the separation of user groups by VLAN allows the application of differentiated services, as shown in Figure 21-9. One common use of user identification and differentiation is to offer guest services. Internal users are identified and authenticated against a user database, and then connected to the internal network. Guest users do not have accounts on the main user database and cannot authenticate to the network. After failing to do so, they are attached to a different logical network. Guest networks may have "splash pages" that require a click-through agreement to not abuse the network; some organizations may also wish to require payment for guest access.

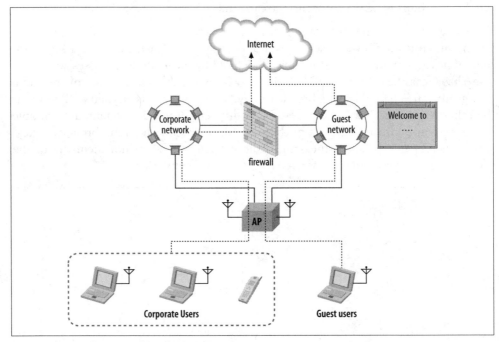

Figure 21-9. Differentiated user services

An additional advantage to link-layer security is that multicast is well-integrated into the security protocol. LAN protocols often make heavy use of multicast or broadcast frames, and the use of multicast LAN frames can only increase. Wireless networks are attractive because of their flexibility and location-independence. Protocols that assist in the automatic discovery and configuration of new devices usually rely heavily on multicast frames.

One downside to this topology relates to bureaucratic requirements around security. At the time this book was written, link-layer security could not comply with FIPS-140, the U.S. federal government's network security standard, because of a subtle flaw with the dynamic key derivation algorithms in 802.11i. Although the encryption mode used by CCMP is approved, a small change to the key derivation algorithm is likely to be required before 802.11i-based networks can meet the FIPS-140 bar.

Performance

This architecture does not necessarily require a choke point. Switching frames at the network edge eliminates the requirement for an oversized packet forwarding device. Wireless LANs are access networks, so by definition, a wireless LAN should not be able to overload a well-built network core. One of the downsides of this architecture, however, is that it is best deployed around a big, fast switched core.

Backbone

Redesigning a network to use VLAN information dynamically can often impose a substantial redesign of the the network backbone. What is required depends on how the wireless LAN connects to the network core. When a wireless LAN connects to the core to attach users to multiple networks, it typically uses an 802.1Q tagged link. Wireless LAN products vary in how widely tagging is used, and to what extent the tags must be pushed across the network. In broad terms, there are two major ways to push VLAN information out to access points.

Direct core connection

When the connection to the network core is made directly, the access points must connect directly to the network core, usually through an 802.1Q-tagged link.

Note that the connection to the core is the logical connection from the access points. With some products, the access points must connect directly to the core, which means that every switch port used to connect to an access point must support any VLAN used by wireless users. Direct core connections for every access point imposes a huge backbone engineering requirement, and may even rule out the use of this topology. If the VLANs do not exist in every closet where APs connect, they must be extended everywhere before the wireless deployment can even begin.

Direct connections to the core may also pose a security risk. Most APs authenticate users, but the APs themselves do not authenticate. An attacker who replaces an AP with his own device may have a direct connection to the network core.

Indirect (tunneled) core connection

Instead of requiring every access point to connect directly to the core, some products allow the use of tunneling protocols to avoid significant changes to the backbone. Users connect to an access point, but the AP tunnels the user's frames to a remote location before they are placed on to the core network. Tunneling can be accomplished between access points, or between an access point and an aggregation device. The tunneling protocol may be proprietary, or it may be based on a simple encapsulation standard like the Generic Routing Encapsulation (GRE), IP in IP, or the Point-to-Point Protocol over Ethernet (PPPoE).

In Figure 21-10 (a), there are two APs on separate VLANs. After user authentication completes, the AP is responsible for connecting the user on to the appropriate VLAN. If the AP is directly attached, then the connection is easy. When the

AP is not directly attached to the VLAN the user must be connected to, the tunnel is built between APs. AP2 locates the VLAN the user should be attached to, and sends user frames through the tunnel to AP1. AP1 then sends frames out on to the network normally. The user's logical attachment remains AP1, no matter what the physical location is. Depending on the implementation, it may be necessary to prevent tunneling across long distances. If the two networks are separated by state lines, or even an ocean, tunneling traffic is likely to result in user dissatisfaction.

In Figure 21-10 (b), the attachment is centralized at the core of the network rather than being distributed at the edge. Frames received by the access points are shuttled up through the tunnel to the concentrator, where they are placed on the appropriate network. VLAN information is only relevant at the end of a frame's journey through the wireless LAN system. Until the frames reach the concentrator, they do not carry VLAN tags. The advantage of a remote tunneling system is that users can be attached to VLANs that are not locally present. The VLANs need to be made available only to the concentrator.

Of the two methods, tunneled connections tend to impose less of a backbone engineering requirement because tags can be distributed on a more local basis. In the direct connect case, every port connected to an access point must carry the complete set of VLANs users may want to work with. The backbone impact is just as great as the first topology for each VLAN. In contrast, indirect connections can span wider areas by operating outside of a spanning tree domain, and configuration of individual switch ports may be easier.

Client

802.1X supplicants are now built-in to the most common client operating systems. Windows 2000, Windows XP, and Mac OS X 10.3 all have 802.1X supplicant software built into the operating system. Provided that you wish to use one of the authentication protocols supported by the operating system's supplicant, there is no client installation to worry about. Furthermore, the built-in supplicant configuration can often be assisted by the use of large-scale system administration tools to distribute the required certificates or configuration information.

Topology 4: Virtual Access Points

A straightforward application of 802.1X and VLAN assignment leads directly to the previous topology. However, it works best when the network has only one class of user—and that is hardly realistic. Most networks are now built to connect employees to internal resources while simultaneously giving guests access to the Internet. Supporting multiple classes of user is becoming much more common, but it creates additional work for security architects. Different logical networks must be run in parallel, often with vastly different security models.

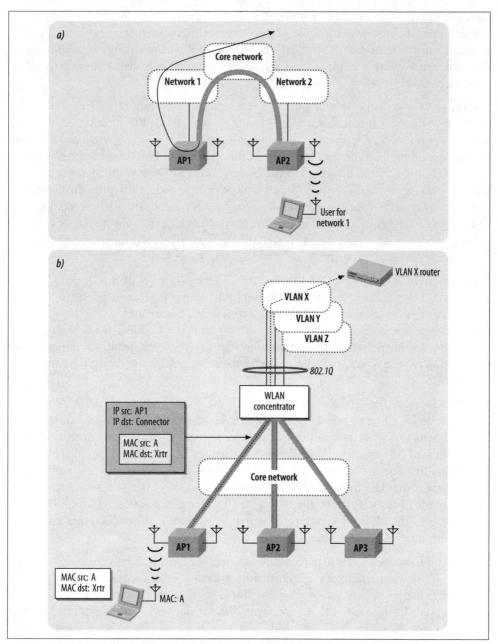

Figure 21-10. Core connections for dynamic VLAN products

One method of building multiple logical networks is to build multiple physical networks, and manage each separately. Competition for network administrator time, access point locations, power and network connections, and radio resources makes building multiple physical networks unproductive. Instead, architects are turning to virtual access points, which enable multiple logical networks to be built on a single physical infrastructure. The physical network owner is responsible for maintaining the infrastructure as a common carrier, and serving as a transit network to other existing networks.

Several years ago, airports woke up to the possibility of using 802.11 as a network medium to connect business travelers (and their wallets) to the Internet. In the first wave, airports worked with specialist integrators to build a single wireless LAN that looked something like the first topology in this chapter. It could be used by business travelers, but was not at all suited to use by anybody else. Many applications of wireless networking went unheeded. Wireless networks are ideal for providing connections that may need to be moved and changed on a regular basis, such as retail kiosks or even the airline equipment at gates. It is easy to understand why a credit-card processing service or an airline would feel that a network designed for road warriors did not provide adequate security.

With a network designed around virtual APs, there is one set of physical infrastructure, owned by the building owner. The building owner is responsible for frequency coordination throughout the building.* From a monetary perspective, the single physical network is also the only game in town, and the building owner can charge for access to the network. In office buildings designed for multiple tenants, the owner may choose to use the wireless network as an amenity to make tenancy more attractive.

Virtual APs may also make a great deal of sense for the network users. With one organization handling physical installation, there is no overlapping installation effort, and it lessens turf wars over radio spectrum. A virtual AP can offer the same services as a dedicated AP, but a virtual AP is often cheaper to install because of the shared infrastructure. The most advanced virtual APs look exactly like multiple standalone APs. I expect that the management of virtual AP systems offer the ability to extend management infrastructure to the users, so that there is a low-level administration interface plus the ability to configure virtual networks for every customer subscribing to a multitenant network service.

Figure 21-11 shows what a network built on virtual access points would look like. In essence, it allows the network administrator to create several copies of the dynamic VLAN topology on one set of physical infrastructure, with each virtual network administered. In the figure, there are three distinct networks to be extended by the wireless LAN. Network A is a typical corporate network. Users who wish to gain access to it must have accounts on the corporate RADIUS server. Network B is a hot-

---

* Newer leases for multitenant buildings are increasingly being written so that the owner retains control of the electromagnetic spectrum and can construct a building-wide network without working around tenant equipment, although the FCC takes a dim view of these provisions.

spot service provider. For device-independence, many service providers use web-based authentication systems that trap user requests until users have identified themselves and made appropriate arrangements to pay for network access. Finally, Network C is designed to support voice over IP, and has an IP PBX system. One set of access points is deployed to support all three networks. One SSID identifies Network A. That SSID has a security configuration that requires 802.1X authentication against the RADIUS server on Network A, and it may be that systems attaching to the network have appropriate client software installed, such as antiviral protection. SSID A may support several different VLANs on Network A, depending on how the RADIUS server is configured. Network A is also configured to support strong encryption. Network B is supported by a second SSID that is configured for web-based authentication. Once users authenticate through the web system, they are allowed Internet access. Network B has no encryption because the service provider does not want to restrict subscriber computing platforms or require special client software beyond a web browser. SSID C is deployed to support voice over IP. Traffic on SSID C is likely prioritized over the other two because of the tighter quality of service requirements for voice traffic. How devices authenticate against SSID C depends on the handsets in use. Many VoIP handsets do not yet support 802.1X, leaving network administrators to rely on MAC filtering and static WEP for security.

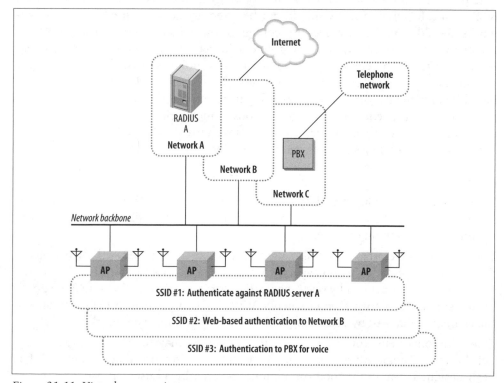

Figure 21-11. Virtual access points

Mobility

This topology provides essentially the same mobility as the previous topology. VLANs can be dynamically instantiated at the edge to connect users, so client stations are dynamically attached to the correct point on the network. As in the previous case, additional protocols may be used to extend mobility across more than a single VLAN domain.

With virtual access points, limiting mobility may be important. This architecture is designed around providing service, and it may be that service should not be ubiquitous. If an office building were to provide connectivity for tenants, the owners may choose to limit where tenants can connect. Rather than connecting anywhere in the building, the service may be limited to a particular floor or wing. If an airport were to deploy a network using virtual access points, the public hot spot service providers would likely be restricted to the public areas, while the airport operational network was available through more of the facility. Different products provide alternate approaches to limiting mobility. As with many other network control functions, your preference should be for centrally-administered access controls.

Security

Due to the tie-in with the link layer, this topology is often used in conjunction with 802.1X and RADIUS. 802.1X should not be a requirement. Each of the virtual networks should have its own security configuration, which would allow every customer to enforce their own security policy. Different customers may have different requirements, and a network built on virtual access points should accommodate any reasonable security policy. For example, most hot spot providers are running web-based login systems. While a web-based login system may be good enough for some applications, legal requirements would impose much stricter handling on a system that accessed personally-identifiable information. Virtual AP-based networks need to accommodate both types of access simultaneously.

Performance

Performance is not constrained by a choke point anywhere. With the wireless network connecting directly into a larger network core, the only performance constraint is congestion on the core.

The biggest problem facing a multitenant network is that the network owner has to design a network with enough capacity for all the users. In the case of a private network owned and operated by one organization for its own purposes, it may be possible to estimate the network requirements. With a network service provided to others, the estimates obtained by consulting with users may be somewhat murky.

One additional item worthy of note is that analyzers may report overloaded channels because a single AP acts as multiple virtual APs. Provided that the network has been designed around the total throughput required by all users, it is acceptable to have multiple networks over the air.

Backbone

Like any other AP, a virtual AP connects a radio network to a wired network. In the case of a virtual AP, both the radio and fixed networks may be created over a shared physical infrastructure. Rather than one wired network, or a set of networks owned by one organization, there may be a need to connect to several customer networks on the back end. When all the networks belong to one organization, they probably have similar security requirements and can be connected easily to wireless networks. Mapping wireless networks on to the wired networks of several different (and possibly competing) customers may require additional measures to ensure security and traffic separation.

Client

As with the other topologies, the client software load depends a great deal on the security protocols. At the easy end of the spectrum, a network can be deployed using web-based authentication without requiring any client software. At the most difficult, the network can use several security protocols, each with its own client software requirement. One of the advantages to virtual AP-based networks is that the virtual APs may be used to create several networks, each with its own special security configuration.

Blurring the Boundaries: Wi-Fi Switching

One of the most talked-about developments in wireless networks in the past few years is the emergence of the new "Wi-Fi switch" architecture. In broad terms, Wi-Fi switches move network functions from access points into an aggregation device that provides control and management functions.

Control and management functions are quite important to a wireless network. Wireless networks often require a great deal of network administration support because they are composed of a herd of small devices. Wi-Fi switches can help administrators build larger networks by providing management support. Rather than managing many autonomous access points, network administrators can work with a handful of switch devices that control access points.

By reducing the time and effort required to control an AP, Wi-Fi switches can make it possible to have more APs on a wireless network. More APs usually means a denser coverage blanket with smaller coverage areas for each AP, and less bandwidth contention.

Wi-Fi switches can be used in any of the topologies discussed in this chapter, although devices from particular manufacturers may adapt better or worse to certain topologies. Different vendors have taken different approaches to easing management pain, as well as providing network-wide mobility, so choose one that fits into your network and supports your selected topology.

Choosing Your Logical Architecture

When choosing a logical architecture, you must weigh several trade-offs. Some of these are security trade-offs are discussed in the next chapter. Many are, however, a matter of balancing performance, simplicity, or functionality.

1. Mobility is a baseline function that should be provided by any architecture you choose. 802.11 provides for mobility within an extended service set, and that ESS must be visible to the client as a single IP subnet. All of the architectures presented here attach clients to a single subnet, although the mechanics of how they do so differ radically.

    a. For small-scale deployments using a handful of APs, any of the architectures work. The first two are easy to set up on a very small scale, and may have the advantage for cost-conscious deployments that will never grow beyond the initial handful of APs.

    b. The IEEE's inter-access point protocol provides link-layer mobility only. Crossing router boundaries into new broadcast domains requires network-layer coordination between wireless LAN access devices. At the time this book was written, subnet mobility generally required picking a single-vendor solution. Mobile IP is an open standard, but it is not widely implemented.

2. Clients must perceive that they are attached to a single IP subnet, no matter what the physical location of their attachment. This does not, however, require that all clients be attached to the same subnet. Multiple subnets may overlap "over the air." Multiple subnets over the air offer the ability to more finely control user access privileges and differentiate between user groups, but require the use of 802.1X.

3. What limitations does the existing network impose? Baggage from past decisions may limit the choices that you can make.

    a. A sprawling network with a large diameter may not be able to extend VLANs across the entire network due to spanning tree limitations. This may rule out the use of a single wireless VLAN, or a dynamic VLAN model where the access points must be connected to the core.

    b. The dynamic VLAN topology may depend on widely distributing 802.1Q tags throughout your network. If VLAN information is not already available, network administrators must find a way to distribute it to all the locations that support a wireless network. Products that require direct connection into the core are incompatible with a routed core network.

    c. Networks may have choke points in a variety of places. Pre-existing choke points may limit the number of wireless devices that can be attached in many locations. If your desired architecture intentionally introduces a choke point, it must be fast enough to not limit throughput.

4. The choice of network topology may be driven in part by the security protocols used on the network. Dynamic VLAN assignment is possible only with 802.1X,

so the last two topologies work best for administrators who want to use link layer security mechanisms. The first two topologies are much more suited to use with network-layer security based on IPsec and personal firewall software. This chapter has not directly explored the trade-off between the different security approaches, but the next chapter does.

5. Static addressing is not necessary. It adds needless complexity with very little benefit in return. Network administrators must manage address allocation, and get directly involved in adding new systems to the wireless LAN.

    a. Static addressing provides only a minimal direct security benefit. Source IP addresses are not authenticated by the sender, and attackers are likely to learn the IP addresses being used on the wireless network unless you employ strong link-layer protection.

    b. Tracking users is better done through the user-based networking that 802.1X provides. With a username available to the network through the RADIUS server, there is no need to associate a user with an IP address. The user can be associated with the username instead.

    c. Dynamic addressing minimizes the chance that two users may accidentally be assigned the same address. Only one DHCP server is needed for several VLANs with judicious use of DHCP helper; if a DHCP server already exists, there may not be any reason to use another one.

Table 21-4 summarizes the different factors discussed in this chapter. Security is too complex to be reduced to a simple table entry, so it receives the full attention of the next chapter. As you consider this table and a purchase decision, keep in mind that some products work with certain topologies better than others.

Table 21-4. Topology comparison chart

	Single subnet	ET phone home	Dynamic VLAN	Virtual AP
Mobility	High if VLAN is large; limited by maximum 802.1D diameter	Depends on size of islands	High	High; but enforcing limitations may be important
Performance	Depends on choke point capacity	Depends on concentrator capacity	High due to distributed encryption	Same as dynamic VLAN
Backbone	High; though may depend on existing network	Varies with range of mobility[a]	Depends on type of connection to network core	Same as dynamic VLAN
Client	Depends on client software[b]	Depends on client software[b]	Built-in to operating system	Same as dynamic VLAN; handles multiple client security models better
IP addressing	High (new subnets and routing)	High (new subnets and routing)	Not required	Same as dynamic VLAN

[a] Newer products may reduce the backbone impact by logically attaching access points to a control device in the network.
[b] Both the single subnet and central concentrator architectures are typically used with VPN software for additional security. Obviously, if VPN software is used, the amount of client integration work is much larger.

CHAPTER 22
Security Architecture

From the time that wireless LANs burst on to the scene, they have been inextricably associated with security, or rather, the lack of security. One of the reasons that wireless LAN deployment is such a significant undertaking is that securing an open network medium is a major challenge. Early wireless networks were, with good reason, likened to leaving an open network jack in the parking lot for public use.

Early solutions for restricting access and protecting data were laughable, in part because the lessons of history did not immediately apply. Traditional network security has focused on securing the physical medium to reduce the risk of network attack, but wireless networks are useful precisely because the medium is not locked behind walls and doors. Short of building a massive RF shield around the building, you must assume that the physical layer is open to anybody who wants to access it.

With a network medium that provides negligible physical security, cryptography must be used to protect user sign-ons and the data that flows over established connections. Encryption can be used to establish trust between devices connected only by radio waves. Cryptography helps to establish the user identity, and assure that access points are part of the network they claim to be. Once a user has been authenticated, cryptography assumes its better-known role of scrambling network traffic to prevent traffic interception.

Network security is intertwined with network architecture. Early fundamental insecurities in 802.11 networks led to an architecture that imposed physical and logical barriers between the existing wired network and any wireless extensions, at a cost of usability. Improved security protocols enable the wireless network to be reintegrated into the existing wired network. The physical network is likely to remain separate because of the radically different physical properties of the wireless medium. For the users and network administrators, it will be part of the same integrated whole. In some respects, it will resemble evolution of the mobile telephone network. Cellular networks are physically separate because they require specialized equipment and management systems to deal with the challenges posed by radio links to subscribers. However, they are logical extensions of the existing telephone network. Users can run the same application (voice) on the cellular network with no retraining, and the mobile telephone network is integrated into the overall management system of telephony. Now that wireless LANs can provide appropriate security, the integration has begun.

Security Definition and Analysis

Informally, data security is defined in terms of three attributes, all of which must be maintained to ensure security. My definition is not meant to be formal. In this section, I'm trying to take a fundamental approach to security by showing how wireless LAN security fails and how some of the failures can be solved by applying solutions the industry has already developed.

Integrity
> Broadly speaking, integrity is compromised when data is modified by unauthorized users. ("Has somebody improperly changed the data?")

Secrecy
> Of the three items, secrecy is perhaps the easiest to understand. We all have secrets and can easily understand the effect of a leak. ("Has the data been improperly disclosed?")

Availability
> Data is only as good as your ability to use it. Denial-of-service attacks are the most common threat to availability. ("Can I read my data when I want to?")

Wireless LAN technology has taken a fair number of knocks for its failures in all three areas. Most of the notable stories have focused on the secrecy aspect, both in terms of the fundamental flaws in early encryption protocols that allowed relatively easy eavesdropping and the lack of strong user authentication. However, other flaws are present. Injecting traffic into wireless LANs has been difficult to prevent before recent protocol developments, and the lack of frame authentication has made service denial too easy.

Network and computer security is often an issue of risk management, and wireless security is no exception. There are many ways to bolster the security of your wireless network, and many products can help meet your needs. Before building anything, start with a roadmap of what you want to do. What network security issues are the most important for your network? Based on the risks that your hot-button issues pose, how much can be spent to mitigate them? This chapter provides a brief sketch of the issues you may wish to consider. More complete treatments can be found in some key government publications, including the National Institute of Standards and Technology's Special Publication series on computer security. Special Publication 800-48 discusses many of the issues related to wireless LANs, although it does not have a great deal of detail on 802.1X.[*] NIST is also responsible for producing Federal Information Processing Standards (FIPS); some FIPS publications address the challenges of building a secure network environment.

Wireless LAN Security Problems

A steady stream of security research and analysis followed the publication of the initial 802.11 standard. Security was not designed into the initial specification, which left networks open to unauthorized users and failed to protect data in flight over the network. By design, wireless LANs are flexible. Flexibility is often a boon; in the case of technology that can be deployed without proper security considerations, flexibility may also be a curse.

Your credentials, please: authentication

Authorizing users depends on identifying them. To make the distinction between people who should have access to data and those who should not, cryptography can be used to provide *authentication*. Only after the network has identified a user can it establish the cryptographic keys used for confidentiality protocols. One of the failings of early protocols is that they authenticated the hardware people used, rather than the users themselves. While there is often a tie between user and machine, it is not as consistent and predictable as it might seem at first glance.

Several approaches have been developed to improve on the initial 802.11 authentication types. One of the most common was to build a transparent proxy that would trap web requests and redirect them to a custom portal page for authentication purposes. Web authentication can successfully improve authentication by using encrypted pages, but it does not provide stronger encryption because it cannot be used to derive keys for link-layer security protocols.

Secrecy over the air: encryption

Keeping data traveling across a wireless link secret is the first challenge that wireless networks of any type must meet. Without physical boundaries, data will be present quite literally "in the air," readily available to anybody with the appropriate receiver equipment. In the case of 802.11 wireless LANs, the appropriate receiver is your favorite 802.11 network interface, perhaps bolstered by a high-gain external antenna.

Keeping data out of the hands of the "wrong" people requires cryptographic controls to keep data out of the wrong hands. Obviously, cryptography must be used to protect all data from interception by attackers passively listening for frames and analyzing data. Like a broad-spectrum antibiotic, cryptography can serve the goal of *confidentiality* by protecting data from everybody who should not have it. Data confidentiality is typically

---

[*] NIST SP 800-48 can be found at *http://csrc.nist.gov/publications/nistpubs/800-48/NIST_SP_800-48.pdf*.

maintained by an encryption protocol that provides only authorized users with the keys to access the data, and ensures the data is not tampered with in-flight.

Secrecy and integrity of the whole network: rogue access points

If you mention the phrase "wireless security" to most network engineers, you will get a response that is heavily focused on securing the radio link by providing appropriate cryptographic operations to secure the link. Secrecy is also a matter of keeping unauthorized users off the network, whether it is the wired network or the wireless network.

Wireless networks have the potential to be a side door into the network that is not protected by appropriate security mechanisms. If access points are connected incorrectly to a secure internal network, they may afford a route into the network that bypasses the perimeter security that is in place. Many network managers also worry about unauthorized (or "rogue") access points that may be connected to the network without permission. Rogue devices are often consumer electronics, with all the security and reliability implied by that statement.

In the end, rogue devices are not a particularly interesting security problem. Every new wave in networking has brought risk, but ultimately, that risk has been addressed. Rogue devices are no different. The linchpin of a rogue strategy is to locate them and limit the damage they can do.

Locating unauthorized devices can be accomplished in several ways. The oldest and crudest location method is to use Netstumbler on a laptop and walk around looking for APs. When unauthorized devices are detected, the laptop carrier can take smaller steps in an attempt to pin down the physical location. Netstumbler is a simplistic tool, and most of the 802.11 interfaces can offer only a rough indication of signal strength. Wireless protocol analyzers offer a step up from simply walking around. Many analyzers offer additional features to help track down unauthorized access points, such as directional antennas to aid in the search, or specialized "find" modes that report the running signal strength in real-time. Even without directional antennas, a search mode that reports rapid change in signal strength can be quite effective in homing in on a device; I have been able to track down an AP in a few minutes using an AirMagnet analyzer.

Walking around to locate devices is problematic, especially since users eventually learn to recognize the AP hunters and turn off unauthorized devices. Rather than using a labor-intensive search process, network engineers are turning increasingly to network-based solutions. By placing radio probes strategically throughout an area, administrators can watch for devices as they are powered on. Multiple listeners can be used to locate devices based on their location and the received signal strength. Probe-based tools can be a special mode in a distributed analyzer, a specialized wireless IDS, or a feature in a centralized AP management system. Some network-based systems even offer the ability to respond to unauthorized devices by jamming or otherwise acting to deny service, but these abilities probably need to be refined before they can see widespread deployment.

Network integrity: traffic injection

As with wired Ethernet, frame spoofing is simple on 802.11. If no encryption protocols are used, a malicious user can simply assign a MAC address to an 802.11 interface and spoof away. Unlike Ethernet, however, 802.11 uses a physical medium that diffuses easily through space. Rather than attaching to the physical medium, 802.11 devices are immersed in it. Ensuring that frames in the air belong and are legitimately authorized network traffic is a difficult proposition that requires a whole suite of cryptographic protocols. In addition to improved encryption, WPA offers encryption protocols that allow each frame to be authenticated to prevent forgery and injection attacks.

As with many other problems, the risk of traffic injection depends may depend on several factors. Many enterprise networks are probably at higher risk for eavesdropping rather than traffic injection. Spoofing frames may be a major risk for service providers, however, because spoofed traffic does not generate revenue.

Network availability: denial of service

There are two major types of denial of service against 802.11 networks. At the radio layer, noise can severely disrupt communications. Any source of radio noise in the 802.11 frequency bands has the potential to interrupt communications. Attackers may use noise that is known to completely disrupt communications to prevent any data from flowing. Short of building a Faraday cage for an entire building, the best that can be done is to track down the noise source and shut it off. In most cases, noise sources are not operated maliciously, and it suffices to track them down. Some handheld devices can report noise levels, which can help to find noise sources.

Even with TKIP and CCMP, only frames that carry user data payloads will have proof of the transmitter address. Management and control frames are not authenticated, and can easily be spoofed. Denial-of-service attacks are trivial because an attacker need only learn the MAC address of an AP to begin sending Disassociation or Deauthentication messages. At some point, it is probably that important control messages will also be authenticated by the 802.11 protocol. Until that point, network administrators can either deploy a tool that will attempt to detect forged control frames, or live with the risk.

Network integrity and availability: rogue clients

Wireless security protocols are designed to authenticate and authorize users, but users often use different machines. Many users like to bring personal machines to the office and connect them to their employer's network. Personal machines usually do not have the full complement of protective software and configuration that employer-owned machines do. At home, personal machines may be connected directly to the unfiltered fury of the Internet and infected with all manner of viruses and worms. When a virus-laden machine is connected to the network, it can easily act as a vector to bypass strong perimeter security.

The "viral vector" often comes up when discussing wireless LAN security, even though it is a generic security problem. Any machine brought into the office and connected to the network can bring malware, whether it is connected to a copper network or a radio network. Two major threads are emerging to deal with viral vectors. One is to push virus scanning out to the edge of the network by incorporating virus scanners and similar tools into network switches. In the long term, this strategy may work; in the short term, I do not understand how the dissimilar requirements of virus scanning and malware detection (high CPU load, large memory requirements) can be reconciled with existing switch hardware, which is typically designed around a set of specialized packet-forwarding chips with only a limited general-purpose processor.

The second thread is now beginning to emerge. Many networks based on Microsoft technology are, practically speaking, required to use Microsoft's machine authentication. To ensure that a user is working with an authorized machine that has appropriate security protections, authentication servers need to tie the user authentication to the machine authentication. Some 802.1X authenticators offer the ability to tie the two authentications together, although doing so is not cryptographically sound because the two authentications are not strongly bound. RADIUS server vendors are beginning to implement similar methods of correlating the two authentications. It seems likely that if the authentication bonding approach is successful, new authentication protocols (or protocol options) will be devised to add proven cryptographic security to the bond.

Network integrity: traffic separation

Networks are usually built to serve multiple groups of users. The groups are often separate and should not share data. User group separation may be enforced on the backbone by VLANs, packet filters, and firewalls. Retaining user group separation on the wireless link requires giving different cryptographic keys to different groups. This concept was discussed in the previous chapter's virtual AP architecture.

Traffic separation works best when it can be enforced at the edge of the network. It is relatively rare for a service provider to be able to dictate software configuration to customers. Very few, if any, service providers could specify a particular vendor's VPN client for use on a public network. However, it is much easier to mandate the use of built-in 802.1X software to enforce privilege separation.

Traffic separation may not have a role in enterprise 802.11 networks, especially when they are new and relatively small. However, the definition of "service provider" can be quite expansive with a flexible network. Many colleges are interested in using 802.11 to save cabling cost in new construction or renovations, as well as enable a third party to sell Internet access to increase revenue. Many cities are working towards the same goal, especially at sites that already provide Internet access, such as libraries. Public users will be placed on an Internet-only network that is already made available to patrons, while a separate network may be used by city employees. It may be desirable to further separate municipal employees by department, especially if some of them handle protected data, such as election returns on public health information. Flexibility may also assist cities in accomplishing their social goals if existing venues such as libraries can be easily used by employees.

Authentication and Access Control

Connecting to wireless networks is designed to be easy. In fact, ease of connection is one of the major advantages to many newer wireless technologies. 802.11 networks announce themselves to anybody willing to listen for the Beacon frames. To protect networks against the threat of unauthorized access, strong access control must be applied. When a wireless station connects to a wireless LAN, there are four ways in which access control can be applied:

Station authentication

> The first step in connecting to a wireless LAN is to perform 802.11 station authentication. Station authentication is either *open system authentication*, in which only trivial authentication is performed, or *shared key authentication*, which depends on the use of a WEP key. (For more details, see Chapter 9.) Many products offer the ability to perform MAC address filtering at the authentication phase to screen out "unauthorized" clients by MAC address.

Association

> After authentication completes, stations attempt to associate with the access point. Generally, this process does not have any security components, though MAC address filtering could also be applied at this step.

Link layer

> Once association has established the virtual network "port" on the access point for the wireless station, link-layer security protocols based on 802.1X can be applied. Authorized users can be connected to resources they are allowed to use, and unauthorized users will be kicked off the network. Wireless networks are open to eavesdropping, so it is necessary to choose an authentication protocol based on strong cryptographic fundamentals.

Network- or transport-layer

> IP-based networks have an unfortunate history of security failings, and a number of higher-layer security products can be applied to critical points in the network. Firewalls can be used to isolate untrusted networks and authenticate users, and VPN termination devices can supply encryption over untrusted networks.

Different authentication protocols work at different layers in the OSI stack. Initially, the native link-layer security mechanisms were quite weak, and network administrators were forced to work at higher layers in the stack. Much of the engineering and design effort in wireless LAN security over the past few years has focused on developing strong link-layer security mechanisms. At this point, network administrators have a choice of protocols to secure the network. In order from weakest to strongest, they are:

WEP shared key authentication
> In shared key authentication, systems seeking network access respond to a challenge from the AP. Shared key authentication is so horribly constructed that it was deprecated (its use was recommended against) by 802.11i.

MAC address filtering
> Every AP in the network is programmed with a list of MAC addresses allowed network access. MAC addresses are easily forged and duplicated, but some older devices may offer nothing better.

WPA preshared key (WPA-PSK or WPA Personal)
> One of WPA's major additions was a preshared key mode that allows stations to authenticate to a network while in possession of only a passphrase. It is significantly stronger than either of the previous approaches, but even stronger methods exist.

802.1X-based protocols
> 802.1X was designed to identify and authenticate users before granting network access. Because it is based on the Extensible Authentication Protocol (EAP), "802.1X" is often used to refer to any one of the extended authentication methods that runs over EAP. Some software may refer to this as WPA Enterprise.

Network-layer authentication
> Insecurity of IP-based networks is hardly a new phenomenon. Many past products have attempted to address authentication of network users in one form or another, and there is a plethora of systems and protocols that can be used once the network (IP) layer is established. Most of the appropriate methods for use with wireless networks will tie in with VPN technology that can also be used to secure the network traffic.

Station Authentication and Association

Applying security at the station authentication phase or the association phase is quite weak. Security mechanisms available at first stages of connection are not strong at all.

An early "security" feature began life as the so-called *closed network*.* In the early days of 802.11, stations had to be configured with the network name (SSID) used by an access point. Client software was so primitive that it searched Beacons in the air for a given network name before associating. The closed network consisted of two components. Access points would send Beacons as required by the standard, but without the SSID information element. Without the SSID in the Beacon frames, there was a minor gain in privacy because some client software would not display an available network. To associate, clients were required to send a Probe Request that includes the SSID, making it function as a hidden "key." APs using the SSID hiding features would only accept Probe Requests from stations that already are configured with the hidden SSID. However, Probe Requests are not encrypted; any station that observes a successful exchange of probe frames can see the SSID and use it in a subsequent association attempt. Attackers who need to know the SSID immediately can even disassociate authorized stations to force transmission of the SSID in the probe exchange when the station reconnects.

One common approach, supported by nearly every product, is *MAC address filtering*. Access points maintain a list of authorized MAC addresses, and deny connection requests from stations not on the list. Screening MAC addresses is better than nothing, but certainly leaves a great deal to be desired. Like wired Ethernet cards, 802.11 cards may change the transmitter MAC address, which undermines the use of the MAC address as an access control token. Attackers equipped with packet sniffers can easily monitor successful associations to acquire a list of allowed MAC addresses.

Practical headaches often compound the use of MAC address filtering. Maintaining the address list is an administrative headache, especially if users are prone to using multiple devices or changing the cards they use. Many products were not designed for large-scale management and require the same information to be entered in to each device individually. Many products that have centralized distribution of address lists require the use of TFTP. TFTP has no place on a secure network.

A second approach to authentication is *WEP shared key authentication*. Access points issue a challenge to a device seeking network access. As discussed in Chapter 5, shared key authentication is broken, and cannot provide any protection from malicious users seeking to authenticate to the network. It is possible to fake a legitimate response to a WEP challenge without any knowledge of the WEP key. (It would, however, be impossible to send traffic without first recovering the WEP key.)

In some products, address filtering and shared key authentication may be combined. However, both are easily defeated. Only consider these two rudimentary methods if you are stuck with wireless client devices that cannot support stronger protocols, and an upgrade is out of the question. Devices that are stuck with crude authentica-

---

* This feature may go by several names, including cloaked network, SSID broadcast suppression, private network name, and several further variations.

tion mechanisms are usually quite old. Logistics applications of 802.11 were an early win for the technology, and the handheld inventory and tracking scanners used in the logistics field typically have limited computing power. Some cannot even do WEP, and quite a few run MS-DOS!

> Address filtering and shared key authentication are awful security, and should only be used when absolutely necessary, such as with devices that do not support anything better.

Link-Layer Authentication

Link-layer authentication, in the form of 802.1X and WPA, is a significant step up from simple filtering approaches. Authenticating users has several advantages. Typical link-layer authentication schemes allow very restricted network access for the purpose of authentication. Full network access is only granted once the user is positively identified. In the wireless LAN world, obtaining user identity early in the network attachment process allows the network to provide much finer access controls because users can be classified and restricted before obtaining network access. Link-layer authentication is transparent to network protocols, and will work for any network protocol you choose. Networks are increasingly homogenous and based on IP, although there may be pockets of older protocols such as IPX. Link-layer authentication can be used to secure both IP and IPX. In many cases, link-layer authentication is also relatively fast because it can happen as the network interface is brought up. Rather than using protocols designed to work across wide-area networks, link-layer authentication can start immediately when the link is established.

WPA Personal (preshared key)

WPA has two modes. The simpler of the two is based on distributing a preshared key (WPA-PSK) to all wireless clients. Key derivation for the wireless link is based on random numbers exchanged along with the preshared key. As with any protocol that uses a preshared key, WPA is vulnerable to dictionary attacks by determined attackers.[*] In essence, WPA PSK is a shortcut. Rather than depending on a computationally intensive multimessage TLS exchange to derive keys, WPA-PSK derives the preshared master key from a passphrase and the SSID.

In most cases, a single preshared key is used for all stations in an SSID. In such networks, all stations share the same master key. With the preshared key, an attacker can monitor the four-way handshake described in Chapter 7 and derive the unique keys for any other station which shares the same preshared key. Attackers can also forge messages that force reauthentication, which enables them to capture the four-way handshake.

---

[*] An attack tool, called coWPAtty, is available from *http://remote-exploit.org*.

Security of WPA-PSK depends a great deal on the quality of the passphrase. 802.11i Annex H discusses passphrase quality, and notes that a passphrase usually only has 2.5 bits of security per character. Very short passphrases are subject to dictionary attack.

The best defense against weak passphrases is to use either the binary preshared key mode and enter the 256-bit preshared key, or to use a strong passphrase. (Not all products support entering the preshared key directly.) The best passphrases will have more than 20 characters, and avoid common phrases and dictionary attacks. Further advice on passphrases and discussion of passphrase quality can be found in the Passphrase FAQ.*

WPA's preshared key mode makes sense for smaller networks that are not stuffed with valuable data. Security is essentially risk management, and many networks may not need anything stronger than WPA PSK because they do not have much of value.

> Use WPA with preshared keys only for small, low-risk networks, or networks which have guest users that do not need maximum protection. Otherwise, use one of the following authentication protocols.

802.1X-based EAP authentication

802.1X is an extensible framework, not a protocol in and of itself. Network administrators can select from a menu of protocols, each with its own strengths and weaknesses. To whittle down the choices to a set of candidates, consider the practical requirements imposed by wireless networks. By transmitting over the air, wireless networks are inherently subject to eavesdropping. Strong encryption to protect credentials is a must. Beyond simply transmitting encrypted user credentials, it is desirable to provide mutual authentication. Obviously, users must be authenticated. In the absence of a physical connection, however, some cryptographic operation is necessary so that users can be sure they are connecting to the legitimate, sanctioned wireless LAN deployment. Finally, automatic WEP key distribution is a no-brainer. Randomly generated keys are more secure than static keys, especially if the random key can be refreshed at regular intervals. Three protocols meet these practical requirements, although a fourth is often considered as well.

Cisco's Lightweight LEAP (LEAP) is an older, prestandard protocol that Cisco designed to address some of the initial security flaws discovered in wireless LANs. It is notable for being the first protocol to dynamically derive keys for each user, but its design fails the other practical requirements. LEAP transmits scrambled credentials using MS-CHAP version 1. Although MS-CHAP version 1 does not transmit credentials in the clear, it is a fundamentally broken protocol that cannot provide signfi-

---

* The Passphrase FAQ is available from *http://www.stack.nl/~galactus/remailers/passphrase-faq.html*. It was written for PGP, but much of the advice applies to any passphrase-based technology, including WPA-PSK.

cant cryptographic protection.* (It remains in use on some embedded devices because of the relatively small amount of CPU power reuqired.) Furthermore, LEAP provides mutual authentication only by running two MS-CHAP exchanges (one in each direction). As a final straw, LEAP is proprietary to Cisco. While there are other options for some of the components in the system, it requires either additional client software or Cisco cards on the client end, and may require Cisco access points in the authenticator role. I have worked with more than one organization that is attempting to move away from LEAP because of its proprietary nature. Client systems must have LEAP software, which can be part of the Cisco driver load or a third-party client; it is not uncommon to see organizations that adopted LEAP heavily to purchase Cisco cards for the LEAP client and put them in portable devices that have built-in wireless cards. LEAP's weaknesses have led to an effort to standardize a replacement protocol, EAP-FAST. At the time this book was written, EAP-FAST was not widely implemented.

The three widely considered standards-based protocols are EAP-Transport Layer Security (EAP-TLS), Protected EAP (PEAP), and Tunneled Transport Layer Security (TTLS). All three use TLS to provide strong cryptographic protection of user credentials, and use the TLS key exchange to provide the seed for link-layer keys. Furthermore, all can provide mutual authentication. Each of them establishes a TLS tunnel with the authentication server, and uses the certificate supplied by the authentication server as the basis for the network-to-user half of mutual authentication.

EAP-TLS uses certificates in both directions for authentication. As part of the TLS tunnel establishment, the network supplies a certificate to the user, which the user will check for validity. Provided the user can validate the server certificate, the client system will transmit the user's certificate for similar validation by the authentication server. EAP-TLS is strong, secure, and easy to understand, but it does have an Achilles heel. The client authentication is provided by a client certificate, which requires the existence of a PKI to generate, sign, and distribute certificates. If you do not already have a certificate system in place, EAP-TLS is probably not for you.

The two remaining protocols, PEAP and TTLS, are quite similar. Both use the server certificate in the TLS tunnel to provide the first-stage network-to-user authentication, and use the TLS tunnel to encrypt the user credentials used for the user-to-network authentication in the second stage. PEAP and TTLS do not depend on extensive use of certificates, but they do require a certificate for each authenticator on the wireless network. Choosing between PEAP and TTLS is more a matter of fitting a protocol to your requirements. TTLS is more flexible in the way it passes data for the user-to-network authentication in the tunnel, and it can be used with nearly any form of second-stage authentication. PEAP is more limited because it requires

---

* See *http://asleap.sourceforge.net/*, a tool used to recover LEAP passwords. It works by forcing users to authenticate, and then brute-forcing their password hash.

that the second stage be performed using an EAP method. In practice, the most commonly used PEAP supplicant is the built-in supplicant in Windows XP/2000, and it only supports one second stage protocol that does not require certificates: MS-CHAP, version 2. For networks that have a large number of Windows clients, PEAP is a good choice because it obviates the need to license and load additional software.

> Avoid LEAP because it is proprietary and relatively weak. Instead, use an authentication protocol based on TLS because it can provide mutual authentication and key distribution.
>
> Three candidates are based on TLS: EAP-TLS, PEAP, and TTLS. EAP-TLS requires client certificates for authentication, and is not likely to be an option unless a PKI already exists. PEAP and TTLS are quite similar, and either makes a fine choice. The former is more useful in monolithic Windows environments, while the latter is more useful with older authentication systems.

Network Layer Authentication

Many early wireless networks were built as separate networks from the existing wired infrastructure, and recycled existing authentication and access control mechanisms. For example, in the single subnet topology in Figure 20-1 in the previous chapter, there is a natural choke point. Firewalls are often deployed at choke points, and may provide some access control functionality. If the choke point device is also capable of terminating VPNs, the VPN software will certainly provide user authentication in addition to traffic encryption.

Firewalls are well-known for providing a number of strong authentication mechanisms, and they have a proven ability to integrate with one-time password systems such as RSA's SecurID tokens. Many IPsec VPN devices also have this capability, although it requires the use of protocol extensions such as eXtended Authentication (XAUTH), Hybrid Mode IKE, or Challenge/Reponse for Authenticated Control Keys (CRACK). XAUTH is quite popular, but it suffers from the compound binding problems discussed in this chapter. High-security networks may wish to avoid some of the problems with protocol extensions by deploying IPsec with user certificates for authentication. Instead of IPsec termination, the VPN device may be an SSL VPN device. Rather than using client software, SSL-based VPN devices may be substantially easier to use because they require only a web browser.

Instead of using a full-blown (and expensive) firewall, many organizations started using web-based authentication systems. The wireless network itself is run with minimal authentication and encryption to enable unrestricted access from potential users. Many networks are run using open 802.11 authentication and no encryption. (Some security-conscious networks are beginning to use WPA-PSK for web-authenticated networks, but it is a relatively new practice.) The first request to a web site is trapped by a proxy and redirected to a secure login page. Before authentication completes, the web system drops any packets from the client. Once authentication succeeds, the client systems packets are allowed through. It is important to note that many web authentication systems do encrypt the login, but have no way of providing strong link-layer encryption.

When wireless LAN security first became a burning issue, several vendors began selling "wireless access controller" devices, which typically combine packet filtering, authentication, authorization, and accounting services (AAA), and a DHCP server; many devices also include a DNS server, VPN termination, and packet shaping or rate limiting. AAA features are typically provided by an interface to an existing corporate infrastructure such as RADIUS, which has already often been configured for remote access purposes. Some products may also include dynamic DNS so that a domain name is assigned to a user, but the IP number can be assigned with DHCP.

Integrating User Authentication Through RADIUS

RADIUS is often used as the authentication back end, no matter where authentication is performed in the protocol stack. Both wireless devices and VPNs can reference external RADIUS servers. Most organizations have a centralized user account system somewhere, and placing a RADIUS server in front of it is a common way to provide access to many network devices. RADIUS servers can also be used to tie together multiple user account systems to present a single integrated view of user accounts in an organization.

Although RADIUS servers have the ability to define local users, the user management tools are not particularly powerful or sophisticated. Most RADIUS servers are deployed in such a way that they refer to other sources of data for user accounts, leaving the RADIUS server to act as protocol translators. Some of the most common forms of external user databases are:

Windows domains
> Most organizations have at least some users in a Windows domain or Active Directory. Integrating a RADIUS server with Windows passwords is easy for users because the Windows password is often the main user credential. End users hate remembering passwords. Referring to a Windows domain allows users to keep using the same credential for a variety of purposes. Windows prevalence varies from the odd departmental network at major universities all the way to huge multinational corporate networks, many of which are built around Windows network technology.

Token cards (such as RSA SecurID, Secure Computing SafeWord)
> Token cards often have RADIUS frontends; many RADIUS servers can also pass credentials directly to a token card server for approval. Integration with token card servers enables administrators to require strong token authentication with wireless networks.

LDAP directories

Directories are highly extensible, and valued by organizations that desire a single user data store for everything. Passwords, access privileges, policies, and contact information can all be stored in a directory. When used to access LDAP directories, RADIUS servers can perform authorization based on information learned from LDAP. For example, universities may identify users as either faculty or students, with students having restricted network privileges.

Kerberos realms

Many universities also have a large investment in Kerberos authentication. RADIUS servers accept credentials from the end user and use them to obtain a Kerberos ticket. If the authentication is succesful, access is granted. Kerberos integration is relatively loose right now. The tickets granted to users are dummy tickets that are not used in authorization, but many universities would like to extend existing Kerberos infrastructure to new wireless networks. I expect to see additional protocol development that uses Kerberos ticket data for authentication in the future.

Unix password systems

Unix password systems include Pluggable Authentication Modules (PAM) and Network Information System (NIS). Organizations with a significant investment in Unix may be able to create single-sign-on by recycling their existing authentication system. RADIUS servers that use these authentication schemes are installed on Unix systems, and attempt to validate user credentials with a system call.

RADIUS proxy

RADIUS servers may pass authentication requests to other RADIUS servers. In environments with distributed user enrollment and account creation, such as most large research universities, it is hopeless to try to create a centralized database. The best solution is to accept the distributed nature of user accounts, and ensure that RADIUS servers can refer authentication requests to other RADIUS servers for processing.

TACACS

TACACS is an alternative access control service. It is used widely by network devices, but is not often used to store accounts for anybody other than network administration staff.

RADIUS authentication and Microsoft Windows databases

There are two ways of looking up Windows user accounts. Operating system API calls can look up user accounts on domain controllers. Network protocols between servers can also be used to look up user accounts. In older Windows NT4-based networks, the domain controllers used an inter-server protocol that has been reverse engineered by the open source community. External RADIUS servers can run software that pretends to be a domain controller, and can therefore look up Windows accounts across the network. In fact, most RADIUS servers developed on Unix systems can use the reverse engineering to perform authentication against NT Domain user accounts. Windows-based RADIUS servers must be installed on a domain controller to look up user accounts.

Networks built around Windows 2000 are largely built with Active Directory. In addition to its many features, Active Directory introduced newer inter-server protocols that have remained proprietary to Microsoft. Internet Authentication Server (IAS), Microsoft's RADIUS server, can use Active Directory communications to look up user accounts stored on any other member server in Active Directory. These protocols have not yet been reverse engineered, and are not available to third-party RADIUS servers. They must instead rely on the system call API on a domain controller. Once an request for user credentials is dispatched to the domain controller via its API, the domain controller may proceed to use Active Directory protocols to look up the user account remotely.[*]

Active Directory can be installed in a native mode, in which the member servers use only the newer Active Directory protocols, or a compatibility mode in which the older, less-secure NT Domain protocols are used as well. Most current installations of Active Directory are now based on the native mode without compatibility options.

The bottom line presents network administrators with a choice: run Microsoft's RADIUS server, run a third-party RADIUS server on a domain controller, or run Active Directory in compatibility mode. The last option is fraught with security problems, and is generally not workable because it also limits the functionality of Active Directory. If you need to authenticate against Active Directory user accounts, the choice is either to use Microsoft's IAS or find a domain controller for a third-party RADIUS server. (Note that not all third-party RADIUS servers can be installed on Windows; most third-party RADIUS appliances, for example, do not run Windows.) In many organizations, both tasks can be quite challenging simply because a large network of domain controllers generally cannot be disturbed without extensive change control procedures.

Most RADIUS server software cannot access Windows user credentials unless installed on a domain controller. If you need to authenticate Windows user accounts, be prepared to set aside a domain controller for that purpose.

[*] The indirect nature of the credential lookup and the domain controller requirement is a subtle advantage for Microsoft's RADIUS server, which is bundled with Windows server operating systems. Third-party RADIUS servers must be installed on a domain controller, and hence, a server installation. Network administrators must therefore justify the additional cost of the third-party RADIUS server over the inexpensive Microsoft RADIUS server.

Ensuring Secrecy Through Encryption

After properly determining user identity and assigning access privileges, the network must protect user transmissions from eavesdropping. Several encryption protocols can be used on wireless LANs:

Static WEP

> With static WEP, a single key is used to secure transmissions between the client and the access point. In most implementations, the same key is used by every station, which dramatically reduces the security.

802.1X-based dynamic WEP

> In late 2001, the flaws in traditional single-key static WEP became impossible to ignore. Fortunately, the 802.1X specification had emerged from the standards committees and provided a way to dynamically send keys to clients. Refreshing WEP keys at short intervals provides defense against many of the attacks against static WEP.

Temporal Key Integrity Protocol (TKIP)

> TKIP is part of 802.11i, and is designed to offer increased security on wireless interfaces with hardware assistance for RC4. To ensure frame integrity, TKIP is used with the Michael integrity check to detect frame tampering during flight. TKIP and Michael are a bandage on the open wound that is WEP. They are more secure, but it is hard to say how much more secure.

Counter Mode CBC-MAC Protocol (CCMP)

> CCMP is the second major component of 802.11i. Rather than using two separate protocols for encryption and integrity, CCMP uses new cryptographic operations to combine both operations into a single protocol. It is a clean break with the checkered RC4-based past of link-layer security. Chipsets now incorporate hardware assistance for AES, which is the cipher that CCMP is based on.

Network-layer encryption

> Instead of protecting the wireless network at the link layer, it is possible to apply long-standing network-layer encryption protocols, such as IPsec, SSL, or SSH.

Static WEP

Static WEP is a horrendous security protocol. It is better than nothing, but that is not saying much. Do not use static WEP unless there is nothing else that can be done to encrypt the network traffic. With most devices, static WEP can be considered obsolete. Nearly all cards have the ability to support improved 802.1X-based link-layer security mechanisms when used with recent drivers on supported operating systems. The only real reason to consider static WEP is the presence of application-specific devices that support nothing better.

You may have some older devices that support nothing better than static WEP due to limited processing power, and the cost of upgrading to a device capable of supporting better security protocols cannot be justified. Many handheld 802.11 inventory scanners and voice over IP telephones fall into this category. If you must use static WEP, first check for the most glaring security hole. Weak IVs are the lifeblood of static WEP tools. When Airsnort first made the news, many vendors updated radio firmware to avoid using weak IVs. Although an IV restricting firmware revision does little to address many of static WEP's flaws, it does dramatically reduce the exposure. Before deployment, check to see whether your static WEP implementations generate weak IVs. If they do, demand a fix. It is unconscionable that any vendor still ships products that are susceptible to this attack.

Static WEP is better than nothing, but it does offer some protection, especially compared to not using it any security measures. It is best at preventing nonhostile users from accidentally associating with the a network next door. However, static WEP will not protect against an even mildly determined attacker. If you are required to use static WEP, take precautions to ensure that the compromise of the WEP network is contained and cannot be used as a launch point for further attacks against your network.

Static WEP is an encryption protocol of last resort. Use it only if you have no other choice, and take appropriate security measures to limit your exposure.

Dynamic WEP Keying with 802.1X

Although 802.1X was designed for user authentication, its improvements to WEP are as important. 802.1X includes messages to distribute keys from the access point to client stations. Dynamic keying does a great deal to address outstanding flaws in WEP, although it is by no means a complete solution.

Dynamic keying has one important dependency. Keys should appear to be random, which means there must be a source of *keying material* or *key entropy* (random bits) somewhere. Keying material may come from an authentication method that generates it, such as one based on TLS, or it may be entered directly as a preshared secret. Through a series of operations that depends on the protocol in use, the keying material is transformed from a collection of random bits into the series of bits used as the link-layer encryption key.

Dynamic link-layer keys must be derived from a master secret. The master secret may be supplied directly, or come from the authentication.

Most importantly from a system administrator's perspective is that the radio link can be keyed dynamically. WEP keys need not be dreamed up by the network administration or distributed to users and network devices. Instead, the user authentication creates a cryptographically secure pool of random data that can be used to derive the WEP key. Stations still do WEP encryption to protect frames, but the key used to encrypt the frame is unique to the user and changes periodically. The rekey interval can be set by the network administrator. Rather than having a single key that is used until it is changed on all devices at the same time, the user's key is created on authentication and refreshed at regular intervals.

Keying messages can be used to distribute either the user keys (key mapping or unicast keys) as well as the broadcast keys (group or default keys). Default keys can be refreshed whenever a station leaves the network, as well as at regular intervals to bolster the protection.

Initialization vectors will repeat over the lifetime of a station association. However, the problem with IVs stems from repeated use of the same IV with the same secret key. By setting a suitably short key regeneration timer, it is possible to avoid repeating the IV+secret key combination. With a 24-bit IV, it will be 16 million (2^{24}) frames before an IV is repeated. By comparing the 16 million frame figure with 802.11 frame rates, you can derive a maximum key length. My analysis of 802.11 frame rates used a traffic load composed of "transactions" consisting of a TCP segment and corresponding TCP ACK.[*] Each transaction consumes two IVs. Based on the 16 million figure, you can calcuate the time until the IV space is exhaused. Table 22-1 presents the results of this calculation for a variety of load factors. In several ways, the table presents an unrealistically short lifetime for the key. For safety, the key lifetime is often set to half an hour, which provides a great deal of protection against IV reuse.

Table 22-1. IV space lifetime

	802.11b	802.11a/g, no protection
Transactions per second	479	2,334
IVs used per second	958	4,668
IV space lifetime, hours		
100% load	4.8 hr	1.0 hr
75% load	6.5 hr	1.3 hr
50% load	9.7 hr	2.0 hr
25% load	19.5 hr	2.4 hr

[*] See the analysis in "When Is 54 Not Equal to 54? An Analysis of the Maximum TCP Throughput of 802.11a, b, and g" (*http://www.oreillynet.com/pub/a/wireless/2003/08/08/wireless_throughput.html*). Note that this analysis assumes a 1:1 ratio between TCP segments and their ACKs, and thus consumes many more IVs than a model that assumes a better ratio of TCP segments to ACKs. However, for the purpose of security, it is useful to use an unrealistically stressful model to engineer a safe limit.

The earliest WEP attack tools based on the Fluhrer-Mantin-Shamir attack, *airsnort* and *wepcrack*, relied on the collection of weak IVs and each required several million frames to recover keys. More recent tools, most notably *aircrack*,* combine the Fluhrer-Mantin-Shamir attack with other attacks and can recover keys much faster, sometimes with less than a million frames.

WEP is still subject to attacks on the frame integrity check, and there is no way to defend against them within the WEP framework. Indeed, the necessity of improving the integrity check was one of the major technical tasks for 802.11i. The only saving grace is that tools that exploit the weak integrity check hardly exist in comparison to their Fluhrer-Mantin-Shamir brethren.

> At best, dynamic WEP is an interim step towards better security protocols, and should only be used when equipment does not support TKIP. When using dynamic WEP, be sure to set a relatively short key lifetime to protect against WEP analysis tools. I recommend no longer than 15 minutes.

Improved RC4-Based Encryption: TKIP

Dynamic WEP is a Band-Aid® that can be used when nothing better is available, or as a way of deploying a link-layer authenticated architecture in a reasonably secure fashion while considering improved alternatives. 802.11i includes two new link-layer security mechanisms. The Temporal Key Integrity Protocol (TKIP) is designed to mitigate known attacks against WEP while retaining backwards compatibility with existing hardware. TKIP is more secure than WEP, but has not yet been extensively analyzed yet.

TKIP's design goal is to be as secure as possible while retaining backwards compatibility. In the first wave of 802.11 chipsets, security was often implemented in software, if at all. To avoid the performance problems of software-based encryption, the second major wave incorporated hardware assistance for many WEP-based frame handling functions, including RC4 encryption. TKIP was designed to work with the WEP frame processing primitives while shoring up a number of the weak points in WEP.

TKIP retains RC4-based frame encryption, which allows it to be retrofitted on to existing 802.11 systems. As with dynamic WEP, TKIP depends on a source of random data to serve as the basis for its keys, so it must be used either with WPA-PSK or an 802.1X EAP method. Beyond the basic similarities, it adds per-frame keying to disrupt attacks against the initialization vector, and replay protection to stop frames from being retransmitted at a later time. TKIP also improves the integrity check by

---

* Available from *http://www.cr0.net:8040/code/network/aircrack/*.

ensuring that the sender of a frame is in possession of the appropriate cryptographic key, and using an improved integrity check.

TKIP and dynamic WEP can coexist on most hardware. Most access points are capable of storing unique link layer keys for every station. If one station uses dynamic WEP and another uses TKIP, the key storage will reflect that. Using both encryption protocols simultaneously does weaken the security of broadcast frames because all stations on the same network must share the broadcast key.

> For most deployments, TKIP should be considered a practical minimum standard unless it is unavailable. However, TKIP is should not be considered a long-term solution.

CCMP: Encryption with AES

TKIP is limited by the baggage of WEP. The Counter Mode with CBC-MAC Protocol (CCMP) in 802.11i was designed from scratch with security in mind. The design goal was to offer security comparable to existing trusted protocols such as IPsec without some of the limitations that IPsec imposes on wireless LANs. Design started with the AES cipher, which is the building block of most of the new security protocols being developed. WEP's legacy will prevent TKIP from being treated as a serious security protocol, but CCMP's underlying structure has been approved for use in sensitive U. S. government applications.

In addition to the efficiency gain from using AES, CCMP improves efficiency over existing cryptographic protocols. Traditional cryptographic protocols can be used either for encryption, which protects data over untrusted paths, or authentication, which ensures that it it was not altered in transit. WEP only provides encryption, and relied on a flawed integrity check algorithm. TKIP uses keys in two distinct ways. Like WEP, keys are used to provide frame encryption. Additional keys are used for a separate integrity check algorithm. CCMP, however, allows a single key to be used for both purposes, which reduces computational overhead and improves efficiency.

The main drawback to CCMP is a common implementation deficiency in client software. Although there is no reason why CCMP cannot coexist on the radio link with the RC4-based encryption protocols, most drivers do not support it. Mixing CCMP with RC4-based encryption requires that the driver support using CCMP for unicast frames and one of the RC4-based encryption protocols for broadcast frames. I do not know of any client vendor that supports this mode of operation. Herein lies the downside to using CCMP: it will result in more complex configurations to support two networks in parallel, and it may require replacing the wireless LAN interfaces in your computing devices.

CCMP is an attractive long-term goal for a link-layer security protocol, but product limitations may require running multiple wireless networks in parallel as well as a forklift upgrade.

Higher Layer Security Protocols (IPsec, SSL, and SSH)

When wireless protocols were first shown to be fundamentally broken, there was a
rush to find a stopgap solution. Network architects turned to proven cryptographic
protocols to encrypt network traffic as it flew through the air. IPsec was a major ben-
eficiary of the attention paid to wireless security, although SSL and SSH are frequently considered. All of these protocols provide a way of identifying users,
encrypting traffic, and ensuring that the packets are not tampered with in flight.

One drawback to using security at higher levels in the stack is that security protocols
can only protect their contents. Protection at the network layer provides security services to the network layer and anything higher in the stack, but cannot do much to
secure lower layers. Security administrators often worry about "turnaround" attacks
that subvert an VPN client and use an established tunnel to access the protected network. To address this potential vulnerability, bolster the standard host-based security with personal firewall software and antivirus software. On the personal firewall
side, several products are available, ranging from inexpensive one-off installations to
robust, feature-rich, centrally managed products. Attacks against VPN client stations are enough of a concern that many VPN vendors bundle personal firewall software as part of the installation.

 Security protocols implemented above the link layer do not offer effective protection to the link layer, so higher-layer security should be aug-
mented with additional host-based security, such as personal firewall
software.

Implementation at higher protocol layers also tends to dictate network architecture.
VPN endpoints are typically bound to IP addresses, and most VPN clients do not
cope well with having the address torn out from under them. Although 802.11 supports roaming by attaching to different networks, those networks may be different IP
subnets. If the IP address changes, the VPN session must be reestablished. More
importantly, users must accept the effects of changing addresses and the need to
reestablish connections.

To keep connections as long-lived as possible, network architects need to maintain
network state as stations move across the network. This can be done with link-layer
identity management tools that provide handoff between APs using 802.1X-based
protocols as in the dynamic VLAN architecture in the previous chapter, or it can be
done by designing the network around the handoff limitations as in the single-subnet

architecture in the previous chapter. The former case is a more complicated architecture for the network administrator to configure, but it is probably easier to build because it does not require extensive backbone engineering.

Many VPN technologies were designed around point-to-point encryption. Multicast applications can be based on IP, but IPsec does not yet include any method for group key distribution to enable the use of many-to-one transmissions. Distributing keys for point-to-point links is an "easy" problem because there are only two parties to the conversation. (By "easy," I mean that the problem is tractable and that a solution exists, not that it is trivial to accomplish.) Keying a point-to-multipoint connection is a "hard" problem because one sender and many receivers must agree on a set of keys, and it may be desirable to update keys as receivers join and leave the multicast session. Multicast data is a natural fit for several applications, most notably streaming media. Large companies may hold internal meetings over internal multicast sessions, and would undoubtedly want to ensure that any data from those sessions is encrypted over wireless networks. Multicast data is also used extensively in financial markets because it is a natural model to distribute market data. Various approaches to IPsec multicast are in progress in the standards communities, but have not been finalized yet.

IPsec is often used because it is implemented at the network layer, and thus is independent of the application with which it is used. As long as the applications can cope with the increased delay for IPsec encapsulation and decryption, it will work. In the most common IPsec architectures, no changes are required to use new applications or new servers located in the protected network. IPsec's wide adoption for remote access also means that there is often an IPsec termination device on the network that provides encryption. Many mobile devices already have clients installed and configured, and users have been trained and are comfortable using them. If an existing VPN concentrator is available and has spare capacity, it may be possible to extend an existing remote access IPsec deployment to internal wireless LAN users.

Adding new tasks to an existing concentrator may cause performance problems, especially if the VPN device was originally specified for remote access. Remote access users do not require significant bandwidth, especially compared to local LAN users. By definition, remote access capacity is defined by your uplink to the Internet. With many organizations still on T-1 lines or the equivalent speed SDSL connection, remote access connections are by definition limited to less than 2 Mbps. Extending a VPN to the wireless LAN may require significant VPN concentrator upgrades, or a wireless LAN system with IPsec termination built-in. IPsec may also cause performance problems. Maximum-size IP packets will become two IP fragments once the IPsec header information is added. One packet will include header information and also be maximum size, but the data that was elbowed out of the packet by the IPsec headers will be a second, minimal size IP fragment. Both fragments must be transmitted before the packet can be reassembled and decrypted.

While the head end of an IPsec solution is under the control of system administrators, the client side is not. Installing and configuring client software in a deployment of any size can be a challenge. That is, if the client software even exists. IPsec client software is targeted at the lowest common platform denominator, so many solutions are available only on Windows. Finding IPsec support for Mac OS and Linux is surprisingly difficult, in large part because of the differentiation on the concentrator side. Vendor X's termination device requires Vendor X's client software to use the features that make remote access easier. A few vendors provide client software for their own termination devices for Mac OS, but Linux clients are hard to find. (Free S/WAN is an IPsec implementation, but it does not support any of the special client features that are usually desirable in deployments.)

Client software loads may not stop with the IPsec client, either. IPsec protects from a wide spectrum of attacks at the network layer, but it is powerless to protect data at the link layer. For example, ARP spoofing or ARP poisoning attacks cannot be stopped by IPsec because it does not encrypt or authenticate ARP frames. IPsec cannot protect against some network layer attacks, either. Because IPsec requires that the client obtain an IP address, many wireless LANs secured by IPsec allow any system to attach to the network and obtain an IP address through DHCP. With that foothold, even casual attackers can launch IP-based denial-of-service attacks against the network infrastructure. Addressing link-layer attacks can be done through personal firewall software, but that presents another client component to install, configure, and manage. Personal firewall software has made great strides in recent years, and there are excellent solutions that can be centrally configured and managed.

IPsec user authentication may also result in a subtle security risk. Site-to-site VPNs use peer systems that are well known to each other and stay in fixed locations. In the leased-line replacement scenario, a handful of systems in well-known locations can be issued certificates for strong authentication. Remote access is a different story, however. IPsec was not designed for user authentication, and it shows. Digital certificates are one option, but are often rejected as an administrative nightmare. A variety of specifications exist to perform legacy user authentication with IPsec, all of which are incompatible. The major protocol, eXtended Authentication (XAUTH), is widely implemented but is not fully standardized. XAUTH requires the disclosure of identity early in the IPsec handshake, and must run in the security-diminishing "aggressive" mode. The security of the handshake and the resulting tunnel to pass user credentials depends on a shared secret. Many implementations of XAUTH allow, or worse, require the same shared secret to be used for all users. Furthermore, XAUTH is poorly designed, and subject to the compound binding problem discussed previously. (The "FIPS mode" on many certified IPsec products disables the use of XAUTH.) Sadly, many vendors continue to use XAUTH because it is implemented by many OEM clients. The major alternative to XAUTH is "Hybrid Mode." Hybrid Mode has a significantly better design, but is not as widely implemented.

An alternative to IPsec is to allow only applications with strong built-in cryptographic systems. Web-based systems can be secured with the secure socket layer (SSL). Host logins can be secured with SSH. SSH can also be used to secure many types of TCP-based network traffic, although the port-forwarding configuration may be too complex for many users. Some environments may have already deployed a framework such as Kerberos for application layer security, in which case it can probably be extended to wireless stations without great difficulty.

Selecting Security Protocols

When selecting security protocols, the first decision is which layer of the networking stack should be secured: the link layer, the network layer, the transport layer, the application layer, or some combination of all of them? 802.1X-based link-layer security and VPNs are used at different layers of the protocol stack, and are not mutually exclusive. Your choice of layer 2 security, layer 3 security, or both will depend on your goals and requirements. Both provide encryption to protect messages from eavesdroppers. Both can provide user authentication. 802.1X protects against many attacks by denying network access before authentication completes, and its authentication is much better thought-out than IPsec remote access authentication methods. 802.1X used in conjunction with improved Layer 2 encryption is likely to meet the security needs of many organizations. In simple terms, the security of an IPsec tunnel is greater than a WEP "session," even one rekeyed frequently using 802.1X protection.

Applying Security in the Protocol Stack

One of the biggest changes in the 802.11 landscape since the first edition of this book is the emergence of a reasonable security architecture in 802.11. First and foremost, the security protocols must keep the network secure. In wireless LANs, security is largely a function of authentication and encryption.

Compound binding vulnerabilities

Most traditional methods of user authentication are not secure. Over time, the resistance of authentication protocols to attack is increasing, but widely-deployed older methods will be used for many years to come. To secure older authentication protocols, it is common to provide some form of encrypted channel to protect the insecure method across an insecure network. The development of strong tunneling technologies such as the Transport Layer Security (TLS) and the IP Security protocols (IPsec) offers an attractive method for protecting older authentication protocols. Using a secure tunnel to protect a much weaker legacy method is referred to as *compound authentication* because the authentication is split into its major tasks of establishing a secure channel and performing user authentication. The most notable examples of compound authentication methods are the TLS tunneling methods used on wireless networks (TTLS and PEAP), as well as the eXtended Authentication (XAUTH) commonly used with IPsec. Designing cryptographically secure protocols is extremely demanding work, and it is easier and safer to use a widely deployed and analyzed protocol such as TLS or IPsec to provide the necessary cryptographic components.

In October 2002, however, research found that the design shared by most compound authentication methods is insufficient to prevent certain types of man-in-the-middle (MITM) attacks. One of the major problems is that the tunneled "inner" authentication method is not strongly associated with, or "bound to," the "outer" protective tunnel. Before exchanging the sensitive "inner" authentication data inside the tunnel, the protocols do not provide for a check that the authentication is occurring with the endpoint of the "outer" tunnel. The compound binding problem does not occur because of weaknesses within the tunnel protocols or inner methods, but rather in the way they are combined. Inner authentication protocols must prove that the endpoints of the inner tunnel use the endpoints of any previous outer tunnels.[*]

At this point, the vulnerabilities associated with weak compound bindings are largely theoretical. Successful use of these vulnerabilities would require active participation on the part of the attacker. To carry out a successful MITM attack, the attacker would need to insert a radio device into the target network, carry out the first phase of authentication with a legitimate authenticator, and then attract a client to steal credentials from. Success requires physical access to the network and facility, as well as numerous active radio transmissions.

XAUTH is no longer subject to active standardization efforts, and may not be fixed to address compound binding vulnerabilities. Compound binding problems in IPsec can be avoided through the use of digital certificates on every client. Wireless LAN protocols have not yet reached the final stage, and are in the process of being modified to address compound binding flaws.

Encryption

An IPsec session probably provides superior encryption strength to any of the RC4-based frame encryption methods, and the age of the standards and most implementations can offer a high degree of trust, especially if static addressing and digital client certificates are used. If it has a weakness, it is that a network-layer protocol cannot provide security for the MAC layer. In most wireless networks secured by IPsec, attackers can easily obtain IP addresses and launch attacks against other network users or denial-of-service attacks against the VPN components because there is no authentication before the network protocol is enabled.

---

[*] IPsec's Quick Mode (phase 2) does this by including signature messages that rely on the results of the IKE (phase 1) exchange protecting it. XAUTH deliberately broke this model.

Security certifications

Depending on the environment, it may be necessary to use products that have passed security certification evaluations. As a rule, many government networks require the use of network products that have been evaluated. In the United States, this process is based on Federal Information Processing Standard (FIPS) 140-2; several major goverments have joined together to replace a patchwork of national standards with the Common Criteria evaluation. Great weight is often given to these security evaluations, but it is worth noting that many products that are certified under meaningful evaluation criteria often have to remove many ease-of-use features.

At this point, link-layer wireless security protocols cannot be given security FIPS 140-2 certification. Several components of the entire link-layer security system must be approved by the National Institute of Standards and Technology (NIST) before the entire system can be certified. For a current list of validated components, see *http://csrc.nist.gov/cryptval/*. The major components of a system that need to gain individual approval before the system can be approved are:

Encryption cipher
> 802.11i's CCMP uses AES, which is approved. RC4 is not approved and almost certainly never will be, which bars TKIP from certification.

Cipher mode of operation
> The CCM mode, which is used by 802.11i's CCMP, was approved in NIST Special Publication 800-38C in May 2004.

Hash algorithms
> The pseudorandom function that expands master keys into key hierarchies is based on HMAC-SHA1, which is approved.

Key wrap
> Keys are sensitive material and need to be encrypted for transport across the network. RFC 3394 defines the NIST key wrap function, which has been approved.

Key derivation
> In January 2005, NIST released implementation guidance (*http://csrc.nist.gov/cryptval/140-1/FIPS1402IG.pdf*). According to the implementation guidance document, NIST is planning to release Special Publication 800-56, which will formally approve key derivation methods.

Even though there are no generally available commercial products that meet security standards, there is an interesting exception. Harris Corporation, a large government contractor (and, coincidentally, the initial developer of the 802.11 PRISM chipset), sells an 802.11 system called SecNet11 that uses a National Security Agency-certified encryption scheme. Buyers must be given approval by the NSA. The price is, not surprisingly, extremely high: over $3,000 per wireless LAN interface, and $1,600 per AP.

Network support

Aside from security itself, other factors influence the decision over how to apply security in the network stack. One of the largest nonsecurity considerations is related to client software. Supporting software is trying, even at the best of times. Working with components built in to the operating system may be a significant advantage. 802.1X-based systems have the advantage, now that 802.1X supplicants are built in to the recent versions of major operating systems. IPsec clients are generally specific to the vendor of termination devices. In both cases, client configuration is a one-time event. 802.1X clients may have slightly better control over when they need to run, provided the corporate SSID is different from other networks. If IPsec is already widely deployed, it may be much easier initially to treat the wireless LAN as a remote access network, especially since that will not require user retraining. Before choosing IPsec, however, ensure that there is enough capacity on the VPN termination device to handle LAN-speed access from the new users.

Support for mobility is likely to be an important consideration. To prevent IPsec tunnels from being torn down, some arrangement must be made to provide IP mobility across the network. Some refer to this task as the creation of a "mobile VPN." IP mobility can be provided by the network itself through the use of a single VLAN for all APs, or through overlay tunnels from every AP to a VPN server, or even 802.1X-based dynamic VLAN assignment. With the ability of 802.11i-compliant devices to move security contexts between APs, it probably has a slight edge for networks with highly mobile users.

Support for network applications may also lead towards a preference for one protocol. Non-IP protocols are not supported by IPsec. Networks that still use IPX or AppleTalk may not have a choice. IP multicast is not supported by IPsec, although it is supported by link-layer security solutions as a series of multicast frames. IPsec is also likely to be too slow for applications that require low latency, such as voice transmission; I am also unaware of any existing phone that supports IPsec, or any plans to introduce an IPsec 802.11 phone.

Different applications may also require protection over different domains. In many cases, it is enough to protect communications over only the most vulnerable part of the path, and radio link encryption is sufficient. In some cases, it will be necessary to use site-to-site encryption to provide security all the way to the border of another network. The distance over which the data needs protection is a function of the security of the network past the radio. If the access points are connected to the same backbone as the destination traffic, radio link encryption is probably sufficient. If the traffic must travel across untrusted networks after leaving the radio, some form of network- or higher-layer encryption is required.

Table 22-2 summarizes many of the factors that come into play when deciding where to implement authentication in your network.

Table 22-2. Summary of major factors in authentication layer decision

Link layer (802.1X)	Network layer (VPN)
Integrated operating system components	May already be deployed with existing capacity on VPN concentrator
Protection of layer 2 network from attack	More familiar for users; less retraining is required
Better mobility architecture	Protects beyond the radio link
Support for IP multicast and non-IP protocols	Security certifications require VPN; e.g., FIPS
Fast handoff support for voice	

Choose Authentication

The choice of authentication technology often depends on the way it will interface with the existing user database. As a first step, identify where the user accounts currently live. Are they in a Windows NT Domain or an Active Directory? Do they live in an LDAP database, or a Kerberos realm? Once you know where to find the users, the choice of system to authenticate them is usually straightforward.

Choosing an EAP method

Practically speaking, it is necessary to use an EAP method based on TLS to provide strong cryptographic keys for frame encryption. This constraint leaves us with three choices: EAP-TLS, PEAP, and TTLS. EAP-TLS is difficult to use because it requires certificates for every client. Without a PKI already installed, using EAP-TLS may be considered a practical impossibility. PEAP and TTLS are quite similar, so the question becomes which one to use. Although the protocols are similar, they support different authentication methods inside the encrypted tunnel. Let the interface to existing user databases make the decision about the authentication method. How the user credentials are accessed for verification determines your EAP method. Three of the authentication methods will work with most authentication databases, with other methods available to cover the remaining few cases.

PAP, the *Password Authentication Protocol*, transmits the username and password without any encryption. It simply submits a username and a password to the authentication server, and the authentication server compares the submitted password to a stored copy. Without any encryption, PAP should not be used across a network connection that does not provide privacy protection. (When PAP is used on wireless LANs, it is used in an encrypted channel, and therefore safely.) PAP is not an EAP method, and is therefore not supported by PEAP. The most common use of PAP is with user databases that one-way encrypt passwords, such as LDAP directories or the Unix */etc/password* file. Rather than store the password itself, or the password in some recoverable form, some systems store a one-way hash of the password such as the SHA-1 or MD5 hash. When a client user or program wishes to prove its identity, the password is processed by the one-way hash, and the resulting hash is compared to stored hash. PAP is commonly used with token cards because the alphanumeric code from the token can be submitted along with a user name. Some supplicants have a "TTLS/Token Card" method that is TTLS/PAP, but without any caching of the password, since token codes expire. Because nearly every legacy authentication database supports password authentication, TTLS/PAP is like Type O blood. If in doubt, it is generally a safe bet.

Microsoft CHAP version 2 (MS-CHAP-V2) performs a challenge/response handshake. The client and server share a secret, and challenge each other to perform computations on challenge values with the secret. The secret is the MD4 hash of the user password. Although it is not reversible, the hash value is used as the secret, which makes it a "password equivalent." MS-CHAP-V2 is widely supported by Microsoft clients, and is commonly supported and used as an inner authentication method with PEAP. If you have an existing authentication database stored in a Windows domain or Active Directory, MS-CHAP-V2 is a logical choice for the inner authentication method. It can either be used "as-is" within TTLS, or it can be used as an EAP method with additional header information (EAP-MSCHAP-V2).

The third common inner authentication method is *EAP-Generic Token Card* (EAP-GTC). EAP-GTC was originally designed to take a username and token code. It does not provide any handshaking or privacy protection. Given its initial intent of shuttling a nonreusable code to a server, the lack of privacy protection is understandable. However, it has seen recent adoption as an EAP method that allows the submission of a username and associated authentication credentials. No EAP method allows the submission of username and password pairs directly, but there is nothing in EAP-GTC that prevents it from being used as a password submission protocol. Nothing, other than implementation, prevents EAP-GTC from being used as a PAP-like authentication method. As an EAP method, EAP-GTC can be used with either TTLS or PAP.

Several other inner authentication methods are available, including the *Challenge Handshake Authentication Protocol* (CHAP), *Microsoft CHAP, version 1* (MS-CHAP), and *EAP-MD5 Challenge* (EAP-MD5). CHAP and Microsoft CHAP are only used by older authentication databases. They should only be used when the existing authentication database does not support one of the newer methods. Both can only be used with TTLS, since neither is an EAP method. EAP-MD5 does not provide security services. It is used for 802.1X on wired networks, but almost never on wireless because of the lack of eavesdropping protection.

It is likely that one of the three inner authentication methods shown in Table 22-3 will work with your user database. Based on the inner authentication method, choose either PEAP or TTLS. The choice of inner method may also depend on the TTLS or PEAP implementation that you consider. The standards allow EAP-GTC to be used within PEAP, but it is not supported by the built-in Windows supplicant.

Table 22-3. Summary of common EAP methods

Inner authentication method	Outer EAP method	Type of account or user database	Comments
PAP	TTLS only	One-way hash systems (most LDAP directories, Unix password format), token cards	Probably the second most common inner authentication method. Most universal; generally works with any database.
MS-CHAP-V2	TTLS or PEAP	Windows user accounts (NT domains, Active Directory) or anything that stores an MD4 hash	Most common form of inner authentication due to the prevalence of Windows
EAP-GTC	TTLS or Cisco PEAP	Same as PAP	Only supported by Cisco supplicant on Windows

After selecting both the EAP method and inner authentication protocol, build the required interface. To work with a set of Windows user accounts, the RADIUS server must access the MD4 hashes of the user passwords. If made a member of a domain, Microsoft's Internet Authentication Server can pull user credentials out of a domain system without additional configuration. Third-party RADIUS servers may need to be installed on domain controllers to access the user account information. Any domain that is trusted can also be accessed through the domain protocols.

LDAP directories are increasingly popular, especially at large sites that require scalability. LDAP directories may be accessed in multiple ways. Some directories may offer RADIUS frontends. Wireless LAN devices can speak directly to the RADIUS frontend, or to the directory's RADIUS server through an alternative RADIUS server performing RADIUS proxy functions. Many RADIUS servers are also capable of working as an LDAP client. When provided with directory credentials, the RADIUS server is able to bind to the directory and validate user credentials directly. The advantage of binding to the directory is that it is usually possible to secure directory access through SSL, which further protects the authentication back-end connections. Less functional RADIUS servers may interface with LDAP by attempting to bind to the directory using the LDAP credentials supplied by the client and checking for success. However, by performing a bind and looking only for success, the RADIUS server is unable to access any user metadata from the directory. If the directory stores privilege information that can be used by the wireless LAN, it is desirable to have the RADIUS server bind to the directory so that the user authorization information can be provided to the wireless devices.

Kerberos servers are popular in many academic environments, and a few RADIUS servers can check user credentials against Kerberos. These RADIUS servers attempt to obtain a ticket from the Kerberos server; if the ticket request is successful, the user is allowed access. However, Kerberos tickets are bound to IP addresses, and are not useful for client authorization.

Authentication architecture

To be successful, an authentication system must interface with the existing user accounts. In many cases, the user account system is small and confined, and the main problem the network administrator has is determining how to build the interface between the wireless LAN and the user account database. Many organizations are large enough, or perhaps divided enough, for the responsibility for maintaining user accounts to be distributed across geographic or administrative boundaries. Users are not members of rival departmental armies, however, and may need to move across geographic or administrative boundaries in the course of work. The end goal of the network design should be to facilitate user mobility and productivity across boundaries. (If you like, call it the Schengen design criterion for distributed wireless LANs.) This design is often found on university campuses, where individual schools, departments, or facilities may run their own networks.

Figure 22-1 shows a portion of a made-up university campus, with five networks: the campus library, a central IT services department that handles networking for common areas and departments that do not need to run their own networks, a school of engineering that prides itself on running an independent network, the campus medical center, and the business school. Each of these departments maintains its own user database, in whatever form they prefer. For wireless LAN access, each of the databases is provided through a RADIUS frontend. In the figure, the user database and RADIUS frontend are shown symbolically.

In designing the authentication architecture, the goal is to provide an authentication facility that allows a single user account to be used across all campus networks. For example, anybody entering the library, whether student or staff, should be able to use the library's network based on the credentials on their home network. If the RADIUS servers in each department have trust relationships and are able to refer authentication requests to each other, only one account is necessary. Accounts are assigned to RADIUS realms, which allow the routing of requests to a defined server. The library's RADIUS server knows that requests for *user@med* must go to the medical center's RADIUS server. If that server accepts the user, access is granted.

Trust relationships between networks are a key component of the architecture. Just as in the cellular world, to get network connectivity anywhere, it is necessary to have a roaming agreement between your "home" network and the network you are "visiting." Network managers depend on the trust because they are granting access to users authenticated by a third party. In a campus environment, the roaming agreeement might be informal. On a larger scale, formal, legally binding agreements may be required. EduRoam, a consortium of European universities, is building a RADIUS mesh on a continental scale, and does require signed formal agreements to join the mesh.

Accounting may also be helpful in this type of environment. Campus libraries devote budget dollars to the acquisition of scholarly material, not to the building of

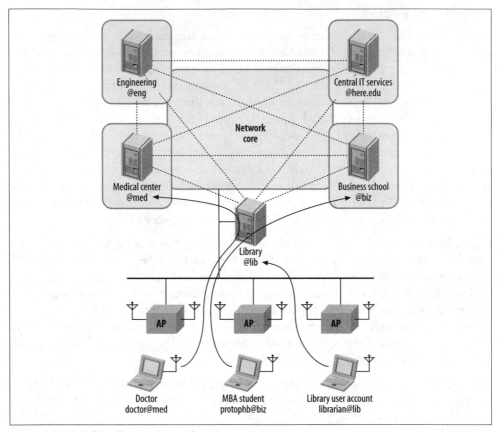

Figure 22-1. Mesh authentication architecture

advanced network services. Through accounting records, a net provider of service (such as the library) can establish that network services are being consumed by users from other networks, which may assist in funding network expansion where service is useful, as opposed to where there is money.

Choose Encryption

After selecting an authentication method, it is usually straightforward to choose a link-layer encryption method because you will be picking the strongest protocol supported on most hardware. Configuration is almost identical between the protocols, and the functionality from the user perspective is identical.

Most of what can be said about static WEP has already been said. Do not use it unless you have no alternative. Nearly all general-purpose devices now support better protocols, leaving only application-specific devices like 802.11 phones or barcode scanners in security limbo. Depending on your security requirements, it may be

---

necessary to shut down deployments of telephony or automation if the security risks cannot be adequately addressed through other means, or if a risk analysis shows that the threat is large.

Using WEP with dynamically derived keys is significantly better because a frequent rekeying interval can mitigate many of the attacks against WEP discussed in Chapter 5. Dynamic WEP should be considered the minimum acceptable level of security for user payload data on general-purpose computing devices. In many cases, manufacturers had to patch drivers, but most drivers from mid-to-late 2002 onwards have support for dynamic keys.

Because of the lingering flaws in WEP, even when used with dynamic keys, TKIP is the target level of security for most networks being built as this book was written. Hardware support requirements for TKIP are identical to WEP, so nearly every 802.11 device has the required hardware. Software support or TKIP is also required, but is increasingly common. TKIP and WPA are built in to the most recent versions of Windows (XP) and MacOS (10.3) WPA is not yet widely available on Linux because the driver framework does not yet have the required level of integration with the supplicant software, although the enhancements are expected in the future.

Most organizations should target TKIP for deployment while making plans for migration to enhanced protocols. Consider dynamic WEP a minimum requirement.

When security is of the utmost importance in link-layer encryption, CCMP is the clear choice. TKIP requires protocol "countermeasures" to detect keys under attack and mitigate the threat. Countermeasures are an admission that there is a fundamental limit on the strength of the protocol. Security does come at a cost, however. CCMP has the most stringent hardware and software support requirements of any of the link-layer encryption protocols. It is only available for use on wireless interfaces that can provide AES hardware assistance. Nearly all recent cards do, but many older cards do not. If you have a significant base of older cards without AES hardware support, the upgrade to AES-capable hardware may be an expensive and daunting challenge.

CCMP is likely to offer the best security. However, it also has the most stringent hardware and software requirements. Many laptop manufacturers choose the cheapest chipsets available, and thus may not support CCMP without external cards.

Multiple SSID support

The 802.11 security protocol architecture allows the simultaneous use of multiple cryptographic protocols on the same AP. Clients are free to use any supported protocol. Encryption of unicast frames is typically done using the strongest protocol supported by a given system, while encryption of frames to group addresses uses the strongest protocol supported by all systems. If an AP has a group of associated stations that support WPA, but there is one station that only supports dynamic WEP, the group key will be dynamic WEP.

The standards do not limit what may be supported, but individual implementations may have problems mixing cryptographic types. One of the most common limitations is that most client software does not support using a CCMP key for unicast frames while simultaneously using a non-CCMP encryption type (TKIP, dynamic WEP, or static WEP) for group frames. Driver support for this type of mix may come in the future. At the time this book was written, supporting CCMP was generally done by providing an additional SSID. One supports the RC4-based encryption protocols, while a second network supports only CCMP. Unfortunately, using two SSIDs does increase the risk of user confusion because the SSID to attach to is a user-controlled parameter.

Client software limitations prevent simultaneous use of CCMP and RC4-based encryption on the same SSID. To use both at the same time, you must use an 802.11 AP that supports multiple SSIDs.

Rogue Access Points

One of the major risks faced by network administrators is the unauthorized installation of 802.11 networks by users. So-called "rogue" access points can pose significant threats. The primary threat is that a device installed by users will not have the full security configuration of an authorized deployment; users probably are not sophisticated enough (and may not be willing) to enable high-security features correctly. Even if they are appropriately secured, unauthorized devices may interfere with the operation of the existing network.

Detection

The first step in dealing with rogue devices is to find out that they exist. Some radio device somewhere must note the existence of an unauthorized device. In the initial years of 802.11 equipment, access points were expensive enough that carrying around a laptop- or handheld-based sniffer was an effective detection mechanism. As more people have become familiar with 802.11, detection needed to become a continuous, automated process. For cost and management reasons, detection is now integrated into most mainstream wireless LAN systems. Depending on the vendor's implementation, the detection component may be implemented through the use of a scanning feature that searches periodically for unauthorized devices or dedicated scanning devices. Scans for unauthorized devices may be passive scans that listen for traffic, Beacons, or Probe Responses, or they may be active scans that use 802.11 Probe Request frames to make unathorized networks reveal themselves.

To be effective, detection must cover all the available 802.11 channels. Initial corporate deployments were largely based on 802.11b, and the radio interface chipsets were not capable of operating in the 802.11a frequency range or with 802.11a modulation. Clever deployers of rogue access points have been known to purchase unauthorized 802.11a devices on the theory that the existing network is not capable of detecting them, and any network analysis tools used by network administrators may be 802.11b-only as well.

Detection capabilities may be built into wireless LAN infrastructure, or it may require standalone devices. There is usually a trade-off between the quality of service provided to users, the quality of detection information, and cost. Dedicated sensors provide the best detection, but also cost the most. Using radios that provide service to users to detect unauthorized devices is much cheaper, but may interrupt or diminish service provided to users.

When a radio searches for unauthorized deployment, it will look for indicators of rogue devices. At the minimum, sensors must search for Beacon frames. All access points and ad hoc networks send Beacons. Some complete 802.11 systems may also observe client traffic and compare the list of clients seen in the radio domain with the clients associated to the infrastructure. Any clients that are present in the former list but not the latter are associated with unauthorized deployments.

Physical Location

Once a rogue AP is detected, network administrators usually want to locate it, usually as a prelude to some sort of response. In many cases, it may be appropriate to simply note the existence of a rogue AP so that an administrator can visit the user and deactivate the device. If active countermeasures are required, it is often best to limit them to rogue devices within a specific area. There are several major types of location technologies in use:

1. Closest AP radius calculations
2. Triangulation
3. RF fingerprinting
4. Differential timing

The easiest method of locating a rogue AP is to use the *radius to the closest AP*, as shown in Figure 22-2 (a). After searching the network for a MAC address, the network system can determine a very rough location based on the location of the AP that detected the device. Radio signal propagation through free space follows a well-known mathematical model. Based on the received signal strength at the detecting AP, the maximum radius can be calculated by finding out how far away a device operating at maximum transmission power would need to be so that the calculated received signal strength would match the measured value. In Figure 22-2 (a), the received signal strength at the AP can be used to detemine the free-space distance to the closest AP, but it does not offer any guidance as to which position on the circle the AP is at.

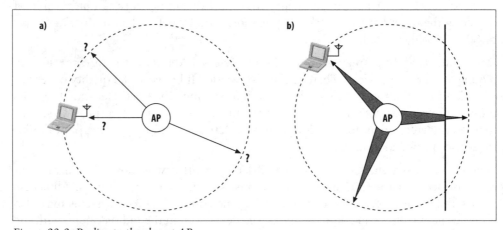

Figure 22-2. Radius to the closest AP

AP radius calculations suffer from a number of flaws. First of all, the free-space radius of a signal transmitted at maximum power is likely to be much larger than the actual radius. While a free-space propagation model may allow for a 100-foot coverage radius, the resulting 30,000 square foot space is too large to be useful. To pinpoint the offending device better, some location tools will build a mathematical model of the radio environment, and take into account any building features along a particular path. In most office buildings, the effective coverage radius is often half the free-space value or less. By reducing the radius from a theoretical 100 feet in free space to an environment-specific value 50 feet or less, the target is reduced to a much smaller 8,000 square feet. 8,000 square feet, however, is still an area of 70–100 cubicles, depending on their size and the office layout. In Figure 22-2 (b), there is a wall on the right-hand side of the diagram, which has the effect of reducing the coverage radius because the radio signals must penetrate the wall. The thickness of the arrow corresponds to signal strength at a given point. When the radio signal encounters the wall, the signal strength drops, which has the effect of reducing the coverage area. Correction of coverage radius for building features works best when there are a large number of them; it is not much of an improvement in typical cubicle-filled offices where the propagation distance is much farther.

AP radius-based approaches can be further refined by using *triangulation*, as shown in Figure 22-3. Triangulation, when used with its original definition, measures the distance from three known points to determine a location. Many of the "triangulation" techniques used in wireless LAN systems can work with more than three measurement points.

Overlapping coverage areas, overlapping radii, and in some cases, probabalistic simulations, are used to come up with likely locations for devices. In Figure 22-3 (a), the overlapping coverage areas of three APs are used to derive a guess at the location. As with the AP radius approach, some triangulation algorithms can be used in conjunction with knowledge of the building construction to further refine the location. In Figure 22-3 (b), the signal deadening effects of two walls are taken into account, which results in a much better prediction.

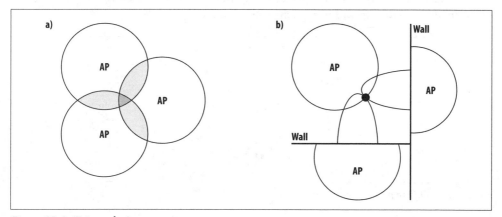

Figure 22-3. Triangulation

Location can be further refined by taking *RF fingerprint* measurements. After generating a set of predictions about how radio waves will interact with the building, the mathematical model is refined with data about how radio waves actually behave. To build a fingerprint database, devices are placed at known locations and then measured. Data on received signal strength and other signal characteristics is then stored as a "fingerprint" for that location. Fingerprints include all the signal propagation characteristics that are hard to calculate, such as reflection off of walls and multi-path interference. When unknown devices are being located, their signal characteristics can be compared to the fingerprint database to refine the location prediction. Improving the quality of location predictions depends on the number of fingerprint locations collected as part of the extended site survey. Although fingerprinting can improve location information, it may require the collection of a great deal of additional data to build a large enough fingerprint database for the desired accuracy.

A final method of location is based on the relative time of received signals. Signal strength depends on a variety of factors, including building construction. Radio waves, however, always travel at the speed of light. Triangulation can be performed based on the relative arrival time of transmissions at measurement locations. Although this technique has the potential to be quite accurate, radio waves are extremely fast, and incredibly precise timing synchronization is required. In Figure 22-4, two APs are measuring the arrival of a transmission from a source. After some amount of time, the signal reaches the first AP. The location system must measure the difference in time between the arrival of the signal at the first measurement device and the second measurement device with extremely high precision. Radio waves travel at approximately one foot per nanosecond, which requires that the location devices be able to discern very small time differences between distributed devices. Although theoretically feasible, the differential time arrival approach typically requires the use of highly specialized devices with timing equipment that is far more accurate than is found in typical access points.

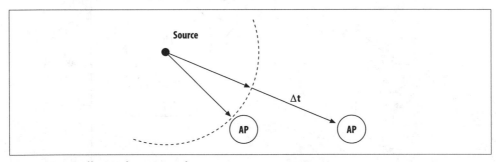

Figure 22-4. Differential timing analysis

Disabling Rogue APs

Many products offer the ability to automatically shut off unauthorized networks, a feature that is often referred to as *containment* or *suppression*. The technical details vary, but some combination of protocol tricks is used to prevent or disrupt connections to rogue APs. Generally speaking, the tricks either prevent associations to rogue APs or disrupt established connections. Many of the tricks depend on the lack of authentication on control frames, which allows infrastructure devices to impersonate rogue APs. It remains to be seen how effective countermeasures will be when the 802.11 protocols authenticate important network control information. Figure 22-5 illustrates the two major techniques for launching denial-of-service attacks on rogue networks.

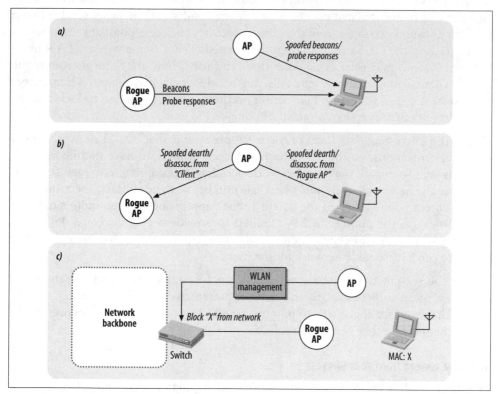

Figure 22-5. Rogue suppression techniques

To disrupt the association process, some devices send spoofed Beacon or Probe Response frames, as shown in Figure 22-5 (a). Without authentication of Beacon or Probe Response frames, an access point can easily impersonate the rogue. The spoofed frames may contain information that contradicts the corresponding frames transmitted by the rogue to confuse client devices. Some clients will be unable to associate to a network that appears to be announcing it is both encrypted (in Beacon frames with the Protected Frame bit set) and not encrypted (with the Protected Frame bit clear). Spoofed Probe Response frames may have the same effect. Some wireless LAN systems may also attempt to capture client association requests by trapping devices associating with rogue clients on to a captive network to prevent damage. To handle stations that are already associated with a rogue AP, Dissasociation and Deauthentication messages can be used, as shown in Figure 22-5 (b). These messages are not signed, which will allow the network infrastructure to kick clients off of rogue networks.

Using messages that are transmitted in response to client communications is not foolproof. Due to multipath coverage, and the placement of infrastructure devices in relation to the clients, it is not always be possible to see all communications initiated on behalf of rogue-attached clients. Some devices will simultaneously send spoofed Deauthentication messages from the client addresses to access points to force access points to drop the connections of rogue associated clients. Some wireless LAN management systems may offer capabilities that can further limit the damage from rogue APs. If clients associated to rogue APs can be identified, a wireless LAN management system could, in theory, take action on the network backbone to lock out the clients from network services on the backbone, as in Figure 22-5 (c).

One of the interesting paradoxes of rogue suppression is that 802.11 networks often spring up in response to the self-determined need of users to have mobile network connectivity. To ensure that supression devices have appropriate coverage scope to disable rogue networks, there must be a fair number of them. In fact, the number of 802.11 access points required for decent rogue suppression is often quite similar, if not identical, to the number of APs required to provide decent coverage. Providing the desired level of supression capabilities often requires deploying enough access points to run a reasonable network for the users.

One of the reasons that some access points are becoming 802.1X supplicants is so that they must authenticate to the network themselves before providing service. Rather than wait for rogue APs to pop up, an 802.1X-enabled wired network simply rejects them before they become a problem.

And now, a word from your lawyers

Interfering with a wireless network through rogue containment may be treated as network tampering or "hacking" under computer crime statutes. (Please consult an attorney who is familiar with all the laws that may apply in your location, especially since I am not a lawyer.) Equipment that is acting to stop rogue devices by spoofing their identity is designed to interfere with the operation of that wireless network. If the network belongs to a neighbor, or coffee shop across the street, your action may be illegal or subject to a civil action.

To avoid creating more work for lawyers, it is an excellent idea to ensure that a rogue AP is in fact connected to the network that you are attempting to protect before launching your counterattack. If the rogue AP is the property of the coffee shop across the street, for example, the owners will almost certainly have a very strong opinion about having their network shut down. A wireless network set up in a large building with many offices may also have several neighboring networks which should be protected from countermeasures. (Enabling unrestricted countermeasures if you rent an office next to a law firm is probably particularly dumb, especially if the law firm is computer savvy.)

Recent FCC regulatory actions prevent property owners from asserting any ownership over the electromagnetic spectrum. Therefore, it is unwise to apply rogue countermeasures to your tenants or neighbors.

CHAPTER 23
Site Planning and Project Management

Wireless LAN deployment is a significant undertaking partly because there is not a great deal of structure to the process, especially when contrasted with a wired LAN deployment. Building an Ethernet network is straightforward these days. Everybody gets a switched Fast Ethernet (or faster) port, and there is a core switching location that is built on even faster, and possibly aggregated, links. For wiring, there are a number of cabling firms that spend a great deal of time pulling the wire for networks, and enough time has passed so that there is general agreement on the principles by which wiring should be structured.

In comparison, radio networks are the Wild West. Service quality from the network to the end user depends on where the user is in relation to the closest network element, and degrades with distance. Network capacity may be based on the sizes of coverage areas, and the physical layout of the building. Every building has its own personality with respect to radio transmissions, and unexpected interference can pop up nearly everywhere because of microwave ovens, electrical conduits, or severe multipath interference. To make matters worse, the quality of the network medium depends not only on what you do for your wireless LAN, but also what your users do, and even what your neighbors do.

When wireless LAN deployment is considered, you start with the obvious questions: "How many access points do I need, and where do I put them?" To answer those questions, you need to conduct a site survey. Site surveys often are done at the beginning of a wireless LAN project, and are usually a significant part of the project plan for the network. This chapter discusses the intertwined nature of the site survey and the project itself, again from a technical perspective. What do you need to do at the planning stage to make a deployment successful? Planning where to put access points is a part of the wireless LAN roll-out itself, so this chapter helps develop your deployment plan, including developing the physical layout plans.

The process of planning a wireless LAN breaks up into several natural stages. Gathering requirements need not be a long drawn-out process involving the production of many lengthy documents; at the end of the planning process, you should be familiar with the coverage and capacity requirements of the network. Refining requirements and translating them into a physical design consistent with the requirements may take a great deal of time and effort at the site.

Project Planning and Requirements

Start planning the wireless LAN as soon as it is clear that you want one. Wireless LANs are still an evolving technology, and the sooner the networking staff is involved, the better it will be. If the wireless LAN is intended for a new building, it would help to involve the network staff as soon as there is a sketch of the basic architecture of the building, especially if there are significant restrictions on the placement of access points. One institution I worked with had a series of tight aesthetic requirements for APs, which forced them to be next to heavy steel structural components, and kept behind paneling. If the network team had been involved earlier, more suitable provision might have been made for AP placement, with a consequent reduction in the amount of money required for the network.

Planning a wired LAN is relatively straightforward at this point. Depending on the size, it may require a fair degree of skill, but fundamentally, the process is well understood. Cable-based network media behave in predictable ways, and the capacity of fixed networks can be upgraded in a straightforward fashion. Wireless LAN technology lacks this level of maturity, which makes the planning process much more important.

Wireless LAN project plans are often referred to as *site surveys*. Site visits are only one component of installing a wireless LAN, and successful wireless LAN installations often require several visits, each for different purposes. Wireless LANs being designed into a building from the beginning will probably require several visits throughout the construction project. As always, begin planning before "breaking cable" on the network expansion.

Site survey work is the heart of installing a wireless LAN. To successfully run a site survey, though, preparation is very important. Before "breaking cable" on a network expansion, gather technical requirements and information to find out which expectations are important. Use the following checklist to flesh out the network requirements; each point is detailed further in a subsequent section:

Throughput considerations
> How much throughput is required? This is partly dependent on the type of device that will be used on the wireless LAN, although if it is a PC-like device with the ability to display large and complex graphics, you will want your wireless LAN to be as fast as possible. In most cases, this will lead to choosing 802.11a- or 802.11g-based networks to use the 54-Mbps physical layer.

Coverage area

Where should coverage be provided? Everywhere? Some areas are much harder to cover than others. Elevator shafts are usually part of a central building core, and very difficult to cover. Providing coverage within elevator cars themselves is not out of the question, but probably not feasible for most users.

User density

In addition to where the users are located, you will need to pay attention to the number of them. Users may gather more closely in public spots, such as conference rooms, lobbies, and the cafeteria.

Mobility

The days in which wireless LANs were a cool new technology populated by power users is long gone. A few years ago, it may have been acceptable during a transition phase to have the network merely facilitate automatic reconfiguration. As wireless LANs become more mature, however, architects must design networks that reflect the ideal of continuous connectivity throughout the coverage area.

User population

How many people will use the wireless network, and what quality of service do they expect? As always, be sure to allow for growth!

Physical considerations

Will new network cabling be needed to supply the wireless LAN backbone, or can you make do with existing cabling? How will the new access points be powered? Can the access points and antennas be installed in the open or must they be hidden?

Aesthetic considerations

To what extent must the wireless LAN hide from public view? Is it acceptable to see the access points, or do they need to be hidden?

Logical network architecture

In most cases, the logical architecture needs to support an IP address block across the entire area of contiguous coverage. Different users may be presented different IP addresses in some of the logical network architectures from Chapter 21. With the recent development of the technology, it is no longer necessary to tailor mobility areas based on IP addressing architecture.

Application characteristics

Are any applications sensitive to high or variable delays? Do any applications provide time-critical data?

Security requirements

Before deployment, you will want to design a network that can address many of the security concerns discussed throughout this book, as well as provide a robust environment that supplies some defense against the possibility of future attacks. Security issues and architecture were discussed in the previous two chapters.

Site environmental considerations

A number of factors can affect radio propagation and signal quality. Building materials, construction, and floor plan all affect how well radio waves can move throughout the building. Interference is a fact of life, but it is more pronounced in some buildings than in others. Temperature and humidity have minor effects. Early site visits can assist in anticipating several factors, and a detailed site survey can spot any real problems before installation begins in earnest.

Project management

As with many other projects, drawing up a schedule and budget is a necessary component. This chapter does not provide any guidance on nontechnical factors because they are often organization-specific.

Network Requirements

Like any other network technology, before deploying a wireless LAN, you must answer three questions: "where?", "how fast?", and "what can I spend?" Typically, the cost is specified independently through a budget process, and what the architect is trying to do is achieve the best possible LAN service within that constraint. The *where* in building an 802.11 network is the set of locations where radio service will be provided. It is usually desirable to have coverage everywhere, but many projects start as scaled-down deployments for conference rooms and public spaces only to hold down cost. The *how fast* refers to the capacity of the radio network. Wireless LAN client speeds depend on distance from the access point and the number and type of obstacles between the access point and the client. Building a high-throughput requires attention to detail to minimize the average distance of a client from its nearest AP. In some physical spaces, the environment can obstruct radio waves to such a degree that a large number of APs are required simply to achieve coverage.

Network architects need to optimize between the trio of variables to get the right network. In some environments, the physical design of the building prevents radio propagation, so the network will need to have a smaller footprint and less capacity. Or perhaps the cost is limited and the objective will be to design as large a network that meets some minimum capacity specification. In rare cases, the network may even be designed around total coverage at high capacity, and cost is allowed to be very high. Optimizing between the three design factors is a continuous process that must occur on a regular basis. As a wireless network grows in popularity, the network will have to grow with it. Initial limited-area deployments will probably need to give way to wall-to-wall coverage. Networks designed for coverage only and based purely on a sparse AP layout to keep costs low may need to move to a higher-capacity deployment to accommodate additional demands for capacity to serve users, or an increased number of users. Finding the balance between the troika of demands is the art of building a wireless network. Fortunately, there are a number of tools available to help make decisions between trade-offs.

Coverage Requirements

All networks cover some area. Wired networks get coverage through network ports placed throughout the facility. To get network coverage, you pull wire and drop in ports. Wireless networks approach coverage planning in a different way because the physical network medium spreads out through space and can penetrate walls. Getting a handle on how radio waves propagate through your space is key to understanding how to cover a network.

The first question to answer is where coverage will be provided. Are you blanketing the whole building or campus, or just putting wireless in select areas? It is often common to start with a pilot deployment that covers a small area while getting familiar with the technology. In many cases, the pilot deployment will cover the IT workspace, though it is also quite common to provide coverage for public areas such as lobbies or conference rooms.

"Ubiquitous" is a popular word for those who are specifying wireless LAN coverage requirements, although it can be a horrific word for those who have to fulfill them. Does that mean that every square inch of the building must be covered? Is it really necessary to have high-quality coverage in, say, the restroom? For public buildings, should escape routes be covered?

The number of access points required to cover an indoor area may depend on several factors. First, there is the matter of building construction. More walls mean more material blocking radio waves, and hence more access points will be required. Different types of material also affect RF in different ways. For a given material, thicker walls cause greater signal loss. Signal power is diminished, or *attenuated*, most by metal, so elevator shafts and air ducts cause significant disruption of communications. Tinted or coated windows frequently cause severe disruption of radio signals. Some buildings may have metal-coated ceilings or significant amounts of metal in the floor. Wood and most glass panes have only small effects, although bulletproof glass can be quite bad.* Brick and concrete have effects somewhere between metal and untreated plain glass.

The second major factor is the desired speed. Simply providing some wireless LAN access throughout an area is different from requiring a certain data rate. 802.11a has speeds that go from 6 Mbps to 54 Mbps, and the coverage provided at the slower speed will be much larger. Building a network that supports the 54 Mbps data rate everywhere will require many, many more access points than a network that simply provides some 802.11 access everywhere. Figure 23-1 is an attempt to show how the distance/data rate trade-off compares for the three major 802.11 physical layers. Higher data rates do not travel as far.

---

* Bulletproof glass is far more common than one might otherwise assume.

Figure 23-1 is based on theoretical calculations of free-space loss. It shows the relative distance at which different speeds are available for 802.11a, 802.11b, and 802.11g. For the calculation, I have assumed a typical transmission power (20 dBm or 100 mW for 802.11b/g, and 11 dBm for 802.11a) and then calculated the distance at which the power would drop to the radio sensitivity for each speed. For typical sensitivity, I used the detailed specifications that Cisco makes available for their a/b/g card. Range is shown relative to the minimum range, which is the top operational rate of 54 Mbps for 802.11a.

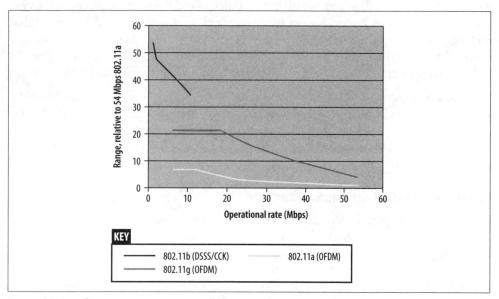

Figure 23-1. Relative range comparison of free space loss

To meet a performance target, it may be necessary to have a lot of of overlap between adjacent APs. If the goal is to have high-speed coverage throughout an area at, say, 36 Mbps, the range of transmissions at lower speeds will significantly overlap. Planning for some overlap to ensure handoff while minimizing the amount necessary to preserve optimum performance is a delicate trade-off in the design of a wireless LAN.

A final factor to consider when designing coverage is the objective of your network. A radio will have a certain coverage area, but the area covered by its transmissions and the area covered by its reception may be different. In general, the latter is a much larger area, especially if you are not using the maximum transmission power the AP is capable of. One of the advantages of deploying a dense network with relatively low power is that there is a great deal of overlap in the reception areas. Any unauthorized APs that are deployed by the user community will be detected by several of the APs in your network, which will enable more precise location.

Outdoor coverage is subject to a different set of trade-offs and engineering requirements than indoor coverage, and is generally only a concern in mild climates where users are likely to be working outside on a regular basis.[*] Certain types of applications are also suited to combined indoor/outdoor coverage; for example, airports may wish to provide outdoor access to the airlines at the curb for skycap equipment. Placing equipment outdoors is often a challenge, in large part because it must be weatherproofed, and there are a number of environmental and safety rules to comply with. Any outdoor equipment should be sturdy enough to work there, which is largely a matter of waterproofing and weather resistance. One solution is to install access points inside and run antennas to outdoor locations, but external antenna cables that are long enough are not always available, and in any case, the cable loss is often severe. Many vendors will have weatherproof enclosures on their price list, especially if they have sold equipment to a large combined indoor/outdoor installation.

Weatherproof enclosures may be subject to some additional safety requirements. International Electrotechnical Commission (IEC) Standard 60529 has test procedures to rate enclosures on protection against water and debris. In the United States, enclosures may also be subject to the National Electric Manufacturer's Association (NEMA) Standard 250.

Coverage and physical installation restrictions

Part of the end-user requirement is a desired coverage area, and possibly some physical restrictions to go along with it. Physical restrictions, such as a lack of available electrical power and network connections, can be mundane. Some institutions may also require that access points and antennas are hidden; this may be done to maintain the physical security of the network infrastructure, or it may be simply to preserve the aesthetic appeal of the building.

It is often desirable to mount access points as high as possible. Just like scouts who try to seize the high ground for a battlefield, APs work best when they are above the typical obstructions that live on the floor. By mounting them above cubicles and other objects, it is often possible to make their signals go farther more reliably. Some access points have mounting kits that enable them to attach to walls, or even the suspension bars for the dropped ceiling tile. Other vendors will recommend installing the AP above the ceiling tiles and using an unobtrusive external antenna through the ceiling tile. Ceiling tile vendors are even getting into the market by producing ceiling tile panels with integrated antennas.[†]

Many commercial buildings use "dropped" ceilings, where the ceiling tile is suspended from the actual ceiling. Network wiring and electrical cables are placed above

---

[*] This chapter does not discuss the use of point-to-point 802.11 links; obviously, they are outdoor links that may be used year-round in any climate.

[†] See, for example, the Armstrong i-ceilings tile at *http://www.armstrong.com/commceilingsna/article7399.html*.

---

the ceiling tile, along with air ducts. In some buildings, the area between the ceiling and the ceiling tiles may be used as part of the building's air-handling system. Safety standards dictate that if objects are placed in the air-handling spaces (plenums), they must not endanger the building's occupants. In case of fire, one of the biggest dangers to people inside the building is that thick black smoke may obscure vision and otherwise obstruct attempts to escape. If an object in the air system were to start giving off smoke, the smoke would be circulated throughout the building. To protect people inside buildings, therefore, there are specific safety standards on how fire-retardant equipment placed in plenums must be. If you wish to mount wireless LAN equipment above the ceiling, ensure that the components placed above the ceiling are *plenum-rated*. In addition to the APs, this would include any support equipment mounted up above the ceiling as well. Power injectors are often not plenum-rated because they can usually be located safely in wiring closets. Any cables used above the ceiling tile almost certainly need to be plenum-rated. Plenum safety standards are developed by Underwriters Laboratories and published as UL standard 2043. UL also tests products for conformance to the standard and certifies those that pass.

Performance Requirements

Coverage is not the end of the story in wireless LAN design. When operating under network load, access points act like hubs. For a given coverage area, there is a fixed amount of radio capacity. An 802.11b access point can move about 6 Mbps of user data to the edge of its coverage range. The physical medium in 802.11 networks is inherently shared. A lone user connected to an access point will be able to obtain speeds of about 6 Mbps because there will be no congestion window backoff. As more users are added to the network, the same 6 Mbps must be divided among the users, and the protocol must work to fairly (or unfairly, as users are sure to contend) allocate transmission capacity between stations.

For a network built to serve users, coverage and quality are an inherent trade-off. It is possible to use fewer access points by attaching high-gain external antennas, but the capacity is shared over larger areas. There is nothing inherently wrong with large coverage areas, especially if the user density is not high. Some deployments may use a single access point with an external antenna to create a huge coverage area because the demand for network capacity is not very high at all. Many K–12 schools with only a few users fall into this category, which is represented by the left-hand side "coverage" picture in Figure 23-2. On the other hand, a network with lots of users may wish to use many small coverage areas. Network engineers will sometimes borrow a term from cellular telephony and refer to such a network as having "microcells." With smaller areas, any given access point is likely (although not guaranteed) to have fewer users than the large-coverage-area case. In Figure 23-2, the right-hand side picture has divided the same area into three separate subareas. As a result, each AP handles a smaller number of stations and the per-station throughput is likely to be better.

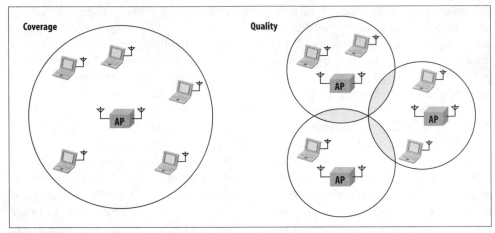

Figure 23-2. Coverage/quality trade-off

One metric that might be useful in evaluating your needs is *total area throughput* (or, its close relative, throughput per unit of area). Both networks in Figure 23-2 cover the same area. However, with three access points, the network on the right provides three times as much throughput. Not all networks need high total area throughput, at least initially. When the wireless LAN proves popular, and the 5 users shown in Figure 23-2 become 10, 15, or even 50 users, the total area throughput may need to be further increased.

How much capacity should be reserved for each user? One answer is to undertake a detailed study of network applications and performance requirements, and to design the network appropriately. In the real world, however, most networks seem to operate on a Schrodinger's Cat sort of principle: as long as packets are moving, the network is working; if we were to inquire too deeply about its operation, it might cease to function. Generally speaking, most wireless network projects are started with only the vaguest idea of required application support, other than perhaps that "it should feel something like a wired connection." In the absence of any countervailing data, I advise to plan for at least 1 Mbps for each user. 802.11a and 802.11g networks allow planning for higher rates per user, especially if you make aggressive assumptions about the burstiness of traffic.

Exploring the coverage/quality trade-off and total area throughput

Under load, an access point will act like a hub, sharing capacity between users throughout its coverage area. Networks built using large AP coverage areas are generally cheaper to build because they use fewer access points, but they may have poor service quality due to lower aggregate capacity. When each AP is responsible for providing connectivity in a large area, there is also a higher likelihood that stations far the edge of the network will communicate using slower speeds.

One way of measuring the quality of coverage is to consider the total aggregate throughput available to the service area, which is in many ways a reflection of the density of the access points. All other things equal, more access points mean that there is more radio capacity. Figure 23-3 shows three networks. On the left, there is a network with one access point. It is capable of offering up to, say, 30 Mbps of user payload data to clients in the service area. In the middle, there is a network built with three access points, operating on lower power. By separating the coverage area into independent radio cells, more throughput is available. Roughly speaking, there will be 90 Mbps available to serve clients. Finally, in the network on the right, there is a single access point with a *sectorized antenna*, which acts like three combined directional antennas. In some implementations, each sector is assigned its own channel, which also reduces the number of collisions between stations attempting to transmit. Done in the most sophisticated manner, each channel on the sectorized antenna will act like an independent access point, and the aggregate throughput available to clients will be 90 Mbps. Throughput quality may also be measured in terms of megabits available per square foot of service area, which is consistent with the total throughput available to the service area.

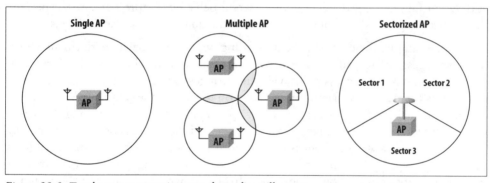

Figure 23-3. Total aggregate service area throughput illustration

In the Ethernet world, Ethernet switches increase network throughput by reducing the contention for the medium. Any approach to increasing the capacity of a wireless network takes the same qualitative approach. By shrinking the coverage area associated with any given access point, more access points can be deployed in a single service area. Although there is a great deal of hype about so-called "Wi-Fi switches," they all share a relatively simple design principle. Network management is harder when there are more elements in the network, so use aggregation devices to concentrate the complexity in a few spots where it can be dealt with, rather than scattered across the network.

Coverage area and coverage quality are an inherent trade-off in wireless LANs. Increasing the quality requires decreasing the coverage of each access point.

Client limitations

One of the major challenges for the industry is that a great deal of 802.11 operations are in control of the client machine and its software, and this may lead to path dependencies and hysteresis in the behavior of clients.

Nearly all of the "interesting" protocol operations that support mobility are in the hands of clients. Client software decides when to roam, how to scan for a new access point, and where to attach. Different machines on the same network may behave differently because 802.11 does not specify an algorithm for deciding when to roam or how to select access points. With so much of the protocol usage up to client implementation, yet unspecified by any standard, the behavior of clients is often a mystery. As a demonstration, get three laptop computers, add 802.11 interfaces, and roll them around your network on a cart. The three computers will move between access points at different times, and generally exhibit different behavior. Future standards, especially the forthcoming 802.11k, should help improve the quality of roaming decisions.

Take, for example, the case of a client deciding where to associate with the network. In most cases, clients will do a relatively intelligent scan when they are first activated, and choose the access point with the strongest signal. For many cards, intelligence ends there. They will continue to hang on to that first access point for dear life, even to the exclusion of much better access points that are nearby. Losing the signal is the only thing that forces many cards to roam. This behavior is often called the *bug light* problem because the client resembles a moth entranced by a flame, unable to move away. Bug light clients are particularly bad for throughput. As they stray far from their point of initial connection, they drop to slower speeds to stay connected.

Not only does this sap the far-ranging client of speed, but it also dramatically reduces the throughput available to other clients on the same access point. A maximum-size network payload of 1,500 bytes encapsulated in an OFDM PHY (802.11a or 802.11g) requires a much greater transmission time at slower speeds. To illustrate the extremes, the maximum size frame at 54 Mbps requires 57 data symbols and 248 microseconds to transmit. At 6 Mbps, however, it requires 512 data symbols for a total time of 2,068 microseconds, or slightly more than 8 times longer. The slower transmission rate robs other clients of the ability to transmit for 1,800 microseconds.

Leaving so much of the overall protocol operation in the hands of the client limits the ability of the network infrastructure to do the "best" thing under some circumstances. Cellular networks, for example, have the ability to direct a mobile telephone to a tower with more capacity. Wireless LAN protocols do not yet have that ability.

Many vendors of wireless LAN systems have implemented "AP load balancing" capabilities that claim to give network administrators the ability to co-locate two access points in close proximity to increase overall network capacity in that location. A common approach is to monitor either the number of associations on each access point, or the amount of transit traffic through each access point, and carefully disassociate active clients on a loaded access point to encourage them to move to an unloaded AP. Without any client cooperation, it is difficult to achieve the optimal balancing because most clients will tend to go right back to the AP they were initially associated with.

 Roaming is always and everywhere a client-driven phenomenon. With the decision in the hands of client software, there is only so much that network equipment can do to improve the user experience.

Realistic throughput expectations

As more users are added to a wireless LAN, the network's capacity is divided between more users and throughput suffers. For networks using the distributed coordination function (DCF), a practical rule of thumb is to expect 50–60% of the nominal bit rate in order to take into account the overhead from elements such as interframe spacing, the preamble and framing headers. Network protocols add additional overhead for network-layer framing and retransmission. An additional problem that most network protocols will impose is that reliable delivery assumes that there will be a transport-layer acknowledgment of transmissions. Every TCP segment must be acknowledged (though not necessarily individually), and the TCP acknowledgments may collide with additional segments in transmission.[*] Table 23-1 shows a rough rule of thumb for the network capacity of an access point.

Table 23-1. Rule of thumb capacity for different 802.11 technologies

Technology	Approximate capacity
802.11 direct sequence	1.3–1.5 Mbps
802.11b	6 Mbps
802.11g, with protection	15 Mbps
802.11g, no protection	30 Mbps, although this will be rare
802.11a	30 Mbps

Quality of service technologies are presently being designed to squeeze more network capacity, but they are not widely deployed. If the history of QoS is any guide, there will be a great deal of talk, followed by standards that very few people use.

---

[*] One estimate I have heard is that you should expect about 10% of frames to be retransmitted if TCP/IP is used as the network and transport protocol combination.

Faster to the Future: 802.11n and beyond

Where do you go past 54 Mbps? Once the standards for 802.11a and 802.11g were finished, and products started appearing on the market, the question of the next leap started to arise.

In 2003, the IEEE 802.11 working group formed a high-throughput study group to study ways to increase the speeds of wireless LANs still farther. Task Group N (TGn) is working on a specification that will offer a net throughput, after subtracting protocol overhead, in excess of 100 Mbps. The task group's goal is to beat 100 Mbps, and it looks likely that the goal will get blown out of the water. There are two competing proposals in the task group right now; both are described in Chapter 15. Both use multiple-input/multiple-output (MIMO) to achieve higher rates. Roughly speaking, one proposal works to dramatically increase the peak data rate as much as possible, while the other keeps the peak rate relatively low and focuses on increasing the efficiency of the radio link.

Number of users per access point

When you are planning a network, you must also ask how many users can be attached to an access point. 802.11 limits the number of associated stations to 2,016, which is for all practical purposes an infinite limit. Practical considerations dictate that you limit the number of users per AP to something much, much smaller.

6 Mbps is a reasonable assumption for the user payload throughput of 802.11b. To engineer a network speed of 1 Mbps for each user, it would at first appear that only six users could be supported on an 802.11b access point. However, network traffic is bursty, so there is a natural oversubscription that can be built into any assumptions about traffic patterns. Engineering 1 Mbps for each user can be done by assuming that there are some times when users will be idle. I have generally found that a ratio in the neighborhood of 3:1 to 5:1 will be reasonable. Given that ratio, an 802.11b access point can support approximately 20 to 30 users.

However, the number of users per access point does not get much better if you go to 802.11a or 802.11g. Speed depends on distance in 802.11. As stations get farther from an AP, they will fall back to more robust but slower encoding methods for transmission. The higher speeds of 802.11a and 802.11g are available only relatively close to the AP, so the 20–30 user per AP number remains reasonable.

If you are using applications that are highly sensitive to network characteristics—for example, voice traffic (VoIP)—the number of stations per access point may be even lower. Wireless networks do not yet have sophisticated quality of service prioritization, and must rely on the medium itself to arbitrate access between stations. Voice traffic and data traffic are at odds with each other. Data throughput is highest when the medium is saturated and the AP transmit queue is pumping out data as fast as possible. Voice frames need to be delivered on time, and queues need to remain relatively free to accept high-priority frames for immediate delivery. Voice traffic, whether run directly on the 802.11 link layer or over IP, is highly sensitive to delay and jitter. To avoid unnecessary delay in frame delivery, you may need to restrict the number of voice handsets even further, down to 8–10 handsets per AP, until the arrival of better QoS technology.

Mobility Requirements

The days in which wireless LANs were a cool new technology populated by power users is long gone. A few years ago, it may have been acceptable to have the network merely facilitate automatic reconfiguration as users moved from one location to another. As wireless LANs have become more mature, however, users have come to expect networks that reflect the ideal of continuous connectivity, regardless of physical location or the convenience of local attachment points.

Continuous coverage and seamless roaming should be the norm throughout a campus environment. Users may move throughout a campus in unpredictable ways, while expecting that the network will just run and support their connection. Generally speaking, users expect that any journey not involving motorized transport should be supported by the wireless LAN. In designing coverage for an entire campus, you may need to engineer the network so that users can cross router boundaries while retaining their addresses, typically through some form of tunneling. Different wireless LAN architectures will accomplish the tunneling in different ways. For a detailed discussion, see Chapter 21.

Network Integration Requirements

There are two components to network planning. The first, physical integration is largely legwork. In addition to the building map, it helps to obtain a physical network map, if one exists. It is much easier to install wireless LAN hardware when no expensive and time-consuming wiring needs to be done. Knowing the location and contents of all the wiring closets is an important first step. The second step, logical integration, consists of hooking your wireless LAN up to the existing network.

Physical integration

Physical integration consists of getting the atoms in the right places. APs need to be mounted according to your plan, and cabled appropriately. Connecting new devices to the network probably requires new cabling if you are concerned with aesthetic appearance. If not, you can run patch cords from existing jacks to the AP locations. Depending on the product and architecture you choose, the cable may be attached to an AP controller, a special wireless VLAN, or the network that exists in the closet.

In addition to supplying connectivity, you must power up the APs. It is possible, though unlikely, that you will power APs directly at service locations. Many enterprise-grade APs are designed to draw power from the Ethernet cable primarily, and may not even offer the option of an external power supply. (Some APs that offer the option of an external power supply draw 48 volt power from their power cords, which indicates that the power circuitry was designed to operate at PoE voltages.) Your switch vendor may offer power over Ethernet, but you need to check and be sure it is compatible. The surest guarantee of power compatibility is compliance with 802.3af, but you may have prestandard products that are vendor-proprietary. If you need to add power to the wiring closet, you can purchase third-party power injectors.

Logical integration

Before attempting the logical integration of your wireless LAN, you must first select its architecture (see Chapter 21). Different architectures will have different integration requirements. Generally speaking, though, you will need to connect at least one network to the wireless LAN. Dynamic network assignment based on AAA may require connecting more than one network. For the most part, these networks will be IP networks. However, in some cases, there may be legacy networking protocols that also need support over the wireless LAN.

The second component of network planning is thinking about changes to the logical network. How will mobile stations be addressed? If all wireless stations will use a single IP subnet, you need to allocate IP address space and ensure it is correctly routed to the wireless subnet. As you allocate new address space, ensure that you leave sufficient extra space for all the access points as well as any support devices. Do not succumb to the temptation to use address translation. Although many applications work through NAT, it is a potential disruption to future applications that are not NAT-aware. It may also break applications that were written before NAT was commonplace.

As part of the network expansion, you will need to add access points. They will probably need IP addresses. If these addresses are being assigned through DHCP, you will probably want to configure your DHCP server to give each access point an assigned address rather than randomly fishing from an address pool. If the access points connect through an IP tunnel back to a centralized controller, you may need to configure filtering rules to allow the communication through, as well as configuring the tunnel on both the AP and centralized device.

Physical Layer Selection and Design

Selection of the 802.11 physical layer is typically driven by user requirements rather than the physical design. In most cases, it is also driven by the need to build the fastest network possible, at least when next to an access point. Choosing a physical layer is a matter of engineering. None of them are inherently superior to the others. In choosing a physical layer, you are trading off many different factors. In a nutshell, the 2.4 GHz ISM band is less affected by obstacles, so 802.11b/g signals will travel farther. However, backwards compatibility can limit throughput, and it difficult to lay out a network with only three channels. Furthermore, many devices use the 2.4 GHz ISM band, and it is likely that there will be some sort of interference from a Bluetooth device, 2.4 GHz cordless phone, X10 video camera, or some similar widget. If not, the use of only three channels will be limit throughput as the channels overlap with each other. 802.11a is ideally suited for high-density, high-capacity networks because it does not have backwards compatibility limitations and the radio spectrum is much larger. Table 23-2 shows a comparison between 2.4 GHz and 5 GHz 802.11 networks.

Table 23-2. Quick reference comparison between 2.4 GHz and 5 GHz 802.11 networks

	802.11b/g (2.4 GHz)	802.11a (5 GHz)
Performance (throughput) per AP	Low for 802.11b; 802.11g may vary from medium to high	Highest throughput per channel
Potential performance per unit area	Low—with only 3 or 4 channels, channel overlap and interference is practically guaranteed	High—greater number of channels means less self-interference between network elements
Range	Lower frequency has longer range	Worse—free-space loss of higher frequencies is higher
Interference	Many other uses of frequency band	Frequency used by many fewer devices
	Very limited channel selection leads to lots of co-channel interference	More channels make layout easier, especially in three dimensions
Backwards compatibility with older hardware	Compatible with 802.11 direct sequence and 802.11b hardware	None

One of the ways to ease the pain of large-scale wireless LAN deployments is to automate as much as possible. Several products offer the ability to automatically lay out channels. One major channel layout approach is based on physical measurements. Network administrators place access points based on expected user density, mounting convenience, and environmental constraints. When the network is powered on, the APs communicate with each other through a wired network to select the optimum channel assignment. Some products continuously monitor the radio space to adjust the channel settings dynamically in response to environmental changes. The major alternative to physical measurements is based on virtual modeling of a building. When creating a virtual model of the building, channels can be assigned based on calculations with the mathematical model to minimize interference. As with may other aspects of wireless LAN design, many products combine both techniques.

2.4 GHz (802.11b/g) Channel Layout

802.11b and 802.11g share the same frequency band. They are subject to the same regulatory requirements, and use an identical channel map (Table 23-3). Although there are 14 channels, each channel is only 5 MHz wide. A direct sequence transmission is spread across a much wider band than its assigned channel. (See Figure 12-5.) For best effect, you will want to keep both the first and second lobes free of interference. Ideally, that leads to a 33 MHz separation between channel assignments.

There is not quite enough radio spectrum assigned to have three fully nonoverlapping channels in most jurisdictions. Rather than have two interference-free channels, most users allow a slight degree of overlap in the second lobe and run on three channels with at least 25 MHz separation; the resulting channel set is 1, 6, and 11. This causes a small amount of interference to each channel, but it is worthwhile to accept a small reduction in throughput per channel to get the third channel.

In some situations, it may make sense to perform a four-channel assignment (1, 4, 8, and 11).[*] The trade-off is that the signal overlap will be more crowded, further reducing peak throughput. Trading peak speed for a higher total area speed may be worthwhile in some circumstances, but I have generally found this to be a poor trade-off.

Table 23-3. Radio channel usage in different regulatory domains

Channel number	Channel frequency (GHz)	US/Canada[a]	ETSI[b]
1	2.412	✓	✓
2	2.417	✓	✓
3	2.422	✓	✓
4	2.427	✓	✓
5	2.432	✓	✓
6	2.437	✓	✓
7	2.442	✓	✓
8	2.447	✓	✓
9	2.452	✓	✓
10[c]	2.457	✓	✓
11	2.462	✓	✓
12	2.467		✓
13	2.472		✓

[a] 802.11 allows different rules regarding the use of radio spectrum in the U.S. and Canada, but the U.S. Federal Communications Commission and Industry Canada have adopted identical rules.

[b] Not all of Europe has adopted the recommendations of the European Telecommunications Standards Institute (ETSI). Spain, which does not appear in the table, allows the use of only channels 10 and 11.

[c] Channel 10 is allowed by all regulatory authorities and is the default channel for most access points when they are initially powered on.

[*] European regulations allow the use of wider-spacing, such as 1, 5, 9, and 13 in a four-channel layout.

Part of the site survey is to lay out coverage areas in a way that minimizes channel overlap. Antennas can be a valuable tool in doing this because they can tailor the coverage area to fit the shape of the building or room. No matter what type of antennas you select, there is a general pattern that can be used. The cellular-telephone industry uses a hex pattern as the background for a channel layout. Figure 23-4 shows the problems in planning out a large coverage area. The center channel, in bold, is set for one of the three nonoverlapping channels. In this case, I chose channel 1 arbitrarily. To avoid overlap, the next set of channels around the center needs to alternate between the two remaining nonoverlapping channels in a circle around the channel. After assigning channels to the ring, successive center channels can be laid out. Two such focal points are shown in Figure 23-4 with circles.

Naturally, Figure 23-4 presents a channel layout under ideal circumstances. Within a building, radio propagation is subject to obstacles, and it is usually impossible to avoid overlapping channels. For example, the first "ring" of channels 6 and 11 around the outside of the center channel 1 may very well interfere with each other, especially if the hexagons represent target operational rates that are much larger than the minimum.

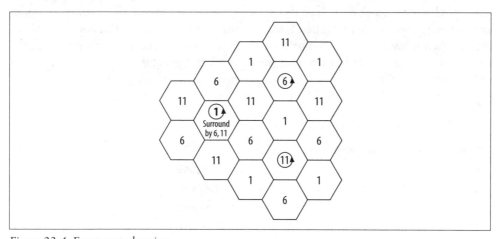

Figure 23-4. Frequency planning

Limitations of the 2.4 GHz channel layout

The inability to perform a channel layout with three channels is not surprising. In mathematics, the general result is known as the *Four-Color Map Theorem*. Map makers discovered in the mid-19th century that an arbitrary two-dimensional map can be filled in with four colors.* Unfortunately, 802.11b/g networks have only three non-

---

* The Four-Color Theorem was finally proved in 1976 with the aid of 1,200 hours of time on a Cray, and was one of the first theorems to be proved with extensive computer assistance.

overlapping channels. Maps where adjacent regions share a color are unsightly. Adjacent AP coverage areas sharing the same channel are not unsightly, unless you can see into the microwave spectrum, but they do suffer from throughput-sapping co-channel interference.

It is often possible to minimize channel overlap by careful AP placement or the use of external antennas, but you will have to devote time and energy to minimizing channel overlap. In three dimensions, it gets even harder. Radio signals may bleed through the floor or the ceiling, requiring you to lay out channels in three dimensions.

Even in large, open, two-dimensional spaces where you would not expect an interference problem, there can be one. In 2002, the Associated Press ran a story about the problems of intereference, and cited a neighborhood in Florida that had formed its own ad-hoc frequency allocation committee to ensure that neighbors were using nonadjacent channels for their home networks!

5 GHz (802.11a) Channel Layout

802.11a has two major advantages when laying out your network. First, there are at least 12 channels, so channel layout is a snap. Table 23-4 shows the channel frequencies. Be aware that some of the first 802.11a cards to hit the market did not support the highest frequency band, so channels 149 and up may not be usable with all cards. Either replace the old cards, or restrict the network to the eight remaining channels. In either case, with 8 or 12 channels, there are more than enough channels for 2-dimensional layouts, and 3-dimensional layouts can be taken care of in most cases.

Table 23-4. a channels (with United States regulatory notes)

Channel number	Frequency (GHz)	Notes
36	5.180	Lowest maximum power
40	5.200	Lowest maximum power
44	5.220	Lowest maximum power
48	5.240	Lowest maximum power
52	5.260	Slightly higher maximum power
56	5.280	Slightly higher maximum power
60	5.300	Slightly higher maximum power
64	5.320	Slightly higher maximum power
149	5.745	Not supported by all cards
153	5.765	Not supported by all cards
157	5.785	Not supported by all cards
161	5.805	Not supported by all cards

Mixed Channel Layouts (802.11a+b/g Networks)

Most networks are being built with a combination of 802.11b/g radios for compatibility with past hardware, while building in 802.11a for future capacity. Dual-radio APs from many vendors are only marginally more expensive than single-radio models. In many cases, the cost of a tri-mode/dual-band network is only a few hundred or thousand dollars more than the cost of an 802.11g-only network. Unless your budget is extremely tight, it is worth paying for more than double the capacity.

For the foreseeable future, most 802.11 devices are likely to operate in the 2.4 GHz band. Most chipset vendors have concentrated on building 802.11g devices. There are several tri-mode chipsets capable of supporting 802.11a and 802.11b/g simultaneously, but they are not yet widely purchased as a built-in laptop option. When I worked on the Supercomputing wireless network, we had 1,300 users at the peak, and only about 100 were using 802.11a. As the price of chipsets and cards continues to drop, and 802.11a becomes more widely appreciated, I expect the balance to shift drastically towards 802.11a for indoor usage. In outdoor environments, transmission range remains the prime concern. Lower frequencies travel much farther, which will enable 802.11b/g to retain its current dominant position.

Planning Access-Point Placement

At this point, most users perceive that wired networks just work. In terms of product maturity and predictability, wireless networks are a step backwards. Protocols still behave somewhat unpredictably, and the relatively young protocols will require you to roll up your sleeves. When planning a network, you need to put in a great deal of work up front. Because wireless networks make user-location transparent to resources, the network itself must be aware of user location.

Once you have an understanding of the requirements and which 802.11 physical layers to use, it is time to figure out where to put the access points themselves. Depending on requirements and budget, figuring out placement may be a quick and dirty project that takes a few hours, or it may involve several visits and a great deal of time and money. This process is often called a site survey because some of the work takes place at the location where the network is being installed, but a new wave of tools is making it possible to do much of the access point placement work with computational models.

Several options exist for determining where to put APs. Vendors may provide site surveys to early adopters who agree to be reference accounts, although the time to be an early adopter of wireless faded long before this book hit the press. Value-added resellers may also have the skills to perform detailed site surveys; resellers may sell site survey consulting services or use site surveys as a way of coming up with a wireless LAN deployment bid. Some companies that specialize in technical education also offer classes on performing site surveys.

The Building

One of the major constraints on where access points are placed is how the building is constructed. Walls, doors, and windows get in the way of radio signals. It is a great help to get blueprints or floor plans and take a tour of the installation site as early as possible. Occasionally, you may get the opportunity to work on a building as it is being constructed. Seize any opportunity for a walkthrough because you will get a much better view of the interior structure before the walls are up. The main drawback to working with a building under construction is that experiments are not possible until the building is finished.

Once you obtain the floor plans, note where coverage must be provided. If the architectural plans are complete and include wiring information, they should also note the location of nearby power and electrical drops. You may also be able to make a preliminary identification of structures that may be problematic, such as ventilation ducts or reinforced concrete walls.

Whether or not you are using an electronic tool to automate the planning process, you should take a walk through the facility. Look for any changes that are not reflected on the blueprints. Verify the type of construction. Unless the building is old and historic, the walls are likely to be made of sheetrock hung from studs, although you can verify this by tapping on the walls. Ask whether there are any firewalls (of the physical sort, not the network sort), since a firewall is likely to be a significant barrier to RF. Structural, or load-bearing, walls are also likely to have reinforcements that pose a significant obstacle to radio waves. If you must conceal APs in certain areas, investigate these areas thoroughly to determine how to hide them, as well as any potential impact to network operations. High ceilings or other difficult mounting should also be investigated. During the walk-through, you are likely to receive a number of strange looks; just keep moving. Thorough walk-throughs will result in a large number of strange looks. Consider it a measure of the quality of the walk-through.

Based on the first walk-through, note any relevant environmental factors. Most importantly, you can correct the blueprints based on any changes made to the structure since the blueprints were drawn. Many minor changes will not be reflected on the blueprints, especially if the building is old. Also note any potential sources of interference. The 2.4-GHz ISM band is unlicensed, so many types of devices using the band can be deployed without central coordination. Newer cordless phones operate in the 2.4 GHz band, as well as Bluetooth-based devices and a number of other unlicensed radio devices. If you anticipate a large amount of interference, testing tools called *spectrum analyzers* can identify the amount of radiation in the wireless LAN frequency band. In practice, spectrum analyzers will not be necessary much of the time unless there is a particularly stubborn source of interference. One handheld analyzer, the Berkeley Varitronics YellowJacket, has a built-in spectrum analyzer for the 2.4 GHz ISM band, and can be useful in tracking down non-802.11 interference.

If your organization does RF testing, it may be necessary to shield any labs where testing is done to avoid interference with the wireless LAN. As a rule of thumb, keep access points at least 25 feet away from any strong interference sources.

Constraints on AP placement

Practically speaking, keeping the APs as high as possible means mounting them around the ceiling level. In many office buildings, the ceiling is a "dropped" or suspended ceiling. APs may be attached to the ceiling mounting bars, or possibly placed above the ceiling tiles. In a pinch, it is possible to mount APs at the top of cubicles. Check with your manufacturer to see what the radiation pattern looks like. If an AP is designed to send radio waves down from the ceiling, it may not work as well when mounted on top of cubicle partitions.

It is relatively common to make adjustments to the AP locations based on physical constraints. One of the primary restrictions is that APs typically connect to the network through an Ethernet cable.* Each AP must be within a 100-meter cable length from the nearest wiring closet. With some flexibility in the specifications, it is occasionally possible to run cables slightly longer than the official limit, although it is never a good idea to rely on it. Depending on the exact configuration of patch panels, risers, and the cabling in the ceiling, the cable run to an AP location may be much larger than it appears.

Electrical power is often a constraint on the AP locations as well. Early APs required standard electrical outlets, but very few organizations had electrical outlets in the ceiling. Installing electrical power is generally quite expensive. With the development of 802.3af, most organizations are powering up their access points over the network cable. Power over Ethernet (PoE) has many advantages; however, the engineering difficulty of pushing 48 volts through 100 meters diminishes your ability to cheat on the cable length.

It is a worth considering installing new wire to support a wireless network, especially if the existing network jacks will not easily support the new APs. When existing wiring is used, it is often run near the baseboards or otherwise less than ideal for use with high-mounted network devices. Running new cable has several advantages. It can be run directly to the area above the ceiling where the APs will be mounted, which removes the need for ugly cable runs up network poles. Older cable systems may have been installed before Category 5 wiring was standard, or modifications may have degraded its capabilites. New cable installations also add a degree of flexibility. In recognition of the need to move APs, some new cable installations will terminate the cable run above the ceiling with a network jack, allowing the use of patch cables to move an AP within short distances.

---

* A few products can use a secondary radio as a "mesh" backhaul, and I expect this option to be more common as time passes.

Depending on the layout of the components above the ceiling, it may be hard to run cabling near ventilation ducts, or hard to mount an AP near a duct. Usually, a relocation of the AP to the next tile over is sufficient and does not radically disturb the coverage of the AP. Likewise, keeping APs away from light fixtures, as well as the electrical conduits to those fixtures, is also important.

A final consideration relates to physical security. Some organizations may feel the need to secure APs against theft. Sometimes, mounting APs above the ceiling may be a sufficient theft-prevention measure because the AP is hidden from view. Many APs now include security slots for physical attachment to an less movable object.[*]

Buildings in progress

With the increasing use of wireless LANs, many are being designed during building construction. Working with a building under construction is both a great deal of fun and a sanity-defying challenge.

One of the first problems is a dependence on the other schedules for the building. Fortunately, it is possible to get an idea of the number of APs necessary by using an modeling tool. Architectural drawings are complete, and generally readily available to the network team even before ground is broken. Start by estimating the various types of material and developing a model.

Walk through each area of the building as it takes shape. Depending on the schedule, it may take shape in several stages or all at once. Gaining access for a walkthrough during construction often requires the permission of the contractor, a hard hat, and a liability waver. In each area of the building, try to determine if the guesses made during the modeling stage were correct. Was the radio loss factor assigned to the walls accurate, or does the model need refining? As areas are finished, it makes sense to spot-check predictions from the modeling tool with a physical test using an AP in its final location.

One of the biggest challenges in working on a building under construction is that the environment is constantly changing. In rare circumstances, the building materials may change due to supply shortages or even last-minute changes driven by aesthetic considerations. Keep the design flexible, and build in a margin for error.

The Preliminary Plan

Determining the number of APs and developing a set of preliminary locations is the first planning milestone. A few years ago, the best way to come up with preliminary locations was to estimate the number of very expensive APs, and place them in open

---

[*] See *http://www.kensington.com/html/1356.html* for more information on the Kensington Security Slot, which is commonly used for this purpose.

areas that were centrally located. Now that APs are much cheaper, there is no longer major pressure to reduce the AP count as far as possible.

To get a very rough ballpark estimate of the number of APs needed, I use two rules of thumb. The first is area-based. At maximum power in a typical open office environment, an AP can provide service to an area of 3,000 to 5,000 square feet (275 to 450 square meters). Simply take the area to be covered, and divide by the AP footprint. Use the higher number if there are lots of open areas and relatively few obstructions; use the lower number if there is a preponderance of closed-wall offices with doors, or significant interior structure to the building. In addition to the area-based number, calculate a user density–based number. Divide the number of users in the organization by 20 to 50. Use a number at the low end if wireless networks are prevalent and widely used, and a number at the high end if wireless networks are new and experimental. By taking the larger of the two numbers, I have a very rough estimate for the number of APs required for an installation.

Knowing roughly how many APs are needed does not provide any information on where they should go. Turning the extremely rough estimate into a preliminary plan requires a bit more work. With enough experience, the AP locations are fairly straightforward. Structural walls or fire-containment walls tend to block a signal, often completely. The central core of a multifloor building is usually the main load-bearing structure, and is often made of reinforced concrete. With attenuation of 10 dB to 20 dB per foot, it is best to consider it an RF shield. Most APs are still usable at greater than the minimum speed after the signal has passed through two to three average-sized offices, depending on the amount of straight-line propagation. Generally speaking, locate APs in open areas with as few obstructions as possible. It always helps to keep them accessible for any needed service, which generally means that areas above cubicles and hallways are preferred.

Developing the preliminary plan has, up to this point, been largely a manual process that requires high skill and extensive experience. In the past few years, modeling tools have emerged that can automate the preliminary planning stage. These tools take an architectural drawing of the building and create a mathematical model of radio propagation. When the network designer changes the location of an AP in the model, the tool recalculates its coverage immediately. Electronic tools can be a valuable asset to reduce the physical validation by deriving a reasonable starting set of AP locations. They are especially valuable when the building does not yet exist because it is still under construction. Depending on the tool, you may be able to use the architectural drawing itself, which will typically be a Computer-Aided Design (CAD) file; some tools will only accept simple graphics files like GIFs or JPEGs. Obtain the physical layout. In most organizations, the facilities department has architectural drawings, or can work with the landlord or building owner to obtain them. In new construction projects, an architect can usually supply them.

As helpful as modeling tools are, it is important not to use them in a vacuum. Radio propagation is very complicated, especially indoors at microwave frequencies. Radio waves may reflect in strange ways off different types of materials, and a few inches here or there can make all the difference in the world to the resulting coverage. Modeling tools also depend on accurate knowledge of the construction of a building, which is not always available to the network staff. Modeling tools are no substitute for actual experimentation.

No matter what technique you employ, use the physical plans to derive a preliminary plan. Detailed radio channel use planning is not yet necessary. If you are using a modeling tool, have it suggest a radio plan, but expect to make some changes after installation. The preliminary plan is, well, preliminary. Expect it to change. The purpose of this stage is not to get everything right, but to get a starting point to work from. Table 23-5 is based on the best-case coverage radius from a typical omnidirectional antenna. If you want to incorporate higher than the minimum data rate, you will probably need smaller radii; the best approach is to use one of the electronic tools discussed briefly in this section.

Table 23-5. "Rule-of-thumb" coverage radius for different types of space

Type of space	Maximum coverage radius (2.4 GHz)	Maximum coverage radius (5 GHz)
Closed office	Up to 50–60 feet	35–40 feet
Open office (cubicles)	Up to 90 feet	60 feet
Hallways and other large rooms	Up to 150 feet	75 feet
Outdoors (without antenna engineering)	Up to 300 feet	Don't even bother!
Outdoors (with custom antennas)	Many miles	Don't even bother!

The preliminary report

The preliminary plan can be used as the basis for further activity. It may be used to provide an estimate for the cost of deploying the wireless LAN in the given area. It may also be used to hire a cabling contractor to perform the physical wiring. The plan itself may include:

1. A brief summary of requirements.

2. Estimated coverage areas based on the site survey measurements. This may be divided into areas with good coverage, marginal coverage, and weak coverage. Reports based on mathematical models may note projected contours for different operational rates.

3. A description of the locations of all access points, along with their configuration. Software tools for automated layout may be able to provide detailed location and configuration information based on the floor maps, such as:

    a. The AP's operating channel.

    b. Approximate coverage area, possibly shown as coverage contours at different speeds.

c. IP configuration, if required. "Lightweight" APs may not have an IP address.

d. Antenna type and configuration, including direction for directional antennas.

e. Any other vendor-specific information that may be useful. Some organizations track devices based on MAC address, so it would be useful to include that in the report.

Radio Resource Management and Channel Layout

Figure 23-4 makes the channel layout appear deceptively simple. When building a network indoors, signal propagation is much more complex. Channel overlap is far more likely indoors because of the need to have higher power directed towards obstacles, which may result in higher than desired power in other directions.

Preliminary plans should include a basic channel map. It is almost certain that adjustments will need to be made to the channel layout. Tuning may be done manually by searching out overlapping channels with handheld tools, or automatically by access points that attempt to find the least busy channel. With only three channels in the 2.4 GHz band, changes may "ripple" through a network and take some time to converge on a final solution.

Refining and Testing the Plan

Depending on the need for accuracy, as well as budgetary constraints, the process of refining the plan may vary a great deal. In small or budget-conscious installations, it may suffice to start with the preliminary plan, turn it on, and see what develops. More methodical deployments may install all or part of the preliminary plan and perform extensive tests to verify it meets requirements. If the preliminary plan is accurate, there may not be much modification required. The major goal of the testing is to discover any unforeseen interference or bad spots and redesign the network accordingly. In most cases, interference problems can usually be repaired by relocating an access point. Adjustments to AP locations are typically not large. Failing that, a different antenna or another AP is usually the answer. In rare cases, multiple design and test phases may be used, although it is quite unusual.

When checking the plan, duplicate the user experience as much as possible. Obstacles between wireless LAN users and access points decrease radio strength, so make an effort to replicate exactly the installation during the site survey. Antennas should be installed for the test exactly as they would be installed on a completed network. If office dwellers are part of the user base, make sure that adequate coverage is obtained in offices when the door is closed. Even more important, close any metal blinds, because metal is the most effective radio screen.

Signal measurements should be identical to the expected use of the network users, with one exception. Most site survey tools attempt to determine the signal quality at a single spatial point throughout a sequence of several points in time, and thus it is important to keep the laptop in one location as the measurement is carried out. Taking large numbers of measurements is important because users will move with untethered laptops, and also because the multipath fading effects may lead to pronounced signal quality differences even between nearby locations.

Extremely thorough organizations may want to test with multiple client devices. Wireless LAN behavior can vary a great deal depending on implementation, and client behavior often varies even with the exact same software. If you need detailed knowledge of how the system will behave, it may be worthwhile to gather several systems with identical software configurations and run them through the same tests at the same time.

The final test report should result in detailed knowledge of the actual coverage of the APs in their final locations. Coverage may be reported as an area, although it is often more useful to report on the area over which a certain transmission rate is reliably obtained. In some cases, it may also be useful to report on performance characteristics, especially if application mix is well-enough known to be characterized.

If the building is under construction, validation may proceed in stages as the building is completed. If the entire building is constructed at the same time, you may want to take basic measurements early in the process to determine if major changes to the radio model are required, with more time-consuming and accurate validation tests at the end.

Validation and test tools

In the past, getting an idea of the coverage of an AP and coming up with an AP layout was time-consuming because it required repeated measurements of signal quality as an AP was placed in a trial location. With the development of automatic layout tools, whether based on modeling or self-tuning capabilities, the validation phase may not require the same extensive set of tools. In-depth analysis of the radio link performance is generally only required when trouble with a test system is discovered.

The most common signal quality measurements are the packet (or, more properly, frame) error rate (PER) and received signal strength (RSSI). Frame error rates need to be kept as low as possible. In the past, an 8% target generally guaranteed acceptable performance. More densely deployed networks should easily be able to achieve 5% or lower. Sophisticated infrastructure devices can often measure the per-client frame error rate directly, as well as the RSSI and signal-to-noise ratio. The RSSI and signal-to-noise ratio are important for achieving higher data rates. To transmit an intelligible frame at a given data rate, there is a given signal-to-noise threshold.

A few tools report multipath time dispersion, which measures the degree to which a signal is spread out in time by path differences. Higher delay spreads make the correlation of the signals more difficult. With a high delay spread, devices need to accept either a higher error rate or fall back to a more conservative coding method. Either way, throughput goes down. The higher the delay spread, the more throughput suffers. Measuring multipath dispersion is generally not important, although it is valuable to have a tool that gathers the data for persistent multipath problems.

When 802.11b was the wireless network of choice, a large number of handheld tools were developed for portable computing platforms such as the Compaq iPAQ. With the increasing adoption of 802.11a and 802.11g, though, handheld devices are falling out of favor and being replaced by Tablet PCs. Most handheld devices have relatively slow external interfaces that are unable to cope with the higher data rates from newer standards. The iPAQ, for example, has an interface for 16-bit PC Cards that run at 8 MHz. While such slow speeds are sufficient for an 11 Mbps 802.11b interface, the higher speed of 802.11a and 802.11g imposes a practical requirement for CardBus. Tablet PCs have a second advantage in the validation phase as well. Many of the planning tools that you might use to develop a preliminary plan include the ability to run a validation client that collects physical measurements and can tie the validation measurements back to the predictions calculated earlier.

Particularly stubborn interference may require the use of a *spectrum analyzer* to locate the source of interference from a non-802.11 network. Devices that can scan a wide frequency band to locate transmissions are not cheap. Expect to pay several thousand dollars, or you can hire a consultant and rent one. As an alternative, it may be possible to use an ISM band-only spectrum analyzer to track interference to its source. In any case, a spectrum analyzer is the tool of last resort, necessary for only the most stubborn problems.

RF fingerprint collection

Some wireless LAN systems require the collection of RF "fingerprints," as discussed in the previous chapter. Fingerprint collection can only proceed once the APs are in their final locations. At that point, test devices can be positioned in common locations so the system can collect the result fingerprints.

Preparing the Final Report

During the planning and testing cycle, you should have prepared preliminary documents that show AP installation locations. When the final test has completed, the network should be documented. If the preliminary plans are in electronic form, modify them to reflect the results of testing, and incorporate the changes into a final report.

In addition to access-point placement, many customers appreciate an estimate of the work necessary to install drivers onto any affected laptops. The scope of this item depends a great deal on the sophistication of the customer's management tools. For many, it will be sufficient to include a copy of the driver installation instructions as an appendix to the report. Some clients may require low-level details on the driver installation so that the driver installation can be completely automated down to any necessary registry changes on Windows systems.

Using Antennas to Tailor Coverage

It may be necessary to provide coverage for a unique area that doesn't "play by the rules" you expect it to follow. Most access points use omnidirectional antennas, which radiate equally in every direction. However, it may be desirable to change the basic radio coverage pattern from a circle to something else for some applications. This is work that is often done in the field to adjust coverage from an AP to match a particular area, or to boost the signal to fill in a hole. With the cost of APs declining rapidly, custom tailoring coverage with antennas is not as necessary as it previously was, although it is still important.

In the past, radio equipment vendors needed to supply antennas and ensure that the capabilities of the combined system would meet the unlicensed spectrum transmission rules. In July 2004, the FCC relaxed the rules to allow a radio device manufacturer to specify a maximum gain and allow the user to select any antenna with the same gain characteristics.[*] Before the ruling, radios and antennas had to be certified as a single unit, and it was technically illegal to attach an antenna from a source other than the radio vendor. With the new rules, manufacturers can certify a system at the limits of the radio rules, and end users can choose any antenna within that outer boundary. If, for example, the radio manufacturer underwent certification testing with a 10 dBi antenna, a buyer is allowed to find a lower gain version of the same type of antenna (say, only 8 dBi), and use it legally.

Antenna Types

Wireless cards all have built-in antennas, but these antennas are, at best, minimally adequate. If you were planning to cover an office—or an even larger area, such as a campus—you will almost certainly want to use external antennas for your access points. When considering specialized antennas, there are only a few specifications that you need to pay attention to:

Antenna type
> The antenna type determines its radiation pattern—is it omnidirectional, bidirectional, or unidirectional? Omnidirectional antennas are good for covering large areas; bidirectional antennas are particularly good at covering corridors; unidirectional antennas are best at setting up point-to-point links between buildings, or even different sites.

Gain
> The gain of the antenna is the extent to which it enhances the signal in its preferred direction. Antenna gain is measured in dBi, which stands for decibels

---

[*] See document 04-165 at *http://hraunfoss.fcc.gov/edocs_public/attachmatch/FCC-04-165A1.pdf*, which modifies the relevant telecommunications rules.

relative to an isotropic radiator. An isotropic radiator is a theoretical beast that radiates equally in all directions. To put some stakes in the ground: I've never seen a specification for the gain of the built-in antenna on a wireless card, but I would guess that it's negative (i.e., worse than an isotropic radiator). Simple external antennas typically have gains of 3 to 7 dBi. Directional antennas can have gains as high as 24 dBi.*

Half-power beam width

This is the width of the antenna's radiation pattern, measured in terms of the points at which the antenna's radiation drops to half of its peak value. Understanding the half-power beam width is important to understanding your antenna's effective coverage area. For a very high-gain antenna, the half-power beam width may be a narrow angle. Once you get outside the half-power beam width, the signal typically drops off fairly quickly, although that depends on the antenna's design. Don't be fooled into thinking that the half-power beam width is irrelevant for an omnidirectional antenna. A typical omnidirectional (vertical) antenna is only omnidirectional in the horizontal plane. As you go above or below the plane on which the antenna is mounted, the signal decreases.

We've discussed antennas entirely in terms of their properties for transmitting, largely because most people find that easier to understand. Fortunately, an antenna's receiving properties are identical to its transmitting properties—an antenna enhances a received signal to the same extent that it enhances the transmitted signal. This result is probably what you would expect, but proving it is beyond the scope of this book. Now, let's talk about some of the antenna types that are available (Figure 23-5 shows a number of different antenna types):

Vertical

This is a garden-variety omnidirectional antenna. Most vendors sell several different types of vertical antenna, differing primarily in their gain; you might see a vertical antenna with a published gain as high as 10 dBi or as low as 3 dBi. How does an omnidirectional antenna generate gain? Remember that a vertical antenna is omnidirectional only in the horizontal plane. In three dimensions, its radiation pattern looks something like a donut. A higher gain means that the donut is squashed. It also means that the antenna is larger and more expensive, although no antennas for 802.11 service are particularly large.

If you want to cover a confined outdoor area—for example, a courtyard between several buildings of a corporate campus—note that the half-power beam width means that a roof-mounted vertical antenna might be less than ideal, particularly if the building is tall. Vertical antennas are good at radiating out horizontally; they're not good at radiating down. In a situation like this, you would be better off mounting the antenna outside a first- or second-story window.

---

* If you want one more stake, the radio telescope at Arecibo has a gain in excess of 80 dBi.

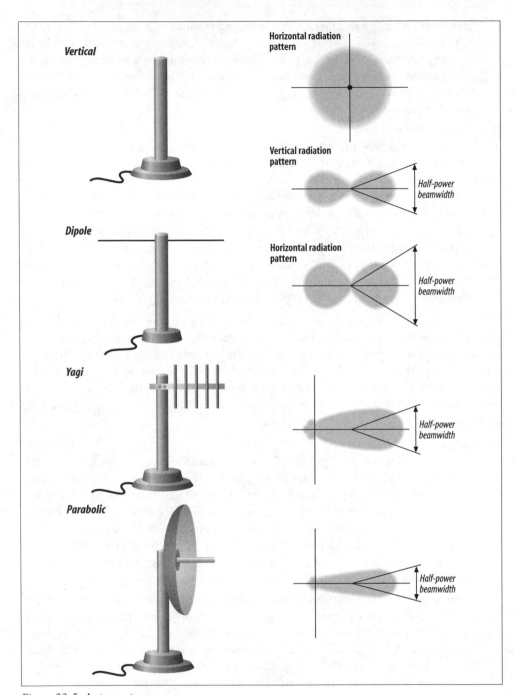

Figure 23-5. Antenna types

Dipole

A dipole antenna has a figure-eight radiation pattern, which means it's ideal for covering a hallway or some other long, thin area. Physically, it won't look much different from a vertical—in fact, some vertical antennas are simply vertically mounted dipoles.

Yagi

A Yagi antenna is a moderately high-gain unidirectional antenna. It looks somewhat like a classic TV antenna. There are a number of parallel metal elements at right angles to a boom. However, you are not likely to see the elements on a Yagi for 802.11 service; the commercially made Yagis that I have seen are all enclosed in a *radome*, which is a plastic shell that protects the antenna from the elements in outdoor deployments. Yagi antennas for 802.11 service have gains between 12 and 18 dBi; aiming them is not as difficult as aiming a parabolic antenna, although it can be tricky.

Parabolic

This is a very high-gain antenna. Because parabolic antennas have very high gains (up to 24 dBi for commercially made 802.11 antennas), they also have very narrow beam widths. You would probably use a parabolic antenna only for a link between buildings; because of the narrow beam width, they are not very useful for providing services to end users. Vendors publish ranges of up to 20 miles for their parabolic antennas. Presumably, both ends of the link are using a similar antenna. Do not underestimate the difficulty of aiming a parabolic antenna properly—one commercial product has a published beam width of only 6.5 degrees. If you decide to install a parabolic antenna, make sure that you have it mounted firmly. You do not want a bad storm to nudge it a bit and take down your connection.

Some vendors make an issue of the distinction between "mesh" or "grid" parabolas (in which the antenna's reflector looks like a bent barbecue grill) and solid parabolas. Don't sweat it—if the antenna is well-designed, the difference in performance between a mesh and a solid reflector is not worth worrying about. A mesh does have an advantage, though, in areas subject to high winds.

Parabolic and Yagi antennas are useful primarily for links between buildings. The biggest problem is aiming them properly. If the two sites are visible to each other, you can play some tricks with gunsights—although if you can see one site from the other, you probably don't need such a sophisticated antenna system. Otherwise, buy a good compass and a topographical map from the U.S. Geological Survey, and compute the heading from one site to the other. Remember to correct for magnetic-North. If you can spend some extra money, you might be able to simplify the setup by installing a high-gain vertical antenna at one site; then you need to aim only one antenna. If the signal is marginal, replace the vertical with a parabolic antenna once you have the first antenna aimed correctly.

High-gain antennas can become a regulatory problem, particularly in Europe, because transmission power limits are lower than in the U.S. The high-gain parabolic antenna sold under the Orinoco brand cannot legally be used at the edges of the ISM band in the U.S. (1, 2, 10, and 11 are excluded) because of signal leakages outside the band.

Antenna cabling

Having put so much effort into thinking about antennas, we have to spend some time thinking about how to connect the antennas to the access points or wireless cards. Most vendors sell two kinds of cable: relatively inexpensive thin cable (typically 0.1 inch in diameter) and "low-loss cable" that's substantially thicker (typically 0.4 inch) and much more expensive. The thin cable is usually available only in lengths of a couple of feet, and that is as it should be: it is very lossy, and more than a few feet can easily eat up your entire signal. One site I worked at concealed APs by mounting them above the ceiling and using an unobtrusive external antenna poking through the ceiling tile. However, the mounting scheme turned out to be a wash. The external antennas had a 2 dB gain, and the cable connecting the antennas to the APs had a 2 dB loss.

Thin cable is intended for connecting a wireless card in a laptop to a portable antenna on your desktop, and that is about all it is good for. To put numbers behind this: one vendor specifies a loss of 2.5 dB for a 2-meter cable. That means that close to half of your signal strength is disappearing in just two meters of cable. One cable vendor, for a cable that would typically be used in this application, specifies a loss of 75 dB per 100 feet at 2.4 GHz. That means that your signal strength will drop by a factor of 2^{25} (roughly 33 million), clearly not something you want to contemplate. I know of one vendor that recommends using RG58 cable with medium-gain antennas. RG58 is better than the really thin cable intended for portable use, but not much better (35 dB per 100 feet); if you use RG58 cable, keep the cable run as short as possible. Better yet, ditch the RG58 and see if you can replace it with LMR-200 (a high-quality equivalent with half the loss).

What does the picture look like when you're using a *real* low-loss cable? Significantly better, but maybe not as much better as you would like. A typical cable for this application—used by at least one 802.11 vendor—is Times Microwave LMR-400. LMR-400 is a very high-quality cable, but it still has a loss of 6.8 dB per 100 feet at 2.4 GHz. This means that, in a 100-foot length of cable, over three quarters of your signal is lost. The moral of the story is clear: keep your access points as close as possible to your antennas. Minimize the length of the transmission line. If you want a roof-mounted antenna, perhaps to cover a courtyard where people frequently have lunch, don't stick your access point in a wiring closet in the basement and run a cable to the roof. If possible, put your access point in a weatherproof enclosure on the roof. If that's not possible, at least put the access point in an attic or crawlspace. There is no substitute for keeping the transmission line as short as possible. Also, keep in mind that transmission lines have a strange ability to shrink when they are routed through walls or conduits. I've never understood why, but no matter how carefully you measure, you are certain to find that your cable is two feet short. More to the point: the straight-line distance from your access point to the antenna may be only 20 feet, but don't be surprised if it takes a 50-foot cable to make the trip. The cable will probably have to go around corners and through conduits and all sorts of other misdirections before it arrives at its destination.

Finally, there's the matter of antenna connectors. All wireless vendors sell cables in various length with the proper connectors and adapters. I strongly recommend taking the easy way out and buying cables with the connectors preinstalled. Connector failure is one of the most common causes for outages in radio systems, particularly if you don't have a lot of experience installing RF connectors.

Antenna diversity

One common method of minimizing multipath fading is to have *antenna diversity*. Rather than making the antenna larger, radio systems can use multiple antennas and choose the signal from the antenna with better reception. Using multiple antennas does not require sophisticated mathematical theory or signal-processing techniques.

Several wireless LAN vendors have built multiple antennas into wireless network cards. Some vendors even offer the ability to connect multiple external antennas to network cards intended for access points. Antenna diversity is recommended by the 802.11 standard, but it is not required. For environments with large amounts of interference, antenna diversity is a worthwhile option to consider when selecting vendors.

Amplifiers: bring on the heat

Amplifiers increase the power of a signal. On the transmission side of a radio network, amplifiers help fling the signal farther to cover more area. Many transmission amplifiers also incorporate preamplifiers for the reception side of the circuit as well, which helps increase the receiver's sensitivity to weak signals.

Indoor deployments of 802.11 typically do not not need amplifiers to increase transmission power. As an AP's transmit power increases, its coverage area can encompass more area, and more stations can join the network. To preserve quality coverage, it is best to design a network consisting of many small APs with relatively low transmit power. Even a wireless LAN deployment focused on providing coverage only, regardless of quality, although a large area is probably able to get by with a high-gain vertical antenna.

Generally speaking, high transmit power sounds like a much better idea than it is in practice, with a few obvious exceptions. Community networks may want to provide coverage for a large area before increasing the density of coverage, and APs may be more expensive than the amplification parts. Point-to-point links built on 802.11 are also a good application for amplification. If the distance is sufficiently large, all the antenna gain in the world won't pull the signal off the noise floor. One of the better-documented outdoor point-to-point shots is the uplink for the Ruby Ranch Internet Cooperative (*http://www.rric.net*).* Remote ISPs building their WANs on 802.11 may also make extensive use of amplification.

SSB Electronics (*www. ssbusa.com/wireless.html*) and HyperLink Technologies (*http:// www.hyperlinktech.com/ web/amplifiers_2400.html*) are two vendors of 802.11 amplifiers. However, if you use amplifiers with 802.11, remember:

- Stay within the legal power limit, both for absolute power and ERP.
- 802.11 is an unlicensed service. If you interfere with another service, it is your problem, by definition. And if a licensed service interferes with you, it is your problem, by definition. Interference is more likely to be a problem if your network covers a large service area and if you are using high power.
- Use equipment that is approved for 802.11 service. Other amplifiers are available that cover the frequency range, but using them is illegal.

 The FCC does enforce their rules, and their fines are large. If you are in violation of the regulations, they will not be amused, particularly if you're in excess of the power limit or using unapproved equipment.

---

* The RRIC is a fascinating site in its own right, and I highly recommend it. The incumbent telephone carrier refused to deliver DSL in the neighborhood, so a group of committed volunteers made it happen.

## CHAPTER 24

802.11 Network Analysis

There is no coming to consciousness without pain.
—Attributed to C.G. Jung

In the 1990s, computer professionals joined doctors as People With Answers. Just as doctors are asked medical questions by complete strangers, computer professionals are asked a bewildering variety of technical questions by complete strangers. When these strangers learn that I work with networks, I am often asked, "Why does the Internet break so often?" The more I contemplate the question, the more I believe that the question should be, "Why doesn't the Internet break *more* often?"

While I could never hope to answer either question in a single chapter of a book, it is obvious that network problems are a fact of life. Networks break, and wireless networks are no exception. Wireless LANs can improve productivity, but they also carry a larger risk of complete outage, and the limited bandwidth is almost sure to be overloaded. After building a wireless LAN, network engineers must be ready to investigate any problems that may arise.

As in many other network types, the trusty network analyzer is a key component in the engineer's toolbox. Network analyzers already exist for the wired backbone side of the wireless network and can be used productively in many troubleshooting scenarios. Wireless network troubleshooting depends on having a network analyzer for exactly the same reason. Sometimes, you just need to have a way of seeing what is on the airwaves. This chapter is devoted to tools that allow network engineers to do just that. Several commercial analyzers are available, and there are free tools that run on Linux. Before diving into the tools, though, it may help to consider why wireless network analyzers are a practical requirement for the network administrator.

Network Analyzers

In spite of the shared heritage, 802.11 is not Ethernet. It has a number of additional protocol features, each of which can cause problems. Fixing problems on 802.11 networks sometimes requires that a network administrator get down to the low-level protocol details and see what is happening over the airwaves. Network analyzers have long been viewed as a useful component of the network administrator's toolkit on wired networks for their ability to report on the low-level details. Analyzers on wireless networks will be just as useful, and possibly even more important. More things can go wrong on an 802.11 network, so a good analyzer is a vital tool for quickly focusing troubleshooting on the likely culprit.

Avoiding problems begins at the planning stages. Some analyzers can report detailed statistics on RF signal strength, which can help place access points. Analyzers can help network administrators avoid creating dead zones by ensuring that there is enough overlap at the edges of BSSs to allow for timely transitions. As wireless networks grow in popularity, they may need to support more users. To avoid performance problems, administrators may consider shrinking the size of access point coverage areas to get more aggregate throughput in a given area. In the process of shrinking the coverage areas, network administrators may go through large parts of the deployment plan all over again and depend once again on their analyzer.

With the limited bit rates of wireless networks, performance is likely to be a problem sooner or later. Performance problems can be caused by cramming too many users into too few access points, or they can be related to problems happening at the radio layer. The designers of 802.11 were aware of the problems that could be caused by the radio transmission medium. Frame transmissions succeed reliably. Most implementations will also retransmit frames with simpler (and slower) encoding methods and fragment frames in the presence of persistent interference.

Interference can be a problem for 802.11 network performance. In addition to the direct effect of trashing transmitted frames that then require retransmission, interference has two indirect effects. Poor transmission quality may cause a station to step down to a lower bit rate in search of more reliable radio link quality. Even if slower transmissions usually succeed, some measure of throughput is lost at the lower bit rates. 802.11 stations may also attempt to fragment pending frames to work around interference, which reduces the percentage of transmissions that carry end-user data. 802.11 headers are quite large compared to other LAN protocols, and fragmentation increases the amount of header information transmitted for a fixed amount of data.

On many networks, however, only a few applications are used. Do performance complaints indicate a general network problem, or a problem with a specific application? Network analyzers can help you find the cause of the problem by examining the distribution of packet sizes. More small packets may indicate excessive use of fragmentation in the face of interference. Some analyzers can also report on the distribution of frames' transmission rates on a wireless network. 802.11b networks are capable of transmitting at 11 Mbps, but frames may be transmitted at slower rates (5. 5 Mbps, 2 Mbps, or even 1 Mbps) if interference is a problem. Stations capable of high-rate operation but nonetheless transmitting at lower rates may be subject to a large amount of interference. Performance depends on radio capacity. Stations that have stepped down to lower rates may not require a great deal of throughput for data service, but the slower rates require a great deal of time on the radio medium. Some analyzers can report the radio utilization as distinct from throughput, which is valuable in tracking down certain types of performance problems.

To solve interference problems, you can attempt to reorient the access point or its antenna, or place a new access point in a zone with poor coverage. Rather than waiting for users to report on their experience with the changes in place, you can use an analyzer to get a quick idea of whether the changes will help alleviate the problem. Some analyzers can provide extensive reports on the RF signal quality of received frames, which can help you place hardware better the first time around. Avoiding repeated experimentation directly with end users makes you look better and makes users happier. Shortening troubleshooting cycles has always been a strength of network analyzers.

Analyzers also help network administrators check on the operation of unique features of the 802.11 MAC. While it is possible to capture traffic once it has been bridged on to a wireless backbone network and analyze it there, the problem could always be on the wireless link. Are frames being acknowledged? If they are not, there will be retransmissions. Are the distribution system bits set correctly? If they are not, then address fields will be misinterpreted. If a malformed packet is seen on the wired side of an access point, it could be mangled at several points. A wireless analyzer can look at frames as they travel through the air to help you pin down the source of the mangled packet. Malformed frames may be transmitted by the client or mangled by the access point, and it is helpful to pin down the problem before requesting assistance from the vendor.

802.11 Network Analyzers

802.11 network analyzers are now quite common and should be a part of any wireless LAN administrator's toolbox. Most 802.11 network analyzers are software packages that use an 802.11 network card. No special hardware is required because 802.11 network cards supply all the RF hardware needed to grab packets.

A network analyzer should be part of the deployment budget for any wireless network. The choice to buy or build is up to you, although I anticipate that most institutions will rely primarily on commercial products and leave development and bug fixes to the network analyzer vendors, especially because commercial analyzers can be purchased, installed, and made useful much more quickly.

AirMagnet (*http://www.airmagnet.com*) and AiroPeek from WildPackets (*http://www. wildpackets.com*) are the two best-known commercial wireless analyzers. I have used both extensively in the Interop Labs when troubleshooting various wireless problems.

Ethereal

Ethereal is the standard open source network analyzer. Like the commercial analyzers, it supports a long list of protocols and can capture live data from a variety of network interfaces. Unlike the proprietary analyzers, Ethereal comes complete with a slogan ("Sniffing the glue that holds the Internet together").

Ethereal runs on most Unix platforms as well as Windows. Source code is freely available for both, but modifications are easier to make on Unix because of the availability of compilers in the Unix programming environment. Like many open source projects, Ethereal is distributed under the terms of the GNU Public License. Protocol decodes are included for many common networking protocols. For the purpose of this section, the important protocols are IEEE 802.11 and LLC, both of which are used on every 802.11 frame. Of course, the TCP/IP suite is included as well.

As 802.11 has become more popular and better supported on Linux, the choice of analysis hardware has opened up. Initially, only Prism-based cards were supported. However, most common interface cards are now supported out of the box. This section was written about Ethereal version 0.10.9, which was released in late January 2005.

Packet Capture on Windows

Ethereal depends on *pcap*, the packet capture library. WinPcap, a port of pcap to Windows, can be used with Ethereal on Windows. Although nearly every Ethernet interface is supported on Windows, wireless cards present different programming interfaces. Many cards cannot capture any frames when using promiscuous mode. By disabling promiscuous mode, many cards are able to capture frames to and from the station only. Wireless packet capture is much more card-dependent on Windows than Linux, so I tend to use Linux instead of Windows.

Compilation and Installation

Building Ethereal for wireless network analysis is much easier than it used to be. Many of the patches formerly required for wireless analysis have been integrated into the main source tree, so wireless analysis works "out of the box."

Ethereal depends on both libpcap, the packet capture library, and the GTK+ display library. Packet capture also requires kernel support to grab packets, in the form of Packet Socket (*CONFIG_PACKET*) support.

Ethereal itself is compiled using the standard open-source routine of downloading the source code from *http://www.ethereal.com*, running *./configure*, *make*, and *make install*.

Setting the Wireless Interface for Monitor Mode

To capture packets, the wireless interface must be put into monitoring mode, which is the equivalent of running an Ethernet interface in promiscuous mode. Each wireless driver has its own method of activating monitor mode.

Cisco Aironet cards

Cisco Aironet cards have two flavors of monitoring mode. In the first mode, called *rfmon*, the driver will pass up any frames in the station's current network. In the second mode, denoted with a simple *y*, the driver will capture any frames on the current channel. Both modes are selected by modifying the driver's running configuration through the proc file system:

```
bloodhound:~# echo "Mode: rfmon" >/proc/driver/aironet/ethX/Config
bloodhound:~# echo "Mode: y" >/proc/driver/aironet/ethX/Config
```

To return to a normal station setting, change the mode back to *ess*:

```
bloodhound:~# echo "Mode: ess" >/proc/driver/aironet/ethX/Config
```

Ethereal requires a network interface name to capture packets. In kernel versions up to 2.4.19, use the Ethernet name of the interface (ethX). In 2.4.20 and later, use wifiX.

Prism cards

Prism-based cards can use one of two drivers: the *linux-wlan-ng* from Absolute Value Systems (*http://www.linux-wlan.org*), and the HostAP driver (*http://hostap.epitest.fi*). Monitoring has been a driver feature of the *linux-wlan-ng* driver since version 0.1.15. It is activated by using the *wlanctl-ng* command, rather than a wireless extensions command:

```
bloodhound:~# wlanctl-ng wlan0 lnxreq_wlansniffer enable=true channel=6
```

To turn off monitor mode, send a request to disable it:

```
bloodhound:~# wlanctl-ng wlan0 enable=false
```

Monitoring with Prism-based cards can also be done with the HostAP driver. It uses a private system call for monitoring mode, similar to wireless extensions. Monitoring is activated by sending a monitor mode command to the card of either 2 or 3, depending on whether you want full monitoring headers (2) or just 802.11 headers (3). Monitoring is deactivated by sending a mode of zero:

```
bloodhound:~# iwpriv eth1 monitor mode
bloodhound:~# iwpriv eth1 monitor 0
```

Orinoco cards

Version 0.15 and later of the orinoco_cs driver supports moinitoring mode without requiring patches. Patches against earlier versions may be found at *http://airsnort. shmoo.com/orinocoinfo.html*. To check that a driver has been patched, run *iwpriv* to look for the monitor control call:

```
bloodhound:~# iwpriv eth1
```

If the driver supports monitoring, it can be activated with *iwpriv* as well. The monitoring driver has two modes. Mode 1 prepends Prism-style monitoring headers that report signal strength and other physical parameters, while Mode 2 has only the 802.11 header. Select one of the two modes, and a channel to monitor. To monitor channel 6 with full Prism-header monitoring information, run this command:

```
bloodhound:~# iwpriv eth1 monitor 1 6
```

To stop monitoring, use a mode of zero:

```
bloodhound:~# iwpriv eth1 monitor 0
```

Atheros-based cards

Atheros-based cards use the MADwifi driver discussed in Chapter 19. With current versions of MADwifi, the card can be placed into monitoring mode with *iwconfig*. If necessary, a channel can also be selected with *iwconfig*, as in the following examples for interface *ath0*:

```
bloodhound:~# iwconfig ath0 mode monitor
bloodhound:~# iwconfig ath0 channel 6
```

With some driver versions, I have found it necessary to assign an IP address to the interface before the interface appears in the capture list. The IP address does not need to be used on the network.

```
bloodhound:~# ifconfig ath0 1.2.3.4
bloodhound:~# ifconfig ath0 up
```

Running Ethereal

Starting Ethereal pops up the main window, which is shown in Figure 24-1. Any user may start Ethereal, but administrator privileges are required to capture packets. (Any user may load files for analysis, however.) The main window has three panes. The top pane, called the *packet list pane*, gives a high-level view of each packet. It displays each packet's capture time, source and destination address, the protocol, and a basic decode of the packet. The Protocol field is filled in with the final decode, or *dissector*, used to analyze the frame. On 802.11 networks, the final decode may be IEEE 802.11 for management frames, or it may go all the way to the final TCP protocol for analysis, as in the case of an 802.11 frame holding an LLC-encapsulated IP packet with a TCP segment carrying HTTP. With the increasing use of link-layer encryption, the end decode is often 802.11 because Ethereal's raw capture cannot decrypt frames and "see" the protected higher-layer protocols.

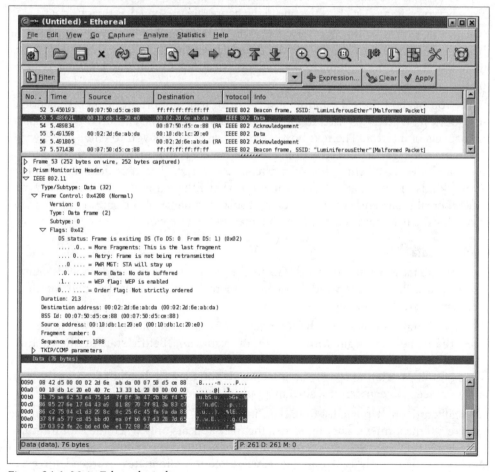

Figure 24-1. Main Ethereal window

The middle pane, called the *tree view pane*, is a detailed view of the packet selected in the packet list. All the major headers in a packet are shown and can be expanded for more detail. All packets have the basic "Frame" tree, which contains details on arrival time and capture length. 802.11 networks may add the Prism Monitoring header, which contains radio-link data. The Prism header was originally developed for use with Prism devices, but has been adopted by most drivers. The capture in Figure 24-1 was taken with an Atheros card, but the MADwifi driver appends the Prism monitoring header. Some drivers have the option of enabling or disabling the Prism header.

The bottom pane is called the *data view pane*. It shows the raw binary data in the selected packet. It also highlights the field selected in the tree view pane. If further dissectors can be called to decode the frame, they will be. For unencrypted traffic, Ethereal can see the Logical Link Control (LLC) header. From there, the LLC may contain ARP packets, IP packets, TCP segments, and so on. Ethereal includes dissectors for all the commonly used protocols, so 802.11 frames are fully decoded when available. However, encrypted frames, such as the one in the figure, are presented as opaque data.

By selecting a field in the tree view pane, the corresponding bits are highlighted in the data view pane. In Figure 24-1, the Data field of the frame is selected, and highlighted at the bottom. I prefer to use a monospace font so that the data view pane at the bottom is presented in columns.

At the top of the Ethereal window is a bar with four important elements. The leftmost button, "Filter:", is used to create filters that reduce the captured packet list to the packets of interest. The text box just to the right allows you to enter filters without going through the construction process. Ethereal maintains a filter history list that enables easy switching between filters. At the right is a text field that displays several kinds of information, depending on what Ethereal is doing. It may indicate that Ethereal is currently capturing data, display the name of the capture file loaded, or display the field name currently highlighted in the tree view.

Capturing data

Capturing data is straightforward. Go to the "Capture" menu and choose "Start". The Capture Preferences window opens. Ethereal can use any detected interface, even wireless LAN interfaces.

The first thing to do is select the interface you want to monitor. For wireless interfaces, the name may begin with *eth*, *ath*, or even *wlan*. Before starting the capture, however, you must place the interface into monitor mode. Ethereal accepts the *–i* command-line option to specify an interface. If you plan to do all of your analysis on one interface, you can define a shell mapping of *ethereal* to *ethereal –i ath0*.

I typically turn on "Update list of packets in real time" and "Automatic scrolling in live capture". If the former is left unselected, the trace appears only when the capture stops. If the latter is left unselected, the trace does not scroll to the bottom. Speed is important to real-time analysis. Disabling name resolution eliminates overhead for every packet captured and may allow a station to avoid missing frames in the air.

Data Reduction

Raw captures can be quite large, and extraneous packets can make finding wheat among the chaff a challenge. One of the keys to successful use of a network analyzer is to winnow the torrent of packets down to the few packets at the heart of the matter. Ethereal provides three ways to reduce the amount of data captured to a manageable amount: capture filters, display filters, and marking packets.

Capture filters

Capture filters are the most efficient way to cut down on the amount of data processed by Ethereal because they are pushed down into the packet sniffing interface. If the packet capture interface discards the packet, that packet does not make it to Ethereal for further processing. Unfortunately, capture filters are not tremendously useful with 802.11. If the Prism monitoring header is appended, capture filters cannot be applied.

Ethereal uses *libpcap*, so the capture filter language is exactly the same as the language used by *tcpdump*. A number of primitives are available, which can be grouped into arbitrarily long expressions. These primitives allow filtering on Ethernet and IP addresses, TCP and UDP ports, and IP or Ethernet protocol numbers. Many can be applied to source or destination numbers. Unfortunately, most of the protocol numbers they apply to are encrypted on many 802.11 networks, and are therefore not useful.

 802.11 frames carry the Ethernet protocol number in the LLC header, so it cannot be filtered on easily if the network is encrypted.

Display filters

Display filters can be used on any field that Ethereal identifies, which makes them far more powerful than capture filters. Display filters inherit the knowledge of all the dissectors compiled into Ethereal, so it is possible to filter on any of the fields in any of the protocols that Ethereal is programmed to recognize. Wireless LAN administrators can filter frames based on anything in the 802.11 or LLC headers. Examples specific to 802.11 are presented later in this chapter.

Using Ethereal for 802.11 Analysis

Several Ethereal features are handy when applied to 802.11 networks. This section lists several tips and tricks for using Ethereal on wireless networks, in no particular order.

Display filters

Ethereal allows filtering on all fields in the 802.11 header. Frame fields are structured hierarchically. All 802.11 fields begin with *wlan*. Two subcategories hold information on the Frame Control field (*wlan.fc*) and the WEP Information (*wlan.wep*) field. Figure 24-2 shows the variable names for 802.11 header components; in the figure, each field is labeled with a data type. Boolean fields are labeled with a B, MAC addresses with MA, and unsigned integers with U plus the number of bits. Table 24-1 shows the same information, omitting the Ethereal display fields that are unlikely to be useful for filtering.

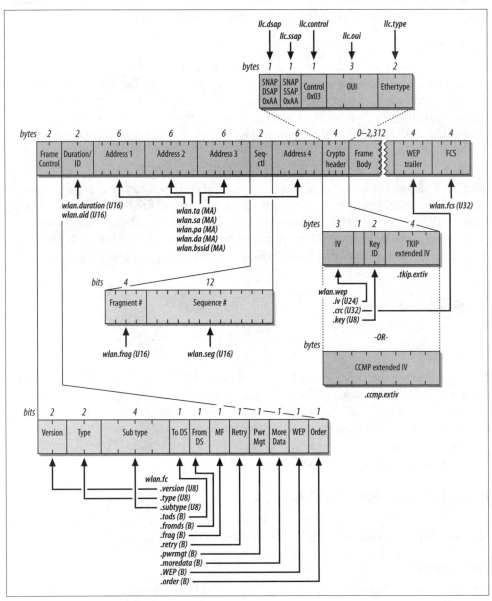

Figure 24-2. Header component variables

Table 24-1. Ethereal fields for 802.11 header components

802.11 header field	Ethereal field
Header fields	
Either source or destination address	*wlan.addr*
Transmitter address	*wlan.ta*
Source address	*wlan.sa*
Receiver address	*wlan.ra*
Destination address	*wlan.da*
BSSID	*wlan.bssid*
Frame control subfields	
Frame type	*wlan.fc.type*
Frame subtype	*wlan.fc.subtype*
ToDS flag	*wlan.fc.tods*
FromDS flag	*wlan.fc.fromds*
Retry flag	*wlan.fc.retry*
Protected frame (WEP) flag	*wlan.fc.wep*
Protection fields	
WEP Initialization vector	*wlan.wep.iv*
TKIP IV	*wlan.tkip.extiv*
CCMP IV	*wlan.ccmp.extiv*
Key identifier	*wlan.wep.key*

Fields can be combined using operators. Ethereal supports a standard set of comparison operators: == for equality, != for inequality, > for greater than, >= for greater than or equal to, < for less than, and <= for less than or equal to. An example of a display filter would be wlan.fc.type==1 to match Control frames.

Logical operators and and or are supported; as in many programming languages, the exclamation point is used for logical negation. Boolean fields can be tested for existence, so Control frames with WEP enabled would be matched by the display filter (wlan.fc.type==1 and wlan.fc.wep).

Figure 24-3 shows a complete 802.11 header in the tree view. Selecting the 802.11 header in the tree view highlights the bits that comprise the 802.11 header in the ASCII view at the bottom. Expanding the 802.11 header tree decodes all the fields in the 802.11 header.

Understanding the LLC header to isolate a protocol

To multiplex higher-level protocol data over the wireless link, 802.11 uses the LLC SNAP encapsulation. SNAP encapsulation is described at the end of Chapter 3. 802.11

Figure 24-3. An 802.11 header in tree view

does not include a protocol field, so receivers cannot discriminate between different types of network protocols directly from the header. To allow multiple protocols, an 8-byte SNAP header is added. The SNAP header is decoded in Ethereal's tree view, as shown in Figure 24-4, for an EAPOL key frame.

Highlighting the LLC header in the tree view shows the corresponding 8-byte header in the packet dump. The eight bytes in the SNAP header are clearly visible in the data view pane. Five fields make up the header:

The destination service access point (DSAP)—llc.dsap
    This is always set to 0xAA for SNAP encapsulation.

The source service access point (SSAP)—llc.ssap
    This is always set to 0xAA for SNAP encapsulation.

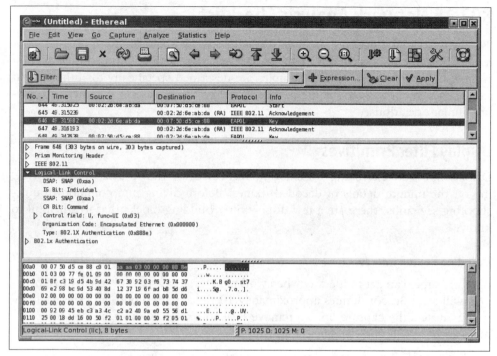

Figure 24-4. LLC SNAP header

Control—llc.control

> This is derived from HDLC. Like all data transfer using HDLC, it labels the data following the LLC header as unnumbered information (0x03). Unnumbered information indicates the use of a connectionless data transport and that the data need not be sequenced or acknowledged.

An organizationally unique identifier (OUI)—llc.oui

> This is used to determine how to interpret the following bytes. IP is encapsulated in LLC using the standard in RFC 1042, which specifies the use of the OUI 0x00-00-00. (Some vendors may use an assigned OUI for proprietary communications.)

Protocol Type—llc.type

> This is copied from the corresponding Ethernet frame. The Type field matches the Ethernet type codes. On IP networks, it will be either 0x08-00 for IP or 0x08006 for ARP. In the figure, it is 0x88-8e because the frame in question is an EAPOL (802.1X) frame.

LLC encapsulation is required by the 802.11 specification because it saves the 802.11 frame from having to carry protocol information directly. In many cases, however, the LLC header is encrypted and is not visible to the sniffer without first decrypting the trace.

802.11 Network Analysis Checklist

To illustrate how a network analyzer can aid network engineers in looking at wireless LAN traffic, this section presents checklists to assist in common authentication troubleshooting scenarios. The examples are described specifically for Ethereal but can be carried out with any of the commercial alternatives described earlier by applying similar operations.

Display Filter Primitives

Display filters are exceedingly useful on 802.11 because they are capable of operating on the minute details of decoded frames. Before diving into common troubleshooting scenarios, there are a few display filter building blocks that it is helpful to know.

Excluding Beacon frames

Beacon frames can get in the way when working with a raw 802.11 trace. Most products will send Beacon frames approximately 10 times per second, and the resulting traffic clutters the capture up. To remove Beacon frames, write a display filter that matches Beacon frames, and negate it.

- Filter on the type code for management with `wlan.fc.type==0`.
- Filter on the subtype code for Beacon with `wlan.fc.subtype==8`.
- Combine the two and negate the operation by using the exclamation point for not with an expression of `!(wlan.fc.type==0 and wlan.fc.subtype==8)`.

Isolating traffic from one station

Often, a packet capture will be targeted at one particular station under test. There are many types of frames that fly between stations, so the method used to isolate just one station depends on what you are looking for.

The first method is to use the *wlan.addr* variable in a display filter, which is shorthand for traffic using that as either a source or destination address.

- Keep only data from one station by using a display filter of `wlan.addr==00:02:2d:6e:ab:da`, where the appropriate MAC address is filled in to the trace. This trace is equivalent to the much longer filter of `wlan.sa==00:02:2d:6e:ab:da or wlan.da==00:02:2d:6e:ab:da`.

Source and destination addresses only appear in 802.11 Data frames. Troubleshooting some problems may require peeking deeper into 802.11 management operations, such as frame acknowledgment. Frame acknowledgments are sent to receiver addresses, not destination addresses. To see anything to or from a station including acknowledgments, use a display filter that includes the receiver address.

- See acknowledgments by adding in the MAC address of the test station as a receiver with wlan.ra==00:02:2d:6e:ab:da, which will show any acknowledgments sent to the station. To see acknowledgments from the station, it will be necessary to add a second receiver clause, for something of the form (wlan.ra==00:02:2d:6e:ab:da or wlan.ra==00:0b:0e:84:32:91), where the second address is the serving access point.

Isolating a protocol

If the body of a data frame is available, the LLC header can be a target for a display filter. Use the *llc.type* variable to look for a specified protocol. Protocol numbers must be entered as hexadecimal digits without a dash.

- Look at a particular Ethernet protocol type with a filter of the form llc.type==0x888e.

The other useful task that can be done with the LLC header is to search for frames sent using 802.1H encapsulation, which uses an OUI of 00-00-F8. The *llc.oui* matches on a hexadecimal number of six digits. On encrypted networks, the only LLC headers that are available are likely to be found on 802.1X frames, so do not be surprised if this filter does not display higher-layer protocols.

- RFC 1042-encapsulated frames can be displayed by llc.oui==0x000000.
- 802.1H-encapsulated frames can be displayed by llc.oui==0x0000F8.

Common Troubleshooting Tasks

With a basic understanding of how to build display filters to isolate frames of interest, we can proceed to discussing common troubleshooting tasks. Rather than present detailed examples with a great number of screenshots, this section will discuss how to isolate frames of interest and give a description of what you should see.

Authentication troubleshooting

- Display filter: isolate EAPOL frames to and from a station, while looking for acknowledgments.

    llc.type==0x888e and wlan.addr==*supplicant-MAC* and (wlan.ra==*supplicant-MAC* or wlan.ra==*AP-MAC*)

All EAPOL frames have an identifier that serves as a sequence counter. Each EAP packet acknowledges the previously received one. Look through the 802.1X session to ensure that each EAPOL frame has a corresponding 802.11 acknowledgment, and that the EAP identifier is incrementing. Some supplicants do not handle retransmissions well, and will crash. (For that reason, many access points must deauthenticate a hung 802.1X session and start over.)

By looking at the contents of the EAP packets, you may be able to learn where the authentication is failing. If it fails after the TLS tunnel establishment, it may be that the supplicant is failing to verify the server certificate. If data is pushed through the TLS tunnel, the authentication is likely failing for another reason. Check your RADIUS server logs for details.

Key distribution troubleshooting

- Display filter: isolate EAPOL key frames to and from a station.

  `llc.type==0x888e and eapol.type==3 and wlan.addr==supplicant-MAC`

There are six steps to correctly distributing keys. A portion of the handshake is shown in Figure 24-5. First, the four-way handshake must complete. As an initial sanity check, make sure that each frame is acknowledged. The quick way to do so is to look at the frame number in Ethereal. If the frame number increases by two, it is likely that the skipped frame is an 802.11 acknowledgment.

One of the most common reasons for key distribution to fail is a mismatch between the supplicant and authenticator security parameters. Ethereal has dissectors built to decode the information elements included in key frames. Figure 24-5 shows the start of an information element decode at the bottom of the tree view pane. In it, the group key is decoded as dynamic WEP. Later on in the decode, there is only one unicast cipher suite. WPA specifies that only one unicast cipher suite should be used, but this stricture is regularly broken by most products. Some supplicants, however, are unable to cope with common practice and will fail partway through the authentication. If the decodes of the information elements in the Association Request do not match those in the key handshake, the authenticator should fail the exchange.

Performance troubleshooting

Resolving performance issues is frequently much easier than identifying them. Generally speaking, performance issues fall into one of the following categories.

- Display filter 1: isolate frames to and from a station, while looking for acknowledgments.

  `wlan.addr==client-MAC and (wlan.ra==supplicant-MAC or wlan.ra==AP-MAC)`

This filter displays all traffic to and from a particular station, along with any acknowledgments. Search through the trace and look for frames that are transmitted repeatedly. If no acknowledgment is received, the frame must be retransmitted in full. When it is not received after multiple attempts, the card will step down its transfer rate to improve reliability. Lower signal to noise ratios are required for slower speeds. One option for resolving this type of performance problem may require increasing the density of access points in the area to improve signal quality. Improving the antenna system on the AP or the client may also help.

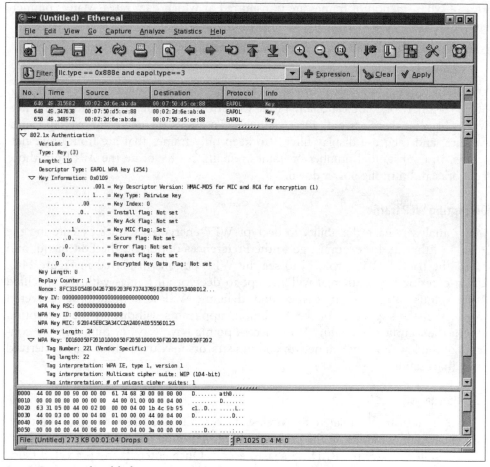

Figure 24-5. Key handshake

- Display filter 2: traffic below a certain speed.

```
prism.rate.data < (speed tag)
```

In conjunction with the previous filter, it may help to look only for frames above or below a certain speed. The prism monitoring header adds a single integer for the speed of the frame. It is reported in units of 500 kbps, so double the value of megabits per second for use in this expression. To see all frames transmitted slower than 2 Mbps, for example, use `prism.rate.data < 4`.

At the very bottom of the Ethereal screen below the data view pane is a window which reports the number of packets along with the number of displayed packets. In Figure 24-1, the capture has 261 frames (noted with the P), and all 261 are displayed (noted with the D). Applications of display filter 2 with a calculator will give you an idea of what fraction of frames are transmitted at which data rates. Many commercial tools report this analysis in real-time through a wizard.

- Display filter 3: data traffic from overlapping networks.

```
wlan.bssid != AP-MAC
```

Users may complain about performance because a different network is overlapping. 802.11b/g networks are especially prone to performance hits from overlapping networks because there are only three channels. To assess the degree of overlap, run a capture, and then use display filter 3 to keep only frames that are from other networks. If a substantial number of frames remain, try to locate the APs from those networks and turn the power down.

Decrypting WEP traffic

Many analyzers have the ability to decrypt WEP-encrypted frames by entering the keys. In Ethereal, for example, go to the Preferences option on the Edit menu, and select the IEEE 802.11 protocol to see the WEP options displayed in Figure 24-6. Upon entering keys, Ethereal will attempt to decrypt all frames with the specified keys. Manual WEP keys are easy to find; dynamic WEP keys need to be recovered from either the supplicant or the AP. Linux supplicants will display the encryption key in the output of *iwconfig*. Many access points have ways of dumping the contents of the key table, which network administrators may use to find the key derived from that station.

RADIUS analysis

Although not strictly related to wireless LANs, Ethereal also has the ability to decrypt RADIUS frames. In the preferences configuration for the RADIUS protocol, it is possible to enter the RADIUS shared secret. Once entered, any protected fields will be recovered automatically. By using RADIUS traffic, it would be possible to automatically recover dynamic keys, although I am not aware of any Ethereal add-ons to do so.

Other Tools

Other tools are often used for network analysis. Although not strictly used as troubleshooting tools, they are often used in assessing coverage.

Finding, Measuring, and Mapping Networks

Searching for 802.11 networks is the first step in connecting to them. Several analysis tools exist to discover networks or assess the coverage area of existing networks. Taken to its extreme, the result of network discovery is "wardriving," in which a user

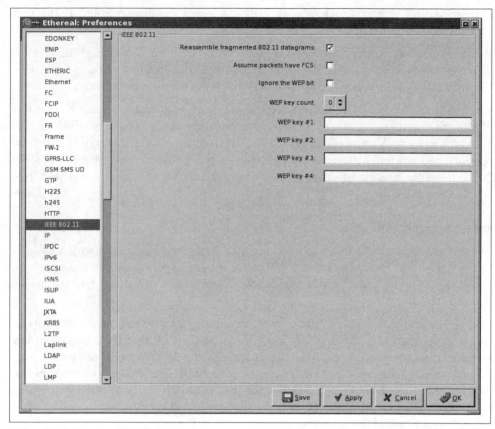

Figure 24-6. Entering WEP keys

with network discovery software logs the locations of access points. NetStumbler (*http://www.netstumbler.com*) and Kismet (*http://www.kismetwireless.net*) are two of the best-known tools.

Network detection is a passive process. Beacon frames can be collected with an 802.11 receiver, and there is nothing that can be done about it. Assuming your network will be discovered is the best policy. Instead of relying on obscurity, either by location, network name, or low transmission power, defend your network with appropriate security tools, such as the authentication and encryption methods discussed in Chapters 6 and 7. Although your network may be discovered, its data need not be.

WEP Key Recovery

Several open source tools are readily available to attack weak WEP keys. The best known is AirSnort, which was released in August 2001. Current code is available from *http://airsnort.shmoo.com/*. AirSnort was the first public implementation of the

Fluhrer-Mantin-Shamir attack against WEP discussed in Chapter 5 and is the best known, but others exist.[*]

WEP key recovery tools depend on certain classes of "weak" initialization vectors. Ethereal has borrowed the AirSnort classification code, and now reports weak IVs. Commercial tools have reported on weak IV usage for many years as well.

To defend against WEP key recovery attacks, network administrators shorten the key lifetime to anywhere between 5 and 15 minutes. Many vendors have patched code to avoid using weak IVs as well. In early 2002, the Interop Labs discovered that several vendors had reacted with surprising speed and prevented the use of weak IVs. By 2004, however, the list of vendors with fixes was almost the same, even with two years to apply the fix.

Key recovery time estimates

There are two components to recovering a key. First, enough frames with weak IVs must be gathered to mount an attack, which I refer to as the *gathering time*. Second, a successful attack must be run against the stored frames, which I refer to as the *analysis time*.[†]

In my experience, the time required to gather enough data to mount the attack is so much larger than the CPU time required to run the attack that the estimate of key recovery time is essentially equal to the gathering time. With enough samples to successfully attack, the analysis time is only a few seconds. The analysis time scales linearly, so the protection afforded by longer keys is only a few seconds. By doubling the key length, the CPU time required for the attack will double, but doubling a few seconds is still only a few seconds.

Authentication

Most 802.1X authentication protocols on wireless networks use TLS tunnels for security. The *ssldump* tool (*http://www.rtfm.com/ssldump/*) can be used to decode a TLS handshake as well as anything passed through the tunnel. Decryption requires a copy of the private keys used with any certificates.

---

[*] See, for example, WEPcrack (*http://wepcrack.sourceforge.net/*) and Aircrack (*http://www.cr0.net:8040/code/network/aircrack/*).

[†] For a discussion of analysis time, see *http://securityfocus.com/infocus/1814*.

## CHAPTER 25

802.11 Performance Tuning

In the past, wireless network administrators have probably received a bit of a free ride. Wireless is new and cool, and people do not know what sort of service they should expect. Users are happy that it works at all, and it is both easy and correct to tell them that they should not expect the same performance they would see on a 100BaseT Ethernet. Many wireless installations do not have large user communities and therefore do not have dozens or hundreds of stations trying to associate with a small number of access points. Furthermore, most wireless networks are logically subordinate to existing wired networks. 802.11 was designed to complement existing LANs, not replace them. When the wired LAN is the primary network, people can still get the job done without the wireless network, and it is seen as less critical. Most likely, your biggest problems are positioning your access points so you have coverage everywhere you want it, installing drivers, and keeping your security configuration up to date.

However, networks have a way of growing, and users have a way of becoming more demanding. Your network's performance "out of the box" is probably fairly poor, even if no one but you notices. Changing the physical environment (by experimenting with access point placement, external antennas, etc.) may alleviate some problems, but others may best be resolved by tuning administrative parameters. This chapter discusses some of the administrative parameters that can tuned to improve the behavior of your wireless network.

802.11 Performance Calculations

Like other network technologies, 802.11 has both a "headline" rate and the actual number of user bits that can be moved through the network. In many cases, the payload throughput is less than the headline rate. In the 802.11 world, the payload throughput is much lower than the headline rate due to the protocol overhead. Payload throughput of half the headline rate is a good rule of thumb.

It is often helpful to calculate a theoretical maximum throughput to compare real-world results to. 802.11 breaks up data transmission into a series of atomic operations. Each atomic operation has several components which must be accounted for; a basic atomic operation is shown in Figure 25-1. The exchange shown is the simplest, consisting of an 802.11 Data frame and its corresponding acknowledgment. Naturally, exchanges can be much more complicated if they involve fragmentation, or are required to use the 802.11g protection mechanism discussed in Chapter 14.

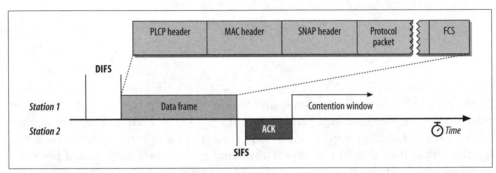

Figure 25-1. Atomic operation

Each atomic operation is composed of multiple frames separated by interframe spacing. To gain access to the medium, the frame sequence generally starts with a Distributed Inter-frame Space (DIFS), and the frames in the sequence are separated by Short Inter-frame Spaces (SIFS). Values for the DIFS and SIFS are dependent on the particular PHY in use, and can be found in the relevant chapters.

Each frame in the air must be transmitted by the physical layer, and therefore has a physical layer header consisting of a preamble plus additional fields to help decode the frame. Generally speaking, the preamble is the dominant component of the physical header transmission time. The physical layer frame's body carries the MAC frame, which is adds 28 bytes. Within the MAC frame, an 8-byte SNAP header brings the total encapsulation overhead of a data frame to 36 bytes. Encryption headers may add additional length to the MAC header.

The higher-layer protocol packet itself is transmitted according to the rules of the particular PHY in use. Each PHY has a minimum block, or symbol, size, in bits. 802.11b networks running at 11 Mbps use 8-bit symbols. 802.11a and 802.11g use symbols that carry much more data, and the symbol size depends on the data rate. At 54 Mbps, the symbol size is 216 bits. (The eventual 802.11n will have even larger block sizes.) Each block of data requires a fixed amount of time to transmit. Different data rates work by packing more or fewer data bits into a block, not by transmitting blocks faster or slower. For example, a 1,536 byte payload for the physical frame consists of 12,288 bits. In the 802.11a PHY, the frame requires the transmission of 57 symbols.

To find the time required for an atomic exchange, break it apart into its constituent pieces, and add up the time required for each. Start by adding up any inter-frame spacing. For many atomic exchanges, there will only be one DIFS and one SIFS in between frames, though the trend is towards more complex frame structures. With the inter-frame spacing accounted for, divide each frame up into its basic components, based on the physical layer that will be used. Frequently, each frame will be divided in the same way, although protection mechanisms are a notable exception because an older transmission type must be used. Each frame has a physical header, followed by the physical payload. The physical payload is the MAC frame, which consists of the MAC header, a SNAP header on any data frame, followed by the higher-layer protocol packet, and concluding with a trailer.

Example Calculation

As an example, consider the transmission of a single 1,500 byte data frame on an 802.11a network. This analysis is intended to be an example of how to dissect the components of the frame, rather than a detailed model, so the discussion neglects any higher-layer protocol effects.

In 802.11a, the SIFS is 16 microseconds, and the DIFS is 34 microseconds. Exchanging a single data frame requires that the station wait for one DIFS, transmit its data frame, and wait for the acknowledgment. The 802.11 acknowledgment is transmitted after one SIFS. There is a total of 50 microseconds of interframe spacing.

Next, break apart the data frame. The preamble and signal field in 802.11a requires 20 microseconds. The 1,500 byte data packet is encapsulated in a MAC frame with SNAP header, pushing the size up to 1,536 bytes. If the frame is protected by CCMP, an additional 16 bytes of encapsulation is added for the header and integrity check, bringing the total payload in the physical frame to 1,552 bytes, or 12,416 bits. At 54 Mbps, the physical frame payload is broken up into 216-bit symbols, so 58 will be required to transmit the data. Each symbol requires 4 microseconds, for a total of 232 microseconds for the data frame.

The 802.11 acknowledgment is only 14 bytes (112 bits) of payload, and can easily fit into a single 54 Mbps symbol. Some chipsets may use lower data rates. At data rates of 36 Mbps and up, only one symbol is required. Extra symbols are required at lower data rates: two for the 18 and 24 Mbps rates, three at 12 Mbps, four at 9 Mbps, and five at 6 Mbps. Say that the acknowledgment is transmitted at 24 Mbps, which is a reasonable balance between minimizing transmission time and retaining reliable transmission. Three symbols require 12 microseconds, for a total of 32 microseconds including the header.

Adding it all together, the 1,500 byte payload requires 50 microseconds of spacing, 232 microseconds to transmit, and 32 microseconds to acknowledge, for a total of 314 microseconds. If no contention ever occurs, 3,184 of these atomic exchanges can occur per second. Each exchange moves 1,500 bytes of payload, for a total payload rate of 38 Mbps. Under nearly ideal conditions, protocol overhead takes 30% of the headline bit rate.

Other components to a performance model

The previous discussion made several assumptions that are exceedingly generous. Most real-world 802.11 networks are lucky to get user payloads of 55–60% of the headline rate. Any serious network would run a higher-layer protocol, adding further encapsulation overhead. TCP/IP, for example, steals 40 payload bytes for its own headers, and requires protocol acknowledgments in the reverse direction. Depending on exactly how TCP/IP is incorporated into the model, it will further diminish throughput.

The previous example also made the implicit assumption that there was never contention for the medium, which is unrealistic. Even though the 802.11 MAC attempts to avoid collisions, they are a fact of life. Some engineers believe that TCP/IP may even exacerbate collisions because it tries to send session-layer acknowledgments back to the sender while the sender may continue to stream data.

Real-world networks also have many other sources of protocol overhead. The previous calculation did not attempt to estimate the overhead of sending Beacon frames, or how typical frame loss rates would diminish throughput.

Block acknowledgments

It is relatively straightforward to build on the previous example to show why block acknowledgments are such a powerful concept. Over 10% of the transmission time for the atomic exchange is required for inter-frame spacing and 802.11 acknowledgment. By changing the 1:1 ratio of data frames to acknowledgments, the proportion of airtime used for overhead operations can be shrunk much farther.

Improving Performance

With limited capacity, wireless networks are often accused of having poor performance. After receiving such a complaint, the first task is to find some way of assessing the performance in some objective manner before developing a strategy to improve performance.

Many commercial network analyzers will report channel utilization. It may be reported either as a percentage of time spent transmitting and receiving frames, or in megabits per second. The former measurement is much more useful because it takes into account the potential variance in speed due to distance from an access point. If all the associated stations are far away, they may only be able to operate at 1 Mbps. A channel fully occupied transmitting at 1 Mbps under the totally ideal conditions described in the previous example will be able to squeak out 0.94 Mbps at 100%

channel utilization. An analyzer that reported only bit transmission rate would not report the high utilization.

If there is contention for radio resources, changes should work to reduce that contention. One of the best ways to increase performance is to reduce the power on access points. By shrinking the coverage areas, stations will be closer to the APs and will (hopefully) operate at higher data rates.

Smaller coverage areas may also help avoid co-channel interference. Capacity for an AP is shared over its entire coverage area. If two APs are on the same channel at high transmission power, it is likely that they will interfere with each other. Although the protocol is designed to gracefully handle two devices transmitting at the same time, it often severely diminishes throughput. Reassigning channel numbers may help avoid interference as well, but capabilities are limited by the number of channels allowed by the technology in use. With 802.11b and 802.11g, there are only three channels, and it is likely that there will be a fair amount of interference from adjacent APs. 802.11a has many more channels, and is therefore much more useful in high-density networks where the AP coverage areas may overlap.

Using better physical layers may also help. 802.11b networks must divide a scant 6 Mbps of radio capacity between all associated stations. 802.11a and 802.11g can offer much higher throughput, often approaching 30 Mbps. If it is possible, it may help to upgrade all stations to better technology. In doing so, beware of 802.11g protection. Protection drastically cuts throughput. Although no precise figure can be offered, a good rule of thumb is that protection may cut throughput by more than 50%.

If protection causes such a throughput hit, the first reaction is to disable it, though preventing protection is harder than it might first appear. Any 802.11b transmission triggers the activation of protection, whether it is associated with the network or not. With the extensive installed base of 802.11b equipment, most 802.11g networks are stuck operating in protected mode, with a consequent reduction in performance.[*]

 For high-capacity, high-density networks, use 802.11a. It has many more channels, and does not need to serve a backwards-compatibility legacy.

In some cases, the network architecture limits performance. Networks that wall off the wireless LAN from the rest of the network force all traffic through a single choke point. If that choke point is not capable of handling the traffic load, performance will suffer. Security protocols may also have a negative effect on perceived performance. IPsec, for example, accepts maximum-size packets for transmission, but the additional IPsec

---

[*] As a user, this also makes your choice clear. When I helped to build the wireless LAN at Supercomputing 2004, there were 1300 802.11b/g users crammed on to 80 APs, but only 100 802.11a users. With my 802.11a card, I did not face contention for the radio medium, and I was able to use the full speed.

headers may require breaking it into a maximum size packet plus a tiny follow-on packet. Both require an 802.11 data frame sequence after contention for the medium, which increases the latency of transmission.

Performance may be perceived as poor due to the application in use. Data transmission is generally quite forgiving. Late arrival of a data frame is not a problem because it means that a web page may load slightly slower. Data transmissions are bursty and lumpy, and it is acceptable for packets to arrive in bursts. If a network needs to support real-time delivery, the engineering becomes much more difficult. Voice is a data stream that must arrive quickly, in order, and with minimal burstiness. Even though a network may support multi-megabit service, it is not acceptable to provide a voice session with what it requires on average. Quality of service on 802.11 networks is based on emerging specifications. While a few voice calls on an AP will work, the quality will suffer as the network load increases and voice traffic cannot be transmitted immediately upon arriving at the radio. Poor voice performance can occur even if the network is not saturated.

As a last resort, it may be possible to squeeze the last drop of performance out of a network by altering various parameters in the 802.11 specification, which is taken up in the next section of this chapter. In my experience, though, 802.11 parameters do not provide large enough performance gains to spend a great deal of time on tuning. Access points are now cheap enough that adding additional network capacity is extremely cost-effective.

Tunable 802.11 Parameters

802.11 provides a number of knobs that can be used to wring extra performance out of a network in dire situations, although a great deal of experimentation is probably required to find the values that work best.

Radio Management

As with other types of wireless networks, radio bandwidth is a precious resource on an 802.11 network. Radio spectrum is constrained by regulatory authority and cannot be easily enlarged. Several parameters allow you to optimize your network's use of the radio resource.

Beacon interval

Beacon frames serve several fundamental purposes in an infrastructure network. At the most basic level, Beacon frames define the coverage area of a basic service set (BSS). All communication in infrastructure networks is through an access point, even if the frame is sent between two stations in the same BSS. Access points are stationary, which means that the distance a Beacon frame can travel reliably won't vary over time.* Stations monitor Beacon frames to determine which Extended Service Sets (ESSs) offer coverage at their physical location and use the received signal strength to monitor the signal quality.

Transmitting Beacon frames, however, eats up radio capacity. Decreasing the Beacon interval makes passive scanning more reliable and faster because Beacon frames announce the network to the radio link more frequently. Smaller Beacon intervals may also make mobility more effective by increasing the coverage information available to mobile nodes. Rapidly moving nodes benefit from more frequent Beacon frames because they can update signal strength information more often.† Increasing the Beacon interval indirectly increases the power-saving capability of attached nodes by altering the listen interval and the DTIM interval, both of which are discussed in the section "Tuning Power Management" later in this chapter. Increasing the Beacon interval may add an incremental amount of throughput by decreasing contention for the medium. Time occupied by Beacon frames is time that can't be used for transmitting data. If you use a network built on virtual APs, each network requires its own set of Beacons, and the overhead can multiply rapidly.

RTS threshold

802.11 includes the RTS/CTS clearing procedure to help with large frames. Any frame larger than the RTS threshold must be cleared for departure from the antenna by transmission of an RTS and reception of a CTS from the target. RTS/CTS exists to combat interference from so-called hidden nodes. The RTS/CTS exchange minimizes interference from hidden nodes by informing all stations in the immediate area that a frame exchange is about to take place. The standard specifies that the RTS threshold should be set to 2,347 bytes. If network throughput is slow or there are high numbers of frame retransmissions, enable RTS clearing by decreasing the RTS threshold.

In Chapter 3, I said that a hidden node was a node that wasn't visible to all the stations on the network. Under what sorts of situations can you expect hidden nodes? Just about any, really. In almost any network, there are bound to be places where two nodes can reach the access point but not each other. Let's consider the simplest network imaginable: one access point in the middle of a large field with nothing to cause reflections or otherwise obstruct the signal. Take one mobile station, start at the access point, and move east until the signal degrades so that communication is

---

* Multipath interference may cause odd time-dependent interference patterns. A particular spot may be within range of an access point at one instant in time and subject to multipath fading seconds later. However, such a spot has marginal coverage and should not be considered a part of a basic service area. 802.16 (WiMax) is also promising for mobile data connectivity.

† 802.11 is not designed to support high-speed mobility, though. Cellular-based, wide-area technologies are more effective.

just barely possible. Now take another station and move west. Both stations can communicate with the access point, but they are invisible to each other.

The previous thought experiment should convince you that invisible nodes are a fact of life, but not very common. Hidden nodes tend to occur in harsh radio environments where stations are very far from the nearest AP. Now that wireless networks have become popular, the AP density is high enough to place a practical limit on the number of hidden nodes.

Fragmentation threshold

MAC-layer fragmentation is controlled by the fragmentation threshold variable. Any frames longer than the fragmentation threshold are sliced into smaller units for transmission. The default fragmentation threshold is the smaller of 2,346 or the maximum MAC frame length permitted by the physical layer. However, the RF-based physical layers usually have a maximum MAC frame length of 4,096 bytes, so this parameter generally defaults to 2,346. The common value immediately implies that fragmentation and RTS/CTS clearing are often used in tandem.

In environments with severe interference, encouraging fragmentation by decreasing this threshold may improve the effective throughput. When single fragments are lost, only the lost fragment must be retransmitted. By definition, the lost fragment is shorter than the entire frame and thus takes a shorter amount of time to transmit. Setting this threshold is a delicate balancing act. If it is decreased too much, the effective throughput falls because of the additional time required to acknowledge each fragment. Likewise, setting this parameter too high may decrease effective throughput by allowing large frames to be corrupted, thus increasing the retransmission load on the radio channel.

Retry limits

Every station in a network has two retry limits associated with it. A retry limit is the number of times a station will attempt to retransmit a frame before discarding it. The *long retry limit*, which applies to frames longer than the RTS threshold, is set to four by default. A frame requiring RTS/CTS clearing is retransmitted four times before it is discarded and reported to higher-level protocols. The *short retry limit*, which applies to frames shorter than the RTS threshold, is set to seven by default.

Decreasing the retry limit reduces the necessary buffer space on the local system. If frames expire quicker, expired frames can be discarded, and the memory can be reclaimed quicker. Increasing the retry limits may decrease throughput due to interactions with higher-layer protocols. When TCP segments are lost, well-behaved TCP implementations perform a slow start. Longer retry limits may increase the amount of time it takes to declare a segment lost.

Tuning Power Management

From the outset, 802.11 was designed for mobile devices. To be useful, though, mobile devices cannot be constrained by a power cord, so they usually rely on an internal battery. 802.11 includes a number of parameters that allow stations to save power, although powersaving is accomplished at the expense of the throughput or latency to the station.

Listen interval

When stations associate with an access point, one of the parameters specified is the listen interval, which is the number of Beacon intervals between instances when the station wakes up to received buffered traffic. Longer listen intervals enable a station to power down the transceiver for long periods. Long power-downs save a great deal of power and can dramatically extend battery life. Each station may have its own listen interval.

Lengthening the listen interval has two drawbacks. Access points must buffer frames for sleeping stations, so a long listen interval may require more packet buffer space on the access point. Large numbers of clients with long listen intervals may overwhelm the limited buffer space in access point hardware. Second, increasing the listen interval delays frame delivery. If a station is sleeping when its access point receives a frame, the frame must be buffered until the sleeping station is awake. After powering up, the station must receive a Beacon frame advertising the buffered frame and send a PS-Poll to retrieve the frame. This buffering and retrieval process can delay the time the frame spends in transit. Whether this is acceptable depends on the traffic requirements. For asynchronous communications such as email, lengthening the listen interval isn't likely to be a problem. But in other applications that require synchronous, time-sensitive communications (such as securities market data feeds today or an IP phone with an 802.11 interface in the future), a longer interval might not be acceptable. Certain applications may also have trouble with the increased latency. Database applications, in particular, are significantly affected by increased latency. A task group is working on MAC enhancements to provide quality of service for transmissions on 802.11 networks, but no standard has emerged yet.

DTIM Period

The DTIM period is a parameter associated with an infrastructure network, shared by all nodes associated with an access point. It is configured by the access point administrator and advertised in Beacon frames. All Beacon frames include a traffic indication map (TIM) to describe any buffered frames. Unicast frames buffered for individual stations are delivered in response to a query from the station. This polled approach is not suitable for multicast and broadcast frames, though, because it takes too much capacity to transmit multicast and broadcast frames multiple times.

Instead of the polled approach, broadcast and multicast frames are delivered after every Delivery TIM (DTIM).

Changing the DTIM has the same effect as changing the listen interval. (That should not be a surprise, given that the DTIM acts like the listen interval for broadcast and multicast frames.) Increasing the DTIM allows mobile stations to conserve power more effectively at the cost of buffer space in the access point and delays in the reception. Before increasing the DTIM, be sure that all applications can handle the increased delay and that broadcasts and multicasts are not used to distribute data to all stations synchronously. If the application uses broadcast or multicast frames to ensure that all mobile stations receive the same blob of data simultaneously, as would be the case with a real-time data feed, increasing the DTIM will likely have adverse effects.

ATIM window

In an infrastructure network, access points provide most of the powersaving support functions. In an independent or ad hoc 802.11 network, many of those functions move into the network interface driver. In ad hoc networks, stations are required to power up for every Beacon transmission and remain powered up for the duration of the Announcement TIM (ATIM) window, which is measured in time units (TUs).

Decreasing the ATIM window increases the power savings because the required power-on time for the mobile stations is reduced. Stations can power down quickly and are not required to be active during a large fraction of the time between Beacons. Increasing the ATIM window increases the probability a powersaving station will be awake when a second station has a frame. Service quality is increased, and the required buffer space is potentially smaller.

Decreasing or disabling the ATIM window would probably have the same effect on synchronous or real-time applications as increasing the DTIM timer on an infrastructure network—that is, it is likely to cause problems with less reliable communications or applications that depend on real-time data. One of the most obvious examples of a real-time application of ad hoc networking is gaming, but it is far more likely that ad hoc gaming networks would be tuned for low-delay and high-throughput than for low-power operation.

Timing Operations

Timing is a key component of 802.11 network operations. Several management operations require multistep processes, and each has its own timer.

Scan timing

To determine which network to join, a station must first scan for available networks. Some products expose timers to allow customization of the scanning process. In products that expose timers, both an *active scan timer* and a *passive scan timer* may be exposed. The active timer is the amount of time, in TUs, that a station waits after sending a Probe Request frame to solicit an active response from access points in the area. Passive scanning is simply listening for Beacon frames and can take place on several radio channels; the passive scan timer specifies the amount of time the receiver spends listening on each channel before switching to the next.

Timers related to joining the network

Once a station has located an infrastructure network to join, it authenticates to an access point and associates with it. Each of these operations has a timeout associated with it. The authentication timeout is reset at each stage of the authentication process; if any step of the process exceeds the timeout, authentication fails. On busy networks, the timeout may need to be increased. The association timeout serves a similar function in the association process.

Dwell time (frequency-hopping networks only)

The amount of time that an FH PHY spends on a single hop channel is called the dwell time. It is set by local regulatory authorities and is generally not tunable, except by changing the network card driver to a different regulatory domain.

Summary of Tunable Parameters

For quick reference, Table 25-1 summarizes the contents of this chapter, including the effect of changing each of the tuning parameters.

Table 25-1. Summary of common tunable parameters

Parameter	Meaning and units	Effect when decreased	Effect when increased
Beacon	Number of TUs between transmission of Beacon frames.	Passive scans complete more quickly, and mobile stations may be able to move more rapidly while maintaining network connectivity.	Small increase in available radio capacity and throughput and increased battery life.
RTS Threshold	Frames larger than the threshold are preceded by RTS/CTS exchange.	Greater effective throughput if there are a large number of hidden node situations .	Maximum theoretical throughput is increased, but an improvement will be realized only if there is no interference.
Fragmentation Threshold	Frames larger than the threshold are transmitted using the fragmentation procedure.	Interference corrupts only fragments, not whole frames, so effective throughput may increase.	Increases throughput in noise-free areas by reducing fragmentation acknowledgment overhead.
Long Retry Limit	Number of retransmission attempts for frames longer than the RTS threshold.	Frames are discarded more quickly, so buffer space requirement is lower.	Retransmitting up to the limit takes longer and may cause TCP to throttle back on the data rate.

Table 25-1. Summary of common tunable parameters (continued)

Parameter	Meaning and units	Effect when decreased	Effect when increased
Short Retry Limit	Number of retransmission attempts for frames shorter than the RTS threshold.	Same as long retry limit.	Same as long retry limit.
Listen Interval	Number of Beacon intervals between awakenings of powersaving stations.	Latency of unicast frames to station is reduced. Also reduces buffer load on access points.	Power savings are increased by keeping transceiver powered off for a larger fraction of the time.
DTIM Window	Number of Beacon intervals between DTIM transmissions (applies only to infrastructure networks).	Latency of multicast and broadcast data to powersaving stations is reduced. Also reduces buffer load on access points.	Power savings are increased by keeping transceiver powered off for a larger fraction of the time.
ATIM Window	Amount of time each station remains awake after a Beacon transmission in an independent network.	Increases power savings by allowing mobile stations to power down more quickly after Beacon transmission.	Latency to powersaving stations is reduced, and the buffer load may be decreased for other stations in the network.
Active Scan Timer	Amount of time a station waits after sending a Probe Response frame to receive a response.	Station moves quickly in its scan.	Scan takes longer but is more likely to succeed.
Passive Scan Timer	Amount of time a station monitors a channel looking for a signal.	Station may not find the intended network if the scan is too short.	Scan takes longer but is more likely to succeed.
Authentication	Maximum amount of time between successive frames in authentication sequence.	Authentications must proceed faster; if the timeout is too low, there may be more retries.	No significant effect.
Association Timeout	Maximum amount of time between successive frames in association sequence.	Associations must proceed faster; if the timeout is too low, there may be more retries.	No significant effect.

## CHAPTER 26

Conclusions and Predictions

It's hard to make predictions,
especially about the future.
—Yogi Berra

This completes our picture of the current state of 802.11 networks. In this chapter, we'll get out a crystal ball and look at where things are heading. First, we'll look at standards that are currently in the works and close to completion. Then we'll take a somewhat longer-term look and try to draw conclusions about where wireless networks are heading.

Standards Work

Publication of the 802.11 standard was only the beginning of wireless LAN standardization efforts. Several compromises were made to get the standard out the door, and a great deal of work was deferred for later. The 802.11 working group conducts its business publicly, and anybody can view their web site at *http://grouper.ieee.org/ groups/802/11/* to get an update on the progress of any of these revisions to 802.11. As standards development progresses, many task groups post detailed reports, including the results of votes on different proposals.

Revisions to the standard are handled by Task Groups. Task Groups are lettered, and any revisions inherit the letter corresponding to the Task Group. For example, the OFDM PHY was standardized by Task Group A (TGa), and their revision was called 802.11a.

In the time since the publication of the first edition of this book, several standards revisions have been approved. 802.11g put the number 54 on boxes throughout the world. 802.11h made the underlying technology of 802.11a suitable for use in Europe, and convinced the U.S. government to open up additional spectrum in a worldwide harmonized band. For now, 802.11i has put security concerns largely to rest, and replaced them with demands for AES-based encryption.

New Standards

Several new standards are worthy of note. 802.11 continues to be a fertile ground for the development of new technology. As a sign of its maturity, it is getting close to rolling over to double letters for its task groups!

Task group E: quality of service extensions

Compared to their wired cousins, wireless networks have limited capacity. Task group E is developing standards to provide quality of service (QoS) by operating multiple queues and reserving the medium. To further provide service quality, 802.11e will define a new coordination function, the hybrid coordination function (HCF), with new means of accessing the network. It will also define the block acknowledgment protocol to reduce the fraction of network operations devoted to overhead.

802.11e is taking a great deal of time to produce. (Originally, it was dedicated to both QoS and security, before security was split off into Task Group I, which has now completed its work.) Rather than hold implementations for the final standard, the industry has selected a subset of the current drafts for interim standardization as Wi-Fi Multi-Media (WMM; see *http://www.wi-fi.org/OpenSection/wmm.asp*). WMM is to 802.11e as WPA was to 802.11i. Both are snapshots of a standard in process.

Task group K: radio resources

Mobile telephone networks make extensive measurements of the radio network to optimize its use of radio capacity. Many 802.11 products make some efforts to monitor radio quality, but there is no standard way of doing so. Task group K is developing a standard for use with 802.11 that will enable access points to collect radio statistics and make intelligent operating decisions based on them. New measurement types are defined to allow 802.11 stations to collect information on noise distribution, the number of hidden stations, and the load on any particular operating channel.

Task group N: high-throughput (100+ Mbps) MIMO PHY

Four complete proposals were initially received by TGn. However, two of the proposals have been withdrawn, leaving only the two described in Chapter 15. In standards-committee votes, TGnSync has been drawing slightly more support than WWiSE. The two standards are quite dissimilar, so expect a fair amount of horse-trading to create the final standard.

Products based on a TGn proposal cannot yet be called "draft 802.11n" since there is no official working draft standard at this time, and it is doubtful that a single proposal will have been selected by the time this book is in print. Products cannot label themselves "pre-N" without risking revocation of Wi-Fi certification. As a result, many products based on one proposal or the other are self-labeled as MIMO.

More distant standards

Task group P is developing extensions to 802.11 for use in automobiles, called Wireless Access in Vehicular Environments (WAVE). Cars move at much higher speed, necessitating handoff improvements. It also includes peer-to-peer networking capabilities to build a mesh between cars. Unlike many other forms of 802.11, it would use licensed spectrum. It is designed initially as a standard method of toll collection and download of safety information, although some observers think that it may eventually replace cellular communications.

Task group R is developing roaming protocols. 802.11i preauthentication is limited in that it does not reduce the computational workload of roaming. TGr is defining protocols that will enhance roaming by moving key material around the network. In the January 2005 meeting, several proposals were eliminated from further consideration, which is an important step in moving towards the final standard.

Task group S is developing mesh networking standards for use in multi-hop environments. Standards development is in a very early stage.

Task group U will modify 802.11 so that it will work with other network technologies. Its goal is similar in scope to the 802.21 working group. TGu modifies 802.11 as necessary to work with other network technologies such as third-generation cellular networks, while 802.21 works on a framework independent of any network technology.

Related standards

802.1X was originally designed for use on wired networks. Its use on wireless networks has been subject to a number of ad hoc standards that are essentially implementation agreements, and the integration of wired access control on wireless networks was messy. 802.1X-2004 specified a new version of EAPOL, and clarified the operation of the two state machines. It has not yet been widely implemented, but it will almost assuredly come to the market soon.

As more users adopt many types of wireless technology, each with its own niche of range and distance, inter-network handoff between complementary networks has moved to the fore. For example, many mobile professionals use 802.11 networks while sitting in hot spots and high-speed cellular data while in the car. Transferring a session between two disparate network types is the focus of the IEEE 802.21 working group.

Current Trends in Wireless Networking

What does the picture look like over the longer term? 802.11 has already killed off other wireless efforts aimed at the home market (such as HomeRF), and has consolidated its lock on short-range data access. As always, the larger issues for the long term are in areas such as mobility and security, both of which present problems that are not easily solved. Security, however, is moving away from a closed model of pure defense to a model that embraces the flexibility of wireless networks and uses them to provide services quickly.

Security

Security has always been the major issue associated with wireless LANs, although recent protocol work has eliminated many of the complaints specific to wireless networks. Mutual cryptographic authentication of the network and the user can now be performed using 802.1X and EAP. 802.11i has given wireless LANs the strong, trusted encryption that network managers were waiting for. WPA has made networks secure enough for practical use, and the industry has made substantial commitments to designing protocols capable of meeting stringent security standards.

Rather than isolate wireless networks, making them less functional, the new approach to network design is to integrate them into the overall network. Wireless networks improve productivity by decoupling user access from location. Early wireless networks gave away a great deal of the increased productivity by imposing access control between the wireless and wired networks, forcing users to learn new procedures for accessing data. Stronger security protocols enable the users to view the network as a single entity. Rather than attaching through cumbersome remote access procedures, users get the same network view as LAN attachment.

Changing the wireless LAN security model has depended a great deal on providing user authentication. With a strong link between the user account and any network activity comes accountability, and accountability may discourage many forms of network misuse. Authentication also shifts the emphasis of wireless LAN security from a general wall to be more like other forms of LAN security.

Authentication protocols

Today, authentication means RADIUS. Wireless LANs have given RADIUS a new lease on life, but the fact is that it was designed for the vacuum tube era of the Internet. Most users no longer use modems for access, but the protocol designed to provide service to modem users underpins the latest LAN medium. RADIUS is unsuited for the complexity being pushed upon it for LAN access. Anybody who has tried to use most RADIUS servers on the market can attest to the increased complexity foisted upon layers of obscure configuration files.

Authentication protocols will need to evolve to cope with the commoditization of IP transport. Wireless networks have driven most organizations to offer some form of network access to guests. As IP transport becomes cheaper and easier to provide, users will expect more access in more places. Authentication protocols need to adapt to more open networks by enabling access in any location. Specialized service providers such as iPass already perform this task; the research universities that have build Internet2 are working on a similar project.*

Building so-called "federated networks" requires authentication systems with extensive proxy capability, so that networks can authenticate guests from arbitrary

---

* See the Internet2 web page at *http://security.internet2.edu/fwna/*.

organizations. I would not be surprised if an Internet authentication system evolved along parallel lines to DNS to enable an organization to find a server to authenticate visitors without having to preconfigure trust relationships.

Admission control

As networks become more open to visitors and other guests, network security takes on a whole new meaning. Ensuring that machines owned by an organization are secure is a difficult task, but one with known solutions. By standardizing on a platform and carefully monitoring for security patches, employing firewalls throughout a network, and keeping antivirus and intrusion detection signatures up to date, it is possible to ensure a reasonable level of security. However, the "keep everything up to date" model breaks down if the infection vector is an external machine. While a corporation can provide access to security software for all the machines it owns, guest machines are on their own. Several new software solutions are extending the concept of network authorization to include the state of a client machine. Machines are only allowed access to the network if they can be verified "clean." Admission control is a way of extending authorization from just the rights of a user to include the state of the user's computing platform as well.

Rogue device control

Controlling the radio spectrum by protecting against unauthorized wireless LAN deployment has been a major thread in the security story of wireless LANs. While there has been a great deal of engineering work, the theory is essentially the same as it always has been. Detect APs that are not part of your network by monitoring the radio spectrum, and take appropriate steps to shut them down if necessary. In recent years, this work has been extended to use radios that are part of your network, or in some cases, data gathered from client devices.

Once unknown devices have been identified, they must be analyzed to determine a threat level. Wireless networks that are attached to some other backbone are not a threat at all, and should not be the target of aggressive attacks. If office space is shared with other organizations, it is certainly possible that signals will bleed through the walls of adjacent offices. In addition to being poor neighbor relations, launching attacks on somebody else's network may qualify as an offense under computer crime laws. To provide network security, some level of threat assessment is required. Unlicensed wireless devices not attached to your network are orthogonal to your administration and security management, and must be left alone. Ad-hoc networks built by visitors or others passing by should also remain undisturbed. Arguably, properly secured access points attached to your network should be left alone as well.

As in other areas of networking, consolidation is the order of the day. Rogue detection and assessment capabilities are increasingly built into wireless infrastructure. Although many companies offer additional equipment that can perform monitoring and security services, the baseline set of functionality required is integrated into most deployments.

Deployment and Management

Wireless LANs have followed the pattern of two previous innovations. Both the personal computer and the local area network started as under-the-radar affairs out of sight of the central IT staff. Eventually, however, they became centrally managed services providing a great deal of information. Wireless LANs have moved out of the under-the-radar phase and are quickly becoming standard connectivity.

The major deployment challenges now come from the effort to move beyond a simple coverage model. Early wireless networks were designed only to cover an area. With increasing usage, however, simple coverage is no longer enough. Ensuring higher capacity, especially in environments where users are accustomed to high-bandwidth wired networks, is at the forefront of protocol development and deployment.

Planning a network

Traditional 802.11 network planning is an arduous process consisting of walking around and taking a vast number of manual measurements. As with many other technological innovations, as the underlying mechanisms are better understood, tools are developed to improve the planning process. These tools are a way of "outsourcing" radio expertise to product developers, since most network administrators will never be radio experts.

One class of tools uses floor plans and architectural knowledge to calculate the number and location for access points, while another approach uses extensive dynamic radio calibration to adapt a network to its environment. Many products use both approaches. In any case, the time in which an expensive, time-consuming site survey was required is fast closing. Site surveys are too labor-intensive and too expensive.

Just as architects needed to learn how to plan for buildings with extensive network wiring, they will learn to incorporate 802.11 into the design process. As always, it helps to set requirements as early in the process as possible. With a basic idea of requirements and walls, preliminary AP locations can be calculated with the help of a modeling tool. By feeding back this information to architects and interior designers, the building's layout can help increase network performance while reducing hassle down the line. If AP locations are decided based purely on aesthetic criteria, or ease of installation, it is likely that network coverage will suffer.

Planning is not the end of the process, either. Computerized models are not perfect, and some changes to the preliminary design should be expected. It is not uncommon to go through multiple test and optimization cycles in building a wireless LAN. Thankfully, however, the dropping cost of access points has lessened the need to use the absolute minimum number of APs possible.

In tandem with planning physical architecture, the logical network architecture must be thought through. As wireless networks have become more common, seamless mobility is expected throughout a facility. The desire for seamless mobility is often independent of the size of the facility, which can lead to interesting challenges in extremely large buildings.

Backhaul

One of the long-standing jokes at the Interop Labs is that the wireless LAN initiatives require a great deal of Ethernet cable to connect all the access points and electrical cords to power them up. As a result, the wireless networking group uses as much wire as other technology initiatives. At this point, wireless networks depend on back-end wiring to supply both network connection and power.

Generally speaking, network connections are easier to supply than electrical power, for a variety of reasons. For simplicity, access points use one wire, and it provides both power and network. However, in some situations, the converse may be true. In large auditoriums, for example, there may be electrical wiring in the ceiling for lighting, but no network connection. Rather than force the installation of network cable for the wireless LAN, several companies are exploring using the wireless network as a backhaul. Dual-radio access points can use one radio to provide service, one radio for uplink, and depend solely on power cable for energy. Mesh backhaul technology is likely to be valuable in a variety of challenging network wiring circumstances. In situtations where meeting the 100-meter Ethernet cable length is a pipe dream, it may be the only solution.

Mini-"regulators" and arbitrators

Disagreements over spectrum can easily erupt in 802.11, especially with the lack of capacity in the 2.4 GHz band used by 802.11b and 802.11g. Unlicensed spectrum means that anybody can use it, and there are no senior rights to the radio waves. In late 2002, an access point was installed by T-Mobile in the same area as an existing AP operated by the Portland-based Personal Telco project as part of a community network effort. There was no technical solution to the interference caused by both devices operating on the same channel, although both sides attempted to assert nonexistent claims.

Although the dispute in Portland was the best-publicized early dispute over spectrum, further problems are almost sure to arise. Many organizations attempt to control radio spectrum in some fashion. Buildings with many small offices may try to manage a single wireless LAN with multiple virtual wireless networks. Several airports have long tried to maintain a single physical wireless network while renting capacity out to the traveling public, airlines, and shops. So many agreements were written in such a way that ceded rights over the electromagnetic spectrum that the FCC declared all such agreements void, with a few minor exceptions.*

---

* See the FCC document DA-04-1844 of June 2004, available for download at *http://hraunfoss.fcc.gov/edocs_public/attachmatch/DA-04-1844A1.pdf*. The order "reaffirm[s] that ... the FCC has exclusive authority to resolve matters involving radio frequency interference [RFI] when unlicensed devices are being used, regardless of venue ... [and that] ... the rights that consumers have under our rules to install and operate customer antennas ... apply to the operation of unlicensed equipment, such as Wi-Fi access points..."

Automatic radio tuning technologies are only part of the solution. With so few channels, resolving interference to the optimum degree may be impossible. (The enthusiasm for building long-haul 802.11 networks may make the problem worse, as more 802.11 signals are sent through crowded areas.) There may be an opportunity here for technically competent individuals to assist with negotiating settlements between users. Some high-tech neighborhoods already have a small version of this problem, as adjacent houses use the same channel. Volunteers have formed neighborhood frequency allocation committees to adjust the channels used by adjacent houses to improve neighborhood performance.* With no legal authority, these arbitrators or "regulators" have no power to force changes, but rely instead on technical authority.

Guest access

Most importantly, though, different access controls are needed for the future. Many early wireless LANs were used just to extend corporate LANs throughout the office. Existing authentication concepts were designed for a known, static user group, such as a group of employees. Providing access to employees is a big task, but it just begins to scratch the surface of what wireless LANs can do. Just as in cellular telephony, the promise of wireless networks is installation in hard-to-reach spots and places where users are on the move, as well as the ability to connect them at an arbitrary destination.

Designing an 802.11 network for a public place such as an airport or train station requires dealing with the question of who is allowed to use the network, and what privileges they have. Network services must be authenticated, and users must be protected from each other. Providing robust services to several disjoint user groups while isolating them from each other requires some thought about network architecture.

Higher education is pushing the envelope on guest access. Research groups often span multiple institutions, and scholars often travel between multiple locations. Rather than require an account at each institution, there is a project to build a "federation" that will allow accounts from any institution in the federation to use networks at other members of the federation. Challenges involved in building the federation range from the purely technical to the nuts-and-bolts intersection of technology and process, to purely policy-related matters. On a technical level, some form of trusted authentication link must be built among federation members.† Federations are stuck using RADIUS, with its limitations.

Once a user account is authenticated against a home institution, however, there may be some need to isolate that user from interior of the visited network. To provide accountability, information that identifies the user needs to be passed from the home

---

* See the Associated Press story at *http://community.bouldernews.com/business/02bwire.html*.

† The EduRoam project (*http://www.eduroam.org*) is one such project. Others are underway in different locations.

institution to the visiting institution. Operations staff at the visited network may want more than just a name, too. If a visitor is hit by a worm or virus, it may be vital to isolate the visitor's computer, contact the visitor, and manually disinfect it. However, if the visitor has come several thousand miles, it may be impossible to contact the visitor's home institution for contact information. Automatic disclosure of, say, a mobile telephone number with the authentication process would assist operations staff. Automatically supplying selected pieces of information without violating privacy, however, is a major technical challenge with current authentication protocols.*

Applications

The first application for wireless networks was freedom—freedom from wires and freedom from worrying about how location affects network services. Users move, but network jacks do not. First-generation applications adopted the Ethernet metaphor and left many applications unchanged. As application developers gained experience, applications began to buffer data and expect that network connections could come and go.

Wireless networks may also have a large part to play in the push for utility computing. As applications reside "out there" on the network, more universal network access methods are required. With improved authentication methods and wireless LAN interfaces on most computing devices, the network becomes the interface to the application. Better authentication systems may also help drive towards single-sign-on capabilities for applications.

Location

Early applications on wireless networks were simply applications from wired networks. Newer applications are likely to make much more out of the location awareness of wireless networks. Conferences often take over huge buildings, and considerable investment is made in signs and guides to keep attendees on the move to wherever they wish to go. Such events are already working on using the wireless network to provide location awareness to enable customized walking directions and "what's near me" navigation applications. IBM Research developed an office system that tracks people and provides location updates at cubicles.† (With luck, future location-based innovations will feel less like Big Brother.)

Voice

After many years of predictions, voice over IP has finally arrived. Several service providers are now able to offer voice quality that is better than cellular to the home over

---

* The Internet2 consortium is developing a software system called Shibboleth (*http://shibboleth.internet2.edu*) precisely because no commercial solution was sufficient.

† The cubicle, codeveloped with office furniture maker Steelcase, is described at *http://www.research.ibm.com/bluespace/*.

DSL. After years of naysaying, consumers are rushing to adopt technology that provides a less-than-stellar call quality, but has additional flexibility.

802.11 is a strong contender for the next-generation cordless phone protocol. Right now, consumers who wish to use both cordless telephones and 802.11 networks need to purchase carefully and ensure that telephones operate in a different frequency band (sometimes by going to garage sales or eBay to hunt down older 900 MHz cordless phones!), or hope that the cordless phone coexists with 802.11. By using VoIP, a cordless phone can share the same network, alleviating worries. Further consumer electronics development using 802.11 will drive down the cost of chips and create a virtuous cycle.

One major shortcoming of 802.11 VoIP devices I expect to see addressed very quickly is the lack of any real authentication capabilities on the handsets. Up until this point, most handsets have not been capable of anything other than MAC filtering. 802.1X authentication with a cryptographic EAP method is a practical minimum security level. If such a phone used the Session Initiation Protocol (SIP), it could be used in an 802.1X-enabled hot spot. Rather than add expensive licensed capacity, mobile telephone carriers could add capacity in dense areas by offloading telephone calls on to a cheaper 802.11 network. Handing calls between two disparate infrastructures is a decidedly nontrivial task, however.

Datacasting

Wireless networks are inherently a broadcast medium. Just as in Ethernet, all frames in an 802.11 network are distributed to all stations and frame filtering rules are applied. The difference between Ethernet and 802.11 is that there is no easy radio analog to switching. 802.11 frames still travel in many directions and cannot be beamed with laser-like focus to a particular receiver. By using multicast frames, it is possible to build applications that provide data broadcasting to multiple receivers. With appropriate reliability protocols, it may be possible to build small-scale broadcasting capabilities into wireless LANs. In a twist on some television stations using spare digital TV bandwidth to send data, wireless LANs might become a short-range video distribution mechanism to many receivers. Several consumer electronics companies have joined the 802.11 standards process, so video distribution over 802.11 is not totally farfetched.

Protocol Architecture

One common theme in 802.11 is that too much is under the control of the client. In 802.11, all stations are created equal. If nineteen users are associated to an access point, the AP is responsible for 5% of the protocol. Arguably, the network infrastructure should be responsible for at least half of the protocol. Recent task groups are moving in that direction, with more centralized control to improve roaming, handoff, and service quality.

Federations and mobility

Federations and mobility are tied in together in terms of protocol architecture because they are both related to network sharing, or the portability of devices between different administrative networks. To borrow a term from mobile telephony, these concepts are driving the separation between the *data plane* (which moves user data) from the *control plane* (which provides authentication and authorization, and sets up the network for the data plane).

When European telephony experts wrote the standards on which modern second-generation cellular networks are built, it was explicitly recognized that no single telecommunications carrier had the financial resources to build a pan-European cellular network. Wireless telephony had previously been held back by a plethora of incompatible standards that offer patchwork coverage throughout parts of Europe. Experts realized that the value of carrying a mobile telephone was proportional to the area in which it could be used. As a result, the GSM standards that were eventually adopted emphasized roaming functions that would enable a subscriber to use several networks while being billed by one network company.

As usage of 802.11 has grown, authentication and cross-network roaming standards have become much more important. When the incredible cost of third-generation licenses pushed a number of cellular carriers to the brink of bankruptcy, they responded by sharing the data-carrying infrastructure to share the cost and risk of an expensive third-generation network build-out. Many 802.11 hot spot providers did the same, grouping into loose federations that allow users to access other providers' networks.

As such arrangements become more common, the utility of federations will extend beyond service providers to include companies with joint ventures and research organizations. Protocols to authenticate manage visiting users will need to be developed because RADIUS does not scale or provide the features necessary.

As 802.11 becomes much more common, its advantages have become clear to organizations that are familiar with other network technologies. Attracted to cheap, unlicensed spectrum, many telephone companies have established their own service provider arms to offer 802.11 services. Incumbent telephone companies use 802.11 networks to sell WAN services. Mobile telephone operators are likely to start using 802.11 as cheap network expansion. The latter is already here, with several 802.11/3G hybrid phones announced. Combining 802.11 with a wider-area technology is quite natural, since it offers cheap abundant capacity in concentrated spots, while leaving the long-range network to a better matched technology.

Enabling quicker mobility while reducing overhead is the focus of several standards groups. Although 802.11i preauthentication can dramatically cut the time required to move from one AP to the next, it does not reduce the workload on the network to do so. A full 802.1X authentication is still required to establish the pairwise master key. As a result, there is still the same workload on the RADIUS server, and preauthentication across the WAN in a federated environment requires responsiveness across potentially large geographic (and networkologic) distances. Finding a way to move keys around the network rather than rederive them on each AP handoff will be very important in Internet-scale mobility. These protocols are being developed in Task Group R.

Future protocols

Wireless networks have a great deal of flexibility. With that flexibility comes a great deal of network administration overhead. Automatic discovery of network capabilities must extend past the low-level wireless parameters so that networks are able to announce how authentication is performed.

Early on, access points were defined by the capabilities of the underlying hardware. Newer radios have much more software functionality, and are embedded in access points that use even more software. As access points continue down the road of becoming almost completely defined by software, the market will further split between the high end and the low end. The low end will be little more than barely-modified reference designs manufactured in large quantities, and the high end will be a reference design that runs highly customized software.

In preparation for the AP becoming a platform for execution of 802.11 code, the IETF has chartered a working group to develop a protocol for the Control and Provisioning of Wireless Access Points (CAPWAP).* CAPWAP has produced a problem statement in RFC 3990, and is in the process of defining architectures and objectives for networks with lightweight access points. The protocol for AP control is expected in January 2006 as of this writing. As access points commoditize and tunneling protocols converge on a standard, it is likely that one of the Linux-based APs will receive a firmware update that enables the use of a standard tunneling protocol. In the meantime, I would not be surprised to see an effort made to develop new firmware for open-source APs that enables them to work with newer controllers.

The End

At this point, there is no way to prevent the spread of Wi-Fi. In the years since the first edition of this book, wireless networking has gone from an interesting toy to a must-have technology. Companies use it to improve productivity and attract employees, just as universities use it to attract students. With the dropping cost of chips and network cards, any laptop owner who wants connectivity can get it.

Network wires will remain for the tasks they are best suited for. Fixed computing resources that do not move will stay wired up, and high capacity networks must be constrained to operate along cables. Wireless networking, however, seems poised to continue its march towards the standard method of network connection, replacing "Where's the network jack?" with "Do you have Wi-Fi?" as the question to ask about network access.

* The working group's home page is *http://www.ietf.org/html.charters/capwap-charter.html*.

Glossary

AAA

Authentication, Authorization, and Accounting. A protocol or system which enables users to prove identity, obtain access to resources, and collect usage statistics. RADIUS is the most common AAA protocol in use with 802.11 networks.

access point

See AP.

ACK

Abbreviation for "Acknowledgment." ACKs are used extensively in 802.11 to provide reliable data transfers over an unreliable medium. For more details, see "Contention-Based Data Service" in Chapter 3.

Acknowledgment

See ACK.

ad hoc

A network characterized by temporary, short-lived relationships between nodes. See also IBSS.

AES

Advanced Encryption Standard. A cipher selected by NIST to replace the older Data Encryption Standard (DES) in 2001 after a five-year evaluation. AES is a 128-bit block cipher which uses either 128-, 192- or 256-bit keys. It has been widely adopted by many protocols requiring the use of a block cipher, including 802.11i's CCMP, though CCMP uses only 128-bit keys. AES is specified in FIPS Publication 197.

AID

Association Identifier. A number that identifies data structures in an access point allocated for a specific mobile node.

AKM

Authentication and Key Management. A set of protocols used to establish user identity and keys. The two currently defined on wireless networks are 802.1X and pre-shared keys.

AP

Access Point. Bridge-like device that attaches wireless 802.11 stations to a wired backbone network. For more information on the general structure of an access point, see Chapter 20.

AS

Authentication Server. The network service that validates user credentials. Usually RADIUS in 802.11 networks.

ASN

Abstract Syntax Notation. The formal description of the grammar used to write MIB files.

association identifier

See AID.

ATIM

Announcement Traffic Indication Message. ATIMs are used in ad hoc (independent) 802.11 networks to announce the existence of buffered frames. For more details, see Chapter 8.

basic service set

See BSS.

BER

Bit Error Rate. The number of bits received in error. Usually, the number is quite low and expressed as a ratio in scientific notation. 10^{-2} means one bit in 100 is received in error.

BPSK

Binary Phase Shift Keying. A modulation method that encodes bits as phase shifts. One of two phase shifts can be selected to encode a single bit.

BSS

Basic Service Set. The building block of 802.11 networks. A BSS is a set of stations that are logically associated with each other.

BSSID

Basic Service Set Identifier. A 48-bit identifier used by all stations in a BSS in frame headers.

CCITT

Comité Consultatif International Télégraphique et Téléphonique. A UN body responsible for telephone standardization. Due to a reorganization, it is now called the International Telecommunication Union-Telecommunication Standardization Sector (ITU-T).

CCK

Complementary Code Keying. A modulation scheme that transforms data blocks into complex codes and is capable of encoding several bits per block.

CCM

Counter Mode with CBC-MAC. An authenticated block cipher mode defined in RFC 3610. It can be used with any 128-bit block cipher, but is commonly used with AES.

CCMP

Counter Mode with CBC-MAC Protocol. 802.11i defines the use of AES with the CCM mode of operation as CCMP. It is the strongest encryption protocol available for use with wireless LANs.

CF

Contention Free. Services that do not involve contention for the medium are contention-free services. Such services are implemented by a Point Coordinator (PC) through the use of the Point Coordination Function (PCF). Contention-free services are not widely implemented.

CFP

Contention-Free Period. Even when 802.11 provides contention-free services, some contention-based access to the wireless medium is allowed. Periods controlled by a central authority are called contention-free periods (CFP).

CRC

Cyclic Redundancy Check. A mathematical checksum that can be used to detect data corruption in transmitted frames. The CRC is a linear hash function, and should not be used for data security assurance.

CSMA

Carrier Sense Multiple Access. A "listen before talk" scheme used to mediate the access to a transmission resource. All stations are allowed to access the resource (multiple access) but are required to make sure the resource is not in use before transmitting (carrier sense).

CSMA/CA

Carrier Sense Multiple Access with Collision Avoidance. A CSMA method that tries to avoid simultaneous access (*collisions*) by deferring access to the medium. 802.11 and AppleTalk's LocalTalk are two protocols that use CSMA/CA.

CTS

Clear to Send. The frame type used to acknowledge receipt of a Request to Send and the second component used in the RTS-CTS clearing exchange used to prevent interference from hidden nodes.

DA

Destination Address. The MAC address of the station the frame should be processed by. Frequently, the destination address is the receiver address. In infrastructure networks, however, frames bridged from the wireless side to the wired side will have a destination address on the wired network and a receiver address of the wireless interface in the access point.

DBPSK
Differential Binary Phase Shift Keying. A modulation method in which bits are encoded as phase shift differences between successive symbol periods. Two phase shifts are possible for an encoding rate of one data bit per symbol.

DCF
Distributed Coordination Function. The rules for contention-based access to the wireless medium in 802.11. The DCF is based on exponentially increasing back-offs in the presence of contention as well as rules for deferring access, frame acknowledgment, and when certain types of frame exchanges or fragmentation may be required.

DFS
Dynamic Frequency Selection. A spectrum management service required by European radio regulations to avoid interfering with 5 GHz radar systems, as well as spread power across all available channels. DFS was also key to the FCC decision to open up the harmonized frequency band in the U.S.

DHCP
Dynamic Host Configuration Protocol. An IETF standard used by network administrators to automatically configure hosts. Hosts needing configuration information may broadcast a request that is responded to by a DHCP server. DHCP was the Internet community's admission that the Internet was growing so fast that network administrators had lost control over what was plugged into networks.

DIFS
Distributed Inter-Frame Space. The inter-frame space used to separate atomic exchanges in contention-based services. See also DCF.

distributed coordination function
See DCF.

distributed inter-frame space
See DIFS.

DQPSK
Differential Quadrature Phase Shift Keying. A modulation method in which bits are encoded as phase shift differences between successive symbol periods. Four phase shifts are possible for an encoding rate of two data bits per symbol.

DS
Distribution System. The set of services that connects access points together. Logically composed of the wired backbone network plus the bridging functions in most commercial access points. See Figure 2-6.

DSSS
Direct-Sequence Spread Spectrum. A transmission technique that spreads a signal over a wide frequency band for transmission. At the receiver, the widespread signal is correlated into a stronger signal; meanwhile, any narrowband noise is spread widely. Most of the 802.11-installed base at 2 Mbps and 11 Mbps is composed of direct-sequence interfaces.

DTIM
Delivery Traffic Indication Map. Beacon frames may contain the DTIM element, which is used to indicate that broadcast and multicast frames buffered by the access point will be delivered shortly.

EAP
Extensible Authentication Protocol. A framework authentication protocol used by 802.1X to provide network authentication. Authentication itself is delegated to sub-protocols called methods.

EIFS
Extended Inter-Frame Space. The longest of the four inter-frame spaces, the EIFS is used when there has been an error in transmission.

EIRP
Effective Isotropic Radiated Power. An antenna system will have a footprint over which the radio waves are distributed. The power inside the footprint is called the effective isotropic radiated power.

ERP

Effective Radiated Power. Used to describe the strength of radio waves transmitted by an antenna.

ESS

Extended Service Set. A logical collection of access points all tied together. Link-layer roaming is possible throughout an ESS, provided all the stations are configured to recognize each other.

ETSI

European Telecommunications Standards Institute. ETSI is a multinational standardization body with regulatory and standardization authority over much of Europe. GSM standardization took place under the auspices of ETSI. ETSI has taken the lead role in standardizing a wireless LAN technology competing with 802.11 called the High Performance Radio LAN (HIPERLAN).

extended inter-frame space

See EIFS.

FCC

Federal Communications Commission. The regulatory agency for the United States. The FCC Rules in Title 47 of the Code of Federal Regulations govern telecommunications in the United States. Wireless LANs must comply with Part 15 of the FCC rules, which are written specifically for RF devices.

FCS

Frame Check Sequence. A checksum appended to frames on IEEE 802 networks to detect corruption. If the receiver calculates a different FCS than the FCS in the frame, it is assumed to have been corrupted in transit and is discarded.

FH

Frequency Hopping. See FHSS.

FHSS

Frequency Hopping Spread Spectrum. A technique that uses a time-varying narrowband signal to spread RF energy over a wide band.

FIPS

Federal Information Processing Standard. Public standards used by nonmilitary agencies of the United States federal government and its contractors.

four-way handshake

The key exchange defined in 802.11i that expands a pairwise master key into the full key hierarchy. The 4-Way Handshake allows a supplicant and an authenticator to agree on dynamically derived encryption keys.

GFSK

Gaussian Frequency Shift Keying. A modulation technique that encodes data based on the frequency of the carrier signal during the symbol time. GFSK is relatively immune to analog noise because most analog noise is amplitude-modulated.

GMK

Group Master Key. The key used by an authenticator to derive the group transient key.

GTK

Group Transient Key. Derived from the group master key by combining with the group random number, the GTK is used to derive the group key hierarchy, which includes keys used to protect broadcast and multicast data.

HR/DSSS

High-Rate Direct-Sequence Spread Spectrum. The abbreviation for signals transmitted by 802.11b equipment. Although similar to the earlier 2-Mbps transmissions in many respects, advanced encoding enables a higher data rate.

IAPP

Inter-Access Point Protocol. The protocol used between access points to enable roaming. 802.11F specifies a standard IAPP, though it is not widely implemented.

IBSS

Independent Basic Service Set. An 802.11 network without an access point. Some vendors refer to IBSSs as ad hoc networks; see also ad hoc.

ICV

Integrity Check Value. The checksum calculated over a frame before encryption by WEP. The ICV is designed to protect a frame against tampering by allowing a receiver to detect alterations to the frame. Unfortunately, WEP uses a flawed algorithm to generate the ICV, which robs WEP of a great deal of tamper-resistance.

IEEE

Institute of Electrical and Electronics Engineers. The professional body that has standardized the ubiquitous IEEE 802 networks.

IR

Infrared. Light with a longer wavelength and lower frequency than visible red light. The wavelength of red light is approximately 700 nm.

ISI

Inter-Symbol Interference. Because of delays over multiple paths, transmitted symbols may interfere with each other and cause corruption. Guarding against ISI is a major consideration for wireless LANs, especially those based on OFDM.

ISM

Industrial, Scientific, and Medical. Part 15 of the FCC Rules sets aside certain frequency bands in the United States for use by unlicensed Industrial, Scientific, and Medical equipment. The 2.4-GHz ISM band was initially set aside for microwave ovens so that home users of microwave ovens would not be required to go through the burdensome FCC licensing process simply to reheat leftover food quickly. Because it is unlicensed, though, many devices operate in the band, including 802.11 wireless LANs.

ITU

International Telecommunications Union. The successor to the CCITT. Technically speaking, the ITU issues recommendations, not regulations or standards. However, many countries give ITU recommendations the force of law.

IV

Initialization Vector. Generally used as a term for exposed keying material in cryptographic headers; most often used with block ciphers. WEP exposes 24 bits of the secret key to the world in the frame header, even though WEP is based on a stream cipher.

LLC

Logical Link Control. An IEEE specification that allows further protocol multiplexing over Ethernet. 802.11 frames carry LLC-encapsulated data units.

KCK

The EAPOL Key Confirmation Key. This key, derived as part of the pairwise hierarchy, is used to create message integrity check values in the four-way handshake. It may also be referred to as the "key MIC key."

KEK

The EAPOL Key Encryption Key. This key, derived as part of the pairwise hierarchy, is used to encrypt keys sent through the 4-Way Handshake. It may also be used as the pairwise key itself.

MAC

Medium Access Control. The function in IEEE networks that arbitrates use of the network capacity and determines which stations are allowed to use the medium for transmission.

MIB

Management Information Base. An ASN specification of the operational and configuration parameters of a device; frequently used with SNMP or other network management systems.

MIC

Message Integrity Code. A hash value calculated over a set of protected data to guard against tampering. In most cryptographic systems, such a hash is called a Message Authentication Code (MAC). 802.11 uses the algorithm MIC to avoid confusion with the Medium Access Control layer.

Michael

The message integrity check algorithm specified as part of TKIP.

MIMO

Multiple-Input/Multiple-Output. An antenna configuration that uses more than one transmission antenna and more than one receiver antenna to transmit multiple data streams. MIMO antenna configurations are often described with the shorthand "YxZ," where Y and Z are integers, used to refer to the number of transmitter antennas and the number of receiver antennas, respectively.

MPDU

MAC Protocol Data Unit. A fancy name for frame. The MPDU does not, however, include PLCP headers.

MSDU

MAC Service Data Unit. The data accepted by the MAC for delivery to another MAC on the network. MSDUs are composed of higher-level data only. For example, an 802.11 management frame does not contain an MSDU.

NAV

Network Allocation Vector. The NAV is used to implement the virtual carrier sensing function. Stations will defer access to the medium if it is busy. For robustness, 802.11 includes two carrier-sensing functions. One is a *physical* function, which is based on energy thresholds, whether a station is decoding a legal 802.11 signal, and similar things that require a physical measurement. The second function is a *virtual* carrier sense, which is based on the NAV. Most frames include a nonzero number in the NAV field, which is used to ask all stations to politely defer from accessing the medium for a certain number of microseconds after the current frame is transmitted. Any receiving stations will process the NAV and defer access, which prevents collisions. For more detail on how the NAV is used, see "Contention-Based Data Service" in Chapter 3.

NIST

National Institute of Standards and Technology. The United States government agency responsible for setting technology standards for the federal government. NIST standards are used by most non classified agencies and have been adopted by many other organizations throughout all types of government.

OFDM

Orthogonal Frequency Division Multiplexing. A technique that splits a wide frequency band into a number of narrow frequency bands and inverse multiplexes data across the subchannels. 802.11a and 802.11g are based on OFDM. 802.11n uses MIMO to transmit multiple OFDM data streams.

OSI

Open Systems Interconnection. A baroque compendium of networking standards that was never implemented because IP networks actually existed.

PBCC

Packet Binary Convolution Coding. An alternative method of encoding data in 802.11b networks that has not been widely implemented. PBCC was also proposed for consideration for 20+ Mbps networks, but was rejected.

PC

Point Coordinator. A function in the access point responsible for central coordination of access to the radio medium during contention-free service.

PCF

Point Coordination Function. The set of rules that provides for centrally coordinated access to the medium by the access point.

PCMCIA

Personal Computer Memory Card International Association. An industry group that standardized the ubiquitous "PCMCIA card" form factor and made it possible to connect a wide variety of peripherals to notebook computers. 802.11 interfaces are available almost exclusively in the PCMCIA form factor.

Also expanded humorously as People Who Can't Manage Computer Industry Acronyms because of its unwieldy length and pronunciation.

PDU

See protocol data unit.

PER

Packet Error Rate. Like the bit error rate, but measured as a fraction of packets with errors.

PHY

Common IEEE abbreviation for the physical layer.

physical-layer convergence procedure

The upper component of the PHY in 802.11 networks. Each PHY has its own PLCP, which provides auxiliary framing to the MAC.

PIFS

PCF Inter-Frame space. During contention-free service, any station is free to transmit if the medium is idle for the duration of one PCF inter-frame space.

PLCP

See physical-layer convergence procedure.

PMD

Physical Medium Dependent. The lower component of the PHY, responsible for transmitting RF signals to other 802.11 stations.

PMK

Pairwise Master Key. The root of all keying data between a supplicant and an authenticator. It may be derived from an EAP method during authentication, or supplied directly as a pre-shared key.

PPDU

PLCP Protocol Data Unit. The complete PLCP frame, including PLCP headers, MAC headers, the MAC data field, and the MAC and PLCP trailers.

PRF

Pseudo-Random Function. An 802.11i function that expands a small amount of data into a larger amount of data. The PRF is used most notably to expand master keys into key hierarchies.

protocol data unit

Layers communicate with each other using protocol data units. For example, the IP protocol data unit is the familiar IP packet. IP implementations communicate with each other using IP packets. See also service data unit.

PS

Power Save. Used as a generic prefix for power-saving operations in 802.11.

PSDU

PLCP Service Data Unit. The data the PLCP is responsible for delivering, i.e., one MAC frame with headers.

PSK - Phase Shift Keying

A method of transmitting data based on phase shifts in the transmitted carrier wave.

PSK - Pre-shared Key

In 802.11i, refers to the authentication method that depends on a statically configured authentication key that must be distributed manually. Also called WPA-PSK.

PTK

Pairwise Transient Key. Key derived from pairwise master key that includes keys used by encryption and integrity protocols, but also includes keys to distribute dynamic keys.

QPSK

Quadrature Phase Shift Keying. A modulation method that encodes bits as phase shifts. One of four phase shifts can be selected to encode two bits.

RA

Receiver Address. MAC address of the station that will receive the frame. The RA may also be the destination address of a frame, but not always. In infrastructure networks, for example, a frame destined for the distribution system is received by an access point.

RADIUS

Remote Authenticated Dial-In User Service. A protocol used to authenticate dial-in users that has become more widely used because of 802.1X authentication. The most common type of authentication server used in 802.1X systems.

RC4

A proprietary cipher algorithm developed by RSA Data Security and licensed for a great deal of money. Also used as the basis for WEP and prevents open source WEP implementations from existing because of the fear of lawsuits by RSA.

RLAN

Radio LAN. A term used by European radio regulations to refer to any wireless network built on radio technology. Although 802.11 is the most popular, others do exist. One of the better known alternative radio network technologies is ETSI'S HIPERLAN.

RF

Radio Frequency. Used as an adjective to indicate that something pertains to the radio interface ("RF modulator," "RF energy," and so on).

RSN

Robust Security Network. A network that uses the security methods of 802.11i and does not provide any support for WEP.

RTS

Request to Send. The frame type used to begin the RTS-CTS clearing exchange. RTS frames are used when the frame that will be transmitted is larger than the RTS threshold.

SA

Source Address; as disinct from TA. Station that generated the frame. Different when frame originates on the distrbution system and goes to the wireless segment.

SDU

See service data unit.

Service Data Unit

When a protocol layer receives data from the next highest layer, it is sending a service data unit. For example, an IP service data unit can be composed of the data in the TCP segment plus the TCP header. Protocol layers access service data units, add the appropriate header, and push them down to the next layer. See also protocol data unit.

SFD

Start of Frame Delimiter. The component of the frame header that indicates when synchronization has concluded and the actual frame is about to start.

SIFS

Short Interframe Space. The shortest of the four interframe spaces. The SIFS is used between frames in an atomic frame exchange.

SSID

Service Set Identity. A string used to identify an extended service set. Typically, the SSID is a recognizable character string for the benefit of users.

SYNC

Short for Synchronize. Bits transmitted by the PLCP to allow senders and receivers to synchronize bit timers.

TA

Transmitter Address. Station that actually put the frame in the air. Often the access point in infrastructure networks.

TIM

Traffic Indication Map. A field transmitted in Beacon frames used to inform associated stations that the access point has buffered. Bits are used to indicate both buffered unicast frames for each associated station as well as the presence of buffered multicast frames.

TK

Temporal Key. 802.11i key hierarchies derive a temporal key to be used for authentication protocols. The temporal key is the main input to link-layer encryption protocols such as TKIP or CCMP.

TKIP

Temporal Key Integrity Protocol. One of the improved encryption protocols in 802.11i, TKIP uses the fundamental operations of WEP with new keying and integrity check mechanisms to offer additional security.

TPC

Transmit Power Control. A spectrum management service required by European regulations to ensure that 5 GHz radios avoid interfering with satellite services.

WEP

Wired Equivalent Privacy. Derided as Wiretap Equivalence Protocol by its critics. A standard for ciphering individual data frames. It was intended to provide minimal privacy and has succeeded in this respect. In August 2001, WEP was soundly defeated, and public code was released.

Wi-Fi

The Wi-Fi Alliance (formerly the Wireless Ethernet Compatibility Alliance) started the Wi-Fi ("wireless fidelity") certification program to test interoperability of 802.11 implementation. Originally, the term was applied to devices that complied with 802.11b (11-Mbps HR/DSSS). It now may include 802.11g and 802.11a interoperability, as well as WPA security.

WPA and WPA2

Wi-Fi Protected Access. A security standard based on 802.11i draft 3. The Wi-Fi Alliance took 802.11i draft 3 and began certifying compliance with early TKIP implementations to accelerate adoption of 802.11 security protocols. WPA2 is based on the full ratified version of 802.11i.

Index

We'd like to hear your suggestions for improving our indexes. Send email to *index@oreilly.com*.

bands
    frequency hopping systems, 242
    ISM, 5
bandwidth, 3
    frequency bands and, 3
Barker words, 255
baseband processors, 344
basic rate set, 62
Beacon frames
    contention-free period, 215
    frequency-hopping networks, 244
    intervals, performance tuning and, 578
    preauthentication, 181
    timing synchronization and, 197
Beacon interval
    scan report, 174
Beacon management frames, 85, 106
BER (Bit Error Rate), 598
block ACKs, 313
block codes, 286
block coding, space-time block coding
        (WWiSE MIMO PHY), 318
Bluetooth, 8
BPSK (Binary Phase Shift Keying), 598
bridges, wireless (WDS), 22
broadcast frames, 56
    DTIM and, 192
broadcast keys, WEP, 120
BSS (basic service set), 16
    BSS transitions, 29
    definition, 598
    IBSS, 16
    infrastructure BSS, 17
    multi-BSS environments, 19
    passive scanning, 172
    scan report, 174
BSSBasicRateSet, scan reports, 175
BSSID (Basic Service Set ID)
    addresses, 52
    definition, 598
    management frames, 83
    overview, 71
    scanning and, 171
BSSType parameter, scanning, 171
buffered frames
    PS-Poll frames, 59
    TIM and, 189–191
bursting
    MAC, TGnSync, 326
    WWiSE, 316

C

cabling, antennas, 550
caching
    pairwise master key (PMK) caching, 168
        preauthentication and, 182
Capability Information field, management
        frames, 86
capture filters, Ethereal, 561
Card Services, PCMCIA, 388
    installation, 390
carrier multiplexing, OFDM and, 277
carrier sensing functions, 37
    physical, 38
catastrophic interference, 245
CCA (clear channel assessment), 309
CCK (complementary code keying), 267, 598
CCM (Counter Mode with CBC-MAC), 598
CCMP (Counter Mode CBC-MAC
        Protocol), 159, 492, 496
    data processing, 161
    data transmission, 162
    input, 161
    reception, 163
certification programs, IOL test, 425
CF (Contention Free), definition, 598
CF Parameter set, 223
    management frames, 97
CF parameters, scan reports, 175
CF-End (Contention-Free End) frame, 221
CF-End+CF-Ack frame, 222
CFP (contention-free period), 215
    definition, 598
Challenge Text information element, 98
channel agility, 275
Channel Agility field, management
        frames, 87
channel layout, access points and, 543
channel pairs, WWiSE, 315
Channel Switch Announcement frame, 212
Channel Switch Announcement information
        element, 100
ChannelList parameter, scanning, 172
channels
    adjacent, rejecting, 257
    clear channel assessment
        ERP PMD, 309
        OFDM PMD, 295
    DS PHY clear channel assessment, 274
    energy spread, 257
    MAC
        TGnSync and, 326
        WWiSE and, 315

About the Author

Matthew S. Gast helps organizations of all types understand wireless network technology and build scalable, standards-based secure wireless LANs. For the past several years, he has volunteered at the Interop Labs as an engineer and instructor, where he works with other leading engineers to understand cutting-edge network security protcols and explain them to conference attendees. Matthew has spoken at numerous conferences across multiple continents and connected to more wireless networks than he cares to count in the preparation of the second edition of this book. Prior to his current "day job" with an advanced wireless LAN systems company, Matthew spent several years with a series of network security companies.

His current professional interests are identity management and authentication protocols, federated networks, and dynamic authorization. In his vanishing free time, Matthew attempts to adapt digital TV to fit his peripatetic lifestyle, as well as occasionally advising start-up companies.

Colophon

Our look is the result of reader comments, our own experimentation, and feedback from distribution channels. Distinctive covers complement our distinctive approach to technical topics, breathing personality and life into potentially dry subjects.

The animal on the cover of *802.11 Wireless Networks: The Definitive Guide*, Second Edition, is a horseshoe bat (*Rhinolophus hipposideros*). This rare and globally endangered species is the smallest of the European horseshoe bats; they typically weigh only 4 to 10 grams and have a wingspan of 19 to 25 centimeters. Horseshoe bats get their name from the horseshoe-shaped, leaflike plate of skin around their noses. This nose-leaf helps modify and direct the ultrasonic sounds they emit through their nostrils (a method of sensory perception known as echolocation) to orient themselves to their surroundings, detect obstacles, communicate with each other, and find food. Bats' echolocation systems are so accurate that they can detect insects the size of gnats and objects as fine as a human hair.

Lesser horseshoe bats are found in a variety of habitats, ranging from the British Isles to the Arabian Peninsula and Central Asia, and from Morocco to Sudan. The lesser horseshoe bat was originally a cave-roosting bat, but many summer maternity colonies now occupy the roofs of old rural houses and farm buildings. These bats also sometimes roost in hedgerows and hollow trees. Maternity colonies of 30 to 70 are normal, but roosting mothers have been known to form colonies of as many as 200 bats. Lesser horseshoe bats hibernate, sometimes in large groups, from October until late April or early May. Their winter roosts are usually underground, in caves or tunnels. They hang by their feet with their wings wrapped around their bodies, often in open and exposed positions but rarely in large clusters.

Colleen Gorman was the production editor and the proofreader for *802.11 Wireless Networks: The Definitive Guide*, Second Edition. Emily Quill and Claire Cloutier provided quality control. Abigail Fox provided production assistance. Johnna VanHoose Dinse wrote the index.

Ellie Volckhausen designed the cover of this book, based on a series design by Edie Freedman. The cover image is a 19th-century engraving from the Dover Pictorial Archive. Karen Montgomery produced the cover layout with Adobe InDesign CS using Adobe's ITC Garamond font.

David Futato designed the interior layout. This book was converted by Judy Hoer to FrameMaker 5.5.6 with a format conversion tool created by Erik Ray, Jason McIntosh, Neil Walls, and Mike Sierra that uses Perl and XML technologies. The text font is Linotype Birka; the heading font is Adobe Myriad Condensed; and the code font is LucasFont's TheSans Mono Condensed. The illustrations that appear in the book were produced by Robert Romano, Jessamyn Read, and Lesley Borash using Macromedia FreeHand MX and Adobe Photoshop CS. The tip and warning icons were drawn by Christopher Bing. This colophon was written by Rachel Wheeler.

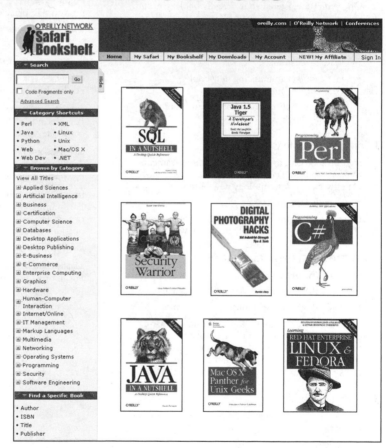

Keep in touch with O'Reilly

1. Download examples from our books

To find example files for a book, go to:

www.oreilly.com/catalog

select the book, and follow the "Examples" link.

2. Register your O'Reilly books

Register your book at *register.oreilly.com*

Why register your books?
Once you've registered your O'Reilly books you can:

- Win O'Reilly books, T-shirts or discount coupons in our monthly drawing.

- Get special offers available only to registered O'Reilly customers.

- Get catalogs announcing new books (US and UK only).

- Get email notification of new editions of the O'Reilly books you own.

3. Join our email lists

Sign up to get topic-specific email announcements of new books and conferences, special offers, and O'Reilly Network technology newsletters at:

elists.oreilly.com

It's easy to customize your free elists subscription so you'll get exactly the O'Reilly news you want.

4. Get the latest news, tips, and tools

www.oreilly.com

- "Top 100 Sites on the Web"—PC Magazine
- CIO Magazine's Web Business 50 Awards

Our web site contains a library of comprehensive product information (including book excerpts and tables of contents), downloadable software, background articles, interviews with technology leaders, links to relevant sites, book cover art, and more.

5. Work for O'Reilly

Check out our web site for current employment opportunities:

jobs.oreilly.com

6. Contact us

O'Reilly Media
1005 Gravenstein Hwy North
Sebastopol, CA 95472 USA

TEL: 707-827-7000 or 800-998-9938
      (6am to 5pm PST)

FAX: 707-829-0104

order@oreilly.com
For answers to problems regarding your order or our products. To place a book order online, visit:

www.oreilly.com/order_new

catalog@oreilly.com
To request a copy of our latest catalog.

booktech@oreilly.com
For book content technical questions or corrections.

corporate@oreilly.com
For educational, library, government, and corporate sales.

proposals@oreilly.com
To submit new book proposals to our editors and product managers.

international@oreilly.com
For information about our international distributors or translation queries. For a list of our distributors outside of North America check out:

international.oreilly.com/distributors.html

adoption@oreilly.com
For information about academic use of O'Reilly books, visit:

academic.oreilly.com

O'REILLY®

Our books are available at most retail and online bookstores.
To order direct: 1-800-998-9938 • *order@oreilly.com* • *www.oreilly.com*
Online editions of most O'Reilly titles are available by subscription at *safari.oreilly.com*